Administration and Development Planning in India

About the Author

Dr. Vishwambhar Nath spent his entire career as a Development Economist in India, the Middle East and Africa.

Born in Lahore on July 14, 1923, Dr. Nath trained as a geographer and economist. He was a Whitbeck fellow at the University of Wisconsin and received his Ph.D. in Geography from the University of Maryland in 1949.

Returning to a recently independent and partitioned India (his hometown, Lahore, now part of Pakistan), Dr. Nath joined the Indian Planning Commission, working with the early leaders of economic development and planning in India—Sir V. T. Krishnamachari, Dr. Tarlok Singh, M. S. Randhawa, Prof. M. S. Thacker, S.K. Dey and others. In the early 1950s Dr. Nath worked on the Census of India, and then he was tasked to lead the Project Evaluation Organization (PEO) of the Planning Commission. As the leader of the PEO, Dr. Nath's work on community development gained international interest. Dr. Nath's academic writings on community and village development are still considered reference works in the field.

In 1957, Dr. Nath joined the Indian Administrative Service (IAS) as part of its Rajasthan cadre. He served as a District Collector in Sawai Madhopur and Pali districts in Rajasthan. In Sawai Madhopur, Dr. Nath was instrumental in creating the Ranthambore tiger preserve as one of several preserves for the already endangered Indian tigers.

Dr. Nath returned to New Delhi in 1963 and rejoined the Planning Commission as the head of its Natural Resources and Urban Planning Division. He was deeply involved with many projects, including the plan for the Calcutta Metropolitan Region.

In 1966, Dr. Nath was deputized to the United Nations Development Programme and began his UN service as a Professor of Economic Development at a newly formed UN Institute for Training in Economics and Social Development in the Middle East located in Kuwait. Later assignments included Development Planning positions in Sierra Leone and Gambia. In these assignments, Dr. Nath's work was primarily focused on creating comprehensive five-year plans for the countries and assisting in the implementation of the plans.

Dr. Nath spent a year as a Visiting Professor of Geography at the University of Kentucky, and, after retiring from the UNDP, he spent two years as a Visiting Scholar at Boston University.

Returning to India in 1986, Dr. Nath was attached to the Centre of Policy Research in Delhi and continued his writing and scholarly work until his passing on September 10, 2002.

A deep intellect and a seasoned administrator, Dr. Nath understood that successful development was a process of change and transformation which required both intellectual analysis of large ideas, and down-to-earth implementation of simple ideas.

Administration and Development Planning in India

Dr. V. Nath

CONCEPT PUBLISHING COMPANY PVT. LTD.
NEW DELHI-110059

ISBN-13: 978-81-8069-811-8

First Published 2011

Published and Printed by

Concept
Since 1974

Concept Publishing Company Pvt. Ltd.
Regd. Office:
A/15-16, Commercial Block, Mohan Garden,
New Delhi-110059 (INDIA)
Phones : 25351460, 25351794, *Fax* : 091-11-25357109
Email : publishing@conceptpub.com
Website: www.conceptpub.com

Editorial Office:
H-13, Bali Nagar, New Delhi-110 015, India.

Cataloging in Publication Data--*Courtesy:* D.K. Agencies (P) Ltd. <docinfo@dkagencies.com>

Nath, Viswambhar, 1923-
Administration and development planning in India / V. Nath.
p. cm.
Includes bibliographical references and index.
ISBN 9788180698118

1. Central planning--India. 2. Public administration--India. 3. India--Economic policy--1947- 4. India--Population--Economic aspects. I. Title.

DDC 338.954 22

of the Community Development Programme as its first Director during the 1950s led to his strong interest in development of rural India, especially its social structures and rural society's response to economic development interventions in post-Independent India. He conducted intensive socio-economic surveys in three villages in Sawai Madhopur district of Eastern Rajasthan in early 1960s, where he was posted as Collector. Simultaneously, he studied the effects of the Green Revolution on social structure in rural Punjab to gauge how far the development in the villages is self-sustainable. Planning and Rural Development is the subject of volume four.

As an administrator (District Collector) and Chief District Development Officer, Dr. Nath observed the problems of administration and implementation of economic development plans in situations created by decentralized planning and local self-government under the Panchayati Raj Institutions. Besides he got an opportunity to give a series of lectures to middle and high level officers of Middle Eastern Countries on Administration and Planning. Also he was interested in following the results of the population censuses and role of population growth on economic development and administrative problems arising out of rapid growth of population and its growing concentration in large cities. All these subjects form part of this volume (Volume Five) Administration and Planning in India. A few articles had to be included in more than one volume in order to make reading on that particular subject complete although it meant repetition of the chapters.

I had the privilege to see Dr. Nath's interest in these areas of development evolve, and how he could knit them together. It is my privilege to bring all his writings together in Volumes so that all his thoughts are available to researchers and planners within these volumes. The author passed away in September 2002 and was involved in academic writing until the last day of his life.

I have received encouragement and assistance in this task from Dr. Surender Aggarwal, Head, Department of Geography, University of Delhi. Dr. Aggarwal, in spite of his very busy schedule, took on the task of editing the first two volumes—Urbanization, Urban Development and Metropolitan Cities in India and Regional Planning and Development in India. Mrs. Suhasini Ramawsamy edited Volume Three—Planning and Development in India. Work on editing the volume, Rural Development and Planning in India has been done in house. In editing this volume Administration and Development Planning in India, Dr. Rakesh Hooja gave important editorial suggestions and has written the Introduction for

Acknowledgements

As mentioned in Volume I, we have made an effort to publish Dr. Nath's writings on Economic Development in FIVE volumes. Each volume focuses on specific area of development and planning in India. The volumes are not being published sequentially but by subject-matter, with the generous assistance of experts on the subjects. During his lifetime, Dr. Vishwambhar Nath had the privilege of working on many important areas of economic development. He was Chief of the Urban Planning Division of the Planning Commission and played a significant role in preparation of the Plans for Calcutta Metropolitan region and wrote extensively on planning for Delhi and national capital region. Urban Development and Planning of Metropolitan Cities is the focus of the first volume in the series.

In a short assignment with the Population Census Commission in the early 1950s, he worked on the idea of demarcation of agro-climatic regions in India and worked with sustained interest on the subject of Regional Development and Planning in India, the focus of the second volume.

Dr. Nath was one of the first two officers appointed by the Planning Commission soon after its Constitution in 1950s. While he had a life long interest in planning and development in developing countries and he worked in this field not only in India but also, on behalf of the United Nations Development Programme (UNDP), in several countries of the Middle East and West Africa. However, his association and several assignments with the Planning Commission of India for almost two decades gave him a deep understanding of planning for economic development in India and he wrote on several issues relating to the subject. Planning and Economic Development in India is the subject of the third volume.

The author's involvement in the Programme Evaluation Organization

endowments can be a major factor in the differences, efficient administration can go a long way in compensating for the disadvantages in natural endowments for development.

Dr. Nath's association with the Indian Planning Commission and as an expert on planning for development in several other developing countries, evaluation of development programmes and participatory democracy at the local level and observing social and economic impact of these developments at the grassroots and as a member of the Indian Administrative Service has made him think and write on several aspects of organization of economic planning processes, implementation of development plans and role of administration in these processes. In this volume he extensively writes about the need for efficient and honest administrative service, change in the political culture which encourages corruption and inefficiency and hinders the full benefits of development programmes reaching the intended beneficiaries, due to political interference and defects in the process of selection and training of the administrators, and politicization of local self-government. During the last four decades of planned economic development, several agencies for implementation of development programmes at the state, district and local levels of administration have become less efficient, politicized and corrupted. This book contains his thoughts, insights, opinions and suggestions expressed through several published and unpublished papers since the early 1950s on several areas of concern on administration and economic development planning in India.

Kamla Nath

ranking. It is a general belief among academicians and public that corruption and inefficient government cannot exist without collusion between the politicians and the administrators. In spite of years of policy changes and institutional reforms the governed, however, seldom trust the intentions of the governance in honesty and efficient implementation of what is contained in the proclamations and a tendency to bypass the policies meant for the general good but might be hurting some. The alibi in this effort are the policy-makers and implementers themselves who can be easily bribed for 'looking the other way' while laws are broken. The general expression "all politicians are thieves" and "babus can be bought" expresses the extreme distrust in the governance. The "trust void" in institutions of political and economic governance is being filled by NGOs.

NGOs are now the single most trusted institution in every country, except China. We should not, however, overlook the mistrust that government has on the work of NGOs, because it sees them as competitors in delivering welfare services to the people which most governments have failed to do well enough. Partly this "jealousy" and partly the fact that NGOs have been found to be misusing funds—particularly those which were in the first place set up by benign protection of the law-makers and religion based groups—the governments have tried to down play the good work of NGOs.

Political Trust and Government Legitimacy

The effect of a government's legitimacy on economic development of a country can find no two stark examples than Singapore and the USSR. Both countries were single party states and both were economically decimated following Second World War. Today, the USSR does not exist as a country, and the people of Singapore are the world's second or third richest. What role good governance and administration has played in differing performance in these two countries will be of interest to readers on the subject.

India, (despite our disagreement with many policies of this and earlier governments) has done quite well on the macro-economic front. Inflation has been kept very much under control, growth rates are high and stable, investment is rising and the fiscal deficit have been kept under control. However, the macro-economic indicators of development do not capture the impact of development planning at the grassroots, which is variable across states and within states. Differences in development resource

Preface

Development and Good Governance

According to Kofi Anan, the ex- Secretary General of the United Nations, "Good governance is perhaps the single most important factor in eradicating poverty and promoting development". The United Nations Millennium Declaration represents the strongest unanimous and explicit Statement to date of UN Member States in support of democratic and participatory governance. The Declaration clearly articulates that the Millennium Development Goals must be achieved through good governance within each country and at the international level. It also states that member States "will spare no effort to promote democracy and strengthen the rule of law" and goes on to resolve "to strengthen the capacity of all countries to implement the principles and practices of democracy and respect for human rights..."

Good governance is recognized as an integral part of sustainable development, key to poverty reduction and development effectiveness. In this task several international financial aid institutions like the IMF and Asian and African Development Banks have insisted on aid receiving countries to improve their financial management and governance. Under the pressure many countries have made sustained efforts at improvement of existing institutions and creation of new ones for macro-economic management; enhancing public accountability through fiscal reforms and financial management; improving budgetary planning processes, strengthening the judiciary, anti-corruption bodies, and legislation to reinforce legal and judicial reforms, public sector reforms — decentralization and local governance and to strengthen institutions of accountability, supporting participation of civil society stakeholders and fighting corruption. But while most domestic legal systems now recognize international norms, implementation has been uneven.

There is also a strong direct correlation between corruption and poverty, with a concentration on impoverished states at the bottom of the this volume—Administration and Planning in India; a senior administrator himself Rakesh Hooja has been engaged in writing on several subjects on which Nath had also keen interest as evidence from his writings.

I am also grateful to Mr. Ashok Kumar Mittal of Concept Publishing Company Pvt. Ltd. for publishing all the volumes and persisting with the task, in spite of delays which would creep in from many unexpected corners.

Last, but not the least I am thankful to my three children, Virendra, Arvind and Jyoti in supporting and encouraging me to undertake the task, in spite of the fact that I am not a student of development planning and it would mean lot of work for me. I on my part have learnt a lot through reading and re-reading Dr. Nath's writings on the subjects contained in these volumes. It has taken me seven years to complete this task and unknowingly lengthened my companionship with him by these many years even when he was not around. This in itself has been a great emotional satisfaction for me.

February, 2010 **Kamla Nath**

Contents

Section III
Land Utilization and Settlement Patterns in India

Section IV
Population, Natural Resource Management and Development in India

Section V
Development Planning and Administration: Theory and Practice in Developing Countries

List of Tables

Introduction : Reviewing the Relationship Between Development Planning and Administration

Rakesh Hooja

Many countries, particularly in the developing world (post-colonial or otherwise) have undertaken some sort of planning with a view to overcoming economic as well as social backwardness and facilitating a change over from the traditional to the modern. Reducing imbalances between various regions within a country and ensuring dispersed growth has also sought to be addressed through planning.

When we talk of planning in the governmental context in India (or what may be called developmental planning), we refer not only to techno-economic or budgetary planning, spatial or area planning, administrative planning, project planning, sector-by-sector and multi-sectoral planning, participatory and decentralized planning, and the like. Such planning can be physical (involving land use and manpower planning, communications, services, utilities), economic (involving production and distribution of goods and services and overall productivity), administrative (involving creation of organizational structures, procedures and rules; preparing programmes and schemes for implementation, determining guidelines, fixing performance targets and norms, etc. and arranging for plan implementation), fiscal (arranging for and providing funds), or socio-political (even including participatory).

We also include in our ambit planning at levels lower than the national, i.e. State (or province), region, district, block, special project area, city or village which are linked in a framework of multi-level planning generated by both 'top down' and 'bottom up' impulses, and systems for both vertical and horizontal coordination of planning (including not only plan formulation but also its implementation). In this context it is clear that planning is not viewed as simply a technical or an economic exercise, not only as a political or administrative device, or a social process, but as an integrated amalgam of all of these.

Another feature is that planning is being practiced in India within a democratic framework and without any centralized controls—though a central planning agency—the Planning Commission of India—was set up for the purpose.

A.H. Hanson, amongst the earliest to comment on the administration of planning, writing at the time when India's Third Five Year Plan document had become available (Hanson "The Administration of Planning, Indian Journal of Public Administration", Vol. 9, 1963, also see A.H. Hanson, "The Process of Planning : A Study of India's Five Year Plans 1950-1964", Oxford University Press, London 1966), however, points out that effective planning cannot be done by a planning agency alone. It is of direct and immediate concern to the legislature, the chief executive, the ministries, the public enterprises and other specialized government agencies, and all lower governmental formations such as local authorities. The draft plan drawn up by the central planning agency incorporates at least some of the ideas and objectives put up by the various executive bodies whose relations with the planner must be close and continuous. As Hanson asserts "Although macro-planning has logical priority, the actual drafting process will inevitably involve a rather complicated interplay between the macro and the micro." The draft plan once formulated has to be approved by the highest political authorities.

Hanson then goes on to state that there is an issue of administrative coordination, which is of the very essence of planning. As Hanson puts it "To break down the Five Year Plan into a series of yearly plans, to translate those into budgetary plans, to ensure that every agency, not only understands its commitments but is determined to fulfil them; to bring about continuous cooperation between the various agencies involved; all these things demand very considerable degrees of administrative sophistication." Hanson goes on to comment that "the really daunting difficulties of planning in a mixed economy arise at the point where the administrator, in order to be effective, has to enlist the cooperation of private groups and individuals."

Issues hinted at by Hanson have been discussed in detail by V. Nath in the first section of the present volume which touches on both the theoretical and practical aspects of the relationship between planning and administration in developing countries and which comprises four chapters.

This first section contains lectures delivered by V. Nath at the UNDP, Kuwait Institute of Economic and Social Planning in the Middle East and thus was aimed at setting forth principles relevant for all the various developing countries. However, this section has special relevance for readers in India since it explains much of why and how development planning has been administered in India. Such an exposition is normally not available either in books of Economics or in books of Public Administration, or in those of Political Science and Government. It could only have been written by someone like Dr. Nath who was both an administrator and an academic and who had worked in the system in both the Planning Commission and in a State Government including working in a district, and thus understood and appreciated all the various nuances concerned.

In the first chapter entitled "Planning and Administration in Developing Countries", Nath reminds us that a large number of countries took to planning, particularly in the period following the Second World War which also witnessed a large number of countries securing independence from colonial rule. Planning has been regarded as an essential instrument for directing the transformation of economies of the countries from underdeveloped to developed, and of their societies from traditional to modern. Planning, through its concomitant definition of the specific goals of development in a country, formulation of the programmes and projects for achievement of the goals, and suggesting the direction of resource allocation and economic activity, offers, according to Nath, the most suitable means of optimizing the development process.

The author of this introduction has long accepted development to mean change plus growth in a desired direction [see for example his articles on Administrative Development in Ramesh K. Arora (ed.) *Perspectives in Administrative Theory*, Associated, New Delhi, 1979 which had drawn from John D. Montgommery and William J. Saffin edited *Approaches to Development : Public Administration and Change*, McGraw Hill, New York 1966]. Thus what constitutes development is dependent upon the subjective assessment of each individual. Accordingly this is an appropriate place to take a slight detour and to refer to Nath's article entitled "Economic Development and Planning in India" in a companion volume (which is the third of five planned volumes of V. Nath's writings, which bears the same name as that of the article, and which has been published in 2010) where Nath has provided his views on the what is the development process. According to him development leads to a multi-faceted change process. The principal changes relate, in addition to economic growth, to (i) use of natural resources; (ii) organization and technology of production; (iii) consumption patterns; (iv) social values, attitudes, patterns of relationships and institutions; (v) political behaviour patterns and institutions; and (vi) motivation of individuals and groups. Keeping in mind that development is a multi-faceted process, the decision models (or projects etc.) have also to be geared to take into account the needs of social, political and the other non-economic (as well, of course, of the economic) aspects of development which may hinder or propel the development process. Amongst those of particular importance (according to Nath) are (i) the social structure, (ii) the political structure, and (iii) external assistance/foreign aid.

Now to return to our examination of the first chapter of the current book. It points out that while most countries which took to development planning set up national or central planning agencies, the nature of the plans formulated in different countries varied greatly ranging from comprehensive national economic development plans (often based on sophisticated programming models), to the delineation of investment programmes of the public and government sectors, to mere collections or compilation of projects.

The introduction of planning had been accompanied by a large increase in the activities of government. Later, Nath indicates (see for example the last chapter of this volume) that from the 1990s a consensus had started developing that most of the industries and infrastructures (power transmission, water supply, telecommunication, etc.) are better managed by private companies rather than government. Nath did not live long enough to see the post-2008 global financial meltdown and the resultant worldwide economic recession which has spurred governments to act to provide stimulus packages and to undertake other measures (including increased spending on various government programmes) to counter the recession. This has led to some reversing of the pendulum and the importance of planning again being appreciated, as government and the Planning Commission have had to become more proactive, and the faith in the markets rather than in planning as the driver of development and growth has weakened.

Nath has echoed Hanson's earlier views (that there was a need for a revolution in public administration to enable it to meet the requirements of successful planning) when he puts forth the concept of administration as a resource for planning keeping in mind that planning for national economic development is a politico-administrative process. A good administration is essential for plan implementation and accordingly there is need for a systematic assessment of administrative capacity for plan implementation (and formulation). Unfortunately the tendency has been not to adequately assess the administrative requirements at the time of plan formulation. Hence sufficient reorganization, reorientation and expansion of administration has not been undertaken to meet the needs of planning. What is required is changes in administrative structures, processes, methods of working, attitudes, as well as patterns of communication, coordination and control within administration.

Administration is not merely a resource for planning. It (along with the political structure) is the immediate environment in which plans are formulated and implemented. The administration itself is a product of the socio-economic and political environment of the country. Accordingly planning, administration and the social-economical-political environment may be regarded as the constituents of a mutually interacting system.

Plan formulation and implementation are responsibilities primarily of the executive within the structure of government. Planning requires structures such as the central planning agency and planning units in the ministries, departments, enterprises and at regional and local levels. It requires establishment of procedures and patterns of interaction among different agencies of the government, and between official agencies and private sector enterprises and the public. It further requires changes in attitudes amongst both officials and non-officials. Planning may significantly alter the relative importance of ministries within government departments and create new foci of power and influence within government's executive.

Plan formulation requires detailed data about various aspects of the economy, sectors, projects, etc. which must be generated, processed and supplied by the various ministries and departments. It also requires intensive communication and consultation amongst ministries/departments and within the ministries resulting in the assessment and formulation of various policies and programmes. Similarly, plan implementation requires coordination both vertical and horizontal at the inter-sectoral, intra-sectoral, regional and local levels which can only be achieved by interaction amongst the different executive agencies concerned with plan implementation.

In the second chapter of this book Nath turns his attention to the administrative structures and processes of plan formulation and implementation, or what he calls "organization of planning".

The Central Planning Agency (CPA) normally formulates both sectoral and territorial plans. However, there is great variation from country to country in terms of its functions, composition, status and its relationship with the executive organs of the government. Such variations primarily relate to differences in the perception about the nature and scope of planning in each country.

Most CPAs are usually associated with the formulation of major economic policies. This is because the plan is normally the most important expression of the economic and social policies of the government as also because the implementation of the plan involves a large amount of detailed policy formulation. However, Nath cautions us that the CPA should not take upon itself the functions of either detailed formulation of policies, or of plan implementation, which are more appropriately the responsibilities of the ministries and other executive organs of government.

The structure of the CPA varies from country to country. The CPA can be located in a Ministry of Planning, it can be a department in an Economic Ministry such as Finance or Economic Affairs, or it can be a Board, Commission or Council which is separate and quasi-independent or which is attached to the office of the Chief Executive of the country's government. Or the CPA function can be entrusted to an academic or research institute. The last option Nath considers the least appropriate. He is also not in favour of the CPA being located in the Finance Ministry because then the Finance related role can subjugate the planning role as also because the CPA should be able to interact freely with all Ministries, including the Finance Ministry. An autonomous CPA may become isolated and faces the danger of being altogether left out of the decision-making. Nath thus considers a Board or Commission attached to the Chief Executive as the most satisfactory arrangement for a CPA as it enables the CPA to take a comprehensive overall view of all things and its link with the Chief Executive greatly facilitates the coordination and advisory roles of the CPA. Nath apparently favoured this model because he himself had worked in such a situation in India and found it to be practicable.

The head of the CPA may be either an economist, or administrator, or public figure (politician).

When the role of the CPA is visualized as one of overall coordination of the planning activity in the country and formulation of a national plan by coordinating the plans made at various levels, then the size of the CPA may remain small, particularly since the CPA is not expected to undertake plan implementation.

The CPA must establish working relationships with (a) the planning units in the sectoral ministries, regional governments and the major public enterprises, (b) the financial institutions like the Ministry of Finance and the Central Bank, and (c) the Central Statistical Agency, which should be independent of the Central Planning Agency. The CPA may also establish relationships with economic organizations like trade unions, chambers of commerce, industries associations, sectoral development councils of concerned stakeholders that may have been set up by the concerned sectoral Ministries, and advisory panels of economists, scientists, and other experts. In India the National Development Council which comprises representatives of both Central Government and the State Governments has come to play an important role with the plan being submitted to it for approval by the CPA at various stages.

Planning structures in the sectoral ministries are the sectoral counterparts of the CPA performing similar functions within the ministry of plan formulation, assessment of progress, providing advice for formulation of policies, etc.

In federal countries, the state or regional or provincial governments have similar systems of a centralized planning unit and planning units in the regional ministries, etc. Some countries with unitary form of government also set up regional planning agencies to deal with special problems at the regional level.

At each level the planning agency is responsible to the corresponding executive government, but it also maintains links with planning agencies at both higher and lower levels.

Nath lists the principle steps in plan formulation as follows: (i) assessment of the needs and of the aspirations of the people, and of resources, and determination of the goals and objectives of the plan, (ii) preliminary formulation of outline plan — examination of alternate strategies, formulation of overall sectoral and long term and medium term growth models, (iii) detailed formulation of sectoral programmes and projects and of regional and local plans within the framework of the outline plan, (iv) aggregation and integration, (v) formulation of the plan, (vi) approval of the plan by the chief executive, and by the legislature, (vii) formulation of annual plans and budgets, (viii) adjustments and revisions based upon appraisal of progress of the plan, domestic and international trends, and other factors.

In turn the detailed work of plan formulation involves: (a) a variety of studies involving assessment of feasibilities and appraisal of impacts, (b) intensive communication amongst different constituents of the planning system, (c) indications by Central Government to regional governments and to sectoral ministries, and by the sectoral ministries to enterprises, etc. and by regional governments to the enterprises under them and to the local governments of the macro-magnitudes of the outline plan, (d) detailed formulation of projects and programmes at enterprise, local government and regional government and sectoral ministry levels, (e) formulation of sectoral plans, (f) formulation of regional and local plans, (g) aggregation and integration of sectoral, regional and local plans into the national plan.

Nath next focuses attention on the administrative aspects of plan implementation. He points out that in mixed economy countries (which nomenclature is itself dated, as today there is no economy in the world which does not have a mix of public and private sector activities) plan implementation is divided between the public sector and the private sector and these have to be coordinated at the national level. Plan implementation in the public sector is controlled directly by decisions relating to resource allocation and executive decisions of the various plan implementation agencies. Plan implementation in the private sector which is dependent upon private decisions is secured through indirect measures which provide the incentives and sanctions to influence private decisions.

In addition to the implementation of sectoral as well as regional and local plans, administrative tasks in plan implementation relate to (i) the formulation and implementation of monetary and fiscal measures related to money supply, prices, taxation, credit, management of foreign exchange etc. so as to achieve investment targets of the plan by directing resource allocation in accordance with the plan, (ii) use of regulatory measures to further the plan objectives, (iii) implementation of the social, economic and political reforms (for example, land reforms and the establishment of democratic institutions for local government and local development) needed for attaining the socio-economic goals of the plan, (iv) appraisal of plan progress and undertaking follow up action as suggested by the appraisal.

Competition among regional governments for locating within a particular region of large enterprises and for allocations of outputs, services and resources (funds), is also an important aspect of planning in most federal countries as are large resource transfers for plan implementation from the federal to the regional governments.

Nath reminds the readers that successful plan implementation involves the availability of suitable managerial personnel, appropriate organizational structures and efficient systems and practices for the carrying out of managerial tasks. Thus he discusses measures required for the planned recruitment, training and organization of the personnel required for both plan formulation and plan implementation. Nath refers to the problem of predominance of traditional social structures and value systems with emphasis on kinship, caste or tribal loyalties, to the absence of modern trained personnel. He also alludes to the importance of cadres of administrators (who tend to become 'generalist' administrators) and how they tend to interact with 'specialists', and the use of devices like multi-disciplinary task forces or pools of officers.

The author then turns to planning and budgeting pointing out that "a budget may be defined as a projection or forecast for a period, of resources and allocations". An effective inter-linkage between the annual plan and the annual budget of government is ensured by framing the resource mobilization part of the budget within the framework of the monetary, fiscal and foreign exchange policies of the plan; by including in the budget all development programmes included in the annual plan so that the development part of the budget corresponds to the plan for the public or governmental sector; and by adoption of the same time period, methods of presentation, concepts and definitions in both the budget and the annual plan. Of course the budget also includes the non-developmental expenditure of the government and relates only to government expenditure and to financial magnitudes. The plan relates to the whole economy and also to physical magnitudes.

Nath reminds us that reclassification of the budget is an important aspect of budgetary reforms to meet the changing needs of planning.

Nath closes this chapter by referring to problems of procedural delays in the approval of projects and programmes or in transfer of funds due to concentration of financial powers while as planning progresses the need for delegation continuously increases. Another set of problems relate to inadequacy of financial scrutiny and analysis which in most countries is confined to purely financial, procedural, or administrative matters, while there is need for much more of financial or economic evaluation, cost benefit analysis and technical evaluation of projects and programmes.

The third chapter on Administrative Aspects of Plan Formulation and Implementation harps back to many issues raised by Nath in the first chapter on Planning and Administration in Developing Countries.

New patterns of communication (between ministries and CPA, between private sector and government, within and between ministries) and coordination need to be established for successful planning. New types of data have to be generated, collected and processed and there is danger of collecting too much data which becomes difficult to handle and may not really be required for effective planning. Generation of too much data may also result in delays in the communication of key data required for planning decisions.

There is the danger of concentration of decision-making at higher levels whereby the problems at the operational level may be inadequately understood at the policy-making levels and which leads to extra long channels of communication.

The need for systematic assessment of the administrative requirements of planning and of the administrative reforms required to meet the needs of planning is now receiving progressively greater attention.

Planning has also led to greater interaction between the administration and the public in terms of (a) involving the people or peoples representatives in formulation and implementation of projects, (b) regulations including controls over production, rationing of resources or goods, control over land use, etc. so as to direct productive activity in accordance with the plan, (c) resource mobilization measures for financing implementation of the plan, (d) corruption whose incidence and magnitude have increased in most countries with planning because of an increase in activities of government and the rapid expansion of staff.

Thus Nath advocates administrative planning as an integral part of the national planning process. Administrative planning encompasses the assessment of administrative capacity for plan formulation and implementation to identify spheres where interventions are required, the consequent formulation of programmes of administrative expansion, reorganization, as well as reforms, and their implementation. Expansion, reorganization and reforms in administration are likely to be constrained by (a) limitations of personnel and financial resources, (b) time required for establishing new administrative agencies, new procedures, patterns of communication, etc., (c) resistance to change within administration when established practices and established patterns of authority are disturbed, and (d) wider social and political factors, including attitudes and values.

Section I is rounded off with a chapter on Organization of Planning in Selected Countries in which Nath has provided descriptions of the organization for planning in four countries, France, India, the Soviet Union and Yugoslavia, having selected these countries to illustrate the organization of planning in both developed and developing countries and in mixed and centrally planned economies.

Till the mid or late 1970s Planning in the 4 above-mentioned countries used to form part of a paper in under-graduate Economics courses in some Indian Universities, and thus it is not surprising that Nath chose to focus on them while lecturing at the UNDP, Kuwait Institute of Economic and Social Planning in the Middle East at the end of the 1960s.

France was taken as a developed West European country which undertook "indicative" planning, the Soviet Union to bring out principal structures and processes in centrally planned economies which undertook comprehensive planning though it was realized that many of its features derived from the size and socio-cultural diversity of the country. Yugoslavia's planning had been modelled after those of the centrally planned economies but had undergone reforms aimed at decentralization and liberalization and focused on local commune structures and workers management of enterprises. India was included as a large federal, underdeveloped, mixed economy country.

The Soviet Union and Yugoslavia have ceased to exist as countries. Centrally planned economies are now a thing of the past. Once the 'Washington Consensus' took hold, all Western Countries including France started moving towards more market oriented policies (though of course the 2008 global economic crisis has discredited the Washington Consensus). Even India has undergone change post 1991 (as Nath himself has indicated in the Companion volume *Economic Development and Planning in India*, Concept, New Delhi, 2010 in a chapter entitled "Role of Economic Planning : Retrospect and Prospect").

In any case the writer of this introduction is a strong believer in contextuality (see for example Rakesh Hooja (i) "The Contextual Character of Good Governance : A View Point" in Ramesh K. Arora and R.M. Khandelwal (ed.) *Good Governance : Initiatives and Impact*, Paragon, New Delhi, 2008; and (ii) "The Contextuality of Social Sciences and Social Science Research" in *Management in Government*, Vol. 33, No. 4, January-March 2007). What is relevant in the context of one country is not likely to be so for another country. What is relevant in a country at a particular point of time may not be so a few years later as the context undergoes change. Nath himself has commented how the French or Soviet schemes could not really be replicated elsewhere even at that time.

Thus what has been described in this chapter has value because it can help us understand how planning was undertaken in four countries at a particular point of time and thus to understand various issues involved in development planning better, rather than in suggesting what can or should be done in those or other countries now.

In the early 1960s, when developmental planning efforts had been started in many developing countries, a number of writings on planning in specific countries had come out. For example, mention may be made of Albert Waterston who followed up studies of development planning in countries like Yugoslavia, Morocco and Pakistan by his then well known book (Albert Waterston, *Development Planning : Lessons of Experience*, Johns Hopkins, Baltimore, 1965).

Many Economics text-books in the 1960s and 1970s contain brief descriptions of the then processes, structures and substance of planning in the Soviet Union, Yugoslavia and France. Thus in this introductory piece it is not proposed to summarize Nath's description of the organization of planning in these countries.

As regards India, the basic organization of planning remains unchanged since Nath's description in this chapter, Nath has briefly commented upon India's federal structure, its Planning Commission (and its status and powers), the relationship between the Planning Commission and the States, planning in the Central Ministries, role of the Ministry of Finance, planning structure in the States, local planning, steps in preparation of Five Year and Annual Plans, implementation of sectoral plans, implementation of fiscal and monetary policies, and direction of private investment.

As already indicated above, the First Section of this book focusing on the relationship between development planning and administration in the context of developing countries contains much that is not easily available in the literature of Economics, Public Administration, or Political Science and Governance. And Dr. Nath has set forth his arguments and descriptions as well as insights in a very clear and concise manner setting forth the relevant issues most comprehensively. In fact few lay readers would have thought that there is a close relationship between administration and development planning as most tend to associate improvements in administration with governance and effective deliveries from the side of government. Hence Nath has done well to emphasize the link between good administration and effective development planning. Accordingly, the contents of this section by itself make this book worth reading, which is also the reason why in this introduction the contents of this section and particularly of the first three chapters have been summarized (though subjectively and selectively) in quite some detail.

Now to turn to the Second Section on Administration and Development Planning in India : Some Areas of Concern. In ten chapters (Chapters 5 to 14) Nath has commented upon some of the major issues of administration in the context of development planning—from the case for smaller States or where that may not be possible then for agro-climatic regions within States having their own decision making-structure, to the issues of area development planning *versus* programme planning and how area planning at block and district levels was initiated in India, to appropriate regions for planning in the Indian context, to district administration and the functions and duties of the Collector to Panchayati Raj and decentralized district planning, as well as the role of technical departments of the State Government *vis-à-vis* Panchayati Raj, to training of officers of the IAS, and the changes in political culture during the 40 years between 1950s and 1990s.

Chapter 5 has assumed great contemporary relevance in the light of the ongoing Telangana agitation and consequent demands for Statehood being expressed in many areas of the country. Nath of course had written the piece as a reaction to the creation of 3 new small States in 2000.

As Nath points out, the issue of reorganization of States dates back to the 1920s when the Indian National Congress indicated its commitment to the formation of linguistic States. He also reminds us that one of the members of the State Reorganization Commission of the 1950s, Shri K. M. Panikar had suggested division of India into 50 small states. He had argued that the small states would be better administered and develop more rapidly because their governments, being closer to the people, would be more responsive to their needs and aspirations—and that the unity of India would be strengthened because small States with limited resources would be in no position to separate from the Union. Neither the other members of the Commission, nor Government of India agreed with him and today, despite the subsequent creation of Haryana, the North Eastern States, Chhattisgarh, Jharkhand, Uttarakhand, Sikkim, etc., India contains 28 States and 7 Union Territories. Nath has reviewed the story of creation of States within the Indian Union since 1948 and gone into some detail regarding the 3 States created in 2000. His recommendation is that all States with a population above 40 million should be bifurcated into smaller States and in case such bifurcation is not possible due to political considerations, then suitably empowered decision-making structures of bureaucrats and popular representatives be created at the level of agro-climatic regions (this is different from the principle of linguistic areas as a sort of proxy for cultural areas normally invoked in all such debates about States' reorganization) in all such States. Nath has found that newly created States normally require time and resources to get over transitional problems. But he has also found that smaller States having comparatively limited resources (both magnitude-wise and in terms of categories of resources) are likely to remain dependent upon Central Assistance for long periods if not for ever. Of course, people of such smaller States have to travel shorter distances to reach the State capital for solutions to their problems, and those in the State capitals may have a better idea of the specific local problems of specific areas in smaller States. Nath has concentrated on administrative and economic or efficiency related aspects, while decisions as to whether or not to create a particular smaller State are more likely to be political.

This chapter should be a must read for all contemporary proponents as well as opponents of smaller States within the country.

Having worked in an integrated Command Area Development Project during its active stage, this commentator has often thought that development through the activities of functionally segmented departments (as is the system in governments the world over) is not likely to be as effective as development through an integrated local area or region based entity which undertakes all aspects of development related to the area in an integrated, and comprehensive manner whereby both preparation of action plans and implementation would be taken up in a thoroughly coordinated manner.

This issue has been taken up in the Sixth Chapter of the present volume where Nath has distinguished between the area development approach and the 'programmes' approach.

In what Nath calls the 'programmes' approach the programmes of various government departments are implemented by each of them in a more or less uniform manner in all areas of the State or country. The area development approach involves both resources development and human development in an integrated manner based upon the physical conditions, available natural resources and the social and economic situation of each specific local area.

Looking at area development experiences and practices followed during the community development era and immediately thereafter, Nath discusses both the block and the district as to which should be the primary unit for planning (he opts for the district), as also which is more appropriate as the unit for implementation and suggests that such a decision should be taken separately for each development programme or major governmental activity.

Nath also looks at district planning as attempted during the Second and Fourth Five Year Plans and at a well known district planning effort of those days the Wardha Plan. The difficulties in district planning identified then by Nath are : (i) tendency towards formulation of plans without regard for the resources likely to become available, i.e. tendency of plans to become mere catalogues of local needs and aspirations, (ii) tendency to emphasize immediate need fulfilment in preference to longer term resources development and tendency to emphasize consumption-oriented activities rather than production-oriented activities, (iii) the emergence of competing claimants for social service facilities and for goods resulting in the tendency to inflate the size of the proposed plans due to a desire to please as many rival claimants as possible, (iv) insufficiency or inaccuracy of factual data regarding locally available resources, local social and economic conditions and technical possibilities, (v) difficulty in providing sufficient technical staff for the purpose. Despite subsequent remedial measures, such problems in district planning have continued to exist in some form or the other to the present day.

It is worth noting that when a selection from the back issues of *Indian Journal of Public Administration* on the theme of multi-level planning was being compiled for publication, then this article by V. Nath written about mid-1960s, and another article 'Regions for Planning' penned a year or two later (and which forms Chapter 13 of the present volume) were both found worthy of being included in that book (*Development Administration and Multi-Level Planning*, edited by Rakesh Hooja and Sunil Dutt, IIPA and Kanishka Publishers & Distributors, New Delhi, 2008).

The next two chapters focus on the functions and duties of the Collector and the Collector's role as a leader. The first was written in mid- 1960, while the second at the turn of the Century in 2000-2001. The changes in the role and functions of the Collector due to the introduction of Parliamentary Democracy and the advent of statutory Panchayati Raj, the Collector's relations with the State Government and how the Collector started functioning as the District Development Officer coordinating all development works in addition to performing his other traditional duties, have been ably brought out. (On one aspect Nath has become outdated. He refers to the land records maintenance being done manually and the system having remained unchanged for 100 years. However, by now most States have computerized their land records.)

The Collector's relations with Panchayati Raj Institutions (PRIs) and how he performs and should perform his development role are issues which continue to be debated even today and the reader may like to refer to the chapter entitled "Pivot of Governance" in Sanjoy Bagachee's book *The Changing Face of Bureaucracy : Fifty Years of the IAS*, Rupa, Delhi, 2007, for a more detailed survey of the changing role of the District Collector and to undertake comparisons with the views expressed by Dr. Nath in this volume.

Despite everything, the Collectors central position as kingpin of administration has remained unchallenged, as the author of this introduction has also brought out in (i) introduction in Rakesh Hooja and Sunil Dutt (ed.) *District Administration : Redefining the Development Role,* Indian Institute of Public Administration and Kanishka, New Delhi, 2008, (ii) two articles by him in Suneel Dhariwal and M. C. Sharma (ed.) *District Level Administration and Role of the District Collector*, Aalekh, Jaipur, 2007. Though the role of the Collector differs somewhat from State to State, broadly speaking the Collector is directly involved in the following spheres (not listed in order of priority): (1) public order, law and order, and crime related administration, (2) land record administration and land revenue court work, land reforms as well as land acquisition, (3) supervision of the district treasury, (4) civil supplies and public distribution, (5) protocol, (6) disaster management and drought/flood relief, (7) district development, (8) conduct of elections, (9) urban and municipal affairs, (10) social welfare and social security, (11) industries and attracting investment, (12) agriculture, (13) cooperatives, (14) district planning and district statistics, (15) registration and stamps, (16) excise, (17) consumer affairs, (18) redressal of public grievances, (19) conduct of census—human, livestock, agricultural, industrial, etc., (20) coordination with banks, (21) supervision of jails, (22) supervision of prosecution staff, (23) MP/MLA Local Area Development Programmes, (24) procurement of agriculture produce, (25) conduct of special campaigns of government, (26) heading special project agencies and trying out new initiatives in various sectors, (27) arms licensing, (28) cinema licensing, (29) regulation of fairs and festivals, (30) e-governance, (31) public relations, (32) various miscellaneous or residual matters which can be grouped under a category of general administration. In some States Collectors are also being associated with programmes related to health, education, water management, etc.

The Chapter on District Administration in Rajasthan in the 1960s (Chapter 8) written in the form of reminiscences as a former Collector has discussed the functioning of the Collector in the context of Dr. Nath's posting as Collector, Sawai Madhopur between 1960 and 1962. This has also been re-printed by the present editor in his book Rakesh Hooja (ed.) *Bureaucracy and Society : The IAS at Work*, Rawat Publications, Jaipur 2010, which comprises 14 mini-memoirs by IAS officers, 7 of which relate to their district tenures as Collector.

In Chapter 9 Nath discusses both the induction level and in-service training of officers of the Indian Administrative Service. He suggests that after about 10 to 12 years of service, officers should be divided into the following four streams based on each officer's aptitude, work experience and potential : (a) management and economic policy stream, (b) agriculture, rural development and environment stream, (c) social services stream, and (d) law and order stream. Once selected for each stream officers should also be extensively trained accordingly both through institutional training and work attachments and study tours within and outside the country related to their particular stream. (Subsequently Government has on its own put into place a system of Phase III and Phase IV mid-career training—which lasts for about 6 to 8 weeks each, but such training is uniform for all IAS officers of a certain seniority). Nath also points to the need for training of IAS officers for postings in urban areas and particularly for senior positions in municipal corporations since the initial induction stage training focuses on district administration and rural postings. However, now the IAS induction training has been reviewed through the Vaidyanathan Aiyar Committee of Government of India which worked from 2005 to 2007 (and with which this commentator had the privilege of being actively associated) and training for postings in municipal areas has also become a part of such training as part of a focus on the likely training requirements of officers for the first 10 odd years of service. Thus newly emerging requirements of training of IAS officers as governance undergoes change are being catered to.

Chapters 10, 11 and 12 of this book are all to do with Panchayati Raj. Nath has earlier discussed Panchayati Raj in its introductory phase in the early 1960s in Chapter 6 (Area Development at the District and Block level) and had dealt in some detail with the Collector's relations with PRIs in Chapter 7 (The Functions and Duties of the Collector). Chapter 10 takes a look at the promise and prospects of Panchayati Raj from the vantage point of the end of the decade of the 1990s when the 73rd Constitutional Amendment had not yet been enacted, though steps to amend the Constitution had been initiated.

For Nath the objectives of Panchayati Raj should be to (i) contribute to meaningful participation by the people in local development, (ii) reduce inter-group economic and social disparities and contribute particularly to alleviation of poverty and unemployment, (iii) not affect adversely existing Centre-State relations, and (iv) promote bottom up planning. (Of course some advocates of Panchayati Raj would like the panchayat bodies to play a much larger role than that suggested by Nath; [see for example George Mathew (ed.) *The Status of Panchayati Raj in the States and Union Territories of India,* Concept Publishing Company Pvt. Ltd., New Delhi, 2000, whose updated and revised edition is now in the press.]

In this context Nath has looked at differences in the socio-economic-political situation between the 1960s and the 1990s, many of which help and others hinder the successful working of Panchayati Raj.

Among the constraints he lists: (a) the unegalitarian structure of rural society, (b) unwillingness of state level political executives and officials to delegate decision-making powers and to transfer resources for implementation of development programmes to the PRIs, (c) paucity of resources of finance and technical manpower with PRIs. Nath points out that while these constraints remain, their intensity and influence have been reduced because of changes during the 30 years till 1989 and there is promise of more successful working in the future.

Twenty years and a Constitutional Amendment later, this observer feels that Nath's conclusion continues to remain valid in today's context.

At about the time India started liberalizing its economy, the author of this introduction had requested Dr. Nath for an article on decentralized district planning for a book then being planned. The resultant piece [originally published in Rakesh Hooja and B.Yerram Raju (ed.) *Decentralized Planning in Multi-Level Framework*, Rawat Publication, Jaipur 1993] has been included in the present book as Chapter 11.

Dr. Nath asserts that "the economic policy regime does not mean the end of planning. On the contrary, planning in India remains very much alive and continues to be the principal instrument of guiding the direction and growth of the national economy." He goes on to state that "besides its role as the central guide to economic development, national and state level planning is also the mechanism through which national goals and objectives of economic, social and political reform are articulated. The statements on the goals and objectives, and on policies and programmes to achieve them, reflect a national consensus arrived at through discussions in various meetings and debates. Thus, planning is also a major instrument of economic, social and political integration of the country."

Nath accordingly reminds us that planning in India is indicative planning for a mixed economy with a small public sector and large organized and unorganized private sectors. The government sector in India aims mainly at providing physical and social infrastructure services—electricity, water, transport, telecommunications, medical and public health, education and training, social welfare, etc. In the public sector, industrial and mining enterprises are confined mainly to coal, steel, heavy engineering and heavy electrical industries—and even in these industries private enterprises are allowed to continue and expand.

For Nath the central objective of decentralized and district planning is to provide basic services and to satisfy urgently felt needs of the people both urban and rural. Decentralized and district planning envisages the maximum participation of the people in both formulation and implementation of the decentralized plans which have to be prepared within the overall framework of the national and state plans.

In Chapter 6 Nath had examined District Planning as attempted in India during the Second and Fourth Five Year Plans. He returns to the theme in the 11th Chapter comparing district planning from below as is being undertaken at village panchayat and Community Development block (taluka/mandal panchayat or panchayat Samiti) levels with the possibility of district planning from above.

Somewhat surprisingly, even though Nath has commented on district planning in many of the chapters of this book, he has not referred to the 1984 Hanumantha Rao report of the Working Group on District Planning of the Planning Commission which has significantly influenced both subsequent efforts at district planning and debates on the subject, and which everyone interested in the subject should take a look at.

Nath did not live long enough to witness the efforts made from 2004-05 onwards at district planning through panchayat bodies based upon new State level guidelines for the same issued by various State Governments at the prodding of the Central Ministry of Panchayati Raj and of the Planning Commission. Readers desirous of an idea of how such exercises have been carried out may like to refer to Rakesh Hooja "Reflections Occasioned by New Guidelines for District Planning by Panchayati Raj Institutions" in *Man and Development*, Vol. 28, No. 4, December 2006 (modified version reprinted along with a group report on District Planning under the same title as an HCM Rajasthan State Institute of Public Administration training reprint, Jaipur 2007). Also relevant in this context is Rakesh Hooja and Meenakshi Hooja, *Democratic Decentralization and Planning : Essays on Panchayati Raj, District Planning and Development Administration*, Rawat Publications, Jaipur 2007.

Some of the deficiencies noted by this commentator over the years in district level plans (especially those emanating from Panchayati Raj Institutions) are: (i) the plans have often been a mere collection of felt needs (wish lists or shopping lists) of the people and resultant demands for financial provisions without taking into account local resources and infrastructure, (ii) the plans have tended to be a mere collection, without much integration of various departmental or sub-departmental proposals and plans which are often indicated or influenced by the State Government, (iii) the so-called district/block plans have been purely rural plans, not taking into account plans for urban areas, (iv) each lower administrative or panchayat unit and planning body has been reluctant to muster any resources at its own level, but has tended to depend upon funds and functionaries being passed down from higher levels, thus limiting its own flexibility while planning, (v) plan formulation and techno-economic appraisal skills have been lacking at district and sub-district levels; thus neither the panchayat bodies nor District Planning Committees have proved to be competent to prepare comprehensive district plans including various activities to be performed by government, panchayat bodies, the private sector and Community Based Organizations (CBOs) which would necessitate district natural resource inventory and use planning, district manpower survey and employment planning, district livelihood planning, district livestock and agriculture planning, district drought proofing planning, district disaster management planning, district industrialization planning, mapping of village-wise infrastructure, facilities and services requirements for spatial or area planning, etc. Some of the deficiencies indicated above by this observer are similar to those mentioned by Dr. Nath in Chapter 6 which has been summarized earlier in this introduction.

The issue of relations between State Governments, technical departments at State headquarters and their functionaries posted in the districts, or even attached to panchayat bodies, and Panchayati Raj Institutions arose immediately upon the introduction of statutory Panchayati Raj in the country in 1959. Writing within 3-4 years of that Dr. Nath identified most of the problems that arise because funds and technical expertise are available with the departments and their district level set-ups, while for implementation certain activities are to be undertaken by panchayat bodies, and others directly by the departmental staff. The insights provided by Dr. Nath in Chapter 12 on the role of technical departments under Panchayati Raj continue to be relevant even today. This is attested to by the fact that when Indian Institute of Public Administration went through the approximately 150 articles on Panchayati Raj published in *Indian Journal of Public Administration* over the last 50 years for selecting and publishing about 30 of them in a single volume, Dr. Nath's article which comprises Chapter 12 in this book was selected and has found place in Rakesh Hooja and Sunil Dutt (ed.) *Fifty Years of Panchayati Raj and Decentralized Development* (IIPA and Kanishka, New Delhi, 2010).

Chapter 13 (Regions for Planning) harps back to Chapter 5 which referred to the need for Agro-Climatic Regions as units of planning and of implementation and to Chapter 6 which talked of area (or regional) planning.

Planning regions have to serve as the spatial units for formulation and implementation of development plans. They must, therefore, be demarcated keeping in view the objectives of planned development and the nature of the principal development programmes. Nath has advocated four sorts of planning regions : (i) administrative regions, (ii) resource development regions (which may also be agro-climatic regions), (iii) metropolitan regions, and (iv) urban regions. Administrative regions comprise the country, the macro-region or zone, the State, the Divisional Commissioner's Division, the district, the block (or panchayat Samiti), and the village, as well as special areas to tackle specific problems like a backward area, an industrial area, irrigation command area, etc.

The Resource Development Region is based on physical features of the areas. Such areas are homogeneous and are demarcated scientifically as opposed to administrative regions which were formed by acts (or may one even call them accidents) of history. The principal usefulness of resource development regions would be in making it easier to relate development programmes more closely to the different physical and socio-economic conditions in different parts of a State.

Nath, writing in the mid-1960s, had identified four metropolitan regions—the hinterlands respectively of the metropolitan cities of Mumbai, Chennai, Delhi and Kolkata which are macro-regions each covering more than one State. He suggested the following as the hierarchy of central places in a metropolitan region : (i) Metropolitan city, (ii) sub-regional centre—the principal town and service centre of the sub-region, (iii) multi-district centre—principal town and service centre of a group of districts (some of those towns could be the headquarters of Divisional Commissioner's Division); (iv) district centre (normally the district headquarters), (v) mandi centre (town with an established permanent market; may be the headquarters of a tehsil or taluka or block), and (vi) Rural Service Centre (a small town or large village serving as a service centre for a group of villages).

This chapter was amongst Nath's various writings that have contributed to the gradual development of a regional science of India. Those wanting to refer to Nath's other writing in this genre are referred to the companion volume *Regional Development and Planning in India by V. Nath* (ed.) by S.K. Aggarwal, Concept Publishing Co. Pvt Ltd., New Delhi, 2009.

Chapter 13 (the last in Section II) is wide ranging in scope. Entitled Changes in Political Culture Between the 1950s and the 1990s it refers to degeneration that has set in within the system after the 1960s when the initial euphoria and idealism following independence had waived. Nath discusses competition amongst politicians and bureaucrats, relations between Ministers and officials, changes in standards of efficiency and accessibility on the part of the administrators, selection of officers and other professionals for more responsible assignments, and the system of rewards, etc.

In some ways this chapter reminds one of the contents of a recent book T.S.R. Subramanian's *Government in India : An Inside View*, (Rupa, Delhi 2009) which however is much more critical about the various self-seeking (selfish) elites in India than Nath's somewhat rambling analysis in this chapter. However, Nath sees signs of hope and revival as he perceives a ground swell for efficiency, and a movement for change amongst India's electorate.

We turn now to the third Section of the book on Land Utilization and Settlement Patterns in India.

In Appendix I to the Chapter 15, Dr. Nath points out that the Revenue Administration (which administers land revenue and land records related matters and works directly under the District Collector) maintains regular records on classification of land, acreage and production of crops, etc. These records are based on periodical field inspection by the local revenue staff, usually the *patwari*. Before 1950 the total geographic area used to be classified as (i) area under forests, (ii) area not available for cultivation, (iii) current fallows, and (iv) other uncultivated land excluding current fallows, and (v) net area sown. Thereafter the area not available for cultivation has been bifurcated into two: (a) barren and uncultivable land and (b) land put to non-agriculture use; the current fallows have been bifurcated into (c) current fallows and (d) other fallow lands; and other uncultivated land excluding current fallows have been further subdivided into (e) cultivable waste, (f) permanent pasture and other grazing land and (g) miscellaneous tree crops and groves not included under net area sown. Thus the earlier 5 categories have been increased to 9.

Nath looks at the general pattern of land utilization in the country; that is the pattern of distribution of land amongst its important uses like cultivation, grazing, forestry, settlements, etc., and the variations in such patterns in different regions of the country.

On improving the pattern of land use, Nath asserts that the objective should be to secure a pattern of land use for each region under which all lands are used according to their land use capability. This implies reduction of idle and waste lands in each region to the minimum by suitable reclamation and land improvement measures on the one hand, and securing such alterations in the existing pattern of land use as are necessary for raising productivity or for conservation of soil and water on the other.

Under improving methods of land use Nath includes provision of irrigation, the whole range of improved agricultural practices, as also effective pasture management and forest management.

Nath next turns to settlement patterns with Chapter 16 being in two parts looking at settlement patterns in various parts of India between 1950 and 2000 and thereafter making related projections for 2021 AD.

Settlement and population densities are linked to level of development. Measures like abolition of *zamindari* and *jagirdari*, development of irrigation facilities and provision of easy credit, and agricultural inputs, steps to encourage adoption of improved practices and enabling of technological enhancements leading to enhanced agriculture production have substantially increased demand for labour in certain areas, as also enabled agro-industrial growth. This naturally effects settlement, migration and population densities. In many areas agriculture extension and social and commercial services (marketing of crops and supply of inputs for high productivity agriculture) are organized from larger villages which become small towns in course of time. There has also been a tendency for urban populations to concentrate in metropolitan cities and their satellite cities. Of course, emigration to the Arabian Gulf has also occurred.

Looking at different regions and states Nath has sketched out a picture of population density differences across the country and discussed various types of sparsely populated areas and why they have remained sparely peopled.

Development during the last 50 years has led to increases in agricultural and industrial output and rise in employment opportunities and incomes. Facilities for education and for preventive health care have also been expended. The aspirations of both the urban and rural populations have undergone change.

However differences in incomes and levels of living between the already developed and comparatively prosperous areas and those of the poor and underdeveloped areas particularly those inhabited by tribal people have increased. Also it has not been possible for government to provide sufficient infrastructure either in metropolitan and other cities, or in the rural areas.

As regards projections for 2021, Nath envisages increasing

urbanization, concentration of population in metropolitan cities, and the growth of large villages into small towns particularly in areas where productivity of land is high, both public sector and private sector units trying to set up units near large cities and locating their headquarters in large cities, the creation of more districts through the bifurcation of large and populous districts and the emergence and development of new district towns, some slowing down in the rate of population increase in large metropolitan cities like Mumbai, Ahmedabad and Delhi and dispersal of some of their population to their satellite cities, an increase in the proportion of urban population, the decline of small villages as large villages become towns, and the increasing importance of rail and road communications.

Nath also expects regional disparities in density of population to continue. This naturally takes us to the next section (Section IV) on Population, Natural Resources Management and Developing Planning in India. Of the five chapters in this Section three (Chapters 17, 18 and 19) look at India's high population and population growth rates and the use of natural resources especially in the agriculture sector to look at the prospects of being able to meet the food etc. needs of the countries increasing population, while two (Chapters 19 and 20) look at the 1991 and 2001, population Censuses in India regarding some results of the decennial censuses and policy issues involved.

Chapter 17 contains a 1967 assessment, along with a longish postscript of 2002, of the relationship between population growth and economic (and particularly agricultural) development in the Indian context. Nath points out that due to India's large and growing population, its development planning and policies have necessarily had to focus on agriculture production not as a means for capital accumulation, but simply to prevent, starvation, maintain a healthier labour force and to discourage rural, and therefore national, unrest. However concern with inadequacy of natural resources as the limiting factor in economic development has progressively diminished as development of new lands and rapid technological advance have made available increasing quantities of food and natural resource based materials or their synthetic substitutes. Nath refers to a low level of per capita income, extremely low levels of food consumption resulting in widespread malnutrition and under nutrition, very small holdings, presence of a large number of landless or near landless cultivators and large scale unemployment among a predominantly agricultural and rural population, and limited natural and social resources resulting in the high pressure of population upon agriculture and agricultural resources.

Initially expansion of cropped area was more emphasized, but gradually attention shifted to increases in productivity with efforts being made as regards developing irrigation, promoting use of modern inputs, attempts at concentration of resources for "intensive cultivation" in some selected areas considered more conducive for agriculture (like Intensive Agriculture District Programme) etc. Nath was concerned with disproving earlier pessimistic assessments of India's capacity to be able to raise its agricultural output to meet future needs of India's rapidly increasing population.

In the 2002 postscript, Nath could vindicate his earlier optimism pointing out how the arrival of high yielding crop varieties, development of irrigation facilities, changes in the geography of crop production, etc. and increases in production of foodgrains and other crops have gone hand in hand with increase in literacy, improved health, access to improved domestic water supply, rural development programmes for building the infrastructure for rapid agriculture development, and improved availability of electricity and means of communications.

Chapter 18 is in some ways an extension of Chapter 17 and looks at both the rapid growth of population and continued concentration of the labour force in agriculture where productivity per worker is much lower than in the non-agriculture sectors. Nath advocates measures to slow down population growth, raise productivity per worker in agriculture, bring about increases in agriculture production, reducing the disparity in productivity between urban and rural workers, reducing the gap between the gross irrigated area and irrigation potential, increasing the efficiency of HYF techniques to increase productivity per hectare and per worker, increasing productivity in unirrigated areas, reducing rural poverty, checking deforestation, undertaking forestry and related soil conservation measures, promoting rural industrialization and the development of industries in small towns, increasing literacy and skill formation as well as diffusion of skills amongst rural workers.

Chapter 19 continues in similar vein focusing on agricultural growth under high population pressure in India. Nath states that India's plan programmes for increasing agriculture output have had four main components: (i) extension of irrigation through programmes ranging from construction of large storage and canal projects to assistance to farmers and rural communities to construct, renovate or modernize small irrigation works such as tanks, wells, tube-wells and the like, (ii) creation of a countrywide extension and supplies system of organizations meant to take to the farmers knowledge of improved techniques and supplies of essential inputs such as good seeds, chemical fertilizers and pesticides, (iii) a major expansion of cooperative credit to provide to the farmers credit at low rates of interest, and (iv) land reforms specifically abolition of intermediary tenure such as *zamindari* and giving rights in lands to the actual cultivators, and providing increased security of tenure to the cultivator land owners.

After examining the official strategy and experience of the Green Revolution and thereafter, Nath concludes that (a) suitable modern capital-and-technology-intensive techniques can be successfully introduced in peasant economies with high population pressures, (b) diffusion of such techniques can be rapid, (c) that the employment reducing and social-polarization effects of adopting the techniques about which much concern has been expressed may have been over-estimated, and (d) the increase in agricultural output and incomes resulting from use of the techniques have created significant new opportunities for raising the economic levels of the poorer groups within agriculture.

Interest in decennial censuses of population is mainly on account of their being the most comprehensive and authoritative records of demographic and associated socio-economic changes in the country during a decade. The census is an administrative undertaking of enormous magnitude and complexity, the largest administrative undertaking in India and one of the largest in the world. The 1991 census of population in India involved participation of 1.7 million volunteer enumerators and supervisors in conducting the enumeration, and staff numbering thousands in the offices of the Registrar General and Census Commissioner of India, the Directors of Census Operations in the States and Union Territories and in census cells in District Collectorates for compilation and analysis of the census data and preparation of various reports and other publications. It also involved willing cooperation of about 200 million heads of households all over the country in furnishing the data about themselves, their household and their houses as required for the census. Nath points out that the enumerators who interview the people often do not understand the significance of many of the questions that they ask the people. The people who respond to the questions may, because of political reasons or social inhibitions, be reluctant to give correct answers to various questions. Despite these limitations, various surveys conducted after every census since 1951 have revealed that the margin of error in the data collected during census is no more than 1 to 1½ per cent.

Nath reminds the readers that in most developed countries of the world the census is a technical undertaking. In India however it is an administrative undertaking and Nath feels there are valid reasons for the preference for getting the census conducted by administrative offices who of course receive advice from Advisory Committees consisting of demographers, economists and other social scientists.

In September 1991 and December 1991, Nath had reviewed in *Economic and Political Weekly* the first two provisional result monographs of the 1991 Census issued by the Registrar General and Census Commissioner of India. Subsequently he analyzed the results of the 1991 Census and some policy implications of the results. These three jointly constitute Chapter 20 of this book. Similarly a research note on the Census in India looking back at the 1991 Census and forward to the 2001 Censuses published in 1998, and Dr. Nath's regional analysis of the first results of the decennial Census 2001 have been combined in Chapter 21. While going through Chapters 20 and 21 readers may also like to refer to the companion volume *Urbanization Urban Development and Metropolitan Cities in India by V. Nath* (ed.) S.K. Aggarwal, Concept Publishing Co. Pvt. Ltd., New Delhi, 2007) and the oft quoted Roy Turner's book *India's Urban Future* (University of California, 1962) which Nath has also cited repeatedly.

Taking Chapter 19 first, Nath informs us that planning for the 1991 Census had commenced in 1987. In addition to consulting a number of advisory and consultative committees of experts etc. the advice of a Data Users Committee comprising representatives of Planning Commission and Central Ministries like education and health and family planning which make the most use of census data was also obtained before census schedules were finalized. House-listing was done in various states and Union Territories between April and September 1990, six to nine months before enumeration. Actual enumeration lasted 3 weeks in February 1991 ending by March 1st. Detailed reports are published 1-3 years after the Census. However, three monographs of preliminary findings were published in 1991 itself.

The provisional total population was found to be 9.1 per cent below projections made by the population division of United Nations in 1988. The average exponential growth rate during 1981-1991 was marginally lower than that of each of the previous two decades. There is large scale inter-State variation in the average exponential growth rate. There was a progressive decline in sex ratio. Some increase was seen in literacy rate. The number of metropolitan cities took a quantum jump from 12 in 1981 to 21 in 1991. The proportion of urban population living in metropolitan cities has risen faster than the proportion of population living is all cities. There is large variation in the populations of various States and Union

Territories as well as great disparity in the levels of economic development among different regions of large states along with differences in ethnic composition of their populations.

This had led Nath to again raise the issue of need for territorial reorganization or creation of smaller states which he had made in Section II of the book. Failing that Nath suggests large and effective devolution of powers and functions along with transfer of funds from State Government to lower levels; and the revitalization of Panchayati Raj. This also had been commented upon by Nath in Section II of this book. Nath also suggests the need for creation of a politico-administrative institution such as a divisional development committee with a wide range of powers—though he realizes that it may not be easy to achieve wide ranging and effective devolution of powers and functions from the State to the divisional level. (This commentator may add that administratively the Divisional Commissioner's division is a somewhat weak link in the administrative chain, and is even non-existent, in some States; similarly integrated Command Area Development divisional structures have failed to emerge in most states—though somewhat effective tribal development divisions to exist in some States).

The provisional 1991 Census figures of urban population is 13 to 19 million lower than the figure of earlier projections. There is however a tendency for the urban population to concentrate in the larger cities leading to increase in both number of cities and of million plus cities. The growth rate of cities and large towns has been significantly higher than the rates of growth of small towns. Part of the increase in the populations of large cities is due to spatial expansion of their agglomerations to include large number of towns and villages. Thus a large number of administrative units become part of each such agglomeration resulting in problems of coordinated planning for them since all the administrative units must be involved in plan formulation for the agglomeration.

There is need to confine the strategy of developing a large number of small towns for accelerating economic growth to less urbanized, relatively backward States where such towns would be developed primarily by upgrading larger villages to become '*mandi*' towns.

The needs for investment in urban development, both total and per capita, are much larger in larger cities than in smaller cities.

Economic liberalization is likely to provide further stimulus to growth of large cities with populations of a million or more, or even of two to five million or more.

Nath also points out that in the early 1960s there had been much discussion by planners and economists concerned with location of industries, and from those preparing urban development plans, on the most appropriate spatial patterns of urbanization for India. This had led to official interventions to promote dispersed industrial development, to accelerate development of backward regions, and to promote small scale and agro-based industries. However, subsequently official interest in this issue of industrial location and urbanization has waned.

Nath has also noted the emergence of a number of urban corridors in the country.

Turning to Chapter 21 and the 2001 Census the average exponential growth rate of the population has been found to be falling for two successive decades. This has been accompanied by progressive decline in total fertility rate. However, there was great variation amongst various states in the annual rates of growth of population during 1991-2001. There has been significant decline in infant mortality and increase in expectation of life at birth. The literacy rate (65.4 per cent) during 2000-2001 was nearly 25 per cent higher than the 1990-91 rate of 52 per cent. One result of the increase in literacy has been the phenomenal growth of print media.

Though the growth rate of population has declined during 1991-2001 there has been a rapid increase in per capita income.

The total urban population increased by 32 per cent during the decade. Urban population in 2000-2001 was 27.8 per cent of the total population, while the corresponding ratio in 1990-91 was 25.7 per cent.

The prospect for the next 15 years (2001-2015) is for significant decline in growth rate of population, and progressive increase in literacy rate and in per capita income. The proportion of urban total population is expected to increase from 28 per cent in 2000-2001 to 35 to 36 per cent by 2015-2016.

Nath indicates that as a result "the average Indian will be living longer, will be better fed, better clothed and probably better housed, and much more informed than his/her predecessor of 15 years ago."

The present volume concludes with a single chapter section (Section V) that looks back at the experience of 50 years of planning between 1950 and 2000.

Nath reminds that through the process of economic development while GDP may increase at a faster rate than earlier, some economic or social groups gain at the expense of others.

With regard to India, Nath reminds us that during the 1930s the National Planning Committee set up by the Indian National Congress had brought out a number of studies on various sectors of the economy. A group of industrialists and businessmen produced the Bombay Plan (a Twenty Year Plan 1945-65) in 1945. The British Government also produced a Ten Year Plan for reconstruction of the economy after the Second World War. Following independence development planning was undertaken officially and the Planning Commission was established in January 1950.

Accordingly to Nath the goals and policies for development at national and state levels have included : (1) increase in Gross Domestic Product through expansion of output in agriculture, industries and services, (2) alleviation/eradication of poverty programmes to supplement incomes and provide employment in non-irrigated areas and to expand and improve rural infrastructures and undertake soil conservation and land reclamation works, (3) eradicate literacy, increase enrolment and attendance in primary schools, undertake programmes of adult education, (4) provide preventive and curative health care for all within easy reach in villages and in cities —providing special health related facilities for women, (5) improvement and expansion of urban infrastructure (electricity, water supply, disposal of solid and liquid wastes, intra-city roads), (6) assistance for self-help housing for people of low and middle income groups in cities and villages—relocation and improvement of slums in cities, (7) provision of vocational education, (8) training for work in traditional handicrafts as well as in sunrise industries, (9) development of large and small scale industries and khadi and village industries, (10) fixing prices of chemical fertilizers, of petroleum products, of minimum support prices, of food-grains to protect incomes of farmers, of items distributed to the poor through the public distribution system, (11) privatization of public enterprise, (12) improve efficiency in operation of nationalized banks, (13) reduce corruption in government at national, state and local levels.

Nath has also described how the focus shifted between sectors from one five year plan to another (for example agriculture and rural development in the First Five Year Plan, industrialization and heavy industries at the cost of agriculture in the Second and Third Five Year Plans) though the State Governments continued to invest in agriculture and rural development including rural infrastructure like roads. How "the fever of nationalization" continued during the 1960s. How during the period 1970 to 1990 efforts of Government were concentrated on minimizing the losses of public enterprises in order to provide funds for expansion of infrastructure. In the 1990s planning got reduced to outlining policies and programmes through whose adoption Government could ensure that balance of payments position remains positive and India does not land in a position similar to the one in 1991 when foreign exchange reserves were exhausted.

Nath states that in India there is now a consensus that most of the industries and infrastructures such as distribution and transmission of power and water supply, and telecommunications are better managed by companies rather than by government. Accordingly the country still persists in making Five Year Plans and fixing targets of achievement in different sectors. The Plans also serve as a means for coordinating the development plans of different States and Union territories. But the Plans have to be moulded as per the balance of payments and fiscal situation in the country, and the international situation.

Nath also indicates that following India's lead most of the developed countries of South and South East Asia and Africa prepared five year plans. Many of them still persist with five year plans. But like in India, there too planning has undergone a change in character.

One wonders what would have been Dr. Nath's reaction had he lived to witness the scenario post the global economic melt down of 2008 which discredited the "Washington Consensus" of relying upon market forces and the private sector along with reducing the role of government. Governments the world over, and in India, had to scramble to put into place stimulus and rescue package. Some observers suggested that the fact that India had a number of nationalized banks helped alleviate the situation in India. The importance of public spending programmes like Mahatma Gandhi National Rural Employment Guarantee Act for the economy has been recognized. Private businesses have contracted. Reliance on export based growth has perforce reduced. Increased governmental regulation and governmental actions to spur the economy as well as increased welfareism is being advocated by many. Thus the pendulum has swung back to quite some extant towards belief in the need for developmental or government planning rather than relying on the market for development.

Thus some of issues raised by Nath throughout this book which had started to appear academic or historic in nature, have again regained relevance.

Many of the insights, views and ideas expressed by Nath throughout this volume need to be understood, reflected upon and debated extensively in today's context. This introduction is meant to whet the appetite of the reader to read the volume and to deliberate upon the contents, which reflect Dr. Nath's useful writings on the subject over a period of 40 years.

Section I

Development Planning and Administration : Theory and Practice in Developing Countries

1

Planning and Administration in Developing Countries

Introduction

National economic development planning has been undertaken in a large number of countries in the post-war period. In the underdeveloped countries, it has been regarded as an essential instrument of directing the transformation of the economies from underdeveloped to developed, and of societies from traditional to modern. It has been believed that planning, with its concomitant definition of goals of development, formulation of programmes and projects for achievement of the goals, and direction of resource allocation and of economic activity, offers the most suitable means of optimizing the development process. Most underdeveloped countries have set up national planning agencies, though the nature of the plans formulated in different countries has varied very greatly, from comprehensive national economic development plans (often based on sophisticated programming models), to investment programmes of the public sector, or even collections of projects.

The introduction of planning has been accompanied in these countries by a large increase in the activities of governments. This has resulted from the following :

(i) Large expansion of existing social services, such as education and health and introduction of new services such as agricultural extension and social security;

(ii) Establishment of industrial, infrastructure (power, transport and communication), foreign trade, and other enterprises by governments, either on their own or in association with private entrepreneurs;

(iii) Introduction of social, political and institutional reforms, such as agrarian reforms; and

(iv) Implementation of monetary, fiscal and regulatory measures, needed for mobilizing resources for plan implementation, directing investment, or for other purposes.

The functions and responsibilities assumed by governments have been so large in the underdeveloped countries, for two reasons :

(i) First, these countries are undergoing development in a social-intellectual environment in which the obligations and responsibilities of governments are expected to be much larger than they were a century ago, when the Western countries were developing. Social services, such as education and health, and infrastructure such as power and transport, in organizing development of which there was considerable private initiative in the Western countries, are now accepted as the responsibilities of governments. Besides, new services and welfare activities such as agricultural extension, and social security, and regulatory activities such as price control and rationing of essential consumer goods, which were not considered important earlier, are now considered essential. Government initiative in planning and its responsibility for national economic development are themselves the products of the changed environment.

(ii) Secondly, governments have to take the initiative in many fields because of absence or extreme shortage of private entrepreneurs. The most notable example is in the field of industry. Governments in many underdeveloped countries undertake industrial projects, not because of ideological reasons, but only because no private entrepreneurs are willing or able to undertake them. Rapid technological advance is also increasing the need for participation of governments in industrial and other enterprises. As a result of the advance, the size and requirements of capital and technical and managerial personnel of the most efficient enterprises are increasing continuously, so much so that the government is often the only agency in an underdeveloped country which can assemble (even with foreign assistance) the capital and the personnel needed for an efficient enterprise.

But the initial enthusiastic introduction of planning and rapid expansion of activities of governments, have been followed, more recently, in many countries by dissatisfaction and disillusionment with planning and development. These have resulted from experiences of shortfalls in achievement of plan targets; delays in completion or overruns in costs of projects; inefficient operation of public services or public sector enterprises, laxity in administration of fiscal, regulatory or reform measures and corruption, etc. The plans have not fulfilled the initial expectations from them and the development process is seen to be considerably longer, more difficult and more costly, than had been anticipated. In some countries, these experiences have been followed by reappraisal of plans and of the planning practice. An important finding of such reappraisals is that the shortfalls, delays, and other deficiencies were due, in large part, to administrative shortcomings, which in turn arose from the fact that the administration was not equipped to undertake the tasks and to fulfil the responsibilities, given to it under the plans. The administrative requirements of plan implementation were not adequately assessed at the timc of plan formulation and appropriate and adequate measures of expansion, reorganization or reorientation of the administration were not taken. The experience has emphasized the importance of the relationship between planning and administration, and of administration as the essential instrument of plan implementation. As a result, the need for systematic assessment of administrative capability for implementation of plan, and formulation of measures of administrative expansion or reform to meet the needs of plan implementation, are coming to be regarded as an essential part of plan formulation.

The relation between planning and administration is close and many-sided. Planning for national economic development is a politico-administrative process. The decision to plan is a political decision of the government, and the goals, objectives, policies, and programmes of the plan also incorporate political, economic and social programmes of the political group or party which is in power in the country. If the party has broad-based political support, the goals and objectives reflect popular aspirations and felt needs; otherwise, they represent the aspirations and objectives of small power elite. The latter is the case in many underdeveloped countries, where the government is composed of small, generally western-educated elites, while the rest of the population is illiterate, ignorant or even primitive.

Implementation of the plan is an administrative task, in which the entire government is involved, directly or indirectly. Even departments and agencies, which are not concerned directly with implementation of any particular programme or project, contribute to it or retard it in important ways, by their attitudes or methods of operation. The judiciary and the law enforcement agencies are two branches of government which have no direct responsibility of plan implementation. But their attitudes and methods have an important influence on plan implementation. A judiciary which is not sympathetic to the objectives and policies of the plan can seriously hinders its implementation, e.g. by rejecting some of the fiscal, regulatory or reform measures taken by the government. Many governments have had to undertake reform of the judiciary or to change its top personnel, in order to implement the plan. The security of life and property, provided by efficient law enforcement agencies are essential for efficient operation of industrial and commercial enterprises, and for stimulating private investment, by local or foreign investors. Inefficient operation of enterprises and low rates of investment are due, in many countries, to the failure of the law enforcement agencies to provide such security.

Reference has been made above to the need for expansion of the administration, to implement the plan. Equally necessary are reorganization, reorientation or reform. These include changes in administrative structures, processes and methods of working, and in attitudes of officials. Not only must new administrative structures (Departments, Bureaus, Enterprises), be set up to undertake new activities, but patterns of communication, coordination and control within the administration must also undergo important changes. Finally, the attitudes of officials and the values that permeate the working of government must change. Such changes are particularly necessary in underdeveloped countries which were colonies or in which the government had been dominated by native feudal elite groups.

The Administrative Problem in the Underdeveloped Countries

The administrative problems of plan formulation and implementation in the underdeveloped countries arise primarily from the vast gap between the administrative requirements of plans of national economic development, and the capabilities, attitudes, and practices of the pre-existing administrations.

In most of the colonial countries, the administrations had very limited functions focused on collection of taxes and creating transport and other facilities needed to facilitate exploitation of the natural and human resources of the countries for the benefit of the metropolitan country. The attitudes of the top civil servants and practices in the administrations, oriented towards ruling subject peoples, were quite inappropriate for economic development. Moreover, the administrations were depleted of their key administrative and technical personnel, when the countries became independent : the higher echelons and technical branches had been manned predominantly by the nationals of the metropolitan countries, most of whom left at this time. Their departure created a serious gap in the administrations, filling which was the first pre-occupation for the new national governments. It proved particularly difficult in countries in which the educational system was undeveloped and the number of educated persons was small. Such a situation was encountered in many countries of Africa and some of Asia: many of them have had to import even teachers and clerks to run public services. But even in countries like India, Pakistan and Ceylon, in which the educational systems were well-developed, the number of educated persons was large, and the administrations had been manned predominantly by the nationals for long periods before Independence, the departure of the colonial administrators left a gap at the top decision-making levels, at which the colonial administrators were predominant. Their places were taken by nationals who, since they had not been used to exercise of so much responsibility and powers, took time in developing appropriate initiative and capacity. The "deficiency of decisions", which is considered by Hirschman (Hirchman, 1964, Chapter 1) to be the most serious deficiency of the LDCs, was encountered for this reason even in these countries.

In non-colonial LDCs, the administrative problem was different, but not necessarily less serious. In most of them, governments, had long been in the hands of small, feudalistic elite groups, which had besides political power and social prestige, control over most economic resources of the country. The functions and attitudes of public administration or/and values of the administrators in these countries were no less growth inhibiting than those of the colonial countries. In most of them the administrative situation was less favourable for economic development than in the colonial countries, because the administrations lacked the method, order, discipline and efficiency characteristic of the latter. Since the education systems were undeveloped and the numbers of educated persons were small, the problems of shortages of educated and trained persons were also not different in most of these countries from those in the former colonies. Of course, they were enormous inter-country differences among them, as among the colonial countries; there was enormous variation—

from Iran and several Latin American countries with relatively developed administrations, to countries such as Yemen, in which administration, in its modern sense, just did not exist.

Administration as a Resource and as the Environment of Planning

The concept of administrations as a resource for planning is useful. It highlights the need for assessment of the administrative capabilities of plan implementation at the time of plan formulation and of proposing measures for increasing the resource and removing deficiencies, as is done in case of the other plan resources. Further, it focuses attention on the need for efficient utilization of the resources, and in particular, its most critical elements, such as top administrative and management personnel. Assessment of administrative capability, along with other resources in plan formulation, will make a major contribution to improving efficiency of plan formulation. For one thing, it will avoid formulation of large, unrealistic plans for implementation of which administrative capability is completely lacking in the underdeveloped countries.

But administration is not merely a resource of planning : it is, along with the political structure, the immediate environment in which plans are formulated and implemented. The procedures, practices, attitudes, and values of the administration affect plan formulation and implementation at every step. The administration is a product of the Social-Economic-and-Political (SEP) environment of the country; but it is that part of the environment, which interacts most directly with the plan. It is true that the administrative practices, attitudes, etc., change in the course of planned development, both as a conscious response to the needs of planning, and as a result of the social, economic and political changes resulting from economic development. Planning, administration, and the social-economic-political environment may, therefore, be regarded as constituents of a mutually interacting system. This broader concept is useful for two reasons :

(i) It helps appreciation of the fact that administration practices, deficiencies and inadequacies are related to the social-economic-and-political environment of the country, and cannot be changed fundamentally without changes in the latter. Thus, in societies in which most social relationships, and patterns of social interaction, are by kinship, tribal or caste groups, it is unrealistic to expect that efficiency or economy criterion will be given precedence over considerations of kin, tribe or caste in such plan implementation decisions as filling a top administrative post, or award of a contract for a project. Similarly, in countries in which salaries of officials are low and the gap between their actual level of living and the desired standard of living is large, a certain amount of corruption is to be expected, especially at the lower levels of government. Appreciation of the relationship helps the policy-makers keep deficiencies like nepotism, corruption and inefficiency in proper perspective, make allowance for them in formulation of plans and programmes and realize both the potential and the limitations of the purely administrative measures that may be taken to remove them.

(ii) It brings out the limitations of purely quantitative assessment of administrative capability, and emphasizes the need for going beyond such an assessment to consideration of vital qualitative aspects, such as decision-making.

Planning and the Structure of Government

I. The Executive

The principal constituents of the structure of government are the executive, the legislature and the judiciary. Plan formulation and implementation are the responsibilities primarily of the executive, and are organized within it. Moreover, the impact of planning by way of expansion, reorganization and re-orientation of the administration, to which reference has been made earlier, is also felt primarily by the executive. The legislature and the judiciary have limited, though extremely important, roles in relation to planning, which are described briefly in a separate section.

Planning is a new activity of governments. It is an intruder in the structures and processes of governance, and requires for its success, major changes in them. Planning requires :

(i) Establishment of new structures such as the central planning agency, and planning units in the ministries, departments, enterprises and at regional and local levels;

(ii) Establishment of new procedures and patterns of interaction, among different agencies of the government, and between official agencies and private sector enterprises and the public; and

(iii) Changes in attitudes among both officials and non-officials. Planning may alter significantly the relative importance of different ministries and departments. It may give new powers or impose new obligations and responsibilities on some ministries/departments and reduce the roles and functions of others, and create new foci of power and influence. The functions and powers of the economic ministries, Finance in particular, increase greatly with planning.

The typical organization of the executive is by ministries or departments, each dealing with a particular function or sector. There are functional ministries/departments such as Finance, and sectoral ones such as Agriculture, Health and Education. Further, within each ministry or department line administration and vertical communication (i.e. downward, or upward, in the chain of authority) are predominant. Planning introduces new pattern of communication and interaction in the system.

Plan formulation requires

(i) Detailed data on various aspects of the economy, sectors industries, projects, etc., which must be supplied by different ministries/departments, either by processing existing data or by conducting new survey, technical and economic studies, feasibility studies of projects, etc.
(ii) Intensive communication and consultation among ministries/departments and branches within each ministry/department.

Plan implementation requires, similarly, coordination at inter-sectoral, intra-sectoral, regional and local levels which can only be achieved by interaction among the different executive agencies concerned with plan implementation.

Accordingly, plan formulation and implementation result in an enormous increase in staff functions (assessment, formulation of policies and programmes, and coordination) and horizontal communication and collection of relevant data for planning.

Planning as an Intruder

The disturbances in established foci on power and departures from established practices and procedures are resented and opposed by the top echelons (ministers, head of departments) of governments in many countries. There is opposition to submission of data to the planning agencies, which is due partly to the additional work involved in collecting and processing the data. There is even greater opposition to coordination by planning agencies. Some ministers/head of departments may be unhappy with increases in the functions and responsibilities of their ministries/departments, finding the increases burdensome. More frequently, there is resentment against the restriction of their own 'freedom' and 'greatly increased power' of the planning agencies and the Ministry of Finance. The Ministry of Finance, on its part, may consider the resource allocation and coordination functions of the Central planning agency, an uncalled for intrusion in its traditional sphere of responsibility. This is particularly the case in countries such as India and Pakistan, in which the Ministries of Finance, patterned after the model of the British Treasury, were performing these functions.

Accordingly, the establishment of the Central planning agency and other planning structures and initiation of planning have evoked serious opposition from the Ministers and top officials of the governments, in many countries and instances of friction between the Ministries/ Departments and the planning agencies are very common. Indeed, smooth introduction of the structures and processes of planning into the government, has been rare. In several countries because of opposition from within the government towards setting up of the Central Planning Agency (CPA) planning has been rendered completely ineffective. In many other countries, planning and the planning agencies have been able to survive in the face of strong opposition from within the government, only because of the support given to them by the chief executive. In some other countries, planning and the planners have survived under administrative arrangements, and in forms which make their survival of limited value.

Part of the difficulty arises from the differences between Ministers and Heads of Department, and the staff of the Central planning agencies in matters of age, training and background. Most frequently, the latter are young foreign-trained economists and econometricians with no experience of administration and with inadequate knowledge of the social and economic conditions of the country, or of the problems of particular sector. Ministers and senior officials are unwilling to accept such persons in the coordination role of planners and of advisers in formulation of policies. The difficulties are increased by the difficulties of communication between the two groups. The Ministers and senior officials have little knowledge (and less appreciation) of the new, sophisticated techniques and models used by the planners, and feel that the latter's ignorance of local conditions is a fatal handicap to their ability to plan.

II. The Legislature and the Judiciary

The Legislature

The role of the Legislature in relation to planning could be summarized as follows:

(i) To influence formulation of goals, objectives, and principal policies and programmes of the plan, by reflecting the needs, aspirations, and expectations of the people;
(ii) To examine, criticize, modify and approve the plan, and to indicate needs for modifications in it, from time to time;
(iii) To approve policy instruments and measures, e.g. legislation for structural reforms, price and distribution controls and establishment of new administrative agencies, needed for plan formulation and implementation; and
(iv) To examine plan implementation.

Detailed examination of the plan by the Legislature is essential for ensuring that the goals and programmes of the plan reflect the needs and aspirations of the people, and are in accord with the Constitution of the country and the broad framework of social and economic policies. However, for meaningful examination by the Legislators and reflection of their views, it is essential that the plan is submitted to it at important stages of formulation, e.g. preliminary formulation of goals and policies, draft and final. Such examination and reflection are not possible if only the final plan is submitted to the Legislature for approval. The scope for changes at this stage is limited, and the Legislators have, rightly, the feeling that they are not really associated with plan formulation and are only expected to rubber stamp their approval of a finished product. This feeling developed in France, because the plans were presented to the Parliament only for final approval.

Detailed examination of the plan, plan implementation, and of the instruments of plan formulation and implementation is generally done in committees of the Legislature. The committees may be general, e.g. for planning and economic policy, or sectoral.

Individual legislators are often interested in the plan only to the extent of getting included in it particular projects or programmes which are of particular benefit to their constituencies. Such interest is legitimate in a democracy even though it is seldom possible for planners to satisfy more than a small proportion of such expectations and desires. Individual legislators (and political parties) have also an important role in explaining to the people the objectives, scope, policies, programmes, benefits, constraints of the plan, preparing them for participation in the plan, both by availing of the benefits (e.g. of schools and health centres, of cooperatives and extension services by farmers) and shouldering their obligations (e.g. payment of taxes, fulfilment of work norms in socialist countries).

The plan may be approved by the legislature through a resolution, as is done in India, or it may be enacted into a Law, as is done in Yugoslavia and several other countries. The practice varies with the socio-institutional structure of the country, and the status of the plan. The Indian practice allows flexibility and facilitates modifications in the plan, because the government, while committed to the plan, is not legally bound to each and every project or detail in it. It is perhaps the most practical procedure under the Constitution of India and framework of judicial institutions. Giving to the plan the status of law, could seriously embarrass the government, and hamper implementation, because every modification could be challenged in the law courts. The Yugoslav practice is based on the fact that the annual plan (which is the operational plan) has the status of the Budget.

Political Parties

Political parties have a vital interest in planning : the plan represents, to a large extent, the economic and social philosophy, and programmes of the party in power. But for success of planning in democratic countries with a multi-party system it is essential also that the plan is accepted as a national plan rather than a party plan. In other words, while different parties may differ on particular programmes (or even policies) there should be broad agreement among them on the basic philosophy, goals, and policies for development, and the plan should be accepted as reflecting these. It is difficult to achieve such agreement and acceptance : the difficulties are particularly serious in underdeveloped countries, in which the party system is just being established; there is little experience with inter-party relations; the distinction between the interests of the party and the nation is imperfectly understood—this is particularly the case in countries where one party had been in power since Independence—and there is a tendency towards formulation of party goals and policies in extremist terms. But achievement of such agreement and acceptance is also particularly important in underdeveloped countries, because most of them are new nations, the feeling of a national identity (as distinct from tribal, regional, or sectarian loyalties) is not well developed, and serious conflicts between political parties can jeopardize the existence of the nation.

In democratic countries, there is no direct contact between the planners and the political parties, and the latter make their viewpoints known and their influence felt through their representatives in legislatures and local government institutions, and the press. But in the centrally planned economies, the Communist Party has direct and intimate contact with planning and a very important role in both plan formulation and implementation. The basic goals, objectives, and programmes of the plan are formulated by the top leadership of the party, acting in concert with the top leadership of the Government. And, party executives at every level are active in formulation of policies and programmes, explaining the plan to the workers and citizens, and ensuring fulfilment of the plan. This is facilitated by the fact that key policy and executive positions at every level are occupied by members of the party. In Yugoslavia, however, while the party had a similar role in the period of centralized administrative planning, its role is now more limited and indirect, and the party members are expected to participate in plan formulation and implementation in their individual capacities, and to facilitate implementation through persuasion.

The Judiciary

The principal role of the judiciary in relation to planning in democratic countries is to act as a custodian of the people, *vis-à-vis* the executive and the legislature. Plan formulation and implementation leads to an enormous increase in legislation and in the activities of the executive. The judiciary must ensure that the new laws are in accordance with the Constitution of the country, and do not limit, curtail or take away the rights of the citizens and that in framing the rules the executive does not go beyond the provisions of the main law.

Planning confers varied benefits on the people, and at the same time imposes obligations and, frequently, restrictions. The latter, such as control over prices, distribution of essential commodities, foreign exchange, and foreign travel are necessary because planning seeks to increase the rates of investment and growth in the economy and is characterized by shortage of resources. The judiciary must ensure that the benefits are equitably distributed, and that no class or group of citizens is unreasonably denied these. Even more, it must ensure that the burdens and obligations are equitably shared, and that implementation of the restrictive measures does not lead to undue curtailment of individual liberty or cause undue hardship.

There are many instances of important legislation passed for implementation of policies not being accepted by the judiciary. Thus, some of the land reform legislation, enacted in India in the early 1950s was declared unconstitutional by the Supreme Court, and the Constitution had to be amended and new legislation passed. Instances of particular actions of the executive being overruled by the judiciary are everyday occurrences in most countries.

An unduly conservative or unhelpful judiciary could seriously obstruct plan implementation. But instances of this kind are rare and this possible disadvantage of judicial review is accepted as the necessary cost of the protection that judicial review gives to the citizens. The main drawback of judicial review is that it is slow, cumbersome and expensive and can only relate to a very small fraction of the cases of executive excess or public grievance. To remedy this defect, and to afford to the public opportunities of complaint against the executive, and redress of grievance outside the judicial system, the institution of ombudsman has been created in many countries.

REFERENCE

Hirchman, A.O. : *The Strategy of Economic Development,* Yale. 1964.

2

Organization of Planning—Administrative Structures and Processes

The administrative structures and processes of plan formulation and plan implementation are described in three sections. The relations among the structures are discussed, very briefly, at the end of the section. The description relates primarily to mixed economy countries; the structures and processes in centrally planned economies have distinctive features, which are brought out best through descriptions of the organization of planning in the Soviet Union and Yugoslavia, given in Chapter 3.

Administrative Structures for Plan Formulation

The principal administrative structures for plan formulation can be listed as follows :

(i) The central planning agency (CPA),
(ii) Planning structures in ministries and enterprises, and
(iii) Planning structures at regional and local levels.

The Central Planning Agency

The central planning agency is at the apex of the planning structures in a country and has the responsibility of formulation of the national development plan, coordinating in the process, sectoral plans on the one hand and territorial plans on the other. Establishment of the central planning agency is usually the first step in initiation of planning in most countries. However, there is great variation in their functions, composition, status and relationships with the executive organs of the governments. These variations are related partly to differences in social and economic conditions, but mainly to differences in the conceptions of the decision-makers on the nature and scope of planning and the role and functions of the planning agency. Faulty conception is, along with opposition to the agency from the existing government agencies, the principal reason for failure of planning in a number of countries.

Functions: The primary function of the CPA is formulation of the national plan. It involves:

(i) Studies of various aspects of the economy, preparation of macro-economic surveys, preparation of growth models (overall and sectoral, long, medium and short-term), and studies of inter-sectoral relationships.

(ii) Coordination of sectoral programmes.

(iii) Assessment of resources—financial, manpower, material and natural—with a view to relating demands with availabilities.

(iv) It is usually associated also with formulation of major economic policies. Such association is essential because
   (a) the plan is the most important expression of the economic and social policies of the government, and
   (b) implementation of the plan involves a large amount of detailed policy formulation.

(v) Appraisal of progress of the plan is another essential function of the CPA; the CPA can indicate the needs for adjustments and revisions in the plan, suggest alternative strategies or draw up alternative plans, only if it has adequate and relevant data on progress.

But the CPA should not take upon itself the functions of either detailed formulation of policies and programmes, or of plan implementation which are, appropriately, the responsibilities of the ministries, and other executive organs of government. Taking up these functions brings the CPA into conflict with the executive organs, and also detracts from its primary functions of plan formulation. It is true that the CPA may find it difficult to adhere to the above rule, for several reasons. The distinction between major and detailed policy-formulation is not always easy to make in practice. If the CPA has advocated a particular policy or programme, in the face of strong opposition from other organs of government, it may wish detailed policy-formulation or implementation of programmes, simply in order to escape the other extreme of being left out of government decision-making altogether. The temptation to participate in detailed policy and implementation decisions is particularly strong in underdeveloped countries, in which administration has long been identified with executive action; staff/advisory functions have been of limited importance and there is no experience with working of essentially coordination and advisory agencies such as the CPA.

The Structure and Status

The structure and status of the CPA vary greatly in different countries. The most common variants are:

- (i) A Ministry of Planning,
- (ii) A Department in an Economic Ministry such as Finance or Economic Affairs,
- (iii) A Board, Commission, Council or Organization, attached to the office of the Chief Executive or an Economic Ministry or having quasi-independent status. The different patterns are a reflection again of differences in economic, political and administrative conditions, the scope of planning and the role and functions of the CPA.

Making the CPA a part of a Ministry like Finance is probably the least satisfactory of the variants listed above. Under it, the CPA is identified with a Ministry—if it is under the Ministry of Finance, planning will come to be considered as an extension of the functions of that Ministry—deprives it of its ability to formulate and express its views freely, and may affect, seriously, its coordinating role.

A Ministry of Planning has better status and acceptability. It also has the advantage of direct access to the Chief Executive and the Legislature. But the Ministry of Planning may not be able to perform the coordination function too well : other Ministries, older and more powerful, may not be too happy to submit their plans for coordination and approval to it.

A Board or Commission, attached to or advisory to the Chief Executive, is perhaps the more satisfactory arrangement, for several reasons. First, since a number of disciplines, backgrounds, or experiences (e.g. Economics, Administration, Science and Technology) can be represented among the members of the organization, it is better equipped to take a comprehensive, overall view of the economy. Second, direct link with the Chief Executive greatly facilitates its coordinational and advisory roles. It enables the CPA to participate in, and advice on, formulation of economic policies; facilitates flow of data on the economy and on projects and programmes, and also makes the task of coordination of development plans easier; the CPA's recommendations on inclusion or exclusion of particular programmes or projects are more acceptable to the other Ministries. Autonomous status gives the CPA greater freedom; but carries with it the danger of getting isolated and left out of decision-making altogether. Such isolation has been the experience of many CPAs, which were set up as autonomous organizations.

In a few countries, planning is entrusted to an academic or research institute. Under this arrangement, the danger of isolation from official decision-making is even greater, because the difficulties of obtaining data, especially on projects and programmes, and the plan may become, or be considered by the government as having become, too theoretical. A more common and advantageous arrangement is to constitute the CPA as an official agency, and to associate an institute with it for studies on various aspects of planning, and preparing and testing different planning models.

The Head of the CPA may be an academic economist, an administrator or a public man. Where the CPA is a Board or Commission, its members would be selected to represent different backgrounds, which are of interest to planning. Below the head or members, most planning agencies have a staff of technical experts—economists, econometricians, statisticians, administrators or management specialists, and specialists in various sectors. In some planning agencies, notably that of France, the civil servants and technicians are carefully selected, and their numbers are kept quite small. However, many central planning agencies have large staffs, including large numbers of middle-and-junior level economists, civil servants and technicians. Large size has the disadvantage of increasing problems (especially within the agency) and may also lead to fall in quality of personnel. Size is related also to size of the country and conception of the roles and functions of the CPA. When the role is visualized as one of overall coordination of the planning activity in the country, and formulation of the national plan by coordination of the plans made at other levels, the size of the organization may remain small. Size increases rapidly only when the organization takes upon itself functions of formulation of sectoral or regional plans or of plan implementation.

Internal Organization

The typical internal organization of a CPA is into a number of divisions or branches, including both sectoral (vertical) and functional or horizontal ones. The sectoral divisions deal with individual sectors of the economy : their principal function is to formulate and review sectoral plans in close collaboration with the planning units in the sectoral ministries. The functional or horizontal divisions are concerned with aspects, such as finance, employment, administration and perspective planning, which concern the entire plan or the economy. The perspective planning division is of particular importance, because it prepares long-term projections, and perspectives of medium and short-term plans. In federal countries, in which formulation of plans by the regional governments is an important part of the planning process, one or more divisions in the CPA deal with coordination of regional plans: the divisions work in close cooperation with the divisions in the Ministry of Finance which have responsibility for transfer of funds for development programmes to the regional governments. The sectoral divisions of the CPA are manned primarily by sectoral specialists, while the functional divisions are manned by economists, statisticians, etc.

Relationships

Reference has been made above to the CPA's relationship with the Chief Executive. This is the most important relationship of the CPA, and affects all aspects of its functioning. The ability of the CPA to perform its functions of macro-economic survey, coordination of sectoral and regional plans and advice on economic policy depends mainly on the nature of its relationship with the Chief Executive. The CPA must establish close working relationships also with (i) the planning units in the sectoral ministries, regional governments, and major public enterprises; (ii) the financial organs, namely the Ministry of Finance and the Central Bank, and (iii) the central statistical agency. The planning units in the ministries, regional governments, etc., should not be subordinate to the CPA; but there should be direct and efficient communication between them and the CPA, and close working relationships between the two. These are essential for efficient plan formulation. The CPA's relationships with the Ministry of Finance and the Central Bank are of great importance because close association between these agencies is essential for macro-economic survey, assessment of financial resources, formulation of cash, credit and foreign exchange budgets, and formulating the monetary and fiscal policies for implementing the plan.

Close relationship with the central statistical agency is essential for providing to the CPA, the data needed for plan formulation. In many countries, where the data were very deficient and/or a central statistical agency did not exist before, one has been established after planning was initiated. In some countries, the central statistical agency forms part of the CPA. This arrangement, while it emphasizes the close relationship between the planning and statistical agencies, is not entirely necessary or even the most efficient. An independent statistical agency can serve the statistical needs of the country better; the CPA should also not be involved in the administrative problems of collection and processing of data.

CPA and the Legislature

If the CPA is a Ministry or part of a Ministry, it will be represented in the Legislature by its Minister. If it is attached to the Chief Executive, it will be represented by the Minister designated for the purpose, by the Chief Executive. The Legislature may constitute one or more committees for more effective contact with the CPA and detailed examination of the plans.

CPA and Economic Organizations

The CPA may establish relationships with economic organizations such as trade unions, chambers of commerce and industry associations, either directly or through the sectoral ministries. Such groups, each representing a particular economic interest or sector, play an important role in plan formulation in many countries, including France, Yugoslavia and India. In France, the bulk of the work of plan formulation is done by the Modernization Commissions, composed of representatives of employers, labour, government and individual specialists. In Yugoslavia, economic organizations, each of which represents the enterprises in a particular sector, assist the federal and republic planning agencies in sectoral planning. In India, Development Councils, consisting of representatives of employers, labour, government and other concerned interests, have been constituted for a number of sectors, and assist in plan formulation for the respective sectors. The CPA (the Planning Commission) is represented on the most important councils.

Advisory Boards, Panels, etc.

The CPA may establish Advisory Panels of economists, scientists, etc., to obtain the advice of independent specialists on various aspects of the plan. The Panels may be permanent, or may be constituted from time to time, as need arises. In addition, working groups, study teams, enquiry committees, etc., may be constituted for advice on particular problems, or detailed study of particular aspects of the plan. Such groups may also be constituted by the sectoral ministries : the practice of constituting such groups is well established in countries in which the administration is patterned on the British model.

Planning Councils and Committees

In many countries, planning or development councils have an important role as consultative or decision-making bodies in relation to the plan. In France, the Planning Council and the Economic and Social Council, large bodies composed of sectoral and regional representatives besides individual experts, have an important advisory role in plan formulation : the advice of the Councils is sought by the Government on basic questions such as the rate of growth, and the plans are examined by them. In India, the National Development Council, on which both the Central Government and the State Governments are represented, has come to acquire a very important role as a decision-making body. The plan is submitted to it for approval at various stages, and its views are obtained on all major questions of economic policy. In the USSR, the National Economic Council has an important role in plan formulation and implementation.

CPA and Total Planning Activity

The permanent staff of the CPA generally undertakes only a small part of the total planning activity in a country : the great bulk of it is undertaken outside the CPA—in planning units in the sectoral ministries and enterprises, and in regional and local governments. The primary and distinctive function of the CPA is to coordinate and interrelate plans for different sectors and territories, and to formulate an integrated development plan for the country. The CPA should encourage (i) establishment of planning structures of appropriate size and strength and of appropriate planning processes at every level, and (ii) development of patterns of communication among the planning structures and between them and the executive organs, so that the different sectoral and territorial plans can be effectively interrelated and coordinated. The CPA is at the apex of the planning system, and has responsibilities of both ensuring development of a planning system of adequate size and strength, and the effective functioning of the system.

Planning Structures in Ministries and Enterprises

Planning structures in the sectoral ministries are the sectoral counterparts of the CPA : they have the same functions of plan formulation, assessment of progress, advice in formulation of policies, etc., for the sectors, which the CPA has for the economy. As a result, they have much in common with the CPA in composition, status, relationships, and manner of functioning. They perform their function of formulation of sectoral plans, by coordinating plans of enterprises, sectoral or sub-sectoral organizations such as industry associations, and the sectoral plans of regions. They must establish patterns of communication and coordination for the sector, similar to those established by the CPA for the economy. The structures need not be large in size, because a large part of the planning activity will be undertaken at enterprise, sectoral organization and regional levels; but they should be close to the decision-makers (the Minister, the Under Secretary) and should have direct access to them. The units are staffed by sectoral specialists, and may also have economists, statisticians and other technicians. The sectoral specialists should be carefully selected for their experience and knowledge of the sector, and their capacity to take on overall view of its needs, problems, and potentials, and its relationships with the other sectors and the whole economy. The ability to take the wider view and grasp inter-sectoral relationships is even more important, than detailed knowledge of the sector. Assessment of progress of the sectoral plans, and modification of plans in the light of trends in progress and other developments, are important activities of these units. They will also be called upon to formulate (or advise on formulation of) policies for implementation of the sectoral plan. However, they should not undertake responsibilities of either detailed formulation of projects and programmes, or plan implementation.

Planning units at the enterprise level must plan for operation, expansion, and modernization, etc., of the enterprise. Like the planning units in the sectoral ministries (and the CPA) these units must be close to the top decision-makers and have access to data relating to all aspects of operation of the enterprise.

Sectoral economic organizations (industry associations, chambers of commerce, modernization commissions, development councils) can make an important contribution to planning. Industry associations and chambers of commerce ascertain the plans, needs and problems of their members, and present them for consideration of the ministries, the CPA and other official agencies. They are representatives of interest groups, and advocacy of the interests of the groups, is quite apparent in the proposals forwarded by them. Organizations like Modernization Commissions in France and Development Councils in India, composed of different interests concerned with a sector, are in a position to take a broader and more objective view of the needs of the sector, and contribute much more to planning for it.

Formulation and evaluation of projects is an important aspect of sectoral planning, which may be organized at the levels of the enterprise, the ministry or at other levels. Large enterprises, public-sector corporations and departments having operational responsibilities for sectors, undertake project formulation, either through their own project units or by giving contracts to consulting firms. Project evaluation, may also be done, in part, at enterprise, corporation or department level; but the final decisions are taken for all major projects at higher level—of the sectoral ministry, the CPA or the Chief Executive.

The Ministry of Finance and the Central Bank have important roles in plan formulation and implementation, by way of :

(i) Assessment of financial resources,
(ii) Formulation of the financial plan,
(iii) Formulation and implementation of the monetary, credit and fiscal measures for plan implementation, and
(iv) Allocation of financial resources for programmes and projects. Where the Ministry of Finance is also the Ministry of Economic Affairs, it keeps watch over major economic trends.

The Central Bank is closely associated with these, and with preparation of annual economic survey and similar studies. After initiation of planning, Planning Divisions are generally established in the Ministry of Finance and the Central Bank, for assessment of financial resources, macro-economic surveys and preparation of the financial plan; they work in close cooperation with the appropriate divisions in the CPA. The resource mobilization and allocation divisions in the Ministry of Finance are often expanded and reorganized to meet the needs of plan implementation. In some cases, Project Evaluation Units have been established to enable the Ministry of Finance to undertake technical and economic evaluation of the projects submitted to it for approval.

Planning Structures at Regional and Local Levels

Regional planning structures are best developed in federal countries, where they form part of regional governments. In countries with unitary governments, these structures are established mostly for (i) regions with special developmental problems or promise (depressed or backward regions, metropolitan regions, regions of water resource development or other major projects), or for (ii) special purposes such as control over land use in UK In recent years, some countries such as France, with unitary governments, have attempted to institute regional planning as an integral part of the planning process and have established regional planning structures.

Planning structures of regional governments may consist of regional planning boards and planning units in the regional ministries, enterprises, etc. These are regional counterparts of the CPA and the other central planning units, and have functions, status and relationships similar to those for the latter. The scope of planning at the regional government level is more restricted, however, because aspects such as foreign trade and monetary policy, and sectors such as defence and heavy industries, which are the responsibility of the Central Government, are not included. On the other hand, there is detailed planning for sectors such as agriculture, small and medium industries and social services, which are of primary interest to the regional governments. An important aspect of planning at the regional government level is coordination of local plans.

The most usual planning structures for special regions are boards, or corporations, manned by full-time members or part-time, ex-officio members. Boards or Corporations, with full-time members are constituted if the responsibilities of the organization include implementation of large projects, e.g. in water resource project regions. But if the responsibilities are primarily those of coordination of plans of a number of executive agencies operating in the region (e.g. in a metropolitan region), the regional organization would consist primarily of representatives of the principal executive agencies concerned, acting as ex-officio members.

Local planning units are adjuncts of the local executive agencies. They are small in size, except in case of municipalities of large cities in the developed countries, which often have large planning units. These units are now constituted for metropolitan regions, which include besides the municipal areas of the cities, other areas affected by urban influence. Local planning is concerned primarily with locations and operational details of the economic activities and services which are the responsibility of the local executive agencies. Physical planning and control over land use are important aspects of local planning, and local planning agencies in UK, Netherlands, etc. are concerned primarily with them.

Relations Between Planning Structures at Different Levels

The most usual and also perhaps the most satisfactory pattern is that the planning agency is responsible to the corresponding executive organ, but is in communication with planning structures at other levels. Thus, the Planning Board of a regional government is under that government—it takes guidance and decisions from the Chief Executive of the regional government—but maintains effective communications with the central planning agency, the planning units in the Central and Regional sectoral ministries, and local, 'special region' and enterprise planning agencies which are under the regional government. In the initial stages of plan formulation, the CPA will communicate to the regional planning board (for guidance of the latter in preparing the regional plan) the principles, priorities, resource allocations and physical accomplishment targets, etc., of the outline plan, as approved by the Central Chief Executive. The regional planning board will communicate to the CPA the regional governments' assessment of resources, and views on sectoral priorities and achievement targets, and the draft plan, when it is formulated. Differences between the two governments will be discussed and the regional plan finalized by the Chief Executives of the governments, with the two planning bodies acting as advisers. When the regional plan is being implemented, the regional planning board will furnish to the CPA (and planning units in the Central sectroal ministries) all relevant data relating to its progress. This pattern ensures that (i) each planning agency reflects in its plan the objectives and policies of the respective executive agency, and (ii) that effective vertical (upward and downward) and lateral communication is established within the planning system, to make possible coordination of sectoral and territorial plans. A large proportion of the problems in plan formulation and implementation arise from failure to achieve such a pattern effectively and, especially, to distinguish between responsibility and communication.

The Process of Plan Formulation Mixed Economies

The principal steps in plan formulation may be summarized as follows :

(i) Assessment of needs, and aspirations of the people, and of resources, and determination of the goals and objectives of the plan.

(ii) Preliminary formulation: examination of alternative strategies; formulation of overall and sectoral, and long-term and medium-term growth models; formulation of the outline plan.
(iii) Detailed formulation of sectoral programmes and projects, and of regional and local plans within the framework of the outline plan.
(iv) Aggregation, integration and successive approximation.
(v) Formulation of the plan.
(vi) Approval of the plan by the Chief Executive and the Legislature.
(vii) Formulation of annual plans.
(viii) Adjustments and revisions, based on appraisal of progress of the plan, domestic and international economic trends and other factors.

Assessment of Needs, Aspirations and Resources, and Determination of Goals and Objectives

The two processes are closely related and are interdependent. The goals and objectives of the plan will flow from the basic social and economic policies of the government, as also from assessments of needs and aspirations of the people, and of the various resources—natural, manpower, material, financial. Needs and aspirations are articulated by the representatives of the people, in the legislatures and local government institutions and in the press. The resources are assessed through surveys and techno-economic studies. A related essential step is preparation of a macro-economic survey, indicating the national income, saving, investment, the structure of production and of employment, foreign trade and balance of payments, levels of development of services, etc. The survey provides the benchmark for the plan.

Data on resources are collected by survey agencies, and are processed for plan formulation by sectoral ministries, the CPA and other planning agencies. The planners also re-analyze and re-combine existing data in a variety of ways. Deficiencies in data can be removed, to a limited extent, by obtaining additional data from the survey agencies at short notice, but have to be removed mainly by undertaking new surveys and expanding or changing the scope of the existing surveys. Detailed data on many aspects, e.g. patterns of consumption and saving, distribution of income, utilization of manpower, energy, and various materials, which were not collected before, begin to be collected to meet the needs of planning. Addition of new survey and statistical agencies, and expansion and reorganization of the existing agencies is the principal impact of planning on these agencies.

Formulation of goals and objectives of the plan is the responsibility of the Chief Executive. They may be approved specifically by the Legislature; more generally, legislative approval relates to the economic and social policies of the government on which the goals and objectives are based.

Preliminary Formulation of the Plan

On the basis of the above assessments and formulation, the CPA will formulate and submit for approval of the Chief Executive, one or more growth models, which set out the principal macro-magnitudes of the plan such as total and per capita output, savings, investment, population, employment, sectoral distribution of resources and sectoral outputs. If a long-term perspective of growth exists already, the model(s) will be formulated within its framework. More than one model may be prepared by the CPA and submitted for consideration of the Chief Executive : selection among the models is a political decision, and represents acceptance by the Chief Executive, of the implications of the selected model. The Chief Executive may not select any one of the models submitted to it, and ask the CPA to repeat the exercise. However, the next step of the detailed formulation of the plan cannot begin until the basic decisions relating to growth models have been taken. The growth models (and the preliminary plan) may also be submitted to advisory bodies such as a Planning Council, or a Panel of Economists, to obtain their views.

The preliminary or outline plan is formulated on the basis of the approved model. It represents the first attempt by the CPA, the sectoral ministries and the financial agencies (the Ministry of Finance and the Central Bank) to sketch the outlines of the Plan. In this plan, the rates of growth, targets for various sectors, financial outlays, and other aspects are outlined briefly and roughly, primarily on basis of the data already available with the various planning agencies. These will be revised in the course of detailed plan formulation; but indication of these at this initial stage of planning is essential to provide to the sectoral and regional planning agencies, guidelines for detailed work.

The outline plan is approved by the Chief Executive and may also be approved by the Legislature. Consideration of the outline plan is an important occasion for the Legislature to indicate its views on the plan and the various economic policies of the government. Detailed discussion of the plan at this stage will give the legislators the feeling of active association with the planning process, and will also make available their views to all the agencies concerned with plan formulation.

Detailed Formulation

The detailed work of plan formulation begins after the outline plan has been approved; it is based on the magnitudes indicated in the outline plan. It is taken up throughout the planning system—from the CPA and the ministries of the central government to regional and local governments and enterprises. It takes up most of the time and resources in plan formulation, because it involves :

(i) A variety of studies ranging from feasibility studies of projects, of appraisal of progress on and impacts of existing programmes, and

(ii) Intensive communication among the different constituents of the planning system. The work can be considered to be divided as follows :—

  (a) Indication by the central government to the regional governments and by the sectoral ministries to enterprises, etc., of the macro-magnitudes of the outline plan relating to regions, sectors, enterprises, etc. similar indication by the regional governments to enterprises under them and to local governments.

  (b) Detailed formulation of projects and programmes at enterprise, local government and regional government levels.

  (c) Formulation of regional plans by regional governments by coordination of local and enterprise plans and submission of plans to the central government.

  (d) Formulation of sectoral plans by the sectoral ministries of the central government on basis of enterprise plans and sectoral plans of regional governments, etc.

Formulation of Regional and Local Plans

Regional plans are drawn up by the planning organs of the regional governments (in federal countries) and other regional planning agencies. The plans are drawn up within the framework of the outline plan and the guidelines, e.g. relating to resource availability given by the CPA and relate primarily to the sectors for which the regional government of the regional planning agency has responsibility. In most countries, regional governments have responsibility for agriculture and allied sectors, small and medium-scale industries, roads, electricity, housing and urban development and social services and regional government plans relate primarily to these. But the plans are frequently comprehensive, make overall and sectoral growth projections for the regions and take into account all programmes and projects located in the regions—of the federal government, the regional and local governments as well as the private sector. Comprehensive plans are made because regional governments consider themselves responsible for overall development of the regions and have to provide infrastructure facilities and services for federal and private sector projects located within them. Regional governments generally exert considerable political pressure on the federal government for location of industrial and other projects (licensed or financed by the federal governments) within their territories and also provide incentives to private sector industrialists for location of industries. Planning agencies, constituted for regions with special problems or promise—backward or depressed regions, metropolitan regions, etc.—also frequently draw up comprehensive regional development plans, which include both programmes and projects to be undertaken by the regional agencies themselves as well those of other public sector agencies and private enterprises.

Local plans are formulated by the planning sections of local government agencies, such as municipalities and district and village councils. They are important in case of large cities and in situations in which the local government agencies have large resources of their own. But in most underdeveloped countries these agencies are poor and weak and have little initiative in formulation of local plans. In these countries, the central or the regional governments prescribe in great detail the guidelines for formulation of local 'plans'. Plans for cities are formulated generally with metropolitan regions (which include besides the municipal area of the city, surrounding areas affected by the city) as the units.

Aggregation and coordination of sectoral and local plans at the regional level, to formulate the regional plan, and fitting in of regional plans into the national plan are important aspects of plan formulation, especially in federal countries, in which the regional governments have an important role in planning.

The regional and local plans prepared at this stage are draft plans. They are modified in the process of aggregation and integration described below. The final plans are prepared, after the integration has been completed and on basis of agreements reached during it.

Both the draft and the final regional plans are approved by the Regional Chief Executives and Legislatures. Local plans are similarly approved by the local government authorities.

Formulation of Sectoral Plans

The sectoral ministries of the federal and regional governments, economic organizations such as industry associations and cooperatives, local government institutions, and enterprises are involved in this process. The process of planning and the participation of different agencies vary in different sectors, depending upon size of enterprise, nature of ownership and other factors; the variations are brought out by Fig. 2.1. In sector 1 Railways, owned by the federal government, only the federal ministry of railways and the individual enterprises (e.g. a regional railway, an equipment manufacturing unit) are involved in planning. Planning at the enterprise level may involve feasibility studies and other aspects of project formulation. The ministry of railways is concerned with evaluation and approval of projects and programmes, coordination of regional and enterprise plans, inter-sectoral coordination, etc. In sector 2, the cement industry, the agencies involved are the federal and regional ministries of industries, the industry association and the enterprises. Formulation of projects or programmes of expansion and modernization takes place at the enterprise level; the industry association aggregates enterprise plans and represents the interests of the industry before the regional and federal governments; the regional and federal ministries approve the sectoral plans, analyze inter-sectoral relationships including those relating to supply of inputs and disposal of outputs (backward and forward linkages). The regional government must provide in its plans for the infrastructure and other facilities needed for implementation of the industry's plan.

In sector 3, Agriculture, in which the individual enterprise is very small, local government institutions and economic organizations such as cooperatives, have an important role in planning. Plans are coordinated at local, regional and federal levels. Project formulation (e.g. for an irrigation project) is done primarily by the sectoral ministries of the regional governments.

Sector	Characteristics	Planning Agencies		
		Primary	*Intermediate*	*Coordinating*
1. Railways	Nationalized Federal	Regional railway, enterprise e.g. equipment manufacturing	—	Federal Ministry
2. Industry: cement	Private, with large enterprise	Enterprise	Industry Association Regional Government	Federal Ministry
3. Agriculture	Private with very small enterprises	(i) Local Government Agencies: Cooperatives etc. for agricultural extension, supplies of credit and input to enterprises and marketing of outputs	Regional Sectoral Ministry	Federal Ministry
		(ii) Regional sectoral Ministry of Irrigation and other infra-structure projects		Federal Ministry

Fig. 2.1: Formulation of Sectoral Plans

Aggregation and Integration of Sectoral, Regional and Local Plans

This is the next step in the planning process, which involves intensive consultation among the officials of the planning agencies, the governments and enterprises; examination of relationships and reconciliation of differences in estimates, points of view and claims and counter-claims through a process of successive approximation. It is frequently observed that the first aggregation of sectoral, regional and local plans gives different figures on inputs and outputs than had been given in the outline plan. In particular, costs are higher than had been estimated earlier. The differences are due partly to better estimation, resulting from detailed formulation of projects and programmes, and partly to the fact that regional and local governments, having different priorities than those of the federal government frequently depart from the guidelines of the outline plan in formulation of their plans. The departures may be significant in democratic countries, in which the regional governments are under pressure to expand social service and welfare programmes rapidly and to attract industries to increase employment and incomes within their territories. Inter-sectoral (and intra-sectoral), inter-regional and sector–region relationships must also be examined in detail in order to iron out discrepancies and inconsistencies in plans and to provide missing links. Finally, estimates of financial and other resources must be made again to take account of price and other changes since the formulation of the outline plan.

Regional plans are finalized in discussions between the representatives of the regional governments and the federal government: the latter includes representatives of the CPA, the Ministry of Finance and the sectoral ministries. Sectoral plans are finalized in discussions between the CPA, the Ministry of Finance and the sectoral ministries : the representatives of major enterprises may also be associated to the extent necessary. The whole process involves successive approximation to reconcile different estimates of inputs and outputs, and different points of view and claims. Frequently, more than one exercise is necessary to reconcile these differences.

The Chief Executive is kept informed throughout the process and may be associated with various steps in it: association of the Chief Executive is essential for finalization of the regional and sectoral plans.

Formulation and Approval of the Plan

On basis of the agreements on regional and sectoral plans, reached through the above process the final plan is now formulated by the CPA. The Ministry of Finance and the Central Bank are closely associated : the financial plan is formulated by them. The plan is submitted for approval, first to the Chief Executive and then to the Legislature. If there is a Planning Council, the plan will be submitted to it also. Major changes will not be suggested by the Chief Executive, because its decisions are already incorporated in the plan, but they may be suggested by the Legislature. In that case, revisions will be necessary, which will involve re-working of sectoral and regional plans, in varying degrees. The Chief Executive and the Ministers will defend the plan in the legislature and attempt to keep the changes to the minimum. Major changes will not be needed at this stage, if the views of the Legislature have been obtained at several intermediate points between the outline plan and final plan, e.g. through discussions on economic policy, sectoral programmes or other aspects of the plan. The Legislature should be kept adequately informed about the plan in various stages of its formulation.

As mentioned above, regional and local plans are also now finally prepared and approved by the appropriate regional and local authorities.

Formulation of the Annual Plans and the Budget

The above processes of preliminary formulation, detailed formulation, aggregation, integration and final preparation, are gone through in case of a medium-term plan, which is the principal plan in most countries. The annual plans are prepared within the framework of the medium-term plan and according to the phasing envisaged in the latter. Departures from the phasing may become inescapable because of domestic or international economic developments, shortfalls or delays in particular programmes and projects and other reasons; but they should be kept to the minimum. Otherwise, the entire structure of the medium-term plan will be disturbed. The process of coordination of sectoral and regional plans, described above for the medium-term plan, is repeated in case of the annual plan, but on a smaller scale. Formulation of the annual plans and the annual budgets are coordinated by the federal and regional ministries of finance, in consultation with the CPA and the regional planning agencies.

Adjustments and revisions in the medium-term plan are made from time to time, on basis of appraisal of progress of plan projects and programmes, domestic and international economic trends and other relevant factors. Delays in execution of key projects having widespread linkages; shortfalls in agricultural or industrial output because of bad weather, labour trouble or other reasons; changes in export earnings because of changes in market conditions of principal export commodities and changes in flow of foreign aid or investment, are some of the factors which necessitate adjustments and revisions in the plan. All major changes in the plan should be made either by or with the knowledge of the central planning agency, so that their intra-sectoral or inter-sectoral effects can be studied and provided for. Minor changes, in case of which such effects are unimportant can however be made by the planning units of sectoral ministries, regional governments etc.

Administrative Aspects of Plan Implementation (Mixed Economy Countries)

Plan implementation in mixed economy countries is divided between the public sector and the private sector. Implementation in the public sector is controlled directly by decisions relating to resource allocation, and executive decisions of the various plan implementation agencies—from the ministries and departments of the federal government and the regional governments, to managements of enterprises, and local government authorities. Plan implementation in the private sector, dependent upon private decisions, is secured primarily through indirect measures which provide the incentives and sanctions to influence private decisions. Implementation of the plans of the public sector and the private sector has to be coordinated at the national level, as well as at the levels of the productive sectors and the regions.

Monetary and fiscal measures have an important role in plan implementation. They are the principal instruments of mobilization of financial resources to achieve the investment targets of the plan, and of allocation of resources between the public and private sectors, and among productive sectors, branches, industries, etc. as envisaged in the medium-term and annual plans. They provide also the principal incentives and sanctions for plan implementation in the private sector.

The principal administrative tasks in plan implementation are the following :

- (i) Formulation and implementation of monetary and fiscal measures,
- (ii) Implementation of sectoral plans, including management of enterprises,
- (iii) Implementation of regional and local plans,
- (iv) Implementation of the social, economic and political reforms, needed for attaining socio-economic goals of the plan, and
- (v) Appraisal of progress and follow-up action.

Monetary and Fiscal Policy Measures

The measures relate to money supply, prices, taxation, credit, management of foreign exchange, etc. The measures have two major objectives :

- (i) To achieve the investment targets of the plan. (This involves, in many underdeveloped countries, raising the level of investment, from 5 to 6 per cent of the national income to 15 to 20 per cent or more, in order to achieve the situation of self-sustaining growth), and
- (ii) To direct resource allocation in accordance with the plan :
  - (a) As between the private sector and the public sector, and
  - (b) Among the different productive sectors (branches and industries), regions, local areas, etc.

The principal agencies, concerned with detailed formulation and implementation of the measures, are the Ministry of Finance and the Central Bank. The central planning agency should be consulted at policy-formulation stage and should be kept informed of major trends in implementation of the measures. But association of the CPA with detailed formulation or implementation of the measures is not desirable, because it involves the CPA in detailed decision-making which detracts from its main functions. In many countries, an economic committee of the Chief Executive (Economic Committee of the Cabinet, Council of Economic Advisers to the President) provides overall direction for formulation of the measures.

Taxation measures are formulated in detail and implemented by the Ministry of Finance. The Central Bank is responsible for management of money supply, credit and, usually also, foreign exchange. Where the Central Bank is under the Ministry of Finance, that Ministry has a dominant position in the field of economic policy. The monetary measures have to be related to the price policy on the one hand and the investment needs of the plan on the other. Most governments of the LDCs resort to deficit financing of investment, because they cannot raise through taxation, borrowing or other measures, all the finance needed for plan implementation.

The Central Bank manages the credit system, directly, and through its control over the commercial banks. It manages the borrowings of the government, gives loans to public sector enterprises and specialized credit institutions, such as industrial banks, and directs commercial banks to increase loans to particular sectors or activities and reduce or stop loans to others. The discount rate, fixed by the Central Bank, influences the level of investment in the economy, and the rules made by the bank, e.g. on the proportion of commercial bank deposits to be invested in government securities, etc., influences the flow of funds in the economy. The directions of the Central Bank to the commercial banks are enforced through a system of inspection.

Management of foreign exchange is also generally the responsibility of the Central Bank : it is done in close cooperation with the Ministry of Foreign Trade. Most LDCs, undertaking planning, experience shortage of foreign exchange and operate systems of control over foreign exchange and imports and exports. The latter are operated by the Ministry of Foreign Trade.

Coordination of different fiscal and monetary policy measures is essential in order to ensure that there is no conflict among them, and that total saving and investment in the economy increase in accordance with plan projections. For example, taxation provides, in most countries, most of the resources needed for implementation of the plans of the public sector. The tax structure is being continuously broadened and modified in these countries by levying new taxes and raising the rates and increasing the coverage of existing taxes, to raise additional resources for plan implementation. But it is necessary to ensure that (a) the additional yields from taxes are not at the expense of private or corporate savings, and (b) they do not affect the incentives to increase individual earnings or corporate profits. Very high rates of tax on personal incomes or corporate profits often have such effect, with the result that, the additional yield from taxes is to a greater or lesser degree offset by lower private or corporate saving. The monetary policy, similarly, has to be devised to meet the resource needs of the plan, but has to be coordinated with price and credit policies. Large scale deficit financing of public sector investment may lead to inflation, which besides causing disturbance to the economy and hardship to the people, would affect levels of private savings and investment and also raise the costs of plan implementation. The benefits from such deficit financing would thus be more than offset by the negative effects of inflation.

Taxation and credit measures are used also as instruments of directing resource allocation to and within the private sector, and as mentioned above, provide incentives and sanctions through which implementation of the plan by the private sector is secured. Investment by private sector enterprises is encouraged by tax incentives such as liberal depreciation allowances, tax holidays to new enterprises for a number of years, etc. Differential taxation, i.e. high rates of taxation for enterprises in some sectors, industries or regions, and low rates in others is often used as a device to direct investment. The taxation measures are usually accompanied by complementary credit measures. Cheap or long-term credit is provided, in addition to tax incentives, to encourage expansion modernization, etc., in the desired sectors, while bank advances for some types of activities (e.g. speculation in real estate or in trading in commodities) are restricted or prohibited to discourage these activities. Credit incentives to the favoured sectors are generally administered by specialized institutions. Loans to industries are generally provided by Industrial Finance Corporations (or Industrial Banks), which understand the particular problems of industrial enterprises and adapt their activities to meet them. Frequently, these agencies develop expertise to evaluate industrial projects and to assist the enterprises (especially small enterprises) with purchase of equipment and raw materials, marketing of output, etc. Agricultural credit is provided most commonly through cooperative societies which also assist the farmers with marketing of output and purchase of inputs.

In the situation of scarcity of resources prevailing in most countries undertaking planning, taxation and credit measures are not adequate to direct investment and economic activity in the private sector, and are supplemented by administrative (regulatory) measures. The most important measures are licensing of new enterprises, and rationing of scarce resources—foreign exchange, materials such as steel and cement and utilities such as electricity and water—and physical planning restrictions on development in particular areas. The measures are generally administered by agencies constituted especially for these purposes.

Implementation of Sectoral Programmes

The programmes are implemented by the sectoral ministries and departments of the federal and regional governments, public sector and private sector enterprises and local governments. The division of responsibilities among the different agencies and the precise functions of each agency depend upon several factors, such as the division of functions among the federal, regional and local governments, the extent of public ownership and the size and nature of enterprises in different sectors. In case of agriculture, the services of agricultural extension, credit and supplies are operated generally by regional and local governments, and the responsibilities of the federal government (Ministry of Agriculture) are limited to formulation of overall policies and programmes, coordination of activities of different agencies and aiding implementation by helping remove bottlenecks, e.g. in supplies of fertilizers. In case of an industry, in which most of the enterprises are in the private sector, the principal function of the ministries is to ensure that the enterprises have the incentives to meet plan targets of investment and output, and have access to the needed financial and material resources, and that they conform to the broad policies relating to prices and distribution of outputs. As mentioned above, these are ensured through fiscal measures supplemented, to the extent necessary, by regulatory measures. In most underdeveloped countries, a number of promotional measures are undertaken to encourage industrial development, particularly small scale. These include provision of technical assistance, cheap credit and other forms of financial assistance (including direct subsidies in some cases);

provision of land and infrastructure facilities at subsidized rates; levying protective import duties and banning of competitive imports, and assured purchases of outputs. The measures may be administered by the ministries, either directly or through specialized institutions such as industrial banks and industrial service institutes. In an industry, in which both private sector and public sector units contribute sizeable proportions of the output, the principal functions of the Ministry/Department are to coordinate formulation and implementation of joint policies and programmes by enterprises of both sectors. If a significant proportion of the investment and expansion of capacity is to be in one of the two sectors, say the public sector, the Ministry must take all the steps needed to achieve this objective. Finally, in nationalized sectors such as railways, electricity and communications, the concerned Ministries/Departments must direct operations and expansion, in accordance with the plan, through the appropriate public sector enterprises.

An important aspect of plan implementation is construction and operation of major development projects—in industry, irrigation, power, transport and other sectors. The projects are undertaken in order to add significantly to productive capacities in industry and agriculture, and to provide the essential infrastructures of development. They involve large investments—in the plans of many countries the greater part of the investment is on major projects—and their construction and operation often create difficult technical and organizational problems. Delays and difficulties in plan implementation, in many countries arise primarily, from major projects.

The Ministry of Finance has a very important role in implementation of sectoral programmes. It allocated resources for all public sector investments, and for operation of all public sector programmes. Secondly, as mentioned above, it is along with the Central Bank the principal agency operating the monetary and fiscal measures through which incentives and sanctions are provided to ensure plan implementation by the private sector.

The principal steps in implementation of public sector programmes may be summarized as follows :

(i) Formulation of the annual programme by the sectoral ministry, enterprise, etc., within the framework of the programme included in the plan.

(ii) Scrutiny and approval of the programme by the Ministry of Finance, and inclusion in the annual budget and the annual plan.

(iii) Approval of the annual budget and the annual plan by the Legislature.
(iv) Authorization of expenditure by the Ministry of Finance; transfer of funds to regional governments and local governments, in case of programmes to be executed by them.
(v) Execution of programmes by the Ministry, Department or Public Enterprises.
(vi) Inspection, appraisal of progress and follow-up action.

Implementation of Regional and Local Plans

In federal countries, plan formulation and implementation are shared between the federal, regional and local governments. Regional and local plans are drawn up within the framework of the objectives, policies and programmes of the national plan, and are coordinated with the latter. They outline resource allocations and achievement targets in sectors in which implementation are the responsibility of the regional governments. Agriculture, small and medium scale industries, power, highways, and social services are the most important such sectors in most countries. The Ministries and Departments of the regional governments implement the plan programmes in these sectors, while those of the federal government provide overall direction and a proportion of the funds, and assist by way of removing bottlenecks (e.g. in supplies of scarce materials), securing inter-regional cooperation, etc. In sectors, such as communications and large industries, in which the implementation responsibility is primarily of the federal government, the regional governments provide important supporting facilities, e.g. land, electricity, water, and link transport for an industrial project. The regional governments are consulted by the federal government in such matters as location of enterprises, distribution of scarce outputs, provision of new services, etc. Competition among regional governments for location of large enterprises and allocations of outputs and services is an important aspect of planning in most federal countries.

In most federal countries, there are large resource transfers for plan implementation from the federal to the regional governments. They become necessary because the most remunerative taxes, e.g. income tax, excise and customs duties are federal, and the federal government has besides, the powers of borrowing and creation of money, while a large port of the expenditure on plan implementation has to be incurred by the regional or local governments. The coordination role of the federal government in plan formulation and implementation is made acceptable to the regional governments partly by the resource transfers. The transfers may be in the form of lump sums, or as proportions of receipts from particular taxes or of outlays on particular programmes. The last practice is adopted in case of programmes (e.g. family planning) in which the federal government is especially interested.

The resources, powers and responsibilities of local government agencies are limited in most underdeveloped countries, and these agencies have limited roles in plan implementation. This is in sharp contrast to the situation in most Western countries, in which local government agencies are important constituents of government, and local governments of metropolitan cities (London, New York, Paris) have vast resources, provide essential services to millions of people, prepare physical plans for large areas, undertake large development projects, and have important functions of regulation of economic activities, e.g. through their zoning laws. In most underdeveloped countries, even the municipalities of large citied are dependent for most of their funds on grants from the regional or the federal government and their activities are regulated in detail by these governments. Urban development and other local plans are drawn up in these countries as part of the plan of the regional government and are implemented by local government agencies, with funds provided mainly by the regional government.

Implementation of social and institutional reforms is an important aspect of plan implementation in most underdeveloped countries. Through such reforms, archaic, growth-inhibiting social, economic or political institutions are abolished or weakened, and are replaced by new, growth-inducing ones. Two important areas of reform relate to land reforms and establishment of democratic institutions for local government and development. Most underdeveloped countries have undertaken land reforms, specifically, break-up of large estates and distribution of the land, held by individuals in access of the size allowed as per the provisions in the newly enacted land reform laws, to the actual tillers of land and/or to landless peasants. The Central Governments in many countries have also passed laws for decentralization of power by strengthening existing local institutions of governance and/or creating new ones through legislative action to be followed by all regional governments.

Management and Organization for Projects

The distinctive role of management is selection, combination and organization of other factors of production—physical and financial capital, labour, raw materials, etc., to achieve the objectives of the enterprise. Efficiency in management consists in producing output at minimum unit coast, through judicious selection and efficient organization of the factors.

Management tasks in relation to operation of an enterprise could be listed as follows :

(i) Making technical decisions—relating to process, design, technical operation, etc.
(ii) Maintaining effective external relations—with customers, suppliers of raw materials, machinery, transport, power and other utilities, bankers, the local community, the government, etc.
(iii) Internal administration—organizing production, selection, training, supervision and control of personnel, and providing necessary auxiliary functions such as accounting, maintenance, research and quality control.
(iv) Integrating various activities into balance, timely and effective action.

A good manager must take into account a variety of factors which are often quite different in nature. Issues relating to technology, external relations and internal administration are interdependent : usually, changes cannot be made in one without affecting the others.

Efficiency in management depends upon factors such as the following :

(i) Personal qualities of top management—enterprise, drive, industry, leadership, coordinating ability, vision, etc.;
(ii) Adequacy and suitability of middle and lower level management;
(iii) Suitable organizational structures, which give the management the needed autonomy, flexibility and resources (external aspects) and make possible coordinated and efficient functioning of the different departments or branches of the enterprise (internal aspects);
(iv) Adequate support of top management by specialist management teams—financial and accounting, personnel, production and quality control, marketing, legal, etc.
(v) Institution of scientific management practices.

Personal qualities of top management are of primary importance; the degree to which other factors are created, or if available, or utilized, depends frequently on these qualities. On the other hand, even the most dynamic and potentially efficient top management would be handicapped by unsuitable organizational structures, or deficiencies in supporting management personnel. Management is fast becoming a science, in which intuitive judgment is being replaced increasingly by scientific analysis. The efficient modern top manager is primarily a coordinator and leader, whose distinctive contribution is in making possible operation at optimum efficiency of (i) groups of specialists in different branches of management and (ii) management teams in different departments of the enterprise.

Managerial and Organizational Appraisal of Projects

Since the success of a project depends primarily upon management and organizational factors listed above, the principal questions relating to managerial and organizational appraisal of projects would be as follows:

(i) The nature of management—personal qualities, background and experience. How are top managers selected?

(ii) The structure of the organization—does it give the management the autonomy and flexibility needed by it for efficient functioning? Is the internal organization conducive to efficient functioning, with adequate coordination between the different departments?

(iii) The suitability of budgetary and financial procedures—do these permit adequate and detailed appraisal of costs and returns, and adequate control of top management on the spending departments? Do they permit efficient operation or do they result in undue delays?

(iv) Does the management have the authority to fix prices for its products, borrow money, and undertake investment? If reference has to be made for these to the policy-makers, are their decisions generally favourable to the views of management? Are the decisions given in time and with sufficient clarity to permit management to take consequent action, speedily and efficiently? In case of public sector enterprises, if the working of the enterprise is expected to contribute to general welfare or development, e.g. through providing essential services at low rates, are these objectives clearly defined, and are the subsidies involved in the process calculated?

(v) The suitability and adequacy of personnel procedures—Do the procedures allow the enterprise to recruit and train suitable personnel in adequate numbers, and to organize them in appropriate cadres? Is sufficient attention paid to recruitment of personnel for senior positions?

(vi) Does top management delegate authority, e.g. to heads of Departments of Divisions adequately, to avoid becoming a bottleneck in operation, without losing control over essential policy-making and direction?

(vii) If the enterprise has been functioning for some time, what has been the record of performance of the present management, and suitability of the present organizational structure? Are these adequate and suitable for undertaking expansion programmes, and for operation of a much larger enterprise? How well has the present project (if prepared by the present management) been prepared?

(viii) Attitude of Government (in case of public sector or joint public-and-private-sector enterprises). Is it enthusiastic, helpful, passive or indifferent? Is management trusted by the Government? Does Government interfere in day-to-day operations or other matters of detail? What are the expectations of the Government from the enterprise? Are these adequately and precisely defined? Is there adequate appreciation within Government of the problems faced by the management? In case of joint enterprises, is there sufficient area of agreement between the objectives of the two partners, or are conflicts in objectives or policies between them, a handicap to efficient functioning of the enterprise?

Role of Development Finance Institutions

Appraisal of suitability and adequacy of management and organization is among the most important aspects of project appraisal by development finance institutions—international or domestic. The World Bank insists that projects aided by it fulfil minimum management efficiency criteria. In cases, where these requirements are not met, the Bank insists before sanctioning a loan that management assistance is obtained for the project and suitable organizational structures is established for its efficient implementation and operation. Development finance institutions frequently insist on the Governments and private firms in removing deficiencies in management, and improve management practices and organizational structures. This is an important part of follow-up of projects, for which loans have been sanctioned. In some cases, continued financial assistance, e.g. disbursement of instalments of sanctioned loans, depends upon removal of defects in management or organization. Some institutions have management and technical assistance groups on their staffs; their assistance is particularly useful to small-or-medium-scale enterprises.

Management Problems in Underdeveloped Countries

The problems arise primarily from extreme shortage of persons with the training, knowledge and experience needed for efficient management of modern enterprises. In some countries, the shortage extends to all levels and branches of management; in others, however, it is confined mainly to top management levels, or to specialized branches such as accounting and personnel management. The shortage is related to the stage of economic development and the social and political conditions in these countries, such as the following:

(a) Existence of small modern sectors and few modern enterprises;

(b) Predominance of traditional social structures and value systems, with emphasis on kinship, cast or tribal loyalties.

Most enterprises in the private sector are family enterprises. Key management positions, in both private and public sector enterprises are filled on considerations of kinship caste or tribe, rather than those of efficiency. Efficiency, drive and enterprise are not rated highly in comparison with traditional virtues such as respect for age, conformity to established norms, etc. There is inadequate appreciation of the value of scientific management even among managers of large enterprises. These conditions often aggravate the shortage of suitable managers. They reduce the incentive for suitable young people to obtain training in management, and compel trained people to seek opportunities outside the country.

(c) Predominance of law-and-order oriented civil servants in key decision-making positions, and limited decision-making opportunities for specialists, including trained managers; the practice of deputing civil servants for top management positions in public enterprises.

Some of these conditions will change as development proceeds. Traditional social structures and value systems will weaken with urbanization spread of modern education, and growth of modern sectors. Experience with successful working of a few enterprises will bring greater appreciation of the value of good management and the importance of efficiency. However, the problem of shortage of trained and experienced management personnel needs further consideration, because it requires action in the way of planned recruitment, training and personnel organization.

Measures for Meeting Shortage of Management Personnel

The measures may be grouped into short-term and long-term. The short-term measures include: (i) deputation of civil servants and recruitment from private enterprises for management positions in public enterprises, and (ii) employment of foreigners, as advisers, consultants or even as managers. Among the long-term measures, planned recruitment, training and organization of personnel cadres are most important.

Deputation of civil servants to management positions in public enterprises is, in spite of its shortcoming, unavoidable in many countries, where civil servants are the only people with any experience of organization and management. Some civil servants make highly successful managers, and the shortcomings of the practice are due to an extent to the attitudes and practices associated with it such as, relatively low regard for such positions among senior civil servants and Ministers; treating such positions as halting places in a civil service career in which persons needing a berth (before they move to suitable positions in the civil service) are posted for short periods, rapid transfers or transfers with the interest of the civil service, rather than of the enterprise, in view. Posting of retired civil servants is particularly harmful. Their appointments are of short duration, so that transfers are frequent. The persons bring with them fixed attitudes, and have little incentive to learn and to adapt themselves to the needs of the enterprises. Moreover, since they are dependent for their appointment on political favours, they are willing to surrender their autonomy and to accept political interference even in matters of detail.

Managers of public enterprises recruited from the private sector, bring with them commercial attitudes and practices—a high regard for economy, flexibility, enterprise, institution of commercial accounting and finance practices, etc. The principal limitations of the practice are :

(a) Limited supply of suitable persons in the private sector. Transfer of very large numbers to public sector enterprises will deplete the private sector and reduce efficiency in it. However, to the extent that trained and capable persons, who had limited opportunities in the private sector, move to positions of greater responsibility in public sector enterprises, the practice leads to more efficient utilization of the available resource of executive manpower.

(b) Many private sector executives find salaries and other emoluments in public sector enterprises unattractive, or political or bureaucratic interference and the need to conform to rules and procedures of public services, irksome.

Foreigners have often been employed as managers of public enterprises with considerable success. The practice is most necessary in case of enterprises in modern, complex-technology industries such as petro-chemicals. It is most useful to the host country, if suitable numbers of its nationals are attached to the foreign managers as under-study, so that they are suitably trained and can takeover when the foreigners leave. The practice has two principal limitations:

(a) Reluctance of governments of underdeveloped countries to employ foreigners in key management positions even for limited periods. The reluctance may be due to political or social reasons or to unfavourable experience with employment of (unsuitable) foreigners in the past.

(b) Difficulty of finding suitable persons. Management skills are scarce, even in the developed, countries. Good managers find lucrative employment within their own countries and are not too anxious to go abroad. Governments of underdeveloped countries wishing to recruit foreign managers often find that they have to pay them very high salaries (or other emoluments). Besides the high cost of such payments, their effect on local salary structures and the morale of local managers have also to be considered, by the Governments. If these disturb local salary structures and lead to dissatisfaction among the local managers, or other staff, the Government may consider the cost of such employment to be too high. Moreover, since decision-makers in the Governments of underdeveloped countries are often not able to distinguish between good and bad managers—the distinction is especially hard to make in complex technology industries for which the need for employment of foreigners is greatest—they have often the unpleasant experience of being cheated by unscrupulous persons.

The problem is being met in various ways, principally through

(i) Collaboration agreements under which the foreign partner supplies its own trained managers and consultants, and
(ii) Foreign aid programmes—bilateral and of the United Nations and its specialized agencies.

Planned Recruitment, Training and Organization of Personnel

Recruitment policies and programmes have to be drawn up within the framework of personal needs and availabilities. The former are assessed from sectoral programmes and projects: the latter depend upon the output of educational (including professional education) institutions. Training may be organized in specialized institutions or on-the-job; within the country or abroad. The decisions will be influenced by the types of training required and the numbers required for each type, and the facilities available within the country and abroad. Crash programmes of training and similar measures are suitable for training large numbers of persons for middle management positions; but they are not suitable for training of top management personnel. Organization of personnel into cadres, task forces, management or technical groups, etc., is the third essential step. Without adequate attention to it, the available personnel are not utilized to maximum advantage, and unemployment among trained personnel and wastage of recruited personnel may appear along with shortages. Cadres are the most common, and perhaps the most suitable form of organization for middle-level personnel. The structure and functioning of the cadres must afford their members, security, as well as opportunities for advancement consistent with their experience and performance. They must also permit a degree of horizontal mobility, e.g. between public sector enterprises. Such mobility is important for efficient utilization of personnel in a period of rapid growth of enterprises. Opportunities should also be provided for in-service, refresher or other professional training. Such training enables the persons concerned to keep abreast of the latest developments in their fields, and is an essential measure of ensuring that the members of permanent cadres, who will constitute the great majority of management personnel, are attuned to modern developments and technological advances. Task forces and management groups are constituted on short or medium term basis for special jobs : they are essential devices for obtaining the participation and advice of the top executives and experts for these jobs. Consultancy groups or firms are composed of experts in different fields—engineering, accounts, economics, tax law, management, etc.,—coming together to work as teams. Such groups (or firms) take up a variety of jobs, large or small ranging from formulation and supervision of implementation of a large project to technical advice on a particular problem. Most consultancy groups are private; but they may also be organized in the public sector. Thus, a large, public sector steel, or petro-chemicals enterprise, may set up its own consultancy groups for formulation of expansion programmes. Consultancy groups from the developed countries are taking up large numbers of jobs of project formulation, appraisal, and supervision of execution in underdeveloped countries : the practice enables underdeveloped countries to obtain the services of qualified and experienced persons for highly specialized jobs. The alternative of training the nationals, or hiring foreign specialists for a wide variety of jobs would be much more expensive.

Personnel for Plan Formulation and Implementation

Formulation and implementation of a plan, providing for repaid economic growth, require large numbers of personnel,—from top-level executives, scientists, and engineers to technicians and skilled workers of all kinds. Assessments of the personnel needs of a plan and formulation of a manpower plan are important tasks in plan formulation. The administrative tasks and problems relating to meeting the personnel needs are primarily in the areas of recruitment, training and organization of personnel into cadres or services, task forces, etc. The tasks and problems are common, to an extent, to the public and the private sectors in mixed economies, but are discussed below with reference particularly to the public sector. The shortage of trained and skilled personnel, common to all underdeveloped countries, can be alleviated or aggravated greatly by the policies and practices followed in relation to organization of personnel. Similarly, efficiency in plan formulation and implementation are also affected greatly by personnel policies.

Personnel for Plan Formulation

The numbers involved are small; but the persons have to be carefully selected for their training, experience and aptitude. Plan formulation within the General Planning Agency requires mainly economists, econometricians, statisticians and sectoral specialists. The latter can be deputed from the sectoral ministries or departments, while the economists, statisticians, etc., can either be transferred from other departments, or more often, are specially recruited. Plan formulation within the ministries, departments, etc., is done mainly by permanent officials, who have detailed knowledge of the concerned sectors, acquired from years of experience in it. Advisers, consultants, etc., are often employed for specialized work. Formulation of projects is done either by individuals or groups of consultants specially hired for the purpose, of by members of project formulation groups working within the ministry, department or enterprise. Large work-executing ministries such as Public Works, Irrigation and Electricity, and large enterprises usually have their own project formulation groups; but hiring of consultants for project formulation or entrusting formulation to consulting groups or firms becomes necessary for most large, advanced technology projects.

The persons entrusted with plan formulation in the CPA and sectoral ministries and departments must possess, in addition to the required technical knowledge, an ability to comprehend the problems of the whole economy or sector and inter-sectoral relationships. Development of planning techniques in recent years has greatly facilitated this task of comprehension, but there is no substitute for the ability and aptitude for it.

To the extent that there are deficiencies of personnel for formulation of plans and projects among the nationals of an underdeveloped country, foreigners have to be employed. In many countries, foreign planning groups from universities and consulting firms have been assisting the planning authorities in formulation of the national plan. A group from Harvard University was assisting the Planning Commission of Pakistan for several years, and groups from several American Universities have assisted or are currently assisting planning authorities in many countries. Training of the nationals in planning techniques and phased termination of its own association is generally a part of the agreement under which such groups are employed. Employment of foreigners for planning for particular sectors, advice on particular problems, or formulation of particular projects is much more common : foreign advisors or consulting groups or firms are employed for some of these tasks in almost every underdeveloped country.

Personnel for Plan Implementation

Most of the personnel requirements of a plan are for implementation, and the principal problem in the underdeveloped countries is one of quantitative shortage. In most countries, the shortage extends to all or most kinds of personnel—from executives, engineers and doctors, to clerks, nurses, laboratory technicians and skilled workers of all kinds. The shortage is often aggravated by unfavourable attitudes, e.g., disinclination for blue-collar jobs. The shortage may be met by importing foreigs. But this is expensive and creates, besides, problems of adjustment between the foreigners and the nationals. In countries like the United Arab Republic (UAR) and India, with relatively developed educational and administrative systems, the shortage is mainly of top-level or highly skilled personnel—managers, scientists, and technologists. These countries have been able to meet their requirements of middle-and-lower-level personnel with relative ease, by suitable expansion of their programmes of training and recruitment. Indeed, there is now a surplus of some categories of personnel (e.g. of engineers in India) and the countries are sending out personnel to other countries. Emigration of personnel, including highly qualified and skilled scientists and technologists, takes place from these countries also because of faulty personnel practices, or because the salaries or working conditions for the personnel are not sufficiently attractive. The resulting ''brain drain'' is a serious problem in these countries, for which no effective solution has been devised so far.

Training and Recruitment

After assessment of personnel needs, training and recruitment programmes of adequate size, and adapted to the varied needs of plan implementation must be evolved. Training may precede recruitment, or follow it. Institutional training is generally before recruitment, while in-service or on-the-job training is after it. Training and recruitment programmes must be closely interrelated; in order to meet personnel needs efficiently, prevent waste of resources and avoid frustration among the persons concerned. Recruitment policies must be so designed as to enable all qualified persons equal opportunities for competing for the job—favouritism on grounds of family, group, region, etc., should be avoided—and also to provide the recruited personnel adequate and appropriate opportunities for promotion and advancement while in service. The latter is difficult to achieve, however, when large numbers of young persons have to be recruited within a short period for a new project or programme. Institutional training furnishes persons with basic education, technical knowledge or skills. It is time-consuming and has to be planned years in advance of requirements. But it can be speeded up through short condensed courses, crash programmes, etc. In-services training prepare persons for particular jobs and is usually of short duration. It cannot, however, be a substitute for institutional training — an adequate structure of training institutions is required to furnishing persons with the basic education and skills, who can be trained for specialized jobs through in-service training.

Organization of Personnel Cadre or Service

The cadre or service is the most common form of personnel organization in government, and is also widely adopted by large private sector firms. It is suitable wherever relatively large numbers of persons, with similar training or skills are employed to perform well defined tasks, which can, moreover, be graded according to skill or responsibility. The armed services, the diplomatic corps, the civil services of Britain, France and other countries, and the former colonial services are prominent examples of higher level services. The service organization is also employed for middle-and-lower-level personnel, ranging from doctors and engineers to stenographers. In underdeveloped countries, which were the colonies or dependencies of European countries, the administration used to be run by the colonial services, which were elite groups of generalists. Recruitment to the services was restricted, and members, besides being assured of financial security (and relative affluence) were given very wide authority. They were the "rulers'' and guardians of the colonial empires. In India, Pakistan and most of the British colonies, there were, in addition, somewhat lower-level services of generalist administrators, (manned by the natives) and also various technical services. The structure of services gave these countries a basic administrative organization and nucleus of trained and disciplined administrators and technicians, which have proved useful to them, especially in providing continuity and stability after the end of colonial rule. Countries like Indonesia and Burma in which such services were very small or were manned mostly by foreigners who left after Independence, have faced much more difficult problems. But dominance of the administrations by members of the former colonial services has had its disadvantages also. The general administrators of the services have been called upon to decide on increasing numbers of complex technical issues for which they have lacked the training and experience. They have taken the wrong decisions, or, more often, delayed decisions, because, feeling ill-equipped to take decisions on their own, they have referred decisions to Committees, Advisory Groups, etc. They have not shown sufficient willingness to refer decisions to qualified technicians;

the latter, denied the decision-making opportunities for which they were equipped, have felt frustrated. As a result, there has been increasing friction between the civil services and the technicians. Finally, the very continuity given by these services has been a disadvantage for economic progress. It has given the people a feeling of lack of change, so that the enthusiasm and sense of participation in a national endeavour for progress which could have been generated with inauguration of planning, after the end of colonial rule, and which could have contributed to economic progress, have not been generated. The conservative policies, advocated by the members of the services have also contributed to the feeling of lack of change.

The principal features of a cadre or service are the following:

(i) Competitive recruitment from among candidates meeting stipulated conditions—age, physical fitness, education, professional skill, mental aptitude, etc.

(ii) Fixed tenure with well defined scales of pay and other benefits and conditions of service.

(iii) Established practices relating to evaluation of performance, reward or punishment, relations between superiors and subordinates, etc.

(iv) A feeling of identification (or belonging) to a selected group, an *esprit de corps*. This feeling is particularly strong among elite groups such as the former colonial services.

The cadre or service is designed primarily for conditions of stability (or slow change), in which jobs can be carefully defined and graded, personnel requirements can be assessed, promotions and mobility, etc., can be regulated, and patterns of interaction between persons at different levels in the cadre can be defined. It is not too suitable for conditions of rapid growth in which the variety of jobs and personnel requirements increase rapidly, and people belonging to different age groups, possessing different kinds of training and skill, have to be recruited.

As mentioned earlier, inauguration of planning has been followed in most countries, with a rapid increase in the numbers of government employees. Most of them have been organized into cadres or services by :

(a) Creation of new cadres, e.g. of agricultural extension workers, social welfare workers and scientists;

(b) Expansion of existing cadres, e.g. of teachers and doctors;
(c) Adding new branches among existing cadres, e.g. of health educators among health workers, of research workers among cadres of engineers, doctors, agricultural workers, etc.

As a result, the number of cadres has increased, and each cadre is larger and has in it people with greater variety of training and skill and doing a greater variety of jobs.

The retention of the cadre organization and its use to meet the needs for organization of an increasing number of employees, reflect appreciation among the decision-makers of its basic usefulness. However, there are a number of problems, for which different solutions are being devised in different countries.

One set of problems relates to association of specialists. The cadre organization is most suitable for doing well defined routine jobs; it is most successful in association with line administration in which there are well defined channels of authority. However, with planning, technological advance and increasing specialization of most activities, there is need for increasing numbers of specialists, as advisers, staff officers, etc., in every ministry and department of government. Even a department such as police in which line administration and cadre organization are most dominant, in crime detection, analysis, intelligence work, etc. recruitment of specialists, fixing their pay scales and service conditions and evolving working relationships between them and the members of the existing cadres has presented problems. Frequently, the permanent cadre have opposed, and often succeeded in blocking, fixation of salary scales for the specialists, higher than or equivalent to their own, which were necessary to obtain specialists of sufficient training and competence. Posting of specialists in top positions, close to the decision-makers has evoked hostility and resentment from members of the permanent cadres.

Where large numbers of specialists with similar training, etc., were required, cadres have been constituted. Thus, in India, new cadres of scientists, economists, statisticians, etc., have been constituted in recent years. In this case also, evolving salary scales, service conditions and working relationships have created new problems. Salary scales and other service conditions have corresponded to (or been somewhat lower than) those of the generalist services. As a result, the best trained and the most competent do not find them sufficiently attractive, and the cadres are, therefore, deprived of the services of the most dynamic and creative persons in the respective fields. Secondly, it is noticed that the structure of the cadre organization is not particularly suitable for these specialized fields. For example, the principle of transferability among a number of similar jobs, a basic principle in the cadre organization, does not apply so well in these fields, as it does in general administration. Transfer of an economist or statistician who has worked for a number of years in one department to another department proves much less satisfactory than a similar transfer of a generalist administrator. In case of the scientist, transferability is even more restricted and the cadre exists only on paper.

The cadre organization has also proved unsuitable for filling highly specialized top-level jobs—managers, and executives in large public sector enterprises, scientists, technologists, etc. It is difficult to fit the most suitable persons into cadres for various reasons—unwillingness of the person to accept the salary scales and other conditions of the cadres (which are generally not too attractive), or to allow themselves to be assigned particular levels in cadres for fear that this would affect their advisory decision-making jobs, short duration of some jobs, etc. Such positions are, therefore, often left outside the cadres, and are filled on an *ad hoc* basis, which creates resentment among members of the cadre (who feel that they are deprived of the chance of getting the top jobs) and leads to accusations of favouritism, etc.

The Task Force and Pool

The deficiencies of the cadre organization have led many countries to experiment with other forms of personnel organization such as the task force and the pool. Task forces composed of groups of persons with different training and skills are constituted for particular jobs—the most common examples are project formulation or implementation teams. The task force brings together the different specialized skills and knowledge required to do a complex, technical job: its other advantages are that it focuses attention on the requirements of the job, so that a sense of urgency and single goal orientation can be maintained. But the success of a task force depends upon the personal qualities of the leaders and personal relations among the members.

The device of the pool or panel is adopted when a number of superior positions requiring similar skills, e.g. of managers, have to be filled. Its principal advantage over the cadre is that it allows much greater flexibility (e.g. in fixation of salary and other service conditions) and mobility. Highly specialized and experienced persons can, therefore, be attracted much more easily than into a cadre.

Financial Procedures for Plan Implementation

The financial procedures for plan implementation relate mainly to budgeting and resource allocations for programmes and projects. They are among the most important aspects of plan implementation, and a large proportion of the problems in plan implementation are related, directly or indirectly, with them.

Budgeting

A budget may be defined as a projection or forecast, for a period, of resources and allocations. Budgets are made for financial, material and other resources; budgets of financial resources, may relate, in turn, to cash, credit, foreign exchange, etc., and may be made for the whole economy or for the government. The most common budget is the annual budget of the Central Government of a country; but there are other important budgets, such as:

(i) Budgets of regional and local governments and enterprises,
(ii) Budgets of credit and foreign exchange, and
(iii) The Budget of the economy.

Government and enterprise budgets are prepared in all countries; the other budgets are also prepared in many countries practicing planning. The different budgets have to be interrelated; interrelation of the different budgets and further relation of the budgets with the plans are important aspects of plan formulation and implementation. Budgeting is not merely a book-keeping exercise : it involves projection, resource allocation and interrelation of different economic variables. Medium term and annual plans could be considered to be budgets of the economy. Increasingly, budgeting is being used also as a device for appraisal of progress of programmes and projects, through preparation of 'programme and performance budgets'.

The Annual Plan and the Budgets

Planning and budgeting are most closely related through the interrelation of the annual plan and the annual budget. The interrelation and the steps in processes of plan formulation and budgeting are discussed below with reference to the annual plan of the public sector and the annual budget of the government. Effective interlinkage of the two is ensured by :

(i) Framing the resource mobilization part of the budget within the framework of the monetary, fiscal and foreign exchange policies of the plan;
(ii) Including in the budget only the development programmes included in the annual plan and all of them. The development part of the budget should correspond to the plan for the public sector.
(iii) Adoption of the same time period, methods of presentation, concepts and definitions in both the budget and the annual plan;
(iv) Close collaboration between the Ministry of Finance and the CPA in various stages of plan formulation and budgeting.

The budget and the annual plan are not identical, however, because :

(a) The budget includes all expenditures of government, developmental as well as non-developmental, while the plan includes only the developmental expenditure;
(b) The budget relates only to the government, while the plan relates to the whole economy; and
(c) The budget relates only to financial magnitudes, while the plan relates also to physical magnitudes.

The principal steps in formulation of the annual plan and the annual budget are the following :

(i) Indication by the Ministry of Finance and the Central Planning Agency, to ministries, enterprises, etc., of the order of development expenditure during the coming year, and of broad guidelines for formulation of development programmes for the year, within the framework of the medium-term plan. The indication and the guidelines are based on analysis of trends during the previous year relating to production, investment, consumption, money-supply, prices, tax and other revenues, etc., and assessment of progress of projects and programmes. To the extent that changes in emphasis on particular programmes, or departures from the agreed phased programmes of execution of projects are desired—these arise from situations like fall in agricultural production due to bad weather, or fall in prices of export products, resulting in shortage of domestic or foreign resources—they should be clearly indicated to the ministries, enterprises, etc.

(ii) Formulation of development programmes and expenditure plans by the ministries, departments, enterprises, etc. The process proceeds in stages and may be spread over some months. The programmes of the enterprises and the departments are scrutinized, modified, coordinated and consolidated by the ministries, and then sent, for approval, to thc Ministry of Finance and the Central Planning Agency.

(iii) Approval of programmes by the Ministry of Finance and the CPA. The process involves : (a) discussion between the Ministry of Finance, the CPA and the ministries concerned, (b) modification of estimates by pruning particular items of expenditure, rephasing of particular programmes, etc., and (c) coordination of programmes of different ministries.

(iv) Consolidation of the approved programmes into the annual plan and the budget.

Approval of Budget and Transfer of Funds

The principal steps are :

(a) Presentation of the budget and the annual plan to the Legislature, and debates on budget proposals relating to taxation, borrowing, deficit financing, etc., and on expenditure proposals of the individual ministries. Modifications by the Legislature of budget proposals relating to taxation etc., are common in most countries. In countries following the American practice, the expenditure proposals of individual ministries are also modified by the Legislature; but this is however not common in countries following British Parliamentary practice.

(b) Approval by the Legislature.

(c) Authorization of expenditure by the Ministry of Finance.

(d) Transmission of authorization by heads of ministries to the heads of department, enterprises, etc. and by the latter to the executive officers working under them.

(e) *Modification of approved expenditure*: Proposals for modifications in approved expenditure have to go through one or more of the steps described above. Modifications within the approved allocations of the ministry, department, enterprise, etc., can be authorized by their respective heads; this practice is essential to avoid delays arising from repeat reference to the Ministry of

Finance. But proposals involving additional expenditure have to be referred to the Ministry of Finance, which in turn seeks approval of the Legislature through 'supplementary demands for grants'.

In countries with regional governments, the same processes—indication of broad guidelines by the (regional) Ministry of Finance and the planning agency; programme formulation by the ministries and enterprises; scrutiny and consolidation of proposals by the Ministry of Finance and the planning agency; formulation of the annual plan and the budget; approval of budget by the Legislature and transfer of funds to the ministries and enterprises—are repeated at the regional level. The processes at the national and regional levels are in progress at the same time. There is also continuous consultation between the national and the regional authorities (Ministries of Finance, Planning Agencies, and Sectoral ministries), to ensure coordination between national and regional plans. The broad indications given by the regional Ministry of Finance and the planning agency to the sectoral ministries fall within the framework of the indications given by the National Ministry of Finance and the CPA. Similarly, programme formulation by the regional sectoral ministries and enterprises is set within the framework of national programmes for each sector. This is because the national and regional plans are closely interrelated. Secondly, implementation of regional plans may involve large transfer of funds from the National Government to the regional governments, and the regional governments may have responsibility for undertaking developments complementary to national projects located within their areas. Regional governments must, therefore, know in detail the central guidelines on programmes and the amounts of the transfer funds likely to be available to them.

A similar relation obtains between local and regional (national in countries with unitary form of government) plans in most countries. Plans of local government authorities are closely related to the regional (or national) plan and their implementation is dependent, in large part, on transfer of funds from the regional (or national) government. One reason for this is that while local authorities have important responsibilities for execution of development programmes and operation of social services, their resources are limited. In most countries, the most remunerative revenue sources, such as income tax, taxes on imports and exports, excise duties, sales tax, etc., are with the national or regional governments, and the local governments have to depend upon revenue sources with limited or inelastic yield. But in countries such as Yugoslavia, in which local authorities have large resources of their own, local plans exhibit considerable initiative and independence, and may not be so closely related to regional and national plans.

Financial Procedure for Projects

The normal budgetary practice of authorization of expenditure for one year is not suitable for most projects, because construction of projects extends over two or more years, and approval of expenditure for a year at a time leads to interruptions in construction at the end of each financial year, and irksome, time-consuming and quite unnecessary requests, each year to the financial authorities for approval of expenditure. The difficulty is resolved by approval, at the initial stage itself, of the entire expenditure on the project, and of the phasing of expenditure during the construction period. The approved expenditure relating to years after the first is then included in the annual budget for each year by the Ministry of Finance, and authorizations are made by it without further examination. Further examination becomes necessary, however, when there are major changes either in total costs or in phasing of expenditure.

Division and Classification of the Budget

Division and classification of the budget are essential for:

(i) Distinguishing between current expenditure and investment, and between non-developmental and developmental expenditure;
(ii) Estimating the obligations for continuous or recurring expenditure; and
(iii) Analysis of expenditure by different ministries, enterprises, etc., or by types of activity.

The principal division of the budget is into 'Revenue' and 'Capital'. The *Revenue budget* relates to expenditure on current activities of the government and is financed from current revenues, mainly tax receipts. The *Capital budget* relates to investment by the government, and is financed from current revenue surpluses, past reserves, borrowings, etc. Most developmental expenditures are included in the capital budget. But 'Revenue' and 'Capital' and 'non-developmental' and 'developmental' are not synonymous. Developmental expenditure may be financed from the Revenue budget; moreover, all of it does not constitute 'capital' expenditure;

expenditure on construction of an administrative office building or a palace is 'capital' expenditure, but it is not 'developmental' expenditure.

The division between developmental and non-developmental expenditure is based partly on conventions. In India, expenditure on running of institutions and maintenance of projects is classified as developmental expenditure during the entire period of the Five Year Plan in which they were started, but as 'non-developmental' expenditure, thereafter. One result of this practice is that the end of each Five Year is accompanied by a very large increase in 'non-developmental' expenditure. The division of expenditure into 'non-recurring' and 'recurring' is essential for indicating the initial expenditure and the continuing or future liability resulting from a particular financial decision, e.g. approval of a project. Expenditure on staff is 'recurring'. In case of buildings and equipment, the principal expenditures, represented by construction and purchase respectively, are 'non-recurring', while the expenditure on maintenance is 'recurring'.

Classification of the budget by heads, sub-heads and further sub-divisions is generally done (i) by ministries, departments and enterprises, and by activities within them, and (ii) according to objects of expenditures—salaries, and other allowances of staff, purchase of equipment, etc. In this way, the classification of the budget divides expenditure by spending agencies, activities and objects of expenditure. In some countries (e.g. Kuwait), classification by objects of expenditure is elevated to the position of primary division of the budget; the primary divisions are :

- Salaries and allowances of staff.
- Equipments, buildings and other expenditures on projects.

The practice is not too suitable for planning, because it does not permit ready and clear separation of 'developmental' and 'non-developmental' expenditure. In many countries, the classification of the budget, designed at an earlier period, has proved to be quite unsuitable for the needs of planning, because large expenditures on projects and other developmental activities are not adequately classified, while minute divisions exist for classification of expenditures which are now unimportant. Reclassification of the budget is an important aspect of the budgetary reforms to meet the needs of planning.

Credit and Foreign Exchange Budgets

In contrast to the general budget, which relates only to the government (or the public sector), the *credit budget* and the *foreign exchange budget* relate to the whole economy, and show allocations of resources between the government and the rest of the economy, and among different sectors of the economy. Both budgets are prepared, in most countries, by the Central Bank, which is the principal agency exercising overall control over credit and foreign exchange. Preparation of the foreign exchange budget is essential in all countries exercising control over foreign exchange. Preparation of the credit budget is essential in centrally planned economies, in which there is direct allocation of credit by the Central Bank to the enterprises, and is an advantage also in mixed economy countries, in which control over credit is exercised primarily through indirect measures, e.g. manipulation of the bank rate. The credit budget enables the Central Bank to keep a watch over credit flows within the economy, and ensures that they are in accordance with the plan. Further, it enables the Bank to supplement, to the extent necessary, indirect measures with measures of direct control, e.g. prohibition on advances (by commercial banks) for purposes such as buying of real estate and speculative buying of agricultural or mineral products.

Programme and Performance Budget

The conventional budget relates only to financial magnitudes; it does not give any indication of physical performance. Full utilization of financial allocations for a programme or project may be accompanied by serious shortfall in physical performance, because of operational inefficiency, rise in costs, etc.; but the conventional budget will not indicate the shortfall. This is a serious deficiency, particularly for plan implementation, because for efficiency in plan implementation it is essential that detailed data on physical performance and the relationship of the latter with financial expenditure should be continuously available. There are two main reasons for this :

(i) The delicate, and often lightly stretched, input-output relationships and material balances underlying many plans, are liable to be completely upset by serious shortfalls in even a few sectors;

(ii) Since planning is accompanied by rapid rise in development expenditure from year-to-year, the possibilities of waste increase greatly, if continuous and close watch cannot be maintained over physical performance, and the latter cannot be related with financial expenditure.

Programme and performance budgeting meets the needs of showing financial and physical magnitudes in one place and interrelating them. The technique of programme and performance budgeting has developed rapidly, in recent years, especially in USA where this system of budgeting is now well established within the government (United Nations, 1965). The system is also being adopted by a number of other countries and its adoption by underdeveloped countries as an important aid to plan implementation is being recommended. Adoption of the system, with suitable modifications to suit the particular needs of each country, is undoubtedly a major budgetary reform to meet the needs of planning. The principal problem, especially in case of the underdeveloped countries, is the difficulty of obtaining data on physical performance, in sufficient detail and simultaneously with data on expenditures. The difficulty arises from deficiencies in the progress reporting systems. Adoption of programme and performance budgeting could, by highlighting the need for detailed and timely progress reports, expedite reforms in progress reporting. If this does not happen, however, it could do more harm than good, because the executive agencies may give vague or incorrect data on performance in order to satisfy the budget authorities.

The Problems of Procedural Delays and Inadequacy of Financial Scrutiny

Perhaps the most serious financial problem in relation to plan implementation is that of procedural delays in approval of projects and programmes, and in transfers of funds. This problem is perhaps greater in countries, which inherited the colonial administrative systems in which the financial authorities were accustomed to minute examination of all financial proposals, than in other countries. It is also greater, because of longer lines of communication and a larger number of processing stages, when approvals and transfers involve regional or local governments, or autonomous public sector or private sector enterprises.

The problem is due, in part to over-concentration of financial powers, and has been sought to be met by progressive delegations of financial powers—from the Ministry of Finance to the sectoral ministries, from the ministries to departments and enterprises under them; and within the latter from heads to operating officials; from the federal government to the regional governments, and from the latter to the local governments, etc. However, it has been noticed in many countries that the need for delegation increases continuously with progress of planning (e.g. with rise in plan expenditure and undertaking of larger and more complex projects and programmes) and that the Ministry of Finance and the other delegating authorities are never able to meet the need adequately. In order to get over delays in transfers of funds, to regional/local governments or enterprises, the device of 'block transfers of funds' is adopted. Under it, transfer of funds for plan implementation from the federal to the regional government are made in one block (e.g. for the entire annual plan), instead of being linked with individual programmes and projects. In case of enterprises, similarly, the occasions for transfer of funds (for projects or for current operations) are reduced to the minimum.

But the delegation of powers remains limited, in many countries and block transfers of funds and other similar devices are not adopted, because the Ministry of Finance and other delegating authorities are afraid of inefficiency and waste at the executive levels, or wish to use their financial powers as instruments of coordination or feel that they must retain the powers to meet their obligations of accountability, e.g. to the Legislature. Where delegations remain limited for fears of waste and inefficiency, the waste and inefficiency resulting from procedural delays should be carefully compared with those that might result from larger delegations. In any case, the remedy for checking waste and inefficiency is to improve efficiency at the executive levels, and not to hamper the initiative of people at these levels through distrust, excessive limitation of powers, and red-tape. Use of financial powers for coordination is neither legitimate nor efficient : coordination can only be secured by building at every point in the planning and administrative system, appropriate structures and processes of coordination and bringing them to an efficient level of functioning. The issue of accountability is more complex, however, and the desire of the ministries, departments and heads of enterprises to retain sufficient financial control to be able to discharge their accountability obligations is legitimate. But the requirements of both accountability and adequate delegation of financial powers can be met through adequate strengthening and improvement of the systems of communication and appraisal of progress. The need for concentration of powers is less, if the directions of the supervisory authorities are conveyed to the executive authorities and the problems and difficulties of the latter are known to the former, and data on progress is available, quickly and in detail. Emergency action can always be taken in such cases by temporary curtailment of the powers of the executive authorities.

A second set of problems relate to the adequacy of financial scrutiny and analysis. Financial scrutiny in most countries is confined to purely financial, procedural or administrative matters such as payment obligations and receipts, salary scales of personnel, etc. It does not extend to financial or economic evaluation of projects, cost/benefit analysis, or technical evaluation of cost estimates, because the Ministry of Finance is not equipped for such analysis. Such analysis is undertaken in many countries at the levels of the sectoral ministries and enterprises. But with progress of planning, as increasing numbers of public sector enterprises have been established and increasing amounts have been given as loans or grants to private sector enterprises, Ministries of Finance in many countries have set up project Divisions to be more adequately equipped for scrutiny of programmes and projects of the enterprises.

REFERENCES

United Nations Department of Economics and Social Affairs: *A Manual of Programme and Performance Budgeting,* New York 1965.

Wn, Chi Yuen : Public Administration for National Development : *International Social Service Journal*, UNESCO, Paris, Vol. XXL, 1969.

3

Administrative Plan Formulation and Implementation

Introduction

References have been made earlier to administrative deficiencies and difficulties in plan formulation and plan implementation, which have affected efficiency of plan formulation and have resulted in serious shortfalls in output and delays or overruns in costs of projects and programmes. These deficiencies and difficulties can be seen as related to one or the other of the following *seven* areas :

1. Communication
2. Coordination
3. Concentration of Decisions
4. Assessment of Administrative Resources
5. Administration and the Public
6. Finance
7. Personnel

The problems relating to Finance and Personnel are discussed in the appropriate sections. The remainder is discussed below.

Communication

Among the problems of communication, those relating to (i) collection and processing of data, and (ii) changes in patterns of communication are the most important.

Problems of Collection and Processing of Data

Plan formulation and implementation are dependent upon supply of a large magnitude and variety of data, e.g. on macro-economic variables such as population, national income and employments, on the various resources (financial, material, manpower and natural) and data on progress of projects and programmes. The data should be adequate and accurate and they should be available in time. It has been mentioned above that: (i) planning has been accompanied, in most countries, by large expansion and reorganization of survey, statistical and other data collecting agencies, (ii) close relations must be established between these agencies and the planning agencies, particularly the central statistical agency and the CPA, and (iii) efficient and adequate systems of progress reporting and inspection must be established to ensure efficiency in plan implementation. Difficulties and deficiencies relating to data result mainly from the failure to meet these essential requirements.

Expansion of the data collecting agencies may not be adequate for various reasons—shortages of personnel, financial difficulties, inadequate appreciation of the need for different kinds of data, etc. The work of the data collecting agencies may not be sufficiently reoriented to meet the needs of planning. Much data, needed for planning, is collected by the executive agencies during the course of their work. Thus data on imports and exports are collected by the customs authorities and on incidence and causes of mortality by the public health authorities. The planning agencies may require changes in the content of data, especially greater detail, or in methods of collection or processing, which may not be made by the data collecting agencies because of administrative difficulties or because there is not sufficient appreciation of the need for the changes. In some cases, the ministries or other agencies are unwilling to furnish data to the planning agencies. This difficulty is serious in countries where the coordinating role of the CPA has not been accepted by the executive agencies.

The problem of obtaining data is much greater in case of the private sector. It arises on the one hand from the unwillingness of managements of large enterprises to reveal details of their operations (to keep them from being known to their competitors and tax authorities) and on the other from the difficulties and the large costs of collecting data on small enterprises, e.g. in agriculture, handicraft industries and retail trade. Collection of data for individuals and households,—on size of population, employment, consumption and savings, etc. required for estimation of the macro-economic variables, also requires much time and expense. Censuses and sample surveys are carried out for collection of such data.

Another set of difficulties relates to delays and defects in communication of data. They may arise again from inadequacy of personnel, lack of modern data-processing devices or other resource deficiencies, and long channels of communications, or simply because too much data is being collected and communicated.

Planners, lacking experience of planning and not sufficiently conscious of the costs of data collection, frequently collect too much data. The same mistake is made by managements of enterprises and supervisory officials in Ministries and Departments, in respect of data on progress of projects and programmes. These data should be selected carefully: they should give to the decision-makers, all information needed for appraisal of progress, they should be capable of verification, e.g. by inspecting officers, quickly and without too much difficulty, and they should not burden the executive officers unduly. Key indicators of progress are particularly useful for this purpose.

New Patterns of Communication

Plan formulation and implementation require new and significantly different patterns of communication, within government and between the government and the private sector, than had prevailed earlier. The earlier patterns within government were predominantly vertical, i.e. between different levels in the administrative hierarchy. But planning brings with it important horizontal and multi-lateral communications, such as between the CPA and the ministries, the ministries and enterprise, and the CPA, and regional planning agencies. Secondly, whereas in the essentially *laissezfaire* situation, which prevailed before the advent of planning, communication between the government and private enterprises was limited, there is now intensive and constant communication between them—for formulation and implementation of monetary, fiscal, resource allocation and various other regulatory measures. But establishing additional channels of communication within the government and between the government and private enterprises and strengthening existing channels is difficult. The difficulties relate, as in case of data, to non-appreciation of the need for additional or stronger communication channels, resistance to establishment of the channels, and deficiencies of staff and other resources. Resistance to establishing new channels of communication is even greater than in case of resistance to collection and transmission of new data, because questions of relative status and importance of different organs are involved. But even when there is no such resistance, adequate and appropriate communication channels may not be established because of lack of realization of the need for them. Usually, such channels are established only after problems have arisen in plan formulation or implementation.

Coordination

Defects of coordination are closely linked with those of communication—much defective coordination results from deficiencies in communication—but they are not entirely due to them. They result also from various other reasons, such as (i) inadequate and inappropriate conception of roles of different agencies, or of the needs of coordination, and (ii) inadequate or inappropriate delegation of powers. The central planning agency is often not able to perform its function of coordination of sectoral and regional plans efficiently, because the chief executive does not fully appreciate the need for it, does not give to the CPA the required political support, and does not set in motion the needed administrative arrangements. Planning units at other levels—ministry, enterprise, region, locality—may be similarly handicapped, because of lack of support from the corresponding executive agencies—ministries, regional governments, heads of enterprises, etc.

Visualizing the coordination needs of formulation and implementation of a comprehensive national plan is extremely difficult for leaders and decision-makers in the underdeveloped countries, in which the activities of the government were limited until recently, and most executive organs were concerned with execution of their limited functions. For instance, analysis of intersectoral and intrasectoral linkages (through input-output, material balances or partial methods) is an important aspect of plan formulation, and success in plan implementation is dependent upon inter-sectoral and intrasectoral flows of inputs and outputs as envisaged in the plan. But efficient and smooth flows can be ensured only through coordination of plan implementation at various levels—enterprise or project, sector, inter-sectoral, locality, region and nation. In case of an industrial project, for instance, construction of the factory buildings, installation of machinery, supply of raw materials, and provision of essential infrastructures such as power and transport must be effectively coordinated. Since such coordination is dependent upon flow of inputs from different enterprises, as well as coordinated action by different agencies at project site, adequate and efficient patterns of communication, coordination and control must be established.

Defects and deficiencies of coordination, relating to projects are brought out more easily (e.g. by delays in completion or in attaining full capacity output) and remedial action is generally taken more rapidly than is the case with those relating to different programmes located in the same area or region. The results of the latter are seen in phenomena like dispensaries without doctors, tube-wells without electricity, lack of facilities for marketing and transport of the larger agricultural output resulting from operation of an irrigation project, or unemployment of technical personnel, trained at high cost. The cost to the community of such defects is no less (perhaps greater) than that of coordination defects relating to projects, but remedial action is often delayed because the consequences of the defects are not so clearly seen. Defective coordination can only be secured by establishing adequate and efficient patterns of coordination and communication at every level. They should be established along with decentralization of operational decisions, so that the maximum number of problems are solved at enterprise, local and regional levels, and only those requiring policy decisions or relating to large magnitudes come up to higher levels.

Concentration of Decisions

Defects of coordination often result from concentration of powers at the top—with the chief executive, central or regional ministries or heads of enterprises—and inadequate delegations to local, project or other operational levels. This leads to long channels of communication, inadequate appreciation of needs and problems of the operational levels by the policy-makers, and of policies by the executive officers, and loss of initiative on the part of the latter. As a result, solutions to coordination problems, which could be easily and quickly reached through direct action by the executive officers, are often delayed or are made more difficult. It is true that top decision-makers often concentrate powers in their own hands and develop patterns of communication at the top, to the detriment of those at lower, operational levels, in order to get over difficulties of coordination. But such attempts at securing coordination only betray lack of appreciation of efficient administrative or management practice, because effective coordination can only be secured by establishing suitable and efficient patterns of communication and decision at every level. Concentration of powers is also the most important cause of the procedural delays which plague all aspects of plan formulation and implementation, especially in the underdeveloped countries, and result in serious shortfalls in output, bottlenecks and other disturbances.

The problems created by concentration of decisions increase with economic development; they are greater in large countries, than in small ones, and in centrally planned economies than in mixed economies. The problems may not be too serious in the early stages of economic development, when the most urgent tasks are clear, the choices are limited; and the top decision-makers, especially in small, mixed economy countries, can make the needed decisions fairly efficiently. But this becomes increasingly difficult as economic development proceeds, the economy gets diversified, and the range of choices increases. The problems are greater in large countries than in small ones for two main reasons: (i) large size leads to long and time-consuming communications, and (ii) large size and socio-economic and physical diversity of the country make it difficult for any group of central decision-makers to visualize and appreciate adequately the needs and problems of different regions. Finally, the problems are greater in the centrally planned economies than in the mixed economies, because in the absence of the market, the volume of decision-making by the planners is so much greater. It will be seen from descriptions of the organization of planning in the Soviet Union and Yugoslavia (in Chapter 4) that a large proportion of the "planning" decisions in these countries relate to operation of enterprises in mixed economies, in response to market conditions.

The problems arising from concentration of power at top levels can be solved by decentralization of administrative and financial powers to operational levels, and by reducing the volume of decision-making in planning. Decentralization of administrative and financial powers should go hand in hand : the former does not become effective in absence of the latter, because if authorities at the operational levels have to seek financial approval from top levels, decentralization of administrative decisions loses much of its value. The volume of decision-making can be reduced by confining planning to key sectors and directing overall economic activity and growth through control over them. This method has been used with success in France and is particularly suitable for planning in developed mixed economy countries. Since large countries are also usually federal countries, building up strong planning and executive agencies at regional levels and maximum decentralization of decisions to them would appear to be the remedy for concentration of powers in these countries. But these steps are either not taken in some federal countries or, if taken, are frustrated, in practice, by the procedures of plan formulation and implementation. Decentralization may not be done if the central planners feel that certain basic objectives of planning, such as high rates of saving and investment, allocation of large resources to heavy industry, powers, transport, etc., will be jeopardized thereby. They may be afraid that regional planners, and political executives, more responsive to popular pressures, will allocate large resources to consumption or investment in consumption goods industries. Decision-making may also remain concentrated at central levels, if resource transfer from the Central Government to regional governments is not made in the form of block grants, but remains tied to individual projects or programmes, because in that case each project or programme has to be approved by central authorities.

Concentration of decisions has remained a major issue in centrally planned economies, and different economies have attempted to meet the problems created by it in different ways. Yugoslavia found concentration of decisions, which had characterized its early period of "centralized administration planning" to be a serious impediment in the way of efficient plan formulation and implementation. It undertook from 1952, a series of economic and political reforms to transfer decision-making powers and financial resources from the central to regional, local and enterprises levels. Moreover, it built strong local and enterprise level institutions, like the commune and the workers' council, for effective exercise of the powers. The decentralization and liberalization, have been progressively extended, so much so that the Yugoslav's economy is now indistinguishable in many ways from market economies. Soviet planning has remained highly centralized, however, though some decentralization measures have been taken, especially in recent years. Two notable measures, taken in 1961-62, are :

(i) Preparation of comprehensive plans by the planning organs of the Union Republics, Autonomous Republics, etc., and greater powers of plan implementation to their governments. Earlier, the republican plans had somewhat restricted scope. They were limited to sectors which were under the control of the republican governments, and sectors such as heavy industry, which were under the control of the central ministries, were excluded from them.

(ii) Constitution of *Sovnarkhozy* for Economic Administration Areas and Regions, for planning and administration of projects in industrial construction and related sectors. The *Sovnarkhozy*

> now perform most of the functions of plan formulation and implementation performed earlier by the central ministries.

Larger decentralization, particularly at the enterprise level, has been advocated in recent years by a group of economists, led by Prof. Lieberman.

Assessment of Administrative Resources
Need for Administrative Reform

The failure to assess the administrative requirements of plan formulation and implementation, the tendency to grossly underestimate these requirements or to omit vital areas from estimation, are common in underdeveloped countries, and constitute perhaps the most important causes of the defects and deficiencies in plan formulation and implementation. The "failure" of plans in many countries has been attributed to the fact that the administrative needs of plan implementation were either not assessed, or the capacity of the administrative system to meet these was grossly overestimated. The main reason for this is that few planning agencies realize that administration is a resource which needs to be, and can be, assessed in the process of plan formulation, along with other resources. The fact that the techniques of assessment, of the administrative resource are not well developed, contributes to the failure to make the assessment or to make a faulty assessment.

The attempts at assessment are usually confined to assessing the needs of technical personnel—such assessments are often made in connection with manpower planning. The needs for lower-level administrative personnel may also be assessed, if there is a shortage of such personnel and there is doubt about the capacity of the educational system to meet the shortage. But assessment of the needs for higher level administrative and managerial personnel is rare, and, the exercise is seldom extended to other administrative resources.

In the plans of a few countries, references are made to the administrative needs and tasks of planning, and qualitative recommendations are made for administrative reforms to meet the needs. But the recommendations are often not followed, and *ad hoc*, individual "reforms" are made from time to time only when problems accumulate, and the need for reforms becomes inescapable. Financial powers are delegated and financial procedures are simplified or improved, and new patterns of communication and coordination are introduced generally under such pressures.

But the need for systematic assessment of the administrative requirements of planning and of administrative reforms to meet the needs is receiving progressively greater attention, as experience is gained with planning, and the planners, administrators, and the political executives appreciate the importance of the administrative factor in successful implementation of plans. Development Administration is emerging as a distinct area of study in public administration. Systematic analyses of administrative problems of plan formulation and implementation in underdeveloped countries has been aided by a number of studies undertaken by the United Nations and associated specialized agencies. Development of techniques of assessment of the administrative resources is also being aided by these agencies : the Public Administration Division of the UN has undertaken a study of the methodology of appraising administrative capability for development (Chi Yuen, 1969 : 121).

Two defects, which are related to assessment of administrative requirements, deserve particular mention. These are :

(i) Drawing up over-ambitious plans and taking up an unduly large number of projects; and
(ii) Transferring to projects in the underdeveloped countries, time schedules and estimates of requirements of personnel and other resources, based on experience in the developed countries.

The first defect may be due to faulty assessment of administrative resources, or it may be due to political pressures for expansion of programmes and inclusion of too many projects. It leads to dispersal of resources, inefficiency, waste and delays in implementation, and slow growth. The second defect is more closely related to faulty assessment. The time schedules and estimates of requirement of personnel and other resources for projects prevailing in the developed countries are a reflection of the high levels of labour and management skills, efficiency of the administrative system, and development of infrastructure facilities of these countries. But when they are transferred to projects in underdeveloped countries, without adjustments for the lower levels in the latter, the results inevitably are delays, overruns in costs, etc. Even when the differences in labour and management skills are minimized (e.g., by giving turnkey contracts to contractors from developed countries) the time and cost turnout to be significantly higher in the underdeveloped countries because of deficiencies in infrastructure or because of various administrative delays and deficiencies. The very fact that the decision-makers and the administrative system are not attuned to an environment of speed and efficiency, characteristic of the developed countries, leads to higher time and costs in the underdeveloped countries.

Administration and the Public

The enlargement of the functions and activities of the administrative agencies, consequent on planning, greatly increase the interaction between the administration and the public. The interaction is primarily in three areas :

(i) Formulation and Implementation of Projects and Programmes.
(ii) Regulation, and
(iii) Resource mobilization.

Formulation and Implementation of Projects and Programmes

It has been mentioned earlier that representatives of the people in legislatures and local institutions reflect their needs and aspirations, which are taken into account by the planners and the chief executive in formulating the goals and objectives of the plan, as well as specific programmes and projects. Members of Legislatures do not generally participate in detailed formulation or implementation of projects or programmes, but those of local institutions do. Local institutions have important responsibilities of detailed formulation and implementation, which range from management of local services and construction activities (education, health, roads, housing, etc.) in most countries, to management of economic enterprises in Yugoslavia. In many countries, participation of the people in programmes of local (community) interest is encouraged through community development programmes. Under these programmes, projects of local interest are formulated in detail and implemented by local communities, which share their costs. This brings forth additional resources for plan implementation, and also makes possible interested and purposeful participation of the people in development activities. Economic organizations, such as cooperatives, which have important functions in modernization of traditional sectors such as agriculture and handicraft industries, or in marketing and distribution, also provide useful opportunities for participation of the people in formulation and implementation of development programmes. Local institutions and cooperatives also provide opportunities to officials and popular representatives to work together. In underdeveloped countries, which have inherited a colonial, law-and-order-and-revenue-collection administration, and in which the great majority of the rural population is illiterate and tradition-bound, such opportunities are invaluable for bringing the administration closer to the people (bridging the intellectual and emotional gap between the people and the officials) and diffusion of modern attitudes and practices among the people.

In many countries, where the local institutions or cooperatives were newly established, or their spheres of activity or responsibility were greatly increased after initiation of planning, implementation of programmes entrusted to these bodies has been marked by considerable inefficiency, waste and corruption. These have resulted from inexperience, incompetence and/or dishonesty of popular representatives, or officials, and have led, in turn, to widespread dissatisfaction among the people. The remedial action, in many countries, has consisted of tightening control of the regional (or national) governments over the working of these institutions, or restricting their functions. A more fruitful approach, which has also been followed in a few countries, is training of members of the institutions and officials in their duties and responsibilities.

Regulation

The regulatory measures include controls over production, employment and income; rationing of scarce consumer goods and productive resources; controls over land use and other regulations connected with physical planning, etc. The measures are undertaken in order to direct productive activity in accordance with the plan, to spread burdens and sacrifices equitably, or to achieve other socio-economic objectives such as distribution of income, and regional distribution of production and employment. The range and nature of the regulatory measures vary greatly in different countries, depending upon the nature of the economy, the scope and nature of planning, and the stage of administrative development. The measures are much greater in number (and are also more comprehensive and more stringent) in centrally planned economies than in mixed economies; they are also more numerous and more stringent if the plan envisages tight resource allocations, or attempts a major structural transformation of the economy and society in a short period. For regulatory measures to be implemented with any degree of success a minimum level of administrative development is required, in its absence, the measures fail to achieve their objectives and only cause (i) delays in plan implementation, and (ii) hardships to the general public and entrepreneurs, and alienate them from the government.

Controls over production are needed in order to achieve the output targets of the plan, and to implement rationing of consumer goods and materials. They are usually accompanied by controls over movement, they can be most easily implemented, and are also most successful in sectors, in which individual enterprises are large in size. Implementation is particularly difficult in case of agriculture, because of the small size and scattered nature of the enterprises, and absence or weakness of sectoral economic organizations. These organizations have a useful role in detailed formulation and implementation of the production control measures. They act as liaison between the government and (their member) enterprises, convey the point of view and problems of the enterprises to the government and persuade the enterprises to accept and conform to regulation of their activities.

Controls over employment are introduced generally in order to allocate scarce manpower resources. They are a characteristic feature of centrally planned economies, but are rare, or have limited scope, in mixed economies. Controls over income are exercised through taxation, fixation of minimum wages is an important measure of welfare of depressed or exploited sections of the community; effective implementation of the measure is difficult, however, in the situation of labour surplus which prevails in many underdeveloped countries.

Rationing

Rationing of scarce productive resources—materials, credit, foreign exchange, etc.—is necessary under most plans, because the plans make rather tight resource allocations. The principal object of the measures is that the needs of "essential users" are met, and consumption by "non-essential users" is kept at a minimum. Consumer goods may be rationed, if there is shortage of such goods at the beginning of the plan or develops because investment in consumer goods sectors under the plan is not adequate to meet the growth of demand (and the deficiency is not met adequately by imports), or if supplies are reduced temporarily by such fortuitous factors as a poor harvest. The scope and nature of the rationing measures depend upon the nature of the resources or goods covered and the degree of scarcity. Efficiency in implementation of the measures depends upon the levels of administrative developments, and previous experience of administration of the measures.

Rationing of essential consumer goods, such as food and clothing, is the most difficult, because the entire population has to be covered, and shortages cause much hardship and discontent. Prolonged and comprehensive rationing of consumer goods had been a characteristic of centrally planned economies : the resultant hardship to the public has been accepted by the planners as the price of attaining high rates of economic growth and industrial development. In Western countries, however, experience with rationing of consumer goods has been limited to war and post-war years, when the restrictions on consumption and the hardship were accepted by the public as a price of the war. In many underdeveloped countries practicing planning, rationing of consumer goods is in force, but the experience is generally unsatisfactory, because of low levels of administrative efficiency and honesty. Rationing measures are, along with resource mobilization measures, the most important cause of corruption and dissatisfaction of the public with the administration and with planning.

Rationing of productive resources (materials, credit and foreign exchange) is less difficult and creates fewer administrative problems than rationing of consumer goods. This is because the number of people to be dealt with by the rationing authorities is relatively small. But the scope for corruption is greater, because administration of the public (the legislature, or the press) and the managers of enterprises and businessmen, who are the ones principally affected by the measures, are willing, in many countries, to pay bribes to obtain concessional or even due allocations of resources.

For successful rationing of consumer foods and scarce materials, effective control over production, imports/exports, movement and distribution are required. To the extent that production, imports and exports, are carried out by private enterprises, the activities of the latter must be regulated. Such regulation is particularly difficult in case of agricultural enterprises, governments in few countries are successful in inducing the farmers to sell to the rationing authorities, food and other agricultural commodities needed for successful operation of the rationing system. The principal reason for the failure is that the prices fixed by the rationing authorities are considered too low by the farmers. But the supplies of products, which do not become available to the rationing authorities, find their way into "black markets". Existence of such markets leads to discontent and often reduces the confidence of the public in the government. However in some situations, the markets are accepted, both by the public and the government, as a necessary safety valve, which keeps the rationing system from breaking down. In some cases, only a part of the available supplies is requisitioned by the rationing authorities, and the remainder is allowed to be distributed through legal "free" markets.

Rationing of credit and foreign exchange are the most important regulatory fiscal measures related to plan implementation in both mixed economies and centrally planned economies. They are implemented primarily by the central bank, with assistance of the commercial banks and specialized agencies such as industrial banks. The public is not directly affected by the measures, except by restrictions on foreign travel, which generally accompany rationing of foreign exchange.

Relatively tight resource allocations and rationing may be accepted as the necessary price of attaining a rapid rate of economic growth. But too tight resource allocations should be avoided, especially in the underdeveloped countries, in which the levels of administrative efficiency and honesty are low and the government's control over production, movement and distribution tends to be loose. Tight resource allocations, apart from causing hardships and discontent among the public, expose the economy to the dangers of widespread disruption of production and distribution, in case of unexpected shortfalls in production in a few key sectors or delays in completion of important projects. Secondly, the control and rationing measures should be confined, to the extent possible, to a few goods or resources, because administration of the measures requires large administrative resources of high quality, and such resources are very scarce in underdeveloped countries.

The primary objective of licensing of enterprises is to implement the sectoral production objectives of the plan. Secondary objectives may include direction of regional location of enterprises, etc. Licensing is often linked with scarce resources : the resources are either reserved for licensed enterprises, or the latter are given preference in their allocation. Control over land use and related physical planning regulations affect both enterprises and the general public. They are administered generally by local or regional planning authorities. The scope and importance of such regulations increases with economic development : much public grievance against "planning" in the developed countries arises primarily from these measures.

Resource Mobilization

Resource mobilization measures for financing implementation of the plan affect the public in a variety of ways : they are a major source of interaction between the public and the administration, and condition, to a large extent, the public image of the administration. Taxation measures are the most important in this respect, because their financial effects are most clearly seen by the public and because tax authorities come in direct contact with the public. Governments in most underdeveloped countries rely primarily on indirect taxes to meet the resource needs of plans; direct taxes have not been given equal importance, because yields are low in comparison with the costs of collection. The difficulties of collection of direct taxes are related in turn to low levels of efficiency and honesty in tax administrations, and unwillingness of the people to pay direct taxes. But indirect taxes are regressive in nature, and the cumulative effect of indirect taxes is inflationary. The rise in prices resulting from indirect taxes also causes dissatisfaction among the people, and planning begins to be identified by them with burdensome taxation and high prices.

High taxation imposes a heavy burden on the public and involves considerable sacrifice. In order that these are borne willingly and without causing social discontent, it is essential that the burdens and sacrifices are distributed equitably, and are also seen by the public to be so distributed. But this can be accomplished only with a high level of administrative efficiency and honesty in the tax departments : few things disturb the burdens of plan implementation or damage the public image of the administration so much as inefficient or corrupt tax departments.

The public impact of borrowing programmes is limited, because the principal participants in the programmes are the financial institutions. The public is directly affected only by the small savings programme, i.e. sale of small savings certificates or bonds. The yield from the programme is not large in most countries, but the governments give considerable importance to it (and spend large resources of finance and manpower on it), because of its educational and public participation effects. The programme induces a sense of participation in the national plan among the public, and can also be used to educate it about the objectives and content of the plan.

Deficit financing has very important effects, which are spread throughout the economy and are felt by all sections of the people. The effects are particularly serious if deficit financing leads to inflation. Inflation greatly increases the tasks and problems of the administration, because a whole array of administrative measures has to be taken to control it. These range from fiscal measures, such as regulation of the bank rate to price controls on consumer goods and materials, controls over wages, rents, etc. A runaway inflation may create serious problems for the administration, e.g. by way of widespread strikes by workers and social tensions. Many economists are opposed to any deficit financing by the underdeveloped countries, because they feel that the governments of the countries lack the administrative capacity to control inflation.

Corruption

Several references have been made in the foregoing paragraphs to corruption. The word is used here for giving or taking of bribes, though it is used also to include favouritism in appointments, or award of contracts, or any infraction of prescribed rules and procedures. Corruption is common in underdeveloped countries, and is, along with administrative inefficiency, the most important cause of public dissatisfaction with the government. The incidence and magnitude of corruption have increased in most countries with planning, because of an increase in activities of governments, and rapid expansion of staff. The latter has led, inevitably, to lowering of quality of staff at all levels, and of standards of supervision and control. Increased participation of popular representatives in formulation and implementation of development programmes has also resulted, in many countries, in diffusion of responsibility and lowering of standards of administrative efficiency, which in turn have encouraged corruption. Finally, regulation of private enterprises by government, controls over production and movement of goods and rationing of scarce resources, open up large opportunities for profit-making for enterprises, which can get necessary authorizations and resource allocations. In this situation, the temptation to offer bribes to officials and decision-makers within government in order to get favourable treatment is strong. The fact that officials exercising regulatory functions are poorly paid in most countries, also encourages corruption.

Corruption may cause large losses to governments, e.g. through leakages of resources or rise in costs of projects and programmes. A more serious consequence is that it reduces efficiency and brings the government and the planning process in disrepute and reduces the willingness of the people to accept the discipline and sacrifices (e.g. in restraining consumption) involved in planning.

Administrative Planning

The foregoing review of the relationships between planning and administration, of the administrative aspects of plan formulation and implementation, and of the administrative problems associated with these, brings out the need and the importance of organizing administrative planning as an integral part of the national planning process. Administrative planning will include the following closely related and interdependent areas :

(i) Assessment of the administrative capability of plan formulation and implementation;
(ii) Formulation of programmes of administrative expansion, reorganization and reform; and
(iii) Implementation of the programmes.

Reference has been made in the section on 'Administrative Problems of Plan Formulation and Implementation' to the need for assessment of administrative capability as part of plan formulation, and to the problems arising from failure to make such an assessment. The assessment will relate primarily to the following areas :

(i) Personnel—technical, managerial, administrative, etc.,
(ii) Finance,
(iii) Procedures—financial, personnel and operative,
(iv) Patterns of communication, coordination and control,
(v) Social, political, and institutional factors, including values and attitudes that affect administrative efficiency and capability.

Assessment will be concerned primarily with plan implementation; but plan formulation should not be neglected. The administrative needs of plan formulation are comparatively small, but since efficiency of plan formulation has a vital influence throughout the implementation process, assessment of these should receive adequate attention. Secondly, particular attention should be given to assessing the capacity for construction and management of large projects, and for undertaking socio-economic reforms. These are the two areas in which administrative inadequacy has been most serious in the underdeveloped countries.

Formulation of programmes of expansion, reorganization and reform will flow from the assessment and will describe the administrative developments required for meeting the needs of the plan. In formulating the programmes, the capability of accomplishing them within the stipulated period, and with the efficiency required to meet the needs of the plan, should also be carefully assessed. The capacity for successful expansion or reorganization of administrative organs is limited by four sets of factors :

(i) Limitations of resources—of personnel and finances;
(ii) The time requirements of establishing new administrative agencies, new procedures, patterns of communication, etc.;

(iii) Resistances to change within the administration, arising from disturbance to established practices, patterns of authority; and
(iv) Wider social/political factors, including attitudes and values.

The size and nature of the existing administrative organs influence also capacity for expansion and reorganization. A relatively large organization is in a much better position to undertake expansion of a given order, such as that needed for implementing a project, than is a small one. The difference is partly a matter of resources; the large organization, having larger personnel and other resources, can divert some of these to serve as nuclei of the expansion. Factors such as previous experience of similar activities and capacity to visualize the needs and problems of the expanded operation also play a part; the management of a large organization is likely to possess an advantage over that of a small organization in these respects. On the other hand resistances to the changes needed for reorganization or reform are much greater in large or old organizations than in small or new ones; the former are particularly ill-equipped to implement programmes of reform. The limited successes with socio-institutional reforms, such as agrarian reforms, in many underdeveloped countries are due in part to the resistance of the established administrative agencies to implementation of the reforms.

To the extent that the capability of implementing programmes of administrative expansion, reorganization or reform falls short of the needs of the plan, the plan should be modified or reduced in scope. Otherwise, plan implementation will be characterized by shortfalls, delays, bottlenecks, waste, etc., arising from various administrative inadequacies.

Expansion, Reorganization and Reform

The principal areas of administration, expansion, reorganization and reform may be listed as follows :

(i) Expansion of existing administrative organs.
(ii) Establishment of new administrative organs.
(iii) Reorganization of administrative organs to equip them for new or expanded functions. Reorganization includes regrouping (of branches or divisions into departments or of departments into ministries).
(iv) Reform of administrative procedures and practices, including introduction of modern administrative techniques.

(v) Other administrative reforms.

Expansion

The need for administrative expansion will be greatest in fields such as education, health, transport, power, etc., in which the plan provides for large expansion of activities; it will be met by expansion of existing administrative organs or establishment of new ones, to undertake new, more specialized functions. But it will be felt throughout the administrative system, including departments and agencies which are not directly connected with the plan. The law enforcement departments are an example of the latter. Expansion will be needed in them because their functions will increase and change with economic development. Law enforcement problems are generally greater among urban non-agricultural populations than among rural-agricultural ones. Secondly, the agencies will need to change their methods, especially in modern techniques (e.g. of crime detection) in order to meet the demands of a population which is more literate and has higher income and greater awareness of its legal rights.

It is necessary to refer particularly to the need for expansion of the finance, personnel and similar basic service agencies of the government. The activities of these agencies are a function of the activities of other agencies of government, and expand with increase in the latter. Thus, the volume of work in the Expenditure Department of the Ministry of Finance increases very greatly under a plan, because of the need to undertake financial appraisal of the development programmes of the Ministries. Moreover, new responsibilities such as financial and economic analysis of projects (cost-benefit analysis) devolve upon the Department. Similarly, the tasks of recruitment, training and organization into cadres, etc., of the very large numbers of personnel required for implementation of the plan, devolve upon the principal personnel agency of the government, such as the civil service commission. But the need for expansion and reorganization of the service departments is often not recognized adequately; expansion is slow, grudging and inadequate in most countries with the result that deficiencies in these departments prove to be a serious bottleneck in implementation of the plan.

The need for expansion in each ministry or agency of the government should be carefully assessed in preparation of the administrative plan, and should be provided in it. The ministries or agencies may be classified for this purpose into these categories :

(i) Those in which expansion is needed as a direct result of the development programmes included in the plan;
(ii) Those in which expansion is needed to meet the larger demands from the other ministries or agencies, and
(iii) Those in which expansion becomes necessary as a result of the economic development and social changes.

Reorganization

Reorganization is closely related to expansion, and both generally go together; large expansion is invariably accompanied by reorganization. The reorganization may be structural, such as conversion of a public utility department (electricity, transport, water supply, etc.) to an autonomous corporation or board, or it may consist in addition of new branches, departments, bureaus, etc., in an existing organization. Structural reorganization is undertaken when size increases greatly or there is major change in objectives or methods of functioning. In the above example of the public utilities, the structural change may be made in order to implement efficiently the large expansion programmes envisaged under the plan, or to affect new emphasis such as on business methods or operations, more efficient services to the consumer, etc. Creation of new departments, branches, etc., within the existing organization is undertaken to meet new needs, implement new programmes, or more efficient implementation of larger programmes. The most common form of such reorganization is addition of new territorial or functional departments, branches, etc.

Reorganization includes regrouping of branches into Departments, of departments into Ministries, etc. Regrouping is common in most countries and is carried out for more efficient communication, coordination, and control. Regrouping becomes necessary as new activities gain importance, older activities acquire new emphasis or orientations, and new relationships have to be established. It is also undertaken, often, in response to the power situation within the political executive. The jurisdiction of a particular ministry may be changed or new ministries may be created in order to satisfy a powerful individual minister or political party. But too rapid or too frequent regrouping should be avoided however, because it leads to instability and confusion. The established patterns of communication, coordination and control are disturbed and new ones cannot be established efficiently.

Reform

Reform is the third essential component of administrative change : the scope for reform may be limited, e.g. to procedures, or it may be wide-ranging and fundamental. As mentioned in the section on Administrative problems of the underdeveloped countries, wide-ranging and fundamental administrative reforms are needed in these countries to enable their governments to formulate and implement plans of national economic development. Administrative reform in these countries must aim at transforming administrative structures and inducing thorough-going changes in administrative practices and procedures. Simultaneously, there must be changes in values and attitudes within the administration. Apart from such basic structural reforms, lesser reforms such as in financial, personnel, and operative decision-making procedures, are needed for improving efficiency of plan formulation and implementation. Moreover, whereas the basic reforms can (or should) be undertaken only at relatively long intervals, (minimum of a few years), the lesser reforms have to be undertaken continuously, as the plan progresses and new needs and problems arise. Administrative expansion and reorganization will itself also necessitate many administrative reform measures which must be carried out speedily in order to take full benefits of expansion and reorganization.

An essential aspect of administrative reform is introduction of modern administrative techniques, e.g. of organization and management work-study, filling and record of information, etc., and providing administrative offices with modern equipment. The output of administrative personnel can increase and the quality of work can improve greatly, as a result of these measures. The administrative plan should provide such reforms in techniques, equipment, etc., to the extent possible within the limitations of finance and other resources.

Reference has been made above to the administrative need of construction and management of projects and of implementation of social and economic reforms. Proposals for administrative reorganization and reform should give particular attention to these two areas. The problems of management and organization of projects have been discussed in the relevant section. Implementation of social and economic reforms is the other important administrative area for which suitable administrative structures and processes must be provided in the administrative plan. The importance of this task cannot be overemphasized, because in spite of limited success with implementation of such reforms by administrative agencies in most underdeveloped countries, these remain the only agencies through which such reforms can be implemented.

In many countries, proposals for administrative reorganization or reform are made primarily by committees or commissions appointed especially for the purpose. The bodies are composed of eminent public men, and non-official experts, besides officials. Appointment of such bodies is common, especially in countries in which the administration is patterned after the British model. The bodies have a useful role in administrative reorganization and reform; they are particularly well equipped to undertake wide-ranging reviews of administrative needs and problems, relate the latter to social, economic and political trends, and to suggest structural changes and new orientations, based on the reviews. But as explained above, such reviews and structural changes should only be made at relatively long intervals, in order to avoid disorganization or confusion. Secondly, appointment of such committees or commissions should not be used as a device for postponing action, as is the experience in some countries, where committees and commissions are appointed one after another, to undertake reviews and suggest reform but their recommendations are not implemented. Such bodies have very useful, but limited functions in the areas of administrative reorganization and reform, and this should be recognized.

Formulation and Implementation of the Administrative Plan

The most suitable agency for formulation of the administrative plan is either an Administration Division in the CPA or a planning division in the Ministry having primary responsibility for administrative matters within the government. If the responsibility is with the latter, it must work in close collaboration with the CPA. Implementation of the administrative plan will involve all agencies, and branches of the government, of course, but the overall responsibility for implementation and coordination must be assumed by the ministry having primary responsibility for administrative matters. The support of the Chief Executive and cooperation of the Finance Ministry and the personnel agency of the government are essential for successful implementation of the administrative plan in many countries, general administration is directly under the Chief Executive—this emphasizes the importance of the link between the two, but where this arrangement does not prevail, special arrangements must be made to obtain adequate support and backing of the Chief Executive for implementation of the administrative plan.

REFERENCE

Chi Yuen Wu: 'Public Administration for National Development', *International Social Science Journal,* UNESCO, Paris, Vol. XXI, 1969.

4

Organization of Planning in Selected Countries

Case descriptions of organization of planning in four countries, France, India, the Soviet Union and Yugoslavia, are given in the following four sections. The countries have been selected to illustrate the organization of planning in developed and underdeveloped countries and in mixed and centrally planned economies.

France is a developed West European country with a mixed economy, in which national planning was initiated after Second World War, with a view to "modernization" and "expansion" of the economy. Planning is "indicative" and plan implementation in the private sector is ensured primarily through fiscal, monetary and other investment influencing measures in mixed economies. The scope of planning has been progressively increased in successive plans, to include a larger number of sectors and aspects such as regional planning; but planning is not comprehensive. The central planning agency remains small, because most of the detailed planning work is done outside it, in ministries and in bodies like the "modernization commissions".

India is a large, federal, underdeveloped, mixed economy country. The important planning structures are at the national and regional (state) levels, and coordination of national and regional plans is a very important aspect of plan formulation and implementation. The scope of planning is larger than in France; this is partly because of the need for modernization of traditional sectors, especially agriculture, and expansion of modern sectors. The planning structures and processes illustrate the characteristics and problems of planning in underdeveloped mixed economy countries.

The principal characteristics of the structures and processes of planning in the centrally planned economies are brought out by the description of organization of planning in the Soviet Union. But Soviet structures and processes have certain distinctive features also, deriving from the very large size of the country, its physical and socio-cultural diversity and its division into a number of political-administrative units. Planning structures have been established at national, republican, local and enterprise levels; the structures at every level are closely related to the corresponding administrative structure. Besides, inter-regional agencies, the *Sovnarkhozy*, have been established at the levels of the economic administration areas and the economic administration regions for planning and administration of industrial, construction and related activities. Planning is comprehensive and a large part of it relates to organization of production and distribution. Inter-enterprise and intersectoral coordination are of crucial importance, and have to be ensured in the absence of the market, by decisions of planners. The credit agencies, such as the Central Bank, have distinctive roles in resource allocation, which supplement those of the executive and planning agencies. Finally, distinctive planning structures have been developed to serve the needs of a collectivized agriculture.

In Yugoslavia, the structures and process of planning were modelled after those of the centrally planned economics, when planning was initiated after Second World War. But they have changed progressively as a result of a succession of reforms aimed at decentralization and liberalization. Planning structures are established at the national, regional (republican), local and enterprise levels. The importance of the local (commune) structures in planning and organization of enterprises and workers' management of enterprises are distinctive features of Yugoslav planning and economic organization. Moreover, enterprises have a freedom of operation which is unusual for a centrally planned socialist economy.

France

Organization of Planning

French planning, initiated in 1946 with the objectives of modernization and expansion of the economy, has been successful; it has helped France to maintain a rapid rate of growth (of about 5 per cent per year) in the post-war years, which is in sharp contrast with stagnation of the French economy in inter-war years and slow growth in neighbouring UK French planning is often referred to as a model for planning in developed countries with mixed economies. But as the following description of the planning structures and processes shows, they represent a distinctive outgrowth of conditions in France in post-war years and bear the mark of unusual personalities. It will not be easy to duplicate them successfully in other countries, particularly the underdeveloped countries.

The Environment of Planning

Urgent need for modernization and expansion. France is a developed West European country, but its economy had been characterized until Second World War, by prevalence of an unusually large number of small, family enterprises. Productivity in these enterprises was low, because of small scale of output and outmoded equipment; costs were high and the products were not competitive with those from neighbouring countries, particularly Germany. The economy went through a long period of stagnation before Second World War, and also suffered extensive damage and disruption during the war. Modernization and expansion were its most urgent needs at the end of the war.

Major government initiative in modernization and expansion was inevitable for several reasons :

(i) Lack of resources, financial or managerial, needed for modernization and expansion, with the small enterprises.
(ii) Existence of a large public sector.
(iii) The tradition of government initiative in economic matters.

The Public Sector

The public sector included, besides social services and traditional activities of government, the following major productive activities and services :

Transport: Railways and Paris Metropolitan Transport; airlines and the aircraft industry, shipping and ship-building, and a proportion of the automobile industry.
Energy and Chemicals: Electricity and gas, coal, including associated chemical works, petroleum and petro-chemicals, atomic energy.
Banking: Bank of France and four other leading commercial banks.
Information: Broadcasting, news agencies, films, etc.

France has always had a larger public sector than UK, and the sector was greatly expanded by successive acts of nationalization under the left-wing governments during the 1930s, and again immediately after Second World War. Nationalization in the latter period was undertaken primarily for modernization and expansion.

Traditions of government initiative in economic matters, of strong centralized administration and decisions by civil servants. The French Government played a much more active role in the economic development of the country (e.g. through encouragement of technical education and expansion of banking) than did the governments in Anglo-Saxon countries, partly because private enterprise failed to achieve the dynamism that it did in the latter. France has also had a strong centralized administration, and local institutions have not had the strength and independence that they have had in the Anglo-Saxon countries. The tradition of decisions by civil servants has kept the administration going during periods of prolonged political instability, such as the inter-war period.

The Planning Structures

Commissariat Du Plan

The central planning agency is the Commissariat du Plan, which is headed by a Planning Commissioner, and is attached to the office of the Prime Minister. But the Commissariat is not a subordinate office, and has large internal autonomy and complete intellectual independence. The Planning Commissioner, generally a distinguished Civil Servant or technocrat, reports directly to the Prime Minister. He is the permanent delegate of the Government in all matters connected with planning. His status is intermediate between that of a Minister and a high civil servant, but since the first three Planning Commissioners were distinguished civil servants, and since they stayed much longer than an average minister, the office acquired considerable prestige and status. The personality of the first Planning Commissioner, M. Monnet, a prestigious civil servant, who later headed the European Coal and Steel Community, has left its mark on the Commissariat and the entire planning system. The First Plan was called the Monnet Plan after him.

The Commissariat has a small, carefully selected staff of civil servants and professionals, who serve essentially as the brains trust and the general staff of planning. Most of the detailed work is done in Modernization Commissions, and sub-committees of these, each of which is constituted for a sector or branch of the economy. The Commissariat reconciles conflicting interests and viewpoints, and coordinates the plans drawn by these bodies. The Commissariat relies on economic and statistical data collected by the Ministry of Finance and other Ministries of Government. It works in particularly close collaboration with the Economic Research Units of the Ministry of Finance for formulating the key magnitudes of the plan—the projections underlying the Plan are prepared by the Unit. No attempt has been made by the Commissariat to collect its own data, or to create a large staff.

Modernization Commissions are constituted for sectors of the economy selected for planning (vertical commissions) or for subjects which affect the entire economy (horizontal commissions). In the First Plan (1946-53), six key sectors—coal, electricity, transport, steel, cement, and agricultural machinery—were selected for detailed planning, and commissions were constituted for them. By the Fourth Plan (1962-65), the number of commissions had increased to 27, of which 22 were vertical (sectoral) commissions; the five horizontal commissions related respectively to employment, finance, productivity, regional development and scientific research. The commissions are composed of the principal interests connected with planning—employers, labour and government—besides independent experts. The members of the commissions are experts in their fields. Most of them have access to detailed data relating to the sector; the representatives of employers, particularly, can draw upon their large organizations for data, results of research, etc. The principal role of the Commissariat is to bring together these experts with different view-points and help them draw up agreed plans, through a process of adjustment and reconciliation of differences. The Chairmen of the Commissions are usually provided by the Commissariat. Sub-committees and Study Groups, on which additional members are co-opted, are constituted for most commissions. The number of members of the Modernization Commissions constituted for the Fourth Plan was about 1000, and including the Sub-committees and Study Groups, the total reached 3000.

The Economic and Social Council and the High Planning Council

The Economic and Social Council is a large quasi-Parliamentary body (about 175 members) consisting of members chosen by Government, or appropriate organizations (of Employers, Labour, etc.) to represent broad interests of the nation. It is predominantly a body of nominated experts, but has also representatives of sectional interests and regions. The Council has, since its reconstitution in 1959, come to have an important role in plan formulation. The macro-magnitudes of the Plan are submitted to it for approval at the start of the process and the sectoral and overall plans are also submitted to it from time to time. In case of the Fourth Plan, three alternative projections, based on different rates of growth, were submitted to the Council and further work on the Plan began after the Council indicated its preference for an annual growth rate of 5½ per cent. The practical work of the Council is done in permanent committees called Sections, of which the Investment and Planning Section is the most important for planning.

The High Planning Council has the Prime Minister as the Chairman, and about 60 members, who include Ministers, the Governor of the Bank of France, Chairman and Vice-Chairman of the Planning and Investment Section of the Economic and Social Council, and representatives of various sectional interests. The Council has responsibilities in both plan formulation and implementation, and is expected to examine and report the execution of the Plan every year.

Planning in the Ministries and Nationalized Enterprises

The large nationalized enterprises, some of which cover entire sectors (e.g. Railways) have their own planning organizations, which prepare plans in consultation with the supervising Ministries. The service Ministries, such as Education and Health, similarly prepare plans for their sector. The plan for each sector is submitted for consideration to the concerned Modernization Commission by the Ministry and forms the basis of the work of the latter. Intersectoral coordination is, of course, the responsibility of the Commissariat du Plan.

Planning at the Regional Level

Although France has had a highly centralized administration, a well developed regional division has existed since the 1920s and the regions have been used for various administrative purposes. Since the Fourth Plan, considerable emphasis has been placed on regional development primarily with a view to reducing concentration in the Paris Region. The principal planning structures at the regional level are the Inter-departmental Conferences. They prepare, in conjunction with the Regional Expansion Committees and regional representatives of the Ministry of Finance, the draft "operational tarnches" for the regions which outline the investment programmes. The work on regional plans is coordinated by the Commissariat du Plan, while policy guidelines are provided by a National Territorial Development Commission.

The Parliament and the Plans

The Parliament has not been actively associated with plan formulation. The first and the third plans were not submitted to it at all, being passed by ordinances, and the second came to it in the third year of its implementation. The fourth plan was submitted to Parliament for ratification, after it had been finalized. Non-association of Parliament with plan formulation is one of the main criticisms of the French planning system.

Implementation of Plans

Implementation of plan is the responsibility of the Ministries and enterprises : the Commissariat du Plan has few formal powers in this respect. Implementation is facilitated by the existence of a very large public sector and the fact that a large proportion of the investment provided in the plans has to be made in this sector. Public sector enterprises prepare their investment programmes in accordance with the plans; control over public investment is exercised by the Board for the Social and Economic Development Fund, attached to the Ministry of Finance. The board, consisting of high finance officials and heads of financial institutions as Members and the Minister of Finance as the Chairman scrutinizes and approves all public sector investments. The Planning Commissioner is a member of the Board. In case of the private sector firms, plan implementation is voluntary. But, since prominent representatives of each industry are associated with plan formulation, there is a moral obligation on the firms to implement the plans. Implementation is facilitated also by a system of incentives and sanctions (e.g. against concentration in the Paris Region). Finally, public sector investment induces private investment in linked industries. Implementation is not a major problem in industries in which the enterprises are large and few in numbers; the problem would arise mainly in case of consumer goods industries in which there are large numbers of small enterprises. But, as mentioned above, French planning has been concerned mainly with key sectors, including producer goods industries, and has not sought to direct in any detail, the consumer goods industries.

The Plans

The principal objectives of the First Plan (1946-53) were modernization and reconstruction, and it concerned itself with only six basic sectors. It was considered that rapid growth in these sectors would stimulate the whole economy, and that control over them was adequate to guide development of the economy. The objectives of planning have changed in subsequent plans and the number of sectors selected for planning has increased progressively. Both the Second Plan (1954-57) and the Third Plan (1958-61) had preparation of the French economy for membership of the European Common Market, and raising the levels of the living as major objectives. In the Fourth Plan (1962-65) there is greater stress on achievement of social objectives, including especially employment, redistribution in incomes, and regional development. The number of sectors selected for planning had increased to 22 by the Fourth Plan. The Fifth Plan (1965-69) continued the shift of emphasis towards social objectives.

Comment

French planning illustrates plan formulation through consultation, and implementation primarily through a system of incentives and sanctions. The scope of planning has been carefully defined and limited : the penchant for careful definition and economy has extended to the selection of sectors for planning, the planning process and the organization of the central planning agency, the Commissariat du Plan. The latter has remained a small group of technocrats performing the central function of coordination; for all other work, ranging from collection of data to preparation of sectoral plans, the resources of the existing agencies—Ministries, public and private sector enterprises, trade associations, etc.—have been exploited. Planning has been successful in its primary objectives—reconstruction and modernization of the economy and maintaining a high rate of growth. But, in recent years, the planning system has been subject to increasing criticism. The principal points of the criticism are :

- Inadequate popular participation in plan formulation, and
- Inadequate attention to social objectives of plans.

Reference has been made above to little or no association of Parliament with plan formulation. It is alleged that the civil servants hold all the strings together and even the Ministers do not have an adequate voice in planning, because the plans come to them in an advanced stage, when making changes is difficult. The structure and methods of functioning of the Modernization Commissions, and the intersectoral coordination procedures do concentrate effective authority in the hands of the civil servants, particularly that of the Commissariat du Plan and the Ministry of Finance. The composition of the Commissions has been criticized on the ground that employers are over-represented while labour is under-represented. Apart from numerical representation, the influence exerted by individual representatives also enters the picture. The employers' representatives, backed by detailed economic and technical data relating to the industry and knowing the thinking of managements have been much more influential than the representatives of labour.

The system worked well in the early years, when the needs for reconstruction and modernization were self-evident, fixation of priorities was relatively easy and the planning process was facilitated by carefully limiting of the sectors selected for planning. But with the passage of time, the area of choice among objectives has widened, attention has had to be given to social objectives, in addition to the economic, and the number of sectors has increased progressively. Fixation of priorities is more difficult—there is much greater room for different views so that more and more decisions have to be political, rather than techno-economic. Accordingly, a system which was very suitable in the early years of planning has been found to be increasingly inadequate and unsatisfactory.

The system was workable in France because it was a developed economy, consisting mainly of organized sectors and had well developed structures of government, trade unions and industry associations, and a developed statistical system. As a result, it was possible for a small group of civil servants and technocrats to bring together the people most concerned with plan implementation and other specialists, to formulate plans, using existing resources of data and personnel and existing channels of communication. Planning was an innovation superimposed on developed organization, and systems of data collection and communication. The system cannot be duplicated with success in underdeveloped countries in which organization, data and communications are also underdeveloped.

India

Organization of Planning

The structures and processes of planning in India illustrate plan formulation and implementation in an underdeveloped country which has a mixed economy with large traditional, unorganized sectors. They also bring out the problems of planning in a large country with a federal constitution and in which there is great physical and social diversity.

India is a large, underdeveloped country with a population of about 550 million[1], predominantly agricultural and rural with 70 per cent of the workforce engaged in agriculture and more than 80 per cent of the population living in villages. Per capita income is under $60 per year, and literacy rate is 24 per cent. There are formidable problems of raising the economic and social levels of a large, rapidly growing population.

Mixed Economy with Large Unorganized Sectors

Agriculture, handicrafts and retail trade, which provide employment to more than 90 per cent of the workforce, are unorganized: they are characterized by prevalence of small, family enterprises, using traditional techniques and having very low productivity. The modern organized sector consists of factory industry, infrastructures (transport, communications, and power) and services such as banking, public administration and education. Most factory industry, general insurance, shipping, etc., are in the organized private sector. The public sector includes rail and air transport, electricity, communications, broadcasting, life insurance, defence industries, etc., beside social services and other traditional activities of the government. Heavy industries (steel, chemicals, and cement), banking, road transport, etc., are partly in the private and partly in the public sector.

Federal structure of government consisting of the Central Government and 17 (22) State Governments

Planning and development are concurrent responsibilities of both the Central and the State Governments under the Constitution. The Central Government has primary responsibility for certain sectors such as transport and communications and defence and heavy industries, while in other sectors such as agriculture, small industries, and social services, the primary responsibility is of the State Governments, and the Central Government has only a coordinating role.

Planning started in 1950 with the establishment of a Planning Commission at the Centre. Three Five Year Plans were completed between 1951 and 1966; the Fourth Plan has begun in 1969, after a three-year interval filled with Annual Plans. The Five Year Plans have been formulated within the framework of long-term perspectives of development and have, in turn, been broken down into Annual Plans. Each Plan is a composite of development programmes and projects of the Central and State Governments and of the public and private sectors.

But planning has not been conspicuously successful. The growth rate of per capita output which was around 1.5 per cent per year in the 1950s had gone down to 0.2 per cent during 1960-1965. The economy is now recovering slowly from the effects of two disastrous droughts (during 1965-67) in which agricultural output suffered a sharp decline, and an industrial recession. Delays in execution of projects and short falls in achievement of Plan targets have been widespread and serious.

Planning Structures in the Central Government : The Planning Commission

The Planning Commission has overall responsibility for formulation of Five Year and Annual Plans and also advises the Central Cabinet on economic and social policies. The Prime Minister is the Chairman of the Commission and the Minister of Finance is a Member; there have been other Minister-Members also in the past. The Non-Minister Members generally include an administrator, an economist, a scientist-educationist and a social worker. The operating head of the Commission is the Deputy Chairman. Some Deputy Chairmen, who were drawn from political life, were also Ministers of Planning, but the present incumbent (1969), a distinguished economist, does not have that position. The composition of the Planning Commission, part-political and part expert, and its functions and methods of working illustrate the need to bring into the planning body decision-making authority and coordination with other agencies of government on the one hand, and expert, objective analysis and freedom from day-to-day working of government, on the other.

The Commission has a large staff of economists, administrators, and sectoral specialists, which is organized into nearly 30 divisions or smaller units. Besides the administrative or service divisions, the divisions are divided almost equally between vertical (sectoral) and horizontal. Among the latter, the Perspective Planning Division, which has responsibility for preparing long-term perspectives of development, and the Division responsible for coordination of plans of the States deserve particular mention. The Planning Commission has close relations with the Central Statistical Organization, and the Indian Statistical Institute; the latter has been particularly active in preparing planning models and undertaking macro-economic studies. The Commission has three other bodies under it : the Programme Evaluation Organization, the Committee on Plan Projects and the Research Programmes Committee. These are responsible, respectively, for evaluation of agricultural and rural development programmes, studies on management, and coordination of research on planning problems through the Universities. Advisory Groups, Panels of Specialists, Study Teams, etc., are set up by the Commission from time to time for advice relating to particular aspects of planning, or detailed study of particular problems.

The National Development Council, consisting of the Prime Minister (Chairman), Members of the Planning Commission, some Central Ministers, and the Chief Ministers of all the States as members, has a central role in policy-making on the plans. The principal magnitudes of each plan—rate of growth, quantum of investment, physical achievement targets, etc.—and policies for achievement of plan objectives are submitted to the Council for approval, at the start of plan formulation, and subsequently from time to time, and the plan is approved by it before being submitted to the Parliament. The constitution of the council and its central role in policy-making bring out the importance of the States as participants in the planning process.

The Planning Commission and the States

The Planning Commission, in collaboration with the Ministry of Finance and the sectoral Ministries of the Central Government reviews and approves the plans of the State Governments. The review is undertaken with the objective of ensuring financial and programme coordination. Financial coordination is of particular importance, because plan implementation involves large transfers of funds from the Central Government to the State Governments. The transfers are necessary because most of the flexible and expanding revenue sources such as income-tax, customs and excise duties are with the Central Government, while execution of most development programmes and maintenance of social services are the responsibility of the State Governments. The association of the Planning Commission, a body having in it non-political experts, has proved very useful for deciding Centre-State resource allocations.

The Planning Commission and the Parliament

The Planning Commission is represented in the Parliament by the Minister of Planning who may be the Prime Minister, or the Finance Minister or the Deputy Chairman. The plan is submitted to the Parliament at several early stages, such as Preliminary Memorandum and Draft, to elicit its views, and at the final stage to obtain its approval. The Plan is examined by the Parliament primarily through its Committees on the Planning Commission and the sectoral Ministries. Approval of the plan is secured through a resolution so that the plan has the status of an approved official programme, but not of law. This practice facilitates revisions and modifications in the plan and avoids rigidity, because while the Government is committed to implementation of the Plan, it is not legally bound to do it.

Status and Powers of the Planning Commission

The official status of the Planning Commission is that of an advisory body to the Central Cabinet : the Commission has no executive authority or responsibility. The effectiveness and influence of the Commission depend entirely upon the importance given to it by the Cabinet and the Prime Minister. The Commission acquired considerable prestige and authority under Prime Minister Nehru, when the Plans were accepted as the principal statements of the development objectives of the Government, and instruments of resource allocation and direction of the economy. Major modifications or changes in the Plans were made only with the approval of the Planning Commission, and the Commission's advice on economic and social policy was highly regarded. The composition of the Planning Commission, with the Prime Minister as the Chairman and Finance Minister as a Member, also contributed to its prestige and authority. These have not been maintained, however, after the death of Nehru, and the Planning Commission, the Plans, and the planning process have been subject to serious attack from both within and outside India. But the planning process is well established in India and constitutes an essential instrument of allocation of resources and coordination of programmes between the Centre and the States and the public and the private sectors.

Planning in the Central Ministries and Enterprises

Sectoral planning is the responsibility of the Ministries. In case of sectors such as agriculture and education, in which operational responsibility is largely that of the States, planning by the Central Ministries consists primarily in formulation of overall programmes and policies, coordination of State programmes and resource allocation among States, programmes and projects. But in case of sectors, such as rail and air transport, communication, steel, chemicals and heavy engineering, in which the Central Ministries have operation responsibilities, detailed planning is done by the Ministries and by the enterprises. Large enterprises, such as Hindustan Steel, have their own well developed planning organizations including divisions for design and formulation of projects.

The Role of the Ministry of Finance

The Ministry of Finance has a particularly important role in the planning process because of its responsibilities for :

- Mobilization and allocation of financial resources, and
- Implementation of economic policies of the Government.

The Ministry of Finance is also the Ministry of Economic Affairs, and the Central Bank is subordinate to it. The Planning Commission and the Ministry of Finance work in close cooperation in overall assessment and allocation of resources, formulation of economic policies and approval of project : maintaining satisfactory relations between the Planning Commission and the Ministry of Finance is a major pre-occupation in the planning process. While these relations have generally been satisfactory (partly because of the association of the Prime Minister and the Finance Minister with the Planning Commission) instances of friction and misunderstanding have not been altogether absent.

Planning Structures in the States

Planning Board and Planning Departments

The principal agencies are the Planning Board and the Planning Department. The Board has the Chief Minister as the Chairman, and all or most Ministers as Members; in some States there are, in addition, non-Minister Members. The Planning Department which is generally under the Chief Minister or the Finance Minister, serves as the Secretariat of the Board. As with the Planning Commission at the Centre, the principal functions of the Planning Board and Department are assessment of resources, formulation of policies and basic guidelines on programmes, and deciding resource allocations and achievement targets. Detailed sectoral planning, intra-sectoral resource allocations or formulation of projects are undertaken by the Sectoral Departments. The composition of the Planning Board and the location of the Planning Department (under the Chief Minister or the Finance Minister) enable these bodies to perform their policy-making, resource allocation and coordination functions. The Department of Finance has an important role in planning, because of its responsibilities of resource allocation and mobilization.

Local Planning

The units of local government or administration are : the district, the town, the community development block and the village. The district is the largest among these; most districts have populations of 1-3 million. Planning for agriculture, rural development and social service sectors is organized mainly at the levels of the district and the community development blocks; it is done either by officials of the Sectoral Department of the State Government or by representative local institutions. The plans follow closely the directions given by the Sectoral Departments. Urban Planning is important only in case of metropolitan cities and other large towns, and is done by local planning agencies under the direction of and assistance from the State Town Planning Departments. In case of cities like Delhi and Calcutta, large metropolitan planning organizations have been created. Excepting the metropolitan cities, however, the principal concern of local authorities urban and rural is with execution of programmes, and "planning" is an adjunct to their executive responsibilities. The Planning Structures of Central, State and local levels and the channels of communication among them and association of private sector agencies with the planning process are important constituents of the process. In case of the unorganized sectors, such as agriculture, the role of the cooperative institutions and elected representatives (from members of local government institutions to those of the State Legislatures and the Parliament) is noteworthy. They participate in planning at various levels and/or bring to the notice of the planners, the needs and aspirations of their constituents.

The Planning Process

Five Year, Perspective and Annual Plans

The Five Year Plan is the principal plan. The first three Five Year Plans were formulated within the framework of long-term (25-30 years) perspectives of development, which indicated only a few key magnitudes such as population, savings, investment and national and per capita income.

A detailed, 15-year, Perspective Plan was prepared to guide formulation of the Fourth and the Fifth Plans which were scheduled to begin in 1966 and 1971 respectively. But the beginning of the Fourth Plan was postponed by three years because of serious economic difficulties during 1965-1968. The draft of the Fourth Plan issued in 1969—the Plan will now cover the period 1969-1974 indicates that a revised perspective up to 1981 has been prepared.

The Annual Plan is formulated within the framework of the Five Year Plan, and is coordinated with the annual budget. Since formulation of the Fourth Five Year Plan was delayed by three years, the period 1966-1969 was filled by annual plans.

The planning process proceeds simultaneously in the Planning Commission, the Central Ministries (and enterprises) and the State Governments. Besides, certain private sector agencies (e.g. industry associations) participate in it. Coordination of Central-State, public-private, and sectoral plans is the essences of the Planning process, which is best seen at the time of formulation of the Five Year Plans. Coordination of Central and State plans is particularly important because the State Governments are equal partners with the Central Governments in the planning process.

Steps in Plan Formulation

The Five Year Plans

(i) Indication of macro-magnitudes of the Plan (population, income, employment, investment, selected physical achievement targets) by the Planning Commission to the Central Ministries and the State Governments. The macro-magnitudes are indicated within the framework of the long-term perspective of development, and against the background of appraisal of trends in the economy and progress on earlier plans. The indication is given after obtaining approval of the National Development Council. The Central Ministries, particularly the Ministry of Finance, are closely associated in formulation of the macro-magnitudes.

(ii) Preparation of sectoral and state plans : This is a long process, which extended over more than one year in case of the Third Plan. A large number of Working Groups and Steering Groups were constituted to prepare sectoral plans and for inter-sectoral coordination. However, the work of the groups represented only the culmination of the process of detailed planning undertaken within each sector at the levels of the Department, and/or enterprise, and in state capitals and local areas. In case of sectors such as industries, representatives of the private sector were encouraged to formulate their own development programmes. Within the states, the process extended to the local level—local government bodies such as Panchayati Raj Institutions and municipalities formulated development plans in the light of guidelines given by the State Governments.

(iii) Discussion of sectoral and State plans, between the Planning Commission, the Ministries, and the State Governments; aggregation and inter-sectoral coordination; reconciliation of estimates relating to investment and physical accomplishments.

(iv) Discussion in the Central Cabinet and the National Development Council to resolve differences and to give guidelines to the Planning Commission for formulation of the Plan.

(v) Formulation of the Plan by the Planning Commission.

(vi) Approval of Plan by Parliament.

It has been customary to publish a Draft Outline or Preliminary Memorandum, incorporating the initial thinking of the Planning Commission on the Plan. These documents besides providing guidance for detailed plan formulation in the Ministries, State Governments, etc., also provide an opportunity to the press and the general public to express their views on the plan.

As indicated earlier, the Parliament discusses the Plan at several stages, and

(vi) Above, relates only to final approval by the Parliament.

The Annual Plans

(i) Indication by the Planning Commission and the Central Ministry of Finance, to the Central Ministries and the State Governments of the investment targets for the year.
(ii) Formulation of annual plans by the Central Ministries and State Governments.
(iii) Centre-State discussions on plans of States : the Planning Commission, the Central Ministry of Finance, the sectoral Ministries, and the State Governments are represented.
(iv) Discussions on plans of the Central Ministries : The Planning Commission, the Central Ministry of the Finance and the Ministry concerned are represented in each discussion.
(v) Incorporating the plans of the public sector in the budgets of the Central and State Governments.
(vi) Formulation of the Annual Plan and coordination with the Annual Budget : these are done jointly by the Planning Commission and the Ministry of Finance at the Centre, and by the Planning Department and the Finance Department in each state.

Implementation of Plans

Implementation of the plans is done by the Central Ministries (through the departments and enterprises subordinate to them). The State Governments and the private sector : the responsibility of the Planning Commission is limited to appraisal of progress and recommending modifications, in the light of progress on the plans and other relevant developments, domestic or foreign. Proposals for modification originate in the enterprises, Department or State Governments; it has been customary to consult the Planning Commission on all proposals relating to modification. The Central Ministry of Finance has a key role in implementation of plans, because it has responsibilities of mobilization and allocation of financial resources, and implementing the economic policies of the Government. All projects and programmes of the Central Ministries must be approved by the Ministry of Finance and allocation for them must be included in the Annual Budget. Implementation of State plans also depends in large part on release of resources by the Central Ministry of Finance.

Implementation of Sectoral Plans

In sectors such as agriculture, small industries, irrigation, power, roads and road transport, education, health, etc., implementation is the responsibility primarily of the State Governments and the roles of the Central Ministries are those of overall coordination and review. In agriculture and rural service sectors, representative (*Panchayati Raj*) institutions have an important role in implementation of development programmes. Municipal bodies, similarly, are responsible for implementation of development programmes within their areas. In case of agriculture, the primary activities of government agencies are development and regulatory. The developmental activities include provision of technical assistance, credit and supplies of modern inputs such as improved seed and chemical fertilizers; cooperatives have an important role in provision of credit and distribution of supplies. The regulatory activities relate primarily to fixation of minimum and maximum prices of output and (compulsory) purchase of output. Purchase of output of foodgrains has for some years been entrusted to a statutory corporation, the Food Corporation of India.

In sectors such as rail and air transport, communications, steel and heavy industries, in which the operational responsibility is of the Central Government, implementation of plans is done either through established Departments (Railways, Posts, and Telegraphs) or through autonomous cooperatives or companies. A large number of new companies have been established in the public sector in the period of the Plans to implement programmes in these sectors.

In sectors such as shipping, international trade, and manufacture of consumer goods, which are largely in the private sector, implementation of plans is ensured through three sets of measures :

(a) Regulatory and resource allocation : licensing of units above a certain size, control over issue of capital, allocations of foreign exchange, scarce materials, etc.;

(b) Fiscal and credit measures for direction of private investment; and

(c) Developmental or promotional measures such as technical and financial assistance, guaranteed purchase of outputs for meeting requirements of Government, etc. These measures are important particularly for small sector enterprises, and for branches in which private entrepreneurs are hesitant to enter because of technical difficulties, uncertainties of demand, etc.

Implementation of Fiscal and Monetary Policies

The principal agencies are the Central Ministry of Finance, the Reserve Bank of India (which is the Central Bank) and the Finance Departments of the States. As explained above, the Central Ministry of Finance is the most important. The taxation programmes are implemented by the Central Ministry of Finance and the State Finance Departments. The monetary and credit policies are implemented by the Reserve Bank of India. The borrowing of the Central and State Governments is managed by the Bank, and the Bank directs and regulates in detail, lending by the commercial banks.

Implementation of credit policies is aided by the fact that life insurance and a large section of banking are nationalized and the commercial banks are subject to detailed regulation by the Reserve Bank of India. The bank is also responsible for allocation of foreign exchange and implementation of foreign exchange controls.

Direction of Private Investment

The principal instruments for direction of private investment are the following :

(i) *Direct control* : This is exercised through licensing of enterprises above a minimum size, control over issue of share capital, and control over operations through the Company Law Administration.

(ii) *Indirect influence* : This is exercised through fiscal, credit, and other measures such as tax holiday for a number of years for new enterprises, liberal depreciation allowance, and development rebates, protective tariffs, together with total ban on imports in many cases, export subsidies (or duties), Government loans, given either directly or through development finance institutions, underwriting by government of foreign borrowings including those from agencies such as the World Bank, preference in purchase of output for meeting requirements of Government, technical assistance, etc.

Soviet Union

Introduction

Soviet planning is the prime example of planning in a socialist country, in which the means of production are owned by the state and the market does not perform (except marginally) the function of resource allocation and direction of economic activity that it does in free enterprise or mixed economies. But it has also distinctive features, not encountered or to the same degree, in other socialist countries, which arise from the immense size of the country, the socio-cultural diversity of the population, the conditions under which planning was initiated in the early 1930s, etc.

The Soviet Union is a very large country (area about 8 million square miles) with great social and cultural diversity in its population of about 250 million (in 1966). The majority of the population is Russian; but there are large ethnic minorities in the European region, and the Asiatic regions are populated predominantly by non-Russian peoples. Most of the Asiatic regions were inhabited until recently by primitive nomadic groups or settled people with their own distinctive cultures.

The country remained quite backward until First World War. It was predominantly agriculture, and agriculture was dominated by an unusually reactionary feudal structure. Serfdom was abolished only in the latter part of the nineteenth century, but the peasants remained illiterate, superstitious and poor. The landlords, powerful and rich, did little to improve their economic and social conditions or to raise productivity through improvement of techniques. Industrial development was very limited; most industries were located in European regions, and were owned or controlled by foreigners. The immense mineral, power and other natural resources of the country were virtually unexploited. Transport and communications were woefully inadequate.

The economy suffered serious disruptions and extensive damage during First World War and the years of civil or political unrest that followed the 1917 revolution. Output on the eve of First Five Year Plan (begun in 1931) was lower than in 1913.

A highly centralized politico-economic structure was established after 1917 revolution. The country was divided into a number of Socialist republics, of which the largest was the Russian (RFSFR). Regions inhabited predominantly by ethnic groups at low socio-cultural level, or with distinctive characteristics were constituted into Autonomous Republics, Regions, etc. Non-agricultural means of production came under state ownership. In agriculture, far reaching changes were made, beginning with elimination of landlords and *Kulaks* (rich peasants) and ended with collectivization in the 1930s. Political and economic power was concentrated in Moscow : planning though initiated for rapid development, was necessary also as an instrument of operation and management of the economy.

The structures, processes and practices of planning were influenced greatly by the above politico-economic, physical and social conditions. They were affected also by basic decisions, such as the decision to industrialize rapidly, with particular emphasis on development of heavy industry. The immense size of the Soviet Union and the variety of its natural resources has given the country a great developmental potential. On the other hand, the size has necessitated very large investment in transport, and size and socio-economic diversity have meant that the problem of communication between the central, regional and local agencies engaged in plan formulation and implementation has been unusually difficult. The issue of centralization *vs.* decentralization of planning decisions has an importance and a complexity in the Soviet Union that it has in a few other countries. Another handicap was lack of previous experience with planning and of development of planning techniques, when planning was started in the 1930s. In contrast, planning in East European socialist countries, undertaken in the post-Second World War years, has been concerned primarily with reconstruction and modernization of developed or semi-developed economies of small, relatively homogenous countries, in a period by which there had been considerable experience with planning and extensive development of planning techniques.

Structures of Planning

The planning structures consist of

(i) General planning agencies, the GOSPLANS, of the USSR the Union Republics, Autonomous Republics, Territories and

Regions, and Planning Units at local levels of the town, district, area etc.,

(ii) Sectoral planning agencies, in the Ministries and Departments of the USSR and the Union Republics, etc.,

(iii) The *Sovnarkhozy*, and

(iv) Planning structures of enterprises.

The organization of the planning structures brings out the close relationship between planning and executive agencies. Beginning with the GOSPLAN of the USSR, which is the Planning Committee of the Council of Ministers of the USSR, each of the general planning agencies is the planning organ (committee) of the corresponding executive agency. Sectoral planning is done in the Ministries and Departments having executive responsibility for the sectors, and the *Sovnarkhozy* are Councils having responsibilities of both administration and planning of industries and construction at the regional level of 'economic administration areas'.

The Central Planning Agency, the GOSPLAN of the USSR, is composed of a Chairman appointed by the Supreme Soviet of the USSR and a Vice-Chairman and members appointed by the Council of Ministers. It has responsibility for formulation of the plan for the national economy, by coordination of territorial and sectoral plans. The GOSPLAN has a number of committees for industrial branches, which investigate technical problems, plan for research and experimentation and carry out uniform technical policies. Since 1962, a National Economic Council of the USSR and a Construction Committee of the Council of the USSR have been constituted. The principal function of the Council is overall coordination of plan implementation, through the Central Ministries and Departments of USSR, the Union Republics, *Sovnarkhozy* etc. The construction Committee has responsibility primarily for coordinating and improving implementation of construction programmes. There are Committees of the Council of Ministers also for labour, wages, scientific research, etc.

Union Republics, Autonomous Republics, Regions and Local Areas

General planning agencies or GOSPLANS exist at each of these levels. The Union Republic GOSPLANS are composed of a Chairman appointed by the Supreme Soviet of the Union Republic and a Vice-Chairman and members appointed by its Council of Ministers. In the largest Union Republics (Russian, Ukrainian and Kazakh) the GOSPLANS are primarily plan formulating agencies; but in the others, they have, in addition, implementation responsibilities relating to supply of materials and solving the operational problems of the *Sovnarkhozy*. The scope of planning by the Union Republic GOSPLANS and their authority has increased considerably in recent years. They now prepare estimates of national income, saving and investment and financial plans for the Union Republics, which were prepared earlier only by the GOSPLAN of the USSR. In the field of industrial planning, their responsibilities now extend to all industries, and to preparation of comprehensive industrial development plans for the Union Republic, whereas earlier these were confined to planning for republican industries only—consumer goods, building materials and timber. The change has given the Union Republic GOSPLANS an important say in decisions relating to location of major industrial enterprises and has brought them in close contact with the *Sovnarkhozy*.

The general planning organs in the Autonomous Republics are the Planning Commissions and in the Regions, the Planning Committees of the Regional (Territorial) Executive Committees. The local planning commissions are committees of the corresponding Soviets and have functions of both plan formulation and implementation.

Sovnarkhozy are regional councils for administration and planning of industry and construction, set up at the level of economic 'administration areas'. In regions, where industry is not important, *Sovnarkhozy* have not been constituted and the industrial units are placed under the *Sovnarkhozy* of a neighbouring area. The number of 'economic administration areas' has been reduced since 1962, through consolidation. In addition, groups of areas have been constituted into 'major economic regions'. The USSR has been divided into 17 major economic regions.

The *Sovnarkhozy* have functions of both planning and administration. They are given all powers to direct the productive, technical and financial activities of the enterprises under them, and can be considered as the regional organs of the industrial Ministries of the USSR. Their functions bring them in close contact with the GOSPLANS and Ministries of the Union Republics, Autonomous Republic, etc., but their jurisdiction frequently extends over the area of more than Republic or region.

Each *Sovnarkhozy* consists of a Chairman, his deputies and members, who are usually selected from the heads of the Chief Administrations and sections. It has usually a large organization, consisting of a number of branches and sections, some of which attend to operational problems, while others are concerned with formulation and implementation of plans, improvement of technical efficiency, etc.

Enterprises

Plan formulation is an important activity at the enterprise level, and a planning unit exists in each enterprise. A large part of the 'planning' activity relates to management of current operation, and the task of the planning unit is primarily one of consolidation and coordination of information relating to different aspects of operation. The annual plan of the enterprise is a detailed statement of different aspects of its operation—technical, financial, output, etc. It is prepared on the basis of a wide range of indicators, technical norms, and practical experience, and forms the basis of allocations of inputs to the enterprise by the supervisory authorities (*Sovnarkhozy*, Ministries, and Departments) as well as of contracts for disposal of output. The long-term plan of the enterprise fixes its general tasks for an extended period. Long-term plans are drawn up on basis of control figures for development of economy of the USSR (transmitted through the *Sovnarkhozy*), and existing economic links, and assessment of techno-economic potential. Design and project formulation units for planning the expansion or modernization of enterprises, exist at the level of the enterprise, groups of enterprises, and the *Suvnarkhozy*.

Planning for Agriculture

Administration and planning of agriculture are under a separate hierarchy, which extends from the agricultural Committees of the USSR and the Union Republics through Production and Procurement Boards and the Territorial Production Boards to the Collective/State farms. The basic supervisory unit is the Territorial Production Board, which is responsible for administration and planning of all the collective farms and state farms within its area. In 1962, there were 960 Territorial Production Boards for a total of 41,300 collective farms and 8300 state farms.

Association of Academies and Individual Specialists

The planning authorities enlist the help of the Academy of Sciences of the USSR, the Academy of Building and Architecture, the V.I. Lenin Academy of Agriculture, etc., in formulating the national economic plan. At the Union Republic level, similarly, the help of the scientific academies of the Union Republic is obtained. In addition, a wide range of scientific workers and specialists (in planning and design) are associated with plan formulation at different levels.

The Process of Plan Formulation (Bor, M. Z. 1963, Annex II, Chapters 1- 4)

"Work on a plan may be divided into the following stages :

Working out of the form of the tables, plan indicators and relevant methodological instructions;

Summing up and implementation analysis of the plan for the current (base) period;

Drawing up of directives (control figures) for plan formulation;

Drawing up and approval of the plan;

Transmission of the state plan targets to those directly responsible for their fulfilment—enterprises, construction agencies and so on.'' p. 130.

"Direct formulation of the national economic plan begins with the preparation of directives, or control figures, for the planning period. These set forth the objectives of economic development in terms of individual branches, determine which basic areas are to enjoy priority in the fixing of targets for the planning period, and also indicate the most important measures for their fulfilment. The draft control figures are prepared by the central planning organs with the help of the republics, ministries and departments and in the light of analysis of plan implementation figures for the preceding period. At the same time, wide use is made of the system of economic balances in order to ensure the coordination of all sections and indicators of the plan at the control figure stage. Control figures approved by the governing organs of the country are fundamental to the formulation of a detailed draft plan......

Enterprises and construction agencies draw up plans, taking the control figures as their point of departure and bearing in mind the direct economic links already established and their further development. The plans are discussed by collectives of enterprises and construction agencies and enter into force after their approval by the *Sovnarkhozy*.

Taking into account the direct links with other economic regions the *Sovnarkhozy* draw up aggregate long-term plans area by area. The Councils of Ministers of the republics check the *Sovnarkhozy* plans to see that they correspond to the control figures and approve the aggregate plan on the republican level. Plan formulation proceeds in much the same way in all parts of the economy, whether they come under the jurisdiction of the Union, Union Republics, Republican Ministries or Republican Department.

The Central Planning organs check the correspondence of the plans of republics, ministries and departments with the approved control figures and decide how far any proposed deviations from the control figures are justified, and then draw up an aggregate plan for the USSR as a whole which they submit to the Government for its approval. An investment list of the most important construction projects is submitted for approval at the same time...'' pp. 131-132.

"The Council of Ministers of the USSR and then the Supreme Soviet of the USSR consider and approve the national economic plan. On the basis of which the ministries, departments, union republics, *sovnarkhozy*, and also the local organs and the enterprises immediately concerned clarify their own plans.

On the basis of the targets they receive, enterprises draw up detailed production plans. At the state enterprises these plans are approved by the directors. On collective farms, the production plans and accounting estimates are approved by general meetings of area (brigade) members.

On the basis of the approved plans economic agreements are concluded between suppliers and consumer enterprises." p. 133.

Financial Planning—Annual Plans and the Budget, Credit and Cash Plans

"Financial planning is an integral part of economic planning. Not only a state plan but also a state budget and the State Bank's credit plans and cash plan must be prepared and approved. The system of financial planning is based on the financial plans of the various economic sectors and enterprises and culminates in the consolidated financial plan, which covers all state revenues and expenditures. . . . .

The state budget is the main state financial plan and serves to combine the various financial plans into a unified system of financial planning. The state budget covers some three-quarters of all financial resources. . . . .

In addition to state budget funds, the funds held by individual enterprises and economic organizations are used to finance the various operations described above. . . . .

Bank credit, as employed by the State, is an important instrument for controlling implementation of the plan and influencing the process of reproduction. Planning of the State Bank's operations takes the form of a credit plan, which is directly geared to the planning of production, supply services and commodity circulation. The expenditure section of the plan lists all credits by recipient (union republics, ministries, etc.) and by type (credits to be used to build-up seasonal stocks of materials, advances made to consignors of goods still en route pending receipt of payment, etc.). The credit plan is helpful in the preparation of monetary outlay balances for the socialist sector of the economy. The State Bank's cash plan, which is directly tied in with the balance of personal income and expenditure, provides the basis for regulation of monetary circulation. . . .

The consolidated financial plan includes the following main items of income—turnover tax, profits, depreciation allowances, receipts from collective farms and cooperatives, state social insurance funds, funds accruing to the State from the general public, savings bank deposits, revenue from foreign trade, etc. The expenditure section of the plan covers outlays on capital works, capital repairs, expansion of the circulating capital of state enterprises and organizations, enlargement of the live-stock reserves of state farms and subsidiary plots, socio-cultural measures, expansion of state stockpiles of materials, defence, administration, replenishment of bank reserves etc.'' pp. 134-136.

Implementation of Plans (Bor M.Z., pp. 137-144)

"The fulfilment of the plan is checked by analysis of returns and statistics and by direct surveys on the spot. These two forms of checking are complementary. The organization of the checking process is based on the actual day-to-day contacts maintained by the planning and economic authorities with enterprises, construction projects, collective farms and state farms; on the application, during the actual process of checking, of specific measures to ensure the attainment of production targets; and on the provision of assistance in efforts to carry out the plan. . . .

An active part in the checking process is played by the local voluntary (Party and trade union) organizations, which keep a day-to-day watch over the progress made in the execution of plans,'' p. 138.

"The central and republican planning authorities are mainly concerned with checking consolidated indicators of the state plans on the basis of the data supplied by the statistical organs and *Sovnarhozy* and through local checks. . . . . In checking the execution of the plan, attention is focused primarily on the key sectors and industries on which the successful development to the entire national economy depends. . .

The planning authorities' and control authorities' work of keeping watch over the fulfilment of economic plans is shared by the financial organs, the banks and the state statistical authorities." pp. 137-38.

"A powerful tool in encouraging the fulfilment and over-fulfilment of production plans is the maximum use of the principle of material incentive, (principally, wages and salaries and bonuses. These are supplemented in various ways by moral stimuli). ...

One of the material incentives used to encourage good work by each enterprise is the establishment and use of a factory fund designed to raise the standard of living of the workers and improve output.'' p. 138.

"Along with the system of encouraging the successful fulfilment of plans, there are also various penalties for non-fulfilment of plans and contracts, for breaches of credit regulations or of economic arrangements between enterprises or organizations, and for putting out shoddy goods. Managers of enterprises are held responsible, both materially and administratively, for poor showing." p. 139.

Accounting and Prices

"The principle of giving workers a material interest in their output is applied with the help of the autonomous internal accounting system, which is one of the basic economic levers of planning. This system ensures that the interests of society are correctly inter-woven with the personal material interests of the workers of socialist enterprises. Outlays must be carefully balanced with production results, the enterprise's expenditure must be covered by its own earnings, and maximum result must be achieved with the minimum expenditure of materials, labour and funds. With this in view, state enterprises are provided with fixed and working capital and are allowed a degree of operational autonomy within the limits of the plan. . . . .

Autonomous accounting calls for a system of contractual relations between enterprises. Contracts give concrete expression to the plan, and serve as an effective means of checking on its fulfilment. They specify the volume, range and quality of items to be produced, delivery dates, terms of settlement, and the liability of the supplier and the consignee for non-performance (fine, forfeit or other penalty)." pp. 139-40.

"The pricing system in industry includes factory wholesale prices, industrial wholesale prices and retail prices. For certain types of industrial products, in addition there are what is known as accounting prices and provisional prices....

A characteristic feature of planned wholesale prices is that they are stable and free from market-economy fluctuations. Another intrinsic feature of wholesale prices is that they are uniform for any given type of output regardless of the enterprise by which it was produced." p. 140.

Role of Credit and Supplies Organizations

"An important function in the successful fulfilment of economic plans is fulfilled by the credit system.....

Enterprises and economic organizations build up funds in their accounts at the State Bank as they sell their output and as their amortization payments, profits, and other deposits accumulate; and these funds are disbursed at definite intervals. Rising incomes of workers, which become available in the form of savings bank deposits, provide another source of substantial free monetary resources. At the same time, the temporary need experienced by enterprises and economic organizations for additional funds (to meet seasonal expenses, procure raw materials, build-up production reserves, finance outlays for the production and movement of finished goods, etc.) can be met through credits extended by the bank. . . . .

Any enterprise which fails to achieve its cost reduction targets or to fulfil its accumulation plans, which permits losses in excess of the plan figures and which fails to husband its own working capital can receive credits from the State Bank only on special conditions and terms of settlement. A short-term credit may not be granted unless the enterprise can obtain the guarantee, the State Bank cuts off its credit facilities and calls in previously granted loans ahead of time." p. 141.

"An important part in the implementation of the plans is played by supply organizations. The enterprises acquire their supplies either from the warehouses of the supply organizations or from other enterprises to which they are directed by the supply organization. In cases where the enterprises have entered into direct commercial relations with each other, they have been bound to notify the supply organizations about their contracts or intended transactions; and these can, if necessary, be invalidated. The supply organizations enjoy a certain degree of freedom in implementation of their plans. A *Sovnarkhozy*, for instance, is entitled to reallocate raw and other materials, etc., among enterprises under its jurisdiction. However, it cannot deviate from the allocation plan for enterprises under other *Sovnarkhozy* unless it obtains the approval of the Government." p. 142.

Agriculture

"In agriculture, however, the problems of plan implementation differ considerably from those encountered in other sectors. These differences arise partly because output is subject to the vagaries of climate and partly because agricultural enterprises are predominantly collective farms, and not state enterprises. The state farms do receive planning directives relating to output of specific commodities and other aspects of their activity. But the collective farms have been free to determine their output, utilization of manpower, volume of investment, and procedure and terms for the remuneration of labour. Apart from the payment of taxes and the statutory formation of depreciation and investment funds, their only obligation has been the fulfilment of sales quotas for specific commodities assigned to them by the State...

Through price and tax policy, the State has influenced the amount of revenue received by farms from the sale of various commodities and, thereby, the pattern of output and sales.

The purchase plan, as well as price and taxation policy has been supplemented by other measures for the implementation of agricultural plans. The State plans the development of production and the supply of tractors, agricultural machinery, transport, chemical and mineral fertilizers and pest control preparations to agriculture, undertakes irrigation and land reclamation schemes, brings virgin and fallow land under the plough, organizes the production of high grade seeds and the breeding of high-productivity livestock and their sale to collective farms, lays out a network of stock-breeding and veterinary institutions, and carries out plans for the training and retraining of specialists and for the dissemination of advanced new experience." p. 143.

Foreign Trade

"The implementation of plans for foreign trade, which is a state monopoly, has been achieved by the use of methods similar to those applied in most other sectors. The overall foreign trade plans have been translated into directives issued to state import and export agencies. They have also been integrated into the purchase and allocation plans of various supply organizations and, frequently, into the production and sales plans of the enterprises producing for export. The fulfilment of these plans has been safeguarded by the existence of the state monopoly of foreign trade and by the long-term trade agreements with other centrally planned economies. These safeguards, however, are not completely effective since trade with the capitalist countries of the world is subject to fluctuations in external demand and prices; and this may influence the implementation of trade and other plans." pp. 143-44.

Yugoslavia

Planning in Yugoslavia is of interest because of its distinctive structures and methods which combine features of socialist and market economies, and which have evolved as a result of trial and error, motivated by a combination of ideology and pragmatism. Planning has helped Yugoslavia, a country with difficult development problems, arising from under-development and ethnic diversity of its population, achieves a rapid rate of economic growth, and has transformed it within about 20 years from an underdeveloped country to a developed one.

Yugoslavia is a medium-sized, South-east European country with a population of about 20 million people (in 1966). There is diversity of religion, language and culture among its people, and a long history of conflict among the principal ethnic groups—Serbs, Croats, Slovenes, etc. There are also large regional differences in levels of economic and social development. In the north-western republic of Slovenia, economic and social levels are comparable to those of neighbouring Italy and Austria; but the southern republics such as Macedonia and Montenegro are much less developed. Reduction of regional disparities has been an important objective of planning.

Yugoslavia was a poor, backward and war-torn economy when planning began after Second World War. Per capita income was below $120; 75 per cent of the population was dependent on agriculture; most farms were small, and farmers, using traditional low productivity techniques, were poor; industry contributed less than 1/3 of GNP, and communications, power, etc., were undeveloped. Moreover, there had been heavy destruction of life and property during Second World War. Nearly 1.7 million lives were lost and damage to property was estimated at $9.1 billion. The Yugoslavs had carried on continuous guerrilla warfare against the German occupation forces. After the War, a Communist regime was established by the leaders of the freedom fighters. A new Constitution was promulgated which established a Federation, consisting of 6 republics and 2 Autonomous Provinces within the Republic of Serbia. The non-agricultural means of production were nationalized, rapid collectivization was begun in agriculture, and systems of centralized administration and planning, patterned after the Soviet model, were established. The period of the First Plan 1947-51, was the period of centralized administrative planning. As in the early Soviet plans, there was great emphasis in this plan on industrialization and on development of heavy industry in particular. Large investments were made in industrial projects. The rate of growth in the Plan period was low, however, - 1.6 per cent overall, and 0.4 per cent per capita. This was due to several reasons : large expenditures on defence following the political break with the Soviet Union in 1948, poor harvests in 1950 and 1951, the inefficiencies of centralized planning, and the mistakes and confusion resulting from lack of experience with planning.

The political break with the Soviet Union provided the background for shifts in economic policies and patterns of economic and political organization; which were accomplished through a succession of reform aimed at decentralization and liberalization. Agriculture was de-collectivized, and only 6 per cent of the land remained in collective farms. But a ceiling of 10 hectares was imposed on individual holdings in order to prevent large economic inequalities from emerging. A structure of cooperative organizations was built-up to provide farmers with facilities of credit marketing, and supplies of inputs. State management of enterprises was replaced by management by workers; the change was justified on the ground that it constituted a further development of communism, in which the State progressively withers away and is replaced by "society". Local authorities were strengthened and the communes were built-up as basic units of local political and economic organization. Authority for planning was decentralized from the Federal level to the levels of the Republic, the district, the commune and the enterprise. A sophisticated system of interpenetration of political and economic representatives was built-up at Federal, Republic, commune and enterprise levels. The Federal Planning Commission (FPC) was replaced by the Federal Planning Institute (later converted to Federal Planning Board) and the planning staff was reduced from 700 to about 50. The FPC had been engaged in formulating detailed plans for each sector, branch, and industry, and deciding resource allocations and supervising plan implementation; its responsibilities were now limited to overall plan formulation and coordination. Detailed plan formulation and implementation were decentralized and entrusted to Republics, communes, and other economic organizations. Detailed direction of operations of enterprises by Federal authorities (FPC, Ministries, and others) was abolished. The enterprises were given considerable freedom in operation, and competition between enterprises in obtaining investment funds and physical inputs and in marketing outputs were encouraged. Enterprises were encouraged to make profits; the earnings of workers were made dependent upon the profits. There were large resource transfers from the Federal level to the Republics and the communes, which made decentralization effective. Fulfilment of key targets of the National Plan was ensured primarily through control over investment, exercised through :

(i) Laws governing the distribution of earnings of enterprises, and

(ii) Activities of the Yugoslav Investment Bank. Republics, communes and enterprises were provided with incentives to exceed the National Plan targets, and large numbers of them did so.

Since the Yugoslav economy attained high rates of investment and growth following these reforms, the initial measures were followed by others, which carried the process further. The movement towards decentralization and liberalization gathered strength progressively. As a result of the successive reform measures, the Yugoslav economic system is now indistinguishable in many ways from a market economy.

Two distinctive features of the Yugoslav system are management of enterprise (i) by workers, and (ii) the commune.

Management of enterprise by workers is based on the principle of "social" ownership and control of enterprises; ownership rests in "society" (as distinct from the State) and the workers manage it as trustees for "society". Management rests in a Workers' Council. This is a large body of 15 to 120 members, depending on the size of the enterprise. The large size of the council, re-election of 1/3rd of the membership every two years and restriction on more than one re-election, are intended to encourage the participation of workers in management and to prevent management from being concentrated in the hands of a group. The council appoints the Director of the enterprise, and decides all matters of policy. It elects a Management Board of 3 to 11 members, including the Director of the enterprise, which is the effective management body.

The earnings of workers and the executives are dependent upon the earnings of the enterprise : they are not regarded as costs, but as "profits", constitute a residual rather than a "first charge" on the receipts of the enterprise. Although the disposition of profits among wages and salaries, investments, depreciation, etc., is decided by the Worker's Council, it is controlled in detail by federal laws (see below). Management of enterprises is supervised by the communes, and the enterprises are in turn represented on one of the two Councils (the council of Producers) of the commune. Activities of individual enterprises in each sector, branch, or industry are coordinated by economic organizations such as chambers of commerce and industry.

The commune is the basic territorial unit in Yugoslavia. There are about 800 communes in the country, and their average population is about 25,000. Besides performing functions of local government and operating services such as health-education and communication, the communes have very important functions of plan formulation and implementation, control over enterprises and investment. The communes prepare the development plans for their areas primarily by integrating the plans of enterprises, participate in appointment of directors of enterprises, and economic organizations; supervise the functioning of the organizations, and make large investments in establishing new enterprises. The communes have large financial resources, which are derived from transfers of proceeds of federal taxes, their own taxes, (which include taxes on personal income and the incomes of enterprises) and revenues from investments. In 1959, 27.6 per cent of the budgetary and planning resources of the country were distributed among the communes (Gigov Kiro, 1961: 409 quoted in Macesich, p.14). Each commune must underwrite the establishment of new firms in its territory and share the responsibility in case of failure. A large proportion of the enterprises are established by the communes.

Structures and Processes of Plan Formulation

The central planning agency is the Federal Planning Bureau (FPB). The Bureau has technical responsibility for preparation of the National Plan, within the framework of policies and objectives laid down by the National Assembly and the Communist Party. It works in close collaboration with the Federal Statistical Institute, the State Secretariats, the National Bank and the Investment Bank, and relies upon these agencies for data needed for plan formulation.

Sectoral planning is done primarily in the State Secretariats, which coordinate the plans of republics, communes and economic organizations. The State Secretariat for Finance and the two Banks are closely associated with formulation of the financial plan. The actual drafting of the plan goes through six stages :

"1. The Planning Institute prepares a detailed analysis of the economic situation with special reference to possibilities for further growth.
2. On the basis of this analysis, the Federal Executive Council and the Federal People's Assembly define the general objectives of the plan.
3. On the basis of items (1) and (2), estimates of the possible development of production, national income, investment and personal income are made.
4. Partial plans for particular branches and sectors of the economy

are then drafted, (e.g., for industry, agriculture, capital investments, personal consumption). At this stage several variants are prepared to indicate alternative possibilities.

5. The most favourable variants and alternatives in the sector plans which are consistent with fixed objectives are next selected, coordinated and linked together into a comprehensive summary plan for the entire economy.
6. In the final drafting stage of the annual (but not in the multi-annual) federal plans, the economic measures by which the plan is to be implemented are formulated" (Waterston, A., pp. 36-37).

Within the Federal Executive Council (Cabinet) the body responsible for most decisions relating to planning is the Committee for General Economic Affairs. The FPB maintains close touch with this Committee, and also with the Committees for Coordination and Perspective Social Plan. Within the Federal People's Assembly (Parliament), the bodies concerned with planning are the Committees for National Economy, of the Federal Council, and the Council of Producers.

The draft plan is submitted for approval first to the Federal Executive Council's (FEC) Committee for Economic Affairs, and thereafter to the FEC. The approved plan is then submitted to the Committees of the Councils of the Federal People's Assembly, and thereafter to the Councils. Changes can be and are, often made at both the Committee and the Council stages of discussion. After the plan has been passed in separate sittings of both Councils, it is published as an act of the FPA and has the force of law. Since the Plan contains the statement of Government economic policies and investment programmes, it has the status of the budget. The Plan is also discussed in the press; but except in case of the Second Plan, which was submitted for discussion to a Panel of Economists, there is no formal procedure for discussion outside official circles.

The structures and processes of plan formulation at the republican level are similar to those described above for the Federal level. The republican plans are also similar to the Federal Plan, except that foreign trade, balance of payments, etc., are not included in them. In 1959, the republics distributed 16.9 per cent of the budgetary and planning resources (Macesich, p. 14). Districts and other regional organizations also have their planning structures and plans but these are of limited importance. The important planning level below the republic is the commune. The plan for the commune represents a detailed programme of action for the economy in its area : it includes the development programme of the commune and integrates the plans of all enterprises and economic organizations. Plans of communes are formulated within the framework of Republican and the national plan, and provide guidance in plan formulation to enterprises and economic organizations. Finally, each enterprise and economic organization formulates its own plan.

The planning agencies at each level are directly responsible to the executive and legislative agencies of that level, and are independent of the planning agencies at higher levels. The relationships between planning agencies at different levels are indirect and are through the corresponding executive agencies.

Five-Year, Annual and Perspective (Long-term) Plans

Both the Five Year Plans and the Annual Plan are important; the latter primarily as an operational blue-print. The stages of plan formulation and approval described above are gone through in case of both. Long-term plans are much less important, however. A long-term, perspective plan was first prepared for the period, 1960-80, though long-term programmes for sectors had been prepared earlier. The 1960-80 Plan was in very general terms, and was intended primarily to provide the perspective for the five year plans.

Implementation of Plans

As mentioned above, in the period of centralized administrative planning, the Federal Planning Commission had extensive powers and responsibilities of plan implementation. But the present responsibilities of the FPB are limited to analysis of plan implementation and of trends in the economy, advising the Federal Executive Council on modifications in the plan, planning methods, and in economic policies, etc. Data on plan implementation and the economic indicators are collected by the State Secretariats (which obtain them from the republics, local authorities, and enterprises), credit agencies, such as the National Bank and the Investment Bank, and the Federal Statistical Institute.

In the period of centralized administrative planning, plan implementation was largely through directives, issued by Federal and Republican authorities, and supplemented by exhortations and propaganda to increase output and achieve plan targets. However, with decentralization and liberalization, directives and centralized resource allocation have been replaced progressively by indirect, primarily fiscal and credit instruments, and the price system and the market have played an increasing role in resource allocation and direction of production, particularly in the consumer goods sectors. Federal and other authorities do not prescribe targets for enterprises; but rely on fiscal and credit instruments for achievements of plan objectives. Monetary incentives are relied upon increasingly to provide incentives for increasing output; the differentials between wages of unskilled workers on the one hand and skilled workers and managers have been progressively increased. Minimum wages have been abolished and family benefits have been reduced and the earnings of workers have been made to depend primarily upon the earnings of the enterprises. Competitive bidding between enterprises for managers and skilled workers further increases the premier on productivity and skill.

Controls over prices and foreign exchange and on distribution of scarce physical inputs are still used to direct resource allocations, influence outputs or achieve certain socio-political objectives. Thus, controls over prices of farm products are used to keep prices low (so that they are not too far out of line from wages) or to support prices. But the scope and importance of the control measures have been progressively reduced, and increasing reliance is placed on the market mechanism for determining prices and allocating resources.

The principal regulatory measures for achievement of plan objective are regulations over distribution of incomes of enterprises. The cost of production includes only the costs of materials, depreciation, interest, and miscellaneous fees and contributions. Wages and salaries, (workers' personal incomes) are included under the income of the enterprise. A large proportion of the income is allocated for payment of taxes, (especially the turnover tax) and for contributions to the various investments, reserve and other funds. The rates of taxes and of contributions to the different funds have varied in different plans; but the very high rate of gross investment under Yugoslav Plans (about 30 per cent of gross domestic product during 1952-61) has been made possible through allocation of large proportions of enterprise incomes to taxes and the various funds.

Taxes are federal, republican and local. The proceeds of federal taxes are divided among federal, republican, and local authorities in prescribed proportions. The federal turnover tax was the most important tax (and means of financing plan investment) in the period of centralized administrative planning; but its importance has decreased progressively. The average rate of the turnover tax has also decreased from about 75 per cent to 15 per cent. Besides the federal turnover tax, there is also a turn-over tax levied by the communes. The proceeds of taxes on personal enterprise incomes are similarly divided among federal, republican and local authorities.

Federal receipts came mainly from the turnover tax, the income-tax, profits on foreign exchange transactions and customs duties. The receipts of communes are derived mainly from taxes on incomes of enterprises, various local taxes, and profits on investments.

Investments are made primarily from "non-budgetary" portions of receipts of federal and local authorities; the "budgetary" receipts are used primarily for financing current expenditure and non-economic investment such as on schools and hospitals. In the period of centralized planning, about 4/5th of the investment was federal; but by the late 1950s the distribution was as follows (Waterston, p. 77):

General Investment Fund	*Per Cent*
Federal	33-35
Republican and Local Government. (including Communes)	35
Enterprises	30-32

Federal Investment funds are transferred to the General Investment Fund, from which loans are made by the Investment Bank. The funds are used primarily for financing large projects, for which the responsibility is of the Federal Government, and for loans to republics, communes, enterprises, and other economic organizations. Loans for projects are given to these on condition that the borrower contributes a proportion of the investment from its own resources. The projects selected for financing are often scrutinized in great detail. The control over investment, exercised by the Investment Bank is powerful instrument of plan implementation. Republican and local governments are free to invest in projects, and the enterprises to expand along lines other than those provided in the plans. It has been estimated that about 10 per cent of the total investment is non-plan investment (*ibid.*, p. 78). The Yugoslav authorities have accepted such investment as the inescapable price of decentralization and liberalization. But the quantum of such investment is kept low by controls over ingestible funds exercised by the Investment Bank and the controls over credit and foreign exchange exercised by the National Bank.

The National Bank, which is the Central Bank, makes allocations of foreign exchange, and also exercises detailed control over the credit system. The Bank directs distribution of credit so as to achieve plan objectives, both by its own loan operations and through its directives to the other banks. In the early years, the bank used to exercise very detailed control over enterprise, and other economic organizations through its system of social accounts, under which they were required to deposit, daily, their balances with a branch of the Bank. The control has been relaxed, but the system of social accounts enables the Bank to have detailed information of the flow of fund within the economy and remains an important instrument of direction of investment.

The Role of Economic and Political Organizations

(i) Chambers of Commerce and Industry

Economic organization such as the Chambers of Commerce and Industry has a very important role in planning. The Chambers have been created for major sectors, branches and industries. They assemble data relating to various aspects of operation and growth in their sectors, etc., advise the planning authorities on sectoral needs, draw up draft plans, and coordinate the activities of enterprises. They are the principal sectoral coordinating agencies, since the abolition of the Ministries.

(ii) The Communist Party and the Trade Unions

The Communist Party plays the central role in plan formulation and implementation in the socialist countries. The basic objectives and policies of the plans are indicated by the top leadership of the party. Members of the party at various levels have very important roles in detailed plan formulation and implementation, by virtue of the positions of authority that they occupy, through their control of the communications media, and through their participation in workers' education. The Communist Party of Yugoslavia had a similar role and importance in the period of centralized administrative planning, but these have decreased and have become progressively more indirect. The interpenetration of Party and management hierarchies, so characteristic of the socialist countries, has become much less; large number of managers are non-members, and the party members' influence on the management and the workers for achievement of plan targets is primarily persuasion. The trade unions organization, with a membership of about 6 million, is another powerful influence on plan formulation and implementation. It also exercises influence on its members, for fulfilment of plan targets and objectives, through education and persuasion.

Volume of Investment, Rate of Growth and Transformation of the Economy

The Yugoslav economy has maintained very high rated of investment (about 30 per cent of the GDP) and economic growth (10 per cent and above) for most of the period since 1952, when the system of centralized administrative planning was abolished. As explained above, the high rates have been made possible primarily by the fiscal and investment obligations on enterprises, and by treating personal income as a residual. Personal consumption has increased less than investment, about 3.2 per cent annually between 1953 and 1956, but 9.9 per cent between 1957 and 1960 (*ibid.*, p. 87).

A large proportion of the total investment has gone to industry : the rate of growth in industry has averaged 13 per cent annually since 1952, as compared with 5 per cent or less, for most of the period, in agriculture. The transformation of the economy from predominantly agricultural, to diversified agricultural-industrial is shown by the following figures (Macesich, pp. 20-21) :

Proportion of national income contributed by	*1947*	*1961*
Industry and Mining	32.7	46.4
Agriculture and Forestry	44.7	26.2

NOTE

1. The problems of project formulation and implementation are discussed in the course on Project Formulation and Evaluation. The administrative problems of construction and operation are discussed in the section of 'Management and Organization of Projects'.

   The data given are as were available in 1966. As per the latest figures the population is above one billion, urban population is more than 30 per cent, literacy rates have also gone up to more than 40 per cent and per capita income has increased more than four times; the proportion of the workforce in the organized sector has also increased substantially since than.

   The data in this section relates to (1966-1970), the period, when the author was delivering these lectures at the U.N. Institute for Economic and Social Planning in the Middle East, Kuwait.

REFERENCES

Bor, M.Z.: *Planning for Economic Development*, United Nations, New York, 1963.

Gigov, Kiro: "The Communal Economy", *International Social Science Journal*, No. 3, 1961. Quoted in George Macesich: *Yugoslavia, The Theory and Practices of Development Planning. p. 14.*

Macesich, George: *Yugoslavia, The Theory and Practices of Development Planning p. 14.*

Waterston, A.: *Planning in Yugoslavia.*

Section II

Administration and Development Planning in India : Areas of Concern

5

Administrative Reforms and Creation of Small States 1947-2000

Introduction

The Indian Union consists of 29 states and 4 Union territories. The population of the states varied in 2001 from 166 million in Uttar Pradesh to less than 1 million in Sikkim and Mizoram. The variation in population of the Union territories was from 974,000 in Pudicherry to 61 thousand in Lakshadweep.

This chapter gives a historical perspective to the present organization of the Indian Union during the period, 1947-2000. It examines the constraints and potentials for economic development and promotion of welfare of the people of the three new states that were created in 2000.

With the examples of Punjab and Haryana, it is explained that although the creations of new states leads to some problems which take long period to solve, but by and large the creation of new states eventually leads to economic development and administrative stability.

It is premised that all states with a population above 40 million should be bifurcated into smaller states and in case it is not possible to divide the large states on political consideration, decision-making structures at levels of agro-climatic regions in all such states should be created.

When India became independent in 1947, it had 3 British administered presidencies, five provinces and about 600 odd princely states. The princely states varied in size from Hyderabad, located in the heart of the Indian peninsula, which had an area and population equal to or greater than that of any one of British administered provinces, to tiny bits of territories, sparsely populated and covering a few sq. kilometres each, located in the western Himalayan region.

The first step in administrative re-organization was accomplished during 1948 with the accession of princely states with the Indian Union and creation of new states by merger of a number of small states. The accession of nearly all the princely states was peaceful. The princes agreed to accede to the Indian Union on assurance of being granted their privy purses and certain other privileges. However, in case of Hyderabad, accession became possible only after the Indian army defeated the Nizam's forces in a brief campaign in October 1948. In case of Jammu and Kashmir, which had a Hindu ruler but a predominantly Moslem population, the accession of the state to India by its ruler has not been accepted by Pakistan. The state has great strategic importance because it borders Pakistan, Afghanistan and Tibet region of China. About two-third of the state is occupied by India and the remaining one-third is under occupation of Pakistan. Four wars have been fought over it, in 1948, 1965, 1971 and 1999 but a resolution of the dispute between the two countries is nowhere in sight.

After the integration of the princely states, the next step was to create new states by merger of numerous small states into union of states. The large number of small states of the Kathiawad peninsula and Kutch were merged to form the new state of Saurashtra. The numerous small hill states in the western Himalayan region, which used to be administered from Punjab, were merged to form Himachal Pradesh. Five small states, which had Sikh rulers, and one, which had a Moslem ruler, were merged to form the new state of PEPSU. Similar unions by merger of small states were created in Madhya Bharat/Vindhyachal. The numerous small states of inland Orissa were merged with the British administered province of Orissa. A number of other small states were merged with the presidencies or provinces within which they were situated.

Six small hill states bordering Assam, which share borders with Myanmar, Tibet or Bangladesh and which have tribal population were created in the 1960s, but only after the Indian army ended years of insurgency in some of them. The former Portuguese possession of Goa, Daman and Diu and the former French enclave of Pondicherry were constituted into separate states in the 1960s when the Portuguese and the French left. The small state of Sikkim which has a strategic location on the route between India and Tibet became a part of India in the early 1970s, just before its ruler was about to declare his independence from India.

The Union territories include the city-state of Chandigarh, capital of Punjab and Haryana, which had a population of about 901,000 in 2001, Andaman and Nicobar islands in the Bay of Bengal, Dadra & Nagar Haveli, a tiny enclave within Gujarat and Lakshadweep, a group of atolls with a population of less than 1 lakh, located in the Arabian sea, about 150 km. from Kerala.

The Union territories are administered directly by the National Government through administrators appointed by it. They have full powers of governance of the territories within guidelines provided by the National Government. Each of the large states has a democratically elected Legislative Assembly and a Council of Ministers headed by the Chief Minister. The Governor of the state, appointed by the National Government assumes executive powers for six months at a time, only when no political party is able to form a government. He relinquishes executive powers and reverts to his position of a non-executive constitutional head only when a political party forms a government.

The State Governments have full powers of maintenance of peace and security within their territories as well as implementation of programmes aimed at increasing agricultural and industrial output, expansion of communications which includes maintaining national and state highways and providing approach roads to villages; rural electrification and providing health care and primary, secondary and higher education. The National Government provides also funds for implementation of these programmes. Thus, the states are the principal units of administration and policy formulation below the level of the National Government.

The process of creation of new states, started in 1948, was completed in the early 1970s after the accession of Sikkim to the Indian Union. But the local demand for creation of Uttaranchal, Jharkhand and Chhattisgarh by separating areas from Uttar Pradesh, Bihar and Madhya Pradesh were supported by the Janata Dal and BJP Governments during the later half of the 1990s. The three new states were created in 2000.

In this Chapter the process of reorganization of states from the 1950s to the 1970s is described at some length. Furthermore, administrative problems and development potential of the three new states that have been created are examined. The point has been made that the creation of the new states shall assist in economic development of their areas and also contributes to making administration in the new states more people oriented. It is argued further that in all the states which have population of more than 40 million, should be divided into small states and if that is not feasible on political grounds, administrative structures should be created at the level of the agro-climatic regions at which level all decisions relating to detailed formulation and implementation of programmes of economic and social development, should be taken. The structures should not be merely bureaucratic but should have popular representation on them. The senior-most Minister of the State Government hailing from the region should be the Chairman of the regional structure.

All the states with population above 40 million have two or more agro-climatic regions within them. The regions are relatively homogenous in physical, economic and social conditions. There is considerable information on agro-climatic regions in the reports of the Population Censuses of 1951 and 1961, the Planning Commission and the Ministry of Agriculture. The ministry formulates and implements its programmes for increasing agricultural output and providing against security of crop failure with agro-climatic region as the unit. Furthermore, it regularly issues reports on the prospects of crop production in different agro-climatic regions. The administrative structures should be created in largest cities in the major agro-climatic regions, so that most of the decisions relating to economic development and welfare of the people can be taken at the regional level.

Against this background the development potential of the three new states that were created in 2000 has been described briefly. It is argued that the poor people of these backward states will benefit by faster, people-oriented economic development. This may be expected because the funds will be in the hands of Ministers and officials resident in the new states that have a much better understanding of the needs and problems of the people than those located in distant capitals.

A Historical Perspective

The issue of reorganization of states dates back to the 1920s when the Indian National Congress indicated its commitment to formation of linguistic states. Creation of such states became unavoidable after the integration of princely states with the Indian Union during 1948. Furthermore, some of the then British provinces had within them people of several linguistic groups. The then Madras presidency, for instance, comprised the whole of present Tamil Nadu, the coastal districts of present Andhra Pradesh, extending north to Vishakhapatnam, four districts of present Karnataka and one district of Malayalam speaking people. Thus it included people speaking four languages, Tamil, Telugu, Kannada and Malayalam. It extended for about a thousand kilometre along the east coast and included, besides, large inland areas. Bombay presidency included western Maharashtra including Konkan, coastal Gujarat and one

Kannada speaking district south of Konkan. It contained people speaking three different languages.

The issue came to a head and early action for reorganization of states became inescapable when a prominent political leader of Andhra Pradesh died after a fast unto death in support of the demand of the people of Andhra Pradesh for creation of a separate state. They had felt that with location of the capital of Madras Presidency in Madras (now renamed Chennai); they were being exploited by the Tamils.

The Government of India then appointed a three-member States Reorganization Commission. It was chaired by Justice Faizl Ali and had Sardar K.M. Panikar and Pandit Hridaya Nath Kunzru as its members. The Commission accepted the principle of creation of linguistic states. Andhra Pradesh was constituted by merging the Telugu speaking districts of the Madras presidency and the Telugu speaking districts of the Nizam's state of Hyderabad. Hyderabad, the largest city in the state which had the buildings for a capital, was made its capital. Karnataka, similarly, was constituted by merging the old Mysore state with the Kannada speaking districts of Hyderabad and of Madras and Bombay presidencies. The capital was located in Bangalore, which had a large number of buildings which house the offices of various departments of the State Government. Kerala was constituted by merging the princely states of Travancore and Cochin and two Malayalam speaking districts of the Madras presidency. Maharashtra was constituted, similarly, by merger of Marathi speaking areas of western Maharashtra, Konkan, Marathwada, which comprised the Marathi speaking districts of Hyderabad and Vidarbha, which had formed part of the British administered province of Central Provinces and Berar. A few small princely states located within its territory were merged in Maharashtra. Gujarat was formed, similarly, by merging the Gujarati speaking districts of Bombay presidency with Saurashtra which had been formed in 1948 by merger of several hundred small princely states of the Kathiawad peninsula and Kutch. The state of Rajasthan had already been formed in 1948 by merger of about 20 Rajput states. The British administered district of Ajmer was merged with it. Two districts of Punjab located in the hills were merged with the new state of Himachal Pradesh.

The largest (in area) and most unwieldy state, resulting from the recommendations of the Commission, was Madhya Pradesh. Its borders extended from the vicinity of Gwaliar, located about 200 km. from Delhi, to the hilly district and inhabited mainly by tribal people of

Bastar which borders Orissa and Andhra Pradesh and which now forms part of Chhattisgarh.

Most of the recommendations of the Commission were accepted by the Government of India. The most notable exception was its recommendation to constitute Bombay into a Union territory. It was opposed so strongly by the Marathi speaking people that the Government of India had to accept their demand for including the city in Maharashtra. It has been the capital of the new state since then.

The process of creation of new states continued through the 1960s and the 1970s. The former Portuguese dominions of Goa, Daman and Diu and the former French enclave of Pondicherry were constituted into separate states when they became part of the Indian Union in the 1960s. This decision was taken at the instance of the Prime Minister, Pandit Nehru, who was keen that the distinctive cultures of these territories should not be changed radically. Six states, each dominated by a separate tribe, were created in the north-east, but only after ending several years of insurgency by the people of some of them. Sikkim, which has a strategic location on the route between India and Tibet, became part of India in the early 1970s just before its ruler was going to declare its independence.

It is of interest to note that the Commission made no recommendation for division of Uttar Pradesh and Bihar despite their very large areas and populations consisting of several ethnic groups. Bihar, for instance, included besides the Hindi speaking areas of north and south Bihar, the mineral-rich forested area, inhabited mainly by tribal people of Chhota Nagpur, which is now constituted into Jharkhand.

Creation of New States

The Government created in year 2000 three new states: Uttaranchal (later renamed Uttarakhand) comprising the hilly and mountainous areas of western Uttar Pradesh; Jharkhand which comprises the hilly, largely forested area, inhabited mainly by tribal people of Bihar, and Chhattisgarh comprising similar hilly, forested area inhabited mainly by tribals of eastern Madhya Pradesh. The decision, after the initial problems of construction of buildings and development of an administrative infrastructure for the capital have been solved, will contribute to faster, people-oriented economic development in these backward new states.

Better governance and more efficient implementation of development programmes are expected because they will be in the hands of officials who belong to the new states and understand and appreciate the needs, problems and aspirations of the people, and also appreciate the impediments to development of the regions.

Uttaranchal

Consider Uttaranchal (later renamed Uttarakhand) : When it was part of U.P., an average resident of the region had to travel for a day, or a day and a half, from his home, say in Pauri Garhwal to Lucknow, the capital of the state, and incur large expenditure for the travel if he or she had a problem with the government. Only an affluent person could afford the time and expense of the travel. However, with the creation of Uttaranchal and location of its capital within it in Dehra Doon, the time and expense of travel from home to the state capital have been reduced greatly. Furthermore, the people have to deal with officials who understand and appreciate their problems and not with those who may have no inkling to them.

The development potential of Uttaranchal is limited, because of its hilly and mountainous terrain and the limited area available for agriculture. No large commercially exploitable minerals have been discovered, thus mining or mineral based industries cannot be developed. The forest resource has been greatly depleted during the last 100 years through thoughtless deforestation. There is need to reverse the process and undertake a programme of re-forestation and construction of small check dams for conservation of soil and water. Local women's groups and some non-governmental organizations have been active in some areas in saving the trees from being cut by rapacious forest contractors. As a result, the trees and the vegetation below them are coming back slowly, yielding fuel and fodder to the villagers and protecting their farms from soil erosion in the monsoon season.

The region has a potential for large and small-scale hydro-power development. However, the controversy over the construction of Tehri dam, a high concrete dam located in Tehri Garhwal district, an earthquake-prone region, indicates such development is not free from risk. Small check dams to conserve the water of the streams flowing down the hills could be built and repaired every year to supply irrigation water and prevent soil erosion. Water wells constructed below the dams will supply water for domestic use throughout the year.

The region has great strategic importance because it borders both Nepal and Tibet. The strategic needs of the country are being met by construction and improvement of roads reaching the borders and posting defence personnel at the borders. Keeping the roads in good repair and meeting the needs of the armed forces provide employment to large number of men. Some sections of the population of the region have a tradition of military service, which has remained an important source of employment for the young men. Large number of young men from these villages joins the army after graduation from higher secondary schools, while others join the police force. Remittances home from soldiers and policemen are a major source of income for many families in the region.

The region has enormous potential for tourism—for pleasure and for satisfying the keen desire of millions of Hindus for pilgrimage to religious places located within it. There are three popular hill stations—Mussoorie, Nainital and Ranikhet—in the new states. The first two have suffered considerable environmental damage in the last 50 years through thoughtless commercial development or disregard of vulnerability of their principal natural resource—forests, to damage through pollution. The lake, the principal attraction of Nainital, is being steadily polluted by dumping into it untreated sewage of the town. Such dumping should be stopped through diversion of the waste water to flow into various *nallahs* (small streams) that flow through the hills. Furthermore, there are a number of villages above Nainital, each located alongside a small lake, which are suitable for development of chalet-type tourism on the Swiss model. Small but clean, medium priced hotels could be built in most of them. In order to make them popular, they need a well thought out programme for educating the people in environmental hygiene and hospitality for the tourists.

The real economic potential of the region is in development of religious tourism. From the Himalayan foothills in Haridwar to its source near the temples of Badrinath and Kedarnath, the valley of the Ganga has been a valley of pilgrimage for millions of Hindus through the centuries. Roads and road transport within the valley have been greatly improved in the post-independence years. The bus service, for instance, which terminated earlier at Rishikesh, a few kilometres above Haridwar, has been extended to Joshi Math, and then up to temples of Badrinath. As a result, the pilgrims, who had to walk for several days to reach the temples of Kedarnath earlier, have now to walk a few hours only. However, there is a dearth of clean, low priced hotels for overnight stay of the pilgrims and the sanitary conditions along the road are less than satisfactory. Removal of these deficiencies will make the pilgrimage to the temples a rewarding experience to be cherished over the years by the pilgrims. Besides it would provide remunerative employment for tens of thousands.

When the proposal for creating Uttaranchal was first announced by the BJP Government in 1999, there were strong protests against it from two groups. The leaders of the Akali Dal, who represented the Sikhs and is an ally of the BJP, wanted that Udham Singh Nagar which forms part of the sub-Himalayan terai sub-mountain area, (to which Sikh farmers migrated from Punjab in the 1950s and the 1960s to establish large, highly productive farms producing wheat, rice and sugarcane), should not be included in Uttaranchal. The area was thinly populated earlier because malaria was endemic in it. With clearing of the land and control over malaria as a result of the national malaria eradication programme in the 1950s, the area has become very productive. A number of rice or wheat flour and sugar mills have been established to process the crops. The Sikhs feared that they would be a small minority in the new state. A more legitimate fear is that their highly productive farms, which average more than 20 hectares in size, would be broken into small farms if the State Government enacts a law limiting the size of individual farms to 1 or 2 hectares, which is the average size of most of the farms in the region. This demand is not being pressed now. Apparently some assurance has been given to the Sikhs by the Central Government that their land would not be subject to the ceiling on size of farms.

The people of Haridwar district also did not wish their district to be included in Uttaranchal. Although Haridwar is the gateway to the valley of the Ganga, it is in the plain and its people feel greater affinity with the people of the plain than with those of the hills. Their demand has also not been accepted and Haridwar is included in Uttaranchal. The capital of the state is in Dehra Doon, which had a number of buildings, which could be acquired and repaired for the offices and the staff quarters of officials and clerks in the state administration. The formation of the state has been remarkably smooth and no major problem of political instability has been experienced so far (2002).

The state has in Dehra Doon and other cities, a large number of High Schools and Colleges. The number of graduates from them is so large that there is a problem of unemployment of the educated. This despite the fact that large numbers of educated men and women work as teachers, nurses and paramedics in their own state. Others go to Dehra Doon to work in offices of the State Government, the Oil and Natural Gas Commission as well as in the Indian Military Academy and the Forest Research Institute. Others migrate to New Delhi to work in the offices of the Central Government and in those of the public sector undertaking and private companies.

The developments mentioned above have resulted in such increase in remunerative employment and income of the people that there is a change in the nature of the migrants from the region. During the 1950s and 1960s, large number of barely educated young men went to Delhi to work as domestic servants, messengers in offices or bearers in small hotels. No longer! The young men who go to Delhi now are all educated; they seek and get jobs of clerks or junior officers in offices of the Government of India or in various public sector undertakings.

The new state of Uttaranchal should have a stable government after the initial troubles about selection of Chief Minister and his cabinet colleagues ended and expenditure on building a capital has been obtained. There are few disparities of caste, or social and economic status among its people. Furthermore, the entire population is aware of the need for building and maintenance of roads to the Indo-Tibetan border and development of leisure and religious tourism, the path of development.

Retaining the three hill stations, Mussourie, Nainital and Ranikhet, keeping them scrupulously clean and maintaining well the roads leading to them are the priority. The same can be said about the roads to temples of Badrinath and Kedarnath and training of local people to take care of these.

Jharkhand

There was strong opposition also to the creation of Jharkhand by separating the hilly, forested, mineral rich part of Bihar, which is inhabited mainly by tribal people, from the rest of the state. The State Government opposed any division of the state although it is very large and populous. It had a population of more than 86 million in 1991 which increased to 98 million by 2001 (Table 5.1). The law and order situation is bad; there is recurring conflict in some parts of the state between the former landlords (*zamindars*) and their tenants who have been given full and heritable rights of ownership in the land that they cultivate, following enactment of land reform legislation in the 1950s.

Implementation of development programmes is ineffective because large proportions of the funds are siphoned away by corrupt officers and political leaders. However, the opposition has been overcome and Jharkhand was created in 2000 along with Uttaranchal and Chhattisgarh.

The leaders of the Jharkhand Mukti Morcha (JMM), who had been agitating for creation of a Jharkhand consisting of the hilly, forested areas, inhabited mainly by tribal people of Bihar, inland Orissa, some districts of West Bengal and a large part of Madhya Pradesh, were also opposed to creation of a much smaller Jharkhand carved only out of Bihar. They are satisfied now with the creation of Jharkhand and Chhattisgarh, hoping that a larger Jharkhand could be formed later, if they keep up their demand.

Jharkhand is rich in mineral resources—coal, iron ore, bauxite, manganese, mica and others. Some of the minerals are exported but most of the production is used in two large integrated steel mills located at Jamshedpur and Bokaro. Two large mills processing bauxite to produce alumina and metallic aluminium and heavy machinery plant is located at Ranchi, which has been made the capital of the state. Plants for manufacturing cement and chemical fertilizers are located in other suitable locations. Furthermore, there are a number of thermal power generation plants based on coal, which supply electricity all over north India, from Kolkata to Delhi and a part of Haryana.

However, despite the riches of the state, the tribal people are very poor and suffer from near starvation, when the rice crop fails and food supplies from outside are delayed, due to poor communication. The small fields in which they grow rice and other food crops are washed away during the monsoon rains. The government of the new state, with assistance from the Central Government, has undertaken a programme of building good motorable roads, so that food, water and blankets can be rushed to these people when their fields and huts are washed away by the floods. Building materials and seed, chemical fertilizers and pesticides are rushed when the floods recede and they can replant their crops and rebuild their huts. The government has also initiated programmes of education of tribal youth—boys and girls, and extended health care to all. An increasing number of tribal young men are able to get jobs as skilled workers in the various factories located in the region and as white-collar workers in the government, which were held earlier by people from other regions.

The economic condition of the tribal people is improving because there is greater emphasis on eradicating poverty and illiteracy among them. The law and order situation will also be improved by controlling, with assistance provided by the Central Government, the activities of the gangs, which live on robbing the mining contractors and executives of various industrial units.

With improvement in the law and order situation, there would be greater incentive to locate various steel fabrication industries in the region. Production of rice and coarse grains can be greatly increased by a sustained programme of construction of check dams on a large number of small streams that flow through the region, to irrigate the fields. The check dams will also reduce soil erosion and flooding of the fields during the rainy season.

Chhattisgarh

Chhattisgarh was carved out of present Madhya Pradesh by including in the new state its southern most districts. Large parts of the region are forested; the tribals are even more backward than those in Jharkhand. Penetration of outsiders such as forest and mining contractors to exploit the region's natural resources and its poor, ignorant tribals will need to be greatly reduced. Furthermore, effective measures will need to be taken for reforestation because the forests have been greatly depleted on account of extensive deforestation during the last 50 years in order to supply timber for construction of houses and other buildings in north-western, western and central India.

The region has large areas of plains in which rice and coarse grains are the main crops. Yields of rice will need to be increased with use of dwarf high yielding varieties of rice, chemical fertilizers and pesticides (as needed) and by providing assured moisture by a large programme of construction of check dams on small streams. Its capital Raipur is located in one such valley.

A large hydro-electric power and irrigation supply dam is located in Andhra Pradesh just outside the region. The hydro-electric and mineral resources of the region need to be surveyed in greater detail than has been done so far, for the establishment of mineral processing industries and power plants in future.

It is of interest to note that in contrast to the misgivings that had been expressed before the creation of the new states, their creation has been remarkably smooth. Even while the problems of creation of an administrative infrastructure (buildings for the secretariat and staff quarters for the employees) are being tackled, stable governments have been formed in all three states.

Needs for Special Central Assistance

Uttaranchal will need special financial assistance for the first two decades. Such assistance will be needed to build a capital, perhaps at Dehradun, and for development of tourism and for alleviation of poverty. Thereafter, however, its revenues from tourism and development of power should finance its administrative infrastructure. Jharkhand too would need special central assistance for the next decade or so for building a state capital probably at Ranchi and a special police force in order to check activity of the gangs that have thrived on robbing the mining and forest contractors or managers of large industrial units. Special assistance will be needed also to impart technical education to tribal youths so that they can be employed in the numerous hills in the region. Assistance will be needed also under the poverty alleviation programmes and irrigation and soil conservation programmes to check ravages of floods during the monsoon. The Government of Bihar has also been demanding compensation for losing its mineral rich portion as a result of formation of new states.

Chhattisgarh will need special financial assistance for building the capital probably at Chhattisgarh. The detailed survey of its forest power and mineral resources would be carried out by the central agencies (Geological Survey, Forest Survey and others). Special assistance will need to be given under tribal welfare, education, health and poverty welfare programmes to raise the economic conditions of the tribal people and prepare the ground for an effective programme of extension education for the farmers, to teach them use of high productivity techniques. The extension officers could be deputed from various districts of coastal Andhra Pradesh or Tamil Nadu where such high productivity techniques are used.

Broadly, financial assistance will be needed to build the administrative infrastructure of building a state capital and creating internal security, taxation and development services. The Geological Survey, the Indian Forest Service and the Ministries of Industry, Power and Agriculture will have to conduct special surveys of the mineral, forest and irrigation and power resources of the three regions. Such assistance will be needed especially for Chhattisgarh; the agricultural, mineral, forest and power resources of the region have not been surveyed in detail. The State Ministry of Agriculture of these states may request for assistance for the above from the Central Government.

The Case for Small States

The idea of small states is not new. Sardar K.M. Panikar had suggested division of India into about 50 small states, each with a population of 10-20 million; the total population of India in 1951 was only 361 million compared to 1027 million in 2001. He had argued that the small states would be better administered and develop more rapidly because their governments, being closer to the people, would be more responsive to their needs and aspirations. The unity of India would be strengthened because small states with limited financial resources would be in no position to separate from the Union. His arguments were not accepted, however, by the other members of the Commission who opted for creation of linguistic states despite the large areas and populations of some of them.

Experience in Creation of Small States in case of Punjab and Haryana

It is necessary to caution that creation of smaller states could create problems, which could be solved only over a period of time with sagacity and a spirit of give and take by the governments of the smaller states. Consider Punjab and Haryana, which were created in 1966, by division of the post-independence East Punjab. There was much opposition to the division of East Punjab in the 1960s despite the strong demand of the people of Haryana for having a state of their own. However, in the nearly four decades after the division, both Punjab and Haryana have developed more rapidly than they would have done as part of a single state. The development of Punjab is based on its highly productive agriculture based on use of modern, high productivity techniques in most of its cropland area which is irrigated by canals, tube-wells or wells fitted with pumps operated by electricity or diesel oil. The principal crops are high yield dwarf varieties of wheat, rice and maize. It has hundreds of small, medium or large scale industrial units located in its cities—Ludhiana, Amritsar and Jalandhar—which provide employment to tens of thousands of workers. It is the state with the highest per capita income in India.

The agriculture of Haryana has also been transformed through adoption of modern, high productivity techniques on lands irrigated by canals or wells fitted with pumps operated by electricity or diesel oil. The area under irrigation increased greatly in Haryana after building of the Bhakra-Nangal dam on Satluj River in the late 1950s. There was large increase also in availability of electricity for agriculture and for industries in both Haryana and Punjab. Yields per hectare of the principal crops—wheat, medium staple cotton and oil seeds in Haryana are somewhat below those in Punjab.

Haryana, which had hardly any industries in the 1960s, has developed an industrial sector particularly in Gurgaon and Faridabad, the two cities located within 30 km. of Delhi. Gurgaon has in its environs, Maruti Udyog, which manufactures India's most popular car and a rapidly increasing number of medium and small-scale industrial units. The Government of Haryana has implemented for more than four decades, a highly remunerative programme of land development for residential, commercial and industrial uses and has also developed an information technology park, which has become a major centre of the information technology industry. A number of large commercial houses including foreign companies, have established their national or regional headquarters offices in the environs of Gurgaon in order to escape the high rents for office space and air and noise pollution of Connaught Place, the central business district of Delhi. Furthermore, much larger office space needed by these companies is available at much lower rents in Gurgaon than in New Delhi.

Faridabad, located about 30 km. south of New Delhi, is another residential-*cum*-industrial satellite city of Delhi. It has a number of factories, making refrigerators, air-conditioners and other appliances and one of the largest factories making tractors, which caters to the demands of farmers in Punjab, Haryana, western U.P. and Rajasthan. The highway linking it with New Delhi is completely lined with small or medium sized industrial units, workshops servicing motor vehicles, refrigerators and air-conditioners. It exhibits ribbon development at its productive best.

Despite rapid economic development in both states, the dispute between them relating to division of water for irrigation from Satluj and Beas rivers in Punjab and location of the capital of Haryana has not been finally settled so far, four decades after the creation of the two states. This has not caused any problems, however, since there is enough water in the two rivers to meet the needs of irrigation of croplands in both states as well as in north-western Rajasthan. The governments of both states have agreed to abide by *ad hoc* arrangements about decisions arrived at between them from time to time. Chandigarh was built in the 1950s as the capital of east Punjab. It serves now as the capital of both Punjab and Haryana states; building of the capital in any other city is just too expensive. The financial resources of the two governments are much better utilized in promoting agricultural and industrial development and providing education and effective healthcare to all their people.

The creation of Himachal Pradesh in 1958 has provided a strong incentive to economic development of the state. Production of food crops (rice, wheat and maize) has increased in its valleys and production of apples, potatoes and tomatoes in other areas has led to increase in remunerative work for small farmers and agricultural labourers. The export of fruit and vegetables to cities in the plains is facilitated by construction of motorable roads to cities. Producers' Cooperatives provide short and medium-term loans to plant the trees, to buy inputs such as chemical fertilizers or pesticides and provide living expenses of the growers until sale of their fruit and vegetables. Cold storages for storing the fruit and vegetables until they are ready for markets in the cities have been built by these cooperatives.

The hill stations—Simla, Kullu and Manali are visited by tens of thousands of tourists in the summer. As a result there is hardly any migration of young men to work as domestic servants as it was in the 1950s and the 1960s. Most of those who go to Delhi, Simla or other cities are educated and work either as white-collar workers or skilled workers such as drivers of motor vehicles. They are paid much more than domestic servants. The government of the state has undertaken an effective programme of rural electrification and extension of telephones to all large villages. As a result, the migrants can keep in touch with their parents or their families when they work in Delhi or Simla.

Need for Division of Uttar Pradesh and Bihar

Uttar Pradesh

After creation of Uttaranchal, the remaining state of U.P. is still too large to be administered from Lucknow. It should be divided into four small states or regional agro-climatic divisions: (i) western U.P. with its headquarters at Meerut; (ii) Central U.P. with its headquarters at Lucknow; (iii) Eastern U.P. with its headquarters at Allahabad; and (iv) Peninsular U.P. with its headquarters at Jhansi. Two of the cities, Lucknow and Allahabad, have already a large number of administrative buildings and large investment will not be needed for establishing capitals or regional headquarters in them. The headquarters of western U.P. should be located in Meerut. It is a large, industrial city and has in its cantonment a large number of buildings constructed by the Indian Army. Some of them could be temporarily requisitioned for the Capital Secretariat or regional structures pending construction of new buildings. The new building structures could be financed easily out of the revenues of the highly productive agriculture and numerous industrial units located in the region.

Much expenditure would not be needed in creating the administrative infrastructure in Jhansi also. Moreover, it could be recovered within one decade through better administration of this underdeveloped region which had been infested with dacoits until the 1970s. The ravines of the Chambal, which sheltered the dacoits, have been steadily reclaimed by construction of check dams on small streams and larger reservoirs to harness the flow of the rivers. The cultivated and irrigated area has increased steadily during the last four decades with consequent increase in agricultural output. Implementation of land reforms and increase in remunerative employment for rural people has put an end to the problem of dacoits more effectively than action by the police.

Bihar

After creation of Jharkhand, division of the remaining parts of Bihar into north and south Bihar should be considered carefully. The two regions would be better administered than at present. The immediate benefit would be in improvement in the law and order situation. The causes of the conflict, related principally to the conflict between the high caste land-owners, who have exploited their low caste tenants and agricultural workers for more than a century would not be eliminated through creation of new states or the regional structures. But it would be reduced in course of time. Patna which would be the capital of north Bihar, has already got the infrastructures of a state capital. Such infrastructures will need to be created at Gaya with financial assistance provided by the Central Government.

The cost of the infrastructure in Gaya will be more than repaid within two to three decades through development of the city for religious tourism. Tens of thousands of tourists from Buddhist countries of South East and East Asia, from Thailand to Japan, visit Gaya, the place of enlightenment of Lord Buddha, every year. His birth place located in Nepal across the border of north Bihar and several other cities in Bihar are associated with his life and work. The great Buddhist University of Nalanda is located near Gaya. The number of tourists and earnings from them would increase rapidly if there were adequate facilities for their reception and stay in Gaya, Nalanda and other places. Roads would need to be greatly improved just as railway and airline connections of Gaya with Kolkota and Varanasi, near which Lord Buddha preached his first sermon. While investment in improving the railway and airline connections will be made by the Government of India, hotels could be made by private entrepreneurs. Suitable hotels could be built to house tourists of different income groups. Rapid increase in the number of tourists will also strengthen India's economic relations with countries of southeast and East Asia. In spite of economic and social advantages in division of the two large states into six or more states, the political leadership is likely to oppose and delay such divisions. In case the division is not possible several administrative agro-climatic regional structures should be created in these states in order for administrative efficiency and balanced development.

Creation of New States and Stability

Respect for the human rights of the people is fundamental for widespread acceptance by the people of the rights of the government to rule over them. The Government must not only claim to be 'of the people' and 'by the people' but also for 'all the people'.

If there are sharp cleavages within a population its government must be seen to be responsive to and meeting the needs of all the people, irrespective of caste, creed and differences of economic/occupation or social status. The Governments of the new states, which were created on popular demand during the 1960s and 1970s appear to be meeting these criteria and are stable despite changes in leadership from time to time.

Punjab, Haryana and Himachal Pradesh in the North, Tamil Nadu, Karnataka, and Kerala and to a large degree Andhra Pradesh, Gujarat and Maharashtra in the West and West Bengal in the East have enjoyed a period of stability for 25 years. The West Bengal, however, had 15 years of turmoil from the mid-1960s to the 1980s. Madhya Pradesh and Rajasthan have enjoyed long periods of stability despite the poverty of the people because the Governments seem to be doing the best they can for promoting the welfare of the people despite the constraints of environment. The unstable governments are Assam, Uttar Pradesh, Bihar and Orissa.

The principal cause of instability in Bihar is the cleavage between the 'other backward castes' and the scheduled castes on the one hand and their high caste landlords on the other.

The cleavages in Uttar Pradesh, confined mainly to the central and eastern Uttar Pradesh, are both of economic status and religion. This largest Indian state has an area of stability, namely in the Western Part but the other regions are unstable. No government can stay in power for long unless these cleavages are resolved.

Orissa is unstable, despite the fact that a particular Chief Minister may have long tenure, because no government seems to be working for the people and people see no use in changing it, because the new government will also be unresponsive to their needs as the previous one.

The present BJP Government of the centre is stable despite its apparent changes in economic policies from time to time because the people see that it is following policies which have yielded rapid economic growth with increasing welfare for the majority of the people. Furthermore, the great majority of the people of the unstable states of the north see that BJP is doing all it can to broker a compromise between the clashing interests of the high and low castes and of Hindus and Moslems.

However, among the new states, Jharkhand and Chhattisgarh, there is likely to be a long period of instability because of cleavages of interest between the people of the plains who have access to well watered plains and others for whom there will be no such advantages but these will be resolved quickly because there are no sharp cleavages of ethnicity or economic interest among their people. Even in the states (which were created on linguistic basis) where there were sharp differences these were settled after a period of conflict.

Creation of Agro-Climatic Regional Structures in Big States

There is a strong case for division of very large and populous states of Uttar Pradesh, Bihar and Madhya Pradesh into smaller states. The process could be considered to have started with creation of the three new states. In U.P., Bihar, M.P. and other large states with populations above 40 million, division into smaller states may, however, be opposed by the political leadership and could create unnecessary difficult problem. If the local sentiment is against creation of small states in these areas there is need for creation of agro-climatic administrative regions.

With decision-making power with the officials of agro-climatic administrative regions, the needs and aspirations of the people would be better understood and local development programmes would be formulated with closer understanding of the development potential and limitations of the regions. The Panchayati Raj Institutions would also work more efficiently since most of the decisions about correcting deficiencies in implementation of rural development programmes could be taken at the regional level instead of being referred to distant state capitals.

The structures (a Council) should not be merely bureaucratic but should have popular representation on them. The senior-most Ministers of the State Governments hailing from the region should be the Chairman of the regional structure and the senior-most Commissioners as its Secretary. Members should include Ministers of the Central and State Government and Members of Parliament and the State Legislature from the region, all Commissioners and Collectors of districts and officers responsible for agricultural and industrial development and social welfare of the people, besides mayors of the municipal corporations of all metropolitan cities of the region. The council should take all decisions relating to agricultural and industrial development of the area and welfare of the people with concurrence of the governments of the states. The creation of these councils is most urgent in U.P. and Bihar which are very large and populous but large areas of which are underdeveloped. Its creation in Marathwada and

Vidarbha regions of Maharashtra will contribute to more rapid development of less developed areas of Maharashtra.

There is the experience of creation in the 1990s of the regional council for Gorkhaland containing Darjeeling and neighbouring districts of West Bengal in which the people of Nepalese or Indo-Nepalese stock form the majority of the population. They felt that they were poor and backward because they were being exploited by the plains people of the state. After the creation of the Council, all funds for agricultural development, education, healthcare and social welfare of the people are earmarked separately for them in the development plans of West Bengal. There is large migration of young men and women from the area, to work as guards, watchmen, etc. (men) and domestic servants (women) in cities in north India from Kolkata to Delhi. Others work in tea gardens; large numbers join the Indian army, usually after graduation from higher secondary schools. They continue a century old tradition of Gorkha regiments which were (and are) considered the most disciplined and valiant in the Indian army.

There is considerable information on agro-climatic regions in the reports of the Population Censuses of 1951 and 1961, the Planning Commission and the Ministry of Agriculture. The Ministry formulates and implements its programmes for increasing agricultural output and providing against security of crop failure with agro-climatic regions as the units. Furthermore, it regularly issues reports on the prospects of crop production in different agro-climatic regions.

Conclusion

This Chapter gives a historical perspective about formation of new states in the Indian Union during 1947-1970. The demand for creation of additional states since 1970 has been met by creation of three new states—Jharkhand, Uttaranchal and Chhattisgarh.

The author reviews the economic and administrative viability of the states created on linguistic basis all of which after an initial period of turmoil and instability have experienced stable governments and economic prosperity during the last 25 years or so. It is expected that the new three states will also lead to economic development in the area after a period of adjustment and support from the national government for creation of additional administrative structures. Investment by the Central Government and other stakeholders in setting up industries, expansion and improvement of roads and communication networks, development of irrigation and power generation plants and boost to tourist industry will all add up and lead to rapid economic development of the new states.

There is need for bifurcation of all the states with a population above 40 millions. Such need is paramount in case of U.P., Bihar, Assam and Orissa, which are economically backward and politically unstable because of their large size and caste and class conflicts. There is no strong demand for this division and it is likely to be opposed by the current political leadership. However, for economic progress and administrative stability it is important to decentralize decisionsmaking by creation of agro-climatic regional administrative structures. The chapter suggests creation of at least four such regional bodies in U.P. and two in Bihar until a consensus for bifurcation of the big states into smaller states is reached.

Table 5.1: Population of States 1991-2001

States	*1991*	*2001*
Andhra Pradesh	66,508	75,728
Arunachal Pradesh	865	1,091
Assam	22,414	26,638
Bihar	86,374	82,879
Delhi	9,421	13,783
Goa	1,170	1,344
Gujarat	41,310	50,597
Haryana	16,464	21,083
Himachal Pradesh	5,171	6,077
Jammu & Kashmir	7,719	10,070
Karnataka	44,977	52,734
Kerala	29,099	31,839
Madhya Pradesh	66,181	60,385
Maharashtra	78,937	96,752
Manipur	1,837	2,389
Meghalaya	1,775	2,306
Mizoram	690	891
Nagaland	1,210	1,989
Orissa	31,660	36,707
Punjab	20,282	24,289
Rajasthan	44,006	56,473
Sikkim	406	541
Tamil Nadu	55,859	62,111
Tripura	2,757	3,191
Uttar Pradesh	139,112	166,053
West Bengal	68,078	80,221
Union Territories:		
Andaman & Nicobar Islands	281	356
Chandigarh	642	901
Dadra & Nagar Haveli	138	220
Daman & Diu	102	158
Lakshadweep	52	61
Pondicherry	808	974
All-India	846,303	1,027,015

Source: Censuses of India 1991 : Paper No. 1, Provisional Population Totals.

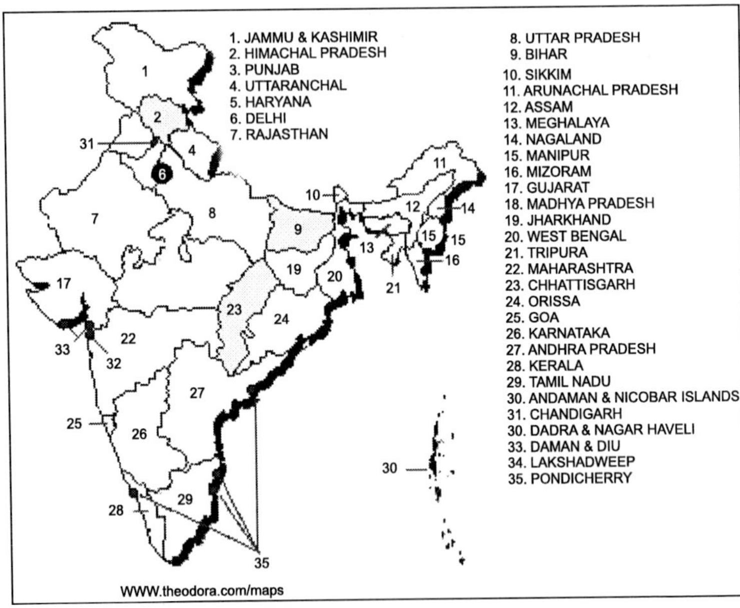

Map 5.1: Territories of Indian States as in 2000

6

Area Development: Planning at District and Block Levels*

Area development relates to development of areas demarcated with a particular objective in view. Areas of large resource development projects—irrigation, power, industrial, areas designated as backward, and units of local administration, district and blocks, are examples of such areas. Area development is a special case of regional development, in which the spatial units of development are defined not on physical or economic considerations, but with particular developmental objectives in view. Usually, such areas are smaller than geographic or economic regions. This chapter outlines, some concepts relating to area development and planning at the district and block levels.

Concepts

A basic concept in area development, as in all regional development, is that the plans for the area are conditioned by its physical conditions, natural resources and social and economic situation. These indicate the development potential, the needs and the problems of the area; the development plan must develop the potential, meet the needs and solve the problems. Accordingly, systematic assessment of resources, needs and problems is the first step in the planning process. The assessment is done by compilation and analysis of existing information, supplemented by fresh surveys, to the extent necessary. The needs are articulated most effectively by the representatives of the people—members of Panchayati Raj Institutions, municipalities and legislatures.

---

* Published in *Indian Journal of Public Administration*, New Delhi, Vol. IX, No. 2, pp. 174-193, April-June 1968.

Area Development and the National Plan

Area development is part of the national planning process. The plans for an area are conditioned by the general framework of the national plan, its policies and programmes, and its resource constraints. These prescribe the framework for "area planning", its overall goals as well as its limitations. The area plan is related also to the plans for larger spatial units of which the area forms part and of the smaller spatial units into which it is divided. The plan for a district has to be related on the one hand to the plans of the state and the regional division in which it is located, and on the other to plans of the block (and other smaller units) which are included within it. This linkage, upwards and downwards, is an essential part of planning for an area.

The development plans for districts and blocks, which came under the influence of an expanding metropolis or of large industrial or resource development projects, must reflect adequately the influence of these major developments. Providing in the local plans adequate complementary inputs, which would enable the local area to obtain full benefits from the resource development project or to withstand the disturbing influence of metropolitan development (unduly large areas in the peripheral regions of cities often get diverted to non-agricultural uses) is one method of reflecting this influence.

Two Approaches to Local Area Planning : "Area Development" and "Programmes"

Here it would be useful to distinguish between the "area development" approach and what may be called "programmes" approach to planning. The latter implies that certain development activities decided at the state or national level are carried out more or less uniformly throughout the area of the state or the country. The plan for a local area, built-up entirely through this approach is an aggregation of such activities—primary and secondary schools, health centres, roads, water supply schemes, etc. The two approaches—"area development" and "programmes"—are not contradictory or mutually exclusive; they are, to an extent, complementary. The "area development" plan has to be formulated within the framework of the objectives and priorities of the national plan, and will have a large component of the national or state programmes mentioned above. On the other hand, even when the "programmes" approach is followed, decision-making in relation to particular programmes in an area has to be related to its local conditions and needs. Thus, the number of primary schools to be opened in an area and the specific location of the schools can be decided only on consideration of local factors. The influence of local factors is much greater in planning of more advanced or specialized services and resource development activities. Elementary service facilities such as primary schools can be created more or less uniformly in all area; but the same cannot be done in case of advanced service facilities such as secondary school, college or polytechnics. Location of the latter has to be decided on careful consideration of various local factors, because faulty location decision will lead to inefficient service to the people and waste of resources. Resource development activities require even greater attention to local factors.

But the "area development" and the "programmes" approach are two different approaches to planning, and emphasis on one or the other leads often to different planning decisions. The "programmes" approach flows from constitution of departments at state or national level for particular development programmes—Education, Health and Agriculture. Exclusive reliance on it often results in inadequate consideration of local needs and problems, because of the inherent tendency of departments to decide the pattern of a programme at headquarters and to follow it in all areas. The result often is that attention is given to less necessary activities in preference to those needed more urgently in the local area; sometimes, unnecessary facilities are created. On the other hand, undue concern with area development would lead to inadequate attention being given to national (and state) objectives and priorities. One could generalize, perhaps, to say that the "programmes" approach is more suitable in planning of social services—especially elementary services such as primary schools, health centres and approach roads. These are needed everywhere and can be planned at the state (or even national) level on basis of criteria and patterns which can be defined with precision, e.g. one primary school for 100 boys of school going age; a metal road within one or two miles of every village. The "area development" approach on the other hand has distinct advantages in planning of resource development programmes. It is also frequently more suitable than the "programmes" approach in planning of more advanced services.

Area development includes both resource development and human development. Expansion of social services, building up the infrastructure of development and institutional reform are the principal instruments of the latter. The relative emphasis on resource development and human development activities in an area, at any point of time, is indicated by its stage of development—status of exploitation of resources and the potential for further development, status of development of social services, etc. However, it is well to point out that development of social services and the infrastructure is an essential prerequisite of resource development, and until these are developed sufficiently, the progress of resource development activities will also remain slow. Thus, a large programme of resource development—mining of coal and iron ore, setting up power stations, steel plants and other industries—appears to be the obvious priority in the resource rich area called the Coal Steel Belt of Eastern India. But the area is backward. It is hilly and forested, has poor communications and few towns and has a large proportion of tribal people. This backwardness of the area hampers resource development activities in various ways. Development of social services and the infrastructure—improvement of communications, opening of schools, hospitals, training centres for craftsmen, modernization of the towns will not only accelerate progress of resource development activities, but will also enable the local people to participate in these activities more actively and to benefit from them. They will be able to obtain employment in new industries and attain higher levels of income and consumption. Similarly, institutional reforms and changes in social attitudes, e.g., in the attitude relating to work, are prerequisites for development of certain areas. The backwardness of area like Eastern U.P. is attributed in part to the tradition of *Zamindari* and prevalence of growth-inhibitive attitudes (e.g., people of high castes should not touch the plough).

Integrated Development

Integration of different development activities undertaken within an area is a fundamental concept in area development. It has been accepted in case of rural development programmes for a long time and was reiterated and reinforced when a unified agency for rural development was created in the Community Development Organization. The structure of the C.D. Organization with a team of subject-matter specialists working under a Block Development Officer, emphasized coordination between developments in different fields—agriculture, animal husbandry, minor irrigation, soil conservation, cooperatives, social education, etc. Constitution of Block and District Development Committees and designating the Collector as the leader of the team of development officers further emphasized coordinated development and creation of Panchayati Raj Institutions has given it a statutory institutional framework.

A primary requisite in coordinated development is securing appropriate relationships in magnitude, space and time between different development activities. Thus the quantum of cooperative credit and supplies of chemical fertilizers, improved, seeds, etc., in a C.D. Block should be related closely to the agricultural extension efforts of the block staff. In other words, if use of chemical fertilizers is being advocated by the staff and is being encouraged by making available supplies on credit given through the cooperatives, it should be ensured that the supplies and credit match the demand created by the efforts of the extension staff. Acceptance of this basic principle underlies the practice of formulating family production plans in the Package Programme districts, and regulating supplies and credit in accordance with these plans.

A second aspect of integrated development concerns the relationship between major resource development projects and local development activities. This relationship may be explained by the examples of power generation and irrigation projects. The villages located near a power project can derive benefit from it only if a programme of rural electrification accompanies the project. Power taken to the villages will, in the present stage of our rural economy, be used for irrigation, cottage and small scale industries, etc., only if adequate loans are given to farmers, artisans or small industrialists for installation of electric motors and purchase of power driven machines. Therefore, in order to carry the benefits of the power project to the villages it is necessary to secure appropriate relationships between programmes of power generation, rural electrification and financial assistance. Similarly, the waters of an irrigation project can be effectively utilized by farmers only if suitable technical assistance is given to them for changing their cropping pattern, from dry crops to irrigated crops, and financial assistance is given for measures like levelling, reclamation and preparation of land. Such assistance should be adequate in magnitude and should be available at the appropriate time and place.

In cases where the interrelationship between the large projects and complementary local developments has been appreciated and the latter have been provided adequately, the result has been rapid resource development and appreciable rise in economic and social levels of the people, (e.g. the Bhakra Canal area of the Punjab). But where this relationship has not been appreciated, and complementary inputs have either not been provided or have been provided inadequately or late, the potential created by the resource development projects has been utilized very slowly or inadequately. This experience emphasizes the need for working out in detail the complementary inputs in case of each major project and ensuring that these are provided adequately, in time and at the right place. In case of irrigation and power projects, sufficient experience has been gained in recent years for working out *norms* of investment on the projects and complementary local development inputs. These norms should be worked out for a few selected projects and should be available for guidance for new projects.

The major industrial and other resource development projects have been called "nuclei of development" in the Third Five Year Plan (Planning Commission, 1961). This concept of the nucleus emphasizes the potential of these projects for attracting various developments to their areas, and initiating a process of area development. Appendix I lists the developmental inputs related to a major irrigation project and a steel plant. These have been divided into three major groups :

- associated,
- complementary, and
- derived.

The associated inputs are essential for the functioning of the project itself. The relation between them and the project is so direct and clear that they are generally provided as part of the project itself. But the complementary and the derived inputs, which are not so directly related, deserve more attention for area development, because it is the adequacy of these inputs and the speed with which they are created in the area that determines the pace of its development. The complementary inputs are necessary for realization of the development potential of the project. The derived inputs have a similar role, but they have been classified separately, because they "derive" from or follow the functioning of the project.

Primary Growth Factors

The major projects could also be called primary growth factors, i.e. primary development activities to which secondary and tertiary activities are attracted. The term could also be used for certain negative factors, presence of which retards development of an area. Prevalence of malaria, bad communications and low literacy are examples of negative growth factors. These too have to be regarded as "primary", because their removal needs first attention in any scheme of development of an area. The importance of removing them is often underestimated. Thus, demands for development of backward areas usually take the form of demands for locating large projects in them. It is not sufficiently appreciated that removal of the negative factors is equally important, though less spectacular. Indeed, as mentioned above, the progress of the large projects will themselves be seriously retarded, if the negative factors are not removed.

Regional Growth

Another useful concept in area development is that of "regional growth". The economies of any area—blocks, districts or larger units—will grow with economic growth in the country. In most cases, this growth will mean change from exclusive dependence on primary industries to diversification of the economy. But in this process, the need for investment will increase progressively. The concept of progressive acceleration of the development process, and of the need for progressively larger investments is well recognized in planning at the national and state levels. The progressive increase in outlays and development activities in successive Five Year Plans is the best evidence of this. But at the level of the small area—the block and the district—the notion that a period of intensive development can be followed by one of lower investment (and development activity), because the area reaches "self-sufficiency" and is less in need of outside investment, seems to recur in Indian planning. The incompatibility of this concept with the dynamics of development was demonstrated by experience of the first community projects and blocks[2] in which an expenditure of about Rs. 22 lakhs per block for three years (or four years if the subsequent extension of time is taken into account) was followed by a post-intensive phase expenditure of about Rs. 1 lakh per year. But the idea seems to persist, as is evident from reference to it in intensive development projects of various kinds (agriculture, small industries, integrated development of districts) which are proposed from time to time. The idea has a certain attraction perhaps—it can be used as an argument to initiate intensive development in a limited number of areas. But there is a danger in adhering to it, because in any project undertaken with this idea there is bound to be a slide-back in development and frustration among the people when the period of intensive development is followed by the normal (slack) period.

It is true that after a period of intensive development, the character of inputs needed in an area changes—from elementary services to more advanced services, from service activities to resource development activities, etc. It is true also that the people's capacity to pay for development activities increase and they are able to undertake themselves many activities, (e.g. drinking water wells) for which they would have required outside assistance earlier. But the savings in investment resulting from this change are more than compensated by the need for larger investments, e.g. in more advanced services, and resource development activities, with the result that the total quantum of investment needed in the area is much larger. The people may not need assistance for irrigation or drinking water wells; but they will want electric motors on wells and piped water supply schemes, which are far more expensive. Therefore, whenever any area is taken up for intensive development, it should be clearly recognized that it is being put on a road on which it will need progressively larger total investment as time passes.

Area Development at District and Block Levels

The need for drawing up plans with districts and other local areas as units has been appreciated from the beginning of planned development. The First Five Year Plan referred to district (and other) plans and the role of local institutions in the planning process. But a concerted effort to formulate plans at district and lower levels was made only at the time of formulation of the Second Five Year Plan. It was symbolized by the phrase "planning from below". As part of this effort, plans with districts and blocks as units were drawn up in a number of States. The Second Plan document defined the scope and content of the local plan (Appendix IIA) and the manner of its preparation in considerable detail. Districts and blocks have since been recognized as important planning units, formulation of plans for them has been recognized as an integral part of the national planning process and an important function of Panchayati Raj Institutions. Plans for districts and blocks were formulated as part of the Third Five Year Plan and similar work has been in progress in most States in connection with formulation of the Fourth Plan. It is of interest to note that the scope of the district plan as defined in the Planning Commission's Memorandum on the Fourth Plan is very similar to the definition contained in the Second Plan.

However, experience with drawing up district plans at the time of the Second Plan and in subsequent years highlights some of the difficulties and problems of such planning (and points to the needs for safeguards), which may be summarized below :

(i) The tendency towards formulation of plans without adequate regard for resources which can be expected to become available—the tendency of plans to become catalogues of local needs and aspirations. This tendency was responsible, in part, for some of the planning effort made at the time of preparation of the Second Plan not yielding the expected results. But as a result of the Second Plan experience, an approximate indication of resources is now given in advance by the State Governments to the local institutions and officers.

(ii) The tendency to emphasize immediate need fulfilment in preference to longer term resources development, to emphasize consumption-oriented activities in preference to production-oriented activities.

(iii) Emergence of competing claimants for social service facilities, works, etc., among which the planning agency must decide. Size-inflation of plans results often from the tendency to please as many rival claimants as possible.

(iv) The need for accurate and adequate factual data—the need for conducting surveys of resources of local, social and economic conditions and technical possibilities.

(v) The need for posting sufficient technical staffs, both for surveys and for plan formulation. The very real difficulty of providing such technical staff constitutes a major constraint in local planning.

Area Development and Programme Planning--Experience of Community Development Programme

The need for local planning has been realized from the beginning of the community development programme and the scope and content of local planning has also been defined fairly clearly. But, within the area of local planning, the present practice is that priorities for different programmes and schemes, and the pattern of each scheme—content, staff, finance, institutional arrangements, etc., are worked out in great detail at the State or even national levels and decision-making at local levels is concerned largely with selecting locations and beneficiaries. The Panchayati Raj Institutions, like their predecessor officials of the community development blocks or other development departments, often function primarily as allocating or distributing agencies, deciding where a primary school or a primary health centre should be located and who should get a *taccavi* loan, the number of schools and health centres to be opened in each block, the details of staff, equipment and buildings for these and the amount of *taccavi* loans to be sanctioned in a block, had been decided at the State level.

This practice of deciding patterns of development activity in detail at the State level and leaving the local institutions only the distributive functions has been the subject of considerable argument. Those opposed to the practice have argued that it does not allow plans to be formulated by local people in accordance with their needs and aspirations or the natural resources and development potential of their areas, with the result that less needed activities are often taken up in preference to those which are needed more and would have given better results—at times money is wasted on schemes which are not needed—and local people are not sufficiently enthusiastic about development programmes. This, they argue, results in development programmes not having the desired effect in terms of participation of people, and retarded economic development of the area. The protagonists of the practice have defended it on grounds of administrative efficiency, securing minimum level of development in all areas and ensuring that National and State priorities are reflected in local plans. Allocation of funds between different heads of development and on individual schemes within each development head is regarded as the chief instrument of securing development according to priorities. Working out detailed patterns of each scheme is considered essential for administrative efficiency and avoidance of waste because it is argued that effective supervision and assessment of performance would be impossible in the absence of these.

It is also pointed out by many that so long as funds for development activities are provided by the State (or Central) Governments and the staff of Panchayati Raj Institutions form part of State cadres, the tendency towards detailed planning of programme at State (and even Central) level will continue. They go on to argue that the Panchayati Raj Institutions can have an effective role in planning for their areas only if they have their own staff and raise their own resources. The argument has some force. There is no doubt that when funds are given by the State Government there is a tendency for it to indicate not merely the schemes on which these may be spent out also in considerable detail the manner in which the schemes may be executed. On the side of Panchayati Raj Institutions also, there is a tendency to regard the schemes as those of the State Government, and to execute them according to the instructions of the latter. The immediate history of Panchayati Raj Institutions—their having been constituted in succession to the C.D. blocks and having inherited the programmes and funds of the blocks and other development departments—strengthens these tendencies. But financing by State Governments and technical staff forming part of State cadres is likely to be continued and the exercise of initiative in local planning by Panchayati Raj Institutions has to be achieved within this situation. The alternative of Panchayati Raj Institutions having their own staff and raising their own resources will, in the present stage of rural development and growth of these institutions, only result in greatly restricting their role in development besides reducing staff efficiency. It will reduce these institutions to the position of former district boards.

The tendency towards planning of programmes at State or Central level has been encouraged by the fact that in much of the rural development activity (of the last thirteen years 1950-1963), the object has been to provide elementary services and facilities—primary schools, primary health centres, drinking water wells and approach roads, co-operative credit societies, a basic agency for agricultural extension—which lends itself very well to planning through "programmes". The second reason for adopting the "programme" approach was that until local consciousness of development needs grew, it was necessary to provide certain leadership from above, and to take up basic activities which were clearly the most urgent needs of most areas.

This approach did create imbalances and difficulties in the community development programme. But since many of these were felt by the State Governments themselves, there was a tendency to resolve them through appropriate action between the State Governments and the Central Ministry of Community Development. Thus, when it was found by some State Governments that many of the activities included in the first community projects were not suitable for their areas, the Central Ministry allowed the States very considerable freedom in deciding the content of the programme within each major field of development activity. But the process was not carried lower, to district or block levels to any appreciable extent, and once the pattern of activity in any field had been decided at the State level, it was applied without major modification to all blocks of the State.

The Need for Shift in Emphasis

As a result mainly of the development that has taken place (during the last 13 years), the situation is changing. Firstly, as the need for elementary facilities has been met, emphasis is shifting to providing more advanced facilities. Planning of these requires much greater attention to local conditions, and it is not possible to apply a uniform pattern to all blocks. Thus, it is not advisable to decide that each block shall have so many secondary schools, marketing societies or centres for training of craftsmen. Block A may need more secondary schools and marketing societies than Block B because it contains a number of small towns in which secondary schools are desired by the people and which serve as *mandi* centres for the villages in their vicinity. Block B on the other hand may be more suitable for location of a training centre for craftsmen or a polytechnic because a large factory located within it could provide employment to the trainees. The need for attention to local factors is even greater in case of resource development activities. Even a comparatively simple activity, e.g. a processing factory (cotton gin or sugar mill) has to be planned primarily on consideration of specific local factors such as availability of raw materials, nearness to market, and advantage of transport. Thirdly, experience with development activities during the last 13 years has created among the local people much greater awareness of the need for development and of the specific development activities needed in their areas. They are more anxious to participate in the planning process and are more vocal in expression of their needs and aspirations. Finally, the "programme pattern" approach cannot provide adequately for inter-sectoral relations or for special planning needs of metropolitan, river valley project or industrial regions. The number of such projects and the areas coming under their influence is growing with economic growth in the country with the result that the need for area development is being felt in an increasing number of districts and blocks.

District as the Primary Unit of Local Planning

The emphasis on resource development activities and provision of more advanced services along with the other factors mentioned above makes the district a more important unit of planning than the community development block. Let us take the examples of education and co-operation again. The community development block was quite a suitable unit for planning a network of primary schools, because the object was to provide every village, (or in case of very small villages or hamlets, a group of two or more neighbouring units) with a primary school. But it is not an equally suitable unit for planning location of middle schools and may have positive disadvantages when adopted as the unit for planning of secondary schools. Similarly, while location of credit co-operatives could be planned with the block as the unit, location of marketing and processing societies has to be planned with a larger area as the unit, because of the need for attention to specific location factors mentioned above.

The need for making the district the major unit of local planning is also felt for other reasons. Effective local planning will require a considerable measure of decentralization of decision-making from the State level to local levels. Such decentralization is more feasible at the district level than at the level of the block. There are several reasons for this. First, the district has the full complement of District Level Officers who can provide the specialist assistance needed for drawing up local plans and making fruitful modifications in schemes drawn up at the State level. On the non-official side, the Zila Parishad has the top-level leadership of the district. Second, for reasons of administrative feasibility, especially maintaining effective communication between the State and local levels, the district is more suitable than the block as a unit of local planning. The State Development Departments or the State Governments find it more feasible to deal with a limited number of Zila Parishads and District Level Officers than with a large number of *Panchayat Samitis* and extension officers. Third, since intra-district variations (in physical or socio-economic conditions are generally not very large, the need for making further modifications in programmes to suit the requirements of particular blocks is comparatively small, after the pattern has been decided at the district level.

Here it is necessary to draw a clear distinction between the units of planning and the unit of implementation of programmes. The fact that the district is accepted as the unit of planning of a particular programme does not mean that it should necessarily be the unit for its implementation also. In some cases, the combination will be useful; but over a large field of development activity covered by the district plan, execution could just as well be done through the *Panchayat Samitis*. The district is a more suitable unit than the block for planning the content of a minor irrigation programme, i.e. deciding the emphasis that minor irrigation should receive in the total agricultural production effort in the district, and the specific schemes which should be taken up, but implementation of a large part of the programme is best done by the *Panchayat Samitis*. The decision regarding the unit of planning and the unit of implementation should be taken separately for each development programme keeping in view its nature, the technical staff and other resources required for it, and the structure of Panchayati Raj Institutions in the State.

Appropriate Interaction between Towns and Villages

Let us consider an average district. Its headquarters is located in a medium-sized town which performs various services for all or most of the villages and small towns located within it. Frequently, the town is also the major commercial centre of the district. The sub-division headquarters towns, important *mandi* towns, and other medium-sized towns have similar roles for parts of the district. Within each block, the block headquarters town has a similar role in relation to villages of the block area. In addition, there are in most blocks one or more small towns (or large villages) which perform similar functions for groups of 25-30 villages.

One effect of the developments of the last 13 years has been that the interaction between these towns and the villages served by them has increased, and the towns have a much more important role in the economy and social life of the villages. The village people come to the towns more frequently and obtain many more of their requirements from them than they did in the past. The very activities of *Panchayat Samitis*—distribution of *taccavi* loans, distribution of permits for supply of chemical fertilizers, cement or corrugated iron sheets, deciding appeals from decisions of *Panchayats*, and various elections have added to the frequency of the town visits. Many village leaders and affluent cultivators visit such towns almost daily. Most of the towns have expanded considerably in recent years, on account of growth of commerce, resulting from larger agricultural production and higher incomes in the surrounding villages, and of their service functions. This expansion will continue as the role of the towns as service centres for the surrounding villages becomes more important, because as agriculture gets modernized and rural electrification and rural industrialization make progress, these towns will have an increasingly important role as centres for distribution of new materials and of servicing and repair of power driven implements and machines. This, for the simple reason that facilities for distribution of new materials and repairs and servicing of machines cannot be created at more than a few central places.

Yet, very little attention has been given so far to examining the inter-relationship between these towns and their surrounding villages and ensuring that development of the two is complementary and mutually beneficial. Indeed there are many instances of defective planning resulting from a failure to appreciate this relationship. The location of facilities like primary health centres and secondary schools has generally been decided on considerations like availability of local contribution, with the result that in many cases the facilities are located not in the place which is the natural centre of the area to be served by it, but in the place which came forward to pay the required contribution. In many blocks, the block headquarters town itself is not well located for serving the needs of the block area.

The first community projects did contain the nucleus of the idea of securing appropriate interaction between towns and villages. The programme of these projects included development of *mandi* centres, improvement of communications between them and the villages and using the centres for providing an increasing range of services and dissemination of new ideas to the villages. But the idea was gradually dropped, because other problems were considered more urgent. Moreover, the C.D. and N.E.S. Blocks which followed the first community projects had such small budgets that these more intensive development activities could not be accommodated within them. However, the time has now come when this relationship should be given adequate attention. The place of the district and block headquarters towns and of the smaller centres within each block, in the development of their service areas should be clearly recognized, and location of various service facilities should be so decided as to enable these centres to perform their service role efficiently. Further, the municipalities of the small towns and Panchayati Raj Institutions should be brought into relations of mutual interaction.

The latter can be done only at the district level : the block is too small a unit for this purpose. The recent recommendation of the Sadiq Ali Report for providing for association of municipalities with the Zilla Parishad in Rajasthan is evidence of recognition of this need. This association will become especially important when integrated area development is accepted as the object of local planning and development of both towns and villages is viewed as part of it.

A Case of Local Planning : The Wardha Plan

The Plan was drawn up jointly by the Gokhale Institute, Poona, the Regional Planning Institute, Wardha and the staff of Wardha Zilla Parishad. It illustrates some of the principles mentioned below :

It is a district plan. The district was selected as the unit of planning for two reasons. First, the district institution, the Zilla Parishad is the most important Panchayati Raj Institution in Maharashtra. Second, the district is considered a more appropriate unit than the block for drawing up a plan of this kind. Plans for blocks and smaller areas fit into the framework of the district plan.

An indication of resources likely to become available for execution of the plan was given by the State Government at the outset.

The plan is based on analysis of existing data, which were supplemented by surveys of socio-economic conditions and technical surveys for location of minor irrigation works, etc.

The plan has been formulated by technical officers of the district and the special staff loaned by the institutes. The technical nature of the planning task has been fully realized in its formulation.

The plan has been formulated with the coordinated efforts of the State Government, the Panchayati Raj Institutions and the specialized institutes.

The plan puts primary emphasis on resource development. Development of certain services (transport, welfare of backward classes etc.) has been emphasized on account of special circumstances of the district.

The plan stresses intersectoral relationships, though these have not been systematically worked out. Further, it recognizes that if a large industrial or other resource development project comes to be located in the district, a major readjustment will be necessary in the plan.

The plan includes a section on rural-urban relationships and development of towns as service centres. Significantly, the centres selected are *mandi* centres and not block headquarters, thus emphasizing the economic rather than the administrative aspects of the relationships.

Efforts similar to the Wardha Plan can be made only in a few selected districts, where special arrangements can be made for institutional assistance. But these plans have considerable methodological value. They bring out the basic principles and the techniques of local area planning; the nature of work involved in it, and the place of local area plans in the National Plan. Appreciation of these will lead to more systematic and fruitful planning efforts in other areas.

Appendix 1

Major Projects and Related Inputs

A. A Major Irrigation Project

(1) *Associated Inputs*

- (i) Transport (road, rail) facilities for movement of equipment, supplies and personnel needed for the project, communication facilities.
- (ii) Housing, water supply, social services (education of children, medical care) facilities for the project staff; creation of a township, if necessary.
- (iii) Soil conservation measures in the catchments area.

(2) *Complementary Inputs*

- (i) Land development and agricultural improvement : reclamation, clearance and levelling of land which is to receive irrigation; reorganization of agriculture, especially switching over from dry to irrigated farming; adoption of improved agricultural practices, e.g. use of improved seed, chemical fertilizers etc.; supplementary minor irrigation—digging of wells, installation of lift irrigation devices etc.; drainage and other steps to prevent water logging in the irrigated area.
- (ii) Improvement of transport and marketing facilities.

Measures of category (i) require creation of services of technical assistance, supplies, etc., and also provisions for loans to cultivators for enabling them to take up land development or agricultural improvement measures.

(3) *Derived Inputs*

As the above measures take effect and agricultural production increase, the area will need agricultural processing industries, agro-industries (e.g. manufacture of improved agricultural implements) and consumer goods industries. These may be called derived inputs, which derive from or follow the earlier developments.

B. Steel Plant

(1) Associated Inputs

Facilities for mining of coal, iron-ore, limestone and construction materials.

Transport, rail and road, for carrying raw materials and intermediate and finished products.

Generation of power.

Supply of water to the plant and to the township.

Urban development—construction of township to house industrial workers and those working in trades and services; organization of various essential services in the township.

(2) Complementary Inputs

Rehabilitation of persons dispossessed of their lands.

Orderly absorption of immigrants and taking steps for ensuring smooth relations between them and the original residents of the area.

Training of craftsmen and other personnel for the plant.

Social education among tribal people, with a view to ensure that they can derive adequate benefits from new economic opportunities within their area.

Reorganization of local agriculture to meet the consumption needs of the larger population, especially for high value perishable products such as milk, vegetables, fruit, meat and poultry products.

(3) Derived Inputs

Industries, which depend upon raw materials supplied by the steel plant or on use of other facilities like power and transport created for it.

Heavy engineering industries, e.g. machine building, manufacture of transport equipment, fabrication of structures, etc.

Heavy chemical industries, e.g. manufacture of chemical fertilizers.

Manufacture of other construction materials.

Light engineering, light chemicals and various consumer goods industries attracted by the raw materials and other facilities available in the area.

Appendix II

Scope and Content of the District Plan as defined in the Second and the Fourth Five Year Plans

Second Five Year Plan

"20. It was recognized that both at the district and at the State level three kinds of programmes sponsored on behalf of public authorities would be included in the plan, namely :

(a) Programmes initiated at the level in question, e.g. taluka, district and State,
(b) Programmes initiated at lower levels and integrated with those in (a), and
(c) Programmes initiated at levels above and integrated with (a), for instance, schemes sponsored by the Central Government but executed through States or schemes sponsored by the State Government and implemented through machinery available in the district.

23. The main constituents of district plan are :

- The community development and national extension programme,
- Social welfare extension projects,
- Agricultural production programme and allied activities in the field of rural development such as animal husbandry, soil conservation, etc.,
- Development of cooperatives,
- Village panchayats,
- Village and small industries,
- Schemes for utilizing effectively resources developed through State projects for irrigation, electricity, communications, industrial development and expansion of training facilities,
- Housing and urban development,
- The programme of small savings,
- Aiding construction projects through labour cooperatives and *shramdan*,
- Programmes for the welfare of backward classes,

- Programmes in rural and urban areas relating to social services, especially expansion of education at primary and secondary levels, health units, health education, sanitation, malaria control, family planning, etc.,
- Utilizing and assisting voluntary organizations engaged in constructive social work,
- Land reform,
- Prohibition work, and
- Dissemination of information about programmes of national, state, regional and local development."

Source: Planning Commission: Second Five Year Plan, 1956, pp. 156-158.

B. Fourth Five Year Plan

"A district development plan should comprehend various activities envisaged in the State Five Year Plan for execution at the district level without respect to the nature of the sponsoring authority or the location of the budget provisions. Some activities undertaken in a district are provided for in the plans of the *Zilla Parishad* and the *Panchayat Samitis*, others in the plans of Departments at the State level. These latter, fall technically outside the field of Panchayati Raj Institutions. The following are the principal sectors in which the local initiative and participation have to be carried as far as possible and can be developed around programmes embodied in the Five Year Plan :

- Agriculture (in its wider sense including animal husbandry, dairying, fisheries, poultry, horticulture, forestry, minor irrigation, etc.),
- Cooperatives,
- Village and small industries in processing industries,
- Elementary and social education,
- Rural water supply and sanitation,
- Rural health and medical services and family planning,
- District and rural roads, including village approach roads (excluding National and State Highways),
- Work programmes for the fuller utilization of rural manpower,
- Development of focal points of growth like market centres, service centres, etc.,
- Social welfare, including welfare of weaker sections, and
- Voluntary organizations."

Source: Planning Commission, Fourth Five Year Plan, 1964, pp. 80-81.

NOTES

1. The typical situation in meetings of the *Panchayat Samitis* is somewhat as follows : The B.D.O. or another Extension Officer reads out a circular from the State Government which informs all *Panchayat Samitis* in the State that a particular scheme is to be implemented and gives the financial pattern and other details of the scheme. The meeting thereupon proceeds to decide which particular villages, persons or groups should benefit from the scheme. There is seldom any attempt to see whether the scheme is not suitable for the area of the *Panchayat Samiti*, whether another scheme would be more suitable or even to attempt to modify the pattern of the scheme in any way. Nor would such attempts be very feasible under the present procedures of sanction and implementation of development programmes.
2. Reference here is to the investment under the budget of the C.D. Block and to the concept which inspired the phasing of this budgetary pattern. It should be made clear, however, that the total quantum of investment and tempo of development activity (including both programmes included within the Community Development budget and others forming part of the development plans of the State) has been accelerated in nearly every area because of general acceleration of development activity under the Five Year Plans.

REFERENCES

Government of India :

- Memorandum on the Fourth Plan, *Planning Commission, New Delhi - 1964.*
- Third Five Year Plan, *Planning Commission -1961.*

Government of Rajasthan: Report of the Study Team in Panchayati Raj, Jaipur 1964

Wardha District Plan Frame (Unpublished).

7

The Functions and Duties of the Collector—The Collector as a Leader*

The institution of the Collector evolved in the hey-day of general administration in the nineteenth century. It was found extremely useful by a colonial power which was governing a predominantly agricultural and rural country, in which it was not interested in forcing the pace of change. The Collector's primary responsibilities were collection of revenues, maintenance of law and order and general administration. But he was the representative of the government in the district, and besides his specific duties, was expected to oversee progress of various other activities of the Government. His role has been summed up admirably by O'Malley :

> "The District Officer was the pivot of the administration combining revenue, magisterial and general administrative duties... He also did much that is now done by local bodies in connection with maintenance of roads, the promotion of education, medical relief and measures of public health... The arrangement by which local executive authority is concentrated in one man has worked well... It is his power to give orders that make the District Officer what he is for it is his function not to do everything himself but to direct and control the work of his staff and to coordinate the different departments of the local administration."
>
> (O'Malley, 1930)

In the years after Independence, the institution has had to adapt to very different conditions and to meet new challenges. The Collectors now work within the framework of a Parliamentary Democracy. Primary

---

* Published in *Indian Journal of Public Administration*, Vol.XI, No. 3, pp. 603-614.

emphasis in administration is on development and the most important movement in the country is social and economic change, directed by Government. Democratic institutions—Panchayati Raj Institutions, co-operatives and others—have been established for local government and development activities. The scope and range of activities undertaken by Government has increased so much and each activity is becoming so specialized that it is becoming difficult for any single officer to keep in touch with all activities in a district, much less comprehend their details or give sensible directions in respect of them. These institutional changes and development activities are essential steps in the transformation of the Indian society, especially Indian rural society, from a static, tradition-oriented, status-dominated, predominantly affluent, modern agro-industrial society. This transformation is the central goal of Indian planning.

In this radically changed situation, the institution of the Collector has been found useful enough to be given new role and responsibilities. This paper describes the new role of the Collector in the field of development. His other roles are undoubtedly important : preservation of law and order for instance is the first requisite of orderly functioning of any civilized community. But development has been selected for detailed analysis here because the new role of the Collector as leader is best seen in this field.

The Collector as District Development Officer

The Collector in his capacity as revenue officer and general administrative officer always had a good deal to do with whatever "development" activity was carried out in the district. Works like repair and construction of small irrigation sources were undertaken by the Revenue Department. In times of famine or scarcity, various relief works including construction and repair of roads, wells and tanks, were undertaken by the Collector. He was also associated with local government institutions—the district boards and the municipalities. He was expected to supervise the work of the District Officers of education, health and other welfare departments. During the inter-War years, as agriculture, co-operation, and other rural development activities began to receive greater attention, he was expected to look after them also. It is this association of the Collector with development activities which accounts for an officer like F. L. Bryane, in Punjab, throwing himself whole-heartedly into rural development work and initiating one of the notable experiments in community development in the country.

But the relation of the Collector with development activities has been greatly strengthened with the inception of the Community Development programme. He has been made the leader of the team of District Level Officers of the departments concerned with the programme—agriculture, animal husbandry, cooperation, minor irrigation, *Panchayats*, small scale and cottage industries, education, health, social welfare, communications and others. Some departments like *Panchayats* may be under his direct control, but for most his role is that of a cocoordinator and guide. The District Level Officers work under their departmental superiors; the Collector gives general guidance, oversees progress and ensures that obstacles and difficulties in implementation of their programmes are removed. In most States, the Collector has been designated as District Development Officer. Since the establishment of Panchayati Raj Institutions, he is expected to serve also as the link between the District Level Officers and the institutions, and the latter and the State Government. These roles may have been given to the Collector partly, because of his traditional links with development activities, and the traditional prestige and status of his post : these things are considered in giving new role to officials. But the step reflects also the judgment that the Collector is best qualified to fulfil them. In the following paragraphs we shall examine the content of these roles, and some requisites of their successful fulfilment.

Coordination of Development Programmes

The Collector has been made leader of the district development team, because of the need for coordination of different development activities at the level of the district and the Community Development Block. The need for coordination of rural development programmes was emphasized by the Grow-More-Food Enquiry Committee which recommended the constitution of a Community Development and National Extension Service for the country.

> "The lesson to be derived from the working of the GMF programmes thus confirms the experience of State and private agencies engaged in village development. It is that all aspects of rural life are interrelated and that no lasting results can be achieved if individual aspects of it are dealt with in isolation.... For many years there have been fairly well organized development departments in the larger States for agriculture, animal husbandry, cooperation etc. These however work independently of one another, following their own

programmes and without a sense of common objectives.... What we have said point inevitably to the need of an organization for intensive rural work which would reach every farmer and assist in the coordinated development of rural life as a whole."

(Government of India, 1950)

The administrative structure of the Community Development Block with a Block Development Officer leading a team of specialist officers and Village Level Workers having responsibility for rendering a variety of services to the rural people was based on the concept of closely co-ordinated development. At the district level, coordination was sought to be achieved by setting up a District Development Committee which had on it all officers concerned with Community Development and related programmes. The Collector was made the Chairman of the Committee. In most States, he was given an assistant called District Planning Officer, or Deputy District Development Officer, who maintained closer touch with the Community Development programme.

The arrangements for coordination of development activities at block and district levels have been strengthened further with the setting up of Panchayati Raj Institutions. The functions of the block level institution, the *Panchayat Samiti*, are broadly similar to those of the C.D. Block organization. But the district level institution, the *Zilla Parishad*, has in some States such as Maharashtra and Gujarat, operational responsibility also for a number of other activities—public works, secondary education, advanced medical care—which were formerly the responsibility of State Departments. In these States, the *Zilla Parishad* and the *Panchayat Samiti* together are responsible for execution of almost all development activities; only major irrigation, power, industrial or other large projects are outside their scope.

The trend towards coordination is being strengthened further with the growing emphasis on drawing up district plans. These plans have been drawn up from the time of the Second Five Year Plan, but they are being given much greater importance now. The district plan covers a much wider field than that represented by the Community Development programmes : it includes all development activities undertaken by the State. Its formulation involves evolving the strategy of development for the district—on the basis of local resources, needs and aspirations, but within the framework of National and State priorities. It involves further, providing appropriate interrelationships between different sectors of development, between major projects and local development activities, and between rural and urban development. (see *Indian Journal of Public Administration*, April-June 1965 and Chapter 8). As the process of formulation of the district plan becomes established, the district will become an important planning unit in addition to the State and Nation.

This movement towards coordination in planning and development at the district level reflects recognition of the fact that there are such large differences in physical, economic and social conditions within the area of each State that decentralization of decision-making below the State level is essential. The district, a unit with a population of one to two million (the population of most districts is within this range) is considered suitable for this purpose because it is small enough for local problems and conditions to be kept constantly in view and yet large enough for building an adequate planning and development organization. Moreover, as most States have a limited number of districts, adequate contact can be maintained between the State and the district level. The very considerations, which led to adoption of the district as the primary unit of administration in the last century, have now led to its selection as the primary unit of local planning and development.

Collector and Panchayati Raj Institutions

The functions of coordination mentioned above have to be exercised by the Collector and the *Zilla Parishad;* the precise apportionment of functions between the two varies in different States depending upon the character of the *Zilla Parishad*. In most States where the *Zilla Parishad* is essentially a non-executive institution, the Collector's role is rather more important. He coordinates the work of the District Level Officers and acts as a link between them and the Panchayati Raj Institutions, especially the *Panchayat Samitis*, which have responsibility for execution of the development programmes at the block level. He must ensure that the *Panchayat Samitis* get the requisite guidance from the District Level Officers, and that the activities of the Extension Officers attached to them are effectively supervised. At the same time he must see that the District Level Officers are given adequate facilities by the *Panchayat Samitis* for supervision of work of their staff and that their advice is followed by the *Samitis*. The *Zilla Parishad* in these States has a limited role in execution of programme; it keeps itself informed about progress and gives general directions from time to time. The district level officers, led by the Collector, assist in this task. But the *Zilla Parishad* has a more important role in planning—the district plan is approved by it. The plan is prepared under the direction of the Collector and he can make an important contribution to it advising on priorities, targets, inter-sectoral balances, etc.

The Collector is also an important link between the Panchayati Raj Institutions and the State Government. He has to bring to the notice of the Government the needs and aspirations of the people, as articulated by the members of the institutions. He must attempt to ensure that these needs and aspirations are given due attention by various departments of the State Government and are reflected in the State. At the same time, he has to see that the priorities and targets laid down by the State Government are adhered to by the institutions and the latter play their full role in obtaining people's participation in development activities. In this process, the Collector has to do much explaining to the State Government and to the Panchayati Raj Institutions. He has often to play the same role between the District Level Officers of other development departments and their heads. This may sound surprising; but is very often the case. The State Level Officers do not often appreciate sufficiently the difficulties of their local officers—in not giving adequate emphasis to particular activities or asking for greater attention (higher priority, larger funds) for other activities. The local officers have particular difficulty in convincing their superiors, when they have low status. But their point of view is likely to be appreciated better when it is reinforced by the views of the Collector who has higher status, has an overall view of the needs of the district, and knows the views of the popular representatives.

In States like Gujarat and Maharashtra where the *Zilla Parishad* is an executive institution and the district level officers are attached to it, the Collector's role as a co-coordinator is a limited one, because most of his functions *vis-à-vis* the district level officers and the *Panchayat Samitis* are performed by the Secretary of the *Zilla Parishad*. The district plan is also prepared by the *Zilla Parishad*. But his role as a link between the local institutions, especially the *Zilla Parishad*, and the State Government is even more important in these States. The responsibility of communicating to the *Zilla Parishad* the views of the State Government and *vice versa* rests primarily on him, because he is the principal representative of the State Government in the district. And, this function has to be exercised by him for practically the entire development programme in the district, because of the wider scope of activities of the *Zilla Parishad*.

The system of Panchayati Raj Institutions provides for direct communication between the local institutions and the State Government. Besides, various individuals—the M.L.As, influential members of the institutions and other local leaders, act as communicators between them, because the State Government must depend upon him for authoritative appreciation of the local situation and must convey its decisions and wishes through him. The importance of effective communication between the State Government and local institutions can hardly be over-emphasized: it is the medium through which national objectives, policies and priorities on the one hand and local aspirations and felt needs on the other are brought together in the planning process and local participation in planning and execution of development programmes is secured. Its importance will increase progressively as local leaders have better understanding of their problems and needs and display greater initiative in mobilizing local resources for implementation of programmes. Taylor and others consider inadequate communication between State and local levels as the major weakness of rural development programmes in India, and have made a powerful plea for strengthening it (Taylor, 1965). There need hardly be any doubt that in the process of strengthening of communications, the Collectors' role as a link between the State and local levels will become more important.

Educator and Guide of Panchayati Raj Institutions

In relation to the Panchayati Raj Institutions, the Collector has another and even more important role—that of an educator and guide. The importance of this role is better appreciated when one keeps in view the role of these institutions in the process of social change in rural India. The institutions have development as their primary responsibility, of course. But they are also training grounds for democratic action. They are throwing up a new leadership which is different in many respects from the older leadership in rural India. It is different to an extent in its social and economic make-up; it is different even more in its aspirations and objectives. The new leaders, and through them the village people, are learning the ways of group politics for control of institutions, the methods of getting things done to benefit particular areas, groups or individuals, and the techniques of focusing attention of higher authorities on their difficulties and problems. There are in many of these institutions, conflicts between groups and individuals, subordination of larger interests of the community to narrow group, caste or even personal interests, complaints, charges and counter-charges. Social scientists are concerned about the influence of caste in these institutions. The working of the institutions and their impact on rural economic development and social change are being studied in a number of places. The Indian Institute of Public Administration is one of these. But the point to emphasize is that the institutions, such as they are, are training grounds in democratic action through which the rural people are learning to make the change from traditional attitudes, socio-economic relations and methods of functioning, to new attitudes and practices based on the concepts of social and political equality and economic progress. In this situation, district and block level officers have an important role to play as educators, moderators and guides of the popular leaders. They must acquaint the latter with Government rules and procedures and the details of various programmes and schemes. They must assist them in obtaining the benefits of particular schemes for their village or group. But, at times they have to advise them to modify, scale down or even give up some aspirations. In doing the latter the Collector's role is particularly important. He may have to explain to an aggrieved leader, that a particular officer, when he does not agree to his demand, is not being obstructive; but is only following Government rules or is doing what he sees as the best way of execution of the programme of his department. He may have to go further and tell a powerful local leader or dominant group in an institution that a particular course of action, while technically correct and permissible under the rules, would not be in the best interest of the community. Often when the decision lies with him, he may have to say "no".

This role cannot but cause difficulties, occasional unpleasantness and misunderstanding. All of us, who have been Collectors in recent years, know of occasions when our actions or motives have been misunderstood. But this is a role which has to be played in the interest of healthy growth of democratic institutions—of ensuring that the community accepts democratic processes, and sees them as being in the best interest of all, instead of being sub-servient to narrow group interests. The Collector has to play this role more than any other officer precisely because he is the leader of the district level officers. One can even say that large numbers of people in the district expect him to play this role. He is considered to be an expert in law and procedure, and his advice is expected to be impartial and in the best interests of the community.

So far we have mentioned only the negative aspect of this role. But there is also a positive aspect. The Collector has many opportunities of giving advice to popular leaders, which will be useful to them in getting things done for their area or group. With his knowledge of State policies and his contacts at the State level, he can help them to take advantage of particular schemes at the appropriate time; he can ask the officers concerned to draw up schemes in a form in which they will be readily accepted. Inadequate knowledge of programmes or failure to present local aspirations in the form of properly worked out schemes often results in popular leaders not succeeding in obtaining the benefits which they want and could get. The Collector's advice and assistance can be invaluable to them.

Some Requisites of Success

The role of the Collector in relation to planning and developments is not easy and, as explained above, playing it holds many possibilities of being misunderstood or disappointed. We shall conclude by referring to some requisites of successful accomplishment of the role. The first and perhaps the most important requisite are adequate recognition among all concerned—the National and State Governments, the local people and their leaders—of the new role and emergence of a new image of the Collector. The old image of the Collector as the ruler of the district no longer prevails; but a new image based on a realistic appreciation of his new role has yet to emerge. Once this new image emerges, various policy and administrative decisions will be taken which will help him in playing the role successfully. The most important of these decisions would relate to selection of persons for the post, their posting and transfer, incentives and methods of work. Selection of suitable persons is of crucial importance because the most important requisites of success in the new role of the Collector are personal qualities like knowledge, understanding and integrity. A Collector can play his leadership role in planning and development and fulfil his function of an educator and guide of popular leaders only if he knows the district and its people well. His knowledge must not be based merely on perusal of reports and papers or be acquired by a quick, jeep-eye view. It must be detailed, intimate, personal knowledge, based on extensive touring, meeting people, and participation with them in various activities. Such knowledge can only be acquired over a period of time, and we would agree with the view that no Collector begins to know his district unless he has been in it for about six months. We would go further and say that a Collector begins to make his most useful contribution in planning and development, after he has been in a district for about a year. The Collector should, therefore, be allowed to remain in a district for a sufficient length of time. The old three-years rule may not be practicable now-a-days; but the practice, all too common, of making frequent transfers of Collectors must be ended.

The Collector should have at his disposal up-to-date and detailed data about the district. In the British days, when primary emphasis was on maintenance of law and order and political stability, the Collector had at his disposal an efficient system of political intelligence. Today, when the emphasis has shifted to development he must be assisted by an efficient system of economic and social intelligence. There has undoubtedly been some improvement in recent years in the methods of data collection at the district level, and the statistical agencies have been strengthened to some extent. But there are still critical deficiencies, the most important being in the agency which works under the Collector himself—*the land records agency*. This agency is still using methods which are antiquated and extremely inefficient. It is unbelievable but true, that in this age of electronic computers the entire work relating to preparation of land records and collection of agricultural statistics in an average district is done by hand and all the calculations are done mentally by the *patwaris* and the *qanungos*. Typewriters and calculating machines are conspicuous by their absence from land records offices. These offices leave one with the impression that they have not seen any change in the last 100 years or more. If the land records system is to play its due role in programmes of economic development and social change—its role in evaluation of our efforts to increase agricultural productions and in implementation of programmes of land reforms is self-evident—it needs to be modernized quickly. Again, lack of appreciation of the need for up-to-date economic and social intelligence is evident from the fact that the results of most of the economic or statistical inquiries conducted in the districts are either not available to the Collectors or become available to them only after long periods. In some cases, the Collectors are not even aware of the existence of the enquiries. Lack of interest among the Collectors themselves is partly responsible for this failure; but here is an area in which immediate change is needed.

Understanding must be mentioned separately from knowledge because it requires, besides knowledge, a certain maturity. The Collector's role in relation to other development officers and popular leaders is very often that of a guide and an adviser. He can be effective only if he is accepted by them in this role. And acceptance requires among other things maturity in the person posted as Collector. Judged purely from this standpoint, the old practice of posting as a Collector, an officer who had been in the service for 8 to 10 years was better than the present practice of posting very young officers.

Integrity, not merely financial but also intellectual and moral is an important requisite. Such integrity is essential for success in any administrative job; it becomes more important in a job like that of the Collector in which contact with people, groups and situations is face to face, and the effects of decisions taken (or avoided) are immediately visible. A man is tested in such a job in a way that is scarcely possible in a secretariat.

Ensuring that officers with the requisite knowledge, understanding and integrity are available for the Collector's posts, requires a number of decisions by the State Governments. Collectors will have to be selected for their personal qualities and the notion that anybody can be Collector, will have to be given up. Selection may have to be confined to officers of a minimum seniority. In the more important districts, such as those with large cities in them, very senior officers may have to be posted as Collectors. The incentives of pay, recognition, etc., will have to be suitably adjusted to make the posts attractive enough for senior officers.

It will also be necessary for the State Governments to give the Collectors the support they need for efficient and effective discharge of their duties. Heads of technical departments must recognize the value of the Collector's advice and give adequate consideration to it, even when it goes counter to their policies or requires modification of their programmes. The Collector must be supported by the State Government when he takes a decision which proves to be locally unpopular. He can do this best only when he is sure of such support. This is a difficult area of action in a young democracy, but it is an area in which healthy conventions have to be established, if the system of political leadership and permanent non-political services is to yield the best results in the districts.

Finally, it is necessary to re-evaluate the importance of the post of the Collector in the Indian Administrative Service and the institution of the Collector evolved in the colonial period. At that time the Collector was the key post in the Indian Civil Service. But in the post-Independence years, other administrative and policy-making tasks have been assuming greater importance. Service officers along with others, have found challenging and rewarding jobs in these. Such opportunities will grow in future and with them the character of the Indian Administrative Service will change. The majority of the members of the IAS are perhaps already doing jobs of economics or social policy-making or of management of various state enterprises, and the proportion in such jobs will increase in future. The question of the relative importance of the post of Collector must, therefore, be asked from time to time and must be answered without sentiment or nostalgia. In answering it, it would be useful to remember that by the latter part of the British period, in the 1920s and the 1930s, the Collector's post was not considered as important as it had been considered earlier. The best men in the Indian Civil Service moved to policy-making jobs in the Secretariats, or to other, more glamorous posts, after a period of stay in the districts. Those who stayed in the districts too long, as Collectors or Commissioners, were considered less than the best. Woodruff calls them "clod-hopping Collector" (Woodruff, 1954). One should not, therefore, be carried away by sentiment. But at the same time one must give adequate recognition to the role of the Collector in planning and development and the growth of local democratic institutions. Rural economic growth and social transformation are most important aspects of national planning—their importance is underlined by the way in which insufficient increase in agriculture output has held back the growth of the rest of the economy in recent years. The Collector occupies a pivotal position of leadership in the field and his performance, especially thc quality of leadership that he provides, has a vital bearing on the speed and efficiency of execution of development programmes and growth of healthy democratic practices. The vital need for speed and efficiency in execution of programmes is recognized at policy-making levels, where the relationship between the programmes (such as those of agricultural improvement) and economic growth is clearly recognized. What is not recognized adequately is the enormous managerial task involved in securing these and the qualities of leadership that it requires. It is not sufficiently recognized also, that until democratic action itself becomes a powerful impetus for securing speed and efficiency—through popular leaders recognizing the importance of the programmes and putting their support behind them—much of the impetus has to be provided by officials in leadership positions, among whom the Collector is the first in the district. Similarly, the guidance provided by the Collector in the initial stages of development of new democratic institutions can influence very materially their growth and their acceptance by the community. Civil servants in developing societies, which are making the change from the traditional to the modern, and from the static to dynamic and growth-oriented, have the unique privilege of acting as catalytic agents of change. And among the men in this position in rural India, the Collector is the foremost.

Annexure I

Collector as a Leader: Some Personal Notes from Stay in Sawai Madhopur

Establishment of Parliamentary Democracy and advent of community development and other rural development programmes had meant a major addition to the Collector's traditional functions of maintenance of law and order, collection of land revenue and intervention in all emergencies. Establishment of Panchayati Raj Institutions had also added to his work because he had to organize and supervise elections to these bodies, as also oversees their functioning. In addition, he had to enquire into complaints about working of the institutions or their office-bearers, particularly chairmen and members of *Panchayat Samitis* and recommend appropriate actions by the State Government, if necessary.

Few of my colleagues were as lucky as I was in Sawai Madhopur to have some spare time at their disposal which Kamla (my wife) and I used for our village studies. Collectors in charge of districts which contained one or more cities or in which there were rival political parties had their hands full with maintenance of law and order, handling strikes and agitations and overseeing working of the municipalities and Panchayati Raj Institutions.

Political Interference and Corruption

I was fortunate in having to experience hardly any interference in my work by Ministers, senior officials of the State Government and Legislators or other political leaders of the district. One reason for it was that no local politician had enough influence in Jaipur to persuade a Minister or senior official to intercede with me in his behalf. The general level of political interference was also lower than what is stated to be now. Interference was confined to a limited number of cases; most political leaders and officials understood and respected the fact that rules and procedures had to be observed and could not be changed to further personal or group interests. Moreover, the tradition established in well-administered state like Jaipur to allow officials to carry out their duties without interference, still had considerable influence. Finally, the Congress Party had a comfortable majority in the State Legislature and the government headed by Shri Sukhadia was quite stable. He had been the architect of the stability and enjoyed a position of pre-eminence within the Congress Party and the

Cabinet. There were dissidents and rival aspirants for his office, of course. But they were not numerous or strong enough to pose a challenge to him.

My good relations with the Chief Minister and the Chief Secretary could also have had something to do with the low level of political interference with my work. They had both known me as a successful Director of the PEO before joining the IAS.

Monetary corruption by both officials and politicians was also much less in both its incidence and the amounts of money involved, than what it is alleged to be now. Petty corruption by clerks, *patwaris*, *tehsildars* and SDOs of the revenue department and similar (low or intermediate) level officials of other departments was widespread. In departments like Public Works, corruption was reported to extend to the top levels of the Superintending Engineer and the Chief Engineer. Many officers of the Rajasthan Administrative Service (RAS) and promoted from it to the IAS were also not above obtaining unauthorized personal benefits or making money. But there was hardly any instance of a direct recruit to the IAS or to one of the central services being corrupt.

Corruption by political leaders was also much less. There was a stigma against it, although the people had begun to realize that monetary corruption was an inescapable part of an administrative system presided over by elected representatives, because there was both need and opportunity for it. They realized that Ministers, MLAs and MPs had to recoup their expenses on elections and of looking after the large number of their constituents who visited them to seek their intervention with the administration for various purposes—from approval of loans and grants for themselves, or for community works such as construction of roads and upgrading of schools, redress personnel or community grievances.

Establishment of Panchayati Raj Institutions had contributed to spread of corruption to the *Zilla Parishads* and *Panchayat Samitis*. I have mentioned earlier *Panchayat Samiti* in Sawai Madhopur, in which a rich grain merchant had paid substantial sums to all voting members of the *samiti* to vote for him. He could afford the expenditure and election to the office of the *Pradhan* was only a matter of prestige for him. But most other *Pradhans* were not rich and had to use the powers and privileges of their office to recoup their election expenses. Their conduct would, of course, breed the usual crop of complaints, against them by their political rivals, particularly the defeated candidates, with the officers. A large number of the complaints against *Pradhans* or other members of the *Panchayat Samiti* or *Sarpanchas* (chairmen) of the village *Panchayat*, that I had to consider in Pali contained allegations of corruption against them.

Conflicts in the Panchayati Raj Institutions—Development takes the Back-seat

The transfer of responsibility for implementation of the community development and some other rural development programmes from officials to the *Panchayat Samitis* gave a setback to the programmes. The morale of the officials placed under the control of the *Samitis*, suffered a significant decline. The BDOs for instance, felt that their status had been reduced because instead of working directly under the State Government they had now to work under the *Pradhans* of *Panchayat Samitis*. Most of them felt that it was more important for them to win the favour of the *Pradhans* (chairmen) or other influential members of the *Samitis* than to achieve higher targets of performance in various development activities. These feelings were shared by the VLWs (Village Level Workers) and the other staff of the *Samitis*. Public participation in community works also fell because the people saw that the greatly reduced loans and grants for the works by the State Government were being given primarily to villages of the *Pradhans* and other influential members of the *Samitis* or of the MLAs and MPs. Most of the *Panchayat Samitis* confined themselves to distributing the grants and loans from the State Government; few made any efforts to levy taxes (for fear of becoming unpopular) or tapping other sources of revenue.

Most important, the *Panchayat Samitis* became arenas for personal, factional and caste conflicts. The majority of the *Pradhans* and the *Sarpanch* members of the *Samitis* were farmers or traders, belonging mainly to the high castes and the dominant cultivating castes. The disadvantaged sections of the rural community—small and marginal farmers and the landless labourers—felt that they could expect little attention to their welfare from the *Panchayat Samitis*. People of the Scheduled Castes and the Scheduled Tribes saw also that the funds provided by the State Government for their exclusive benefit were being allocated mainly to villages of the Scheduled Caste and Scheduled Tribe members of the *Samitis* who maintained good personal relations with the *Pradhans* and the influential *Sarpanchas*.

The conflicts in *Panchayati Raj* institutions were not too numerous or too serious in Sawai Madhopur district. But they were very numerous in Pali and a significant proportion of them were so serious as to bring the working of the *Panchayat Samitis* or the *Panchayats* concerned to a standstill.

I had always been an enthusiastic supporter of active participation of the people in planning and implementation of rural development programmes. It was my strong conviction that the programmes should not be prepared and implemented indefinitely by the officials, and that the rural people should be closely associated with them at every stage. Without such association, 'public participation' in the programmes had no meaning. Furthermore, I felt that without public participation the programmes could not be implemented successfully or their benefits would remain limited. In particular, the basic service facilities established under them would continue to function below capacity and the community works constructed at such great cost to the government and the people would deteriorate for lack of adequate attention to their maintenance and repair.

But I was depressed by these developments because I had seen the enthusiasm and the high hopes that had been raised among the rural people and among the officials about the potential of the community development and other rural development programmes for improving the economic and social conditions of the villagers in its early years. The programmes had initiated a movement for rural development, through their agricultural extension activities and provision to the rural people of basic services particularly primary or secondary schools, primary health care facilities, approach roads and drinking water wells. The village people had responded by large contributions of labour, materials and cash towards construction of the community works which were most needed by them.

But I had reservations about the structure, organization, functions and powers of the PRIs and particularly about statewide coverage by them within a few years of initiation of the community development programme. I felt strongly that expansion of the PRIs and transfer of responsibility for rural development programmes to them should have been slower and spread over an extended period. This would have allowed sufficient time for evaluation of experience of working of the *samitis*, and for making the changes needed for removing the deficiencies. But with simultaneous state-wide coverage that had been affected, the deficiencies would persist and maintenance and repairs of the community works by the official agencies or by the people would suffer.

I had seen too many instances of the latter during my tours while working for the Programme Evaluation Organization. Finally, I felt that the economic development and social welfare components of the community development and other rural development programmes, entrusted to the PRIs would receive a serious setback. Since the *Panchayat Samitis* were essentially political institutions, they would be concerned more with political than with developmental matters and that in the institutions which were ridden by individual, factional or caste conflicts, implementation of development programmes would come to a standstill. I was dismayed to see these fears being realized so soon after establishment of the PRIs.

Starting with Rajasthan in October 1959, most of the State Governments established these institutions in the early 1960s. But after seeing their unsatisfactory working, the governments of most of the states abolished them in the early 1970s. They have been revived in the 1990s, and with the enactment of an Amendment to the Constitution, establishment of these institutions has been made a statutory obligation of the State Governments. The institutions have been established in all the states but it will be several years before they fulfil the role envisaged for them.

Another widespread practice was giving feasts in which all men of their caste and their friends and relatives from neighbouring villages were fed soon after death of an elderly person. It was common for a relatively well to do Meena cultivator to feed a few hundred men after the death of his father or respected uncle. Since the expenses of such large feasts meant that the host would be indebted for life, the government of Rajasthan had banned them. But no collector or officer of the police dared to enforce the ban. The officers in my office and leaders in one of the villages that I visited were fond of telling the story of a young police officer who was murdered along with his small party of policemen while trying to enforce the ban in a village in the extreme northern part of the district. The *Gujars* (herdsman) of the village had made arrangements for giving a feast in which about 10,000 men of their caste, resident in the village and neighbouring villages would be fed after the death of a much respected elderly leader of the caste. The leaders of the village had informed the Collector and the Superintendent of Police about the feast and also warned them that they or their subordinates should not interfere with it. This young officer chose to ignore the warning. As soon as he went to the village, the organizers of the feast asked him to go back. But ignoring the advice, when he tried to arrest the leaders, he, all the policemen accompanying him were shot dead.

This true story brought home to me the wisdom of the British policy of minimum interference with the social customs of the Indians, after their bitter experience of the consequences of ignoring this principle in the first war of independence (which they called the Sepoy Mutiny) of 1857.

REFERENCES

Government of India 'Ministry of Food & Agriculture' India : Report of the *Grow-More-Food Enquiry Committee*,, 1952, pp. 50 and 53.

Nath, V. : "*Area Development, Planning at District and Block Levels*", Indian Journal of Public Administration : April-June, 1965.

O' Malley L.S.S.O'.: *The Indian Civil Service* : 1601-1930, London, 1963, pp. 68-70.

Taylor, Carl C., Douglas Ensminger, Helen Johnson and Jean Joyce, *India's Roots of Democracy*, Calcutta, Oxford University Press, 1965, Chapter 22.

Woodruff, Philip, *The Men Who Ruled India*, Vol. II, The Guardians, London, 1954.

8

District Administration in Rajasthan in the 1960s : Reminiscences of a Former Collector*

Introduction

Although written mainly for personal use, these reminiscences of my two years tenure as Collector of two districts, Sawai Madhopur and Pali, describe and comment on the major social, economic and institutional reforms, the development programmes and the social and economic changes, that the rural areas of Rajasthan districts witnessed during the 1950s and the early 1960s. They contain observations also on the administration during the period, in which under the outstanding leadership provided by the Prime Minister, Pandit Nehru at the Centre and the Chief Minister, Shri Sukhadia in the State, there was political and economic stability and it was possible to undertake far reaching institutional and administrative reforms including abolition of the feudal tenure system of *Jagirdari* and conferment of permanent and heritable rights in land of the cultivators and establishment of a planning process aimed at achieving rapid rural development and social change. The administration experienced a progressive increase in its role of initiating and leading the process, without suffering serious conflict or cleavages. At the same time, its efficiency and effectiveness increased steadily.

There was much scope for conflict within the administration because it was led and dominated by officers of the former princely states for the great majority of whom implementing programmes of economic development and social change was a new and daunting experience. Furthermore, all officers, old and young, had to maintain good working

---

* Published in *Prashansika : A Journal of Administrative Processes*. Vol. XXVIII, Number 2, June-July 2001, Rajasthan State Institute of Public Administration, Jaipur.

and personal relations with elected representatives of the people and to meet their demands, as far as possible within the laws of the state and administrative rules and procedures. They had to understand and appreciate the fact that the elected representatives might make demands on them under pressure from the people, who had elected them and on whose continued support they depended in order to remain in office, and that the representatives would often ask the officers to bend the rules in order to meet the demands. These had to be refused politely without offending the representatives.

The Chapter describes experience of the author in district Sawai Madhopur, since 20 months of his two years of district experience were spent in it. Description of his two months stay in Pali has been omitted because it would have meant merely an Appendix to the main paper. (The description is in first person),

Sawai Madhopur

My wife and I recall our stay in Sawai Madhopur with fondness mixed with nostalgia. I had requested the Chief Secretary, Mr. B.S. Mehta, for being posted in a district in preference to being posted in the Secretariat in Jaipur. This was a somewhat unusual request : most IAS officers preferred then (and perhaps do now) to be posted in the Secretariat. But I wanted a district posting for reasons explained below and I have never regretted the choice. My wife and I learnt more about rural life and rural development in Rajasthan (and to an extent also in India) through my district postings, than we would have ever done otherwise.

I had joined the IAS in 1958 after spending eight years on the staff of the Planning Commission; five of which had been with the Programme Evaluation Organization (PEO) of the Commission. The PEO had been established to evaluate the effects of the community development and other rural development programmes of the government on the life of rural people. It carried out its duties through :

(a) Concurrent, independent evaluation of working of the programmes by its own almost 25 Project Evaluation Officers posted in community projects and blocks located in different states and regions of the country, and
(b) Surveys and studies designed to measure the social and economic effects of the programmes on rural people.

After completing my 9-months training for the IAS in Shimla and Jodhpur, I had spent a year (1959-60) as Vice-Principal and Director of Research of the newly established Central Institute of Community Development, Mussooree, U.P.[1]

After all these years of study and research on rural development programmes, I was keen to acquire first hand knowledge of their working in the field, and felt that it would be obtained best through a district posting. The then Rajasthan Government was keen on the Collectors giving first priority in the duties to direction and overall supervision of community development and other rural development programmes in their districts. The government considered the Collector's duties as a District Development Officer to be the most important. It had implemented the community development programme with great enthusiasm and success, and had been the first government in the country to establish in October 1959, the 3-tier structure of Panchayati Raj Institutions consisting of village level *panchayats*, block level *panchayat samitis* and district level *Zilla Parishads*, which had been recommended by the Balwant Rai Mehta Team.[2]

The District

Sawai Madhopur is a medium-sized district which had an area of about 5,000 sq.km. and a population of 875,000 in 1991. It is situated south-east of Jaipur and Tonk district in eastern Rajasthan and borders Madhya Pradesh to its east. It had formed part of the former Jaipur state and had the reputation of being a peaceful, almost somnolent district where "nothing much ever happened". There was no city in the district. Sawai Madhopur itself and the sub-divisional headquarter town of Gangapur were small towns with populations of around 20,000 in 1961.

Sawai Madhopur's only claim to distinction within Rajasthan was that a large cement factory was located near its suburb Maantown in which the offices of the Collector and other officers were located and its railway station was the meeting point of the broad gauge Delhi-Bombay railway line of the western railway and its metre gauge branch line to Jaipur, located about 130 km. away. The factory has now been closed for more than a decade. Sawai Madhopur and its sub-division town of Gangapur are connected by a metalled road and also served by the broad gauge railway.

Sawai Madhopur town and Maantown are located at the southern end of the district. River Banas, located about 20 km. north of Maantown has to be crossed for going both to Jaipur and to Gangapur town. The crossing was not a problem during the dry months of January to June when water level in the river was low and it could be crossed by jeep. But during July to December, the water level was too high for the crossing. During these months the bridge on the river at Tonk, about 60 km. west of Sawai Madhopur had to be used for going to Jaipur. Gangapur could be reached during these months only by the Delhi-Mumbai line of the western railway.

Almost two-third of the district is a plain from which small hillocks, each topped by a fortress emerge as islands out of a sea. Each fortress was the residence of a former Jagirdar with the principal village of his jagir spread around the base of the hillock. The eastern third of the district is hilly and has extensive thorn forests in which there is much wildlife. The historic Ranthambhore fort is located about 15 km. from both Maantown and Sawai Madhopur. The Ranthambhore Wild Life Sanctuary and Tiger Reserve are located in the forest surrounding the fort.

Sawai Madhopur is not a dry district. Average annual rainfall of 62 cm. is adequate and reliable enough for growing the kharif (monsoon) crops of sorghum, millets, groundnuts and cotton without irrigation. The rabi (post-monsoon) crops of wheat, mustard, barley and gram can also be produced without irrigation because the heavy black soil retains moisture. They do best however under irrigation. Wells, powered by diesel operated pumps and tanks are the principal sources of irrigation. Less than 10 per cent of the cropped area of the district was irrigated in 1961; the proportion had increased to 60 per cent in Sawai Madhopur tehsil by 2001 because of widespread use of diesel operated pumps on the wells. The increase in yield per hectare of dwarf high yielding variety of wheat and mustard, the principal cash crops justified the high expense on diesel oil for operating the pumps.

The irrigated fields in which vegetables and fruits are grown, are heavily manured, intensively cultivated and are also surrounded by two to three feet high mud walls for protection against dry summer winds, soil erosion and damage by animals. In case of tanks, both the areas below them and those in their beds, which become dry during the dry season, are cultivated.

In 1961, however the district was twice its present size. It had an area of 10,000 sq. km. and a population of just over 1 million. Karauli and Hindon, sub-divisions of the district were constituted into a separate district during the 1980s. It is much more compact now than it was in 1961. It would take me six hours by train to reach Hindon and a similar time to reach Karauli. It would take up to seven hours to reach the tehsil headquarters town Dausa, located about hundred miles north of Sawai Madhopur. Dausa was closer to Jaipur than to Sawai Madhopur.

It was convenient to tour the district by road during January to June when the Banas River would be crossed by jeep. In the rainy season, the roads were so bad that one tehsil headquarters of Sawai Madhopur sub-division and most of those of the other sub-divisions were almost unapproachable.

I visited Dausa only twice during my entire stay in Sawai Madhopur, once at the time of Panchayat elections of January 1961 and again on general election of 1962. The first visit was to get a feel of the district and see the arrangements for the election. The second was to reassure myself that the arrangements for the general election had been made strictly in accordance with the instructions issued by the Chief Electoral Officer. I was somewhat surprised to find that in contrast to the other tehsils, where most of the farmers were Meenas, in Dausa there were Gujjars and Jats. They could become violent if any officer tried to interfere with the decisions of their caste Panchayats. I was lucky that both elections went off peacefully and there was no untoward incident anywhere. My successor was not so lucky, however, there was some violence in Dausa, and he was blamed for not being able to prevent it and was transferred soon after the election. Such transfers, rare in those days in Rajasthan, are perhaps more frequent now.

The People

More than 90 per cent of the population was rural in 1961. The proportion had been reduced to 83 per cent in 1991. For most of it, agriculture was the principal or secondary means of livelihood. The principal castes were (and are) the Meenas, the Malis, the Jats and the Gujjars among the cultivators, and the Jatavas (Chamaars) among the Scheduled Castes. Sawai Madhopur is often called a Meena district because the Meenas constitute the majority of the cultivators in it. They and the Jats are classic, dry land farmers. The Malis, originally vegetable growers, specialize in intensive cultivation of irrigated lands in which they produce wheat, mustard, sugarcane, vegetables and fruits (guava, papaya and banana). The Gujjars are also dry land farmers. But their inclination is towards pastoral pursuits; they depend mainly on sale of milk and meat of cattle or sheep and goats that they graze in the forests.

The Jatavas, called Chamaars earlier, are petty cultivators-*cum*-agricultural or non-agricultural labourers. Large numbers of them used to migrate until the mid-1950s to forests of Madhya Pradesh during the dry season to make wood charcoal there. But the migration had stopped by the end of the 1950s. Most of the rural Jatavas had become cultivators-*cum*-labourers. They had been allotted small plots of land for cultivation which had become available after abolition of *Jagirdari*. They supplemented their income from cultivation with working as agricultural labourers or as workers on construction works located at short distances (up to 20 km.) of their villages. They had stopped their traditional practices of lifting dead cattle, flaying their hides and eating their meat, in a bid to raise their ritual and social status. Large numbers among them had become vegetarians. The Jatavas of the hamlet that I had selected for my study were cultivators-*cum*-labourers. But most of those whom my wife studied, worked as unskilled workers for contractors because their village was located close to the factory, or in the factory itself.

Employees in the factory had much higher incomes than the others, and this was reflected in their more diversified and urbanised consumption. Consumption of milk, vegetables, fruit, meat, sugar, tea and oil was much higher among them than among other villagers. One reason for this was that they bought most of their food whereas the farmers produced most of it themselves. The educated sons of factory workers wore western style clothes (bush shirts and trousers) outside their homes and had become quite assertive of their rights and privileges, such as award by the Government of Rajasthan of scholarships for attending schools and colleges, reservations of jobs in government service, and of seats in the State Legislature and the Parliament for them. Some of them had become clerks and school teachers and many more were aspiring to get such white collar jobs.

The Meenas, who were classified as a Scheduled Tribe, were also entitled to these privileges. But they rarely mentioned them in our discussions with them because the privileges meant little to them. They were much more interested in the opportunities for employment on various construction works, located within cycling distance of their villages, which had opened up since the mid-fifties. In the Meena village, located closest (4 km.) to Sawai Madhopur railway station, which we had selected for study, one or more young men from every household worked on public works, which included periodic repair of the road connecting the village with the railway station and keeping the railway station and the double line track of the Delhi-Mumbai railway line and the metre gauge railway line to Jaipur. Wages from labour on these works provided a useful supplement to their meagre income from agriculture.

The Period—Institutional and Socio-Economic Reforms, Development Programmes and Social Changes

The two years 1960-62 of our stay in the districts came towards the end of the Nehru era. During the 1950s the country had enjoyed political stability, after the trauma of the partition of former British India into India and Pakistan in 1947. Political integration of the country was achieved between 1946 and 1948 through accession of almost 600 former princely states to the Indian Union. Organization of cadres of all-India, central and state services during 1948-49 provided the administrative infrastructure for orderly government and social and economic progress.

The decade of the 1950s was also a period of major institutional, political and social reforms and steady economic growth. The Constitution of India which provided for Parliamentary Democracy and separation of the legislative, executive and judicial wings of government was adopted in January 1950. It was followed by establishment in March 1952 of an elected, bicameral Parliament at the Centre and Legislative Assemblies in all the states. The peaceful orderly and efficient conduct of election in 1952 as well as the two that followed it in 1957 and 1962 had demonstrated to the world, India's capacity to conduct this major operation in the democratic process peacefully and efficiently despite the handicaps of extreme poverty and low literacy of its predominantly rural electorate.

Among the social and economic reforms, abolition of *Zamindari* and *Jagirdari*[3] was perhaps the most important. Others related to statutory abolition of untouchability, and special measures for uplift of the Scheduled Castes, the Scheduled Tribes and other backward classes. Rapid economic development and social change were perceived to be the most important national goals, to be achieved through national development planning. Two Five Year Plans had been implemented during the 1950s and the Third Plan (1961-66) had been launched in April 1961.

Rajasthan was among the states, most affected by the political changes and social and economic reforms. It had been formed in 1948-49 by integration of about 20 former princely states and the British administered district of Ajmer. This was followed by organization of cadres of the IAS, the Rajasthan Administrative Service (RAS) and various technical or developmental services. The services were manned at the beginning almost exclusively by officers of former princely states, who had the qualifications and experience needed for absorption in the services. Even in the early 1960s, most of the officers in many services belonged to this category. The senior-most positions in all the services—almost 20 per cent in the

IAS—were occupied by them. Their numbers and proportions in the services would go down rapidly, however, during the 1960s as a result of their retirement and increase in number of young, direct recruits to the services.

The principal political and socio-economic reforms, and development programmes undertaken in Rajasthan during the 1950s were the following :

(i) Establishment of the State Legislature followed by orderly and peaceful conduct of the general elections of 1952 and 1957;
(ii) Abolition of *Jagirdari* which had been the dominant system of land tenure in former princely states;
(iii) Establishment in the early 1950s of village Panchayats after elections based on the principle of adult suffrage, and of *Nyaya* (judicial) *Panchayats*. The village (or multi-village) panchayats became part of the 3-tier structure of Panchayati Raj Institutions from October 1959; and
(iv) Implementation of the community development and other rural development programmes.

Abolition of *Jagirdari* was accompanied by conferment of full and heritable rights in the cultivated lands on the actual cultivators. Furthermore, large areas of cultivable lands, which had been retained by the *Jagirdars* as their *khud kasht* (self-cultivation) or *shikar* (hunting preserve) lands, became available for allotment to the landless, belonging mainly to the Scheduled Castes or the artisans. The area which a *Jagirdar* could retain for self-cultivation was limited by a ceiling on it.

The village *Panchayats* were given important administrative and developmental functions, as also the right to levy taxes and other duties. They had responsibility for management of the common lands of the village, which included woodlots, pastures and other uncultivated lands and the small but very valuable area on which the village abadi (inhabited area) stood and that reserved for extension of the abadi in future. Their responsibilities related to maintenance of sanitation within the villages, periodic repair of village tanks and approach roads. They had responsibility also of construction or repair of drinking water wells, construction of buildings for schools, panchayat ghars (buildings in which the panchayats met), and offices of cooperative societies. They had to make contributions towards construction of these works to match the grants given by the State Government or to undertake the construction with their own funds. This role became very important under the community development programme through which large grants became available for construction of the works from the State Government. The Panchayats were expected to make matching contributions in money, labour and locally available materials. The three high castes—Brahmin, Rajput and Mahajan (traders) contributed money; the contributions of the farmers and the Scheduled Castes were in labour or locally available materials.

The judicial *panchayats* had powers of hearing and deciding complaints about petty crime, intra-family quarrels and disputes relating to land or other property among the villagers. Appeals against their decisions could be made to the law courts or to the Collector.

The principal effect of the community development programme, launched in 1953, was to extend to the villages a network of developmental and welfare services, provided either by the government itself or by institutions like the cooperatives. Extension services for agriculture, animal husbandry, cottage industries and handicrafts; veterinary services, primary and secondary schools and primary health centres, were the principal services/facilities provided by the State Government. The government also gave grants for construction or repair of approach roads, reclamation of waste lands; construction, repair or improvement of sources of drinking water (wells and tanks) and other land improvement measures. Short and medium-term credit, supplies of improved seed, chemical fertilizers and other inputs of improved agriculture, and facilities for marketing and processing of crops were provided by cooperative institutions. The community development and other programmes provided also funds for welfare of the disadvantaged sections of the rural community, particularly the Scheduled Castes, the Scheduled Tribes and women.

Implementation of development programmes and extension of basic services to the rural people had been started by the State Government immediately after formation of Rajasthan. The process received great impetus, however, with the start of the community development programme. By the end of the 1950s, the network of services was almost complete. The 1960s and later decades would see further extension of the network, improvement in functioning of some services and provision of specialized services relating especially to agriculture.

Political Stability

The background to this steady progress and emphasis on implementation of development programmes was provided by political stability under the leadership of Shri M.L. Sukhadia, who was the Chief Minister of Rajasthan during most of the 1950s and the 1960s. He and the Chief Secretary, Mr. Mehta, led an administration marked by stability and progress in all directions. These, in turn were major factors in fostering among all concerned—Ministers, Legislators, officials and the people—the feeling of belonging to Rajasthan, instead of to the princely states of which they had been officials or subjects earlier. This was perhaps the greatest achievement of the two men.

I cannot help recalling a remark made to me during his visit to Sawai Madhopur by Mr. Barkatullah Khan, then Minister of Forests (and Chief Minister in the early 1970s) which showed the intensity of the parochial feelings among the older residents of former states. He was a native of Jodhpur and had gone to live in Jaipur only after he joined the Rajasthan Cabinet. He told me that his old mother had never visited him in Jaipur because she considered it to be a city of a ruler, Sawai Man Singh I, who had betrayed the Rajput cause by giving his sister in marriage to the Mughal Emperor Akbar. The rulers of Jodhpur who had submitted to the emperor much latter considered themselves superior to them. Those of Udaipur considered themselves superior to all others because their forbearer Rana Pratap had never submitted to the emperor.

Village Studies

Our twenty months in Sawai Madhopur were uneventful[4]. My work at the office was quite light and I had plenty of time to devote to study of three villages located three to eight kilometres. from my office which I had selected for the purpose. My wife joined me in the studies when she saw the abject poverty of the Meena women in one village.

They would thank their stars if they could get enough cereals to eat through the year and avoid hunger during the lean season (July-September) before the monsoon season crop of sorghum or millet was harvested. They could not afford to keep milch animals—buffaloes to provide milk for their children or themselves. They worked hard in the fields; they did more work in the fields than the men. They bathed in the pond located next to the village in which their livestock bathed also. They were too poor to afford use of soap or hair oil. As a result, they were not much cleaner after the bath, than they were before it. They neglected their children and household duties because they were busy in the fields. As a result infant and maternal mortality was so high that they could never think of family planning.

There have been dramatic changes in all these respects by 2001. Now they bathed in two wells located in the village, or with water which is piped in many houses. They can afford to drink milk and have vegetables and fruit as part of their diet. Maternal and child mortality has gone down so much that many couples in the reproductive age group practice family planning. Advice for it is given by an auxiliary nurse mid-wife living in a village or by nurses in a multi-facility hospital with 40 beds located in a suburb of Maantown.

During my stay in the district, I had to conduct election to *Panchayats* in January 1961 and the General Election of March 1962. Detailed instructions for conducting the elections were given by the Chief Electoral Officer in Jaipur. The polls were peaceful. We were surprised to see that the villagers—both men and women—came out in large numbers, dressed in their best clothes and singing and dancing, to exercise their votes for election of members of the *Panchayats*. But, few people bothered to vote for elections of the MLAs and MPs. The villagers concluded, correctly, that the decisions of members of village *Panchayats* would affect their welfare far more than those of the MLAs or MPs. Jaipur was 130 km. away; and Delhi might as well be in another country as far as they were concerned!

Visit of Queen Elizabeth II and Prince Philip Mountbatten

The only other notable event of my stay was the visit of Queen Elizabeth II and her husband Prince Philip Mountbatten for a tiger shoot in the forest of the Ranthambhore Game Sanctuary. Invitation for the visit had been extended by the former Maharaja of Jaipur, without reference to but with the concurrence of the Government of Rajasthan and India. All arrangements for the stay of the royal couple and the shoot were made also by the Maharaja. The royal couple went away satisfied because the Duke shot a tiger and his secretary shot a tigress. My only contribution to the visit was to make fool-proof arrangements for their security. I had to relocate about 40 shops located at the junction station where the railway lines connecting Sawai Madhopur with Mumbai and Jaipur met. This mini market of 40 odd shops in 1961 had about 800 shops in 2001. Plots for location of additional shops were sold for a long time by the *Panchayat Samiti* of Sawai Madhopur and later by the *Nagar Palika* (Municipal Committee) of Maantown at prices which made a handsome contribution to their budgets.

Mr. Sukhadia and Mr. Mehta

One of the secrets of Mr. Sukhadia's success as a Chief Minister was that he did not interfere with day-to-day work of the Collectors. During my twenty-months stay in Sawai Madhopur, I received only one telephone call from him at the time of a strike by workers in the cement factory. He enquired whether everything was under control. When I replied that it was, he said no more.

Mr. Mehta was superb as a trainer of young recruits to the service. Most of them belonged to other states—U.P., Punjab, Tamil Nadu or West Bengal. Yet, by the time they had finished their one-year probation, and were posted to the Secretariat or a district they would forget their native states and would have a feeling of belonging to Rajasthan.

Training of I.A.S. Officers

New Recruits—Bridegrooms

The new recruits would be treated like bridegrooms at the welcome dinner given for them by senior officers—Secretaries and Deputy Secretaries to various Departments of the Government; the Commissioner, the Collector, the Deputy Collectors and the City Magistrate of Jaipur. Before the dinner, they would be introduced to the senior officers including the Chief Secretary. After the dinner they would be regaled to music by the best musicians in Jaipur. On their next day, they would call on the Chief Secretary and senior officers in the Secretariat as well as the Commissioner, the Collector and the City Magistrate of Jaipur. They would not meet them again until after their nine months of training in a district when they would come back to Jaipur for their first posting in the Secretariat but preferably in a district as the Collectors or Sub-Divisional magistrates. They would be posted to the district in which they had been trained, unless they had any problems in staying in a district too far from Jaipur.

Annual Conferences of Collectors and Commissioners

These conferences which were held in March were another occasion when all the Collectors, Commissioners and many Secretaries and Deputy Secretaries to Government would meet young officers. The conference would be inaugurated by the Chief Minister and addressed by the Ministers of Planning and Development, Finance, Health, Education and Welfare of the Scheduled Castes and the Scheduled Tribes. Every Collector had to make a presentation of about one hour to explain working of development programmes in his on her district and the problems that he or she faced. The Ministers and Secretaries to government and Heads of Departments would take measures to solve the problems. In both evenings of these meetings, there would be dinner parties attended by the Chief Secretary and other senior officers stationed in Jaipur, besides the Collectors and Commissioners. After the dinner and playing of music by professional musicians, by some officers or their wives, polite conversation would extend into the small hours of the morning. The dinner meetings were held invariably in some historic buildings, the architecture of which was of particular interest for the invitees.

Mr. Mehta would compare favourably or perform any British officer of the ICS in his capacity for training of young officers. Whenever he was in Jaipur, about twenty young officers posted in the Secretariat or visiting Jaipur would gather at his home in the evening. He would take two drinks (no more) over two to three hours at which he would be joined by the young officers present. The young officers would seek his advice on any problems that they faced. The subjects discussed ranged over a wide area, even personal problems that they faced would be discussed also. However, even the gossip was never malicious.

Whenever Mr. Mehta was in Jaipur, there was 'open house' at his house for 2-3 hours at the evening for drinks and conversation. After two drinks, there would be conversation for 2-3 hours. Young officers were encouraged to discuss their problems and were advised on how to get over them by Mr. Mehta. There would also be dinner almost every night at the house of one or other senior officer. He would himself visit most of the districts himself during the course of a year.

The 'training' given by Mr. Mehta through these evening meetings has been so effective that two officers of the cadre have held posts of Secretary to the Government of India with much distinction. One went on to become the Governor of Tamil Nadu while the other was until recently the Ambassador of India to the United States. The number of those who went on to become Chairman or Directors of public sector undertakings after serving as Secretaries to the Government of India would be two dozen or more.

The observations in the previous paragraphs are based on the village studies that my wife and I did during our stay in the district. My official work was not heavy and I could devote much time to village studies and my wife could join me in the studies, because she has an M.A. in Economics and became interested in the studies when she saw the abject poverty of women of the Meenas and the Jatavas. Furthermore, the values and the superstitions that the women had, appeared incredible to a woman who had spent all her life in Delhi or in district or sub-divisional towns in Punjab; her father was a physician whose various postings were in these towns.

Although I stayed in Rajasthan for only two years, the stay was so happy and instructive that I have acquired affection for the state which is unbelievable. The two Chief Ministers that have been as interested in economic and social development as Mr. Sukhadia have belonged to different political parties but their commitment to development was such that there is great certainty in its development. Almost half of the state suffers from periodic scarcity of food, fodder and water (for people and livestock). Despite this, it has an exportable surplus of cereals; adult and female literacy rates have increased remarkably rapidly; total literacy rate doubled between 1991 and 2001. Maternal, infant and child mortality have also been reduced.

The Attraction of Rajasthan

The attraction of Rajasthan is such that three of my friends who trained for the IAS in Simla, decided to settle down in Jaipur. One is from Punjab, the other is from Kerala and the third was from belts of Uttar Pradesh. I stayed in Rajasthan for only a few years, but I have such pleasant memories of my stay that during the last 16 years, that I have been in India after return from abroad, I have followed developments in the state with great interest.

NOTES

1. The Institute now called the 'National Institute of Rural Development' is located in Rajendra Nagar, Hyderabad in Andhra Pradesh.
2. A committee to evaluate progress of Community Development and National Extension Service Programmes, Ministry of Community Development and Cooperation, New Delhi, 1957.
3. *Jagirdars* in former princely states were intermediary tenure-holders. Their principal duties included collection of land revenue from the tenant-farmers, preservation of law and order and other duties specified by the princes. A large proportion of the land revenue had to be deposited by them into the treasury of the state.
4. We had a large house in the yard of which was an orchard, which had been bearing most delicious papayas. The house was located almost next to my office, in the building which housed the office of the Collector, the two

deputies—the additional District Magistrate and the Development Officer who looked after the Panchayati Raj Institution. My next-door neighbour, the Superintendent of Police also had his office in the building, which had also a lock-up, a sub-treasury, office of the Judicial Magistrate. The Block Development Officer and about 30-odd sub-divisional officers posted in Maantown lived in the street adjoining our house. Most of them had kept their families in Jaipur or their home towns because there was no facility for education of their children. Furthermore, the small hospital with two doctors was located in Sawai Madhopur town, about 15 km. from Maantown. Several of district level officers—the executive engineer (buildings and roads), the district agricultural and veterinary officers and the district forest officers lived in Tonk; the district medical and public health officer lived in Karauli, which was then a sub-division of the district, but is now a separate district. They would all come to Sawai Madhopur to attend the monthly meetings of the *Zilla Parishad* when they would attend to the problems in working of their respective departments which had been pointed out by the members of the *Zilla Parishad*. By 2001, they were all living with their families in Maantown, because there were two multi-facility hospitals with large number of doctors, one in suburbs of Maantown and the other about 8 km. from it. There was also a college and a polytechnique and a higher secondary school in the suburb of Maantown.

9

Training of Officers of the Indian Administrative Services

I. The Present Training Programme

Training of officers of the IAS and other All India and Central services starts with a stay of 18 months at the National Academy of Administration located in Mussoorie in Uttar Pradesh. In this period, besides attending lectures, seminars and group discussions, the trainees participate in a tour of India which provides them an opportunity to see the immense variety in physical, economic and social conditions in different parts of the country. Thus the trainee, whose world view may have been conditioned by what he or she saw in their home state, gets a much wider all India view.

Furthermore, the opportunity to live and make friends with trainees from different states gives him or her, an opportunity to know about and appreciate the life style and customs of people of different regions. This knowledge would be invaluable to them when they work in Ministries of the Government of India or as executives of parastatals whose operations extend all over the country.

The training programme at the Academy includes lectures in public administration, criminal law, economics, rural sociology, history of India, the environment and other subjects which provide to the trainees the basic equipment needed to work as administrative officers.

It should enable the trainees to become proficient also in use of computers, fax machines, e-mail and internet. This is essential because they will need this proficiency throughout their service career. In Andhra Pradesh, the Chief Minister has established in all districts, a computerized office, so that he can get detailed reports from the Collectors about conditions in their district and ensure that effective action is taken to counter any untoward development. Governments of other states could follow his lead. Revenue records could be computerized in the next decade or more. This will increase their accuracy and reduce the cost of compiling and sharing them. Furthermore, use of these techniques will greatly improve communications between the State Governments and the Districts. Information on success or failure of different development programmes will be available to the various departments of the State Governments more rapidly and in greater detail than at present, so that changes in the content of various development programmes can be made more rapidly, keeping in view the problems in their implementation in different districts than at present.

After they reach the state to which they are posted, IAS officers would be under training for about 18 months in a district and at the State Academy of Administration, if the state has one. The first object of training in the field and at the academy is to provide the basic knowledge needed to become successful Collector. Thus, they would attend at the state academy, a course in revenue law, and lectures on the economy of the state, its history, art and architecture, its natural resources and environmental problems. Those who come from states different from the state of posting must learn to speak fluently and read and write the official language of the state. Ability to understand at least one dialect, which could come later, would also be useful.

Training in the field requires living at the district headquarters town/ city and inquest of towns to villages and small towns. In this period, the trainees would spend time going round the cultivators' fields and seeing the conditions under which they live and work. They would also see the working of the Revenue administration, the police, the Panchayati Raj Institutions and the different development departments of the state at rural area level. This period provides them also an opportunity to know the social customs of different castes, inter-personal or inter-caste conflicts in Panchayat Raj Institutions and various economic and social problems of the rural people. They would observe how effective or acceptable to the rural people various rural development programmes have been. They would get to know also, the various financial leakages and administrative lapses in implementation of these programmes.

Although land revenue is no longer an important source of income for the governments of most of the states, revenue records are of the utmost importance. They show the ownership or other rights in every plot of land; the state of the crops the prospects of a shortfall in production of foodgrains or cash crops. In states like Bihar, which have implemented land reform laws in recent years, they would hear innumerable complaints from poor cultivators about how they have been deprived of their rights to the land which the reform conferred on them through connivance between the former landlords and corrupt Revenue Department officials, so that they remain agricultural labourers for their former landlords.

If they are observant they would find also that many customs of the rural people are very different from the prevailing stereotypes. During my stay as a Collector in a district of Rajasthan in the 1960s (1960-62), I found that the customs of giving a dowry on the marriage of a daughter and ban on marriage of widows were observed only by people of three high castes—Brahmins, Rajputs and Mahajans (traders). The prevailing custom among the cultivating castes and the Scheduled Castes was that a man had to pay a bride price to the parents of the woman he wanted to marry. She would leave him and go back to her parents' home if he did not treat her well. The caste *Panchayat* would then decide if the bride price should be returned to him or not. Women did more work in the fields than men in those days so that by marrying, a man acquired a valuable worker and he must pay her parents a price for raising her.

It is only after the training in the field and the state academy of administration that the officers would get their first posting as Assistant Magistrates or sub-divisional officers. In this position, they would try cases relating to payment of land revenue or rights to land or of petty crime. Furthermore, they would help the Collector in his various duties from maintenance of peace and security in the district, to overseeing implementation of various development programmes, the working of Panchayati Raj Institutions, supervising relief work in case of natural calamities such as floods and conducting elections to P.R. Institutions, the State Legislature and the Parliament. He or she would observe that much of the Collectors' time is spent in facilitating coordination between various departments that undertake rural development programmes and in working of different departments concerning with rural development.

Posting as a Collector, which may be preceded by a period of service in the Secretariat of the state would come after five to eight years of work in the state.

Refresher training programmes are organized at the National Academy after ten to twelve years of service. Before it or soon after it, it would be useful to divide the officers in the following four streams :

1. Management and economic policy formulation stream,
2. Agriculture, rural development and environment stream,

3. Social services stream, and
4. Law and order stream.

The division should be done by the Chief Secretary and a Committee of Secretaries of the State Government with concurrence of the Chief Minister, the Finance Minister, the Home Minister and the Ministers of Health, Education and Social Welfare. It should be based on the officers' aptitude, work experience and potential.

Specialized Training Programmes

Management and Economic Policy Stream

Officers selected for this stream should have worked in the Departments of Finance, Industries, Tourism, etc. of the State Government and participated in management of a parastatal owned by the State Government. They should preferably have held a position also in one of the economic Ministries of the Government of India. The number of officers in this stream would be quite large and the stream would appear to be most attractive to young officers because it offers the prospect of holding senior and admittedly glamorous positions in the Ministry of Finance, Commerce, Industry, Tourism, Surface Transport, or Civil Aviation, etc. or as executives in some successful parastatals of the Government of India such as the Indian Oil Corporation. However, not all officers are equipped for such positions because of educational background and aptitude. After selection, officers of this stream should receive refresher training in the National Academy in principles of management, basic principles of cost accounting and short courses in Economics, Company Law, Labour Relations, etc. After the refresher training there should be :

- A short period of training in one of the reputed management institutes—Ahmedabad, Barrackpur or Bangalore;
- Attachment for a few months with a successfully managed Indian company. The company managed by the Tatas, Kirloskars, Godrej or Bajaj Auto, Ranbaxy Laboratories, Hindustan Lever, and the Indian Tobacco Company are some of the companies, which would be suitable for such attachment. The attachment will give the trainees an opportunity to see what does or does not succeed in Indian business and industry, how companies grow and how managements cope with the problems of falling sales or profits. Officers of this stream should also have an opportunity at some stage in their service

careers to go abroad, for a short course in management, at a reputed school of management located in Harvard, MIT or Stanford University in the USA or in a school in the UK or France. They should be attached for a few months with the World Bank or the Asian Development Bank to observe the working of these development and finance institutions. They should be followed at some stage with a short period of attachment with the World Bank or the Asian Development Bank. They would know the criteria which the World Bank and the ADB have for determining suitability of projects to be financed by them in developing countries. Management consultants such as Arthur Anderson or Price Water House would give them an opportunity to see how foreign businesses work, the working of the international development finance institutions and understand and evaluate the reports of management consultants.

Agricultural, Rural Development and Environment Stream

The number of officers in this stream would also be quite large. Some of the most successful Collectors, or Deputy Development Commissioners would be included in this stream. They will work in agriculture, rural development, irrigation, environment, etc., in departments of the State Government or in Ministries of the Central Government concerned with these subjects. Some of them would have had degrees in an agricultural science, agricultural economics or rural sociology. For their refresher training they should attend short courses in these subjects at the National Academy or the Indian Institute of Public Administration, New Delhi. While working in the Ministries of the Government of India, they should have an opportunity to travel to countries like Israel, China, Indonesia, Thailand or Malaysia to see how these countries have tackled problems of rural development or conservation and efficient utilization of their land and water resources and minimize soil erosion and related problems. They should also have a capacity to interact well with experts who can provide ingenious and low cost methods of conserving water and controlling pollution of air and water.

Social Service Stream

The number of officers in this stream would also be quite large. A large number could be of women. They would work in the Departments of Education, Health, Family Planning, Social Welfare, Welfare of Women and Youth etc. of the State Governments and in the Ministries of the Government of India dealing with these subjects. They should understand why programmes of eradicating illiteracy, providing universal primary education and primary health care to all or acceptance of family planning, have not been accepted by rural people in some states, while they have been accepted widely in other states such as Kerala and Goa. They would have to interact with workers of the NGOs (non-governmental organizations) who undertake similar programmes. The interaction will help them understand methods of work of these organizations and help to assure them that no organization indulges in anti-national propaganda, as some Christian Missionaries during British days and also after independence have done.

Officers in both the rural development and social service streams would have an opportunity also of studying closely the working of Panchayat Raj Institutions and observing the leakages and inefficiency in rural development and social welfare programmes. Some officers in this stream may have to work in emergencies, as Vice-Chancellors of Universities. In these positions they would have to deal often with strikes by teachers or staff of hospitals. Refresher training for them should include short courses in human relations and personnel management at the IIPA. They should be given an opportunity to travel to see the working of the programmes in Kerala and other countries like Indonesia and China which have had particularly successful programmes of extension of education and health services for the rural people. Closer to home a study of the Grameen Bank in Bangladesh would be useful.

The Law and Order Stream

The number of officers in this stream would be much smaller than in the other streams. They would occupy the top positions in the State Governments in the Home Department and the Chief Ministers' Secretariat. In the Central Government, they would work in the Prime Minister's secretariat and Ministries of Home Affairs and Defence. Refresher training for them should include brief periods of attachment with the police and the armed forces so that they have an adequate knowledge and appreciation of the organization and methods of working of these services and the motivations of the men and women who work in them. This knowledge is of vital importance to maintenance of internal security and defence of the country. Officers in this stream should also have an opportunity to travel abroad to see the organization, method of work and equipment used in some developed countries such as Britain or France.

They should have one or more short courses in project evaluation, so that they are equipped to process cases of purchases of equipment by the armed forces or the police with some knowledge of the criteria used by the forces to decide on purchase of equipment.

Commissioners and Other Senior Positions in Municipal Corporations

The number of metropolitan cities, viz. cities with populations of one million and above, is increasing rapidly. It increased from 5 in 1951 to 23 in 1991 and further to 35 by 2001. The cities are the political, commercial and cultural centres of the regions in which they are located. Furthermore, large numbers of large, medium or small industrial units are located within them or in their peri-urban areas.

The State or Municipal Governments of the cities face serious problem of financing expansion of electricity and water supply for their growing populations, expanding the sewerage system and public transport systems. The corporations depend upon loans or grants from the State Governments to finance expansion of housing and infrastructure facilities since their own resources are barely adequate for performing basic municipal functions such as lighting and cleaning of streets and keeping them in good repair.

Most of the positions of Commissioners of Municipal Corporations are filled at present by officers of the I.A.S. Deputy Commissioners in some departments belong also to the service. The number of such positions is expected to increase progressively as the number of metropolitan cities.

The Municipal Corporation of the cities and even governments of the States in which they are located face serious problems in providing security of life and property to the residence, or providing them basic amenities—electricity, drinking water and intra-urban transport. Provision of electricity became difficult because of widespread theft, in connivance with some officials by slum dwellers, owners of industrial units or other large users. Provision of security of life and properly to citizens becomes difficult because of activities of criminals in some cities in collusion with corrupt officers. Privatization of distribution of electricity is being advocated, judging by experience in Mumbai and other cities in which private distributors make profits by checking theft. Intra-urban public transport has been provided efficiently in many cities by private or public companies. The experience in these cities should be studied by Commissioners of Municipal Corporations. They should attend, preferably before appointment as Commissioner or Deputy Commissioners short courses in personne management and human relations, because they would have to deal often with strikes or other graft of municipal employees.

Officers selected for these positions would be drawn primarily from those in the social service or agriculture, rural development and environment streams. They should be good at maintaining good relations with local political leaders and employees of the corporations. This is essential because they would have to interact continually with local political leaders and meet their demands as far as possible. Furthermore, they should be able to maintain good relations with leaders of unions of various categories of employees in the sanitation departments, skilled and white collar workers such as drivers of buses, meter readers and clerks of the property tax departments, the electricity board or the water supply board. They would have to ensure that the employees of the various boards do their work efficiently and that monetary corruption is curbed without provoking strikes. Frequent strikes by any group of workers can ruin the reputation of any Commissioner. In doing their work, they should seek cooperation of civic minded leaders in various neighbourhoods. They would find many such socially concerned citizens in every neighbourhood or market and also find them quite willing to extend their cooperation to the Commissioners.

The Indian Institute of Public Administration (IIPA) organizes short term courses in municipal administration and municipal finance. Officers to be selected for these positions should be required to attend these courses. They should, have prior to or in the first year of posting as Commissioners, have a short period (2-4 weeks of attachment) with an institute of urban planning. This will help them understand the methods used by the institute of preparing development plans for cities and the context of development plans.

During their tenure as Commissioner, the officers should have opportunity to visit capitals of countries such as the Philippines, Thailand, Malaysia, or Indonesia to see how the corporations of these cities which have also witnessed expansion and growth of population and economic activities during the last few decades and have managed to cope with these problems and financed needed for expansion of infrastructures.

Location of the Refresher Training Programme

The refresher training wing of the National Academy should be located in New Delhi and should work in close cooperation with the Indian Institute of Public Administration. Location of the programme in New Delhi will ensure that the trainees in various streams are addressed from time to time by Ministers and Secretaries of the Government of India, heads of parastatals and eminent economists, sociologists and experts in public administration. They could also be addressed from time to time by visiting foreign scholars.

Cooperation with the IIPA will ensure that while comprehensive training programme are organized by the National Academy, short six to eight weeks courses are organized by the IIPA.

Concluding Remarks

The country depends upon officers of the IAS, IIAS and other All India and Central Services for running various administrative and technical services of the Central and State Governments. In view of the increasing complexity of the political, social and economic problems being faced by the country, it is essential that the officers recruited for these services have the capacity to deal with the problems later in the service. Furthermore, their training—basic and refresher should equip them to face them. However, in order to ensure that officers possessing the qualities mentioned above are attracted to enter the service and are retained, their remuneration, basic and throughout their service courses should be comparable with those in private sector corporations and multi-nationals.

II. The Training of Indian Administrative Officers : Some Glimpses from Rajasthan—and Personal Notes on Training in Villages

The New Recruits—Bridegrooms

In Rajasthan, the new recruits of IAS would be treated like bridegrooms at the welcome dinner given for them by senior officers—Secretaries and Deputy Secretaries to various departments of the Government, the Commissioner, the Collector, the Deputy Collectors and the City Magistrate of Jaipur. Before the dinner, they would be introduced to the senior officers including the Chief Secretary. After the dinner the best musicians in Jaipur would regale them to music. On their next day, they would call on the Chief Secretary and senior officers in the Secretariat as well as the Commissioner, the Collector and the City Magistrate of Jaipur. They would not meet them again until after their 9 months of training in a district when they would come back to Jaipur for their first posting in the Secretariat but preferably in a district as the Collectors or Sub-Divisional Magistrates. They would be posted to the district in which they had been trained, unless they had any problems in staying in a district too for from Jaipur.

Annual Conferences of Collectors and Commissioners

These conferences, which were held in March, were another occasion when all the Collectors, Commissioners and many Secretaries and Deputy Secretaries to Government would meet young officers. The conference would be inaugurated by the Chief Minister and addressed by the Ministers of Planning and Development, Finance, Health, Education and Welfare of Scheduled Castes and the Scheduled Tribes. Every Collector had to make a presentation of about one hour to explain working of development programmes in his or her district and the problems that he or she faced. The Ministers and Secretaries to Government and Heads of Departments would take measures to solve the problems. In both evenings of these meetings, there would be dinner parties attended by the Chief Secretaries and other senior officers stationed in Jaipur, besides the Collectors and Commissioners. After the dinner and playing of music by professional musicians, by some officers or their wives, polite conversation would extend into the small hours of the mornings. The dinner meetings were held invariable in some historic buildings, the architecture of which was of particular interest for the invitees.

Mr. Mehta, the then Chief Secretary, would compare favourably with British officers of the ICS in his capacity for training of young officers. Whenever he was in Jaipur, about 20 young officers posted in the Secretariat or visiting Jaipur would gather at his office and home in the evening. He would take two drinks (no more) over two to two-and-a-half-hours at which the young officers present would join him.

The young officers would seek his advice on any problems that they faced. The subjects discussed ranged over a wide area, even personal problems that they faced would be discussed also. However, even the gossip was never malicious.

The 'training' given by Mr. Mehta through these evening meetings has been so effective that two officers of the cadre have held posts of Secretary to the Government of India with such distinction. One went on to become the Governor of Tamil Nadu while the other was until recently Ambassador of India to the United States. The number of them who went on to become Chairmen or Directors of public sector undertakings after serving as Secretaries to the Government of India would be two dozen or more.

Three Months (January-March 1959) in the Sands of Nagaur and Jodhpur Districts of Rajasthan

There were four of us who had joined the Indian Administrative Service in 1958, as a result of the Special Recruitment made by the Union Public Service Commission and we had selected Rajasthan as the state in which we were to work arrived in Jaipur early in January 1959. The Chief Secretary, Mr. B. Mehta, decided that for our training in the field we should spend three months in the villages of Nagaur and Jodhpur districts and six months in Jodhpur city working as Assistant Magistrates. The four included, Mr. B. Hooja, the Chief Editor of the Journal *Indian Book Chronicle*, Mr. R.C. Sood who had been a successful businessman in Delhi, Mr. R. Mukherjee who had worked as a Solicitor in Calcutta with a company which had been owned by Scots earlier but was now owned by an Indian and me.

Our first month in the field was spent in Jayal a large village, located a few miles from the district headquarter town, Nagaur. We stayed in a rest house which had four rooms, one for each of us, a large drawing room, electricity and running water and sanitary fittings in the bath rooms for our stay in comfort. The Collector visited us often and instructed the clerk in-charge of the rest house to ensure that we got all the groceries and other supplies from Nagaur town that we needed. After a long morning and two hours in the evening, going round the farmers' fields, measuring their areas, assessing the state of the crops, with the help of the *patwaries* (village level functionaries of the revenue department) to determine the land revenue or tax that the farmers should pay to the government, we would come back exhausted, even in January it was hot in the fields, have our bath, and spend 2-3 hours in conversation, enlivened by glasses of beer before taking our dinner and going to sleep.

Mr. Sood had wisely brought with him a servant who cooked our meals and a plentiful supply of beer. B. Hooja, always a book lover, had brought a small collection of books. The Collector lent us a copy of the Gazetteer of Nagaur and Jodhpur districts which had been written by a British officer at the turn of the century. We would spend two-three hours reading in the long afternoons. The most interesting fact that we learnt from the Gazetteer was that Meera Bai, the queen of the Rana of Chittore who had left her husband to become a mendicant poetess and had settled down in Vrindavan, the place where Lord Krishna had spent his childhood, and who like millions of other Hindus, regarded Krishna as God, was born in village Merta of Nagaur district.

Nagaur was an interesting town. About one-third of its population of about 15,000, were Moslems. Most of the houses were built of mud-bricks; their walls were plastered with brown clay which kept them cool in the long hot summer and protected them from damage by rain. From its numerous mosques and turrets on the houses of the affluent, it looked more like a Middle Eastern than a Rajasthan town. It was known throughout Rajasthan for its cattle fair, held in February, in which were bought and sold thousands of cattle (bullocks, cows and buffaloes), horses, camels, sheep and goats.

During the second month, we lived in a rest house in Phalodi, a town of Jodhpur district, located about 200 km. from Pokharan, the site of India's nuclear tests. Our daily routine was not very different from that in Jayal. We learnt the details of the land records maintained by the *patwaries*, so that we would be able to decide, when we worked as Collectors or Sub-Divisional Officers, disputes among farmers about rights in land or cases of default in payment of land revenue.

Here, we saw the effect of acute shortage of drinking water on the lives of the inhabitants. In this large semi-desert area with numerous villages and hamlets there ware very few wells which had potable (sweet) water for drinking and domestic use throughout the year. We would see men who lived in a hamlet, 6-8 km. from a drinking water well, riding their camels to fetch drinking water. They would fill two large leather buckets perched on both sides of the beasts with water which would last them a week. The men were *swarthy*, tall, well built and handsome. They would be accompanied sometimes by their women, who were also tall, well built and good looking. Most of them were *Bishnois*, followers of a faith, started by one Jambaji, whom they regard as their prophet, some three centuries earlier. The 29 tenets of their faith constitute a masterly treatise in conservation of soil and water, flora and fauna in a harsh semi-desert environment. Thus they do not allow any one to kill a deer or a peacock or any other animal or cut a tree in the woodland around their villages or hamlets. They would pounce on any one who did. There was an incident widely reported in the media almost eighteen months ago when the Bishnois held prisoner of one of the most famous film actor of Bollywood, because they alleged that he and his companion had killed two deer. He vehemently denied the charge and was released on intervention by the Government of Rajasthan. But I am not sure that he had not killed, because the Bishnois do not lie.

Kheenchan

One day we visited Kheenchan, a village of about 5000 people, most residents of which are women, children or old folks of Marwari merchants who work as shop-keepers in Mumbai or towns in Maharashtra. Most of the men, who work outside the village, live without their families whom they visit for two-three months in the year. They come home also when there is a marriage or a death in their family or that of one of their near relatives.

They have constructed large houses, called *havelies*. Built of rust or light brown sandstone, these are beautiful two-three storey houses, with richly done doors and windows. During the course of this month, B. Hooja and I spent four or five days in Mathania, a village of about 2000 people about a third of whom were Mahajans (traders) or Brahmins. Here we saw (i) very efficient traditional water harvesting about which there is so much talk these days and (ii) an equally efficient, simple method of preventing ingress of dust or eggs of guinea worm from entering drinking water. Most of the houses of the Mahajans are built of sandstone. They have tanks for storage of rain water immediately below the roof. The rainwater falling on the roof of the house during the few rain showers is collected in the tank and used for drinking or other domestic use for a part of the year. The village has a large number of *bawries* (step wells) which have potable water. Before filling their pitchers the women of Mahajan or Brahmin families tie a piece of Muslin around the mouth of the pitchers to prevent ingress of dirt or any insect. Farmers or Scheduled Castes do not follow this practice. Guinea worm is a long, slimy worm. If its eggs enter the body, they breed there. The process of extracting the mature worms is very painful; often the limb (an arm or a leg) has to be cut by a surgeon to save the patient from dying through poisoning by gangrine. There are large numbers of people among the Scheduled Castes or farmers who have lost a limb in this area, but almost none among the Mahajans or Brahmins.

We spent the third month of our field training in the Bilore community development block in order to study working of the CD programme. The area receives more rainfall than in two areas in which we had lived earlier. However, the scarcity of drinking water is as acute in this as in the other two areas because most of the wells have brackish water. We accompanied the Block Development Officer on his visits to the villages to see the working of the programme. The BDO, who appeared to be a conscientious enough man, complained that some of his extension officers did not cooperate with him because they took their orders not from him but from their departmental superiors. The interesting part of our visit would appear to have ended with our stay in Mathania. The stay at Bilore was not interesting; we learnt nothing that we did not know already.

After three months in the field, we stayed for six months in Jodhpur working as Assistant Magistrates. Our principal job in this period was to try cases of petty crimes such as burglary or disputes about rights in land. Our families joined us here. Jodhpur was an interesting city in those days. It had a population of about 150,000, three-fourth of which was Hindus or Jains and the remaining were Moslems. While the Hindus or Jains were merchants or white-collar workers, most of the Moslems were artisans. They were the poorer one-quarter of the population. They specialized in printing tie-and-dye designs on cotton or silk fabrics used for women's skirts or *saris* or men's turbans. The design consists in printing small white dots within a coloured background. The work is time consuming, but the Moslem men and women do it because there is a large market for tie-and-dye fashion in Rajasthan, Delhi and abroad.

The old city is built at the back of a fort, located on a low hill on top of which was the palace of the Mahajan. After Second World War, a number of well planned neighbourhoods had been built to house the increasing population of the city. The city became important during the 1950s with location in it of a college for training of pilots, starting of a division of the Indian army and establishment of the Central Arid Zone Research Institute. The Director of the Institute, a very pleasant gentleman from Coorg, became a friend.

I had read much about the piccalillis of the princes and the fact that their people tolerated them only because they had the protection of the British forces and could not be removed. My experience both in Jodhpur and later in Sawai Madhopur which had been a part of Jaipur state is different. I, however, found that in both states, the people not only respected but revered their rulers for what they had done for them.

Maharaja of Jodhpur, when he became the ruler of the state was only twelve years old and was studying in Britain. He ruled the state in the 1920s to the late 1940s, was an enlightened ruler who did much for the welfare of his subjects. He built in Jodhpur a first class multi-facility hospital and a degree college. To relieve scarcity of water in the frequent dry year, he had dug or repaired a large number of wells. The beautiful Ummed Palace, built of light brown sandstone and located about three kilometres. outside the city, shines like a gem out of the bleak landscape, was built by him as a famine relief work in the 1930s. Since the palace was empty at the time, our families and we had a conducted tour of it, courtesy the caretaker, a kindly, retired IAS officer coming from Uttar Pradesh.

Designed like the palaces of 19th century Europe, Ummed palace has a large number of state rooms which have beautiful frescoes paintings on the walls and ceilings and richly embroidered tapestries. It is being used now as a deluxe hotel by the Taj Group of hotel managers of Mumbai and is very popular with the tourists. Later (during 1960-62) when I worked as Collector of Sawai Madhopur district which had formed part of the erstwhile Jaipur state, I noticed the same respect and reverence for Sawai Mansing II who had been the ruler of Jaipur state during the 1930s and the 1940s. On becoming the Maharaja, he invited Sir Mirza Ismail, the town planner—Prime Minister of Mysore to be his Prime Minister in order to build a new, modern city, outside the old pink city. Sir Mirza designed a city with wide roads and well planned residential neighbourhoods. He built also in the new city, a multi-facility hospital, a post-graduate college for men, which later formed the nucleus of Rajasthan University, a public school for women and a large public garden with a museum and a zoo inside it. The administration of the state was modernized so that it compared favourably with that in many British administered provinces.

I shall never forget the three months that the four of us spent in Nagaur and Jodhpur districts. We got to know one another intimately which we could never have done otherwise. Furthermore, we got to know the harsh semi-desert environment in which the farmers and peasants work. The success or failure of the corps that they grow and availability of pastures for their flocks is a gamble with the rains. If the rains fail, both the farmers and their herds must leave to save themselves and their flocks from starvation. The peasant farmers and cattle grazers leave for greener pastures in eastern Rajasthan while the usually migrate to cities in eastern Rajasthan or Madhya Pradesh in search of employment.

Appendix – I

Personal Doubts and Expectations from Joining the IAS in the Special Recruitment 1957—Excerpts from Diary Notes Left as Precious Reminiscences of the Author

Misgiving and Uncertainties of Joining IAS

Simla Staff College October-November 1958

I sometimes wonder if I haven't made a hash of my life, anyway. (i) I lost two years during college days, when on persuasion from my father I left college on health grounds. They were an utter waste. (ii) Then I did Geography, doing an M.A. in Economics would have been so much better. (iii) I could have gone to Cambridge after my M.A. and done something real nice. (iv) If I hadn't gone to USA to do my Ph.D. I might have taken the I.A.S. exam in 1947 and been really something by now. (v) Then, after coming back with a Geography Ph.D., if I had picked up an Economics M.A. I could have stayed on in the Economic Division in the

Planning Commission and been a Director by now, and on my way to being a chief or something, instead I became a Private Secretary. (vi) K. N. Raj had advised me not to leave University of Ceylon, where I had been promoted as a Reader within three months of joining the service. I might have made an outstanding Geographer by now; I could have been an honoured professor at Delhi University by now and respected all over the country. Instead, I am here in the IAS to go in a back of beyond place in the heart of Rajasthan.

I spent five years in the Programme Evaluation Organization (PEO) from the Private Secretary's post that was the only escape possible. I have now joined the service, from the PEO. From that standpoint again, this was the only course possible. What else could I have done having been in the Government for eight years and not getting anywhere in terms of permanent service prospects etc. At every stage the decision one took appeared to be the best under the circumstances. The only real mistakes were: leaving college in 1940; taking Geography in 1944; leaving Wisconsin in 1948, without an M.A. in Economics and perhaps not taking an M.A. degree in 1951.

I have been too much carried away with what people have said is good and profitable at the time, and haven't paid enough attention to my own inclinations. Those that I have done and I had really wanted to have been really good; but these have been few. One of them was writing the 3rd Evaluation Report in 1956. This has been perhaps the outstanding achievement of my life so far. I left Evaluation because I had ceased to like it any more. I knew I was getting stale and needed a new life; new experiences.

However, now in my 36th year, I stand in the middle of my life with about 3/4th of the productive life ahead of me. It is not too late to make a fresh start. The circumstances are more favourable. There are no pressing family commitments; I can make my own decisions. There is no problem of insecurity, a minimum income is guaranteed. Now is the time to do my best, and to achieve, rather than be lost in the morass of introspection and self-doubt I haven't made much money. The bank balance after paying for the car is *nil*.

Now in the IAS, it is true that I look upon my immediate job not without misgivings. I don't like court-work; I don't like the useless running about which the district job often implies. I hate the small corruption and snobbery that goes with it. It is also true that I think often that I shall be wasting my time in a backward, unknown place, while others like I.G. Patel, K.N. Raj and other colleagues are doing important, exciting work, which I could also be doing. Part of the misery may be due to the physical discomfort of not having a house to live in, and not having the family here. But it is not merely that: it is that I am afraid that my time is going to be wasted. Wasted in useless pursuits, wasted like the time in Simla Training School! I have been unhappy in Simla because of this very thing. We are tired of this and want this to be over with as soon as possible. The reasons for this feeling are mainly two: (i) the way in which the training is being conducted, and (ii) the fact that most of us do not have our families here.

However, I have chosen my objective now I shall stick to it and do my very best to succeed. God will help me.

As for the immediate, what I must do is to write on :

1. The Geography and History of Jodhpur State.
2. The Administrative pattern of the district, before and now, and the process of transformation.
3. The structure of the development organization—official and non-official.
4. The agricultural economy,—land utilization, etc.
5. The land situation : Agrarian & land reforms; the social changes as a result of this, particularly its impact on the landed, the *Jagirdars* on the one hand, and the landless on the other.
6. The working of the District Administration :
   (i) Judicial,
   (ii) Development,
   (iii) Revenue and Settlement.
7. Take two blocks and within it take about 5 villages and make a real thorough study of the village economy, social and economic structure; change and working of the development programmes. Make a study of the Community Development (C.D.) Programme in these two blocks, as has not been done by the PEO and as have always been wanted to do.
8. During the revenue and settlement training, write detailed studies on all aspects, and particularly on the C.D.

Must finish the Community Development monograph, with the experience and the leisure that I will get here.

I have been in the staff college for a little more than three months.

We are being treated exactly like under-graduates. As far as I am personally concerned, I don't find anything in the training except Law and District Administration. The greatest pity of it all is that many of my colleagues have not only willingly submitted to this but have well nigh insisted that they be treated like under-graduates. The amount of cramming which some of them have done for the exams, the importance they have attached to them; the pains which some of them take to please the lecturers, and the petty jealousies that have developed as a result are simply unbelievable.

The main purpose of this training should have been to enable us to get acquainted with each other, get some basic ideas about the kind of job which we have to do; and how to do it, and finally and most importantly to imbibe by living together some of the spirit of the service and a sense of camaraderie for each other. True, it is not right that we should consider ourselves apart from the rest of the people. But that does not mean that we should not consider ourselves part of a group having a common approach to common problems; sharing the spirit of service to the country; sharing our ideals and standards of character and professional work and conscious of being engaged in a common endeavour. This was the main thing this course should have done. It has failed to do that, by and large. We have begun to know each other; some friendships which may last for a long time have been formed. Something by way of becoming friends and colleagues has been done but not enough. The emphasis has been too much on book learning and cramming. If there had been more travelling, we might have got to know each other better. I got to know my 17 colleagues of the service through the three days trip much better than I had done in three months, and I feel a certain sense of oneness with them, as I don't quite feel for the others. The decision to have very little travelling (taken no doubt in interest of economy) has been an unfortunate one.

The main saving grace of the training and in fact of our entire training is the Vice-Principal. He is great; splendid lecturer, an enthusiastic and competent administrator and a first class man—kind, understanding, sympathetic. But I am sure, even he wouldn't be very happy about this method of training a group like ours, which consists of people hand-picked, as a result of a stiff all-India exam and who have varied, and in many cases distinguished experience. The V.P. said one day that any amongst us could run the staff college. I am sure not all could run it, but many could, and at least do darned sides better job of lecturing than some of our lecturers.

And of course he is with us as far as our main grievance is concerned. Seven months ago, our results were announced. Four months ago, the training started, and to this day we don't know, which states we are going to, what seniorities and pays we shall get. I am sure the Home Ministry has its own difficulties in the matter. The states are alleged to have backed out of their commitments to take people from this batch. I don't know what the other difficulties are. But the failure to give out the terms and conditions under which we have to work is to say the least, undermining the morale of the people. There are so many selfish interests working against new entrants to the service that they are lucky if they can get a fair deal. The play of selfish interests completely blinds people including the Ministers apparently, to the fact that quality is needed to keep the reputation and efficiency of the service. The people in this batch are infinitely superior to the State service *wallahs* who have been promoted to the IAS, and to the C.S.S. *wallahs* who occupy positions in the Central Secretariat. The coming in of our batch will raise the tone of the services wherever they go. It is not always realized that services are what people manning them make them. If the I.C.S. is respected today, and C.S.S. is looked down upon, it is because of the quality of the people in them. If the IAS is to retain its prestige not only as the first service in the country, but more so as a group of people who can shoulder the most onerous administrative responsibilities, it must get the right kind of people into itself. The Special Recruitment was a splendid idea. Apart from a few people, the entrants through this method have brought different experience, excellent performances in their respective sphere of work, and intellectual ability into the service. On an average, because of their experience, they are better than the Metcalf House crowd. Yet they are being treated as if they were not wanted. I feel that such a method of recruitment should become a regular feature : a certain number of people, between the ages of 25 to 35, who have done good work in non-administrative fields or fields allied to administration should be regularly brought into the administration. They will enrich the Service and increase its capacity to handle the varied responsibilities which it will necessarily have to face in future.

I know that this idea is against the accepted pattern of recruitment to the Service and most of us being tradition minded could never appreciate it. That is why we feel very safe in increasing the Metcalf House quota, but extremely reluctant to introduce any innovation like this. We don't think out our own solutions to our needs and problems.

Once these questions of seniority pay etc. are settled, we shall all feel very much better. Personally, I am quite satisfied if I get my present pay and 7 years' seniority. This will give me a handicap of 3 years in comparison with chaps like Bhagat who joined in 1948 (as a result of 1947 exam) and perhaps five years in comparison to Bhatia and Pasricha.

But in life everything can't be by calculation. I won't mind that I have had varied and worthwhile experience. The American trip and the 8 years' experience with the Planning Commission have been very good. I wouldn't give them up; the varied experience which I have had will make me a better administrator, and of course, I am a happier man, with a broader vision, as a result of them when I go up in the administrative ladder. I am sure I shall need and shall be able to use everyone of the experiences—geography, population, regional planning, land use and soil conservations, community development, socio-economic investigations,—which I have had. I must conclude that God has been very kind and I am sure he will be kinder still in future. During the coming years, I shall be able to use my creative ability and capacity for performing whatever duties are assigned to me even better than so far. I am sure these duties will be much more significant and responsible than they have been so far. I am sure, I shall have to undertake administrative responsibilities and fill positions which will fully tax every ability, capacity and resource which I have. I shall be happy, if I get such opportunities. I think I shall do well in the administrative service, and shall be able to make a contribution to it and to the welfare of the people where I am posted.

I have heard a report from Hooja that the Rajasthan chaps are going to be given two years training in U.P. I am sure it is wrong. I can't see myself spending two years in U.P. in O.F.S. B.K.T. and some petty sub-divisions. I am sure this won't happen. I won't mind doing another short training course in revenue law in Rajasthan. But really, I would like to be just straight on the job in a sub-division in Rajasthan, and after sometime of this I would like to do something worthwhile. I want to do work in the Development Department, Census, Directorate of Economics and Statistics, etc. where I can with my experience make some contribution. The Census job I particularly want to do. I participated in the last Census (1951), and as it turned out, very significantly; I would like to this time also. If I became the Census Superintendent or Additional, I can make a real contribution and also keep up my interest. I wouldn't mind doing a planning job in the Development Department. They need such people in Rajasthan. The present Chief Minister is enthusiastic and means well. I hope they won't waste my talents; I won't waste my talents. I shall not fear and make the best of my twenty years in the service. The population/resources picture is about as bright in Rajasthan as anywhere, except Punjab. I forgot to mention two things I have desired very much to be Secretary of Rajasthan Canal Project. Irrigation will be the boon of Rajasthan and that canal will perhaps be the best irrigation project in

Rajasthan. As Secretary of the Project, I can do some regional planning, which I have always wanted, I can try out my ideas perfect techniques. This is one job which I look forward to. This was one reason, why I chose Rajasthan. It is possible to make Rajasthan another California. It is not easy: for one thing the people appear to be much less enterprising and enthusiastic, for another the pressure of population is greater in India. The Punjab example proves incidentally that people are greater than politics and that they may steadily forge ahead, while their politics is moribund and their Government comparatively inefficient.

Materially, I hope I shall be comfortable. I have been so far, with God's grace. I haven't much money but have always had enough. I am hoping that my pay will be protected. It is not possible to live on Rs. 600 a month. At 35, I must save something, and I have no right to make my children poor, and give them a handicap in life.

During the past year, I have been to the Food and Agriculture Organization (FAO) of the United Nations for a month. I am hoping to go again early next year. I want at some time in the future spend some years working in a responsible capacity in a U.N. Organization. It will be good, and I want to do it. I shall be able to make a solid contribution, I am sure, and in the process raise the prestige of my country also. If I go now, complete the Evaluation manual, and complete my advice to them on Evaluation techniques. I want this Evaluation paper to become a Manual on Evaluation. Hope Prof. Ghosh prints it as such. I should have explored my idea of writing the manual with Banners. If I go now, for the short assignment to FAO, I shall have much better chances of going later. I shall be known there and I shall be respected better here. If I do, this will mean a good financial gain. This will also enable me to strengthen the contacts with the F.A.O. which I have made. They must at least have the best possible education and training, and must have sufficient money to start them in life. Schieweli, Dr. Wahlem Aykroyd, Rao, and Autret—all these contacts can be very useful. Jacoby will be there for more than twenty years in the service of the FAO. Perhaps, by the fifties I shall be in a position within the UNO where I would be doing top level and really significant jobs. I would like to continue doing these for some time longer.

I don't know what I shall do about my desire to teach and do some independent research, write some books etc. I must do some of that before I retire. I have been working on a little monograph on Community Development. I haven't made much progress. I wanted to complete it before December. I want to make some contribution to my first love Geography also. But perhaps my more significant contribution will be to community development, population, regional planning, provided of course I get started.

New Delhi, January 1958

Increasingly, I am beginning to feel that as the ICS fellows leave, the rot which has already set in the administration will become evident, unless some strong remedial action is taken, and in time. The stark fact is that the administration is just not attracting the top quality young men who are needed to run it at even a minimum level of efficiency. Too many of the responsible positions at every level are being filled by promoted people who do not have the capacity for them. They are just very small, very incompetent men in very responsible positions. Giants like Tarlok, Goswami are becoming rare, and their places are being taken by figure heads—men who don't matter—who exist merely to occupy a room in the Secretariat and to have a name plate outside it.

I left Simla on December 19th, 1958. During the last few weeks, I was very homesick. I would have left a week earlier, if I had got the money from the Bank. Narainswamy's lethargy delayed everything and if it had not been for the almost heroic effort of Nangia—a young clerk from N.W.F.P.—we would never have got our pay.

From the 22nd to the 29th December, I underwent Secretariat training in the Ministry of Food and Agriculture. It was a joke in my case, but I renewed and reinforced my contacts with Nehemial, the Agricultural Extension Commissioner.

The chances of getting the senior scale and starting work which I like appeared bright. Mr. Dey had a few days earlier offered me a job as Vice Principle and Director of Research at the Institute of Community Development at Mussoorie, and had said that he would see to it that my field training in Rajasthan is expedited. Prof. Ghosh had repeated his desire to have me back in the P.E.O. I am not sure whether I shall take the Mussoorie job—I have been advised against by Prof. Karve and Dewan, persons whose advice I value very greatly. But it offers an opportunity of getting away from the field, if I want to do so. Coming to the P.E.O. has distinct disadvantages; both to the organization and to me. What I would like to do most, after a brief period in the field is to participate in making the Third Five Year Plan of Rajasthan. I have worked for eight years in the Planning Commission but have not been at the centre of plan making. I should like to be now. If I start with it in Rajasthan I can look forward to continuing the same kind of work at the centre, after some years. Dewan tells me that the post of Deputy Secretary Planning will fall vacant in March and that the Chief Secretary is already thinking of a few names for it. Tarlok Singh says that I must come back to Delhi after a few years in Rajasthan. I should like to do this job, and then get into the Central Pool. I think I must be there: nobody is better qualified, and I shall be able to do an excellent job there. I am looking forward to my work in Rajasthan—particularly planning and development work. But after a time, my place is in Delhi. And from Delhi, I must go for a few years to a good UN job and it shall not be evaluation of nutrition or something marginal. It shall be important, vital and at the centre of things.

For the moment, the Rome trip has receded into the background.[1] This has been another disadvantage of joining the service thanks to S.K. Dey who refused my release without even telling me. If I hadn't joined the IAS, I could have gone to Rome, and made perhaps Rs. 10,000, besides strengthening my contacts there. I also understand that three of the Directors in the Planning Commission—Mitra, Datar and Vyasulu are shortly being promoted to the posts of chiefs in the scale of Rs.1500 to 2000. If I had stayed in the P.E.O., I could have looked forward to a similar promotion, perhaps in another year. Monetarily, therefore, I haven't gained from the change at least not at present. But I hope that the monetary loss or lack of gain will be more than compensated by the opportunity of more creative work and better prospects in future.

On coming to Jodhpur, on the 1st of February, 1959, I was confronted with the order directing me to go to Nagaur for settlement training from the 1st February.

The order was conveyed by Mathur on phone to the Collector on the 30th January. This is a typical instance of how things are done, with utter disregard of the convenience of those concerned. True, as members of the Executive, we must be prepared to move any time; but we are also people, with families. As it is, I had just brought Kamla and the children along that very day, and we felt very disturbed, about having to go to Nagaur. The place has no accommodation; the teacher's house which I had arranged for my family in Jodhpur was not quite ready, and Kamla was completely unprepared for living alone, without me in this strange place. We had nearly decided that she and the children should go back to Delhi, when Hooja offered that the two families could stay together in their house. I am very glad about it, because it makes it possible for Kamla to stay.

Soon after my field training, on insistence from S.K. Dey, I was posted at the Central Institute for Community Development at Mussorie. After a few months stay at Mussorie, the author sought a posting as Collector where he could do research on social and economic change in village India. Dr. Nath was posted at Sawai Madhopur from 1960-62, where he along with his wife did intensive studies on 'Social and Economic Change in Village India'; based on the research he wrote several articles in various journals and the study based on a resurvey of the villages after 40 years, i.e. 2001, is included in the Volume '*Rural Development and Planning in India*' (forthcoming).

From 1963-66 he worked with the Natural resources and Urban Planning Divisions of the Planning Commission. He went on deputation with the UN from 1966-1970 to Kuwait. On being offered further assignments from the United Nations and refusal from the Government of India to allow him to take up another assignment, the author resigned from IAS. His experiences in the IAS and the United Nations are interestingly described in the publication— *Development a Saga of Two Worlds* (Concept Publishing Company Pvt. Ltd., 2002).

REFERENCE

1. The offer from the FAO came in 1959 and was turned down by the then Minster for Community Development, Mr. S.K. Dey, under whom the author was working then as Vice-Principal of the Institute of Community Development without even informing the author; this would have never happened if he was not an IAS officer.

10

Panchayati Raj—The Promise and the Prospects*

Introduction

Panchayati Raj with a three-tier structure of democratic institutions at the district, village and intermediate levels is proposed to be revived or rejuvenated through the central legislation which is before Parliament. This development follows three decades of mixed experience with the earlier institutions that were established in different states between 1959 and the early 1960s. Successful working of the earlier institutions would have contributed significantly to India's progress towards social and economic change and political development. But serious problems in their working or other reasons, led to disillusionment with them and their super session in a large number of states during the 1960s or the 1970s. Central legislation and the structural reforms in the institutions, undertaken in recent years in some states, hold the promise of greater success in the 1990s than in the 1960s, and of the institutions becoming a vital and vibrant component of Indian polity. The legislation and the reforms are reflection of the fact that, backed by appropriate statutory safeguards and endowed with adequate resources of finance and manpower, and decision-making powers, the institutions can achieve their enormous potential of contributing to social, economic and political change.

---

* The article was published in *The Journal of Institute of Public Administration.* A draft of the paper was also presented at the Symposium, "Panchayati Raj" held by the Centre for Area Development Action Research Studies, New Delhi in August 1989.

Objectives

Establishment of Panchayati Raj Institutions (PRIs) through the legislative process should have three principal objectives:

(i) It should contribute to meaningful participation by the people in local development;
(ii) It should reduce inter-group economic and social disparities and contribute particularly to alleviation of poverty and unemployment;
(iii) It should not affect adversely Centre-State relations, preservation of which forms the basis of our federal polity; and
(iv) It should promote bottom-up planning.

Some Preliminary Points

The context of 1989 and the early 1990s is very different from that of 30 years earlier. However, some of the structural constraints that led to disillusionment with the PRIs and abandonment of several earlier attempts at decentralized planning still remain. But their intensity and influence have weakened enough to warrant hope for more successful working of the new institutions. The differences and constraints are summarized below.

The Differences in Socio-Economic-Political Situation Between 1960s and 1990s, Conducive to Success of PRIs

(i) Much higher literacy and awareness among the rural people of both the potential and constraints of rural development programmes and of their own rights in a democratic state. Improvements in transport, greater rural-urban linkages, experience with the political process, over a period of more than four decades and widespread exposure to communication media—newspapers, radio and TV—are other factors contributing to the awareness.
(ii) 40 years of experience with working of rural development programmes—community development, IADP, Integrated Rural Development Programme (IRDP), national employment programme and others which have been undertaken in the last four decades.

The experience has demonstrated the potential and constraints on growth of output and income and improvements in levels of living of the rural people.

(iii) And the noteworthy success, perhaps the most upstart is IADP and extended green revolution which have contributed to spectacular increases in agricultural output in some areas (Punjab, Haryana, Western U.P.) and steady increases in output in others' such as the irrigated areas producing rice or other crops. On the other hand IADP and the NEP seem to have had negative limited influence on the position of rural-unemployment and under-unemployment.

(iv) Expansion of infrastructures and basic service facilities in most areas.

(v) Generally higher levels of living of large sections of the rural population.

(vi) Much greater rural-urban interaction, principally through greater participation of rural people, particularly the youth, in jobs in towns, and greatly increased production by the farmers of perishable foods for urban markets. The interaction is greatest in villages located within 15 km. of large towns.

On the other hand the hindrances are:

(i) Little redistribution of rural assets. Land reforms were stopped midstream due to strong opposition of large and middle level farmers.

(ii) Numbers of landless and marginal farmers are much higher due to increase in population and labour force, without significant increases in the cultivated area, or redistribution of the latter.

(iii) Increase in unemployment—rural and urban; replacement of hidden underemployment by open unemployment due to relatively slow growth in both the rural and urban economies.

(iv) Continuance (or increase) in economic disparities between the large and middle level farmers on the one hand and the marginal farmers and the landless labourers on the other. The large and middle farmers have benefited much more from increase in agricultural output and from most other rural development programmes, than have the small farmers and the landless. The latter have remained the rural poor.

(v) Greater awareness and discontent among the poor of the increasing economic disparities and unemployment.

(vi) The political process is well established, but is devoid of its post-Independence enthusiasm and idealism. Its means and ends are widely understood, and are regarded by the public objectively. It is now seen, rightly, as the principal means of obtaining and exercising political power. Obtaining economic benefits through it, including satisfaction of personal greed by the political executives, is recognized (though not accepted) as an inevitable accompaniment of the process.

(vii) The bureaucracy, state and local, is no longer seen as being independent or impartial. It is recognized and accepted as the hand maiden of the political executive. Its inefficiency, delays and greed are also recognized and largely accepted.

The Structural Constraints

(i) Among the constraints two are most important : those arising from the unegalitarian structure of our rural society, and those due to the unwillingness of the state level political executives and officials to delegate decision-making powers and transfer resources for implementation of development programmes to the PRIs.

The political, social and economic inequalities of rural society are well known. The large or middle level farmers, belonging generally to the dominating cultivating castes, are in positions of political power—as Sarpanches of village panchayats and as heads of Zilla Parishads and intermediate level institutions in most of the states. They have also economic power and social primacy. They controlled the earlier (or existing) Panchayati Raj Institutions and used them for their personal and class benefits and will, undoubtedly, try to control and use the new ones.

(ii) The rural elites have intimate linkages with higher level elites—Ministers, MLAs and MPs, most of whom have similar socio-economic backgrounds. But the linkages of leaders of the rural poor with their representatives at the State and Central levels have also increased and could increase more rapidly in future.

The provisions in the Central legislation for larger representation in the PRIs for the Scheduled Castes and

Scheduled Tribes could mitigate the constraint, but could not eliminate it.

State Level Constraints

(i) Unwillingness (or opposition) of the state level political executive—MLAs and Ministers—to decentralize decision-making to the heads of district or lower levels, particularly the heads of the Zilla Parishads or intermediate level institutions. Regardless of whether the heads belong to their own or other political parties, they are seen as potential competitors or antagonists.

And who wants competitors and antagonists?

(ii) Unwillingness of state level officials to decentralize decision-making to the PRIs. Within the technical departments, the unwillingness is stated to be due to lack of the specialized technical knowledge, which is essential for efficient and effective working of projects among the elected representatives. They maintain that their own departmental functionaries alone have the knowledge. The stock reply is, "the elected representatives cannot make the right decisions because they do not understand technical subjects".

On the contrary, there are trends towards further centralization among both the political executive and the bureaucracy. The trend extends to the Central Government. The proposed amendments in the Constitution of India and enactment by Parliament of the legislation on Panchayati Raj and Nagarpalikas, which are state subjects under the Constitution, is itself, being interpreted as evidence of the centralizing trend.

Paucity of Resources of Finance and Technical Manpower

Finance

(i) The taxes with the greatest yield and high potential for growth with economic development, such as central excise, import and export duties and income-tax, are with the Central Government. The Central Government raises also very large resources through domestic or external borrowings and deficit financing.

The State Governments have the remaining taxes with high yield and growth potential, notably the sales tax. They also receive large grants or loans from the Central Government for meeting their deficits on current or capital accounts. Grants or loans for centrally sponsored schemes are a major constituent of such transfers. Their proportion in the content of state plans has increased from about 44 per cent in 1980 to almost 75 per cent in 1987-88.

The scope for raising resources by the PRIs is limited. For them property tax is the main source of revenue with high yield and potential for steady growth. But these attributes of the tax are important only in urban areas where property values are high; both yield and growth potential are low in the rural areas.

(ii) The PRIs (and *Nagarpalikas*) are not willing to tax heavily their constituents for reasons that are well known. The elites which control them do not want to tax themselves, while the poor have low assets and incomes.

Manpower

Technical personnel, including executives of Zilla Parishads are deputed in most states from the revenue or technical departments of the State Governments. Creation of separate cadres of officials for these institutions has to be examined in depth and decisions taken, preferably through a consensus between the Central and State Governments.

There has been some real decentralization of power and resources to Panchayati Raj Institutions in recent years in a few states, notably, Karnataka, West Bengal, Andhra Pradesh and Kerala. The experience of these states will be of great interest for the future development of the PRIs. The initial experience with the reforms is encouraging, although an objective assessment of their potential and constraints (success or failure) and the factors contributing to these will become possible only after another two or three years.

The Prospect

These constraints remain, but their intensity and influence have been reduced because of the changes of the last 30 years. The rural elites see the need, indeed the compulsion, of accommodating the interest and aspirations of the Scheduled Castes, the Scheduled Tribes and other weaker sections of the community. They realize that accommodation is the only way to avoid confrontation and violent conflicts. The widespread conflicts in rural Bihar, as also those in parts of other states are a pointer in this direction.

The provisions relating to larger representation for the Scheduled Castes and Scheduled Tribes in the Central legislation could also contribute to greater accommodation between them and the rural elites.

There is greater appreciation with the State Governments also of the need for decentralization of decision-making powers and larger transfers of resources to the PRIs. The examples of the four states mentioned above, in which such decentralization has been effected, cannot be overlooked by the other State Governments. Increasing proportions of MLAs and Ministers in all states will progressively see the need for working through the leaders and members of the PRIs to retain and strengthen their local political bases. They may have to refine their techniques or forge new ones for such working, to achieve their objective.

Successful working of the new PRIs is by no means assured. But the changes of the last 30 years do hold the promise of more successful working now than in the 1960s. There will, of course, be large inter-state and intra-state variations in performance of the institutions; they are inevitable in a country of such large size and such regional diversity. But the differences in performance should lead to efforts for structural reforms to remove the weaknesses of the PRIs which are not doing well, rather than reversal of the whole process of democratic decentralization.

11

Decentralized District Planning under Economic Liberalization*

Introduction

The economic liberalization policy regime does not mean the end of planning. On the contrary, planning in India remains very much alive and continues to be the principal instrument of guiding the direction and growth of the national economy. The Eighth Five-Year Plan, 1992-97 was started in April 1992[1] and will, hopefully, be followed by the Ninth-Five Year Plan, 1997-2002.

The objectives, priorities and thrust areas of the Eighth Plan, its macro economic aggregates—level of public and private investments, rate of growth of GDP (total, sectoral and per capita), distribution of investment by sectors, programmes and major projects, target of increase in output in various sectors and financing—were decided by the National Development Council, which is presided over by the Prime Minister and has as its members, Chief Ministers of all the states and Union Territories and Central Ministers of Finance, Commerce, Industry, Agriculture, etc., who are most concerned with economic development. Similarly, macro economic and sectoral aggregates and allocation of public investment by sectors and projects have been or are being decided for the plans of States and Union Territories which have been formulated within the framework of the National plan.

Besides its role as the central guide to economic development, national and state level planning is also the mechanism through which national

---

* Published in "*Decentralized Planning in Multi-level Framework*", Eds. Rakesh Hooja & B. Yerram Raju, 1993, Rawat Publication, Jaipur.

goals and objectives of economic, social and political reform are articulated. The statements on the goals and objectives, and on policies and programmes to achieve them, reflect a national consensus, arrived at through discussions in various meetings and debates. Thus, planning is also a major instrument of economic, social and political integration of the country.

Annual Plans

Annual plans are the annual components of the five-year plans and are formulated every year by the same process of discussion between the Central Government and the Governments of States and Union Territories. The discussions on the annual plan for 1992-93, the first year of the Eighth Five-Year Plan, were held during February and March 1992, and implementation of the plan had also begun in April 1992. The content of the annual plans is similar to that of the five-year plan. However, trends in agricultural and industrial output, exports and imports, employment and availability of financial resources are given primary consideration in determining of the priorities and contents of the annual plan. Allocations for individual projects and programmes are decided keeping in view the variables mentioned above, as also progress on on-going projects and programmes, and on detailed preparation of new ones.

Economic Liberalization

Economic liberalization policies comprise industrial, trade and fiscal policies. Their central objective is to increase efficiency in the productive and service sectors of the economy by removing, or reducing progressively, the impediments to these. In case of the manufacturing sector, this objective is sought to be achieved by removing restrictions on location, capacity, output and pattern of equity participation of larger private sector industrial enterprises which had been imposed by the system of industrial licensing. The latter has been abolished for all but eighteen industries which include sensitive industries such as defense production and atomic energy.[2]

Economic liberalization policies also envisage greater private sector participation both in basic industries such as steel, coal and heavy engineering and in infrastructures such as power, transport and telecommunications (the outputs of which can be sold), which has been the preserve of the public sector since the mid-1960s. A number of public enterprises are proposed to be partly privatized, while several loss-making enterprises may be closed or sold. A number of private sector power generation projects have been approved in recent months and others are being examined. Mini and medium-sized pig iron and steel plants have all along been in the private sector. However, the private sector is also being encouraged to establish large steel plants with capacities of one million tons or more. A number of projects have been cleared by the concerned Ministries while others are being examined. On the other hand, several public enterprises are proposed to be privatized, wholly or in part, and several loss-making enterprises may be closed[3]. A National Renewal Fund has been established to take care of the interests of the effected workers.

A third objective of economic liberalization policies is to increase foreign investment in India both by transnational corporations and individuals, particularly non-resident Indians, with a view to increase the quantum of investment in the economy and also facilitate import of the most efficient industrial technology. The restrictions on such investment have been abolished and private foreign investment is being actively encouraged.

The trade policy package involved removing progressively the restrictions on imports and exports. The fiscal policies aim at reducing budgetary and balance of payment deficits. The budgetary deficit is sought to be reduced by curbs on expenditures, particularly non-developmental expenditures of the Central and the State Governments and the losses of public enterprises. Reduction of the budgetary deficit will reduce the inflationary pressures generated by the large budgetary deficits particularly during 1988-89 to 1990-91 and devaluation of the Indian rupee in July 1991.

It is hoped that (a) these measures will help make Indian industrial enterprises more efficient and competitive in the export markets, (b) India's exports will increase progressively with reduction in the trade and payment deficits, and (c) the Indian consumer will be served with manufactures of improved quality at international or lower prices and more efficient infrastructures and other services.

Three important points have to be noted in this connection :

(i) The new industrial policy announced by the present government in July 1991, constituted a quantum leap in a process that had been started in 1979. One indication of the latter is provided by progressive increase in the number of industrial enterprises that had been subject to licensing. A great majority of small and medium scale industrial enterprises were already outside the scope of industrial licensing.

(ii) The ELP package is being unfolded in stages. The budgets for 1991-92 (formulated in July 1991) and 1992-93 marked important stages in this process of unfolding. The import policies for the second half of 1991-92 and the first half of 1992-93 constitute similarly two stages in the unfolding of trade policies. Furthermore, the various statements in Parliament by the Finance Minister and the Prime Minister spell out their details and implications, which are elaborated further by the Governor of the Reserve Bank of India.

(iii) The price and trade policy packages would undergo further changes in the light of domestic and international developments. Two important factors militating against expansion of India's exports at present are the global recession and the economic collapse of the Soviet Union which was the most important market for India's exports.

Planning and Economic Liberalization

The relationship between planning and economic liberalization is better understood if we keep in view the fact that planning in India is indicative planning for a mixed economy with a small public sector and large organized and unorganized private sectors. It is not central planning for a command economy in which the entire productive and distributive system is controlled by the state. The public sector in India aims mainly at providing physical and social infrastructure services—electricity, water, transport, telecommunications, medical and public health, education and training, social welfare, etc. The public sector industrial and mining enterprises are confined mainly to coal, steel, heavy engineering and the heavy electrical industries. And even in some of these industries, private sector enterprises were allowed to continue and expand;[4] the share of the private sector in steel, heavy engineering and heavy electrical industries, in transport, power generation and other infrastructures, the outputs of which can be sold would increase progressively under economic liberalization. This is because private sector participation in these areas is not only being allowed but is also encouraged through various facilities and incentives provided to the prospective entrepreneurs.

Decentralized and District Planning

The central objective of decentralized and district planning is to provide basic services and satisfy urgently felt needs of the people, both rural and urban. It envisages their maximum participation in both formulation and implementation of the plans. Decentralized plans have also to be prepared within the overall framework of the national and state plans. Thus, their objectives, priorities, policies and programmes must be in conformity with those of the latter. Furthermore, their requirements of finance and manpower should be within the availability of these, from the local bodies and from the State Governments. Overlooking this aspect would undermine the entire planning process because there would be difficulties and delays in approval of the plans by State Governments and further delays and shortfalls in their implementation.

Plans for districts, community development blocks/talukas/mandals and villages are prepared for their respective jurisdictions by the Zilla Parishads, the intermediate level institutions (CD block/taluka/mandal), *samitis* and the village panchayats in predominantly rural districts. However, in about 150 districts, one-third of the total of 446 districts in the country, in which the proportion of the urban population is higher than the national average of 25.7 per cent (the actual proportions vary from 25 to 100 per cent), the municipal bodies—municipal corporations, municipal committees, cantonment boards, notified area committees, etc., have also an important role in planning for their respective jurisdictions.

Moreover, in the large metropolitan cities (with population of 500,000 or more) for which development authorities have been established, they have the principal role in development planning. Indeed, the long-term development plans prepared by the authorities have pre-eminence in the areas covered by them. The latter include besides the agglomeration of the large cities, considerable rural areas. The panchayats of the rural areas covered by the plans may not engage in any activity which constitutes a violation of the development plan drawn up by the development authority. The most common violation is sale by panchayats and/or individuals for residential, industrial, commercial or other uses of lands which had been reserved under the development plan for public purposes such as location of educational and medical institutions, parks and other recreation areas[5].

History of Decentralized and District Planning

Formulation of district plans goes back to the mid-fifties when the second Five-Year Plan was being formulated by the Planning Commission. The Commission asked the State Governments to get district plans prepared through the Development Advisory Committees to be constituted especially for this purpose[6]. However, since the total expenditure projected in these plans was several times greater than the funds available for them, the plans were not implemented and the idea of preparation of district plans itself was given up.

But, there is no alternative to formulation of district plans in the radically changed context of the early 1990s. There is a national consensus among all political parties on revival or revitalization of both the Panchayati Raj Institutions and urban local bodies which have remained under suspension for long periods in several states. Formulation of plans for their respective jurisdictions is, or should be, an important function of these institutions. In a number of states notably Karnataka, West Bengal and Kerala, Panchayati Raj Institutions with greatly enhanced functions and resources were established during the 1980s and have been encouraged to formulate development plans for their respective areas. Elections to municipal bodies have also been held during the last two or three years in a number of states, including Uttar Pradesh and Haryana, where they had not been held for almost two decades and the municipal areas had been administered by administrators appointed by the State Governments.

Plans for districts and lower level aeria units must contain a programme for employment generation[7], keeping in view the magnitude of unemployment and underemployment. The programme will also contribute to alleviation of poverty by providing gainful employment and income to the poor. Such programmes should be undertaken in both the rural and urban areas.

The Process of Decentralized Planning : Planning from Below and Planning from Above

Plans for districts, villages and intermediate units such as talukas mandals or community development blocks can be formulated either through planning from below or planning from above. Planning from below involves preparation of plans by panchayats or villages or multi-village circles in consultation with the leaders of the villages concerned. They would be formulated by assessment of local needs, development potential, resources and constraints. Decentralized planning is most meaningful—it meets the urgently felt needs of the people best and can elicit their maximum cooperation through contribution of cash, labour, materials, etc. in construction works and effective use of service facilities—if planning from below is the dominant process in it. But planning from below is not easy and it is time-consuming. Obtaining agreement of all the leaders and groups involved in preparation of the plan for a village or multi-village circle takes time. Furthermore, personnel from the technical departments have to be deputed to the panchayats to assist them in preparation of the plans. They must ensure that the plans keep in view the guidelines of their departments in respect of availability of finance and manpower and achievement of targets etc. Finally, the village or multi-village plans need to be modified and adjusted before they can be included in the plan for the CD block/taluka/ mandal. A similar process of adjustment of plans for these units has to be undertaken to formulate the district plan.

Planning from above means breakdown by districts and smaller units of state level targets of accomplishments, allocation of resources of finance, technical personnel, etc., and is done mainly by the district and lower level officials of various technical departments on the basis of their assessment of the needs and development potentials of the units within their jurisdiction. Thus, the agricultural development plans for districts and CD blocks would be prepared by the district and block level agricultural officers by breaking down, for their respective districts and blocks, the state level agricultural plan. A similar procedure would be followed by district and block level officials of industrial, educational, medical and public health, and social welfare departments. The plans would be prepared in consultation with the PRIs, of course. But they would be governed by the detailed directives for their preparation issued by the heads of the respective technical departments.

Planning from above has the following advantages :

(i) It is expeditious;
(ii) Technical personnel, viz., the district, block and lower level officials of technical departments are generally available;
(iii) There is no problem of adjustment of district and lower level plans with the state plan; and
(iv) Implementation of the plans is virtually assured.

Decentralized Planning under Economic Liberalization

Decentralized planning and economic liberalization have such different objectives and levels of operation that, at first sight, it appears that economic liberalization would have little, if any, effect on decentralized planning. However, a little reflection will show that the effects are profound and far-reaching.

If economic liberalization policies are successful, they would lead to faster economic growth, particularly through more rapid expansion in the non-agricultural sectors—industries and services—which would mean larger employment in these sectors. The greatest spatial effects would be in the large metropolitan cities and their peripheral regions, which stretch long distances along the principal highways radiating from them. Expansion of industrial enterprises, particularly large and medium-sized enterprises, would take place mainly in the peripheral regions : enterprises would seek peripheral locations in order to avail of relatively lower cost of land while retaining the advantages of linkage with the cities, provided by their physical, economic and social infrastructures.

Most small and medium-sized enterprises would, however, continue to be concentrated in the metropolitan cities.[8] Small enterprises having backward and forward linkages with large enterprises could be located both in the cities and in the peripheral regions in the vicinity of large enterprises. Examples of the latter would be enterprises providing components and spares and repair and maintenance services to the larger enterprise, or those processing their outputs. Industrial expansion would mean corresponding or greater employment in the service sectors.

Effects on the Rural Areas

Manufacturing and service sector enterprises would draw, especially at the beginning, skilled labour and professional personnel mainly from the cities[9] and only unskilled labour from the surrounding villages. But with the spread of industrial and service skills in the rural areas, more and more skilled workers would also be drawn from them.

Employment in industries and services would mean higher incomes for the rural people who would lead, in turn, to higher and more diversified consumption and spread of urban life styles among them. The positive effects of these changes on consumption would range from quantitative increase and qualitative improvement in food such as milk, vegetables and fruit through acquisition of durable consumer goods such as gas stoves, refrigerators, and TV sets, to living in *pucca* houses having electricity, water and indoor toilet facilities. Other effects would include increase in literacy and education (including vocational and technical education), improvement in health and nutrition, primarily through use of modern medicine, greater attention to personal hygiene and weakening of traditional taboos and social restrictions. The negative effects would range from increase in drinking and use of drugs to prostitution, crime and other social evils.

Since industrial entrepreneurs would be under little obligation to locate in backward regions, regional disparities in economic development could increase in the short-to-medium terms. Over a longer period, however, industry would go to backward regions also partly to avail of the incentives offered by the State Governments for locating there. There would also be greater rural-to-urban migration and combination of rural living and urban work in the peripheral regions of the metropolitan cities.

Effects on Decentralized Planning

The PRIs for the districts which form part of urban agglomeration have to prepare development plans for their respective jurisdictions keeping these trends and developments in view. Thus, the *zilla parishad*, the *panchayat samitis* and *panchayats* of a district like Khera in Gujarat or Gurgaon in Haryana must prepare the development plan for the district keeping in view the expansion in industries and services that are taking place and those that are expected in the foreseeable future. The plans will also have to be flexible so that they can be rapidly adjusted to accommodate new developments such as the location of a large manufacturing unit or training institute. The industries and service enterprises located in these districts would mean larger revenues for the PRIs. But they would also make greater demands on their finances and technical manpower to meet their needs for land and physical and social infrastructures.

Appendix I

That economic liberalization and planning can proceed simultaneously as illustrated by the following four news items appearing in *The Times of India*, New Delhi of March 8, 1992. p. 7.

- Prime Minister's call to increase exports.
- Government clears three major coal projects.
- Outlay for Punjab (Annual Plan 1992-93) fixed at Rs. 1,500 crores.
- Rs. 3,853 crores annual plan (1992-93) for U.P.

The first item relates to the Prime Minister's speech on the occasion of laying the foundation stone for a large private sector project which has a large potential for export promotion and import substitution. The second item relates to three major projects for expansion of output of coal for meeting the needs of coal-burning thermal plants. The last two items are self-explanatory.

PM's Call to Increase Exports

(*The Times of India News Service*, Nagpur. March 7,1992)

Nagpur, March 7 : The Prime Minister, Mr. P.V. Narasimha Rao, today urged industrialists to increase their export targets.

The Prime Minister arrived here on a day's visit. He addressed a public meeting at Maudha, about 33 km. from here, after dedicating two industrial plants to the nation and laying the foundation stone of a third.

Mr. Rao said that though the present foreign exchange position was comfortable, it was not enough to meet the country's requirements.

He said petroleum products, fertilizers and edible oils were still imported. The country's production of these items was not enough to meet the requirements.

Mr. Rao arrived at Maudha by helicopter after landing at Nagpur airport and drove straight to the Rs. 23 crore Visakha Industries plant manufacturing synthetic blended yarn. The plant is already commissioned and this year would reach the export figure of $ 5 million.

From there, Mr. Rao arrived at the sprawling 120 acre Pennar Aluminium Company Limited which is putting up a Rs. 90 crore plant which will manufacture sophisticated value added aluminium products.

From Maudha, the Prime Minister flew to Kalameshwar where he laid the foundation stone of a cold rolling mill, a Rs. 250 crore plant of Nippon Denso Ispat Complex, a Mittal group company. Incidentally, all the three plants are promoted by industrialists from the PM's home state, Andhra Pradesh.

Government Clears three Major Coal Projects

(The Times of India News Service)

New Delhi, March 7 : The Government has cleared three major coal projects to be implemented at a total cost of Rs. 2,137.93 crore.

A new project approved by the Government is the Kalinga opencast of the South-Eastern Coalfields. The project, located in the Talcher coalfields in Orissa, will cost Rs. 485.77 crore and will have an annual output of eight million tonnes of coal when completed. Coal from this project will be supplied to coastal thermal plants.

The Government has also cleared the expansion of Nyvelli Lignite mine-I at a cost of Rs. 1,336.93 crore. With this expansion, coal output from this mine will go up to 10.5 m.t. from the present level of 6.5 million tonnes per annum.

The third project concerns the extension of the service life of the 600-MW thermal power plant of the Nyvelli Lignite Corporation for another fifteen years. This project will cost Rs. 315.23 crore.

Coal production in the country during 1990-91 was estimated at 201.73 million tonnes. It is projected to go up to 306 million tonnes by the terminal year of the Eighth Plan.

The Union Budget for 1992-93 provides for an allocation of Rs. 14,998 crore for the energy sector of which the share of the coal sector is Rs. 2,683 crore.

Rs. 3,853 crore Annual Plan for Uttar Pradesh
(The Times of India News Service)

New Delhi, March 7 : The annual plan of U.P. for 1992-93 has been fixed at Rs. 3,853 crore, Rs. 150 crore more than last year's plan in money terms.

The plan was finalized at a meeting yesterday between the Deputy Chairman of the Planning Commission, Mr. Pranab Mukherjee and the Chief Minister, Mr. Kalyan Singh, who gave an assurance that the state would mobilize additional revenue to the tune of Rs. 150 crore in 1992-93.

The additional tax effort will reflect on the 1992-93 Budget to be presented by the State Finance Minister on March 12.

Outlay for Punjab Fixed at Rs. 1,500 crore

New Delhi, March 7. P.T.I. : Punjab will have a plan outlay of Rs. 1,500 crores, including Rs. 90 crore as loan from financial institutions for 1992-93.

This was decided at a meeting here today between the Planning Commission, Deputy Chairman, Mr. Pranab Mukherjee and the Chief Minister, Mr. Beant Singh.

The current year's revised plan outlay of the state is Rs. 1,000 crore.

In his introductory remarks, the Deputy Chairman stressed the need to complete the ongoing projects instead of taking up new projects.

Punjab, he said, had tremendous development potential and should be able to regain its position among the front ranking states.

The Chief Minister referred to the special problems of the state, especially those relating to power and irrigation, transport and education.

The meeting also discussed the crucial point in development like utilization of groundwater resources and forestation.

NOTES

1. The two-year interval between completion of the Seventh Five-Year Plan, 1985-90 and beginning of the Eighth Plan was filled in by annual plans for 1990-91 and 1991-92.
2. The industries are listed in Annex II. p. 22 of The Statement on Industrial Policy, issued by the Ministry of Industry on July 24, 1991. Annex I of the statement gives the proposed list of eight industries to be reserved for the public sector. Annex III lists thirty-four industries for which there will be automatic approval of foreign technology agreements and for foreign quality participation. The statement contains a detailed survey of the industrial policies followed since Independence. The survey concentrates on explaining the progressive changes in the policies keeping in view the national priorities and needs. It also emphasized how the new industrial policy constitutes a continuation of the same process of evolution and why the changes incorporated in it are needed keeping in view national and international developments.
3. Statement on Industrial Policy, pp. 18-19.
4. Along with establishment of five public sector steel plants, the two existing plants—the Tata's located at Jamshedpur and of the Indian Iron and Steel Company—were modernized and allowed to expand.
5. This practice is widespread and constitutes a serious impediment in the implementation of the second development plan for Delhi and the Regional Plan 2001 of the National Capital Region. The principal reason for the practice is high prices of land in the DMA, so much so that sales of even small areas of land by a Panchayat would bring amounts far in excess of the annual revenues of the panchayats.
6. In states like U.P., a Planning and Development Department was created to consolidate the district plans into a plan for the state and overseeing implementation of the district plan becomes the most important responsibility of the Planning Department.
7. The programmes, such as the national employment programme, which aimed at providing gainful employment and income to the landless and the marginal farmer and other rural poor, have been implemented for long periods. The

Jawahar Rozgar Yojana, started in 1989 constituted a major intensification of the programme. However, similar programmes have not been undertaken in the urban areas in most states despite the fact that the problems of unemployment and underemployment of the urban poor, especially recent migrants to the cities are widespread. The programmes in the urban areas should concentrate on providing shelter and basic service facilities to the urban poor. The land development and housing programmes, particularly the slum improvement programme, are the most suitable for the urban areas.

8. The reasons for the concentration are explained in the author's Goa University lecture, "Growth of Metropolitan Cities", January 1991 (Unpublished).
9. The author's field survey in 1990 of two new industrial centres, Bhiwadi (Rajasthan) and Dharu Heda (Haryana), located about 25 km. from Delhi and producing a wide variety of products for the Delhi market, revealed that nearly all the skilled workers and professionals commuted to work from Delhi and only unskilled workers came from the surrounding villages.

REFERENCE

Government of India, Ministry of Industry : *The Statement on Industrial Policy*, July 24, 1991.

12

The Role of Technical Departments under Panchayati Raj*

With the establishment of Panchayati Raj Institutions, the rural development activities of the State which were hitherto being carried out by the Community Development Organization have been transferred to the former. In addition, in most States certain activities formerly carried out by the departments of the State or by local bodies like District Boards have also been transferred. Thus in Rajasthan, the *Panchayat Samitis* have been given responsibility for primary education which was formerly under the Education Department and certain rural works earlier carried out by the District Boards (where they existed), besides the activities of the C.D. agency. The resources—technical personnel, supplies and most of the funds—needed for carrying out all these activities are provided by the technical departments of the State Government which also provide guidance in regard to major policies as well as the specific schemes to be taken up in their respective fields. In other words, the role of the departments is one of providing technical, organizational and financial support to the local institutions for carrying out their developmental responsibilities, and giving policy directions in respect of these. This chapter is confined to the experience of Panchayati Raj Institutions in Rajasthan.

Nature of Relationships

The precise nature of this relationship and the extent, to which the departments and local institutions interact in execution of development programmes, will be clear from the following example of the Agriculture Department :

---

* Published in *Indian Journal of Public Administration*, Vol. VIII, No. 4, pp. 512-521.

Staff

The Department provides to the *Panchayat Samitis* Agricultural Extension Officers, Compost Inspectors and other technical staff needed for the agricultural extension programme. These are recruited by the Department, are borne on its cadres, and are deputed to work in *Panchayat Samitis* for specified periods. During the period of deputation, however operational control over them rests entirely with *Samiti* to which they are deputed, which also exercises considerable administrative control over them. Their departmental superiors—the District Agricultural Officers—are concerned primarily with providing technical guidance and other assistance needed by them in carrying out their extension activities.

Supplies

The Department, as the technical adviser to the *Samitis*, recommends particular varieties of improved seeds, fertilizers, pesticides, improved implements, etc., to be used in the *Samiti* areas. These recommendations are made by the District Agricultural Officers keeping in view the physical conditions, cropping patterns and previous experience with improved practices in the area of each *Samiti*. The Department also assists the *Panchayat Samitis* in securing supplies of these. In case of improved seed, where the quantities involved are large, the responsibility for purchase and distribution has been transferred entirely to the *Samitis* and cooperative agencies; the Department's role being confined to the giving of technical advice. But in case of supplies like pesticides, for which the demand is limited and subject to fluctuations because usage is not widespread, the Department may itself procure supplies and distribute them to the *Samitis*. The policy of the State is that the entire supplies work should be handled by cooperative institutions, that each *Panchayat Samiti* should make arrangements with them for obtaining its supplies and that the role of the Department should be only that of a technical adviser. However, until these arrangements are fully developed or in case of commodities which are in limited demand, the Department has often to assume greater responsibility.

Finance

All the funds required for salaries of extension staff and other administrative expenses, and loans and subsidies for various schemes are provided by the State Government. As regards funds for supplies, the actual financial arrangements are often quite elaborate, because a number of agencies are involved; but the chief point is that financial responsibility for supplies does not fall on the *Panchayat Samitis*, but is borne by the State Government either directly or through appropriate arrangements with the cooperative institutions.

Planning of Programmes

The Department has an important role in the planning of agricultural programmes in the *Samiti* areas. The specific development schemes to be taken up in *Samiti* areas are indicated by it. The magnitudes (targets) for each scheme are also decided by the Department on the recommendations of Extension Officers working in the *Samitis* and the District Level Officers, which in turn are based on experience of working of the schemes in the *Samiti* areas and attitudes of the *Samiti* members towards them. Other factors like availability of funds for a scheme with the department and the place which it occupies in the priorities of the Department play even more important part in the final determination of targets. The result is that the targets do not always reflect the demands of the *Samitis* and it is found that demands in respect of some schemes remain unsatisfied while there are unutilized funds under others.

This pattern of relationship between the technical departments and the administrative agency executing rural development programmes was evolved in the Community Development Blocks and has been inherited by the *Panchayat Samitis* as successors to the Blocks. The principal object in establishing this relationship was to secure inter-departmental coordination in execution of development programmes in the block areas. It was argued that different departments are approaching the cultivators for adoption of their programmes independently, there is no coordination between them; he cannot adopt improvements or facilities propagated by one department and support services for which fall within the sphere of another department, also become available. Thus, recommended agricultural practices cannot be adopted unless credit is made available by the cooperative societies; the quality of livestock cannot improve unless the cropping pattern is changed and fodder crops are grown, etc. Therefore, the best results can be achieved if the activities of the different development departments are cocoordinated by a single administrative agency and the cultivator is reached only through it. The administrative structure of the C.D. Block with the multi-purpose Village Level Worker at the bottom, a team of Extension Officers, one for each field to guide him, and a Block Development Officer having control over them all, was designed with this object in view.

But, this arrangement under which the entire resources of a technical department of the State are placed at the disposal of a local institution and the department has to work through it for carrying out programmes for which it is responsible at the State level, has certain problems inherent in it. These are discussed below. Two points may however be noted at the outset :

(i) Some arrangement of this kind is essential if the local institutions are to be enabled to discharge their development responsibilities at all; because in the present stage of their development, it is inconceivable that they could either raise adequate finances or build up the technical staff and organization needed for executing the development programmes. Resources have to be organized by the State Government and transferred to local institutions. As regards finance, the difficulties being experienced by the *Panchayat Samitis* in raising even the small resources assigned to them bring out the very real problem of taxation by local bodies having jurisdiction over small areas. The situation will undoubtedly improve in course of time, and as these institutions get established and grow in strength they will be able to raise larger revenues than they can do at present. But even then, the major portion of the funds required for implementation of development programmes will have to be transferred to them by the State Government. This is so even in advanced countries like the U.K. where local institutions are much better developed than in India. The entire modern trend in public finance appears to favour "central" as opposed to "local" taxation, with the result that transfer of resources from a central agency (National or State Government) to local institutions becomes inevitable.

(ii) The technical cadres and organizations have similarly to be built up at the State level and then placed at the disposal of the local institutions. Because of the technical nature of the tasks involved, employment of well trained and fairly highly paid staff becomes necessary. Moreover, these have to be supported by technical specialists and institutions like research stations and workshops, so that they can function effectively. All this can be done only at the State level under the auspices of the technical department concerned.

This is not to argue that the present pattern of relationship between the *Panchayat Samitis* and technical departments is the only possible one or that there is no room for improvements or even structural changes in it. These are possible and will undoubtedly be made as more experience is gained with the working of the pattern in different States. The main point of the argument is that some such pattern has to be evolved because the premises on which it is based are inevitable in the present situation.

Acceptance of this fact and adoption of similar patterns is essential for solving the problems of municipalities and other local bodies for urban areas. The major weakness of these bodies also is inadequacy of funds, staff and organization for carrying out their civic, administrative and developmental responsibilities. At present, each urban local institution has to raise its own funds and build up its own administrative and technical organization; but since most of them are quite unable to do so an atmosphere of helplessness, stagnation, inefficiency and frequently corruption prevails in them. This situation is not likely to change radically in the near future, because the difficulties about raising resources and building up technical and administrative organizations which have been mentioned above for *Panchayat Samitis* apply also to all but the largest municipalities. Therefore, State initiative in raising resources and building up technical and administrative cadres is just as necessary in their case as in that of the *Panchayat Samitis*.

Problems

The problems and disadvantages of this system of relationships between the technical departments and local institutions can be classified into two main categories :

(i) From the point of view of the technical departments, the main drawback is loss of advantages of 'line administration';

unity and directness of supervision; simplicity of staff relationships; direct responsibility for execution of programmes, etc.

(ii) For the local institution, the main disadvantage is limitation of its initiative, self-reliance and if one may use the word "independence".

The various difficulties and problems which one hears so much about in the field and some of which are discussed below are seen on analysis to be related to one or the other of these two categories of problems.

It should be made quite clear that these problems are inherent in the system. Their magnitude can be reduced by appropriate improvements in administrative procedures and through better understanding of the mechanics of the system by officials and non-officials. Thus development policies, methods of programme planning, procedures for coordination between the technical departments and local institutions, delegation of powers to departmental functionaries at different levels can be constantly reviewed and improved so as to meet the need of the system better. Training programmes can be organized for members of the local institutions and for officials of the departments so that there is better understanding of objectives of development programmes, of the specific role of departments and local institutions in these, and of the ways in which officials and non-officials can cooperate most effectively. It is the responsibility of the Development Department of the State Government to organize such training programmes as also to take the initiative in bringing about the necessary improvements in administrative procedures. Considerable work has been done in both these directions in Rajasthan, as in other State, but further action is constantly required.

However, all these steps while they will improve the efficiency of the system, and reduce the magnitude of the problems, cannot eliminate them altogether. The existence of these problems has to be accepted as a necessary part of the system. If in case of any particular programme it is found that working through this system continues to be unsatisfactory and the only remedy is direct working by the technical department concerned, such a programme should be transferred to that department. Similarly, an activity for which the local institutions are in a position to take complete responsibility should be transferred to them. But for most development programmes, joint participation of technical departments and local institutions will be necessary and the problems of the system will continue to be faced. In order to bring out the kinds of difficulties which arise in the field, let us examine a problem each from the major categories mentioned above and two other problems, relating to organizational deficiency of technical departments and the staffing pattern of the *Panchayat Samitis*. The first guidance to Extension Officers is primarily an administrative problem for the departments; while the second, allocation of funds for programmes, is concerned mainly with autonomy of the *Panchayat Samitis*. The last two do not arise from the relationship between the departments and the *Samitis* but they affect the working of development programmes and influence the attitudes of officials and non-officials about this system of relationships. Discussion of these two problems has, therefore, been included to obtain a better understanding of the field situation in which this system is functioning.

(i) Guidance to Extension Officers

The pattern envisages that operational and administrative control over Extension Officers should rest with *Panchayat Samitis* while technical guidance is provided to them by the District Level Officers. For the latter, this necessarily means a considerable dilution in authority over Extension Officers because not only can they not order their movements or ask them directly to undertake specific tasks (they must request the *Vikas Adhikaris* for this purpose), but their power to pull up the inefficient, sluggish or the indifferent workers and to reward the efficient ones for good work also gets limited. They may not, therefore, feel as much responsibility for the performance of the Extension Officers as they would when they were directly under their control. The Extension Officers on their part may feel that they do not have enough support of District Level Officers. Many may feel insecure that they are subject to control of a political body which judges them not so much by their technical competence or efficiency as by the relationship which they can establish with influential members of the body. Some Extension Officers establish good relations with powerful people in *Panchayat Samiti* and use this fact to short circuit the authority of the District Level Officers and *Vikas Adhikaris*. Those who fail to do so find that their work comes in for frequent criticism in the *Panchayat Samiti* which they feel is unmerited. Secondly, the

District Level Officers have to get their recommendations accepted by the *Samiti* before it will take action on them. There are occasions when they find that the *Samiti's* decision depends upon its internal group politics, and their technical advice does not get full acceptance. These political factors are particularly important in such matters as grant of *taccavi* loans or subsidies for various schemes, and purchase of supplies or equipment, i.e. matters in which individuals or groups are benefited. The District Level Officer may find that these benefits are given not to people who are most deserving or best able to make the necessary effort to execute the particular scheme but to those who are supporters of powerful persons in the *Samiti*. He may also find that the *Samiti* does not take the prescribed action against these people when they fail to abide by the conditions of the grant, or even to execute the scheme at all. He may in consequence, feel that technical considerations are sacrificed to local group politics, that resources are being wasted and that his technical advice is not heeded.

All these difficulties do arise in one *Panchayat Samiti* or another, and there are District Level Officers whose thinking is dominated by the increased difficulties of supervising their Extension Officers and getting their technical recommendations accepted by the *Samitis*. On the other hand, it must be stated also that with the greater awareness of developmental needs among the rural people, the interest in development activities, the competition between villages to secure benefits from development schemes, the vigilant supervision over activities of Extension Officers which many *Sarpanches* display, the more realistic appraisal of field problems, the eagerness with which a scheme which is wanted is taken up and that which is not wanted is ignored, are also appreciated by many District Level Officers who feel that their task has been facilitated after the formation of the *Panchayat Samitis*.

(ii) Allocation of Funds for Programmes

On the side of the *Panchayat Samitis*, the complaint is often heard that all planning is done at the State level, that schemes along with all their details are decided by the departments and that all that they are required to do is to execute them. However, whenever this complaint is discussed in some detail with members of the *Samitis* it is frequently found that the grievance is not against detailed guidance. Most of the responsible members of *Samitis* realize that such guidance is essential and that there would be enormous wastage of funds if it were not there. The grievance is really against non-availability of adequate funds for the keenly felt needs of the local people while funds and other resources are available for other schemes which are not wanted. Thus a *Panchayat Samiti* may find that only limited funds are available for *taccavi* loans for irrigation wells for which there is keen demand and large number of applications have to be rejected or kept pending for long periods, or that grants are not available for school buildings even though these are badly needed and many *Panchayats* are willing to contribute their share for these; but funds are available for contour bunding or assistance to certain village industries for which there is very little demand. This difficulty is due partly to the fact that National or State planning priorities are often different from local aspirations and needs. Thus, if increase in food production has been given higher priority over local works, there may be unutilized funds in the schemes under the former while the demands remain unsatisfied in the latter schemes. To the extent that this is so, a disparity between availability of resources and local needs cannot be avoided. But within this broad limitation, there is always considerable scope for closer adjustment of resources to local needs and every effort should be made to achieve this. One way of achieving this is, of course, delegation of powers of reappropriation of funds from one scheme to another to the *Panchayat Samitis* themselves. Several important steps have already been taken in this direction in Rajasthan. But there is need for constant review and taking further steps as and when necessary.

(iii) Organizational Deficiency of Technical Departments

There is continued inadequacy of organization and resources for meeting the demands placed on them in case of several important technical departments. Take the example of the Department of Agriculture again. With the progressive expansion of the extension organization under the C.D. agency (not *Panchayat Samitis*), the responsibility of the Agriculture Department to provide technical guidance to extension staff in finding solutions to problems of cultivators, in arranging supplies and equipment needed for adoption of improved practices, and in providing basic facilities and institutions to serve the needs of extension workers have increased enormously. The departmental organization has, of course, been considerably strengthened in recent years to meet all these needs. However, important deficiencies still remain and the organization is nowhere equal to the tasks that it has to perform. In

Rajasthan, as in most other States, the Department has only one District Level Officer in each district. During the last few years, specialists of the level of agricultural assistants have been added to his staff to provide guidance in specialized branches like agronomy, soil science, plant protection, etc. Most of these are young men, fresh from universities with little experience of field problems. The number, calibre and status of these specialists will have to be progressively raised in future so that specialist advice in these branches is available to cultivators near enough to the field. Similarly, experiment and research facilities of the Department will have to be progressively increased in order to meet more adequately the needs of the extension staff and in order especially to ensure that the cultivators' problems are quickly brought for solution to the research workers and the results of research are taken back to the cultivators.

The supply organization has been greatly expanded and strengthened with the development of co-operative agencies but further strengthening is necessary.

(iv) Staffing Pattern of the Panchayat Samitis

Another difficulty arises from continuance without adequate modification of the basic staffing pattern of one Extension Officer for each field of development activity—agriculture, animal husbandry, cooperation, village industries, etc. This pattern was evolved in the C.D. Blocks and served the very useful purpose of ensuring that all fields of development activity comprising within the scope of the block agency, received attention. However, modifications are needed in this basic pattern in the light of experience and changing quantum of work in different fields or in the same field in different *Samitis*.[1] Thus in an average *Panchayat Samiti*, there is serious disparity between the work-load carried by the Sub-Deputy Inspector of Schools (S.D.I.) or the Agricultural Extension Officer on the one hand and the Industries Extension Officer, Sheep and Wool Extension Officer or Compost Inspector on the other. An average *Samiti* has 60 to 80 primary schools with 100 to 150 (in some cases even more) school teachers. The routine administrative work connected with supervision of functioning of so many schools is so large that one S.D.I. can barely cope with it. As a result, the quality of supervision suffers, and what is more, there is no time left for giving technical guidance to teachers in improving the quality of instruction. The Agricultural Extension Officer is similarly heavily worked. Agriculture being the most important field of extension activity, he has to bear the greater share of responsibility for supervision of *Gram Sewaks*. Secondly, the administrative tasks connected with supplies of seed and fertilizers, and grant of loans and subsidies are sufficient to keep him quite busy. The other Extension Officers mentioned above have comparatively little work. Some of them who are posted in *Samitis*, in which the schemes of their Department are not proving acceptable for one reason or the other, have very little work indeed.

These disparities are not likely to disappear with passage of time; on the contrary, they are more likely to be accentuated. Thus, the workload in the field of primary education will increase progressively as the goal of universal primary education is approached. Similarly, in case of agriculture the workload is likely to increase. There is need, therefore, for making a realistic re-assessment of present and expected future work-loads in each field of development activity and making adjustments in the staffing pattern in the light of this re-assessment.

Conclusion

The pattern of relationships which has been evolved between the Technical Departments of the State Governments and the Panchayati Raj Institutions is a response to the situation in which the institutions have to assume responsibility for development programmes, but the resources for implementing these programmes have to be built up by the State Governments and transferred to them. This pattern is one way of solving this problem; other countries have evolved other ways of meeting the same situation. Certain problems and difficulties are inherent in the present pattern of relationships. Nevertheless, acceptance of the fact that some such pattern is inevitable in all fields of development activity in which joint participation of the departments and local institutions is desired, and constant work towards reducing the problems arising from this pattern are necessary for its smooth functioning. The scope of the pattern could, of course, be carefully defined, and activities in which the disadvantages of joint participation continue to outweigh its advantages, could be taken out of the system and carried out directly by the Technical Department or the local institution as the case may be. But in all fields to which the system is applied it should be accepted with all its implications by all concerned.

Appendix I

Major Projects and Related Inputs

I. Major Irrigation Project

A. Associated Inputs

(i) Transport (road, rail) facilities needed for movement of equipment, supplies and personnel needed for the project, communication facilities.

(ii) Housing, water supply, social services (education of children, medical care) facilities for the project staff; creation of a township, if necessary.

(iii) Soil conservation measures in the catchment area.

B. Complementary Inputs

(iv) Land development and agricultural improvement: reclamation, clearance and levelling of land which is to receive irrigation; reorganization of agriculture, especially switching over from dry to irrigated farming; adoption of improved agricultural practices, e.g. use of improved seed, chemical fertilizers, etc.

(v) Supplementary minor irrigation—digging of wells, installation of lift irrigation devices, etc.; drainage and other steps to prevent water logging in the irrigated area.

(vi) Improvement of transport and marketing facilities.

Measures for category A require creation of services of technical assistance, supplies, etc., and also provisions for loans to cultivators for enabling them to take up land development or agricultural improvement measures.

C. Derived Inputs

(vii) As the above measures take effect and agricultural production increase, the area will need agricultural processing industries, agro-industries (e.g., manufacture of improved agricultural implements) and consumer goods industries. These may be called derived inputs, which derive from or follow the earlier developments.

II. Steel Plant

A. Associated Inputs

(i) Facilities for mining of coal, iron-ore, limestone and construction materials.
(ii) Transport, rail and road, for carrying raw materials and intermediate and finished products.
(iii) Generation of power.
(iv) Supply of water to the plant and to the township.
(v) Urban development—construction of township to house industrial workers and those working in trades and services.
(vi) Organization of various essential services in the township.

B. Complementary Inputs

(vii) Rehabilitation of persons dispossessed of their lands.
(viii) Orderly absorption of immigrants and taking steps for ensuring smooth relations between them and the original residents of the area.
(ix) Training of craftsmen and other personnel for the plant.
(x) Social education among tribal people with a view to ensure that they can derive adequate benefits from new economic opportunities within their area.
(xi) Reorganization of local agriculture to meet the consumption needs of the larger population, especially for high value perishable products such as milk, vegetables, fruit, meat and poultry products.

C. Derived Inputs

(xii) Industries, which depend upon raw materials supplied by the steel plant or on use of other facilities like power and transport created for it.
(xiii) Heavy engineering industries, e.g. machine building, manufacture of transport equipment, fabrication of structures, etc.
(xiv) Heavy chemical industries, e.g. manufacture of chemical fertilizers.
(xv) Manufacture of other construction materials.
(xvi) Light engineering, light chemicals and various consumer goods industries attracted by the raw materials and other facilities available in the area.

Appendix II

Scope and Content of the District Plan as Defined in the Second and the Fourth Five Year Plans

A. Second Five Year Plan

"20. It was recognized that both at the district and at the State level three kinds of programmes sponsored on behalf of public authorities would be included in the plan, namely :

- (a) Programmes initiated at the level in question, e.g. taluka, district and state,
- (b) Programmes initiated at lower levels and integrated with those in (a), and
- (c) Programmes initiated at levels above and integrated with (a), for instance, schemes sponsored by the Central Government but executed through States or schemes sponsored by the State Government and implemented through machinery available in the district.

23. The main constituents of district plan are :

- (a) The community development and national extension programme, social welfare extension projects,
- (b) Agricultural production programme and allied activities in the field of rural development such as animal husbandry, soil conservation, etc.,
- (c) Development of cooperatives,
- (d) Village panchayats,
- (e) Village and small industries,
- (f) Schemes for utilizing effectively resources developed through State projects for irrigation, electricity, communications, industrial development and expansion of training facilities,
- (g) Housing and urban development,
- (h) The programme of small savings,
- (i) Aiding construction projects through labour cooperatives and shramdan,
- (j) Programmes for the welfare of backward classes,
- (k) Programmes in rural and urban areas relating to social services, especially expansion of education at primary and secondary

levels, health units, health education, sanitation, malaria consciousness, family planning, etc.,

(l) Utilizing and assisting voluntary organizations engaged in constructive social work,

(m) Land reform,

(n) Prohibition work, and

(o) Dissemination of information about programmes of national, state, regional and local development."

Source: Planning Commission: *Second Five Year Plan*, 1956, pages 156 and 158.

B. Fourth Five Year Plan

"A district development plan should comprehend various activities envisaged in the State Five Year Plan for execution at the district level without respect to the nature of the sponsoring authority or the location of the budget provisions. Some activities undertaken in a district are provided for in the plans of the Zilla Parishad and the Panchayat Samitis, others in the plans of Departments at the State level. This latter fall technically outside the field of *Panchayati Raj Institutions*. The following are the principal sectors in which the local initiative and participation have to be carried as far as possible and can be developed around programmes embodied in the Five Year Plan :

(i) Agriculture (in its wider sense including animal husbandry, dairying, fisheries, poultry, horticulture, forestry, minor irrigation, etc.),

(ii) Cooperatives,

(iii) Village and small industries in processing industries,

(iv) Elementary and social education,

(v) Rural water supply and sanitation,

(vi) Rural health and medical services and family planning,

(vii) District and rural roads, including village approach roads (excluding National and State Highways),

(viii) Work programmes for the fuller utilization of rural manpower,

(ix) Development of focal points of growth like market centres, service centres, etc.,

(x) Social Welfare, including welfare of weaker sections,

(xi) Voluntary organizations."

Source: Planning Commission: *Memorandum on the Fourth Plan*, New Delhi, 1964. pp. 80-81.

NOTE

1. Some modifications have been made. The Cooperative Department, for instance, has added Assistant Inspectors to assist the Cooperative Extension Officers and the number of these varies with the number of Cooperative Societies in the Samiti areas.

13

Regions for Planning*

The region is a conceptual tool for understanding the diversity in space and for organizing space for particular purposes. Every science has its regional scheme based on distribution of the phenomena in which it is interested. Thus in medical science, there are regions showing distribution of cholera, malaria and other diseases. Frequently, regions are based on distribution of a group of related phenomena. Climatic regions are an example. The concept of regions based on multiple related phenomena is found to be particularly useful in sciences such as geography, economics and sociology. Geographers distinguish regions based on distribution of the physical phenomena—geological structure, topography, climate, hydrology, soils and natural vegetation—or regions based on distribution of these phenomena and human phenomena such as agricultural land-use, population density and the settlement pattern. Sociologists and cultural anthropologists distinguish cultural regions based on distribution of various cultural phenomena. All such regions are demarcated on the basis of internal homogeneity and external contrast; the areas included within them have certain common characteristics which set them off from areas outside. The economists also distinguish regions on the basis of homogeneity in economic characteristics. Industrial regions are an example. But the concept of economic regions based on the principle of interrelationship is also used in economics. An economic area has been defined by Losch as the market area of a commodity, and an economic region as a system of such market areas (Losch 1964, and J. Friedman, and W. Alonso 1964, p. 115). Such an economic region may include areas with widely divergent economic characteristics. Typically, it will include an industrial producing

---

* Published in *Indian Journal of Public Administration*, New Delhi. Vol XII, No. 1, pp 1-17, 1966.

centre and a consumption area which may be largely rural. The two are considered as forming part of an economic region because of their economic relationship.

These principles, homogeneity and interrelationship, have their utility in demarcating regions for planning.

Planning Regions

Planning regions have to serve as the spatial units for formulation and implementation of development plans. They must, therefore, be demarcated, keeping in view the objectives of planned development and the nature of the principal development programmes. Secondly, since institutional and administrative arrangements for plan formulation and execution will have to be made with these regions as the units, they must be related to the existing politico-administrative structure of the country, its territorial divisions. Since most planning is done by government (or by agencies established by government), it is most convenient to adopt the territorial divisions or administrative regions as the planning regions. Planning and development agencies can be established for these regions simply by expanding the existing departments or adding new ones. Secondly, arrangements for association of the people's representatives with the planning process can also be made most conveniently with them as units, because Legislatures, local bodies and other democratic institutions are already established for them. Other planning regions have undoubtedly to be adopted for particular purposes. But the need for them must be clearly established, because their acceptance involves supplementing or replacing the administrative regions.

Planning in India is the concurrent responsibility of the Central and the State Governments. It is being done with the States (and Union Territories) as the primary units. Below the State level the principal units of administration and planning are the district, the block and the village. Administrative and institutional arrangements exist at these units for formulation and execution of plans, and for association of popular leaders with planning. These administrative regions are in fact the principal planning regions of the country. However, they are not adequate for all planning purposes and have to be supplemented by other regions for some purposes of planning, and may even have to be replaced for other purposes. Thus, for development of water resources it is convenient to adopt a river valley or a river system as the region; in metropolitan planning it is necessary to plan with the metropolitan area of the city as the unit.

Similarly, for planning of transport or development of power resources, regions may have to be specially delineated keeping in view the particular requirements of the planning task. Secondly, even when administrative units are adopted as the planning regions, it is useful for the planners to be aware of similarities, contrasts or economic relationships between areas situated in different administrative units. Thus, the Himalayan areas of U.P., Punjab, Himachal Pradesh and Jammu and Kashmir have certain common physical features of topography, climate and soils and common patterns of resource use and economic activity. In all these hilly areas arable land is limited, specialized forms of agriculture (e.g. horticulture), and grazing and exploitation of forest resources are important economic activities. Population is sparse, water supply and communications are difficult problems, and there is urgent need for programmes of conservation of soil and water. These common features, problems and needs have to be kept in view and arrangements for cooperation in plan formulation or implementation have to be devised between the States and Union Territories concerned. A regional scheme which expresses the common links between these areas is, therefore, useful for planners.

The Planning Tasks in India can be divided into the following four categories :

(i) Agricultural and related development programmes—land reclamation, soil conservation, irrigation, animal husbandry, forestry and fisheries;
(ii) Development of industries, power, transport and communications;
(iii) Development of social services—education, medical care, social welfare, etc.; and
(iv) Urban development.

The classification follows broadly the sectoral classification in the Five Year Plans. Urban development has been added. It is not a separate sector of development but it has been listed here because urbanization affects the economy in such a variety of ways and urban development is a task of such importance that it was felt that it should be listed separately in order to focus attention on it.

In agricultural and related development programmes, primary emphasis is on scientific and more intensive exploitation of the resources of land and water. This has to be done by changing present production techniques and by undertaking various resource development programmes.

Since regional variations in the methods of resource use and the resource development economy—patterns of agricultural land-use and cropping, development of livestock husbandry, forestry or fishing—are related primarily to the physical factors. Regional schemes based on analysis of the physical factors and associated human factors of agricultural land-use and rural settlement; furnish the basic mosaic for planning the development programmes. Such schemes bring out the contrasts within the country and within individual States which are most significant for planning purposes. Further, they bring out for each region (and its smaller divisions) the basic physical and human factors, and the potential and limitations of the physical environment. The scheme of "Regions for Resource Planning" developed by the Regional Planning Unit of the Indian Statistical Institute (Unpublished) and the scheme of Resource Development Regions and Divisions recently published by the Planning Commission (Government of India, 1964) are both schemes of this type. The latter is described below.

Such schemes are useful also for planning of social service programmes, especially in the rural areas, because planning of these programmes has to be related primarily to the rural settlement pattern. They are useful to a limited extent for planning of industrial, power, transport and associated development programmes. They furnish the basic facts on location of mineral and power resources, and agricultural raw materials, and of distribution of population which have to be taken into account in planning of these programmes. Thus, the scheme of Resource Development Regions and Divisions published by the Planning Commission distinguishes the Eastern Plateau and Hills Region. This region, consisting of the plateau areas of Bihar, Orissa, West Bengal, Eastern Madhya Pradesh and two districts of the Maharashtra, has been demarcated primarily on basis of geological and topographic factors. But by distinguishing it the highly mineralized areas which contain most of the coal, iron ore, manganese and other mineral resources of the country, have been separated from the adjoining areas of the Gangetic Plain or of the Deccan which are poor in minerals. Visualizing this mineral-rich area as one region is very useful in planning of industrial, power and transport programmes. However, it appears that regional schemes based on the principle of homogeneity are not adequate for planning of such programmes and that schemes based on the principle of interrelationship have to be used. The latter are useful because they indicate how regions are related with one another and with the national economy and the potential or limitations for development which these relationships hold. Thus for any region the scheme of Resource Development Regions and Divisions would indicate only its agricultural, mineral, forest and other resources, but it would not indicate the potential or limitations for development which its location with reference to other regions creates. Consider the South Bihar Plain area (consisting of the districts of Shahabad, Patna, Gaya, Monghyr and Bhagalpur) as an example. It has a very large population in relation to its agricultural land, has few mineral resources and would appear to have a limited potential for industrial and urban development. But its location next to the coal and steel centres of Bihar and West Bengal and athwart the principal transport routes of Northern India hold for it enormous possibilities of industrial and urban growth.

As an illustration of schemes based on the principle of inter-relationship, a scheme of metropolitan regions has been described in Part II. The scheme distinguishes four metropolitan regions, which are the hinterlands respectively of the metropolitan cities of Calcutta, Madras, Bombay and Delhi. The scheme is based on the concept of central places; (For a discussion of the hierarchical order of Central places see Isard, 1960, pp. 222-227) each metropolitan city is regarded as an apex central place, which is linked through a system of secondary and lower order central places to every part of its hinterland.

Accordingly, we consider four sets of regions:

(i) Administrative Regions,
(ii) Resource Development Regions,
(iii) Metropolitan Regions, and
(iv) Urban Corridors.

Administrative Regions

States (and Union Territories), districts, blocks, and villages constitute the different units in the structure of administrative regions. The planning process in India provides for formulation of plans with them as units and interrelation of plans of different units. The plan of each State is drawn up within the framework of the goals, investment magnitudes and physical achievement targets of the national plan : but it reflects in its details—the financial and physical magnitudes of different sectors and the particular projects included in it—the development potential of the State and the needs and aspirations of its people. The plans of districts are related similarly to the plan of the State, and of smaller units to the plan of the district. Such interrelationship between plans of different units is an essential aspect of the national planning process. It enables plans to reflect national goals and objectives on the one hand and local needs and aspirations on the other. Institutional arrangements have been established at various area levels for participation of the people's representatives in the planning process. The National and State Legislators frame the policies for planning; the local leaders participate in detailed planning and implementation of programmes for their areas. The responsibilities of the local leaders in planning have increased, and much greater attention has begun to be given to local planning after the establishment of the Panchayati Raj Institutions. The district plan particularly is being given increasing attention, because it is felt that the area of the district is sufficiently large for formulation of an integrated development plan and officials and non-officials of sufficient calibre and experience are available for preparation of the plan. If the present trends continue the district will in time emerge as a distinct unit of planning in addition to the Nation and the state.

The administrative regions have some characteristics which enhance their claims to being accepted as planning regions. Most States of the Indian Union are quite large in size so that adequate planning organizations can be built up for them. Secondly, the areas of most States are coterminus with the linguistic regions of the country and their people have a certain sense of linguistic-cultural unity. The importance of linguistic regions as basic planning regions can scarcely be overemphasized in a large, multilingual country. The districts similarly are of sufficient size to be adopted as primary units of local planning. The population of most districts ranges between one and two million and their area ranges between two and five thousand square miles. Secondly, since the boundaries of most districts follow natural features such as rivers or hill ranges and have remained unchanged for long periods and the district headquarters town is the principal administrative, commercial and educational centre of the area, there is among their people a well-developed feeling of "belonging to the district". There are of course districts which are quite unsuitable for local planning because they are too large or too small or contain areas of sharply contrasted physical and economic characteristics.[1] But the number of such districts is small.

Among the administrative units below the district level, the community development block is the most important for the purpose of planning because the institutional and administrative structure of planning and development—the *Panchayat Samiti* and the community development organization—have been built up round it. A typical block consists of about 100 villages with a population of 50,000 to 100,000 but there are variations in different areas. Below the block level, the traditional unit of rural community life, the village, has also a certain importance in planning. The aspirations and needs of the rural people are articulated first through the village Panchayat and agricultural and rural development programmes must be formulated in the first instance with the village as the unit.

Supplement to Administrative Regions

(i) *Special Areas* : This structure of administrative regions is used mainly for planning of agricultural and related development programmes, social service programmes and others which are the responsibility of the State Governments. It is useful for planning of these programmes because it enables planners to relate programmes for successively smaller areas to local conditions and the needs and aspirations of the local people. But it has to be supplemented in various ways in order to meet planning needs for which it is found to be inadequate. One set of supplements consists of areas of special problems or promise for which special development programmes have to be undertaken and special administrative or institutional arrangements have to be established. Metropolitan areas of cities, industrial complexes, areas of river valley projects or other resource development projects, and backward areas are the most important among such special areas. In each case the boundaries have to be demarcated keeping in view the particular objects of planning and development. They have to be defined precisely in some cases but not in others. The boundaries of "metropolitan areas" have to be defined with precision because they have to be given the force of law. Control over urban land-use which is an essential element in metropolitan planning cannot be enforced without legal sanctions. The boundaries of areas of irrigation and other resource development projects may also have to be defined precisely, because the areas which will receive irrigation or other benefits and those which will not receive such benefits have to be clearly distinguished. On the other hand, boundaries of backward areas need not be defined so precisely. The boundaries of special areas may change relatively quickly. The metropolitan area of a city may have to be enlarged from time to time as the city expands. The areas of irrigation projects may also be enlarged as the scope of the projects is enlarged. On the other hand, backward areas may be reduced progressively in size as backwardness is liquidated.

(ii) *Zones, Macro-regions and Commissioners' Divisions :* Another set of supplements to administrative regions consists of groups of States and districts and are useful for planning at inter-State and inter-district levels. Inter-State action is required for water resource development, power generation and distribution, and various other development programmes. There is considerable experience of inter-State co-operation for water resource development in India; the river valley projects undertaken during the last 15 years are outstanding recent examples of such cooperation. But as each case requires agreement among the States concerned, adequate institutional arrangements are essential for securing inter-State cooperation. The need for inter-State action in power generation and distribution has also begun to be recognized increasingly. The power systems of most adjoining States are already inter-linked. Formation of regional power grids has been under consideration for some time: the grids are visualized as the first step in the establishment (eventually) of a national power grid.

Since the re-organization of the States in 1956, an institutional arrangement for inter-State action has existed in the Zonal Councils. These Councils have been constituted for the five Zones—Northern, Central, Eastern, Southern and Western—into which the country is divided. Each Zone consists of two or more States and adjoining Union Territories. The agency of the Zonal Councils could be used for planning and co-coordinated execution of programmes of development of inter-State interest more effectively than has been done so far.

Zones also provide a useful conceptual framework for macro-regional divisions of the country : most macro-regional divisions are variations on the Zonal scheme. (Government of India: Report of the Energy Survey of India Committee, 1965, p. 85)[2] Macro-regions are useful for planning of various activities of the Central Government and for regional economic and social analysis. They can be very useful in planning flows of basic commodities—coal, iron and steel, cement, petroleum products, chemical fertilizers, foodgrains and agricultural raw materials—and deciding locations of industrial units keeping the flow patterns in view. This concept has been best developed in U.S.S.R., which has been divided into a number of "major economic regions" each based on one or more major industrial complexes. However, the related Soviet concept of self-sufficiency at major economic region level, very attractive in a country with long distances, sparse population and relatively underdeveloped transport has distinct limitations in India. As the bulk of the coal and iron ore deposits of India are located in Eastern India, this region must remain the premier iron and steel producing region of the country and large flows of coal, steel and heavy engineering goods from the region to other parts of the country must remain an essential feature of the Indian economy. Ignoring these facts and attempting to achieve self-sufficiency at macro-regional level could lead to a distorted and wasteful pattern of resource development. Macro-regional schemes are useful for regional economic and social analysis because they make possible presentation of data on regional differences within a large country in terms of a limited number of units. In U.S.A., the Census Divisions are used extensively for this purpose, and the practice of using macro-regions is growing in India. The National Sample Survey, the Energy Survey and various studies of the National Council of Applied Economic Research present data on regional differences within India primarily by macro-regions.

In most of the larger States of India there has existed for a long time an intermediate unit between the State and the districts—the Commissioner's Division. These Divisions, consisting of 5 or 6 districts were formed for coordination of work in the districts; but many of them express also the most significant differences in physical and economic conditions within a State. In any case, these Divisions furnish as the Zones do at the macro-regional level, the starting point for dividing large States into a limited number of relatively homogeneous units. Distinguishing such units is useful in planning for a large State because it provides to the State and the local planners a frame of reference for comprehending the diversity within the State and for modifying the development programmes accordingly. Such modification is particularly necessary in agricultural and related programmes which have to be adapted to the physical conditions and agricultural and settlement patterns of each area.

With these two sets of supplements, the structure of administrative regions consists of : nation, macro-region or zone, state, division, district, block and village, and the special areas. The latter cannot be integrated into the administrative structure, because their boundaries would frequently cut across the boundaries of states and districts. But since planning arrangements for them can be made without serious disturbance to the administrative structure, they can also be considered along with the administrative regions.

Resource Development Regions

The scheme of Resource Development Regions and Divisions of India published by the Planning Commission is based on analysis of data of topography, geological formations, soils, rainfall, and agricultural land use, cropping pattern, population density and occurrence of mineral resources. The data have been analyzed for each district of the country. The district has been adopted as the minimum unit for classification partly because the data for most of these variables were not available for smaller units and partly in order to make the scheme more useful for planning. It is considered that "the district is of such overwhelming importance as a unit for execution of most development programmes that a classification in which districts are not divided has a certain usefulness which is lost as soon as districts are divided." (Planning Commission, 1964, p. 3)

The scheme recognizes five primary or major natural regions of the country : the Himalayas, the Northern Plain, the Peninsular Plateau and Hills, the East Coast Plain, and the West Coast Plain. Each of these is divided into one or more regions to make a total of 14 regions on the mainland of India. The fifteenth region is formed by the Islands in the Bay of Bengal and the Arabian Sea. The regions are divided further into sub-regions, divisions and sub-divisions. But the important units below the regions are the divisions; sub-regions and sub-divisions are units of secondary importance and have been distinguished in a very few cases. Only one region, the Eastern Himalayan, has been divided into sub-regions and only five divisions have been divided into sub-divisions. The scheme distinguishes 61 divisions, each of which is located entirely within the territory of a State. The divisions are formed by intersection of boundaries of the regions and the States or by further division of the area of a region located within a State. Each division is a unit, homogeneous in physical and socio-economic characteristics, and located entirely within the territory of one State which can be adopted as a planning unit by the State Government. The objects of the scheme are :

"(i) to provide a framework for understanding the variety of physical conditions and resource development potentials in different parts of the country to those concerned with planning at the Centre and in the States, so that these differences are given due consideration in planning of programmes, and adjustments in programme content and patterns are made to meet these, wherever necessary; and

(ii) to furnish to those concerned with planning at the State level, a scheme of division of their States into internally homogeneous units, each of which can be used as a unit for planning of most of the programmes included in State Plans." (Government of India, Planning Commission, 1964, p. 2).

The reference to State planning will be readily understood because agricultural and related development programmes for which the scheme is particularly useful are the responsibility primarily of the State Governments. Since the resource development division consists of a group of districts, it can be easily integrated into the structure of State planning. It can serve as an intermediate unit between the State and the districts and is in fact a better unit than the Commissioner's because it is demarcated scientifically. Its principal usefulness is in relating development programmes more closely to the different physical and socio-economic conditions of different parts of a State. Such relation is particularly important in large States such as U.P., Maharashtra, and Madhya Pradesh within which there is such diversity of physical and socio-economic conditions. The content of the plan of each sector can be decided first at the resource development division level and district plans can then be made within the framework of these decisions. The scheme also enables planners to keep in view the similarities between areas located in adjacent States. The example of the Eastern Plateau and Hills Region and of the Himalayan Region of U.P., Punjab, Himachal Pradesh and Jammu and Kashmir, given above, illustrate this point.

Metropolitan Regions

In this scheme the country is divided into four metropolitan regions—the hinterlands respectively of the metropolitan cities of Calcutta, Bombay, Madras and Delhi. Each hinterland is a macro-region consisting of two or more States together with Union Territories or parts of States. It can be divided further into sub-regions, divisions and smaller units going down to the service area of the small town (or large village) with population between 5,000 and 10,000, which performs various commercial and other service functions for a group of villages. Towns of different sizes located in a metropolitan region are considered to be central places of different orders; the metropolitan city is considered to be the apex central place of the region.

The areas included within a metropolitan region are dissimilar in physical features, land-use and cropping pattern, population density and various other characteristics. The metropolitan region of Delhi includes the Himalayan areas of Jammu and Kashmir and Himachal Pradesh, the Punjab plain as well as the desert of western Rajasthan. The region of Calcutta includes areas as dissimilar as NEFA and North Bihar. But all parts of a metropolitan region are bound together by the bonds of functional relations with the metropolitan city. The relations are primarily commercial—distribution of goods is the principal element in them,—but they are also cultural and administrative. Three of the metropolitan cities are ports but the fourth, Delhi, is an inland city. The external trade functions which the port cities perform for their metropolitan regions are shared in case of the Delhi region between Calcutta and Bombay. But the concept of the metropolitan region does not involve as a necessary condition that the metropolitan city be a port or that it be the only port in the region. It only involves that the metropolitan city be so important as a commercial, administrative and social service centre that it can be recognized as the apex centre of the region. Each of the four cities has this position in its metropolitan region. The cities are connected with every part of the hinterland through a succession of smaller towns—sub-regional centres, district towns, *mandi* centres, etc. These are central places of different orders, each of which is connected upwards with higher order central places and downwards with lower order places; it is also connected with its own particular hinterland (service area) for the specific services that it performs for it. In this way, a whole system of functional relationships—economic, socio-cultural, and administrative—focuses eventually on the sub-regional and the metropolitan cities, and the influences emanating from these cities travel to every part of the hinterland.

Formulating such a scheme of metropolitan regions has many limitations at present. First, because of virtual lack of data on economic relationships between the metropolitan cities and their hinterlands, the regions cannot be demarcated precisely. Studies on demarcation of the hinterland have been carried out most extensively for Calcutta (see Green Lastie) and the boundaries of the Calcutta region can be drawn somewhat more precisely than those of the other regions. The regional transport surveys now being conducted under the auspices of the Planning Commission are expected to make available considerable data which will make possible more precise demarcation of the other three hinterlands. Similarly, studies on the economic relationships between cities and towns of different sizes within a metropolitan region and between them and their service areas, needed for dividing the metropolitan regions into sub-regions, divisions and smaller units, are virtually lacking. In Appendix I, central places of six classes have been listed, which implies that it should be possible to have a size hierarchy of six units, going down from the metropolitan region to the service area of the very small town or large village which functions as rural service centre. But this classification is only illustrative and will need to be verified by studies in the different metropolitan regions. It is most likely that central places of all the six categories are not fully developed in every region. However, the hierarchical order provides the framework for seeing the cities and towns of different sizes as linked parts of a spatial system.

As important as the paucity of data is the fact that the city-region relationship is not as well developed in India as it is in industrially advanced countries. Since the bulk of the population is rural, depends upon subsistence agriculture and has limited extra-village economic relationships, the influence of the metropolitan city, or of any urban area for that matter, is quite weak. But this influence is increasing as means of communication improve and modern social services and consumer goods are used by the rural people to an increasing extent. One visible result of this increase is use by large commercial firms of the four metropolitan cities as focal points for distribution of products within the regions. Various agencies of government and such institutions as the Life Insurance Corporation are also using these cities as regional headquarters for their activities. The smaller cities are similarly beginning to be used increasingly as focal points for distribution of products or radiation of various activities, within their respective influence areas.

The metropolitan regions may be roughly indicated as follows :

(1) The Calcutta Metropolitan Region—Assam, Nagaland and the Union Territories in North East India; West Bengal, Bihar, Eastern U.P., and Eastern Madhya Pradesh, except the extreme Southern portion.

(2) The Madras Metropolitan Region—Madras, Kerala, most of Mysore and most of Andhra Pradesh.

(3) The Bombay Metropolitan Region—Maharashtra, Gujarat, Southern Madhya Pradesh.

(4) The Delhi Metropolitan Region—Punjab, Jammu and Kashmir, Himachal Pradesh, most of Rajasthan, Western U.P., and Northern Madhya Pradesh.

Urban Corridors

Transition Zones or Corridors: It is useful to distinguish transition zones or corridors between the metropolitan regions. These are areas in which the influence of two metropolitan cities overlaps, i.e. the advantages of obtaining services from the two cities are nearly competitive and the local people have a choice of obtaining services from one or the other city. The choices are exercised in favour of different cities at different times or for different commodities. Central U.P. is such a transitional zone between the metropolitan regions of Delhi and Calcutta. The transition zones are roughly indicated below, they can also be indicated more precisely when more detailed data become available :

(1) Between the Calcutta and the Madras Regions—extreme South Eastern Madhya Pradesh and North Eastern Andhra Pradesh (the hinterland of Visakhapatnam).
(2) Between the Madras and the Bombay Regions—the Northern fringe of Mysore.
(3) Between the Bombay and the Delhi Region—Southern Rajasthan, and Central Madhya Pradesh.
(4) Between the Delhi and the Calcutta Regions—Central U.P.

The transition zones will be seen on an all-India map as arc-shaped belts of varying widths. Their northern apex is in Central U.P. in the vicinity of Allahabad. From this point they go southwards dividing in Central Madhya Pradesh into three arcs going North-West, South-West and South-East respectively.

The metropolitan regions are units of the same size order as the macro-regions. In some cases they are very close to the zones or other commonly used macro-regions. The Madras Metropolitan Region is coterminus with the South India Region of many macro-regional schemes. The Bombay Metropolitan Region differs only slightly from the Western India Region of macro-regional schemes—it includes Southern Madhya Pradesh. The metropolitan regions based as they are on the economic fact of exchange of goods and services are even more useful than the macro-regions for planning, production and distribution of basic commodities. They are useful also for planning of power, transport and similar programmes. In fact they appear to be the most useful macro-units for working out the regional implications of the long-term perspective of development. The national projections of population, its distribution between urban and rural areas and among various economic activities, of supply and demand of basic commodities and of requirements of power and transport can most conveniently be broken down in terms of the metropolitan regions. Programmes for attaining the targets of development can then be formulated with each metropolitan region as the unit. It appears also that inter-State relationships for purposes of resource development are also visualized most fruitfully in terms of metropolitan regions.

But the metropolitan regions have their greatest utility in urban planning which will have to move in the not distant future from planning for cities to planning of entire hinterlands as units. The need for adopting in case of the large cities, a sufficiently large "metropolitan area" as the unit of detailed land-use planning, and a still larger "peripheral region" as the unit of less detailed, directional planning has, already been recognized. The "metropolitan area" concept, first used in the Delhi Plan, is now being used in the plans of all major cities of India. The Delhi Plan also visualized planning for its peripheral region which is now being called the National Capital Region. This is an area of about 400 square miles located in U.P. and Punjab. In case of Calcutta, the CMPO has demarcated outside the Calcutta metropolitan district a Southern Plain Region, as the unit for less detailed, directional planning. The Maharashtra planners are already thinking in terms of planning with the Bombay-Poona Region as the Unit. In Gujarat, the entire strip between Ahmedabad and Surat, which is experiencing rapid urban-industrial growth, may be adopted as a planning unit. The process has to be carried further and entire hinterlands of metropolitan cities have to be viewed as planning regions. For each such region, the likely growth of the urban population can be forecast within the national perspective of economic development. This total can then be distributed in towns of different sizes located in different parts of the region. The location and size of some towns will, no doubt, be determined by such factors as distribution of natural resources and topographic conditions. Thus, the steel and heavy engineering centres of the Calcutta metropolitan region will be located mainly near the coal fields or iron ore deposits. But location and size of most of the towns in a metropolitan region can be planned in accordance with accepted policies of dispersal of economic activity and balanced regional development.

Growth of local, district and multi-district centres can be planned in the perspective of the expected growth in the economy of their service areas. In fact, each such town can be built up as a focal point of modernization of agriculture and of the rural economy, which provides a constellation of services, ranging from distribution of supplies required for modern agriculture (chemical fertilizers, steel, petroleum products, and power-driven implements) to facilities of modern education, medical care and recreation. The relations between these towns and their service areas can be improved through improvement of means of transport and communications. The more suitable among them can be developed as local growth points by establishment of various agro-industries and other industries. Some towns can be planned deliberately as growth points to stimulate the economy of stagnant regions or to serve as counter-magnets which will relieve the pressure on large cities. As one city or area approaches saturation point, growth can be transferred to other cities or areas within the metropolitan region.

Urban planning of this kind, with metropolitan hinterlands as units, is an essential counterpart of perspective economic planning. The metropolitan regions furnish the most useful conceptual framework for such planning, because the different cities and towns within each region can be viewed as interlinked and mutually interacting parts of a spatial system.

Appendix

Hierarchy of Central Places in a Metropolitan Region

1. Metropolitan City.
2. Sub-regional centre—the principal town and service centre of the sub-region.
3. Multi-district centre—principal town and service centre of a group of districts. Some of these towns are also headquarters of Commissioners' Divisions.
4. District centre—the principal town and service centre for the whole or a major part of the district. Most of these towns are also district headquarters.
5. *Mandi* centre—town with an established permanent market (not weekly *hat*) serving an area approximating a community development block or a taluk. It may also be the headquarters of the block or taluk.

6. Rural service centre—small town or large village functioning as a service centre for a group of villages.

NOTES

1. Some districts of Bihar and Madras with population of three to four million are recognized as being too large for efficient local planning. The Madras districts have been bifurcated for purposes of planning and a similar bifurcation of the Bihar districts will be useful. On the other hand many of the districts of Rajasthan, Madhya Pradesh and Himachal Pradesh are very small.
2. One such scheme is that used by the Energy Survey Committee (Government of India: *Report of the Energy Survey of India Committee*, New Delhi, 1965, p. 85) which divides the country into the following six energy regions:
   (i) Northern: Punjab, Himachal Pradesh, Delhi, Rajasthan and Jammu and Kashmir.
   (ii) Central: U.P. and Madhya Pradesh.
   (iii) Eastern: Bihar, West Bengal and Orissa.
   (iv) Assam: Assam, Tripura and Manipur.
   (v) Southern: Andhra Pradesh, Mysore, Madras and Kerala.
   (vi) Western: Maharashtra and Gujarat.

   The only unsatisfactory feature of the scheme is inclusion of U.P. and Madhya Pradesh in one region. There are marked physical and socio-economic differences between the two States which are marked by their inclusion in one region. Each State is large enough to constitute a region by itself.

REFERENCES

Friedman, J. and Alonso, W. : *Regional Development and Planning: A Reader*, Cambridge, the M.I.T. Press, Mass. 1964.

Green, Lassie : *The Economic Hinterland of Calcutta*, to be published by Asia Publishing House, Bombay.

Government of India, Planning Commission, *Resource Development Regions and Divisions of India*. 1964.

Government of India : *Report of the Energy Survey of India Committee*, New Delhi, 1965.

Isard, W : *Methods of Regional Analysis*, Cambridge, M.I.T. Press, 1960..

Losch, August : "The Nature of Economic Regions," in J. Friedman, and W. Alonso: *Regional Development and Planning : A Reader*, Cambridge, The M.I.T. Press, Mass., 1964, p. 115.

14

Changes in Political Culture Between the 1950s and the 1990s

This chapter reviews changes in political culture and complex institutional development during the five decades of economic development of the country, since Independence which has led to increase in corruption and inefficient administration. Poor administration has forced the state and national level apex courts to take on the role of activists to ensure not only human rights but the rights of people to live in clean environment and decent living conditions by provision of clean air, water, sewage and housing, for citizens and poor migrants in metropolitan cities.

Politics and Administration

When Pandit Nehru was the Prime Minister, he chose as Ministers in his cabinet, persons who had qualities of leadership, or expertise in their subjects, efficient administration and/or for the part that they had played in the movement for Independence. Not all of them were members of the Congress Party. Two outstanding non-Congressmen in his first cabinet, formed in 1950 after adoption of the Constitution of India, were Dr. B.R. Ambedkar, Minister of Law who was an expert in Constitutional Law and had been the principal draftsman of the Constitution of the country, and the Minister of Finance, Dr. John Mathai, who was an eminent Economist. After Dr. Mathai resigned in 1950 on a difference of views with him, Pandit Nehru appointed Mr. (formerly Sir) C.D. Deshmukh, who had just retired from his post of the first Indian Governor of the Reserve Bank of India, after a long and distinguished career as an officer of the Indian Civil Service. He continued in this post for eight years, 1950-1958, and resigned again on account of some differences with the Prime Minister. Pandit Nehru was the Minister of External Affairs himself, but his principal adviser for many years was Sir Girija Shankar Bajpai, who had a distinguished career as an officer of the Indian Foreign and Political Service under the British Government.

His readiness to appoint non-Congressmen is reflected also in appointment of members of the Planning Commission. Development planning was his first love and he remained the Chairman of the Commission from 1950 when it was established until his death in 1964. The members of the first Commission were : Mr. Gulzari Lal Nanda, a successful labour leader of Ahmedabad; Mr. G.L. Mehta, who had been the Chairman of the Scindia Steam Navigation Company; Mr. C.D. Deshmukh; Mr. (formerly Sir) V.T. Krishnamachari who had a long and distinguished career as the Dewan (Prime Minister) of two princely states—Baroda and Jaipur; Mr. R.K. Patil, who had joined the Congress Party after he resigned from the ICS in 1943 when he refused to order firing on a procession of freedom fighters at the height of the Quit India Movement of 1942-43 and Mrs. Durgabai, a distinguished social worker of Andhra Pradesh, who had worked with great success for the welfare of women and children in her home state. Thus while Mr. Nanda and Mr. Patil were members of the Congress Party, the other four were not. They were appointed because of their expertise.

He continued this policy until his death. The members of the Planning Commission at that time were : Mr. Ashok Mehta, a labour leader of Mumbai and a member of the Socialist Party; Mr. (formerly Sir) Chandu Lal Trivedi who had retired from the ICS after a successful tenure as the Governor of Punjab; Prof. V.K.R.V. Rao, an Economist; S. Tarlok Singh, ICS, who had been associated with the Commission since its formation; Prof. M.S. Thacker, a Scientist who had long experience of work as Chairman of the Calcutta Electric Supply Company and Prof. Mahalanobis an eminent Economist and Statistician. Thus not a single member represented the Congress Party.

The Chief Ministers and the majority of Ministers in the cabinets of the State Governments in the 1950s and the 1960s were also political leaders of great administrative ability. Pandit Govind Vallabh Pant in UP, Mr. C. Rajagopalachari and Mr. Kamraj Nadar in Madras (now Tamil Nadu) Dr. Bidhan Chandar Roy in West Bengal and Mr. Mohan Lal Sukhadia in Rajasthan were notable among them. They administered their states with ability, introducing much needed economic or social reforms and contributed to economic development of their states.

An outstanding administrator of a different kind was Sardar Partap Singh Kairon in Punjab. He was a no-nonsense achiever who could not tolerate expression of any difference of views by any official. He had spent many years in his youth in the USA and his style of administration resembled in many ways that of a Governor of an American State in the 1930s. During his tenure as Chief Minister from the late 1950s to the mid-1960s he ensured that most of the villages in the state had electricity and water for irrigation and drinking. His work laid the foundation for the Green Revolution in Punjab in the late 1960s. Despite his shortcomings, which Pandit Nehru knew very well, he tolerated him because of his outstanding contribution to economic development of the state.

Although its magnitude was much smaller than now, monetary corruption among the political executive was not absent in Pandit Nehru's time[1]. Although scrupulously honest himself, he tolerated monetary corruption in the State Governments because he realized that it was an inescapable consequence of a system of government in which election, as a member of a State Legislature or of Parliament, costs millions of rupees. Although, he lived in the palace like Teen Murti house, which had been the residence of the Commander-in-Chief of the Indian Army during British days, Pandit Nehru had only one armed motor cyclist ahead of his Hindustan 13 car, the only car made in India in the 1950s, and one car full of security men following it, when he travelled from his office in South Block to his house. His complete disregard for personal safety and his habit of jumping into a crowd, to ask it to get back and observe the cordon made by volunteers of the Congress Party during pre-Independence days and by the police when he was the Prime Minister, are well known. The Chief Ministers and Ministers of states similarly had no great concern for their personal safety. I remember that when the Chief Ministers came to see members of the Planning Commission, they would be accompanied by their private secretaries and one or two security men. A personal experience, when I was working with Mr. Krishnamachari illustrates the point. One morning, a slim man of medium stature, dressed in spotless white *khadi* came to me and said, "I am U.N. Dhebar and wish to see Mr. Krishnamachari. Would you please tell him that I am here." I did and he went in immediately. I was stunned by his courtesy and utter simplicity of manner. Mr. Dhebar was the Chief Minister of Saurashtra, a state which had been formed in 1949 by merger of more than 400 princely states of Kathiawar, but his manner did not give any indication of his high office. The practice of a motorcade of security men accompanying the Prime Minister and smaller motorcades of security men accompanying Ministers of the Cabinet in the Central Government started in the late 1960s. It reached its height in 1990s when there was a motorcade of about forty vehicles accompanying the Prime Minister. The size of Prime Minister's and Ministers' motorcades has been greatly reduced since then. But after the assassination of Mrs. Indira Gandhi and Mr. Rajiv Gandhi, no Prime Minister or Minister can be unconcerned about the need for his or her personal security.

Self-Reliance

In Pandit Nehru's time, emphasis in construction of large irrigation-power-flood-control projects or exploitation of natural resources was on self-reliance. Three examples illustrate the point. A French consortium had offered to build on a turnkey basis, the Bhakra Dam, a high concrete dam constructed in Punjab during 1952-1960. Indian engineers had no experience of building high concrete dams at that time, but the Government of India declined the French offer, because the engineers assured the government that they would build the dam themselves, obtaining foreign technical assistance on the most difficult aspects of construction. They invited a team of American consultants who had built in the 1930s the Boulder dam, a nearly 700 ft. high concrete dam on the Colorado River in south-western United States, to assist them. The dam was built at a higher cost and the time taken for its construction was more than that estimated by the French consortium. But the Indian engineers gained valuable experience which enabled them to build later in the 1960s and 1970s two other high concrete dams in Punjab without any foreign assistance.

The Oil and Natural Gas Commission was established in the late 1950s when geophysical surveys and preliminary exploration indicated the prospect of location of large off-shore petroleum deposits in the coastal strip stretching from the vicinity of Mumbai (formerly Bombay) north along the coast of Gujarat. There were offers of detailed exploration and exploitation of the reserves by foreign multinationals. However, these offers were declined because the Minister for Oil and Natural Gas assured the Cabinet that the exploration and exploitation would be done by the Commission. There was much criticism in the press, inspired apparently by the multinationals against the Minister, but he was firm in his decision. In the subsequent four decades, the Commission has successfully explored and exploited these resources. Indigenous output of crude oil has increased steadily; it meets at present half or more of the total requirements of crude oil. The engineers and other experts have obtained the best available foreign expert advice when there have been problems which they could not handle. Thus an American who is the world's best expert in capping burning oil wells has been invited several times when there has been a fire in one of the oil wells in the off-shore areas where the oil is being exploited by the Commission. During the last two decades, as also earlier, sizeable off-shore and on-shore areas have been entrusted for exploration and exploitation to foreign oil companies. However, discovery of a commercially viable deposit has yet to be made by any of them.

Refining and distribution of petroleum products had been the monopoly of foreign multinationals until the late 1950s, when the Indian Oil Company was formed to undertake these activities. During the intervening four decades the foreign multinationals have been allowed to increase progressively the refining capacity in their refineries which they had constructed near Mumbai (formerly Bombay) in the 1950s, to participate in the building of new refineries and to greatly increase the number of stations that distribute their products. Yet, the I.O.C. has for more than three decades been by far the largest company refining crude oil and distributing petroleum products. The number of stations distributing its products is far higher than the combined total of the stations distributing products of the multinationals.

Large foreign economic and technical assistance was obtained during the 1950s and 1960s, for construction of steel mills, a heavy machinery manufacturing factory, factories for making heavy electrical machinery, machine tools, telephone receivers, and electrical equipment. Economic assistance was obtained principally from the Soviet Union, West Germany and Britain, while technical assistance was obtained from them and other European countries. However, the emphasis on self-reliance enabled Bharat Heavy Electrical and Hindustan Machine Tools to build, by the 1970s, new plants within India without external technical assistance. Bharat Heavy Electrical has successfully constructed since than electricity generating plants and laid down transmission lines in other developing countries.

The first fertilizer and locomotive manufacturing units were built in the 1950s with foreign technical assistance. However, in the following decades a number of fertilizer manufacturing units have been constructed and a locomotive manufacturing unit has been expanded without foreign assistance. One could give other examples.

Today, however, emphasis is on foreign participation. Foreign multinationals are being invited to participate in construction of sorely needed infrastructure projects—electricity generating stations, ports, highways, airports—all areas in which there is very considerable indigenous experience already available. They are being given guarantees of repatriation of their capital and high rates of return on their investment which would be the envy of Indian companies. An example is the guarantees given to Enron, an American multinational which is constructing a large electricity generating station in Maharashtra. At the same time, the Tatas were forced to withdraw their proposals for (i) construction of a sorely needed international class airport in Bangalore and (ii) starting an airline that would be competitive with global airlines after long delays in approving their proposals in the Ministry of Civil Aviation. Bangalore has become the computer software export capital of India during the last two decades; the turnover of the industry runs into billions of rupees. However, for the expansion of the industry to meet rapidly increasing foreign and domestic demand the existence of an international airport is essential. The present small poorly maintained airport could stifle the growth of this industry. However, the Civil Aviation Ministry is oblivious of this prospect.

Indian industrialists seeking to establish steel mills are eagerly seeking participation of foreign multinationals for their projects. It is interesting to note, however, that the biggest manufacturer of steel in the world is an Indian resident in Britain. Despite the repeated claims of successive Governments that they are doing their best to encourage investment by non-resident Indians in India, he will not invest in India because he finds delays in decision-making by Ministers and bureaucrats too exasperating.

Manufacture of motor vehicles and consumer durables—air-conditioners, refrigerators, television receiving sets and washing machines are some of the products for which foreign multinationals have set up manufacturing or assembly facilities. Their stated objectives are to exploit the expanding market for those products, or as in case of motor vehicles, to gain an entry into the expanding Indian market.

The Tatas established a factory for manufacturing trucks, buses and passenger cars in Jamshedpur with technical assistance from Daimler Benz of Germany. Another Indian company established a factory for manufacture of trucks and buses near Chennai (formerly Madras) with technical assistance from Leyland Motors of Britain. The Tatas completely indigenized production of trucks and ended collaboration with Daimler Benz within a decade. Furthermore, the quality of their trucks and buses is so high, that they have a virtual monopoly in supply of these vehicles in North India and have also been exporting vehicles to African and neighbouring countries of South and South East Asia. They are now planning to enter the expanding market for small passenger cars. Maruti Udyog was established in the 1980s with the Government of India and

Suzuki Motors of Japan as equal partners for manufacture of passenger cars and jeeps and started production in the mid-1980s. It has become during the intervening 15 years by far the biggest manufacturer of passenger cars in India. However, despite tall claims by Suzuki Motors of virtual indigenization of production, Maruti Udyog continues to import vital components for gear boxes from Suzuki Motors at prices which make a handsome profit for the company.

Korean and other motor vehicles manufacturers have established assembling plants in India during the last decade with the explicit object of gaining entry into the expanding Indian market. Other multinationals have entered banking, trading on the stock exchange, manufacture of soft drinks, Ice cream, breakfast cereals and other processed foods, building and operating luxury hotels and restaurants and manufacturing brand name clothing and shoes that pander to the tastes of youth of the urban *noveau riche*. The manufacturers of soft drinks have not fulfilled the guarantees of earning foreign exchange by export of their products which they gave to the government at the time of entry into the Indian market. Furthermore, they have killed Indian manufacturers of soft drinks. The manufacturers of breakfast cereals and ice cream have similarly killed or stifled growth of Indian companies manufacturing them. Foreign banks are making such large profits on their operations in India that their number is increasing rapidly. An Anglo-American financial company which started trading on the Bombay stock exchange triggered a bear market and caused a large outflow of foreign exchange from India earlier this year by offloading its shares. *It is difficult to find one multinational which has entered India in recent years and which has contributed to increasing the country's foreign exchange earnings or contributed to its industrial or economic development.* The examples given above of Tata Commercial Vehicles, Bharat Heavy Electrical and Hindustan Machine Tools show that participation of foreign multinationals in industrial projects is most beneficial to the economy if there are strong Indian counterparts which can quickly dispense with their assistance.

To come back to the Planning Commission, as stated earlier, the members of the Commission including the Deputy Chairman in the 1950s and the 1960s were experts. Furthermore, the Prime Minister ensured that no decision on major economic or developmental policies or on implementation of large public sector projects was taken without the approval of the Commission. It lost that position in the late 1960s after Mrs. Gandhi became the Prime Minister and has never regained it. Mrs. Gandhi did not give the importance to the views of the Commission that had been given earlier. Decisions on economic and developmental policies or implementation of public sector projects began to be taken exclusively by the Ministries and reference to the Commission for its views became virtually a formality.

Most of the members of the Commission are still experts. However, its Deputy Chairman has for nearly two decades been a senior member of the ruling party. The present Deputy Chairman is no exception (2002).[2] Furthermore, his more important role appears to be that of a political emissary of the Prime Minister in negotiations with foreign governments. During the seven months of rule of the Bharatiya Janata Party, the Deputy Chairman has spent more time abroad than in India. The Prime Minister's Council of Economic Advisers which contains besides economists some of the biggest industrialists in the country is far more important than the Commission in advising the government on economic and developmental policies. The principal function of the Commission at present is to coordinate plans of the Central and State Governments, formulate annual plans within the framework of the Five Year Plans and to review progress of state plans.

Monetary Corruption

As mentioned earlier, monetary corruption was not absent in Pandit Nehru's time. However its magnitude was miniscule in comparison with what it is today. Large contributions were made by industrial and business houses and other wealthy men towards the election expenses of the Congress Party as also of other parties including the Communist Party. They were duly recorded in the accounts of the companies as well as by the treasurers of the political parties. This practice was discontinued in the late 1960s and has not been revived, so that it is not easy to trace the sources of funds of election campaigns of different political parties or of individual candidates. Furthermore, while there was an election every five years until 1977, there have been three elections already in the two years following the fall of the Congress Government led by Mr. P.V. Narasimha Rao in 1996.

Expenses on elections are incomparably larger now than in the 1960s. The practice of serving liquor to the 'volunteers' canvassing for election of a candidate or participating in the election campaign of a party, in addition to providing them food and some compensation for their loss of earnings during the days that they spend in campaigning, rarc in the 1960s, has become common. The inevitable result is increase in monetary corruption. Those who get elected as members of Parliament or of State Legislatures have both an urgent need and ample opportunities for monetary corruption. Their salaries are adequate only to meet their day to day living expenses. How are they to recover the large expenditure that they incurred in getting elected except through monetary corruption? Furthermore, the opportunities are legion. A vote in favour of or against a proposal of a large business or industrial house could mean a gain or loss of millions to the company. The company would, therefore, ensure that the maximum numbers of MPs and/or MLAs are in favour of its proposal and would not hesitate to offer them money to obtain their support.

Many Chief Ministers who are unsure of remaining in power, reward half of the MLAs supporting them with posts of Ministers, Ministers of State or Deputy Ministers in their Cabinet, and reward others with positions in public sector enterprises in which they have opportunities for making money. The almost endemic campaigns by dissidents to dislodge ruling Chief Ministers in many states appear to be motivated by the craving for political power so that they can enrich themselves.

In the 1950s or 1960s, hardly any MLA or MP had a criminal record.[3] However the number of those with cases pending in the courts for criminal offences has become so large that both the biggest political parties and the Election Commission are trying hard to keep their number to the minimum. The Election Commission is also trying hard to ensure that the election expenses of candidates do not exceed the prescribed limits.

The Bureaucracy

There has been a sea change in the character of the bureaucracy. Monetary corruption was not absent in British times. In some department such as Public Works, it affected all but the highest members of the service. However, the middle and high level officials of the provincial civil services and the members of Indian Civil Service were people who were competent and free from corruption. They were well paid, had much prestige and power and came usually from affluent or upper middle income group families.

The position remained unchanged during the 1950s to the 1970s. Most of the direct recruits to the Indian Administrative Service were the best graduates of the Universities, came from upper middle income group families and prided themselves on doing their job honestly and well. A member who indulged in monetary corruption was regarded as a 'black sheep' and held in contempt by his service colleagues.

The top officials of the Ministries of the Government of India and of large public sector units were recruited in the 1960s or early 1970s and are still honest, hard working and efficient. However, their number is bound to decline progressively because of the pressures under which they work. Consider one example. The salary of the top officials in the Government of India, Secretaries to the Government, is Rs. 30,000 p.m. (1990). The take home salary, after deducting income-tax, and pension and provident fund contributions etc. is much less. Assuming a hundred times increase in prices since the mid-1930s, the current salary has the purchasing power of a salary of Rs. 250 to Rs. 300 p.m., which was the salary of a middle level official in the 1960s. Even the starting salary of an ICS officer was only Rs. 350 p.m. in those days. High ranking officials in the Government of India and the public sector units have small families of one to three children. However, they must ensure that their children go to the best schools and colleges so that they are educated well enough to get remunerative jobs in companies or become professionals like physicians, chartered accountants or engineers in which they are assured an upper middle class level of living and that their daughters are married in upper middle income group families. Furthermore the officials must have enough savings at the end of their service to build or buy a flat in Delhi or in the metropolitan city near their place of origin where they choose to live. Middle level officials have similar needs and aspirations. The emoluments of top-level and middle level officials must be such that their legitimate needs and aspirations such as those mentioned above are satisfied and they have no inescapable pressure to indulge in monetary corruption.

Relations between Ministers and Officials

Pandit Nehru himself and most of the Ministers in his Cabinet had great consideration for their senior officers. They had respect for their expert advice in order to ensure that there was no serious contravention of the economic or social policies of the government. Outstanding work by senior officials, by heads of public sector enterprises or experts—engineers, scientists, doctors, economists and others—was rewarded by conferment of honours. The officers reciprocated by doing their best in implementation of policies indicated by the Ministers. Sardar Patel relied so much on his secretaries that the rulers of small princely states signed the instrument of accession to the Indian Union by meeting his secretaries alone.

The system of conferring honours on high ranking officials, executives of public sector enterprises and experts working in the government departments was discontinued in the 1960s and has unfortunately not been revived. Thus one strong incentive for doing one's best has been eliminated. Furthermore, many Chief Ministers and ministers in both the Central and State Governments have developed an increasing tendency to have 'yes men' or officials belonging to their caste or community to work under them. Asking the officials or heads of nationalized banks to bend the rules in pursuit of populist policies promulgated by Ministers to consolidate their position became common in the 1970s. One result of the policy was that the losses of nationalized banks mounted rapidly during the 1970s and 1980s when they were asked to open branches in small towns or villages in which business was not enough to pay the expenses of running a branch and advance loans to farmers who were encouraged not to repay them. There has fortunately been a reversal of this policy in the last 20 years. Most of the nationalized banks are now making profits and steadily writing off their bad debts because they have been allowed to close uneconomic branches and not to give loans to non-creditworthy borrowers. The better banks such as the State Bank of India are also trying to increase operational efficiency because they see that they lose the most lucrative business to foreign banks which have much higher operational efficiency, undertake aggressive marketing and adopt modern technology to increase productivity of their employees. There is increasing respect, in the most important Ministries in the Government of India for efficient top-level officers, economists, scientists and other professionals. Many top-level officials are given extensions of one-two years beyond their statutory retirement age in order to ensure that their expertise continues to be available in the policy areas in which they have specialized. These welcome changes are unfortunately confined so far only to the Central Government. In some states on the other hand wholesale transfers of collectors and superintendents of police with changes in Chief Ministers have been witnessed in recent years. In affecting these transfers the CMs have given little thought to the difficulties such transfers create for the officers and the demoralizing effect that they have on them. It is not a coincidence that these states are among the most backward and poorly administered states in the country.

A number of examples have been given above to illustrate the changes in political culture and the bureaucracy during the last four to five decades. Some of the changes were inescapable. The idealism generated by the movement for independence could not be sustained for ever. Furthermore, leaders of the upper castes and relatively affluent groups who were in power in the first two decades after Independence had inevitably to yield power to leaders of the dominant caste and other backward castes, because these castes form the majority of the population. The ethos, motivation and thinking of the new leaders are very different from those of the earlier leaders. It is the credit of Indian society that this drastic change in the caste and class structure of the ruling elite has been accomplished without violence. It is to its credit also that some aberrations such as violence in elections and some economically debilitating populist policies have been reversed. There is need for more such changes because despite being illiterate, ignorant and desperately poor for the most part, the electorate has demonstrated in election after election that it will not tolerate inefficient governments.

There is urgent need for revival of the spirit of self-reliance in the efforts for economic development. A number of examples have been given to demonstrate that the red carpet treatment given to foreign multinationals will not assist economic development. The multinationals can contribute to economic development only if there are strong Indian collaborators who can quickly borrow the advanced technology from them and become self-reliant. Decision-making at ministerial and top bureaucratic levels has to be streamlined so that non-resident Indian businessmen and industrialists are encouraged to invest in India and Indian business houses are encouraged to invest in sorely needed infrastructure projects and also to invest in sunshine industries with potential for rapid growth such as the information technology related industries.

Political Development, Accessibility of Government

The government was accessible to the common people in some ways during British rule. The Collector, who was the district officer regularly toured his district in the cool season and listened to the grievances of the peasants in order to redress them. He was accessible also to the big landlords and businessmen and professionals such as physicians and surgeons and conferred honours on them in order to retain their loyalty. Such accessibility had been greatly reduced for some years after independence, but it has been restored after the inauguration of the Community Development (CD) programme. The Block Development Officers toured their CD blocks regularly listened to the demands of the rural people and urged them to contribute their labour and locally available materials for construction of much needed facilities such as approach roads, improving water supply sources and construction of buildings for primary and secondary schools. They conveyed also to the State Governments any complaints that the rural people had about functioning of the government. However, there is not enough contact between the Collector and the rural people. The collectors are so busy with other duties that they do not have the time to visit most of the villages in their districts. Their knowledge of the area they administer and socio-economic needs of its people are based on jeep-eyeview.

In the army, similarly the British captain of a regiment participated regularly in the games of the soldiers and had tea with them after the games. Once a month he dined with them. This contact created a bond between the officers and the men which induced the men to obey the orders of the captain implicitly even if it meant dying in battle. The men who had fought valiantly during a battle were given monetary rewards and widows of those who had died were given a pension for life which was enough to meet their living expenses. Their sons were given first preference in joining army. Such contact has been greatly reduced after independence because Indian officers do not establish the *bon homie* with their men that the British officers did.

Government should be accessible to the people through their elected representatives. Every legislator (member of the State Assembly or Parliament) is visited regularly by his constituents who present to him grievances and seek his intervention with local officials to remove them and if not to request the government to redress them. The legislators convey the demands to the Ministers and try to ensure that these are met.

There is less contact between the government and the people in the urban areas particularly in large metropolitan cities. The population of the cities is too large for the Municipal Commissioners to try to listen to the needs and problems of the people, particularly the poor. The government becomes accessible to the people only in a crisis such as outbreak of an epidemic disease or if there is a serious shortage of water, electricity or foodgrains, sugar, kerosene, which are distributed through the public distribution system. However, in order to avoid such crisis, it is essential to establish regular contact between the government and the people of metropolitan cities and the lobbies of big business such as the Federation of Indian Chambers of Commerce and Industry and Confederation of Indian Engineering Industries. The latter are consulted now in important economic policy discussions.

Political Development and Inefficiency

A major weakness of our political development is increase in corruption among several Legislators and Ministers in many State Governments, which has led to inefficiency and corruption among officials and workers in municipal, state and even some national services.

The Situation in the British Period

The British Government placed great emphasis on efficiency in all branches of public service and honesty among top ranking members of the All India and provincial civil, judicial and medical services. They were expected to deal competently with a crisis situation such as a communal riot or a flood in the area of their responsibility.

They were paid handsomely and had besides perquisites which enabled them to have a comfortable life style. Their pensions were also high enough to enable them to live comfortably in retirement. Officers who showed exceptional efficiency were knighted or given some Indian titles. Similar honours were conferred on wealthy businessmen and big landlords especially if they had taken some steps for benefit of the public or helped the British to recruit men for the armed forces. This practice ensured their loyalty to the government and gave them an incentive to do some work such as financing maintenance of a charitable hospital or a secondary school or college.

Highly successful lawyers were promoted as judges of the High Courts. One of them ended his career as Chief Justice of the Supreme Court of India.

Doctors in the provincial medical service were paid salaries which enabled them to have a comfortable life style. In addition, they were allowed private practice without prejudice to their duties in the hospitals to which they were attached. The professors and lecturers in colleges of humanities and sciences, medicine, engineering and other services were also paid well enough not to need to augment their incomes by private work. They too were honoured if they made major contributions to increasing efficiency in their service or by their research.

The Situation after Independence and up to Early 1960s

India had inherited well paid competent incorruptible civil and military services from the British. The Prime Minister, Pandit Nehru, the Home Minister, Sardar Patel, the Finance Minister and the Defense Minister relied on their advice in formulation and implementation of their policies. Integration of princely states the most important achievement of Sardar Patel was achieved with assistance from highly competent civil servants.

He used also their experience in restoring peace and order in Punjab, Delhi and Western Uttar Pradesh after the communal riots of 1947-48.

Pandit Nehru was his own Foreign Minister. But the top officers in his Ministry were those who had worked in the political affairs department of the British Government or were senior ICS officers. Pandit Nehru appointed several of them as Ambassadors or High Commissioners in European countries and others in which India had established its Embassies and High Commissions.

The Defence Ministers similarly relied on the advice of Chiefs of the defence forces in all matters relating to the defence of India. Going against their advice in 1962 led to the ignominious defeat of the Indian forces by the Chinese during October-November 1962, this only restored their prestige. Indira Gandhi relied entirely on the ability of the Commanders of the Indian Army during the war with Pakistan in 1971, which India won handsomely.

Mr. C.D. Deshmukh, the Finance Minister of India during 1950-1958 and Governor of Reserve Bank before that, was a distinguished civil servant himself. He appointed as his secretaries and governors and deputy governors of the reserve bank, officers who had shown an exceptional ability to help him formulate monetary and fiscal policies needed to promote economic development without serious strain on the balance of payments. Many of the research officers in the bank had distinguished themselves in studies in the best English or American Universities. The Deputy Governors of the Reserve Bank if not working in the bank were expected to have such ability as to command the respect of the officers of the bank.

This policy continues till today. The Governor is an eminent economist or an experienced banker. He does carry out the policies initiated by the Finance Minister but at the same time warns him against the dangers of any measures taken in response to political demands. The Governor being India's representative in the IMF, the World Bank and other international financial institutions has to enjoy also confidence of these organizations.

The higher echelons of the civil and military services remained honest up to the end of Nehru era despite effective reduction in their emoluments due to inflation. Officers of the Indian Administrative Service and other all-India and central services who succeeded the ICS remained honest because although the purchasing power of their emoluments was declining they could afford a comfortable life style in service and after retirement. Officers of the IAS whose salaries were much lower than those of the ICS were proud to belong to a distinguished service. Their emoluments, a highly subsidized house and medical care allowed them to have a comfortable life style while in service. The pensions were also adequate to allow them to live comfortably after retirement. Most of them retired after spending a decade or more in Delhi, where they could put their children through college and if they are lucky marry the sons and daughters to IAS officers or executives in corporation.

However, since some Chief Ministers were overbearing many IAS officers migrated to the Central Government in order to avoid incurring the displeasure of the Chief Ministers. The overbearing attitude of Chief Ministers and most important Ministers in Government of several large states has led to a progressive decline in the quality and efficiency of the civil services. This was understood by Pandit Nehru and his successor Mr. Lal Bahadur Shastri who was Prime Minister during 1964-66. His Finance Minister Mr. T.T. Krishnamachary, a successful businessman picked up some reliable IAS officers to fill up top positions in his Ministry and the Reserve Bank of India.

Deterioration—1962 to today

The ICS (Indian Civil Service) and other services were succeeded after Independence by the Indian Administrative Service, the Indian Foreign Service, the Indian Police Service and other central services which followed their predecessors of the British period. With this change, the emoluments and other perquisites of the officers suffered a drastic decline. However, even in the 1950s, the emoluments were high enough to attract the best graduates of Indian Universities. The members of the IAS had to work under Ministers who did not put important faith in their advice. The position is so bad now that in several states most of the IAS officers prefer to work in the Central Government and the Secretariats of states to working as Collectors or Commissioners. Today, a collector who does not bend the rules to satisfy a Minister or an influential MLA (Member Legislative Assembly) may find himself transferred to a district in which conditions of living are really bad.

The Home Ministry still depends upon the advice of the bureaucrats recruited from the Indian Administrative Service. At the other extreme the position in the Defence Ministry is so bad that the Chiefs of the armed forces routinely protest about advancement to the top position in the services of people who are junior to those whose claims have been unjustly overlooked in the promotion. They complain also that the Defence Minister relies more on the advice of the Defence Secretary, a civilian then on them. Successive Railway Ministers have routinely announced opening of new railway lines which are uneconomic, neglecting the expenditure for maintenance of the railway tract, supply of wagons, conversion of single railway track to double track and maintenance of those already constructed. The accidents resulting from such neglect are routinely put down to human error. The policy is then changed and a belated and inadequate effort is put into essential maintenance.

Competent, well-paid well-trained and uncorrupted administrative and technical services are essential for efficiency in government and avoidance of serious errors of policy and programme formulation and implementation.

Main Causes of Deterioration

One of the main causes of corruption in the political executives is that the practice of duly recording contributions to the election expenses of political parties by companies was abandoned in 1969 for political expediency and has not been restored. The result is that moneys for fighting elections are obtained from various sources—companies, big businessmen and even smugglers and other criminals. After having financed the elections of various parties and of the Ministers these criminals have no hesitation in continuing their criminal activities. The Chief Minister of one large state has been in and out of jail during the last 3 years because there are proved charges of corruption against him. However, when in jail he runs the administration through his wife who has been elected as the Chief Minister. His following among the poor people of the state is so large that every time he is sent to jail his followers start rioting.

A former Chief Minister of another large state has been convicted of massive corruption. However her political following is so large that every time her case came up for trial in the courts, her followers started a riot which was curbed with some difficulty.

Both the Chief Ministers are secure in their positions; there is no strong movement for their resignation. On the other hand there is great instability in Government in U.P. which is one of the most inefficiently administered state in India.

Corruption in some departments of the Central Government, such as Income Tax and Excise and of State Governments such as sales tax is so widespread that all officers from the inspectors to the Assistant Commissioners or even many Commissioners are presumed to be corrupt. The lowest officers in these departments can line their pockets without any fear of being persecuted by their superiors. The position is worse among employees of the municipal bodies and state electricity boards which supply electricity to both urban and rural areas. Under-payment or non-payment of municipal taxes or not attending to their duties for days together by the lowest staff such as sanitation workers is common. They do it because they have protection of influential councillors. Many councillors connive with the staff to permit encroachment on municipal lands by the slum dwellers. Theft of electricity by the slum dwellers as also by high income households, by farmers who use electric motors on surface wells is so great that most of the state electricity boards incur large losses every year. As a result, privatization of transmission and distribution of electricity is being actively considered by the Central Government. The argument is that the companies which take over the responsibility for transmission and distribution of electricity will curb theft in order to earn an adequate return on their investment. Privatization of other municipal services such as water supply and waste disposal is also being advocated for the same reason.

Movement for Change

The Indian electorate can tolerate a degree of corruption but would not tolerate when it goes beyond a limit. The Government headed by Mr. Rajiv Gandhi (1984-1989) was forced to resign because there were credible charges of corruption against it. It was followed by two unstable coalitions which were headed by inefficient Prime Ministers. The Government headed by Mr. P.V. Narsimha Rao which lasted for five years, 1991-1996, made sweeping changes in economic and fiscal policies as a result of which growth of GDP went up from 3-4 per cent per annum to 5-7 per cent per annum. India's balance of payments deficit was wiped out and has not been negative since then. But he lost the election in 1996 because there were credible charges of corruption against him and some of his Ministers. They are being tried in courts and some of them have been convicted by a Special Judge.

The present (NDA) Government which followed two unstable coalitions expects to complete its five year tenure of office, because the Prime Minister and several other Senior Ministers in the Cabinet are known to be scrupulously honest and efficient.

A determined Election Commissioner decided about six years ago to ensure that there was minimum violence in the election process. As a result, there has been little violence in the three elections to Parliament which have been held after 1996; there has been significant reduction in violence in elections to many States Legislatures also.

Ground Swell for Efficiency

The desire of the Indian electorate for honesty in government has been mentioned above. There is a similar keen desire for efficiency. Among the most popular Chief Ministers today are of Andhra Pradesh, Karnataka, Tamil Nadu. They may not all be honest but they are making determined efforts for economic development of their states. The Chief Ministers of these states are in competition to provide the most suitable infrastructure for information technology industries which are experiencing such rapid growth in India that exports of computer software services to the USA and Europe makes a major contribution to Indian export earnings. The Chief Minister of Haryana similarly, is making all out efforts to attract information technology and various consumer durable industries and offices of multinationals to the two satellite towns of Delhi—Gurgaon and Faridabad.

The Chief Ministers of Maharashtra and Gujarat are doing their best to preserve the primacy of their states in industry. Besides, there are no credible charges of corruption against any of these Chief Ministers. The Chief Minister of Andhra Pradesh, a computer buff has established a practice of receiving information everyday about events in their districts from all collectors. As a result of his system of communications governments could provide relief and ensure rehabilitation of the thousands of people who were affected by floods during a cyclone earlier this year (2000) within a week. As a result loss of life and property was reduced to the minimum. On the other hand, the Government of Orissa could not provide such relief or arrange rehabilitation of the cyclone hit people for several months; thousands died and many thousands remained homeless for months.

The Chief Minister of Punjab, a farmer himself, has persuaded or literally forced the Central Government to pay prices for wheat and rice which would provide to the farmers in his state an adequate income besides an adequate return on their investment. Due to the joint efforts of the Chief Ministers of Punjab and Haryana the environment of Chandigarh is attractive enough for it to be a most suitable location for two most rapidly growing industries—information technology and manufacture of pharmaceutical drugs.

The Chief Minister of West Bengal during 1970-1990, a wealthy barrister before he joined politics, carried out land reforms, viz. abolition of *zamindari* which had been resisted by the *Zamindars* for three decades after Independence. His government, led by the Communist Party of India has been in office for more than six decades and is secure. The principal reason for this is that the peasants vote for him (or his present successor) because the government has conferred on them full and heritable rights in lands that they cultivate. Output of rice, the main food crop has doubled after the reform and that of jute, the main cash crop also increased. The government brought peace to the industry sector of Calcutta and Howrah which had been so badly affected by the activity of militant trade unions, that most of the leading industrialist shifted their factories to Maharashtra or Tamil Nadu. Although the industries have not come back, despite the strenuous efforts of his government to woo the industrialist, the flight of capital from Calcutta and Howrah has stopped. Most important, the civil service can do their job efficiently without fear of incurring the wrath of the Chief Ministers or other Ministers.

The efficient Chief Ministers insist that the collectors in various districts of the state are efficient enough to report any untoward happening in their districts immediately to the State Government and request it to obtain financial assistance from the Government of India to provide funds for coping with a disaster such as a flood.

Dr. Manmohan Singh, an able economist himself was, as Finance Minister in the Government headed by Mr. P. V. Narasimha Rao, responsible for formulating economic policies that contributed to increasing the growth of Gross Domestic Product (GDP) by more than 50 per cent during the decade 1991-2000. He had some very able secretaries in his Ministry. This practice has been continued by the present Prime Minister and his Senior Ministers.

Civil servants who have distinguished themselves in service are not yet conferred honours but making efficient IAS or IPS officers, governors of small states has become routine.

Respect for Human Rights

The Indian administration has not been responsive to human rights for a long time. The British administrators, although trained in the liberal traditions of Oxford and Cambridge thought nothing of throwing thousands of freedom fighters in jails. Death or serious injury in police custody was also overlooked sometimes. The position is not much better today. The law and order situation in states like Bihar and the Telengana regions of Andhra Pradesh is chaotic. Burning of villages of the Scheduled Castes and hundreds of their leaders by armed gangs of high castes is common. In Telengana villages, similarly burning of villages of the Scheduled Castes and killing of particular landlords is common. Murder or kidnapping of leaders of one gang by a group of others in Mumbai is routine and the police is powerless to stop it.

The British however maintained law and order at all costs. This is no longer possible now as mentioned above. For the situation to improve, it is essential first that all those against whom there are charges of any serious crime, such as murder, or rape should be debarred from contesting elections to the State Legislators or from holding any other elective office. Second, any police officer against whom there are charges of causing death or serious injury to any person in judicial custody or overlooking such a death should be immediately suspended and then tried like any other criminals. Members against whom there are such charges have to resign because of unrelenting criticism against their continuance in the State Governments. A government like that of Orissa in which hundreds died due to lack of food or shelter for weeks after the cyclone in 1998 due to its inefficiency should be dismissed by the President. These and similar other steps should continue so that the State Governments have grater respect for human rights.

Change in Governance—the Role of the Courts and the Electorate

Respect for efficiency and honesty of senior officers is being slowly restored after three decades of decline in it. Increase in their emoluments and other perquisites so that they can have a comfortable life style without resort to corruption is a matter of time. The electorate realizes that a certain degree of corruption among the Ministers is inescapable. But there is a keen desire for honesty and efficiency among government officers. The elections in Punjab earlier this year (2001) replaced an unpopular and corrupt government of Akali Dal which had been in office for more than two decades, and replaced it with one headed by a Chief Minister who is known to be honest and efficient. The electorate of Tamil Nadu has similarly dismissed a corrupt and inefficient government but has replaced it with another who is not scrupulously honest but is efficient and is assisting rapid economic development in the state.

Some of the improvements in governance through intervention of courts and demand of the voters has led to improvement in governance as illustrated by the example of Delhi—the capital of India.

Safety Nets in the Sea of Corruption and Inefficiency Independent Judiciary and Judicial Activism

The judiciary was not independent during the British period. Despite promises to the contrary the courts assisted in implementation of policies of the administration. During the Quit India Movement of 1942 thousands including the top most leaders of the Congress Party were sent to jail without trial and remained there till the duration of the Second World War.

Independence of the judiciary is a basic principal of the Constitution of India. Furthermore, all citizens of India have a right to fair trial, if accused of any crime. This position continued till the Emergency which lasted between 1974 and 1977. Hundreds were put in jails without trial. Torture of those in jails was common. But most of those guilty of such crimes were not convicted until after the emergency ended. After the emergency the Supreme Court and the High Courts in most of the important states have regained their independence, regaining of the independence is a most hopeful development in the process of India's development of a vibrant democracy.

The courts routinely blame the governments for wilful neglect or inefficiency in performance of some of their essential functions. In Delhi, public interest petitions are filed by concerned citizens for the failure of the state electricity or water supply boards to guarantee uninterrupted supplies of electricity and water in metropolitan cities. The Supreme Court or the High Courts pass strictures against them and order them to take action to improve performance. Its role in ensuring cleaner and safer Delhi described below is indeed commendable

Some Recent Interventions by the Supreme Court

During the two months (October-November 2000) the Supreme Court has passed an order to raise the height of the Sardar Sarovar Dam by five metres and asked the states to ensure resettlement of the persons, whose homes will be submerged, without delays. Madhya Pradesh and other states are taking action accordingly. Through another order, the court has forced the Government of Karnataka and Tamil Nadu to desist from freeing TADA accused headed by forest brigand Veerapan in exchange for release of the actor Rajkumar. The states have complied. Meanwhile, Rajkumar has been released.

The Working of the Supreme Court, Electoral Process and Creation of Additional Institutions of Governance : The Case of Delhi National Capital Region.

Towards a Cleaner and Safer Delhi—Role of the Courts

Delhi, Capital of India, has a number of bodies for providing municipal services and land development for provision of housing for its rapidly increasing population. Except the area under the jurisdiction of New Delhi Municipal Committee (NDMC), the Municipal Corporation of Delhi (MCD) performs municipal functions in the contiguously urbanized area of the city, located within Delhi state. The area had a population of more than 8 million in 1991, which is projected to increase to almost 13 million by 2001.

The two municipal bodies have responsibility for lighting and cleaning of streets (including removal of garbage), maintenance, widening and repair of roads, ensuring that vacant areas of government land are not encroached upon and demolishing unauthorized structures. Besides, they run a number of primary and secondary schools and health care centres. The Municipal Corporation manages also three hospitals.

The Delhi Development Authority (DDA) was created in the late 1950s to oversee implementation of Delhi's long-term Master Plan 1962-1981. It has developed large areas of land for house building by individuals and by cooperative housing societies and for location of markets, parks, schools, hospitals and other public purposes. Furthermore, it has built tens of thousands of dwelling units for housing people of low and middle-income groups in the capital.

Role of the Government

In addition, Delhi has a democratically elected State Government, which has among its responsibilities development of industries and agriculture, provision of education, health and welfare services and ensuring supplies of food at reasonable prices. Finally, since Delhi is the capital, the National government and the Delhi Government have responsibility for providing security of life and property to the citizens. The bodies which are responsible for providing water and electricity to Delhi and operating the sewerage system and providing public transport are affiliated to the Municipal Corporation of Delhi or are autonomous.

Problems of Delhi

Pollution

Delhi has very high levels of pollution of air and water. Since the public transport system consisting of buses is totally inadequate to meet the needs of the people, Delhi has a very large number of bicycles, motor bicycles, and passenger cars for personal transport and three-wheeler and four-wheeler taxis for public transport. Pollution of air is due primarily to the solid particulate matter emitted by the exhausts of the motor vehicles.

Pollution of water is due to inefficient maintenance of the sewerage system and large areas of the city not being served by the sewerage system at all. Several sewerage treatment plants are not functioning at all or are functioning much below capacity.

Yet it has been left to the Supreme Court, which has responsibility for upholding the Constitution of India to ensure that the levels of pollution of air and water are reduced so that Delhi does not become the most polluted and filthiest capital in the world.

In two judgments delivered almost two years ago (in 2000), in response to public interest petitions, the court ordered that : (i) all three-wheeler and four-wheeler taxis which were more than 15 years old should go off Delhi's roads; and (ii) only 1500 new vehicles which meet Euro I standards should be registered up to June 2000 and those that meet Euro II standards should only be registered after this date.

The foreign (Korean) manufacturers of passenger cars claimed that their cars already met the standards laid down by the court. However, Maruti Udyog, the biggest supplier of passenger cars in India, petitioned the court that it needed more time in order to manufacture cars which met the standards laid down by the court. The court granted its request but observed that Suzuki Motors, which owns fifty per cent of the equity in Maruti Udyog—the balance is owned by the Government of India—has been making cars meeting Euro II standard in Japan for several years but has transferred an obsolete technology to India, a practice which is common among multinational corporations investing in developing countries. Now in order to save its market share, Maruti Udyog has also brought out new models, which meet Euro II standards. The State Government implemented the orders despite strikes by owners of three-wheeler and four-wheeler taxis. The old vehicles have gone off the roads.

The beneficial effect of the court's order is already apparent. There is significantly less solid particular matter and other pollutants in Delhi's air, although the number of motor vehicles has increased.

Delhi has a large number of industrial units that discharge pollutants including poisons such as chemicals containing mercury and nickel into the water of the Yamuna turning the river into a virtual sewer and making its water unfit for drinking for long distances downstream of Delhi. The court had ordered sometime back that these units be closed. The State Government has belatedly begun to seal these units but has allowed some units to reopen under pressure from the owners.

A large number of large or medium sized industrial units making consumer goods and consumer durables—garments, bed and table linen, pharmaceutical drugs, refrigerators, air conditioners and passenger cars are located in four satellite cities of Delhi-Ghaziabad and NOIDA in Uttar Pradesh and Gurgaon and Faridabad in Haryana. The workshops and service facilities for repair of the consumer durables sold in Delhi are also located in them or along the highways connecting them with Delhi. Their owners have chosen these locations because labour is much cheaper than in Delhi. Furthermore, they can get land for location of their units and for their expansion with increase in demand at much lower prices than in Delhi.

The workers in these units live in the satellite cities, although the proprietors may commute from Delhi. Maruti Udyog has a worker's colony within its large compound.

A large number of multinational corporations are locating their regional offices in Gurgaon where suitable air-conditioned office space and apartments or houses for their employees and executives have been built by private builders in preference to location in the central business district of Connaught Place. Office space in the latter is too expensive and is not large enough for the needs of the multinationals. Furthermore, Connaught Place has very high levels of air and noise pollution and is so congested that there are traffic jams, which take several minutes to clear. Gurgaon is free from all these problems.

If the large and medium scale polluting units located in Delhi were to move out, they would find larger space for expansion. Installation of effluent treatment plants can often be self-financing because the treated effluent can be sold as valuable manure or as construction material.

Slums and Littering

Creation of Slums

That squatting on public land is done with the connivance of politicians is indicated by an event, which is in progress at present (May 2000). The railways wanted to remove about 30,000 squatters whose huts are located on railway land alongside railway tracks. Their removal is essential in order to increase safety of railway travel. However, a former Prime Minister of India has stepped in on behalf of the slum dwellers saying that he would undertake a fast unto death if the slum dwellers were removed without providing an alternative site for their huts. The Railway Board is now looking frantically for an alternative site for location of the huts.

In a major judgment delivered on 17th February, 2000, affecting at least 30 lakhs (3 million) people living in the capital's slums, the Supreme Court has asked the authorities to remove their shelters and stop further growth of unauthorized hutments on public land.

Asking the authorities to file compliance reports within eight weeks, the Court warned that violation of the directives would be viewed seriously. Explaining the order, the court observed :

> "When a large number of inhabitants live in unauthorized colonies with no proper means of dealing with domestic effluents or live in slums with no care for hygiene, the problem becomes more complex."

On the mushrooming growth of the slums the court stressed that, "establishment or creation of slums appears to be good business and is well organized. Large areas of public land are usurped in this way for private use free of cost. It is difficult to believe this can happen without the passive or active connivance of the land owning agencies and the municipal authorities."

Some Solutions for Problems of the Slums

It is difficult to see how 30 lakh (3 million) people who constitute nearly one-fourth of population of the city can be moved out of Delhi. It is difficult also to stop in-migration of the rural poor into Delhi when about 400,000 people are estimated to come into Delhi every year. Here they find jobs as construction workers, as unskilled and skilled industrial workers, domestic servants, watchmen, gardeners and artisans—carpenters, masons, drivers and repairmen of motor vehicles, electricians and repairmen of electrical or electronic goods. They come from all over the country. The construction labourers come mainly from Rajasthan; the gardeners come from U.P., the watchmen come from Haryana, Bihar and U.P., the unskilled industrial workers come from U.P., Bihar, Orissa and even Bangladesh. The skilled workers come mainly from Punjab and Haryana. The incomes of all except artisans or repairmen are too low to allow them to afford proper housing. The architects have yet to evolve low cost housing with arrangements for supply of drinking water and its drainage that can be rented or owned in course of time by the present slum dwellers.

The earnings of the artisans and repairmen are high enough for them to live in colonies with brick and mortar houses and electricity and drinking water supply connection. They could be provided sewerage facilities if the system was expanded. They could pay the necessary connection fees because most of them drive motorcycles or scooters for personal transport and some even have cars. The number of domestic servants living in slums could be reduced, if the middle income and affluent households that employ them provided them housing within their own dwelling units. Similarly, the security agencies that employ watchmen should provide housing for them in Delhi or its outskirts next to their own offices.

Littering

Egged on by the Supreme Court, the Delhi State Government is appointing 108 Area Magistrates who will fine on the spot, individual pedestrians or motorists caught littering the roads by throwing banana skins or a bunch of groundnut shells. Citizen activists are also proposed to be involved in preventing littering. The Magistrates are finding it difficult to carry out their duties. There have already been fist fights between the Magistrates and litterbugs outside fruit juice stands and wayside eateries whose customers litter the roads. The police have had to intervene to bring the situation under control. The habit of tolerating littering is so deeply ingrained among the sanitary inspectors who fine the litterbugs that they say they are doing this only in order to carry out the orders of the Supreme Court. Apparently they themselves are not concerned about the utility of what they are doing.

The time of the court is most valuable. There is such a large backlog of cases pending decisions of the Supreme Court and of the High Courts in the states that they should be allowed to concentrate on this work. As a people, we adopt quickly to the 'no littering' norm, as soon as we go abroad. There is no reason why we should live in filth and litter in our own country. (*Times of India*, February 18, 2000)

Clean Water and Air

The various orders of the Supreme Court have already begun to clean Delhi's air and water. Reduction in the pollutants in the air has been mentioned earlier. There is some evidence also of reduction in pollution of water of the river as it leaves Delhi. But it would be far better if the job of ensuring reduction in pollution was done by the State Government or the municipal bodies and did not require intervention of the Supreme Court.

It is the strength of India's system of domestic governance that when one branch of government fails to protect the public welfare, another steps in. Egged on by the strictures of the Supreme Court the Delhi State

Government has already taken a number of initiatives to reduce pollution of air and water in Delhi and is contemplating others.

The initiative of the Supreme Court has created awareness among the public about the dangers of high levels of air and water pollution in Delhi. It is unlikely that the politicians would find it as easy as they have done until now to encourage squatting on public land.

Shifting of Markets of Fruit and Vegetables and Hazardous Materials

Two years ago (in 2000), there was a fire in a crowded locality at the northern edge of Shahjahanabad (old Delhi) that has godowns that store hazardous materials such as paints and offices of truck companies that bring these materials into Delhi. About fifty people died and about a hundred were injured. This loss of life could have been much greater because of the inflammable nature of the materials. However, neither the MCD nor the State Government has taken any action to shift the market to a safer location on the outskirts of Delhi. The shift would result in saving of time and cost of bringing these materials into the heart of Delhi. The old market for fruit and vegetables located in an extension of Shahjahanabad has been shifted to two locations on the northern and southern outskirts. The result is reduced wastage of the produce, due to larger space for storage of fruits and vegetables now available in the new locations, needed to meet the much larger demands of the increasing population of Delhi, than was available in the old market.

Besides valuable land has been made available for housing, schools and health centres in the centre of Delhi which was occupied by the market. Similarly, the markets for building materials—timber, cement, marble and steel have been shifted to various other locations from their own locations in Paharganj. Perhaps it will take an order of the Supreme Court to induce the State Government of Delhi to shift the markets for hazardous materials.

The case of Delhi illustrates that the Supreme Court has to intervene to effect improvements in essential civil services. Apparently despite or because of the multiplicities of various authorities to provide essential services, the level of efficiency of the services remains low despite the claims to the contrary. Political pressure by various groups—polluting industries, the Delhi Jal Board or the Sewerage Board nullifies several attempts at a cleaner and greener Delhi. True rapid growth of economic activities and population's lack of pride of belonging to a city, majority of who are temporary migrants, is a major problem.

NOTES

1. The famous Mudra case when T.T. Krishnamachari was the Finance Minister.
2. An exception has been made by the present Prime Minister, Dr. Manmohan Singh in appointment of Dr. Montek Ahluwalia as the Deputy Chairman of the Planning Commission.
3. The issue of tainted Ministers in the present government raised by the opposition party has stalled the Parliament for hours since 2002.

Section III

Land Utilization and Settlement Patterns in India

15

Land Utilization in India (1953)*

Introduction

The main objective of this chapter is to analyse, from the data available, the general pattern of land utilization in this country, i.e. the pattern of distribution of land among its important uses like cultivation, grazing, forestry, settlements, etc. An attempt has also been made to assess the possibilities of securing more intensive use of the land resources, and in particular of increasing the area under cultivation and analyze problems connected with land utilization. However, it is not possible in a paper of this type to treat these problems at length, or to make detailed suggestions for the improvement of land use. These are beyond the scope of this paper and belong to the wider fields of agriculture, forest or pasture management.

Cultivation, grazing and forestry are the three main uses of land. Most of the land in any country is occupied by these three uses. Other uses of land, e.g. towns and villages, factories, roads, railways, canals, etc., although very important from the economic standpoint, occupy relatively small areas. Of the three main uses, cultivation is the most intensive, and there is a tendency in all countries, as population increases and demands of food supply grow, to bring as large areas as possible under cultivation. This tendency is particularly strong in old and densely populated countries like India, China and Japan in which the pressure of population on land is very high. However, the possibilities of cultivation are limited by physical factors like inadequate or badly distributed rainfall, low temperatures, hilly and mountainous terrain, thin or infertile soils, so that large areas in every country are under forests or grazing lands, or lie

---

* Published in *Journal of Soil and Water Conservation in India*, 1953, Vol. I, No. 2, pp. 4-18.

barren and unproductive. The pattern of land utilization in a country is thus conditioned by two sets of factors :

(i) The physical factors like climate, topography and soils which set the broad limits upon the capabilities of the land, and

(ii) The human factors like length of occupation of the area, density of population, social and economic institutions (especially systems of land tenure) and the technological levels of the people, which determine the extent to which the physical capacities of land are utilized.

In newly settled sparsely populated countries like the countries of North and South America, Australia and New Zealand there are still considerable areas in which land utilization can be more intensive. Large areas which are at present used for grazing or are under forests can be brought under cultivation, if populations increase and the demands on land are greater than they are today. But, in old densely populated countries like India, China, Japan and most countries of Europe, where adjustment to the physical environment has been going on for ages and the pressure of growing populations has operated to bring under use all land that is usable, the pattern of land utilization comes much closer to the physical capabilities of the land. In such countries possibilities of making land use more intensive are dependent in the main upon measures like large scale irrigation; reclamation of land with the aid of heavy machinery; drainage; correction of soil defects like salinity and alkalinity through chemical means, which involve application of modern scientific and engineering techniques.

Also, it should be emphasized that in these old countries possibilities of increasing production from land are much more in the direction of improved agricultural, forest or pasture management techniques than in securing a more intensive land use pattern. Thus in India, increases in agricultural production have to come mainly through increased production from the lands already under cultivation. Increases resulting from increased area under cultivation can only be limited for the simple reason that the additional acreages which can be brought under cultivation are comparatively small. Improvements in the pattern of land use are essential not only for increasing production but also for improving physical and hydrographic conditions and for controlling soil erosion, floods and other problems.

The general pattern of land utilization in different regions of the world is shown in Table 15.1. It will be seen from this table that the highest proportions of arable land are in South Central Asia (Indian Union, Ceylon

Table 15.1 : Land Utilization in the World (by Regional Divisions)

(Figures in 1000 hectares)

	Total Area	Arable Land including Current Fallows and Orchards	Per cent of Total Area	Permanent Meadows and Pastures	Per cent of Total Area	Forests and Wood Lands	Per cent of Total Area	Unused but Potentially Productive	Per cent of Total Area	Built on Area Waste Land and Other	Per cent of Total Area
		I		II		III		IV		V	
1	2	3	4	5	6	7	8	9	10	11	12
(i) Europe	493,00	147,000	29.8	96,000	19.5	128,000	26.0	10,000	2.0	112,000	22.7
(ii) USSR*	2,227,000	225,000	10.1	124,000	5.6	920,000	41.3	12,000	0.5	946,000	42.5
(iii) USA & Canada	1,930,293	221,068	11.4	314,206	16.3	653,259	33.8	93,100	5.0	648,085	33.5
(iv) Central America	497,707	19,932	4.0	106,794	21.4	110,741	22.2	13,900	2.7	246,915	49.6
(v) South America	1,779,000	64,000	3.6	343,000	19.3	746,000	41.9	66,000	3.7	560,000	31.5
(vi) Africa	3,042,000	187,000	6.2	579,000	19.0	918,000	30.2	80,000	2.6	1,278,000	42.0
(vii) Oceania	856,000	19,000	2.2	368,000	43.0	76,000	8.9	12,000	1.4	381,000	44.5
(viii) Asia (excl. USSR)	2,684,000	346,000	12.9	257,000	9.6	472,000	17.6	92,000	3.4	1,517,000	56.5
(a) The Far East	1,193,556	101,493	8.5	194,639	16.3	124,229	10.4	23	Neg.	772,465	64.7
(b) South East Asia	449,318	42,190	9.4	966	0.2	266,811	59.4	9,218	2.0	130,133	29.0
(c) South Central Asia	435,600	159,326	36.6	—	—	45,091	10.3	46,759	10.7	184,424	42.3
(d) South West Asia	605,179	39,814	6.6	61,707	10.2	34,283	5.7	36,388	6.0	403,057	66.6
World Total	13,509,000	1,230,000	9.1	2,187,000	16.2	4,024,000	29.8	379,000	2.8	5,689,000	42.1

*Unofficial figures.

Source : "Year Book of Food and Agriculture Statistics", 1950, Vol. IV, Part I, FAO, Washington DC, 1951.

and Pakistan) and Europe. In the latter, favourable natural factors like moderate temperatures, adequate and well-distributed rainfall, large areas of plains with fairly fertile soils, combined with the high levels of cultural and technological development attained by the people account for the very large percentage of arable land and relatively small areas of barren and unproductive lands. In South Central Asia, the high proportions are due primarily to the existence of large areas of fertile plains. Climatic conditions in this region are not so favourable as in Europe. Rainfall in most of the region is concentrated in a short period of the year, is precarious and over large areas (especially in the north-west) insufficient for cultivation. In India, sown area is about 33 per cent of the total land area. Although due to the high density of population, sown area per capita is very low in India (about three-fourths of an acre), it is nevertheless true that among the large countries of the world, India has about the highest percentage of land devoted to cultivation.

At the other extreme from Europe and South Central Asia are regions like South America and Oceania (composed mainly of Australia and New Zealand), in which proportions of arable lands are very low and large areas are barren and unproductive. A large part of Australia is desert and other large areas are used for grazing as rainfall is too low for agriculture. In South America, large areas are occupied by forests and grasslands. In both continents, the short length of occupation is also an important reason for the proportions of arable land being low. Considerable possibilities of extension of cultivation exist in both, and as populations grow and demands on land increase, the areas under cultivation will undoubtedly increase.

The Land Use Pattern in India

The main source of information on land utilization is statistics on classification of land in the "Agricultural Statistics of India". Land is divided into five classes : forests, areas not available for cultivation, current fallows, other uncultivated land excluding current fallows, and net area sown. Figures on areas sown more than once and areas irrigated are also given. The figures for Indian Union for the year 1949-50 are given in Table 15.2. State-wise figures are given in Table 15.3.

Statistics from the different parts of the country are not of the same degree of reliability and accuracy. In areas of temporary settlement, in which a regular reporting agency has existed, the statistics are based on field to field inspection and are fairly reliable. But in areas of permanent settlement, where such agency did not exist, the statistics are much less

Table 15.2 : Classification of Land in the Indian Union in 1949-50

	Area (1000 acres)	*Per cent of total*
Gross area	810,809	100.0
Unclassified area	196,199	24.2
Classified area	614,610	75.8
Net area sown	266,372	32.9
Current fallows	58,171	7.2
Other uncultivated land excluding current fallows	98,400	12.2
Not available for cultivation	96,024	11.9
Forests	93,143	11.5
Area sown more than once	35,514	—
Gross area sown	301,886	—
Irrigated area	48,652	—

reliable. Statistics for areas forming part of the former Indian States are similarly very variable. The position regarding classification of land statistics and the steps which have been taken in recent years for their improvement are discussed at somewhat greater length in Appendix I.

Unclassified Areas

Out of a total land area of 810.8 million acres, statistics on classification of land cover about 614.6 million acres. The remaining 196.2 million acres or 24 per cent of the total land area are unclassified. The unclassified areas are located mostly in the territories of the former Indian States. They have been held mostly as *jagirs* or other forms of privileged tenures, and are also unsurveyed for the most part. More than 90 per cent of the area of unclassified lands is in seven States, mostly Part B and Part C States, as shown in the figures in Table 15.4.

Nearly a third of the total unclassified area is in Rajasthan, most of it forming part of the Thar Desert. Over 27 per cent is in Jammu and Kashmir and is hilly and mountainous for the most part. In the other States also, the unclassified areas are located mostly in the hilly, dry or inaccessible sections. Thus in Assam and Orissa, these are located in the hilly sections covered by jungles and inhabited mostly by tribal people. From this distribution, it appears that most of the unclassified areas are either barren or unproductive or are suitable only for forests or grazing; the proportions suitable for cultivation are not large. Reporting is being gradually extended into the unclassified lands. Within the last two years their acreage has been reduced by about 19 million acres, from 214.84 million acres in 1947-48 to 196.2 million acres in 1949-50.

Table 15.3 : Classification of Land in the Indian Union (By States), 1949-50

(Figures in 1000 acres)

Name of the State	Gross Area	Classified Area (area according to village papers for which returns exist)	Forest	Not Available for cultivation	Other Uncult-vated land excluding current fallows	Current Fallows	Net area sown	Area sown more than once	Gross area sown	Cultivable area included in (6)	Net Area Irrigated	% Sown area of Total area (8/2)	% Irrigated area of net area sown (12/8)
1	2	3	4	5	6	7	8	9	10	11	12	13	14
Part A States													
Assam	54,404	33,400	4,002	4,248	16,946	1,739	5,570	823	6,393	—	1,327	10.23	23.6
Bihar	45,011	44,790	7,884	3,747	5,574	4,737	22,848	6,285	29,133	N.A.	5,595	50.76	25.3
Bombay	71,213	70,212	9,914	8,473	2,098	7,042	41,082	1,281	42,363	1,058	1,761	57.69	4.3
Madhya Pradesh	83,375	83,104	23,645	5,817	20,267	4,919	28,456	3,738	32,194	5,764	1,691	34.13	5.9
Madras	81,786	80,757	13,814	14,647	11,272	9,716	31,308	5,037	36,345	245	9,850	38.28	31.5
Orissa	38,487	18,264	2,502	4,736	3,498	1,169	6,359	965	7,324	—	1,672	16.52	26.3
Punjab (I)	23,922	23,208	759	6,034	2,587	1,880	11,948	2,183	14,136	307	4,790	49.95	40.2
Uttar Pradesh	72,597	72,224	7,819	11,834	10,240	2,562	39,769	9,459	49,228	—	10,878	54.78	27.3
West Bengal	19,696	19,549	1,713	3,046	1,919	1,159	11,720	1,291	13,011	N.A.	2,329	59.50	19.8
Total	490,491	445,508	72,052	62,582	74,401	34,923	199,060	31,062	230,127	7,374	39,893	40.58	20.0
Part B States													
Hyderabad	52,572	52,927	6,187	8,572	985	13,119	24,064	135	24,199	N.A.	1,488	45.77	6.2
Jammu & Kashmir	59,379	5,799*	1,472*	1,801*	564*	406*	1,556*	108*	1,664*	74*	701*	—	45.0
Madhya Bharat	29,785	27,625	2,880	6,215	6,669	1,109	10,752	688	11,440	—	462	36.70	4.3
Mysore	18,873	17,385	1,957	5,705	1,460	1,807	6,456	140	6,596	—	1,152	34.20	17.8
PEPSU	6,431	6,371	46	398	936	876	4,115	675	4,790	—	1,845	63.98	44.8
Rajasthan	83,332	20,669	655	4,223	4,544	2,862	8,385	1,065	9,450	10	1,503	10.06	16.9
Saurashtra	13,655	1,397	7	155	222	—	1,013	—	1,013	N.A.	54	7.42	5.3

(Contd.)

(Contd.)

Name of the State	Gross Area	Classified Area (area according to village papers for which returns exist)	Forest	Not Available for cultivation	Other Uncult-vated land excluding current fallows	Current Fallows	Net Area sown	Area sown more than once	Gross area sown	Cultivable area included in (6)	Net Area Irrigated	% Sown area of Total area (8/2)	% Irrigated area of net area sown (12/8)
1	2	3	4	5	6	7	8	9	10	11	12	13	14
Travancore-Cochin	5,852	5,350	1,542	482	429	68	2,829	217	3,046	N.A.	940	48.34	33.2
Total	269,879	137,523	14,746	27,551	15,809	20,247	59,170	3,028	62,198	84	8,145	21.92	13.7
Part C States													
Ajmer	1,547	1,561	47	595	303	247	369	37	406	N.A.	117	23.54	31.8
Bhopal	4,402	4,406	953	937	858	107	1,551	57	1,608	N.A.	17	36.14	1.1
Bilaspur	290	285	30	29	136	15	75	45	120	N.A.	5	25.98	6.6
Coorg	1,015	1,012	331	250	226	35	170	1	171	N.A.	7	16.76	4.1
Delhi	370	366	(a)	80	50	11	225	49	274	N.A.	68	60.81	30.2
Himachal Pradesh	6,692	1,956	342	365	627	60	562	349	911	—	135	8.28	24.0
Cutch	10,864	5,003	127	1,407	1,200	1,466	741	23	764	599	69	6.98	9.3
Manipur	5,522	—	—	—	—	—	—	—	—	—	—	—	—
Tripura	2,580	2,634	1,715	17	501	14	387	70	457	13	—	15.00	—
Vindhya Pradesh	15,104	14,356	2,740	2,211	4,297	1,046	4,062	788	4,850	3,484	196	26.89	4.8
Total	48,386	31,579	6,285	5,891	8,198	3,001	8,142	1,419	9,561	4,096	614	16.81	7.5
Part D Areas													
Andamans & Nicobar Islands	2,058	—	—	—	—	—	—	—	—	—	—	—	—
Grand Total	810,809	614,610	93,143	96,024	98,400	58,171	266,372	35,514	301,886	11,554	48,652	32.85	18.5

* Excluding enemy-held areas. (a) Less than 500 acres.

Table 15.4 : Distribution of Unclassified Areas

State	*Unclassified area (thousand acres)*	*Per cent of total for Indian Union*
Rajasthan	62,663	31.6
Jammu and Kashmir	53,580	27.3
Assam	21,004	10.7
Orissa	20,223	10.4
Saurashtra	12,258	6.2
Cutch	5,861	3.0
Himachal Pradesh	4,736	2.4
Madhya Bharat	2,160	1.1
Total Seven States	182,485	92.7
Total Indian Union	196,199	100.0

Net Area Sown

Net area sown totals 266.37 million acres. This is 33 per cent of the land area of the country, but 43 per cent of the classified area. The term "net area sown" refers to the physical area sown to crops. To arrive at the total acreage of crops sown or what is called "gross area sown", figures for areas sown more than once must be added to the net area sown. In 1949-50, 35.5 million acres were sown more than once, bringing the gross sown area to 301.9 million acres.

Area sown more than once forms about 13 per cent of the net sown area. This proportion is rather low especially in view of the fact that in practically all parts of India temperatures are high enough for plant growth to continue uninterrupted throughout the year. There is no period of cessation of plant growth as is experienced in winter in temperate lands like those of Europe and North America. The main limiting factor in case of India is deficiency of moisture. Rainfall in most parts of the country is concentrated in a short period of 3 to 6 months. In the remaining months of the year, there is very little rain, and crops have to depend on irrigation or moisture available from the sub-soil. One of the main functions of irrigation in India, therefore, is to make possible production of two or more crops in the year from lands which could produce only one crop otherwise. Secondly, the fertility levels of most of our crop-lands are low, because applications of farm-yard manure are generally inadequate and the use of chemical fertilizers has been practically non-existent. This is also an important reason for large areas being able to grow only one crop in the year. The large programme of extension of irrigation facilities which is being undertaken as part of the Five Year Plan and the increasing emphasis on use of manures and fertilizers should result in considerable increases in areas sown more than once.

Distribution of Sown Area

The percentage of sown area to the total land area varies greatly in different parts of the country, depending mainly upon physical conditions of climate, topography and soils. The highest percentages are in the Indo-Gangetic Plain and in the plains along the east and west coasts. In many parts of these plains, as much as 80 to 90 per cent of the land is under cultivation. On the other hand, in mountainous or arid areas, the proportion of crop-land to the total may drop to 10 per cent or even lower. It will be seen from Table 15.3 that in the five States of West Bengal, Bihar, U.P., Punjab and PEPSU, which have most of their area in the Indo-Gangetic plain, the proportions of sown area to the total vary between 50 and 65 per cent. The proportions would be much higher if the hilly and mountainous sections of these States are excluded. These five States together have about 34 per cent of the net sown area of the country, although their land area is only 20 per cent of the country's total. Their share in the gross sown area is even higher—37 per cent—because the proportions of areas sown more than once are higher in these States than in most other parts of the country. These latter range from about 20 per cent in the Punjab and PEPSU to more than 30 per cent in Bihar, while the average for the whole country is only 13 per cent.

In the States situated in Peninsular India, the proportions of crop-land to the total vary generally between 30 and 50 per cent, and are much lower than in the plains. In Madhya Bharat, Madhya Pradesh and Mysore, about 35 per cent of the land area is sown, in Madras the proportion is 38 per cent and in Hyderabad 46 per cent.

Comparisons with mountainous and arid States are rendered somewhat difficult because of the existence of large areas of unclassified lands in these. But the acreages reported under crops are quite low and generally range between 10 and 20 per cent of the land area. In Cutch, the proportion is only 7 per cent shown in Table 15.5. The Part A States have generally much higher proportions of lands under cultivation than the Part B and Part C States. The reason for this is mainly historical. British rule spread over most of the fertile plains of the country, leaving the hilly, mountainous, and arid sections, and large parts of the peninsular plateau under Indian princes. Most of the Part B and Part C States have large areas of hilly, mountainous or dry lands. States like Travancore-Cochin and PEPSU which are situated in the plains are the exception rather than the rule among them. On the other hand, the Part A

States include large areas of plains. The area of the Part A States is only three-fifths of the country's total area, but they have nearly four-fifths of the sown area. On the other hand, the Part B States with 33 per cent of the land area, have 22 per cent of the sown area and the C States with 6 per cent of the land area have only 3 per cent of the sown area.

Table 15.5 : Total Area and Area Sown by States Grouped as A, B & C of the Indian Union

	Total Area (million acres)	*Per Cent of Indian Union*	*Sown Area (million acres)*	*Per Cent of Indian Union*	*Sown Area Total Area per cent*
Part A States	490.49	60.5	199.06	78.4	40.6
Part B States	269.88	33.3	59.17	22.1	21.8
Part C States	48.39	5.9	8.14	3.0	16.6
Total Indian Union	810.81	100.0	266.37	100.0	32.9

Current Fallows

The term "current fallows" is applied to lands which were not under crops at the time of reporting but which had been sown in the recent past. The definitions of "current fallows", however, vary greatly in different parts of the country so that the figures on "current fallows" from different States are not comparable. In the Punjab, for instance, land is classified as "current fallows" if it has been left uncultivated for less than two years. Land lying uncultivated for more than two years is classified as "other uncultivated land excluding current fallows". In Bombay, on the other hand, land continues to be classified as "current fallows" if it has remained uncultivated for less than ten years. Definitions of "current fallows" as adopted in some of the States are given in Appendix II.

The total area reported under "current fallows" was 58.1 million acres, or 7.5 per cent of the total land area in 1949-50. States having the largest acreages were : Hyderabad, Madras, Bombay, Madhya Pradesh and Bihar. Together, these five States accounted for about three-fifths of the total acreage under "current fallows", Hyderabad alone having almost one-fifth of the total. How far the large areas reported under this class in these States is due to physical conditions or the nature of the farming system, and how far do these result from the particular methods of classification, it is difficult to say. Under the system of dry farming, which is followed in many parts of Bombay and some other States, a plot of land is cultivated only once in two, three or more years, so that large areas of fallow should be expected wherever this system is followed. On the other hand, Hyderabad, which reports such large areas under "current fallows", and also Bombay, have very small acreages under "other uncultivated land excluding current fallows", indicating that considerable acreages which are reported under the latter class in other States may be reported as "current fallows" in these States. In Hyderabad, there has been a marked increase in the acreage reported as "current fallows" in recent years. The area has increased steadily from 4.6 million acres in 1940-41 to 13.4 million acres in 1947-48 and again 13.3 million acres in 1949-50. The reasons for this increase are not clear, however.

Other Uncultivated Land Excluding Current Fallows

In this class are included all uncultivated lands which are not reported under other heads, viz. "forests", "not available for cultivation" and "current fallows". Thus most of the areas under village groves and pastures, areas covered with jungle scrubs and bamboos as also large areas of private forests are included in this class. Some of these lands have been cultivated in the recent past, for, as mentioned above, land under "current fallows" is brought under this class if it remains uncultivated beyond a specified period. But large areas may have remained uncultivated since long. Formerly, the term "cultivable waste" was used for these lands, but this term had to be given up because it was realized that large areas were not fit for cultivation due to rough terrain, thin or eroded soils or for other reasons. Figures for areas suitable for cultivation within this class are reported for some States but not for others. The total area so reported is 15 million acres of which about two-fifths is in Madhya Pradesh and the remainder mostly in Madhya Bharat and Vindhya Pradesh. Table 15.6 shows the distribution of "other uncultivated lands except current fallows" and the areas reported as cultivable in certain States.

Table 15.6 : Total Area Cultivated and Uncultivated in Some States

	Other Uncultivated Land Excluding Current Fallows (in 1000 acres)	*Cultivable Area (in 1000 acres)*
Madhya Pradesh	20,267	5,764
Assam	16,946	N.A.
Madras	11,272	245
U.P.	10,240	N.A.
Madhya Bharat	6,699	N.A.*
Bihar	5,574	N.A.
Rajasthan	4,544	N.A.
Vindhya Pradesh	4,297	3,484
Orissa	3,498	N.A.
Punjab	2,587	307
Bombay	2,098	1,058
Cutch	1,200	599

*3,367,000 acres in 1947-48.

A proper classification of lands included in this class is essential because this is a sort of residual class including within it lands of different types ranging from those which are very useful as pastures and village groves to those which are practically barren and useless. Such a classification is especially necessary because the possibilities of extending cultivation are mainly in lands of this class or in those under "current fallows". In the new scheme of classification, which has been brought into force from 1950-51, lands of this class have been sub-divided into three categories—village groves and pastures, cultivable waste and other uncultivated area. This classification would bring about a great improvement on the present position and would give a much clearer picture of the types of land included in this class than is available at present.

Areas not Available for Cultivation

This class includes land occupied by towns, villages, roads, railways and other non-agricultural uses, lands under beds of streams, rivers and other water bodies and barren lands in hilly, mountainous or desert areas. Thus, this class includes on the one hand lands which are being used for highly productive purposes (some of these command very high prices also) and on the other those which are practically useless. This lumping together of very different kinds of lands is obviously very unsatisfactory. In the new scheme of classification, lands of this class have been sub-divided into "barren and unproductive" and "lands used for non-agricultural purposes". The total area included in this class is 96.0 million acres. Madras with 14.6 million acres and U.P. with 11.8 million acres have the largest acreages under this class.

Forests

According to the figure of Agricultural Statistics, the total area under forests in the Indian Union are about 93 million acres or 11.5 per cent of the land area of the country. Statistics on area under forests appear also in the Forest Administration Reports. The figures from the two sources do not agree, however, in some States, especially in those having large areas of private forests, the difference is fairly large; in others it is rather small. The main reasons for differences in the figures from the two sources appear to be the following:

Most of the area included under private forests and forests managed by corporate bodies in the Forest Administration Reports appear under the heads "other uncultivated land excluding current fallows", and "not available for cultivation" in the Agricultural Statistics. The differences in Madhya Pradesh, Bengal and Madras are mainly due to this reason,

In Agricultural Statistics, wherever figures are based on plot to plot inspection, the area not actually under forests is shown under other appropriate heads. Thus cultivated area is returned under "net area sown", lands covered with scrub, bamboos, jungles, etc., are returned mostly as "other uncultivated land excluding current fallows". But in the Forest Administration Reports such areas, if they are included in lands under the control of the Forest Department, are returned as forests. The differences in the case of Punjab and U.P. arise mainly from this factor,

Unprofitable and inaccessible forests, which are included under "forests" in the Forest Administration Reports, are in many States shown as "areas not available for cultivation" or "other uncultivated land excluding current fallows" in Agricultural Statistics. Thus in the case of Assam most of the "unclassified forests" of the Forest Administration are returned as "other uncultivated land excluding current fallows" in Agricultural Statistics.

The figures in Agricultural Statistics and Forest Administration Reports relate in many cases to different periods. The figures given in Table 15.7 for forest areas in the former provinces in 1946-47 give a comparative idea of the data available from the two sources.

Table 15.7 : Areas under Forests in the Provinces in 1946-47

(Figures in 1000 acres)

Province	*A. According to Forest Administration Report (Statement XX)*				*B. According to Agricultural Statistics*	*Differences*
	State forests	*Forests owned by corporate bodies*	*Private forests*	*Total*		
1	2	3	4	5	6	7
Ajmer	47	147	186	380	47	333
Assam	13,612	33	203	13,848	4,056	9,792
Bihar	1,320		5,046	6,366	6,612	246
Bombay	8,127	3	108	8,238	7,933	305
C.P. and Berar	14,754		15,363	30,117	15,829	14,288
Coorg	534		218	752	331	421
E. Punjab	2,333	61	652	3,046	769*	2,277
Madras	12,029		9,517	21,546	13,515	8,031
Orissa	1,801		1,074	2,875	2,606	269
U.P.	9,136	13	1,969	11,118	6,963	4,155
West Bengal	1,697		1,044	2,741	1,708*	1,033
Total	65,390	257	35,380	101,027	60,369	40,658
Andaman and Nicobar Islands	1,600	—	—	—	—	—

*1947-48.

Distribution of Forests

Most of the forests of the country are situated in hilly and mountainous areas. The Himalayas and their foothills and the hill ranges of Peninsular India (the Western and Eastern Ghats, the Vindhyas, the Satpuras, and associated ranges of these) are the main forested areas of the country. In the States of Peninsular India, as there are large areas of hills and plateaus, the area under forests is fairly large. Madhya Pradesh with 23.6 million acres and Madras with 13.8 million acres are the two States with large areas under forests. In the States of Northern India, on the other hand, areas under forests are comparatively small and these too are located either in the Himalayan sections to the north or in the plateau sections to the south of the plains. In the plains sections proper, areas under forests are very small indeed because most of the land is taken up by agriculture. The problem of shortage of forest produce, especially fuel, which is encountered over large parts of India, is seen in an acute form in the plains. The demand for forest produce is very large because of the large populations, but the supply is limited, because areas under forests are small. As a result, a large part of the demand, especially that of the village consumers, remains unsatisfied and the practice of burning cow dung is so widespread. The possibilities of increasing areas under forests are very limited, however, as most of the lands in the plains must continue to be used for cultivation. The people in the plains must remain dependent on forests in adjacent areas of hills and plateaus for a large part of their requirements of forest produce. Their needs can be met to some extent (to a large extent in areas where the density of population is not too high) by the creation and efficient management of small plantations of trees near the villages. The importance of such village tree-plantations has long been realized and the new forest policy enunciated by the Government of India also especially emphasizes the need for such tree-plantations. But it should be mentioned that in many densely populated areas these plantations cannot be large enough to meet the fuel needs : use of alternative fuels like soft coke is essential for supplying the fuel needs and for stopping the practice of burning cowdung.

Grazing Lands

Areas used for grazing are not at present shown separately in the classification of land statistics. Grazing takes place mostly in forests and other uncultivated lands (including "current fallows") wherever pasturage is available. In most of the private forests, as also in forests managed by local bodies and the Revenue Departments, grazing is practically unrestricted. Even in the reserved forests of the Forest Departments in which grazing is regulated, it is allowed for a large part of the year. Provision of grazing at concessional rates to the people living close to the forests has been an important principle of forest policy in India.

The total pasturage available in the country is not sufficient for the needs of the large livestock population. According to the Livestock Census of 1945, there were about 177 million cattle and buffaloes in the Indian Union (present territories). The area devoted to production of fodder crops is, however, only about ten million acres. This large bovine population, therefore, subsists mainly upon pasturage, supplemented by stalks of grains like millets, wheat and rice straw or any grains that can be spared. The grazing lands have to support, in addition, about 85 million sheep and goats for which there is practically no other feed available. In the rainy season, there is sufficient pasturage in most parts of the country. But the rainy season is short and for the remainder of the year, the supply is very low. As a result of large numbers of animals depending upon them, most of the areas used for grazing are heavily over-grazed. Over-grazing is one of the main causes of destruction of forests and other natural vegetation and of soil erosion in this country.

Possibilities of Increasing the Area under Cultivation

At this point, when the various classes of land have been considered, it is possible to discuss the question of possibilities of increasing the area under cultivation. The question is of considerable significance, as increasing the cultivated area is one of the two major means (the other being increase in productivity per acre) of raising agricultural production. Unfortunately, however, in the existing state of information on land utilization it is not possible to make any definite statement on this subject. The available statistics do not cover the whole area of the country, and the classification is not sufficiently detailed to bring out all the informations that is required. Moreover, statistics from different parts of the country vary greatly in accuracy. Definitions of "current fallows" and "other uncultivated lands excluding current fallows", the two classes with which we are most concerned in making such an estimate, vary in different States. There have been no detailed surveys of uncultivated lands to determine which of them are suitable for cultivation and which are not. At present, therefore, we can only note certain points which emerge from the available data and which may indicate what the position is likely to be.

The "unclassified areas" are situated mostly in arid, mountainous or other regions of low productivity, so that the possibilities of increasing areas under cultivation in these can only be limited.

In areas classified as "not available for cultivation", similarly, the possibilities cannot be large as most of these areas are also hilly, mountainous or arid.

As for forests, there is undoubtedly scope for extending cultivation to a limited extent in forest areas in some parts. But against this, there are much larger areas of cultivated land which should be retired from cultivation and brought under forests in order to afford protection from soil erosion, desiccation, floods, etc. The net result would most probably be a decrease in cultivated area and not an increase. The area under forests is insufficient and has to be increased. Any decrease from the present totals cannot be contemplated.

"Current fallows" and "other uncultivated lands excluding current fallows" remain the two classes in which scope for expansion for cultivation is appreciable. As has been mentioned above, substantial reduction can be made in "current fallows" if more intensive cropping methods including raising the moisture status of soils are adopted and soils are properly manured and fertilized, so that there is less need for keeping lands fallow. As a considerable portion of the land classified as "current fallows" is in the dry areas of Peninsular India, extension of irrigation facilities and improvements in dry farming methods are other important steps necessary for reducing acreages of fallow lands.

Of the 98.4 million acres under "other uncultivated lands excluding current fallows", about 15 millions are reported as cultivable. How much of the remainder is cultivable is not known. However, it is clear that in many areas, lands under this class are mostly uncultivable. Thus in Assam, most of the lands are covered by jungle, and would probably remain so. Such uncultivable lands have to be maintained as forests or grazing lands, though by proper land utilization practices they can be made much more productive than they are at present. Finally, most of the grazing lands and village groves are included in this class and additions which must be made in these categories to meet the needs for forest produce and pasturage must come from lands of this class. Accordingly, in estimating the acreages which can be available for cultivation from land in this class, due allowance should be made for unfavourable physical conditions and the demands for forest produce and grazing.

To conclude among the uncultivated lands, the acreage at present reported as cultivable is only about 15 million acres. To this figure may be added areas from "other uncultivated lands excluding current fallows", "current fallows" and some areas from unclassified lands to make up the total acreage of additional lands which can be brought under cultivation. What the precise figures would be it is not possible to say—this can only be determined by surveys which should classify lands according to their land use capability. But it is quite clear that the total, whatever it might be, cannot be more than a small fraction of the area already under cultivation. The 15 million acres reported as cultivable amount to less than 6 per cent of the sown area. It would, therefore, be reasonable to conclude that the possibilities of increasing the cultivated area are limited, and that the major increases in agricultural production have to come through raising productivity of the lands already under cultivation.

The conclusion that the scope for expansion of cultivation is not very large, appears to be supported by the trends of the last 40 years. Statistics on net area sown in British India are available from 1911-12 onwards and these show that there has been no significant increase in sown area in this period. As the population of the country has been rapidly increasing, sown area per capita has markedly decreased as shown in Table 15.8.

Table 15.8 : Change in Per Capita Net Sown Area in India 1911-1951

Year	*Population (in million)*	*Net Area Sown (in million acres)*	*Net Sown Area per capita (in acres)*
	British India*		
1911-12	231.6	202.0	0.88
1921-22	233.6	207.2	0.89
1931-32	256.8	211.4	0.82
1941-42	295.8	214.0	0.72
	Indian Union†		
1951	356.9	266.4	0.75

* Compiled from: W. Burns—"Technological Possibilities of Agricultural Development in India", pp. xiv and xvii.

† The larger figure for the Indian Union is due entirely to larger area coverage. Figures for "net area sown" in the Indian provinces ranged between 170 and 175 million acres during the period 1936-37 to 1946-47, showing that the trend of the earlier decades continues in this period also.

There seems to be considerable justification for the view that, as in other old and densely populated countries, farmers in most parts of this country also have pushed the limits of cultivation as far as they could with the technological means and resources at their command. If certain cultivable lands remain uncultivated, it is mainly because they suffer from defects like deficiency of moisture, infestation with weeds or pests, prevalence of diseases like malaria which, though they can be corrected with modern scientific methods and engineering techniques, could not be tackled with the limited resources and rather simple techniques of the average Indian farmer. Extension of cultivation into uncultivated lands would, therefore, involve in most cases removal of defects from which the lands suffer and as a result of which they have remained uncultivated. This process is bound to be both expensive and slow. The Central Tractor Organization's scheme for reclamation of 2 million acres[*2] of *kans*-infested wastelands in Central India (Madhya Pradesh, Bhopal, Madhya Bharat), for instance, is scheduled to take 7 years, which means a rate of progress of about 3 lakh acres per year. The cost is at present about Rs. 52 per acre. Costs of reclamation may well be higher and progress slower in other areas which need to be reclaimed, because the area selected for this scheme is one of the more favourable areas for reclamation purposes.

The Problem of Land Utilization

The main conclusion which emerges from the above analysis of the pattern of land utilization in the country is that with our present methods of land use the available area is very insufficient for our needs. Even though as much as one-third of the land is under crops—a fairly high percentage in comparison with other large countries of the world—crop-land per capita is only about three-fourths of an acre. And as most of it is of low productivity, agricultural production is not adequate to meet our needs even at the present very low standards of consumption.[*3] For example, although 80 per cent of the crop-land is under foodgrains, production of foodgrains falls short of consumption by 3 to 4 million tonnes. The available pasturage is insufficient for the needs of the large livestock population, and most of the areas used for grazing are heavily over-grazed. Supply of forest produce is similarly much less than the demand, although most of the forests are over-exploited and over large areas forests have been depleted in recent decades.

Our demands on the products of the land—agricultural, forest and pastoral—are moreover, likely to increase greatly in the future. The population of the country is increasing very rapidly, at the rate of 4 to 4½ million persons per year. A fairly rapid rate of economic development is essential if the economy is to be strengthened at the base, and standards of living of the population are to be raised. This rapid economic development will place heavy demands on the land resources. To mention just one small example : industries like paper, rayon, paints and varnishes, which are based on utilization of forest produce, are still in their infancy in this country. In Europe and North America these industries are very well developed and large areas of forests are devoted almost entirely to supplying raw materials for these industries. The paper and allied industries for instance are the largest users of wood from the Canadian forests. When these industries develop in India also, their demands for timber and other forest produce will be tens of times greater than it is today, and considerable areas of forests will have to be devoted to meet these demands.

There is no possibility of our being able to make up the current shortages and to meet the increasing needs unless our techniques of land utilization are greatly improved. We have seen for instance that cultivated area has failed to keep pace with the increasing population in recent decades, that in future also it can be expected to increase to only a limited extent, and that the requisite increases in agricultural production must come mainly through increased productivity of lands already under cultivation. The situation for pastures and forests is basically similar; areas under these uses cannot be increased sufficiently to meet the requirements, and a very large part of the requisite increases in production must come by scientific management of forests and grazing lands.

Aside from the need of increasing production, there is the vital question of preservation of our natural resources of soil, water and vegetation. That we have been very wasteful in the use of these resources, there is not the least doubt. Although quantitative data is lacking, there is evidence everywhere to impress upon us the gravity and the vast magnitude of the problems arising from the wasteful use of our natural resources. Over large areas in the hilly and mountainous regions of the country the protective cover of forests has been destroyed. The causes for this destruction are varied. Over-grazing by cattle, sheep and goats is one major cause. Unrestricted felling to meet demands of fuel and timber, and clearing of forests to make room for cultivation are other important factors. In some areas, as in parts of Assam, Bihar and Orissa, shifting cultivation, which is practiced by the tribal people, is a principal cause of destruction of forests. As a result largely of destruction of forests and other natural vegetation, large areas in all parts of the country are suffering from soil erosion which has become one of the most serious problems facing the country. Large areas, especially in the hilly regions, have been rendered barren and unproductive by soil erosion. Sheet erosion causes enormous losses to agriculture every year by washing off the top layers of the soil and reducing productivity of the land, while gully erosion ruins considerable acreages of productive lands. Increasingly frequent and severe floods in the rivers; covering of large areas in the foothill zones with coarse sands and gravels; silting up of rivers, lakes and reservoirs; fall in ground water levels and gradual desiccation of lands close to the margins of the Thar Desert are other consequences of our misuse of the land resources. The damage caused by these to the Indian economy every year in the way of reduced productivity in agriculture, and physical destruction of life and property (through floods, etc.) is staggering. And the very existence of agriculture and settlement in many areas is threatened by erosion and other problems.

Improvement of Land Use

As already mentioned in the beginning, it is not possible in a paper of this type to treat in any detail the question of improvements in land use practices as this would extend over the whole field of agriculture, pasture and forest management. We may only mention here the two aspects of the problem : (a) the extensive aspect which deals with improving the pattern of land use, i.e. distribution of land among its various uses, and (b) the intensive aspect which aims at improving practices within each use.

(a) *Improving the Pattern of Land Use*—The objective should be to secure a pattern of land use for each region under which all lands are used according to their land use capability. This means on the one hand reduction of idle and wastelands in each region to the minimum by suitable reclamation and land improvement measures, and on the other securing such alterations in the existing pattern of land use as are necessary for raising productivity or for conservation of soil and water. Retiring certain marginal and highly erodible areas from cultivation, restriction or closure of grazing in certain grazing lands, settlement of shifting cultivators on permanent cultivation arc some examples of the kinds of alterations needed in land use patterns. The reclamation and land improvement and the restriction programmes should be combined as far as possible, so that suitable alternative opportunities are provided for the persons affected by the restrictions. In order to attain such a pattern of balanced land use, it is necessary to classify the lands according to their land use capability. Surveys of soils and land use capability are needed for this purpose. Such surveys should be conducted in selected areas, e.g. areas suffering from serious soil erosion or areas in which large blocks of cultivable wastelands are available for reclamation, so that the results of the surveys can be applied to development programmes already in progress or proposed to be undertaken in the near future.

(b) *Improving Methods of Land Use*—Under this are included provision of irrigation and the whole range of agricultural improvement practices (use of improved seeds, application of manures and fertilizers, proper crop rotations, control of pests and plant diseases, etc.) as also efficient pasture management and forest management. This is much the larger problem of the two, embracing as it does nearly the whole field of agricultural improvement. It is not necessary to discuss the measures which are needed for improvement of agriculture, pasture or forest management or which are being taken by the Central or State Governments at the present time. These are too well known. However, an idea of the importance which this problem has received in the nation's development effort can be had from the fact that nearly half the expenditure in the Five Year Plan is for irrigation and agricultural and rural development work. The first problem, which is related more to the long-term aspect of conservation of resources, has not received adequate attention so far, but emphasis on this will have to increase in the near future, if our natural resources of soil and water are to be conserved and if a high level of productivity is to be maintained over a long period.

Appendix I

Note on Land Utilization Statistics

Agricultural statistics from different parts of the country are of varying degrees of accuracy and reliability. In those areas of the former "provinces" which are under temporary settlement, the Revenue Administration maintains regular records on classification of land, acreage and production of crops, etc. These records are based on periodical field inspection by the local revenue staff, usually the *patwari*. But in areas of permanent settlement like Bengal, parts of Bihar and Assam, no such agency existed until recently, and the statistics are based on estimates made by local authorities like the village *chowkidars*. These estimates are much less reliable than those of the *patwaris*. Data from the former Indian States are also of varying degrees of accuracy. Attempts are now being made by the Central Government and the State Governments to improve the accuracy of agricultural statistics and to set up proper administrative machinery for their collection in areas where it has not existed so far. In 1948, the Government of India appointed a committee in the Ministry of Agriculture for examining the position regarding agricultural statistics. The report of this committee (Agricultural Statistics in India,1949) contains a comprehensive survey of the present methods of collection of statistics in the different parts of the country and makes detailed suggestion for their improvement. The work of improving agricultural statistics has been entrusted to the Directorate of Economics and Statistics, Ministry of Agriculture.

Apart from the general drawbacks of agricultural statistics, the land classification statistics proper suffer from the following defects :

The system of classification is not sufficiently detailed. Very different kinds of land are lumped together in the same class. Thus the class "other uncultivated land excluding current fallows" includes forests (private forests, and other forests like the un-classed forests of Assam), grazing lands, village groves, land covered with scrub, coarse grasses, bamboos, etc. The class "not available for cultivation" includes land used for towns, villages, railways, roads, land occupied by water bodies, and also barren lands.

Definitions of the terms vary greatly in the different States. The best example of this is of "current fallows", whose definition varies from State to State.

In order to remove these defects, the Directorate of Economics and Statistics, Ministry of Food and Agriculture, has evolved a new scheme for classification of land and has issued instructions to the States to compile statistics, beginning with 1950-51, according to the new scheme. Standard definitions of the various terms to be followed by all States have also been adopted. The new scheme of classification is as follows :

	New Classification	*Old Classification*
1.	Total geographical area	Same
2.	Area under forests	Same
3.	Barren and uncultivable land	Not available for cultivation
4.	Land put to non-agricultural uses	
5.	Current fallows	Current fallows
6.	Other fallow lands	
7.	Cultivable waste	
8.	Permanent pasture and other grazing land	Other uncultivated land
9.	Miscellaneous tree crops and groves not included under net area sown	excluding current fallows
10.	Net area sown	Same

Appendix II

Definitions of "current fallows" and "other uncultivated lands excluding current fallows "as followed in the different States before the adoption of the revised classification (Source—"Indian Agricultural Statistics", Vol. I, 1938-39).

State	*Current Fallows*	*Other uncultivated lands excluding current fallows*
Assam	Includes all lands which are thrown out of cultivation or are not cultivated for 3 years.	—
Bombay	Maximum period for which lands thrown out of cultivation is reckoned as fallow is 10 years.	—
Madhya Pradesh	Land which has been fallow for not more than 3 years is reckoned as current fallows. For Berar, it includes occupied cultivable land left fallow for private reasons such as grazing, etc.	Includes: (i) The waste area within holdings (including fallows of more than 3 years), (ii) Land under tree forests which is not administered under any Act dealing with forests, (iii) Land under scrubs jungle, or grass, and (iv) Groves not included in holdings. For Berar, it includes land available for cultivation but not given out.

State	*Current Fallows*	*Other uncultivated lands excluding current fallows*
Madras	Includes all occupied waste, e.g. waste portions of land for which revenue is paid.	Includes areas occupied by babul and casurina trees when they do not form parts of forest areas.
Punjab	The maximum period for which land is reckoned as fallow is 2 years, but as a change in classification is not generally made until the year for quadrennial statements comes round, the old classification may be retained from 1 to 3 years longer than the prescribed period.	Includes areas of waste not allotted for cultivation.
U.P.	The maximum period for which land left uncultivated is reckoned as fallow is 3 years.	—
Coorg	Gives (i) the estimated area of cultivable banes, and (ii) the difference between area sown and the gross area of the actual holdings (exclusive of banes).	Gives the estimated area of cultivable waste.
Mysore	1. All lands whether a full survey number or a portion thereof except, extents shown as 'phut kharab' left uncultivated in the lands under holdings (khate), are classed as "current fallows" (*vide* their letter in reply to the circular). 2. The difference between the areas of the lands occupied by individuals and of those actually cultivated by them is taken as fallow. Stat., Vol. II, 1939-40 to 1942-43).	Gives unoccupied assessed waste.

*Appendix III**

A Method to indicate the percentage of land which should be under forest: Some Comments

1. In his article of the above title in the Indian Forester, the editor has made some very useful suggestions on determination of the proportions of land which should remain under forests in hilly and plain areas* . The method suggested by him for hilly areas would prove to be a useful guide for foresters, administrators and others who need to have an approximate idea of the areas which should be under

forests and other uses in particular areas. The method, as the author has himself pointed out, can give only approximate results. But its value will be appreciated when it is borne in mind that data on soils and other characteristics by which land use capability may be accurately determined are very meager (virtually non-existent in most areas), and it will take several years before the necessary Surveys are conducted, and such data become available. Two observations on this method may, however, be made:

The method is designed to give an approximate idea, on a regional basis, of the proportions of land which should remain under forests. It is not meant to be, and should not be used for determining whether a particular piece of land should or should not be under forests. The method relies only upon determination of slopes. Slope is undoubtedly a very important factor in determining land use capability, and perhaps the most important on a regional basis. But where specific locations are concerned, and the most suitable land use for particular areas is to be determined, one or more of the other factors determining land use capability like character of the underlying geologic formations, nature and depth of soils, drainage, etc., may be of equal or even greater importance than slope.

The figure of 12 per cent slope which has been used in the article is merely illustrative. It should not be taken as a criterion on the basis of which one could demarcate forest and non-forest areas. The figures of 12 to 20 per cent are, as explained by the author, based upon American experience, and he has also explained why he has chosen the former figure. In case of India, the figures would most probably be lower than these. There are two main reasons for this. Firstly, in the tropical climates of India weathering is more rapid than in the sub-tropical and temperate climates of U.S.A. Secondly, the monsoon rainfall of India is of a torrential character and is more erosive than rainfall in large parts of U.S.A. (especially Northern U.S.A.) which comes in long, gentle showers. The critical percentages would vary also in different parts of India itself. They will have to be determined by actual tests in different areas. It will not do to apply figures derived under different conditions of another country.

2. Calculations on the area which should be maintained under

forests in the plains are most interesting. Here, the main consideration is supplying the needs of the population for forest produce; physical considerations like slope are less important. According to the author, in areas having a population density of 500 persons per square mile, about 20 per cent of the land should be under forests in order that the needs of the population for fuel and other forest produce may be adequately met. These calculations lead to one conclusion; the forests and tree lands (including village plantations) located within the densely populated plains can supply only a portion of the needs for forest produce; a large part of the needs must be met by imports from other areas (or by alternative fuels, in case of fuel needs), and the higher the population density, the greater this dependence upon imports or alternative fuels. The reason for this conclusion is obvious. In most of the plains areas, where the density of population is 500 or above, a very large part of the land is taken up for cultivation (up to 80-90 per cent in many parts) and the balance is occupied mainly by grazing lands, fallows or non-agricultural uses like towns and villages, roads, canals, railways, industries, etc. The area under forests is very small, and even under a well planned system of land use, it can be increased only to a limited extent. Take West Bengal plain for an example. Population density is nearly 1,000 per square mile. On the basis of the above calculations, nearly 40 per cent of the land would be needed for forests. But the area at present reported under forests is only 6 per cent of the total. 61 per cent of the land is under cultivation, 6 per cent is under fallows and the balance is waste or is occupied by non-agricultural uses. Obviously, it is not possible to obtain any thing like the requisite percentage of 40 per cent under forests in this area as the needs of agriculture, settlements, industries and transport are much more important. The situation in other densely populated areas, like UP, Bihar and the plains of East and West Coast is essentially similar. Requirements of fuel and forest produce are very large because of the large populations, but as very high proportions of land are occupied by agriculture and other uses areas under forests are small and cannot be greatly increased.

3. This is not to deny the need for creation of tree plantation close

to villages, or of bringing under forests all waste or idle lands in the plains. These measures are very necessary both for reducing dependence upon imports and for preservation of proper physical conditions and conservation of the resources of soil and water. But it must be recognized that these measures, necessary though they are, provide only a partial solution of the problem of supplies of fuel and other forest products in most densely populated plains.

4. It is but natural, that the demand for forest produce from the plains should impinge first and most heavily on forests in the marginal zones between the plains and the mountains or plateaus (the foot-hill zone of the Himalayas and the lower slopes of the plateaus and hills of Peninsular India), which are nearest the concentrations of populations. Forests in these zones would be the first to be exploited and would also be under constant pressure for larger and larger supplies, because supplies from such forests would be the cheapest. These forests would quickly disappear, as they have done in many parts of the country, unless exploitation is carefully regulated, and constant vigilance is exercised for their protection. But preservation of forests in these areas is most urgent in order to protect the plains from soil erosion, floods, silting of streams and fertile croplands, desiccation, etc. The problem is thus a complex one. The short term interest of getting supplies at the lowest price possible and the long term need for conservation of natural resources are in conflict in these marginal zones, and only with the most careful regulation can forests in such areas be protected from depletion.

5. The solution of the problem of supplies of fuel and other forest produce has to be worked out separately for each region, depending upon the particular conditions in the region. In those regions, where large tracts of forested lands in the plateau or hilly areas are located close to the plains, these lands can supply the needs of the plains to a large extent. The plains and their adjoining plateau or hill lands can thus be visualized as composing one unit, the two parts of which are complementary to each other. The Malabar-Konkan Coastal Plain and the Western Ghats, the Chota Nagpur Plateau and the plains that surround it in North Bihar and West Bengal are examples of such complementary regions.

As the demands for fuel especially are very large, use of alternative fuels to supplement fire-wood appears to be necessary in most areas. In Bengal, Bihar, U.P. and other areas situated close to the coalfields, soft coke provides a suitable alternative fuel and its use should be encouraged as much as possible. In southern and western India, however, where distances from the coalfields are long and the cost of transport of soft coke is very high, the problem is more difficult. Development of hydro-electricity and of locally available fuel deposits, like the south Arcot lignite, offer fruitful lines of approach for these areas.

Source: Indian Forester, March 1953, pp. 192-194.

16

Settlement Pattern of India 1950-2000 and Projections 2021*

A Historical Perspective

It should be mentioned that the irrigated valleys of Western Maharashtra which produce large crops of high yield sugarcane with high sucrose content and high yield rice, have a number of sugar and rice mills and other industries making machine tools for various uses, were drought prone until the late 1950s and needed 'food for work' programme from time to time. They were transformed into their present status by effective use of their underground and surface resources of water for irrigation. The farmers who are organized into cooperatives, which provide them improved seed, chemical fertilizers and other inputs and market and process the crops, have become so rich that their leaders dominate the politics of Maharashtra. There is enough work and income for even small farmers in growing the crops and for agricultural labourers both in the sugar and rice mills and other industrial units that manufacture machine tools. The farmers and agricultural labourers in the valley around Nasik have more than enough work in growing fruit and vegetables and packaging it for consumption in Mumbai, Pune and cities all over north west India and also for export to the Gulf countries for consumption of Indians working there. All these areas attract workers from south-east and south-west Maharashtra (Marathwada) and Vidarbha, which were drought prone, when under their former ruler, the Nizam of Hyderabad. The same can be said about large parts of Gujarat, Haryana and North Western and Eastern Rajasthan. They too have large surpluses of wheat, medium staple cotton and oilseeds (mustard and groundnut) after extension

---

* Unpublished

of irrigation from canals; wells fitted with diesel oil or electrically operated pumps. The area around Nagpur has a large irrigated area under orchards which produce the best loose jacket oranges in India.

The recommendation for agricultural and agro-industrial development in central and eastern Uttar Pradesh and Bihar, in order to reduce poverty and emigration of their most productive workers to cities of Punjab and Haryana in the cool season (November to April) along with West Bengal, is not unrealistic when viewed in historical perspective or in the context of developments in West Bengal during the last 3 decades.

These areas were the most productive and densely populated areas of the country until the 1870s. Their productivity was reduced first by indigo planters (all British) who made large profits growing indigo for making dyes, until development of synthetic (aniline) dyes by the Germans after the 1870s. The indigo planters did nothing to restore the fertility of the land on which they had grown fat. The Scots, who owned tea gardens in Assam, wanted labour for work in the gardens, because the local people of Assam and the tribal living in the hills were unable or unwilling to do the arduous labour for long hours that was required in the gardens. The British who owned sugar plantations in Natal, South Africa, Trinidad and British Guinea in the Caribbean recruited workers for plantations in this area and Fiji in the South Pacific because the local population was unwilling or unable to do the arduous work required in the plantations. The recruited workers established colonies of Indians in these distant lands to the extent that they form majority of the population in some of them; but their home areas were bereft of their most productive labour.

In the 1930s when immigration to these lands was stopped, young men from these areas started going to Kolkata and Mumbai in order to work as unskilled or skilled workers in jute mills that line the Hoogly river, or in various industrial works in Kolkata or Howrah. They did also the most arduous jobs such as of rickshaw-pullers in the residential and commercial areas of Kolkata, as porters in Howrah railway station or in commercial establishments. They worked as unskilled industrial workers also in Mumbai or its satellite cities or in the port.

Late in the 1960s when there was a shortage of labour in sowing and harvesting of the *rabi* (cool) season crops in Punjab and Haryana, young men from these areas filled the gap. They stayed in the villages of Punjab and Haryana from November to April, and returned home when the cool season crop had been harvested. Those who were literate and well built became doormen and guards in banks and other offices and flats of the affluent in Kolkata and Mumbai.

The present Government of West Bengal has reversed the process of migration of rural workers from central and northern West Bengal to Kolkata and Howrah. It has expedited construction of a dam on Teesta River, the monsoon floods of which used to cover large areas with sand and silt. The farmers have been given low interest loans to buy livestock and ploughs to clear farm lands of sand and silt, and to buy seed fertilizers and pesticides to plant high yield rice and jute. Full and heritable rights have been conferred on the actual cultivators on lands that they had been cultivating by extinguishing the rights of the *zamindars*. The latter have been given loans to buy tractors to reclaim the land that has been left to them for self-cultivation and to install pumps operated by electricity or diesel oil on wells to irrigate the areas that could be irrigated. There is full employment for both farmers including former *zamindars* and agricultural labourers and there is little need for either to migrate to Kolkata in search of work. Production of rice has increased so much that the state that had very often a deficit of rice now has a surplus in some years. Production of jute has increased and its quality has improved so much that imports from Bangladesh have been reduced.

Agricultural and agro-industrial development in Bihar started in the 1960s by :

(i) Completing the land reform of extinguishing the rights of the *zamindars* and conferring full and heritable rights in land on the actual cultivators. The incidents of violence against their former tenants by the *zamindars* such as burning their villages and causing deaths or injuries to many have been effectively ended by the Government. Loans at low interest have been given to the farmers to buy seed, chemical fertilizers and pesticides (as needed) to grow crops of high yield rice, wheat, chick peas, peas and pulses. The former *zamindars* have also been given loans to buy tractors to reclaim the lands which were left to them for self-cultivation by clearing the land of coarse sand and silt brought down, by Kosi, Gandak and other rivers. The former *zamindars* have been given loans also to install pump sets on wells to irrigate areas that are irrigable. Small farmers, who cannot afford to keep their own tractors, rent them from those who have them for getting their lands ploughed by tractors. The rate for hiring tractors is fixed. Construction of a dam on Kosi River in Nepal has greatly reduced the damage to croplands caused by floods of the river.

(ii) Some of the areas are suitable for growing high quality mangoes, which are in great demand in Kolkata, Patna and other cities. Growing and packaging the mangoes and potatoes, another cash crop, has created much work and income, for landless agricultural labourers so that there is much less need for them to migrate to Kolkata, Mumbai, Delhi or other cities. The former *zamindars* have in cooperation with the traders built cold storages to keep potatoes and mangoes.

Production in south Bihar has increased greatly in recent years since the farmers including former *zamindars* have been given loans to buy pump sets for irrigation of land, which is irrigated by bullocks earlier. The irrigated area has increased and the lands are being irrigated more effectively. More effective cultivation by tractors has been another reason for increase in production of food crops, which has increased so much that north and south Bihar produce enough foodgrains to feed Jharkhand and inland Orissa which being hilly and forested and inhabited by tribal have often a large deficit of foodgrains.

There is a potential for increasing agricultural output much further because the process of upgrading the degraded lands and providing physical and social infrastructures (motorable roads, electricity, telecommunications, education and health care) to the rural population has just begun.

In U.P. the land reform of abolition of *zamindari* and conferring full and heritable rights in land that they cultivate has been completed. Farmers who own lands that are covered with sand and silt brought down by Sarda, Gomti and other rivers have been given loans or subsidies to clear the land by manual methods and to plant high yield wheat, rice, coarse grains and pulses or cash crops, sugar cane and mangoes; the latter grown in orchards around Lucknow and Varanasi. The former *zamindars* have been given loans to buy tractors for reclamation of the lands left to them for self-cultivation and to buy pump sets for irrigation of the lands that need irrigation.

Most of the orchards are owned by former *zamindars*. They have taken medium-term loans to plant the trees and to build cold storages to store them until they are ready for market. Potatoes, another cash crop are also stored in the cold storages.

Renting tractors by small farmers, by paying a fixed charge to the tractor owners is common in both UP and Bihar because cultivation by tractors is more economic than that by bullocks.

As a result of these measures there have been major increases in agricultural output in both U.P. and Bihar. Thus there is much less need for small farmers or agricultural labourers to migrate to metropolitan cities (Kolkata, Mumbai, Delhi, Lucknow, Patna or others). However, since the migration is a century old, most of the small farmers and agricultural labourers do migrate to these cities (or to Punjab and Haryana in the cool season) to supplement their income in farming.

Increasing proportions of the migrants is educated and have basic skills to work as skilled workers in industrial units. Those who work as guards or gateman on banks or offices of large companies or houses or flats of the affluent have enough skills to use firearms given to them effectively in case of attacks by robbers.

With these measures there has been major increase in agricultural output, remunerative work for farmers and agricultural labourers in growing foodgrains and packaging the commercial crops for markets that there is much less need for small farmers and agricultural labourers to migrate to the cities in search of work. The overall results are:

(i) Increase in production of food and cash crops,
(ii) Greater income from agriculture and agro-processing to small farmers and even agricultural labourers,
(iii) Increase in productivity of the land, and
(iv) Fewer migrants from these areas to live in the slums of large metropolitan cities.

Mini urbanization, i.e. growth of large villages to small towns is facilitated in areas in which the tightly nucleated village with a population of 1000 or more is the norm. Most of the rural people in Punjab, Haryana, western Uttar Pradesh and adjoining areas of Rajasthan and north-western Madhya Pradesh live in such villages. In them, the high castes [Brahmins, Rajput or Jat farmers and the Mahajans (traders)] live in the central areas of the villages and the Scheduled Castes live on the outskirts. The areas have been invaded and their cities destroyed by invaders so many times that the people saw safety in numbers.

The experience in West Bengal and the projected experience in Bihar and U.P. indicates that abolition of the exploitative system of land tenure, i.e. *zamindari* gives a powerful impetus to the actual cultivators to maximize agricultural output by optimum use of their land and labour. Availability of low interest loans by cooperatives to buy improved seed, chemical fertilizers and pesticides (as needed) in order to plant high yield wheat and rice and of medium-term loans from land mortgage banks to buy tractors and pumps on wells and other machines enable the farmers to make their farming capital-intensive. The marked increase in agricultural output in Rajasthan after abolition of the exploitative system of land tenure, i.e. *Jagirdari* proves also that abolition of exploitative systems of land tenure—*zamindari* and *jagirdari*—gives a powerful incentive to the actual cultivators to maximize agricultural output by optimum use of their land and labour. Almost all the areas which had the '*ryotwari*' system of land tenure, described above, in which the farmers paid land revenue directly to the State Government the farmers were not exploited.

The tightly nucleated village is the norm also in Gujarat, Maharashtra and adjoining areas of Madhya Pradesh or Rajasthan because potable water sufficient to support a village with population of 1000 or more is available only in a limited number of places. In coastal Andhra Pradesh, Tamil Nadu and parts of Karnataka, where potable water is available almost everywhere such villages became the norm because collection of land revenue, administration of criminal justice and maintenance of peace in the rural areas could be organized most effectively by state personnel posted in such villages. The population of such villages has increased after the 1950s because agricultural extension, social and commercial services to farmers has been organized efficiently in them. Inputs of improved agriculture are supplied through them. The crops are marketed or processed through small/medium sized towns most of which are headquarters of talukas or community development blocks.

In such villages, the Brahmins and the majority of the farmers live in the centre of the villages while the Scheduled Castes that do agricultural labour or load or unload crops in the markets or work in rice, sugar or oil mills live in the outskirts or in one or two hamlets located close to large villages. In all these areas agricultural extension, social and commercial services (marketing of crops and supply of inputs of high productivity agriculture) are organized from larger villages some of which have become small towns in course of time. Agro-processing activities are organized, however, in medium sized towns with population of 25,000 or more.

In Kerala and adjoining area of south-west Karnataka, most of the farmers with small or larger landholdings live in individual compounds surrounded by their field of rice, a patch of tapioca, a few coconut trees and a drinking water well. The Scheduled Castes and landless labourers live also in individual houses, which would have a few trees around it and a well. Commercial and Social service facilities are organized in large villages, which have population ranging between 5 and 10 thousand.

Marketing and processing the crops (e.g. of coir to make various goods of household or decorative use) and distribution of consumer goods and consumer durables and building materials is organized in relatively large villages or towns which have a population of ten thousand or more. Such villages or small towns generally have a Church or a Temple as their focal point. They are located along motorable roads. Agro-processing activities are located in the larger towns.

In eastern India (West Bengal, Orissa and Assam), however, the tightly nucleated village disappears, here potable water free from dissolved impurities is not available anywhere. Most of the high caste households live in their own compounds adjoining their tanks in which they grow fish and draw water for irrigation of crops. Potable water is obtained from shallow wells located next to the tanks. In this area, as in Kerala, agricultural extension, social service and commercial activities are organized in large villages, which have access to motorable roads. Agro-processing activities are organized often in the towns many of which were centres of traditional cottage industries. Most of the large villages or towns/ cities are headquarters of district or mauza administration.

The Influence of Land Tenure

All the areas which produce most of the wheat, rice, sugarcane, medium staple cotton or oilseeds in the country, described above, were under the *ryotwari* system of land tenure under which the farmers paid land revenue directly to the State Governments and administration of criminal justice and maintenance of peace and security was organized by the state.

On the other hand, the areas in which productivity of land is low and there has been a history of migration to cities or to distant lands were under the *zamindari* system of land tenure in British ruled provinces and *jagirdari* in princely states. It has been mentioned that effective land reforms, i.e. conferring full and heritable rights in land on actual cultivators that they cultivate and extinguishing the rights of the zamindars has resulted in dramatic increase in production of rice and jute in West Bengal. Apparently abolition of the rights of *zamindars* and conferring full and heritable rights in land that they cultivate has provided the farmers a strong incentive to increase agricultural output with optimum use of their land and labour. It encourages also making agricultural operation capital intensive because tractors for cultivation and pump sets powered by diesel oil or electricity are used for irrigation of most of the croplands in these areas. Low interest loans are given for the purchase of the machines or inputs of high productivity agriculture by Cooperative Societies and Land Mortgage Banks.

A similar development has occurred in eastern Rajasthan following abolition of *jagirdari* in the early 1950s. There has been such a large increase in production of wheat that the state which was deficit in cereals for two decades after its formation has a surplus of cereals in most of the years; the areas irrigated by canals in western Rajasthan have large exportable surplus of cotton and groundnut and of 'mustard' in the irrigated areas of eastern Rajasthan which are irrigated by wells fitted with pumps operated by electricity or diesel oil in Eastern Rajasthan have a large exportable surplus of mustard. The state has reached this position despite the fact that almost half of the state suffers from serious drought in two out of three years.

Density of Population

A map published by the Census Commissioner of India in the publication, "Census of India 2001, Paper No. 1, Provisional Population Totals", shows that the most densely populated states are : U.P., Bihar and West Bengal in the north and Kerala in the south. A medium high density belt extends from Gujarat and Maharashtra in the west to Tamil Nadu in the south. Andhra Pradesh and Karnataka are included also in it. Punjab and Haryana are the only states with medium high densities in the north.

At the other extreme states with low densities of population are Jammu and Kashmir, Uttaranchal (renamed Uttarakhand) and Himachal Pradesh in the Western Himalayan Region and Arunachal Pradesh and seven hill states of the North-East which are populated by tribes.

Jharkhand, Chhattisgarh, inland Orissa and eastern Madhya Pradesh which are forested and inhabited largely by tribal populations also have relatively low densities. Rajasthan, half of which is semi-arid or arid and suffers from frequent draught also has a low density of population. The densities are related to agricultural and agro-industrial development in different regions.

This pattern of high and low population densities is unlikely to be altered in the foreseeable future because it is based on the facts of topography, climate, and vegetation. Development of irrigation, however, in the last 50 years has increased population densities in the areas described in (i), (ii), and (iv) under 'Sparsely' Populated Areas. In (iii), the population densities in the hilly and forested areas of Peninsular India or in the Himalayan regions cannot increase because of limited availability of arable lands to support large populations.

Centralization and Decentralization of the Urban Population

Centralization and decentralization of the urban population are proceeding at the same time. On the one hand, there is a tendency for the urban population to concentrate in the metropolitan cities and their satellite cities— There were 5 metropolitan cities (with populations of 1 million or more) in 1951 and populations resident in them constituted 17 per cent of the total urban. The number has increased progressively to 35 by 2001 and their population of 108 million constitutes 38 per cent of the total urban population. The 42 million resident in Greater Mumbai, Kolkata-Howrah and Delhi which have populations above 10 million have 15 per cent of the total urban population in the cities themselves or the satellite cities.

At the same time, a large number of relatively large villages are becoming small towns because agricultural extension, social service, commercial distribution of inputs of high productivity agriculture and supply of short-term loan to buy improved seed, chemical fertilizers and pesticides for current cultivation by cooperative societies and of medium-term loans to buy tractors, pump sets or other machines by land mortgage banks or nationalized banks are also organized through relatively large villages or small towns. Marketing of crops is also organized through them, because they have access to motorable roads. Processing of crops to make rice or wheat, flour, sugar, cooking oil or ginning of cotton are also concentrated in the large towns.

Both processes are most active in the areas in which productivity of land is high and has increased rapidly as a result of extension of irrigation and effective land reforms. The reasons for such contradictory developments in the distribution of urban population have to be explored.

The foregoing discussion has concentrated on areas which have medium to high density of population. In most of them there is large in-migration of workers from villages to the cities. In other areas Kerala, South Kanara district of Karnataka and Goa, there is large emigration of young men (and/or women) to the Gulf countries and to cities within India. In two other states there is large seasonal or longer term migration to metropolitan cities, from Punjab and Haryana. Most of the foodgrains (rice, wheat, coarse grains, pulses), sugar, medium staple cotton, oil seeds and jute are produced in these areas. Most of the manufacturing industries and service sector activities are also located in them, mainly within or the peri-urban areas of large cities.

Sparsely Populated Areas

This section deals with sparsely populated areas and discusses economic changes in them as a result of development programmes undertaken by the Central or State Government or other developments.

These areas are discussed under the following regional heads :

(i) Western Himalayan Region comprising Uttaranchal (renamed Uttarakhand), Himachal Pradesh and Jammu & Kashmir;
(ii) Eastern Himalayan Region comprising Assam, the six hill states of the north-east and Sikkim and inland Orissa;
(iii) Hilly and forested areas of Peninsular India inhabited mainly by tribal and located in Jharkhand, inland Orissa, Chhattisgarh, central and eastern Madhya Pradesh and small areas in the hilly forested areas of Maharashtra, Gujarat, Telengana region of Andhra Pradesh and southern Rajasthan; and
(iv) Desert or semi-desert areas of western Rajasthan.

(i) The Western Himalayan Region

There have been major economic developments in the region as a result of which there is much more remunerative employment for small farmers and agricultural labourers and also in the cities. The change influences have been the following :

- Posting of large contingents of armed forces on the border of India with Nepal and Tibet;
- Rapid growth of religious and pleasure tourism;
- Expansion of the irrigated area through cooperative efforts of the farmers and the State Governments;
- Rural electrification and expansion of facilities for telecommunications; and
- Major expansion of facilities for education to school and college levels and for preventive health and medical care.

Posting of large contingents of armed forces has created much remunerative employment for large number of agricultural labourers and small farmers. They work in building and repair of roads and in producing food (vegetables, poultry products, pulses and some rice or wheat) for the armed forces. The labourers have employment also in looking after officers and men of the forces. Large numbers of young men from Garhwal and Kumaon regions of Uttaranchal join the armed forces or the police force usually after graduating from higher secondary schools. The Garhwal and Kumaon regiments were important components of the Indian army during British days also.

Pleasure tourism in the summer provides gainful employment to a large number of people. Tens of thousands of tourists visit the hill stations in Himachal Pradesh—Simla, Kullu and Manali, and Mussoorie, Nainital and Ranikhet in Uttaranchal while the affluent live in luxury hotels, the great majority in small hotels managed by local people.

Looking after Hindu pilgrims, to the temples of Badri Nath and Kedar Nath, Hardwar, Rishikesh in Uttaranchal and the holy places of Hindus and Sikhs in Himachal Pradesh, provides employment to tens of thousands for 6 months to a year. While the temples are visited for three to four months of early summer; Hardwar and Rishikesh in Uttaranchal and holy places of the Hindus and Sikhs in Himachal Pradesh attract pilgrims throughout the year.

Most of the towns in these states are district headquarters. However, the capitals are Simla in Himachal Pradesh, Dehra Doon in Uttaranchal and Srinagar in Jammu and Kashmir are all cities which had more than 200,000 people in 1991.

Growth in population of Simla has been due mainly to the location of the capital of the Himachal Pradesh in it. The State Government has located most of the offices in buildings which had been constructed by the Government of India before 1947, when Simla was the summer capital of British India.

Growth in population of Dehra Doon pre-dates to location of Uttaranchal in it. It was due to location in it of the headquarters of the Oil and Natural Gas Commission (ONGC) and location in its vicinity, manufacturing facility of the Bharat Heavy Electricals. Both of them provide employment to several thousand white collar and skilled workers.

No comments are made for Jammu and Kashmir. While posting of large contingents of the Indian Army has created large employment for local people in Jammu and Ladakh regions of the state but its tourist industry has been adversely affected by continual warfare between the armed forces and militants operating from their bases in Pakistan.

Agricultural output—grains (rice, wheat or maize, and pulses), oilseeds and fruit and vegetables has increased of both Uttaranchal and Himachal Pradesh. The State Governments assisted the increase by giving technical and economic assistance to farmers for increase in the irrigated area and for soil conservation. They have also been provided to farmers through cooperative societies providing short and medium-term loans for buying seed of improved dwarf high yielding varieties of wheat or rice, chemical fertilizers and pesticides. Some areas in Himachal Pradesh specialize in production of apples; in others production of potatoes, tomatoes and winter vegetables (peas, beans, etc.) are important cash crops. The State Governments have assisted the producers by construction of motorable roads. Producers' cooperatives assist them by providing loans for buying various inputs, and renting space in cold storages for storing the fruit, and vegetables pending its export to markets in the cities.

As a result, there is much less migration of young men to go to the cities to work as domestic servants or as messengers in offices than it was until the 1960s. Those who do migrate seek jobs of white collar workers in the Government of India or in offices of companies. Working as domestic servants is now considered *infra dig* by young men or women of these states.

There has been rapid increase in communications and social service facilities. Large number of boys are attending high schools and colleges; they seek and get white collar jobs in offices of the Government of India in Delhi or their own State Governments or in institutions such as the Forest Research Institute, the Indian Military Academy and the head office of Oil and Natural Gas Commission, all are located in Dehra Doon. Others who are educated to high schools or college levels become teachers in schools and colleges and para-medics. Despite this, there is the problem of unemployment among the educated youth. Most of the large villages have access to motorized roads and telephone and postal facilities. They have electricity also; thus their isolation is broken. As a result of these developments, the income and level of living of most of the people has increased.

(ii) The Eastern Himalayan Region

In Assam and the Hill States, production of rice, the principal foodgrain, is concentrated in the valley of the Brahmaputra. Despite occasional loss of the planted crop by floods of the Brahmaputra and other rivers, there is enough production to feed all the people of Assam, the six hill states inhabited by tribal and Sikkim which are deficient in rice. The main problem is to reach the rice to the people of the hill states when they are flooded during the monsoon.

The problem of insurgency in Nagaland has been nearly solved although occasional attacks by the armed forces on the Naga militants still persist. There is also the problem of conflict between the native

Assamese or tribal farmers and agricultural labourers who are immigrants from Bangladesh. Their number has increased so rapidly in recent decades that the Assamese are afraid that they would form a majority of the population and they would lose the land of their birth. No solution to the problem has been found so far. There are occasional clashes between the Assamese and the Bangladeshis in which thousands are killed or injured.

(iii) Hilly and Forested Areas of Peninsular India

Hilly and forested areas of Peninsular India inhabited mainly by tribal and located in Jharkhand, inland Orissa, Chhattisgarh, eastern and central Madhya Pradesh and small areas in Telengana region of Andhra Pradesh and hilly areas of Maharashtra, Gujarat and southern Rajasthan. In all these areas, land available for cropping is limited and the tribal populations have been exploited by mining and forest contractors, since the areas were opened up by the British for export of minerals (coal, iron ore or others) during the last century, and for location of steel mills and other industrial and power plants after the 1950s.

The first priority in development of these areas has been building of good motorable roads so that food, water, blankets and medicines can be rushed to the people when their habitation areas are flooded in the monsoon season. After the floods recede, seeds fertilizers, plough and building materials are sent so that they can rebuild their homes and clear the croplands of sand and silt, and plant their crops.

Tribal in many of these areas have a serious complaint that when their homes and croplands are acquired for location of mines or large industrial units or power plants. They are neither given enough compensation for their lands nor allotted enough cultivable land and habitable areas in which to build their new fields and homes. As a result they are rendered penniless and have to work on low wages for mining or forest contractors or those building these mills.

This grievance should be removed. Another grievance is that funds allotted for their welfare by the Central Government are utilized by the State Governments for other uses. This grievance should also be removed.

Voluntary associations of tribal should be encouraged to manage the forests located around their villages and on which they depend for fuel, fodder, medicinal herbs and some food. They will manage the forests much better than forest contractors whose main interest is to maximize their profits by extracting timber.

Formation in 2000 AD of the new states of Jharkhand and Chhattisgarh will assist economic development in these states because decisions relating to development and welfare of the people will not be taken by Ministers and implemented by officials located in Patna or distant Bhopal but by those located in their midst in Ranchi and Raipur.

The unrest in the tribal areas of Telengana region of Andhra Pradesh is due to the fact that full and heritable rights in the croplands that they cultivate have not yet been given the actual cultivators.

The reform should be implemented without delay so that the unrest is ended. Finally, location of secondary and technical schools for boys and girls and provision of facilities for preventive health and medical care for all will assist economic development in all the areas. Tribal youth, educated to secondary school level and having basic skills can find employment in various industrial units located in their areas. They can become white collar workers in offices of the State Governments or in companies managing the industrial units. Others can work as teachers and para-medics. Educated tribal girls having knowledge of principles of nutrition and preventive health would help rural women make cleaner homes and raise healthy children. Some of them will become nurses and para-medics in hospitals or dispensaries located near their homes. The present Government of Madhya Pradesh has during the last few years implemented a successful programme of management of rural hospitals and dispensaries jointly by physicians, and representatives of the beneficiary populations.

As a result of these measures, the economic conditions, and health of the people should improve progressively. However, the areas will remain thinly populated because industrial units that manufacture steel, chemical fertilizers, cement, etc. provide employment to far fewer workers than those located in and around metropolitan areas.

In the foregoing sections are described the measures taken during the last 50 years through which the proportion of poor has been progressively reduced and there has been major improvements in education, awareness, health and productivity of residents of all these areas except of the residents of arid regions of west Rajasthan. It has been mentioned also that emigration of small or large proportion of the young to cities located within the region or adjoining them will be an on-going process. Furthermore, increasing proportion of the migrants will be young men who are educated and have basic skills so that they can get jobs of white collar and skilled workers. The young migrant workers would be felicitated and will be the leaders of economic development and social change in the regions from where they come.

Agricultural development in Assam, the hill states of the North East and inland Orissa : While Assam is self-sufficient in rice, the principal food crop; other hill states have deficits. However, because of small populations rice can be supplied easily from the Assam valley except during the monsoon season when the roads are broken and food has to be supplied to some areas by air, which is of course quite insufficient. The activities of the rebels (Nagas and Bodos) also disrupt communications. Production in the Assam valley could be increased greatly by control over the floods of the Brahmaputra and other small streams that flow down the Himalayan slopes and cover large areas with sand and silt during the monsoon season. Possibilities of industrial development are limited because of absence of any raw materials. Development of petro-chemical industries around the Khasi and Jaintia hills is possible; however, refinery at Nunmati is inhibited by the activities of Nagas and Bodos, whose raids disrupt often the working of the refinery.

The only 'industry' at present is handloom weaving of Assam silk and of cotton cloth by women of various tribes to produce garments for skirts and upper garments of designs which show the identity of their tribes. Low interest loans should be given to Manipuri women to increase production of garments of various Manipuri designs for which there is a high demand in metropolitan cities. These measures will reduce the activities of Naga and Bodo revels and set the stage for faster economic development of the Assam valley and of tribal areas. Farmers in areas which produce lose jacket oranges should be given loans to increase output for the markets of Kolkata and other cities.

Inland Orissa is about the most backward areas of the country. The principal reason for it that it was ruled until integration of states in the late 1940s, by princelings who were too poor to undertake any economic development programmes or even to build and maintain roads in forested areas which is full of hills and valleys. The first priority in the area is to build and maintain motorable roads so that food, medicines and blankets (and later building materials) can be sent to the area for use by people whose homes and crops have been destroyed by floods that follow the frequent visitations of cyclones during the monsoon and post-monsoon seasons. With these measures casualties from various diseases of the marooned people would be minimized and the people can be assisted to rebuild their homes.

Good motorable roads will facilitate inflow of rice and other foods throughout the year and prevent semi-starvation that is endemic in this area. With improvement in their health the farmers would plant their crops more efficiently and minimize the damage to them during cyclones.

(iv) Desert or Semi-Desert Areas of Western Rajasthan

These areas are inhabited by (a) small numbers of farmers concentrated in villages near which potable water is available throughout the year, and (b) pastoralists who graze their herds of cattle, goats and sheep on the scanty pasturage available in the cool season or spring. The areas are visited by more or less serious droughts in two years out of three. In these years, the pastoralists emigrate with their herds to eastern Rajasthan and adjoining areas of Madhya Pradesh to save themselves and their animals from starvation and thirst.

Food for work programmes are undertaken to provide people with food, water and money for buying clothes and other needs. They work on building roads, repair of old sources of water such as wells or step wells and building new ones discovered with modern sensor based techniques. However, emigration of young men to cities or of families to rural areas of eastern Rajasthan or western Madhya Pradesh will remain an important part of the development strategy for the region.

Concluding Remarks

The discussion in the foregoing sections can be divided into two parts :

(i) Discussion of developments in most of the densely populated areas of the country which produce most of the foodgrains (rice, wheat, coarse grains, maize and pulses), sugar, oilseeds, short and medium staple cotton, jute, tea, milk, poultry products, fruit and vegetables. All the metropolitan cities are located in them and most of the manufactured goods are produced in them. Most of these areas attract migrants from other regions to work in their industrial units or in various services in their cities. From other areas, however, there is emigration of young men to the countries of the Arabian Gulf or to metropolitan cities within India or seasonal migration to farms in some areas to meet the shortage of labour there.

The developments during the last 50 years which have led to rapid increase in agricultural and industrial output and rise in employment opportunities and income of the rural people in most of these regions have been reviewed. It has been explained that the measures to increase the irrigated area, provision of short and medium-term loans to farmers through cooperative societies to buy inputs of improved high productivity agriculture and to subsist while their crops are marketed has greatly assisted economic development in these areas.

(ii) Expansion of facilities for education and for preventive health and medical care has resulted in a better educated and healthier rural population. Furthermore, the initiatives taken by the State Governments by way of increase in irrigated areas, expansion of facilities for secondary education, preventive health and medical care, and communication including telecommunication facilities assisted the development process. Agricultural and agro-industrial development in some areas which had been retarded by prevalence of intermediary land tenures under which the farmers had to give a part of their produce to intermediary tenure holders (zamindars and jagirdars) has risen greatly after abolition of these tenures. Both the *zamindars* and *jagirdars* and their former tenants and agricultural labourers have contributed to the increase. Two other factors contributing to the increase have been :

- Major increase in the irrigated areas partly as a result of construction of canals and partly by installation of pump sets operated by diesel oil or electricity on irrigation wells;
- Much greater use of capital in agriculture. This has taken the form of use of new dwarf high yielding varieties of seed of wheat and rice; higher yield and improved varieties of sugarcane, cotton and jute; chemical fertilizers and pesticides and finally, machines (tractors, diesel oil or electrically operated pump sets on irrigation from of wells). Even farmers with small holdings use these inputs and hire tractors from those who have them.
- Short and medium-term loans given at rate of interest which they can afford to pay has made a major contribution to this development.

Another noteworthy development has been a major change in aspiration of both the rural and urban populations. There has been major increase in male and female literacy; even small farmers can repair small defects in the tractors and pump sets that they use. All of them want that their sons should be educated and become white collar or skilled industrial workers and their daughters should be married to such workers.

The principal problem to which no solution has yet been found so far is to provide tradable and non-tradable infrastructure facilities (electricity, clean and adequate water, arrangements for disposal of solid and liquid wastes, roads, primary and secondary school facilities and preventive health and medical care) telecommunications, news and entertainment (through print and electronic media) to residents of metropolitan cities. There is need for large investment in providing some of them; in others difficult technical, managerial or political problems have to be solved before the required level of efficiency can be achieved.

Unless satisfactory solution to these problems is found, large number of people in metropolitan cities will remain deprived of facilities which will impair their health and productivity. Recent developments in Ahmedabad have been mentioned to illustrate the problem.

The developments of the last 50 years which have increased agricultural output and associated employment and increase in some areas have increased differences in income and level of living between the already developed and comparatively prosperous areas and those in poor and underdeveloped areas particularly those inhabited by tribal people. Appropriate measures will need to be taken to reduce this disparity in the interest of equality and social justice.

Settlement Pattern of India in 2021—a Projection*

It is useful for geographers and urban planners to reflect on the probable settlement pattern of India's population in 2021.

The population of India in 2001 has been estimated at 1027 million by the Census Commissioner of India (Census of India 2001). The rate of growth during 1991-2001 had declined to 19.4 per cent per decade from 21.4 per cent per decade during 1981-91. Assuming that the declining growth trend continues and the rate of growth of population averages 16 per cent per decade during the next two decades, the population of India would be 1382 million by 2021. The figure could be lower because according to a projection of the Population Division of the United Nations, the population of India would be 1235 million by 2015. It is useful for geographers and physical planners to reflect on the probable settlement pattern by 2021. The following observations are meant to stimulate discussion on the subject.

---

*Unpublished

Increasing Urbanization

The proportion urban/total population would increase significantly from 28 per cent during 2001 to anywhere between 35 and 40 per cent by 2021; UNDP, New Delhi has projected that the proportion would be 36 per cent by 2015.

The increase in urban population would be due mainly to the following reasons :

Increase, perhaps slower than during 1981-1991 and 1991-2001 of population of the largest metropolitan cities; Mumbai, Kolkata, Delhi, Bangalore, Chennai, Hyderabad, Ahmedabad and others. The sharp decline in growth rate, experienced by Kolkata during 1981-1991 could be experienced by a number of other large cities. The principal reason for this is that with the expertise and finance available with the municipal corporations of most of the metropolitan cities and the governments of the states in which they are located, it is extremely difficult and expensive to ensure dependable supplies of electricity and drinking water and provide facilities for disposal of solid and liquid waste, school or college education and preventive health and medical care facilities for such large concentrations of people.

An indication of the difficulties is provided by the recent (January 2001) experience in Ahmedabad after the earthquake in Kutch in which about 20,000 people are estimated to have been killed. Ahmedabad (population 4.5 million in 2001) is the capital of Gujarat, one of the most developed and progressive states in India most of the people of middle and high-income groups of the city live in multi-storey flats. These developed large cracks, which had to be repaired after the quake.

Ahmedabad has good architects and town planners and the fact that the region is subject to high intensity earthquakes is also well known. The architects and engineers could have ensured and the corporation could have insisted that the multi-story buildings, which have been built in thousands in recent decades, were earthquake proof. The principal reason for not doing this was to maximize the profits of the builders who deliberately violated the standards prescribed by the architects and engineers for construction of earthquake proof buildings. Yet no builder has been punished by the corporation for such deliberate violation of safety standards.

An increasing proportion of the population of most of the metropolitan cities will be living in their suburbs and satellite towns/cities. In Mumbai, along with growth of population in the main city, located on the island, there has been rapid growth in the last four decades of population in the satellite cities of Nhavi Mumbai and Thane, and in the areas appropriated by factories along the Mumbai-Pune rail-*cum*-road strip and along the highway going from Mumbai to Delhi.

In Delhi metropolitan area similarly, a significant proportion of the population lives in five satellite cities—Shahdara, Ghaziabad and NOIDA in Uttar Pradesh and Faridabad and Gurgaon in Haryana. In the satellite cities are located hundreds of small, medium scale and large industrial units that manufacture motor vehicles, machine tools, various consumer durables and consumer goods—cloth, clothing, processed foods and drugs. The plant manufacturing India's largest selling passenger car is located just off the road between Gurgaon and Delhi. NOIDA and Gurgaon have become also centres of the information technology industries because the governments of the states have created the infrastructure for such development. National and regional offices of a large number of multi-national corporations are located in Gurgaon in preference to the Central Business District (CBD) Connaught Circus of New Delhi. Private builders have built buildings suitable for their offices with dependable supplies of electricity and water on land developed by HUDA (Haryana Urban Development Authority). Rents are lower in these buildings than in the CBD; large office space required by the corporations is available and there is freedom from congestion and pollution of air and water that are the bane of the CBD.

The villages located between Gurgaon, Faridabad and Delhi have become urbanized because large proportions of their populations work in industrial units located along the highways between these two cities and New Delhi. Many workers in New Delhi and retired persons who need education facilities for their children and health care facilities for the children and themselves live in these satellite cities. The same is true of villages located between Old Delhi and the satellite cities in U.P. mentioned above. Similar trends can be described for other metropolitan cities. All of them have a number of satellite towns/cities extending over long distances along the highways radiating from the metropolitan cities.

The principal reasons for concentration of population in metropolitan cities are :

(i) Metropolitan cities are cultural capitals of the regions in which they are located. Mumbai, Pune, Kolkata, Chennai, Hyderabad, Bangalore and Trivandrum are the cultural centres for Marathi, Bengali, Tamil, Telugu, Kannada and Malayalam respectively.

Best writers in these languages are located in their cultural centres mentioned above. The same can be said for the other cities. The film-makers, writers, artists and musicians have decided that these cities provide them with the best facilities and largest audiences for expressions of their sentiments. Mumbai is also the most important centre for production of films and television serials which provide employment to large numbers of workers.

(ii) Availability of employment for both white-collar workers as well as skilled and semi-skilled workers is in metropolitan cities and their satellite cities/towns. Besides, Delhi, the national capital, ten metropolitan cities are capitals of the states in which they are located. As a result there are opportunities for employment for large numbers of people in the offices of the government (central, state and local) and of the public or private sector in industrial or service sector units that are located in them and/or in their satellite cities/towns.

(iii) Most of the metropolitan cities are commercial capitals of the regions in which they are located. Delhi is the principal centre for distribution of consumer goods and consumer durables in its entire hinterland which includes Punjab, Haryana, western Uttar Pradesh, Uttaranchal, Himachal Pradesh and Jammu and Kashmir. More than 12 million people living in it and its satellite towns/cities constitute a large market for provisions (foodgrains, spices, milk, fruit and vegetables), medicinal drugs, textiles, clothes, furnishings for homes and offices and consumer durables—refrigerators, air-conditioners, electrically operated kitchen gadgets and motor vehicles. As a result, some of the refrigerators and air-conditioners are assembled or manufactured in a satellite city—Faridabad; others are imported. The factory producing India's largest selling passenger car is located in a suburb of Gurgaon, a satellite city of Delhi. A large number of industrial units, located in the outskirts of Gurgaon, manufacture spare parts for the car; others make machine tools and building materials. A factory for manufacturing motor bicycles is also located in a satellite city. Located in another satellite city is a factory for producing tractors.

Ghaziabad, a satellite city located in UP, is a principal centre for production of furnishings for homes and offices and processed foods.

Located in NOIDA, another satellite city in U.P., are a large number of Industrial units which manufacture machine tools.

The owners of all these factories have decided correctly that these are the best locations for distribution of the goods produced by them. Mumbai, Kolkata, Chennai, Bangalore, Hyderabad, Pune, Ahmedabad and Jaipur have similar roles in the states in which they are located. All of them except Jaipur and Kolkata have become also important centres of information technology industry. All, except Jaipur and Ahmedabad, are centres also for producing films and television serials in Hindi and different regional languages.

Both processes; growth of metropolitan cities and growth of large villages with market facilities are concentrated in areas in which productivity of land is high due to adequate and dependable rainfall and/ or irrigation provided by canals and/or wells powered by diesel oil or electricity.

It is interesting to note that the metropolitan cities and large villages which have developed into small towns are all concentrated in areas in which productivity of land is high. The areas have been described above. All the 35 metropolitan cities are located in these areas, or at their margin, such as Mumbai, Kolkata and Chennai. Readers will read the old adage, 'a town exists to market the surplus of a fertile area around it'; the larger the fertile area the larger the surplus and larger the town/city. Mumbai, Kolkata, Chennai became large cities because they were the main parts from which the agricultural surplus of India—foodgrains, cotton, tea, sugar or its minerals were exported and manufactured goods needed, were imported. They meet the needs of the British and Indians and the smaller metropolitan cities attained this size because of various reasons described in the foregoing sections.

On the other hand, Bhilai (in Madhya Pradesh), Rourkela (in Orissa), Bokaro and Jamshedpur (in Bihar) and Durgapur-Asansol (in West Bengal) have failed to become metropolitan cities despite location of large steel plants and associated chemical fertilizers or cement plants in them in which there is large employment and in which thousands are engaged in providing various consumer goods and services to the workers in the plants. These areas are all located in hilly and forested areas which are inhabited mainly by tribal.

Many industries which use high weight, low value raw materials such as steel to manufacture goods such as motor vehicles are located near metropolitan cities. The manufacturers calculate correctly that the costs of assembling the raw materials are more than offset by the savings in distribution of the high value finished products. This saving is vital when different manufacturers (e.g. in motor vehicles, air-conditioners, refrigerators, electrically operated kitchen appliances, television receivers) compete for limited but expanding markets.

Even the first three petroleum refineries established in India were located in Mumbai with no regard for the problem of pollution of air or water that their location caused. Most of the later ones have also been located near large cities.

The attraction of large cities as headquarters of public sector or private sector units engaged in development of mineral resources, steel, manufacture of heavy electrical goods, machine tools, or transport equipment is so great that the headquarter of BHEL (Bharat Heavy Electricals) which manufactures turbines and other equipment for electricity generator stations is located in Bhopal, a metropolitan city. The headquarter of Oil and Natural Gas Commission engaged in exploration and development of oil fields off and on-shore Mumbai and Gujarat is located in Dehra Doon, which is 1500 km. from the oil fields. The headquarter of Steel Authority of India which manages all the five public sector steel plants is located in Kolkata with a strong regional office in Delhi. Hindustan Machine Tools which makes light machine tools is located in Bangalore as is Indian Telephone Industries (ITI) which makes telephone receivers and telecommunication equipment. One reason for location of the offices in large cities is that the education, and health facilities and housing required by the executives of these enterprises are available only in large cities. The regional offices are located in Delhi because the Ministers and bureaucrats that exercise, or need to exercise remote control on the operation of these enterprises, are all located in Delhi.

Reasons for Growth of Large Towns and Cities

(i) *Growth of District Headquarters Towns* : India had over 700 districts during 2001; the number could increase to 800 during the next two decades. This would be for political and administrative reasons and large populations of several populous districts will lead to their division into smaller districts.

Every district headquarter would be a small city or large town because with the coverage, already achieved, with rural electrification, provision of access to motorable roads, telecommunication services and growth of the market economy in most of the rural areas. There would be enough education, health and commercial service activities to provide gainful employment to workers in these cities. The existing urban corridors would increase in size and would also widen because the problem of capitals' skilled labour and developed land are located in them. The Delhi Metropolitan District would expand to include a highly developed Gurgaon, NOIDA, Ghaziabad, and Faridabad. Such higher expansion and widening would also occur between Mysore and Bangalore in Karnataka around Hyderabad in Andhra Pradesh and Coimbatore and Chennai in Tamil Nadu and Pune in Maharashtra. New corridors could develop.

The largest metropolitan cities such as Mumbai, Ahmedabad, and Delhi probably would not increase as rapidly as in the last two decades. This is because of the difficulties and high expense of providing adequately the physical and social infrastructures needed to service such large concentration of people. On the other hand, the proportion of people in smaller metropolitan cities could increase. Transport of goods to prosperous villages and export of their produce to markets would itself provide enough, business, for a large town or small city.

(ii) *Decline of Small Villages* : In the rural areas, the number of very small villages could decline and that of relatively large villages with populations between 2000-5000 could increase. Such concentration could result from concentration of road and telecommunication facilities and social services (education, health) in the larger villages. These villages would be reclassified as small towns which would automatically increase the proportion of urban/total population. Cultivators with highly productive irrigated landholdings could live in large villages to take advantages of the service facilities in them and commute to their lands by tractors, mopeds and scooter, etc. Their tenants and agricultural labourers could also commute to the farms on bicycles and scooters. Such villages are already the norm in several relatively developed northern, western and southern states—Punjab, Haryana, western U.P., Rajasthan, Gujarat, Maharashtra, Tamil Nadu, Karnataka and Andhra Pradesh—in which the number of large villages are already urbanized due to industrial development. They would increase also as agricultural production increases in areas such as eastern Rajasthan and parts of western Madhya Pradesh in which the number of villages are large. These could become small towns with increase in agricultural productivity. On the other hand the population of the largest cities such as Mumbai, Kolkata and Delhi would increase much slower than during recent decades and could even decrease.

Thus two facts may be highlighted at this stage. First, the proportion of urban/total population would increase. Second, the number of large villages and small towns would increase at the expense of the small villages. The increase would be sharpest in U.P., Bihar, West Bengal, Madhya Pradesh and east Rajasthan with more rapid growth of agricultural output following effective land reforms in Bihar.

(iii) *Relatively Large Villages becoming Small Towns* : Another reason for increasing urbanization would be that tens of thousands of villages that had populations between 3000 and 5000 in 1991 would become small towns by or much before 2021. This would be due to both natural increase of the population resident in them and in-migration of people from small villages.

The principal reason for the latter is that the infrastructure and service facilities essential for high productivity agriculture and healthy living—dependable supplies of electricity, adequate and clean drinking water, motorable roads, telecommunication and postal services, banks, stores for improved seed, chemical fertilizers and pesticides, facilities for purchase and repair of tractors, electric or diesel operated pumps for irrigation and supply of fuel and spare parts for them can be provided at reasonable cost only in large villages. Cooperative societies that provide short-term credit for current cultivation and branches of Land Mortgage and nationalized banks that give credit for buying tractors, pump sets and other machines for land reclamation and improvement of homes can be located also in relatively large villages. Secondary education and preventive health and medical care facilities can also be provided in them. Farmers living in them can commute to their farms located within one to three kilometres by tractors, scooters or mopeds. Agricultural labourers can commute to the farms by bicycles or mopeds. A large percentage will have work on loading or unloading crops in the mini market towns or working in the processing units located in the larger ones as a secondary source of income. Finally, the marketable surpluses of the crops can be carried to regional markets at low cost only from large villages.

The development has occurred and will occur in the immediate future in areas in which productivity of agriculture is high and there are already a large number of towns and relatively large villages.

Living in Large Villages is an Advantage for two Reasons

(i) There is possibility of defense against invaders. This may have been part of the reason for this pattern to emerge in Punjab, western U.P. and Haryana which were invaded by a succession of invaders throughout the Moslem period of Indian history when Delhi was the capital of north India and large parts of peninsular India.

(ii) Another reason for this pattern in these areas as well as in Rajasthan, north-west Madhya Pradesh, Gujarat and Maharashtra is that potable water adequate to support a village is available in only a limited number of villages. This pattern has persisted after advent of irrigation also because family and agricultural labour can be combined easily in such villages. Marketing and processing of crops for sale in cities can be also best organized in relatively large villages. The stores for improved seed, chemical fertilizers, pesticides; cooperative societies and Land Mortgage Banks that give loans can be located in them.

(iii) Furthermore, various social services—education, health—commercial infrastructure facilities, and telecommunications, reliable supply of electricity motorable roads can be provided best in these villages. Farmers can reach their farms located at one to two kilometres from their homes in 15-20 minutes by bicycles and mopeds. People can live in brick and mortar houses provided with piped water from overhead tanks or wells fitted with pumps, in which sanitation is maintained by them only in such villages.

The areas in which relatively large villages are becoming small towns are :

(i) *Punjab, Haryana and Western Uttar Pradesh* : The principal crops in the area are dwarf, very high yielding rice and wheat in Punjab; wheat, oil seeds and cotton in Haryana and wheat, sugarcane and oilseeds in western Uttar Pradesh. There are a large number of towns in which the crops are processed and which serve also as centres for marketing the crops. Furthermore, small, medium scale and large industrial units are located in a number of towns and cities of central Punjab. Large number of workers in the factories live in villages closest to them and commute to them from their villages. Production of milk, vegetables and poultry products for industrial workers and residents of cities is a major source of income for farmers or their women.

Conditions are similar in western Uttar Pradesh. The area is irrigated by (a) canals from Yamuna and Ganga rivers; (b) deep tube-wells, owned and run by the State Electricity Board; and (c) surface wells powered by electric or diesel operated pumps owned by farmers themselves.

There are a number of sugar mills located in towns in the strip between Saharanpur and Ghaziabad. At its southern end Shahdara, Ghaziabad and NOIDA are the principal cities. They have high concentrations of industrial units and large number of industrial workers. They are also important dormitory cities of Delhi. Sahibabad, located a few kilometres east of Ghaziabad is also becoming a dormitory town.

In Haryana, high productivity agricultural and agro-industrial development has occurred in the western part of the state following extension of canal irrigation in the 1950s, after construction of the Bhakra-Nangal dam. There are a number of towns, which have facilities for marketing the principal crops—wheat, oilseeds (mainly mustard or groundnut and cotton. Several town/cities have mills for processing wheat and oilseeds, cotton gins and textile mills.

The environs of Delhi have Gurgaon and Faridabad as satellite or dormitory cities of Delhi; both of them have a large number of industrial units. Two factories manufacturing passenger cars are located in the region, one in the environs of Gurgaon and the other at some distance from NOIDA. A large number of units located near the factory in Gurgaon manufacture parts for motor vehicles.

(ii) *Coastal Andhra Pradesh* : High yield rice and sugarcane are the principal crops. There are a large number of rice flour and sugar mills, located in a number of small market towns or cities. The present government has organized an efficient system of telecommunications through which all information about any untoward development in any part of the state can reach the capital within an hour. With this development, disaster relief after visitation of cyclones can be organized quickly with minimal loss of life and property.

(iii) *Coastal Tamil Nadu :* Especially the delta of Kaveri River, which is irrigated by canals from the river. High yield rice, of which two crops are grown in the year, is the principal crop. There are a large number of rice and flour mills and market towns in which the mills are located. The towns have also facilities for supplying inputs of high productivity agriculture, and needs of the population for consumer goods. Road and rail communications are good. Besides, Chennai, there are a number of smaller cities such as Trichy, Madurai and Tuticorin a port town in the extreme south. All of them have several industrial units.

(iv) *Coimbatore and its environs in Western Tamil Nadu* : High yield medium staple cotton is grown under irrigation from a canal from Pykara River. There are a large number of textile mills as well as industrial units manufacturing spare parts for the mills and machine tools. Coimbatore has in recent decades, become a multi-industry city. A number of villages around it have become dormitory towns for workers in factories and offices located in the Coimbatore Metropolitan Area. A major increase in irrigated area has followed rural electrification and growth of large number of mini market towns.

(v) *South-west Karnataka* : The rail-*cum*-road strip between Mysore city and Bangalore and the Mangalore Metropolitan area and its extension north to cover the whole of south Kanara district. The farmland located between Mysore city and Bangalore is irrigated by a canal from Kaveri River. There are a large number of relatively large villages which perform market town functions for farmers living in small villages. The functions are performed also by the towns in which rice, flour and sugar mills are located. The Bangalore Metropolitan Area, with its extension to Hossoor along thc road to Chennai, has one of the largest concentrations of factory industries in India. These range from manufacture or repair of aircraft, assembling trucks, production of precision machine tools, manufacture of pumps and compressors for refrigerators and air-conditioners to information technology. A large number of villages in it are urbanized because they serve as dormitories for workers in the factories located in the metropolitan area. Several large industrial units such as Hindustan Aircraft have their own workers' colonies.

South Kanara district also has a number of towns and urbanized villages from which hundreds of thousands of young men and women have gone out to work in the Gulf countries and in Mumbai, Chennai and other southern cities. The Mangalore Metropolitan Area with its port, petroleum refinery, banks and other offices is a magnet for in-migration of rural people.

(vi) *Kerala* : The percentage of urban/total population is low in Kerala but this is due partly to the definition of villages and towns adopted by the State Government. Most of the households live in their own compounds surrounded by their rice fields and/or groves of coconut and tapioca. A village may have a population of up to 10,000. However, if the upper limit were reduced to 5,000, there would be a large increase in the number of small towns and in the proportion urban/total population. The increase would be highest in North Kerala—in Kochi and north of it in Kozhikode and Mopalapuzham districts. Hundreds of thousands of young men from these districts work in the Gulf countries. Their remittances home are the principal source of income for their families. There are a large number of relatively large villages, which perform market town functions. They supply food and other provisions—drugs, clothes and other factory made consumer goods and building materials—to rural people. There is brisk construction activity in reconstruction or expansion of the houses of the families of the emigrants.

(vii) *Coastal Gujarat* : The area is relatively urbanized. There is a number of cities and towns of various sizes, between Ahmedabad and Surat. Processing of crops, principally groundnut and making an enormous variety of manufactured goods—textiles, clothes, jewellery, machine tools and drugs—provide employment to millions of workers. A variety of consumer durables such as air-conditioners and electrically operated kitchen gadgets are manufactured or assembled in towns in the area. Discovery of crude oil off and on-shore

Gujarat, has added oil refining and petro-chemical industries including manufacture of plastic goods for the households as major industries. Development of dairying around Anand in central Gujarat to produce liquid milk for Mumbai and cities in Gujarat and milk products—butter, cheese and baby food—throughout India provides employment to women of thousands of small farmers who keep one-to-three buffaloes to produce milk for the dairy.

(viii) *Western Maharashtra :* There are a large number of towns located in valleys in which high yield rice and sugarcane with high sucrose content are the principal crops on lands irrigated by small streams flowing west from the western Ghats to the Arabian sea. There are a large number of small or medium sized towns or cities in which rice, flour and sugar mills are located along with factories that make machine tools for the mills and other uses.

Mumbai, its environs and those of Pune have the largest concentration of factory industries in India. They include petroleum-refining, manufacture of motor vehicles, textiles, clothing, a large variety of machine tools, consumer durables, furniture for homes, offices and hospitals and pharmaceutical drugs.

The declared policy of the Governments of both Gujarat and Maharashtra is to secure dispersal of industries from coastal Gujarat and Western Maharashtra to less developed regions of the states—Saurashtra and Kutch in Gujarat and Marathwada and Vidarbha in Maharashtra. The object is to reduce environmental pollution in coastal Gujarat and Western Maharashtra and to secure balanced regional development of the states. However, the policies have not been successful so far due to various reasons including lack of measures to achieve decentralized development.

Industrial development in Saurashtra would become feasible only after irrigation is extended to the area from the Sardar Sarover dam located on Narbada River in Madhya Pradesh. With removal of the constraint of scarcity of water, agricultural output would increase and agro-processing and other industries could be located in a number of small or medium sized towns or small cities which were capitals of former princely states.

The factories located in the market towns or cities of Vidarbha and Marathwada at present, are concerned primarily with processing of crops grown in the regions, cotton gins and oil mills in Marathwada and oil mills and cotton textile mills in Vidarbha. Development of other industries in the two regions will become possible if fiscal and other incentives are offered to industrialists to locate their factories in them in preference to western Maharashtra. The development will occur first in Vidarbha, which has a number of towns/cities in which processing of cotton, and groundnuts, manufacture of cloth and production of oil are the principal industries. Furthermore, road and rail communications and telecommunication facilities are well developed. The infrastructure for industrial development—adequate and dependable supplies of electricity and water, good road and rail communications and telecommunications—must be available in selected cities or towns in Marathwada before significant industrial development can be expected in it.

(ix) *Goa*, with a population of just over a million, is relatively urbanized. Besides Panaji the capital, there are a number of small towns. High yield rice, coconuts and mangoes are the principal crops. The mangoes and fish are sent to Mumbai. Tens of thousands of young men and women work in the Gulf countries or in Mumbai or Pune. There is brisk construction activity in repair of old houses or building new ones for the families of the migrants. Thousands of young men and women work in the large number of hotels and cafes that are visited by tens of thousands of visitors from Mumbai, Pune or other cities during weekends and holidays.

The university attracts students from Maharashtra and Karnataka besides those from Goa itself. The port handles millions of tonnes of export of iron ore every year. Building of the Konkan railway has added a railway link to Mumbai and Pune and facilitated export of mangoes and fish to the two cities and entry of tourists.

Agricultural and Agro Industrial Development

Uttar Pradesh and Bihar

The area under irrigation in central and eastern Uttar Pradesh could be increased significantly through rapid increase in the number of surface wells fitted with electric or diesel oil operated pumps. The Rihand and other large power stations located in Jharkhand or in Madhya Pradesh are closer to central and eastern U.P. than they are to western U.P. or Delhi in which most of their power is used at present. The capacity of these plants could be increased to serve the needs of central and eastern U.P. Thousands of small tanks located in the area could be repaired and renovated to increase the area under irrigation.

Increase in agricultural output would be both in foodgrains—wheat, rice, gram (chick peas), peas and pulses—and cash crops—sugarcane, oilseeds, potatoes and mangoes. Location of factories processing the crops, manufacture of potato chips and mango *chutneys* would be the logical next step.

A similar development could be initiated in Bihar by a government determined to end the class war between the former landlords and their tenants that is preventing modernization of agriculture and development of agro-processing industries in the state. This would however, be a later development than in U.P. There is great potential for increasing agricultural output in north Bihar by reclamation of the lands which are covered with coarse sand and silt by the monsoon floods of the Kosi, Gandak and other rivers. Agricultural output in South Bihar would increase following replacement of thousands of wells worked by animal power by those operated by diesel oil or electric pumps.

One of the beneficial effects of development of high productivity agriculture and agro-industrial development in U.P. and Bihar would be that millions of young men who are working at present in metropolitan cities—Mumbai, Kolkata, Delhi and others—would return to their home villages. Hard working and disciplined, they would contribute the needed labour for high productivity agriculture and agro-processing industries. Furthermore, with incomes relatively higher than that of most of the other villagers, they together with farmers with relatively large holdings will constitute the principal buyers of consumer goods and consumer durables—processed foods, drugs, black and white and color television sets, fans and building materials.

A large percentage of the medium-sized villages in which markets for the output of high productivity agriculture and supply of inputs for it would be located would become small towns.

Rajasthan and Madhya Pradesh

Output of cereals has increased in Rajasthan by more than 50 per cent between 1976 and 1992. Output of commercial crops—mainly oilseeds—

has increased also (SIDA 1997, p. 36). The increase in agricultural output is due partly to reclamation for cultivation of the cultivable wastelands and partly to use of high yielding varieties of wheat along with chemical fertilizers and pesticides in areas having assured moisture provided by irrigation from canals or wells fitted with pumps operated by electricity or diesel oil. Consumption of chemical fertilizers for instance has increased from 7.42 kg. per hectare in 1981-82 to 20.19 kg. in 1993-94, i.e. nearly three times. The increased output is being processed by a number of wheat flour and oil mills located in a number of market towns in eastern and south-eastern Rajasthan and in the area irrigated by canals in the extreme north western part of the state.

As a result of this development, the state has a surplus of foodgrains and a large exportable surplus of oilseeds. The literacy rate has increased by 57 per cent between 1991 and 2001. Female literacy rate has more than doubled. Per capita income has increased by 83 per cent during 1980-81 to 1996-97 (Tables 16.1 and 16.2).

Similar but less spectacular development has occurred in Madhya Pradesh as the data for literacy and per capita income in Tables 16.1 and 16.2 indicate. While agricultural and economic growth in Rajasthan is constrained by environmental hazards—semi-arid and arid conditions—in nearly half of the state; there is no such constraint in Madhya Pradesh. Such development will follow increase in education and improvement in health of the population through effective programmes of providing education and health care to the population. The state has launched effective programmes in which the beneficiary populations cooperate with the officials in managing the facilities that provide education and preventive and curative health services.

Table 16.1: Literacy Rates 1991-2001

Sl. No.	*State*	*Literacy rate in 1991 (per cent)*			*Literacy rate in 2001 (per cent)*		
		Total	*Male*	*Female*	*Total*	*Male*	*Female*
1.	Bihar	38.5	52.6	23.5	47.5	60.3	31.6
2.	U.P.	41.7	55.4	26.0	57.4	70.2	43.0
3.	Rajasthan	38.5	55.1	20.8	61.0	76.5	44.3
4.	M.P.	43.4	57.4	28.4	64.1	76.8	50.3

Source: Registrar General of India: Census of India, 2001. Paper No. 1, Provisional Population Tables, New Delhi, 2001.

Table 16.2 : Growth Rate of Population, 1981-1991 and 1991-2001 and Growth Rate of Per Capita Income 1980-81 to 1996-97

India and States	*Population in 1990-91*	*Population in 2000-01*	*Growth rate of population Per cent per annum*		*Literacy rate*			*Per capita income rupees at 1980-81 prices (Rupees)*		
					Person	*Male*	*Female*			
	(Millions)	*(Millions)*	*1981-91*	*1991-2001*	*2001*			*1980-81*	*1996-97*	*Increase (%)*
1	*2*	*3*	*4*	*5*	*6*	*7*	*8*	*9*	*10*	*11*
India	846.4	1027.5	2.01	1.93	65.4	75.9	54.2	1625	2814	70.5
Andhra Pradesh	66.5	75.7	2.37	1.30	61.1	70.9	51.2	1380	2134	54.6
Assam	22.4	26.6	2.17	1.73	64.3	72.0	56.0	—	—	—
Bihar	64.5	82.9	2.10	2.50	47.5	60.3	33.6	917	1010	10.1
Goa	1.2	1.3	1.47	1.39	82.3	88.9	75.5	3145	6550	97.8
Gujarat	41.3	50.6	1.92	2.03	70.0	80.5	58.6	1940	3717	91.6
Haryana	16.5	21.0	2.42	2.47	68.6	79.3	56.3	2330	3996	71.5
Jharkhand	21.8	26.9	2.15	2.09	54.1	67.9	39.4	—	—	—
Karnataka	45.0	52.7	1.92	1.59	67.0	76.3	57.5	1380	2518	64.5
Kerala	29.1	31.8	1.34	0.90	90.9	94.2	87.9	1568	2274	45.0
Madhya Pradesh	48.6	60.4	2.41	2.18	64.1	76.8	50.3	1358	1877	38.0
Maharashtra	78.9	96.8	2.29	2.04	77.3	86.3	67.5	2425	4853	100.1
Orissa	31.7	36.7	1.83	1.48	63.6	76.0	51.0	1314	1595	21.4
Punjab	20.3	24.3	1.89	1.80	70.0	75.6	63.6	2674	4171	56.0
Rajasthan	44.0	56.5	2.80	2.49	61.0	76.5	44.3	1228	2247	83.0
Tamil Nadu	55.9	62.1	1.43	1.06	73.5	82.3	64.6	1448	2876	98.6
Uttar Pradesh	132.0	166.0	2.28	2.30	57.4	70.2	43.0	1278	1628	27.4
West Bengal	68.0	80.2	2.14	1.64	69.2	78.0	60.2	1773	2641	49.0

Note: The 1991 populations of Uttar Pradesh, Bihar and Madhya Pradesh have been reduced to take into account the separation of Uttaranchal, Jharkhand and Chhattisgarh respectively from the three states.

Sources: Registrar General of India: Provisional Population Totals Paper No. 1 of 1991 and Provisional Population Totals, paper 1 of 2001, New Delhi, India.

For per capita income : E.P.W. Research Foundation : National Accounts Statistics of India 1950-51 - 1996-97, Mumbai, 1998, p. 84.

Increase in agricultural output and development of agro-processing industries will occur first in the north-western part of the state. There are a large number of small and medium sized towns or cities, besides the three large cities of Gwaliar, Indore and Bhopal all of which have several industrial units. Such development in the eastern and central parts of the state which are rich in agricultural, mineral or forest resources and have a number of large industrial units and power plants but have large tribal populations will be a later development which would follow effective extension of education and health care facilities to the population and training the young men and women to become skilled industrial or white-collar workers.

West Bengal

Output of rice and jute has increased so much that the state which had a deficit of rice even a few years ago, has a surplus now. More important, most of the small cultivators and agricultural labourers have much higher income than they used to have. The government of the state has assisted increase in output of rice and jute during the last three decades. The land reform of abolition of *zamindari* has been accomplished in fact; full and heritable rights in land have been conferred on the actual cultivators and those of the *zamindars* have been extinguished. Short and medium-term loans have been given to the former zamindars to buy tractors to reclaim the land left to them for self-cultivation but which used to be covered by silt, sand and boulders brought down by the floods of Teesta River, and to buy seed of improved dwarf high yielding varieties of rice, chemical fertilizers and pesticides, as needed. The degradation of land has been reduced greatly by construction of a dam on the river.

Similar loans have been given to the former tenants to buy improved seed of rice and jute, chemical fertilizers and pesticides (as needed) to increase production of rice, other grains (pulses and oil seeds) and jute on land that has been given to them.

The farmers, freed from the obligation of surrendering a proportion of their produce to the zamindars, have made strenuous effort to maximize returns on their land, labour and capital. The need for import of jute from Bangladesh to make jute goods has been reduced also. More important, most of the small farmers and agricultural labourers have so much work in agriculture that the need to migrate to Kolkata to find work has been reduced greatly. They have been uplifted from poverty to middle income status.

Western Maharashtra

It should be mentioned that the irrigated valleys of western Maharashtra, which produce large crops of high yield sugarcane with high sucrose content and high yield rice, have a number of sugar and rice mills and other industries making machine tools for various uses, were drought prone until the late 1950s. They were transformed into their present status, by effective use of their underground and surface resource of water for irrigation. The farmers who are organized in cooperatives which provide them improved seed, chemical fertilizers and other inputs, and market and process the crops have become so rich that their leaders dominate the politics of Maharashtra. There is enough work and income for even small farmers in growing the crops, and for agricultural labourers both in agriculture and in the sugar and rice mills and other industrial units that manufacture machine tools. The farmers and agriculture labourers in the valley around north have more than enough work in growing fruit and vegetables and packaging it for consumption in Mumbai, Pune and cities all over north west India and also for export to the Gulf countries for consumption of Indians working there. All these areas attract workers from south-east and south-west Maharashtra, Marathwada and a part of Vidarbha which are drought prone and development of which was neglected by their former ruler, the Nizam of Hyderabad.

Central and Eastern Uttar Pradesh and Bihar

The recommendation for agricultural and agro-industrial development in central and eastern U.P. and Bihar in order to reduce poverty and emigration of their most productive workers is not unrealistic when viewed in historical context or in the context of developments in West Bengal during the last 3 decades.

These areas were the most productive and densely populated areas of the country until the 1870s. Their productivity was reduced first by indigo planters (all British) who made large profits growing indigo for making dyes, until development of synthetic (anilines) dyes by the Germans after the 1870s. The indigo planters did nothing to restore the fertility of the land on which they had grown indigo. The Scots, who owned tea gardens in Assam wanted labour for work in the gardens, because the local people—Assamese and the tribal living in the hills were unable or unwilling to do the arduous labour for long hours which was required in the gardens. The British who owned Sugar plantations in Natal South Africa, Trinidad and British Guiana in the Caribbean, and Fiji in south Pacific also recruited labour from eastern U.P. and Bihar to work in the plantations. The workers established Indians' colonies in these lands to the extent that they form the majority of the population in some of them, but their area of origin was bereft of its most productive manpower.

Emigration

Since a tradition of emigration has been established young men from these areas migrated to Kolkata to work in jute mills and various industrial units to do such arduous and back-breaking jobs as porters at the Howrah and Sealdah railway stations, labourers in the shops in the Central Business District, and as rickshaw pullers in the city. In the 1960s they began to migrate to Punjab and Haryana, to work as agricultural labourers because there was a shortage of workers for harvesting the monsoon season crop of coarse grains (and rice in Punjab), oilseeds and medium staple cotton in Haryana and planting and later harvesting of the cool season crops of wheat and mustard. They started migrating to Mumbai and Delhi to work as unskilled workers in the industrial units in these cities or in their satellite cities. Their remittances home remained the main source of income for their families.

The present Government of West Bengal has reversed the process of migration of rural workers from central and northern West Bengal to Kolkata and Howrah. It has expedited construction of a dam on Teesta River, the monsoon floods of which used to cover large areas with sand and silt. The farmers have been given low interest loans to buy livestock and ploughs to reclaim their landholdings and to buy seed fertilizers and pesticides to plant high yield rice and jute. Full and heritable rights have been confirmed on them on land which they cultivated by extinguishing the rights of the *zamindars*. The former *zamindars* have been given loans to buy tractors to reclaim the land that has been left to them for self-cultivation and to install pumps operated by electricity or diesel oil to irrigate the area that could be irrigated. There is full time employment for both farmers (including former *zamindars*) and agricultural labourers and there is little need for either to migration to Kolkata in search of work. Meanwhile production of rice has increased so much that the state which had a deficit of rice in some years, has always a surplus. Production of jute has increased and its quality improved so much that imports from Bangladesh have been reduced.

Agricultural and agro-industrial development in Bihar should start by :

(i) Completing the land reform of extinguishing the rights of the *zamindars* and conferring full and heritable rights in land on the actual cultivators;

(ii) Loans at low interest should be given to the farmers to buy seed, chemical fertilizers and pesticides (as needed) to plant crops of high yield rice, wheat, chick peas, peas and pulses;

(iii) The former *zamindars* should be given loans to buy tractors to reclaim the lands which have been left to them for self-cultivation, clearing the land of coarse sand and silt brought down by Kosi, Gandak and other rivers. They should be given loans also to install pump sets on wells to irrigate areas that are irrigable.

Some of these areas are suitable for growing high quality mangoes, which are in great demand in Kolkata, Patna and other cities. Growing and packaging the mangoes, and potatoes, another cash crop will create so much work and income that there would be little need for small farmers and agricultural labourers to migrate to Kolkata and Delhi or other cities. The former *zamindars* would in cooperation with the traders, build cold storages to keep potatoes (another cash crop) until they are ready for the market. Production in South Bihar would increase greatly if the farmers, including former *zamindars*, were given loans to buy pump sets for irrigation on land which is irrigated by bullocks at present. The irrigated area would increase and the land would be irrigated more effectively.

In U.P., the land reform of abolition of *zamindari* and conferring full and heritable rights in land to farmers that they cultivate has been completed. Farmers who own lands that are covered with sand and silt should be given loans and subsidies to clear the land and to plant high yield wheat, rice, coarse grains, and pulses or cash crops—sugarcane and mangoes; the latter in the areas around Lucknow and Varanasi. The former *zamindars* should be given loans to buy tractors for reclamation of the lands left to them for self-cultivation and to buy pump sets for irrigation of the lands that need irrigation.

With these measures there will be much greater remunerative work for farmers and agricultural labourers in growing foodgrains and packaging the commercial crops for markets that there would be much less need for them to migrate to the cities in search of work.

System of Land Tenure

It should be mentioned that all the areas except those under *zamindari* and *jagirdari* and Kerala, were under the '*ryotwari*' system of land tenure in which farmers paid land revenue directly to the provincial governments, which also had direct responsibility for maintaining peace and security in the area. There were no intermediary tenure holders such as *zamindars* in

British ruled provinces and *jagirdars* in princely states. On the other hand, areas in which productivity of land is low and there has been a history of migration to cities or to distant lands were under the *zamindari* system of land tenure in provinces and jagirdari in princely states.

The dramatic increase in output of rice and jute following abolition of *zamindari* in West Bengal and of wheat and other cereals and oilseeds (mustard and groundnut) in parts of Rajasthan and western Madhya Pradesh following abolition of *jagirdari*, indicates that the effective abolition of intermediary tenure holders gives a powerful incentive to the actual cultivators to increase agricultural output by optimum use of their land and labour.

Since short-term credit is provided to them to buy improved seed, chemical fertilizers and pesticides for current cultivation and medium-term loans are given for buying tractors and pump sets for reclamation or intensive cultivation of croplands and irrigation of areas that need irrigation, it has made agriculture in these areas more capital intensive. The farmers are much richer than they used to be and much better educated and informed to make economic use of capital.

It is contended that the reform will lead similarly to large increase in output of rice and wheat and other cash crops in U.P. and Bihar. Another advantage would be improvement in health and aspirations of the actual cultivators. The governments must ensure that there is no conflict between the high caste cultivators and their former tenants who have become actual owners of the lands. This conflict is the main reason why agriculture is not getting modernized in Bihar to maximize agricultural output.

Nucleated Residential Living

Most of the people lived in tightly nucleated villages with population of 1000 and more in north-west India (Punjab, Haryana, western U.P. and adjoining areas of Rajasthan) partly for reasons of defence. The area has been invaded so many times that the people saw safety in numbers. While the Brahmins, Mahajans and Jats or Rajput cultivators lived in the centre of such villages, the Scheduled Castes, most of them agricultural labourers, and others who performed various services for the high castes and the farmers lived on the outskirts rather than in hamlets separated from the main village. In semi-arid Maharashtra and Gujarat and adjoining areas of Madhya Pradesh, and Telengana area of Andhra Pradesh the tightly nucleated village has been the norms because potable water sufficient to support a village is available in a limited number of places.

Urbanization is facilitated in areas having tightly nucleated villages, most of them semi-arid areas when with irrigation, production increase and facilities for agricultural extension, credit and markets and processing the crops are located in relatively large villages (small towns) most of which were tightly nucleated villages earlier. Health care and secondary, technical and higher education are also located in such settlements. It is hampered in Eastern India partly because of paucity or absence of roads, waterways which were the principal means of communication and were displaced by the railways and roads, and cannot be revived now.

In eastern India and parts of Karnataka and Tamil Nadu where potable water is available everywhere, the central village (with population of 1000 or more was the settlement of the Brahmins, Mahajans (Chettiars) and high caste farmers; the Scheduled Castes lived in various hamlets which fringe the central habitation area after which the village is named. There are at least two temples one of the high castes and the other of the Scheduled Castes. In Kerala the majority of the household live in individual compounds in which the house is surrounded by its fields of rice patch of tapioca and groves of coconut and other palms. Commerce and social services (education, medical care) and to an extent religious services are concentrated in both large settlements with populations of 5000 and more and smaller centres with populations as low as 1000.

In eastern India, the habitation area of high castes is small; not much larger than one of its several hamlets each of which houses a particular service caste.

Importance of Rail and Road Communications

All the areas of high agricultural output and agro-industrial development discussed above have good railway and road communications. Even in Rajasthan and Western Madhya Pradesh, all the towns and cities have good railway and road communications.

The same is true of the coastal plain of Eastern India. In Peninsular India, railways had to be constructed in order to extract minerals—coal and iron ore for export. The steel and heavy industry cities developed around the steel plants have had very little impact on the surrounding areas which are inhabited by tribal. Roads have been constructed along the valleys in which the Adivasis live. It could be said that the railways were constructed to connect the existing productive areas and cities to the ports in order to facilitate foreign trade. But their maintenance is poor, mainly because of underdevelopment of the area. The formation of the new states of Jharkhand and Chhattisgarh should provide a stimulus to development of the states, after the initial problems of establishment of a new state have been overcome. Production of rice should increase rapidly in Chhattisgarh in which there are a number of valleys in which large quantities of rice and other grains can be produced.

Urbanization is facilitated in areas having tightly nucleated villages with populations of 1000 and more with increase in agricultural output, cooperative societies which give short-term loans for current cultivation; branches of Land Mortgage Bank and nationalized banks that give medium-term (3-5 years) or larger credit for buying tractors, pumps for irrigation and land reclamation can also be located in the larger villages with populations of 2000-3000 and more. Smaller cities can be more livable than huge metropolitan areas, if the people share a common culture and the disparities in income are not too large. Chandigarh, capital of Punjab and Haryana is much more livable than Delhi, because it is a planned city of less than a million people, not more then half a million if the slum dwellers are excluded. It has a University, a world-class hospital, a stadium for cricket in one of its suburbs and small parks galore in its various neighbourhoods. Most people are working or retired civil servants.

There is a very large class of professionals who speak the same language and take delight in similar things. Punjabi songs and dance are the rage. It has a salubrious climate. The town planner surrounded a large part of it by a lake which cools the city when it is hot. Furthermore, it is so close to hill stations—Solan, Kasouli and others—that one could spend a long weekend there. Warm personal relationships develop between people who were posted in the same department. The Haryanvis are concentrated in their own neighbourhoods.

On the other hand, Delhi is a huge megalopolis which has large disparities in income and consumption and great diversity in the activities of the residents. The civil servants are no longer the dominant group as it was even in the 1970s.

There are large numbers of businessmen; where super affluence is to be seen in the parties that they gave in their farm-houses and night-clubs. There are Ministers and their staff and numerous followers and other hangers-on who want to get some advantage out of him, if one is from Punjab, the next-door neighbourhood may be from Kerala. One cannot move about freely without a vehicle of one's own. The alternative of riding a bus is not pleasant because they are so crowded. As a result, for a large number of people, it is 9 to 6 at the office (with 1½ hours for travelling to and fro in the bus) and watching TV and sleep thereafter. Summers are hot; winters are cold so that outdoor activity is reduced to a minimum. The maximum health-conscious persons (young or middle aged) can manage is a walk or jog in a park or even on a road in the mornings or early evenings.

Pune a much smaller city than Mumbai is the centre of Gujarati culture—Rohtak a relatively small city is the centre of Haryanvi culture, Varanasi is the centre of Oudh culture, Lucknow is the centre of Dance and Music, and keeps its tradition, Kanpur renowned industrial centre with a concentration of slums of poor industrial workers. It is perhaps the filthiest city in India. Chennai a metropolis must yield place to Madurai as the centre of Tamil Culture. Similarly, Hyderabad once a centre of culture of the Nawabs has not yet been a centre of Andhra culture. The centre of Karnataka culture is Mysore, the seat of the Maharajah, and Bangalore a city of the foreign British. Jaipur is the centre of Rajasthan culture, which has Jodhpur and Udaipur as strong centres as well of the culture. Gwaliar and Indore each represents their own source of cultures of the regions in which there is a mixture of the Marathi and Hindi.

Conclusion

The Settlement Pattern described in the foregoing sections is unlikely to change in the foreseeable future. The principal changes would be along the lines proposed above.

The most important change would be:

1. Dispersal of population of some of the largest metropolitan cities—Mumbai, Kolkata, Delhi—to their satellite cities because of difficulties of providing water, electricity, facilities for disposal of solid and liquid waste in most cities. This has been noticed to a certain degree already but its full development awaits improvement of road and rail communications between the Central Business District in the main city and the satellite cities.

   The growth of Nhavi Mumbai and Thane would have been much faster if the Maharashtra Government had not kept its Secretariat in Mumbai. In Delhi, despite the uncongested nature of Lutyens' New Delhi all the development is in the satellite cities because both the MCD and the NDMC are unable to make adequate arrangements for supply of electricity and water, disposal of solid and liquid waste that is already there. A metropolitan railway is being constructed because the roads are unable to carry all the traffic.

2. Inter-regional disparities in density of population : A map published by the Census Commissioner of India—2001, shows that the states with (i) the highest densities of population extend from Delhi to Kolkata—They include U.P., Bihar and West Bengal. This is the traditional 'Heartland of Hindustan' the most productive and densely populated part of the country. Kerala is the only state in the south which has similar high density, (ii) a belt of states with medium high densities includes Punjab and Haryana in the north, Gujarat and Maharashtra in the west and Tamil Nadu, Karnataka and Andhra Pradesh in the south.

   The rural populations in these areas have access to assured and adequate supplies of water for irrigation provided by canals and/or wells fitted with pumps powered by electricity or diesel oil. In these areas are grown dwarf high yield varieties of wheat and rice, sugarcane and medium staple cotton, mustard and groundnut for local consumption and for export to other areas. These states have the highest agricultural production and have high levels of urbanization with large number of small towns and urbanized villages in which crops are marketed or processed and various small scale industries are located near the metropolitan cities.

   While the areas mentioned in (i) above are densely populated, they do not have, with the exception of West Bengal, export of any commercial crop. They are barely able to feed themselves or have large export (seasonal or longer-term) of persons to Gulf countries and other regions.

   The areas mentioned in (ii) above produce most of the surpluses of wheat, rice, medium staple cotton, sugarcane, cooking oil and tobacco. Most of the manufacturing industries are located in them and level of income and consumption of the rural people is much higher in them.

3. Agricultural extension, Commercial and Social service facilities are organized in large villages which could have population ranging between 5 and 10 thousands. Such 'villages' or small towns generally have a Church or a Temple as their focal point. They are located along motorable roads which are the principal means of communication. Agro-processing activities rice mills,

plants manufacturing goods for household and industrial use and supply of building materials and various consumer durables (refrigerators, air-conditioners, washing machines and others) are supplied from the larger towns.

In eastern India (West Bengal, Orissa and Assam), the tightly nucleated village disappears. Potable water free from dissolved impurities is not available anywhere. Most of the high caste households live in their own compounds, adjoining their tank in which they grow fish, and draw water for irrigation of crops. Potable water is obtained from shallow wells located next to the tank. In this area, as in Kerala, agricultural extension, social service and commercial activities are organized in large villages which have access to motorable roads. Agro-processing activities are organized often in the same towns which were centres of traditional cottage industries.

Many of the larger villages become mini-market towns by acquiring functions of agro-marketing, agro-processing and social service facilities. In Kerala where most of the household lived in their own compounds surrounded by a patch of rice, a grove of cocoanut and tapioca, the village is a place where commercial, agro-industrial and social service facilities are organized. Such 'villages' could have a population of 10,000 or more or 5000 or less. Every such village had a temple or a church as its focal point.

In eastern India (West Bengal, Orissa, Assam) the 'village' as a tightly nucleated settlement unit disappears. Most of the people live in hamlets surrounded by their tanks from which they get fish and irrigate their fields of rice. Stores for agricultural crops and distribution of consumer goods, durables and building materials are also located in them. They are also the places from which crops are marketed and are processed in larger ones. The village is a purely administrative concept which relates to a somewhat larger settlement which houses the zamindars or sub-zamindars surrounded by scheduled castes each of which do agricultural labour for the high caste *zamindars*, some of whom may be non-resident.

With land reform and end of the rights of the *zamindars*, the Scheduled Caste agricultural labourers have become the actual cultivators. They manage their own small holding; do agricultural labour on the lands of the largest farmers and repair tanks, repair roads and community works such as offices of cooperative societies and panchayats and of administrative buildings such as offices of block development committees, police stations and offices of taluka, sub-division and district offices.

The administrative offices were established long ago and have committed labourers for maintenance of their buildings and approach roads to them. The works needed for rural development have to be planned and implemented by voluntary or state-sponsored 'Panchayati Raj' Institutions.

The discussion in the foregoing sections can be divided into two parts:

1. Discussion of development in most of the densely populated areas of the country which produce most of the food crops (rice, wheat, coarse grains, maize and pulses), sugar, protective foods (milk, poultry products, fruit and vegetables), oilseeds, short and medium staple cotton, jute and tea. All the metropolitan cities are located in them and most of the manufactured goods (consumer goods, consumer durable, machine tools, transport and electrical equipment and others) are produced in them while some of these areas attract migrants from other regions to work in their industrial/service units, from others there is emigration of young men to the Gulf countries or to metropolitan cities within India or seasonal migration to farms in some areas to meet the shortage of labour there.

   The developments during the last 50 years which have led to rapid increase in agricultural output and industrial development and not in employment opportunities and income of the rural people have been reviewed.

   Furthermore, the measures which have been taken by the State Governments by way of agricultural extension, expansion of short and medium-term loans, building roads, facilities for education, preventive health and medical care, communication including telecommunication facility have been described.

2. It has been noted that agricultural and agro-industrial development in some areas which had been retarded by prevalence of intermediary land tenures, under which the farmers had to give a proportion of their produce to intermediary tenure-holders (*zamindars* and *jagirdars*), has risen greatly after abolition of these tenures. Both the *zamindars* and *jagirdars* their former tenants and agricultural labourers have contributed to the increase. Two important features of the increase have been :

   (i) Major increase in the irrigated area partly as a result of construction of canals and partly by installation of pump sets operated by diesel oil or electricity or irrigation wells.

(ii) As a result there is much greater use of capital in agriculture. This has taken the form of use of new dwarf high yielding varieties of seed of wheat and rice, higher yield and improved varieties of sugarcane, cotton and jute, chemical fertilizers and pesticides, and finally, machines (tractors, diesel oil or electrically operated pump sets on irrigation wells). Even small farmers use these inputs, hiring tractors from those who have them. Short and medium-term loans given at rates of interest which even small farmers can afford to pay has made a major contribution to this development.

Other noteworthy developments have been major changes in the level of education, skills, health and aspirations of both the rural and urban population. There has been major increase in male and female literacy; even small farmers can repair small defects in the pump sets that they use. All of them want that their sons should be educated and become white-collar or skilled industrial workers and their daughters should be married to them.

There is need for large investment in providing some of them; in others difficult technical managerial or political problems have to be solved before the required level of efficiency can be achieved. Unless a satisfactory solution to these problems is found, large numbers of people in metropolitan cities will remain deprived of these facilities which will impair their health and productivity.

The developments of the last fifty years, while have increased agricultural output and associated employment and income in some areas, differences in income and level of living between the already developed and comparatively prosperous areas and those in the poor and under-developed areas, particularly those inhabited by tribal people have increased. Appropriate measures will need to be taken to reduce this disparity in the interest of equity and social justice.

Prospect

1. Regional disparities in density of population will remain unchanged in the foreseeable future. Furthermore most of the rural people in the densely populated areas will continue to

have higher levels of income and consumption than those in the sparsely populated areas. These disparities will continue despite the developments in the sparsely populated areas.

2. Urbanization of the population and increase in the number of metropolitan cities will also continue. Furthermore, most of the manufacturing activities and service sector activities will continue to be concentrated in and around metropolitan cities or other large cities. The reasons for this have been explained.
3. The principal problems to which no solutions have been found so far are : (i) to provide tradable and non-tradable inputs to the residents of the metropolitan cities. The tradable inputs include supply of electricity, potable water, and housing. (ii) The others some of which are tradable in parts include disposal of solid or liquid waste; education to secondary school, colleges for humanities, sciences and professions, motorable roads, and ensuring security of life and property for the citizens.

Private profit-making companies or public sector companies contribute to providing some of these inputs. The former have been so efficient in supply of electricity in some cities that they are being encouraged to provide it in others. The companies which have been supplying electricity to Mumbai have been entrusted recently (June 2002) with the responsibility of distributing it to residents of Delhi. The companies hope to make a profit on their investment after two to three years of operation, in which they will have to check theft of electricity by a proportion of industrialists, owners of small hotels as well as by slum dwellers.

Life Insurance Corporation has provided loans for middle income housing almost since its inception in 1958. Its contribution is likely to remain at present levels. Most of its loans will be given to people of middle or upper middle income groups although the government may contribute through urban development authorities in construction of houses for low income groups especially the residents of slums.

Provision of education to secondary school level has been the responsibility of state and local governments which they have fulfilled with assistance from voluntary denominational or non-denominational organizations. Provision of preventive health and medical care has similarly been the responsibilitics of state and local governments.

Denominational organizations and charitable trusts participate in providing such care for the poor residents of cities. Private medical practitioners and profit-making multi-facility hospitals provide such assistance for people of middle and high-income groups. Health insurance companies are coming forward with schemes under which they pay (on payment of their premiums) the costs of prolonged treatment or surgery for people of middle or high-income people. Such treatment remains, however, beyond the reach of the large proportion of people with low incomes who cannot avail of these.

The State Governments provide primary medical care to poor patients free of cost. As incomes of most of the residents of rural and urban areas increase, levying a nominal charge for the care has been accepted mainly in order to ensure that the beneficiaries realize its value. However, treatments of prolonged sicknesses and of cases involving surgery are not available to the poor. Besides, the hospitals run by the state or municipal governments or some charitable organizations cannot cater to the needs of more than a fraction of people of low-income groups.

Another problem to which no solution has been found so far is to reduce the number of illiterate, unskilled people in poor health who live in the slums of metropolitan cities. It has been argued that there has been major increase in agricultural and agro-industrial output in U.P., Bihar, West Bengal and most of the other large states, with the result that there is far more remunerative employment for landless labourers than it was in the 1950s. It has been argued also that the level of education and skills of the small farmers and agricultural labourers in densely populated areas has increased considerably.

It has been explained also that there has been such rapid increase in remunerative employment in Uttaranchal and Himachal Pradesh that there is far less need for their people to go to cities to work as domestic servants. They come mainly to work as white-collar workers and live in brick and mortar houses.

Then who are the slum dwellers? Most of them are not from the tribal areas; in Delhi, Kolkata and Mumbai they are from U.P. and Bihar. Would their numbers decrease in the foreseeable future?

Local and State Governments of the southern states Kerala, Tamil Nadu, Karnataka and Andhra Pradesh have in general been more successful in providing adequate housing and the other infrastructures in their cities than governments in western, northern and north central states.

The Governments of Gujarat, Maharashtra, Punjab and Haryana all of which are relatively developed and have much larger financial resources have been more successful in providing these infrastructures then the Governments of U.P., Bihar and West Bengal. The reasons for this difference can only be identified in consultation with state and local governments in these states.

It is not clear for instance why the Government of U.P., which is so efficient in looking after millions of pilgrims at the Kumbha Melas which are held in it at intervals of six years, should allow large proportion of the population of its principal industrial city Kanpur or its holy city Varanasi live in slums without adequate provisions for potable water or disposal of liquid or solid waste. The second problem to which solution must be found is to reduce the number of slum dwellers in metropolitan cities.

Increasing urbanization and increase in the number of large villages and small towns at the expense of small villages were experienced during the latter half of the 19th century and before Second World War in the large number of countries that are now developed. It has been experienced also in a number of countries in South East and East Asia that have undergone rapid economic development during the last fifty years. Similar development has been experienced in a number of areas in several states in the south, west and north-west of India in which agricultural output has increased rapidly and a large number of agro-processing, consumer goods and consumer durable industries have been established. The areas have been detailed in this paper. It is argued that similar development would occur also in the Indo-Gangetic plain states of U.P. and Bihar in which agricultural development and development of agro-processing industries has been hampered by their neglect by the governments of these large states. The development could increase significantly the proportion of urban/total population in the country. Besides, it would accelerate economic growth with welfare in the two large states, which contain nearly 25 per cent of the population of the country. Another factor contributing to slow progress was prevalence of the *zamindari* system of land tenures under which the farmers had to surrender a part of their produce to *zamindars* who were intermediary tenure holders. Many of them lived in the cities.

This survey points to emergence of four Indias : (i) relatively Developed States with high levels of urbanization—Punjab, Haryana, Coastal Gujarat, West Maharashtra, Tamil Nadu, Coastal Andhra Pradesh, Kerala, Karnataka and West Bengal; (ii) relatively under-developed but populous States—Uttar Pradesh, Bihar; (iii) relatively underdeveloped States with physiographic handicaps : Mountainous hilly and forested in the west and east Himalayan Region—Orissa, Western Rajasthan, Assam, Jharkhand, Chhattisgarh, Eastern Madhya Pradesh, Telengana Region of Andhra Pradesh, Saurashtra, Kutch; and (iv) semi-desert to hilly and forested in peninsular India—Rajasthan, Western Madhya Pradesh, Himachal Pradesh, Uttaranchal, Jammu and Kashmir, hill States of North East.

Connected with history (i) and (ii) were under British India, (iii) and (iv) were largely under princely states or were inhabited by autonomous tribes.

Government is stable, regardless of party affiliations, wherever this disparity has been reduced, e.g. Malaysia, South Korea, Taiwan. In India similarly, Governments are most stable in the states in which disparities in income and consumption levels between different classes have been reduced, primarily by increasing agricultural output and remunerative employment to agricultural labourers of the Scheduled Caste and traditional farmers of the other backward and Scheduled Tribes.

Appendix I

The total urban population of India in 2001 was 285.4 million and formed 27.8 per cent of the total population. The gross increase during the decade was almost 69 million; the figure for 1991 was 217.0 million. Urban population increased by just over 30 per cent during the decade. If this rate continues during the next two decades, the total urban population would be 440 million and its proportion in the total population of 1382 million would be just over 32 per cent. Assuming that the growth rate of population is as low as 1.3 per cent per annum during 2001-2015 as projected by UNDP and the total population rises to 1235 million by 2015, the urban population could be close to 360 million (as projected by UNDP). It is hoped that growth rate of urban population in the next two decades would not be faster than 30 per cent per decade because it would be difficult for a poor country to support too rapid growth of urban population.

Inter-state differences in proportion of urban population could persist at the two extremes. Moreover, the rates for growth of urban population could be quite high in some States such as Rajasthan, Madhya Pradesh, Haryana and Kerala, which could support much larger urban populations.

Among the 16 States with populations of more than 20 million in 2001, the ranking by urbanization is given in Table 16.3.

Tamil Nadu and Maharashtra are the two most urbanized states with 43.9 per cent and 42.4 per cent of urban populations. Maharashtra with 41 million has the largest size of urban population, which accounts for almost 14 per cent of the urban population of the country. It has also the largest number (4) of million-plus cities. The other three most urbanized States are listed in the table.

Bihar is the least urbanized state with 10.5 per cent of its urban population (Table 16.3). U.P. the most populous state with 166 million population in 2001 also ranks low (20.8 per cent) in urbanization (Table 16.3).

Table 16.3 : Rural Urban Distribution of Population—India and Selected States/Union Territories, 2001

Sl.No.	*States/UTs*	*Total population (million)*	*Urban Population (million)*	*Per cent Urban/ Total*
1.	Tamil Nadu	62.1	27.4	43.9
2.	Maharashtra	96.8	41.0	42.4
3.	Gujarat	50.6	18.8	37.4
4.	Karnataka	52.7	17.9	34.8
5.	Punjab	24.3	8.2	34.0
6.	Haryana	21.0	6.1	29.0
7.	West Bengal	80.2	22.5	28.0
8.	Andhra Pradesh	75.2	20.5	27.0
9.	Kerala	31.8	8.3	26.0
10.	Madhya Pradesh	60.4	16.1	26.6
11.	Jharkhand	26.9	6.0	22.3
12.	Rajasthan	56.5	13.2	23.4
13.	Uttar Pradesh	166.0(?)	34.5	20.8
14.	Orissa	36.7	5.5	15.0
15.	Assam	26.6	3.4	12.7
16.	Bihar	82.9	8.7	10.5

Source : Rural/Urban Distribution of Population—India, States and Union Territories, 2001. Registrar General of India : Press Note, New Delhi, 20th July, 2001.

The percentage of urban population would be even lower in U.P. if the figures for the 25 odd districts of western Uttar Pradesh were excluded. The figure for Haryana, 29.0 per cent, shows the low weight of the satellite cities of Delhi and the towns and cities of western part of the state in a predominantly rural state. The figure for West Bengal, 28.0 per cent, reflects the low weight of the Kolkata Metropolitan District and the Asansol—Durgapur industrial complex in a predominantly rural state.

Other states, which have low level of urban population, are Rajasthan, Madhya Pradesh and Kerala. Orissa and Assam have even lower levels of urbanization.

The total number of metropolitan cities (with population of 1 million and above, has increased from 23 to 35 (over 50 per cent), thus confirming the projections of the Population Advisory Council of the Registrar General. Greater Mumbai, Kolkata and Delhi urban agglomerations have more than 10 million people each. Another 4 cities, capitals respectively of Tamil Nadu (Chennai), Karnataka (Bangalore), Andhra Pradesh (Hyderabad) and Gujarat (Ahmedabad) have populations of more than 4 million. These seven cities can be considered mega cities with the most difficult problems of providing essential services—dependable supplies of electricity and water, adequate arrangements for disposal of solid and liquid waste, efficient management of traffic and control of pollution of water and air—for their populations. The three 10 million cities have additional problems of flooding of their low-lying areas during the monsoon season.

The growth rate of urban population of Delhi urban agglomeration, more than 50 per cent during 1991—2001, experienced during 3 of the previous 5 decades. The population of Mumbai urban agglomeration however, increased by 33 per cent during the decade.

The above figures confirm by and large the statements made in various sections of this chapter. Andhra Pradesh strikes the only discordant note. The relatively low figure of 27.0 per cent of urban population for the state reflects the large weight of largely rural Telengana, which affects the higher level of coastal Andhra Pradesh.

Appendix II

As the Mounds of Mohen-jodaro and other places in North West India—Punjab to Gujarat—show that the settlement is several thousands years old in this region. As might be expected in a semi-desert region, the settlements were along the rivers of Punjab—Ravi, Chenab, Jhelum, Sindh, and Beas.

The purpose of this note is to describe a distinctive type of urban settlement which may be found in other regions of the world, but is not found in India outside north western India.

This note relates to the towns on mounds. Several small towns with populations of up to 10,000 were located on mounds. Among the most famous is Pak Pathan, in south-western Punjab which houses the shrine of one of the most famous Sufi Saint Baba Farid, a prominent holy man who preached in the Punjab in the 14th Century. At the shrine there is a small piece of wood with two tooth marks which were supposed to have been made by the saint. The Punjabi verse accompanying it says, "O Farid, your bread is made of wood and the seasoning on it is your epitaph. Those who indulge in richly buttered bread (pleasures of the flesh) do not go to God but suffer."

After the British conquered Punjab, modern administration, courts, post offices, telegraphs, a railway station, a bank and a shopping centre for British officers and affluent Indians had to be built. These all got ground below the town on the mound as close to the railway station as possible.

As the population grows and the new town expands a typical 2-town pattern comes into being. Examples of such mound-towns are Gujarat, a sizeable district town, Pak pattern mentioned above and several large villages.

The reasons for the location of the towns on the mounds are :

- an assured water supply for the small population,
- defence from invaders.

As the hold of the British grew in the century 1847-1947 the population of civil station grew and the old town was reduced in importance. But the old town remained the symbol of urban settlement. Streets in the town on the mounds were very narrow. But there was relative process of expansion of the new settlements surrounding the mounds.

NOTES

1. In the tables attached to the Human Development Report : Statement on India published by UNDP, New Delhi, the population of India is projected at 1235 million by 2015 and the proportion of urban/total population is given as 36 per cent. UNDP has assumed a growth rate of 1.3 per cent per annum during 2000—2015. This is unrealistic however because the growth rate was 1.9 per cent during 1991—2001 and a more gradual decline to 16 per cent per decade projected in this paper is more realistic. The proportion urban/total population 36 per cent in 2015 corresponds however to the projection of this paper.

REFERENCES

Economic and Political Weekly : EPW Research Foundation: National Accounts Statistics of India 1950-51—1996-97, Mumbai, 1998, p. 84.

Human Development Report 2001: Statement on India, UNDP, New Delhi, 2001.

Swedish International Development Agency (SIDA): *Rajasthan, a Statistical Study*, New Delhi 1997.

Registrar General India:

- Census of India 1991, Provisional Population Totals, Paper I of 1991.
- Census of India 2001, Paper No. I, Provisional Population Totals, New Delhi 2001.
- Rural/Urban Distribution of Population—India, States and Union Territories, 2001, Press Note, New Delhi, 20th July, 2001.

Section IV

Population, Natural Resource Management and Development in India

17

Population, Natural Resources and Economic Development in India (1967) with a Postscript of July 2002*

Introduction

Rapid increase of the world's population is among the most important phenomena of our time. In the underdeveloped countries the "population explosion" is accompanied by an explosion of expectations. Governments and elite groups want and expect to attain a high (Western) level of living—for themselves and for the mass of the people. Because economic development is considered the means to this goal, most underdeveloped countries have initiated economic development programmes. But the relationship between population growth and economic growth is far from clear. Although the demographic sequence accompanying economic development—decline in mortality, acceleration of population growth, decline in fertility—has been described in detail and the socio-economic changes accompanying it adequately documented, there is as yet no accepted theory which relates the two, nor is it possible "to deduce the set or sets of conditions necessary and sufficient to achieve secular fertility declines" (Leibenstein, 1957, p.158).

In the absence of an accepted theory of population growth and economic development, two different, almost conflicting views on the demographic prospects of the underdeveloped countries are sustained.

---

* The contents of this Chapter were presented at an International symposium on the "*Geography of Population Pressure on Physical and Social Resources*", held at Pennsylvania State University in September 1967. The conference papers were published by Oxford University Press, 1970. The author wrote a rejoinder to the paper in 2002 given at the end of the Chapter.

First, there is the view that if contraceptives are developed and made available in these countries, they will be used, with significant effects on birth rates. Indeed, Ohlin goes so far as to regard the development of oral and intra-uterine contraceptives as a major technological breakthrough which has "affected the prospects of fertility control the world over" (Ohlin, 1967, p. 8). But this belief in the "power" of new contraceptives is contested by others who place greater emphasize on the importance of social and economic changes as prerequisites for decline in fertility. According to this view, "the possession of advanced contraceptive technology is an incidental matter, while the truly crucial question is whether the potential users of contraceptives genuinely wish to achieve the small family pattern" (Zelinsky, 1966, p. 13).

It is not impossible that both points of view are vindicated in different underdeveloped countries. The fertility-decline experience of countries such as India and China, with large populations but limited natural resources, could be significantly different from the experience of, for example, most countries of Africa and Latin America in which the relationship between population and natural resources is more favourable. But natural resource is an area in which relationships are even less clearly understood, and there is the additional lack of satisfactory definition or measures of the relationship between population and natural resources. Measures such as density of population, man-land ratio, and cropland per capita, once used extensively are now considered inadequate or defective. The search for more adequate measures is under way (Ackerman, 1959, pp.127-152).

In terms of natural resources, the view is widely held among geographers that economic development of countries such as India and China will be more difficult than in countries where the relationship between population and natural resources is more favourable. Ackerman has divided the "technology-deficient" countries into the China-type (high population-resource ratio) and the Brazil-type (low population-resource ratio), and has listed for the former "continued consciousness of impending crisis and increasing pressure for attachment to foreign resources" as characteristics of the development process (*ibid*, p.149). Ginsburg expresses a similar view when discussing the development prospects of China and India :

"Their greatest similarity, however, lies in the inflexibility imposed upon their development planning and policies by the necessity for increased agricultural production, not as means for capital accumulation, but simply to prevent starvation, maintain a healthier labour force and discourage rural and therefore national unrest. Both illustrate the degree to which high man-land ratios act as deterrents to accelerated economic development" (Ginsburg, 1965, p. 420). This view reflects the thinking of the classical economists who regarded scarcity of fertile land as the major limitation to economic development—Ricardo's law of diminishing returns in agriculture, for example. But concern with inadequacy of natural resources as the limiting factor in economic development has progressively diminished as development of new lands and rapid technological advance have made available increasing quantities of food and natural-resources-based materials or their synthetic substitutes. Moreover, economic development has taken place in countries with abundant as well as limited natural resources—Ackerman's U.S. and European types (Ackerman, 1959, p. 149). However, two roles of natural resources in economic development have been important in the past and remain so today. First, abundant natural resources attract capital investment. Most of the foreign investments of the European countries in the 19th century were either in resource development enterprises such as mines and plantations, or in railways which made resource development possible. Until recently, most of the U.S. investment in underdeveloped countries was of this type: in 1948, fifty-nine per cent was in extractive industries and sixteen per cent in public utilities (Nurkse, 1953, p. 84). Second, the presence of natural resources, which can be exploited without major changes in existing technology and socio-economic structures, facilitates economic development through local means, especially in the early stages when capital, organization, and technology are scarce and society is not oriented towards change. Recent Indian experience with agricultural development, reviewed in this Chapter, shows that increase in agricultural output was quite rapid during the 1950s, when large areas could be reclaimed for cultivation by the farmers, but has been slow in the 1960s. Such areas are no longer available and increase in agricultural output is dependent on improvements in agricultural techniques.

Economic development is a multi-faceted, complex process. Many of the factors contributing to it and the relationships connected with it are inadequately understood. Some of them, such as the relationship between population and natural resources, have begun to be explored only in recent years. This study of population growth and economic development may be regarded as a case description of development under a particular relationship between population and natural resources. Comparative studies of other regions will contribute to a better understanding of the role of this factor in economic development[1].

The Economic Setting of Population Growth

The population of India is currently increasing at an annual rate of 2.5 per cent. As a result of the eradication of malaria and improvement in medical and public health services (Census of India, 1961, pp. x-xi), the rate of growth has accelerated significantly in recent years—averaging about 2 per cent in the 1950s compared with 1.0 to 1.25 per cent in the previous three decades. The current rate of increase is not high in comparison with other underdeveloped countries, but the economic setting in which it is taking place has created serious problems, principally of raising output of food. This problem, dramatized by widespread scarcity of food and local famine during the recent drought years, 1965-67, has forced Indian planners to give the highest priority to increasing agricultural output and especially food. It has also furthered the gradual recognition of rapid population growth as a handicap to adequate economic growth. The family planning programme, which has existed since the 1950s, has since 1965-66 been expanded into a nation-wide effort whose objective is "reducing the birth rate from 40 per cent at present to 25 per cent as expeditiously as possible" (Planning Commission, 1966, p. 346).

The economic setting of population growth in India may be outlined as follows :

(i) A very low level of per capita income—$ 69 per year in 1965, compared with an average of $100 for East and South East Asia excluding Japan, which itself was lowest among the major regions of the world (United Nations, 1967, p. 727);

(ii) Extremely low levels of food consumption, resulting in widespread malnutrition and under-nutrition. Seventy-five per cent of the calories in the Indian diet are provided by cereals; consumption of foods supplying protein, fats, and minerals is very low. Average calorie intake—1970 per capita in 1961—is below the minimum requirement of 2100 calories for a tropical country, with the result that large sections of the population are chronically undernourished. The incidence of "hunger" (calorie intake below the minimum requirement) was estimated at 33 per cent for the rural population in 1961 (Madalgi, 1968, p. 65);

(iii) Very small agricultural holdings, presence of a large number of landless or near-landless cultivators, and large-scale underemployment among a predominantly agricultural and rural population.

To understand this situation fully, it is necessary to review demographic and economic trends in the half-century which preceded the beginning of planning.

The Historical Setting

Population Growth without Significant Economic Development

The population of India increased by more than 50 per cent between 1901 and 1951 (Table 17.1), most of it occurring between 1921 and 1951. Increase from 1901 to 1921 was curtailed by high mortality from malaria and other tropical diseases, as well as by frequent famines and epidemics. The last two years of the 19th century witnessed one of the severest famines in India's history; loss of life was estimated at about 3 million (Census of India, 1955, p. 275). During the first decade of the 20th century, there were a number of epidemics of bubonic plague and in 1918-19 the influenza epidemic took the lives of an estimated 12-13 million, affecting a net decline in population during the decade 1911-1921. After 1921, however, famines and epidemics were held in check, and a period of uninterrupted population growth began. Even the Bengal famine of 1942-43 with an estimated mortality of about 1.5 million (*ibid,* p. 292), and the loss of life during disturbances following the Partition of British India into India and Pakistan only marginally affected population growth from 1941-1951. The Census Commissioner of 1951 called 1921 the year of "the great divide" in India's recent demographic history, separating a period of uninterrupted growth from an earlier period of uneven and in the aggregate slow growth (Census of India ,1953, p. xiii).

Table 17.1 : Population of India, 1901-1961 (Present boundaries)

Year	*Population (000's)*	*Decennial variation in per cent*
1901	236,281	
1911	252,122	+5.73
1921	251,352	-0.31
1931	279,015	+11.01
1941	318,701	+14.22
1951	361,130	+13.31
1961	439,235	+21.50

Source: Census of India 1961, Paper No. 1 of 1962, Final Population Totals, Delhi, 1962, p. x.

But population growth occurred throughout the entire period 1901-1961 under conditions best described as "overall economic stagnation."

Perhaps the most telling evidence of this is the absence of significant change in the occupational structure. The proportion of male workers in agriculture and other primary activities fluctuated between 70 and 75 per cent and the proportion in manufacturing (both household and factory) remained at 10-12 per cent[2] (Table 17.2). Indeed, between 1901 and 1931 changes were regressive : the proportion of male workers increased in agriculture and declined in manufacturing. Although there was considerable growth of modern industry as indicated by a five-fold increase in output between 1900-01 and 1944-45 (Siva Subramonian, 1965, p. 347), the employment provided by factories was small, less than 3 million in 1951 when the total labour force was more than 142 million. Moreover, since the factories were concentrated in a few areas, notably Calcutta and Bombay, the modernizing and growth-inducing effects of industrial development were limited. On the other hand, the principal effect of contact with modern factory industry (first foreign, but later also Indian) on the village economy was a decline in local crafts. The decline, which had begun in the nineteenth century, continued throughout this period, forcing large numbers of village artisans out of their traditional occupation and into agriculture (Gadgil, 1942).

Urbanization was negligible until the 1930s. The proportion of urban population to total population remained between 10 and 12 per cent between 1901 and 1931 (Table 17.2), began to gather momentum in the 1930s, increased during the 1940s from 13.9 per cent to 17.3 per cent partly as a result of the exceptional conditions of war and Partition, and then slowed down in the 1950s. The slower growth of urbanization is linked with the inability of the Indian economy to expand employment opportunities and housing rapidly enough to sustain the process of rapid urban growth. The point that Indian urbanization has not entirely been the result of economic growth, but has represented, at least in part, a transfer of population pressure from rural to urban areas has been developed by the debate between the proponents of the "pull" and "push" explanations of Indian urbanization.

Historical comparisons of national income for developing countries are subject to serious limitations because of deficiencies of data. The principal difficulty in comparisons for the late British period of India's history was the existence of a large number of Princely States, most of whom had very inadequate and poor statistics. One of the more careful estimates, however, reports per capita income in Undivided India in the early 1940s as only 18 per cent higher than at the turn of the century, the average annual income figures being Rs. 42.2 for 1900-01—1904-05; and Rs. 49.6 for 1940-41—1944-45 (Sukhatme, 1965, p. 340). In spite of considerable growth of manufacturing and some urbanization, the growth

Table 17.2 : Trends in occupational distribution of male workers and growth of urban population, 1901-1961

(Per cent of male workers)

Year	*Agriculture*	*Primary sector*	*Manufacturing (household and factory)*	*Secondary sector*	*Tertiary sector*	*% of urban population*
1	*2*	*3*	*4*	*5*	*6*	*7*
1901	65.61	70.37	11.37	12.31	17.32	10.91
1911	68.50	73.66	9.62	10.97	15.37	10.57
1921	69.87	74.54	9.33	10.51	14.95	11.38
1931	68.73	74.08	8.99	10.43	15.49	12.13
1951	66.85	69.08	9.84	11.59	19.33	17.34
1961	64.88	67.98	11.27	12.68	19.44	18.00

Note : Primary sector includes agriculture, livestock husbandry, forestry, fishing, and mining and quarrying (Industrial Categories I, II and III of 1961 Census).

- Secondary sector includes manufacturing (household and factory) and construction (Industrial Categories IV, V and VI of 1961 Census).
- Tertiary sector includes trade and commerce, transport, storage and communication and all other services (industrial categories VII, VIII, and IX of 1961 Census).

Source: Census of India, 1961, Paper No. 1 of 1962, Final Population Totals, Delhi, 1962. p. xxvi.

rate for the period works out to less than 0.5 per cent per year, a direct result of stagnation in agriculture. This fact emerges from a number of studies of population growth and trends in agricultural output (Table 17.3). Table 17.3, based on the study of Mukherjee and Sivasubramonian, shows that during 45 years, crop output increased by only 12.6 per cent, while population increased by 37.9 per cent; output per capita declined by almost 18 per cent for all crops and as much as 26.5 per cent for food crops. In fact, the entire increase in crop output was due to increase in output of non-foodgrain crops. It should be noticed that increase in crop output was less than increase in cropped area, indicating a net decline in average crop yields.

Essentially similar results emerge from Blyn's study, which covers the period 1891-92 to 1946-47. Although Blyn confines his study to the British provinces and does not include the Princely States (Table 17.4), both studies include West Punjab and Sind, now in Pakistan, where rapid increase in agricultural output followed construction of irrigation canals.

Table 17.3 : Growth of Population and Crop Output in Undivided India, 1900-01 to 1944-45

Average of quinquennium	*Population index*	*Index of area cultivated*	*Index of average annual output*			*Index of crop output adjusted for population*		
			*Food**	*Non-food***	*All crops*	*Food**	*Non-food***	*All crops*
1	2	3	4	5	6	7	8	9
1900-01—1904-05	100.0		100.0	100.0	100.0	100.0	100.0	100.0
1905-06—1909-10	103.1	105.8	97.5	106.8	99.6	94.6	103.6	96.6
1910-11—1914-15	105.1	109.8	105.6	121.7	109.1	100.5	155.8	103.8
1915-16—1919-20	105.6	108.8	107.2	102.8	110.5	101.5	97.3	104.6
1920-21—1924-25	108.0	108.9	101.8	124.7	106.8	94.3	45.5	98.9
1925-26—1929-30	113.6	111.8	97.3	138.7	106.3	85.7	122.1	93.6
1930-31—1934-35	120.5	114.8	100.3	137.9	108.5	85.2	114.4	90.0
1935-36—1939-40	129.2	115.3	97.9	159.1	111.1	75.8	123.1	86.0
1940-41—1944-45	137.9	118.4	100.9	155.3	112.6	73.5	113.2	82.1

* Food item includes rice, wheat, jowar, bajra, maize, barley and gram.

** Non-food includes sugarcane, sesame, rape and mustard, linseed, cotton, jute, tea, coffee and tobacco.

Source: Mukherjee, P.K. and Sivasubramonian, S: Agricultural Output and National Income in India : in Bhattacharjee, J. P. (ed.). *Studies in Indian Agricultural Economics.* Indian Society of Agricultural Economics, Bombay 1958, p. 24.

Table 17.4 : Changes in Population and Agricultural Production in British Provinces of India in 1891-92—1946-47

(Annual average in per cent)

Population	*0.67*
Cropped area	0.40
Output: all crops	0.37
Food grains	0.11
Non-food grains	1.31

Source: G. Blyn, *Agricultural Trends in India*, 1891-1947, Philadelphia, 1966, Chapter 5.

As a result, figures for the areas which now form part of the Indian Union would be less favourable. For the 1951 Census an estimate of trends in population, cropped area, and irrigated area for the period 1891-1951 was made for 61 districts in the North, West and South, representing about 1/3rd of India's total population in 1951, and a similar proportion of the cropped area. Districts whose boundaries had not changed during the period and whose agricultural statistics were good were selected for this analysis. The results, summarized in Table 17.5, indicate that gross cropped area per capita declined by 21.5 per cent between 1891 and 1951, while gross irrigated area per capita declined by 12.5 per cent. These declines were not compensated by increased crop yields. On the contrary, data on yields of rice, wheat, and other crops for the period 1910-11 to 1945-46 show a decline in most cases. The one outstanding exception is rice in Madras, whose yield showed an increase of 15 per cent during the period (Census of India, 1955, pp. 61-71).

Table 17.5 : Trend of Cultivation and Irrigation 1891-1951

	1891	*1921*	*1951*
Gross area sown* (in million hectares)	40.4	41.9	45.2
Net area sown** (in million hectares)	36.4	37.5	40.1
Irrigated area (in million hectares)	5.2	6.2	6.8
Gross area sown per capita (in per cent)	121	124	95
Net area sown per capita* (in per cent)	109	111	84
Irrigated area per capita (in per cent)	16	18	14

* Gross area sown includes net area sown and those cropped areas which are sown more than once.

** Net area sown is the physical area under crop.

Source: Census of India, 1951, Vol. 1, Part I B. Appendices to the Census Report 1951, Delhi, 1955, pp. 48-49.

Decline in Food Consumption

The most disturbing result of the failure of agricultural and foodgrain output to keep pace with growth of population was the decline in per capita consumption of food. Although India became for the first time a net importer of foodgrains in the 1920s (mainly rice from Burma), and progressively increased these imports (Table 17.6), per capita consumption of foodgrains declined by 20 per cent from 1900-01 to 1944-45. This percentage does not even include the exceptionally low figure during Second World War, resulting from the interruption of rice imports after the Japanese occupation of Burma in 1942. The interruption was followed by famine in Bengal in 1943 and scarcity of foodgrains over large parts of South India in 1945 and 1946. Since foodgrains provide most of the calories in the Indian diet, fall in per capita consumption meant chronic under-nutrition for large sections of the population.

Table 17.6 : Production, Net Imports (or Exports) and Consumption of Foodgrains in Undivided India : 1900-01 to 1944-45

Quinquennium	*Population (million)*	*Foodgrains*				
		Production (million tonnes)		*Net imports (+) or net exports (-) (million tonnes)*	*Net availability for consumption (million tonnes)*	*Consumption per capita per day in gramms*
		Gross	*Net*			
1	2	3	4	5	6	7
1900-01—1904-05	288.8	63.6	55.6	-1.1	54.6	536
1905-06—1909-10	300.4	62.0	54.2	-0.6	53.6	505
1910-11—1914-15	313.8	70.8	61.9	-2.0	60.0	541
1915-16—1919-20	315.0	70.3	61.5	-0.4	61.9	558
1920-21—1924-25	312.0	66.1	58.4	+0.8	59.2	539
1925-26—1929-30	328.4	63.3	55.6	+0.8	56.4	485
1930-31—1934-35	348.0	66.5	57.7	+1.2	58.9	497
1935-36—1939-40	373.2	63.4	55.3	+1.4	56.6	431
1940-41—1944-45	397.2	65.8	57.6	+0.5	58.2	417

Source : Bhattacharjee, J.P. and Roy, S.M.: Trend of Consumption of Food and Foodgrains in India in Bhattacharjee, J.P. (Ed.) *Studies in Indian Agricultural Economics*, Bombay, 1958, p. 202.

Small Agricultural Holdings and Widespread Underemployment

The great majority of the agricultural population subsisted by cultivation of very small holdings, but there were also large numbers of landless or near-landless agricultural labourers.

About 4/5th of all agricultural holdings were below 4 hectares (Planning Commission, 1959, p. 3). "Agricultural labour" families defined as "ones in which either the head of the family or 50 per cent or more of the earners reported agricultural labour as their main occupation" accounted for 30 per cent of all rural families (*Ibid*, Table 17.7). Half of these families cultivated small bits of land in addition to labouring for wages, but the remainder were completely landless. The existence of such large numbers of landless or near-landless agriculturalists is an indication of the extent of land hunger in India. The working members of the "agricultural labour" families averaged employment about seven months in the year. For women, the period of employment averaged only 134 days in a year. There was also widespread underemployment among the small cultivators. Datar, using the data of the Agricultural Labour Enquiry conducted by the Government of India, and sample surveys of unemployment conducted in a number of states, estimated in 1956 that 31.1 million agricultural workers were unemployed for more than half the year (*Ibid*, Table 17.8). This number represented 28.5 per cent of the total agricultural labour force, which was estimated at 109 million at that time (Datar, 1955, pp. 195 and 288). A number of attempts have been made to estimate the size of the surplus agricultural labour population. One, based on continuation of cultivation with human and bullock labour and the family farm enterprise, put the surplus in the 1950s at 20 million (Lewis, 1954, p. 116).

Table 17.7 : Categories of Agricultural Labour Families.

Census zone	*% Agricultural labour families to total rural families*	*% to total agricultural labour families*		*% to total agricultural labour families*	
		With land	*Without land*	*Casual*	*Attached*
North India	14.3	40.6	59.4	78.3	21.7
East India	32.7	58.0	42.0	76.1	23.9
South India	50.1	54.4	45.6	95.0	5.0
West India	20.4	43.2	56.8	90.2	9.8
Central	36.7	39.9	60.1	81.6	18.4
North-West	9.8	28.5	71.5	69.0	31.0
India	30.4	50.0	50.0	84.6	15.4

Source : Ministry of Labour, Government of India : Report on Intensive Survey of Agricultural Labour : All India, Vol. 1. Delhi, 1954.

Table 17.8 : Unemployment in India

Rural agricultural	30.3 million persons for 7 months
Rural non-agricultural	4.8 million persons for 6 months
Urban agricultural	0.8 million persons for 7 months
Urban non-agricultural	2.1 million persons for 6 months

Source: B.N. Datar, The Second Five-Year Plan—Employment Approach, in : Papers Relating to the Formulation of the Second Five-Year Plan, Planning Commission, New Delhi, 1955, p. 208.

Paucity of Other Natural Resources

India's other natural resources do not materially alter this picture of high pressure of population upon the agricultural resource. The mineral and energy resources, while they do provide a basis for an industrial structure of adequate size and diversity, do not include any large export-revenue earning item, such as petroleum in the Middle East, which could help finance economic development. On the contrary, there are major deficiencies in fuels and minerals, the effect of which has been felt increasingly in recent years as demands have gone up with expansion of industry. It will be felt even more in the future. Imports of minerals and fuels which accounted for 21.8 per cent of the total value of imports in 1960-61 are expected to increase to 34.2 per cent by 1975-76. In contrast, exports of minerals and fuels represented only 6 per cent of the total value of exports in 1960-61 (Table 17.9).

Table 17.9 : Contribution of Agricultural and Mineral Products to Imports and Exports in 1960-61, and Projections for 1970-71 and 1975-76, in India

	1960-61		*1970-71*		*1975-76*	
	Value Million Rupees*	*%*	*Value* Million Rupees*	*%*	*Value* Million Rupees*	*%*
A. Imports						
Agricultural products (Cereals, fibres and vegetable oils)	3,368**	29.9	1,840	13.5	2,000	12.4
Mineral products (Metal, Petroleum products, sulphur, and rock phosphate)	2,332**	21.8	4,140	30.5	5,500	34.2
Total	11,216**	100.0	13,600	100.0	16,100	100.0
B. Exports						
Agricultural and animal-based products	5,092	75.8	7,224	59.0	8,503	52.4
Minerals (including coal)	401	6.0	1,713	14.0	2,300	14.2
Total	6,719	100.0	12,251	100.0	16,243	100.0

*$1= Rupees 7.5

**1961-62

Source : Planning Commission : Notes on Perspective of Development India 1960-61 to 1975-76, New Delhi, April 1964, pp. 164-173.

The principal assets of India's mineral and energy resources are large reserves of high grade iron ore, fairly large reserves of medium-to-poor grade coal, a substantial hydro-power potential (estimated at about 41 million kW.), and sizeable deposits of manganese, mica, bauxite, and thorium-bearing sands (Nath, 1970). A liability are the lack of non-ferrous metals—copper, lead, zinc, and tin; raw materials of the chemical industry such as sulphur and rock phosphate, and most important, petroleum. The petroleum position has improved somewhat with the discovery of oil in Gujarat and may well be transformed if there are large oil finds in the off-shore area of the Gulf of Cambay where preliminary explorations have been promising. But excluding this area, the proved reserves have been estimated at only about 100 m.t. Although consumption of petroleum is still small—about 8 m.t. in 1960-61—it is increasing rapidly and is expected to range between 45 and 65 m.t. annually by 1980-81 (Govt. of India, 1965, p. 116). India also has large reserves of nuclear fuels, especially thorium-bearing sands, and development of processes for generation of power from them at economic cost could provide almost unlimited amounts of energy. But until then, energy supplies will remain limited and expensive.

Inadequate Social Resources

Underdeveloped countries have very limited supplies of the social resources needed for development—capital, technology and organization—and India in 1951 was no exception. Very low per capita income meant low savings, estimated at about 5 per cent of the national income in 1950-51 (Planning Commission, 1956, p. 8), and very limited supplies of capital. In technological skills and organization, India was undoubtedly more fortunate then most underdeveloped countries. There were large numbers of educated, trained and experienced people, especially in the cities. The administrative and technical services, which had a fair level of efficiency, had been manned predominantly by Indians for a long time. Business and industry were managed by Indian entrepreneurs, and the skilled workers were all Indians. India also had well-organized political parties headed by leaders of outstanding ability, political acumen, and stature. Large numbers of Indian civil servants, technicians, skilled workers, and traders left the country to work in neighbouring countries of Asia and Africa. This, and the prevalence of unemployment among the educated, seemed to indicate that the number of educated and skilled persons was in excess of the requirements of the country. But this supply of education, skill, and entrepreneurial ability, concentrated in the cities, must be viewed alongside the illiterate and apathetic mass of the Indian population if a proper measure of India's social resource endowment is to be obtained. The percentage of literate persons, even with the very liberal definition of literacy adopted in the Indian Censuses, was only 16.6 per cent in 1951. In rural India the knowledge and experience of most people were limited to their village and small local area, and they had little awareness of or interest in the outside world. Modern technical skills were virtually non-existent; except for a flour or rice mill in larger villages, or an occasional pump for irrigation there was little use of power driven machines. Finally, except for small groups, such as the Marwari and Gujarati traders and Punjabi Sikhs, the rural population did not show the dynamism needed to escape the local environment. Migration was small in volume. The 1951 Census showed only 3.1 per cent of the population living outside its State of birth and most of the migrants, whether they went to other parts of India such as the tea plantations of Assam and the coalfields of Bihar or to foreign countries, were content to remain unskilled labourers. The dynamism of the rural population of the Punjab described by several researchers, however, was rare.

Many explanations have been given for both the lack of dynamism and the prevalence of an attitude of stoic (or apathetic) acceptance of fate. The value system of the Hindu religion is one explanation; the effects of the monsoon, another. Malenbaum attributes them to the rigid social system of the Indian village (Malenbaum, 1962, pp. 133-143).

A discussion of the influence of such social factors on economic development would take us far beyond the scope of this paper, but it is pertinent to add that static resource-use techniques and low levels of consumption (including food) persisting over long periods, with little visible prospect of improvement, contribute to the formation and strengthening of such attitudes. This is suggested by the dynamic attitudes and behavioural patterns which emerge in villages, in various parts of India, where efficient resource use results in economic development. For example, the development of remunerative, progressive agriculture in the canal colonies of the West Punjab produced in the 1920s a new, dynamic group of peasants (Darling, 1947). More recently, Scarlett Epstein has described a similar phenomenon in the Mysore villages (Epstein, 1962).

If we are to understand fully the magnitude of India's task of economic development, we must add to this list of natural and social resource limitations, her decision to use democratic methods. The choice was made consciously and deliberately, and over the years the Government of India has consistently enlarged the area of democratic action in development. In agricultural and rural development, this is best seen in the rapid expansion of cooperatives and the constitution of representative institutions for management of development programmes. But development through democratic methods is harder and slower, especially in its early stages, than development through authoritarian methods. Modernization of agriculture, for instance, will have to be achieved in India by voluntary decisions of some sixty million heads of agricultural families. Most of them are illiterate and tradition-bound and too poor to take risks. These "decision-makers" require dynamic leadership and intensive education by trained personnel. But both trained personnel and dynamic leaders are desperately short in India. The pace of development could be accelerated if decision-making was concentrated in the hands of trained workers or executives of development institutions. Similarly, the utilization of surplus labour for the creation of physical capital (irrigation works, roads, schools, etc.) advocated by some economists (Lewis, 1954) as a method of accelerating development requires organizational resources of larger magnitude and perhaps also of higher quality, when the workers have to be organized on a voluntary rather then compulsory basis. China has adopted such programmes on a large scale; but in India their use has been very limited. A rural manpower programme aimed at utilizing surplus rural labour for construction of development works was started only in the Third Five-Year Plan; earlier, the only opportunities for labour were through voluntary contributions. But the programme was small—the target was to provide by the end of the Plan employment for 100 days to each of 2.5 million persons. This number, it will be recalled is only seven per cent of Datar's estimate made 10 years earlier, of the total number of underemployed persons in rural areas. Furthermore, achievement has been only 16 per cent of the meagre target (Planning Commission, 1966, p. 111).

Experience with Planning

The First Five-Year Plan was drawn up under conditions of acute stress—food shortage, disruption of the economy, and the influx of about seven million displaced persons following the Partition. Primary emphasis was given to increasing agricultural output and to rehabilitation of displaced persons of the economies of Punjab and West Bengal, which had been affected most by the Partition, and of sectors, such as railways, in which equipment had been depleted as a result of over-use during Second World War. But the planners also recognized the prime need for removing the causes of long-term stagnation in the economy and initiating a "process of development" (Planning Commission, 1951, p. 14; and Planning Commission, 1956, p. 1).

The Plan set forth a model of long-term development, which provided for a doubling of total national income in 21 years (by 1971-72) and per capita income in 27 years (by 1977-78). The rate of population increase assumed in the model was the 1941-51 rate of 1.25 per cent per year. The model was subsequently revised in later Plans, in the light of emerging demographic and economic trends. The Second Plan, keeping in view the favourable performance of the economy under the First Plan, brought forward the target dates of doubling national and per capita income to 1967-68 and 1973-74 respectively (Planning Commission, 1956, p. 11). It revised the rate of population growth slightly, to 13.3 per cent per decade in 1961-1970 and 14.0 per cent per decade in 1971-1980. But during the 1950s this rate was in fact much higher than predicted—2 per cent per year, instead of 1.25 per cent—and it became clear that the earlier models of economic development would have to be revised. The Third Five-Year Plan put forward a new model of growth for the period 1960-61 to 1975-76, in which the rate of growth of national income was raised to about 6 per cent, so that after providing for the more rapid population increase, per capita income could still increase by about 4 per cent per year (Planning Commission, 1961, p. 27).

The period of the three Plans witnessed the beginnings of economic growth. National income increased by more than 60 per cent and per capita income rose by nearly 20 per cent (Planning Commission, 1966, pp. 419-20). In agriculture, long-term stagnation was broken and output began to increase steadily: agricultural output was 58 per cent higher in 1964-65 than at the beginning of the First Five-Year Plan (*ibid*). Industrial output increased nearly 2½ times. There was also considerable expansion of social services, the best indication of which was the near trebling of enrollment in primary schools (*ibid*, p. 422). By the end of the Third Plan, nearly 80 per cent of the boys and girls in the age group of 6-11 years were in schools (*ibid,* p. 313).

Within the 15-year period, however, growth was more rapid in the first ten years than in the last five; in the latter, growth of national income was barely adequate to keep pace with growth of population :

Growth (per cent per year)	*1950-60*	*1960-65*
National income	3.6	2.6
Population	2.0	2.4
Per capita income	1.6	0.2

The slower growth rate of the 1960s was due mainly to the slowing down of growth in agriculture. The average rate of increase of agricultural output during the period 1949-50 to 1964-65 was 3.2 per cent per year (Table 17.10); but the rate for the period 1960-61 to 1964-65 was only 1.06 per cent per year, as compared with 3.94 per cent in the earlier 12-year period. Moreover, examination of annual index numbers of agricultural output shows that during the three years 1961-62 to 1963-64 output fluctuated around the level of 1960-61 (Table 17.11). It rose by 11 per cent in 1964-65, but the high output of that year was followed by an exceptionally low one, owing to widespread drought in 1965-66 and again in 1966-67. The year, 1967-68, is reported to have been a good one, and according to preliminary indications, output will exceed the previous high level of 1964-65 by about 5 per cent. But it is clear that the steady growth of agricultural production begun in the 1950s has not been maintained during the 1960s.

Table 17.10 : India-Growth Rates in Agriculture 1949-50 to 1964-65 (Compound Growth Rates in %)

	Agricultural production	*Area under crops*	*Agricultural productivity*
1949-1950 – 1964-65			
(i) Foodgrains	2.98	1.34	1.61
(ii) Non-foodgrains	3.61	2.52	1.06
(iii) All crops	3.19	1.55	1.60
1949-50—1958-59 All crops*	3.8	2.3	1.32
1955-56—1964-65 All crops*	3.9	1.1	1.9

* Growth rates calculated from annual index numbers given in Appendices 1.1 to 1.3 of above.

Source: Economic and Statistical Advisor, Ministry of Food and Agriculture, Government of India, Growth Rates in Agriculture, New Delhi, March 1966, p. 21.

Output of foodgrains increased less rapidly than total agricultural output—the average rate of increase during the period 1949-50 to 1964-65 being 2.98 per cent per year (Table 17.10). But like total agricultural output, output of foodgrains was also stagnant between 1960-61 and 1963-64 and has been characterized since then by marked fluctuations. The rate of increase of foodgrain output in the 1950s, though higher than the rate of increase of population, was not high enough to terminate imports, which continued at 2-4 m.t. per year (Table 17.11). One reason for this was the rise in per capita consumption with increase in income : per capita availability of foodstuffs is estimated to have increased from 1759 calories per day in 1950-51 to 2145 calories in 1964-65, (Planning Commission, 1966, p. 9). The income elasticity of demand for foodgrains is high in India; it is estimated at 0.81 for the rural population and 0.64 for the urban population (Planning Commission, 1964, Appendix C, p. 14). But as domestic output began to stagnate, imports increased rapidly to 10 m.t. in 1966 and decreased only slightly to 9 m.t. in 1967. Large imports of foodgrains were necessary in 1966 and 1967 to avert famine; but they were made without drastic reduction in other imports only because a large proportion was obtained under P.L. 480 assistance from U.S.A. The value of imports of "cereals and cereal preparations" represented nearly 40 per cent of the total export earnings of India during 1965-66 and 52.2 per cent during 1966-67. But 77.5 per cent of the imports during 1965-66 and 55.0 per cent of those in 1966-67 were obtained under P.L. 480 assistance (Government of India, Ministry of Finance, p.24). In the absence of such assistance, an additional 30 per cent of the export earnings in each year would have had to be spent on imports of foodgrains.[3] Moreover, continuation of rapid population increase and slow growth of foodgrain output for any length of time will push import requirements to impossibly high levels. The Panel on World Food Supply of the Science Advisory Committee of the U.S. President has calculated import requirements of foodgrains given in Table 17.12; the calculation is based on the assumption that the population growth rate increases progressively from 2.42 per cent per year during 1960-64 to 2.80 per cent per year in the late 1970s and early 1980s, while foodgrain output increases at "no more than its 14-year (1950-64) trend line rate of 2.36 per cent per year" (Holst, 1967, p. 687)[4]. The cost of the imports projected for 1971 is 65.5 per cent of the total export earnings for that year, as projected by the Planning Commission; the figure for 1976 is 77.5 per cent.

Even apart from the need to avoid an impossible international trade situation, rapid increase in agricultural output is essential for maintaining a satisfactory rate of economic growth. The close connection between agricultural growth and overall economic growth is indicated by the foregoing review of economic trends.

Table 17.11 : Agricultural Production, Foodgrain Production and Foodgrain Imports

A. Production				*B. Imports (on Government of India's account)*		
Year	*Index of agricultural production (1949-50 = 100)*	*Index of foodgrain production (1949-50 = 100)*	*Quantity of foodgrain production (million t.)*	*Year*	*Quantity (million t.)*	*Value (million rupees)***
				Average of quinquennium		
				1951-55	*2.46*	*1,166.9*
				1956-60	*3.46*	*1,347.0*
				Annual		
1960-61	142	137	82.02	1961	3.50	1,295.6
1961-62	145	140	82.71	1962	3.64	1,410.9
1962-63	140	134	78.45	1963	4.56	1,830.6
1963-64	143	137	80.24	1964	6.27	2,662.5
1964-65	159	150	88.95	1965	7.46	2,903.2
1965-66	133*	121*	72.29*	1966	10*	n.a.
1966-67	132*	125*	n.a.	1967	9*	n.a.

* Provisional.

** $1 = Rupees. 7.5

Source : Up to 1965: Economic and Statistical Advisor, Government of India, Ministry of Food and Agriculture, New Delhi, 1966.

1966 & 1967 : Government of India, Ministry of Finance, Economic Survey 1967-68, New Delhi, 1968.

Table 17.12 : Projections of Foodgrain Requirements and Value of Exports.

Year	*Import requirement of food grains*			
	Quantity (million t.)	*Value (billion U.S.$)*	*Value of total exports (billion U.S.$)*	*Proportion of value of foodgrain imports to value of exports (col. 3/col. 4) in %*
1	*2*	*3*	*4*	*5*
1965-66 (Actual)	7.46	0.62	1.69	36.41
1971	15.3	1.07	1.63	65.50
1976	24.0	1.68	2.17	77.50
1981	32.5	2.28	n.a.	—
1986	42.8	3.00	n.a.	—

Source : 1965-66: Government of India, Ministry of Finance, 1968.

1971-86 :

Cols. 2 and 3 : Holst W., Evaluation of Population and Food Production Problems of India, in : The World Food Problems, Report of the Panel on World Food Supply of the President's Science Advisory Committee, The White House, 1967, p. 687.

1971-76 :

Col. 4 Planning Commission, Notes on Perspective of Development of India: 1960-61—1975-76, New Delhi, April 1964, p. 167.

The importance of increasing agricultural output has been recognized in India's Plans. In the First Five-Year Plan, it was given top priority and as much as 36.94 per cent of the total development expenditure was on agricultural development and irrigation programmes (Saran and Chawla, 1967, p. 480). But the proportion fell to 22.26 per cent during the Second Plan and 21.84 per cent during the Third Plan (*ibid*). In both the Second and Third Plans, large investments were made in industry; less emphasis on agriculture and irrigation was due also to steady growth of agricultural output in the 1950s and the relatively comfortable food supplies. But stagnation of agricultural output during 1960-64 and the sharp fall during 1965-67 have again focused attention on agriculture. The draft outline of the Fourth Plan, issued in 1966, reiterated the need for giving the highest priority to increased agricultural output (Planning Commission 1966, p. 30); and the Government of India adopted in the same year a "New Agricultural Strategy" for increasing output of foodgrains. The strategy is a significant departure from earlier official programmes and relies heavily on high yield, hybrid and dwarf seed varieties, chemical fertilizers, and pesticides—and provides for concentration of resources in areas with assured and adequate irrigation facilities, where such concentration will produce the maximum results. By 1970-71, 25.30 million hectares of cropland will be brought under intensive cultivation of foodgrains; they are expected to produce 63.35 m.t. of foodgrains, out of the total projected output of 120 m.t. (Sivaraman, 1967, p. 440).

Strategies of Agricultural Development

The "New Agricultural Strategy" is based on recognition, on the one hand, of certain natural-resource-based limitations on increasing agricultural output and, on the other hand, of the possibilities opened up by agricultural research. These limitations and possibilities are discussed below at some length because they point to the directions which development of agriculture in India must take in the future. The discussion is based on a comparative analysis of three programmes : the New Agricultural Strategy, the Perspective Plan for "Development of Agriculture 1960-61 to 1975-76" drawn up by the Planning Commission in 1964 (Planning Commission, 1964), and the USPSAC Panel programme (Holst, 1967). The Planning Commission's plan represents official thinking on increasing agricultural output before adoption of the "New Agricultural Strategy"; the programme of the Panel appears to have had a considerable influence on the Strategy. The projections of the three programmes are given in Tables 17.14, 17.15, and 17.16.

Expansion of Cropped Area vs. Increase in Productivity

Over the period 1949-50 to 1964-65, the rates of increase of cropped area and productivity of croplands were almost equal (Table 17.10). But calculation of the rates for two reference decades, 1949-50 to 1958-59 and 1955-56 to 1964-65, shows that increase in cropped area was more rapid in the first decade, while increase in productivity was exactly the reverse. Rapid expansion of cropped area in the early 1950s was the result of land reform. With the abolition of feudal systems of land tenure (*Zamindari* and *Jagirdari*) and the enactment of policies favouring reclamation of cultivable wastelands adopted by the government,[5] large areas of wastelands, now transferred to private or village control, were brought under cultivation by the former *Zamindars* and *Jagirdars*, who wanted to become "cultivators", and by their former tenants, who had acquired rights in land; the process was assisted by loans and grants from the government. Also, large areas of government-owned wastelands were allotted to landless cultivators. However, as reclamation of the more marginal wastelands became increasingly difficult and expensive, the rate of expansion of cropped area slowed down after the middle 1950s. The "net sown area" which had increased by 12 million hectares between 1950-51 and 1956-57, increased between 1956-57 and 1962-63 by only 6 million hectares (Table 17.13).

Table 17.13 : Land Utilization, India 1950-51 to 1962-63

(in 000 hectares)

	1950-51	*1956-57*	*1962-63*
Geographical area	326,287	326,287	326,287
Area according to village papers	284,315	292,435	299,912
Forests	40,482	51,702	55,448
Not available for cultivation	47,517	47,024	50,308
Permanent pastures and grazing lands	6,675	12,190	14,127
Land under miscellaneous tree crops and groves (not included in net area sown)	19,828	5,510	4,589
Cultivable waste	22,943	21,846	17,971
Fallow land : Other than current	17,445	11,965	10,263
Current	10,679	11,705	10,962
Net area sown	118,747	130,493	136,244
Area sown more than once	13,146	18,582	20,492
Total cropped area	131,893	149,075	156,736
Irrigation			
Net irrigated area	20,853	22,533	25,663
Area irrigated more than once	1,710	3,174	3,935
Gross irrigated area	22,563	25,707	29,598

Source : Government of India : Directorate of Economics and Statistics, Ministry of Food and Agriculture, New Delhi, 1966.

Both the Planning Commission (1964) and USPSAC Panel (Holst, 1967) recognize that expansion of cropped area can make only a limited contribution to the future increase of agricultural output and that most of the increase must come from increase in productivity. But whereas the Planning Commission has visualized an increase of 20 per cent in gross cropped area between 1960-61 and 1975-76 (Table 17.14) which would contribute more than one-fourth to the total increase in agricultural output in this period, the USPSAC Panel has projected only a marginal increase of 10 per cent in the cropped area underfood grains during a 22-year period, 1964-86, in which total foodgrains output would be more than double (Table 17.15). An examination of the projection of the Planning Commission, however, reveals that most of the increase in gross cropped area will come from multiple cropping over a larger proportion of the cropland—increase in area sown more than once—whereas increase in cropland or "net sown area" will be small. Out of a total increase of nearly 30 million hectares in gross cropped area, as much as 21.6 million hectares will be from areas "sown more than once" (Table 17.14). Increase in these areas is to come from an expansion of irrigation—by 27.54 million hectares—and consequent second crop growth.

Table 17.14 : Projections of the Perspective Plan, Planning Commission

	1960-61	*1965-66*	*1970-71*	*1975-76*
Population (million)	*439*	*492*	*555*	*625*
Growth rate (%) per year				
Population	2.4	2.5	2.5	
National income	5.0	7.7	7.5	
Per capita income	2.6	5.0	5.0	
Agricultural production	2.3	5.1	4.3	
Industrial production	8.6	12.3	10.0	
Gross cropped area (million hectares)	152.25		171.66	182.19
Net sown area (million hectares)	132.74		137.78	141.05
Area sown more than once (million hectares)*	19.51		33.88	41.14
Gross irrigated area (million hectares)	27.93		45.75	55.47
Area under foodgrains (million hectares)	113.24		127.53	134.41
Production of foodgrains (million tonnes)	82.0		122.0	151.0
Consumption of chemical fertilizers (million tonnes, NPK)	0.3		2.45	

* Post script - 2002 : With the expansion of irrigation facilities, area sown more than once can be increased sizeably and net area sown can also be extended up to some extent.

Source : Planning Commission : Development of Agriculture, India 1960-61 to 1975-76, New Delhi, January 1964 (Mimeographed) and Notes on Perspective of Development India 1960-61 to 1975-76, New Delhi, April 1964.

The possibilities of increasing the "net sown area" are in fact quite limited, even though large areas continue to be recorded in the statistics on land utilization, under the three categories, "cultivable waste", "current fallows", and "fallows other than current". The total area under these categories was nearly 40 million hectares in 1962-63 (Table 17.13). "Current fallows" form an integral part of the cropping system on unirrigated lands in the low rainfall zone (below 762 mm annually) as well as on the other lands of low productivity and probably cannot be reduced much; the area under "current fallows" changed little between 1950-51 and 1962-63. In the other two categories, there are large areas which suffer from soil erosion, weeds, salinity, alkalinity, or other soil defects and are either unsuitable for cultivation or can be reclaimed only at high cost. In 1960 a team of agricultural experts investigated the possibilities of extension of cultivation into cultivable wastelands and concluded that: "Ten million acres (4 million hectares) might be the upper limit of the additional area that might become available for arable farming itself out of the existing cultivable waste during the period of about fifteen years beyond 1960-61" (Planning Commission, 1963, p. 4). When considering the possibilities of extension one must also remember that these areas, as well as most of the areas classified as "forest" are used for grazing. The large livestock population of India—226.8 million bovine animals and 101.1 million sheep and goats in 1961—depends mainly upon grazing these lands because the area actually classified as "permanent pasture and grazing land" is very small—14.13 million hectares in 1962-63 (Table 17.13). Diversion of large areas of cultivable wastelands or fallow lands for cultivation will only accentuate the problem of subsistence of livestock.

The area under forest also cannot be reduced without further reducing the supplies of wood and other forest products and exposing large areas to serious soil erosion. Supplies of industrial wood, pulp for paper and other industries, and fuelwood are already inadequate, and the demands are growing rapidly. Production of timber and other industrial wood was estimated at 8.0 million c.m. in 1965. The demand in that year was estimated at 11.0 million c.m. and was expected to increase to 24.0 million c.m. by 1975-76 (Planning Commission, 1966, p. 205). The demand for pulp, derived mainly from bamboo, was expected to increase more than 5 times, from 450,000 tonnes to 2,275,000 tonnes between 1960-61 and 1975-76 (Planning Commission, 1964, p. 125). The demand for fuelwood, which is the principal domestic fuel in both rural and urban areas, was expected to increase by more than 30 per cent during this period

(Government of India, 1965, p. 77). The Planning Commission has come to the conclusion that these rapidly growing demands can be met only by a radical change in forestry practices from the existing conservation-management to modern plantation-management (Planning Commission, 1966, p. 205). Any large reduction in the area under forests is out of the question.

Absence of areas of cultivable land which could be reclaimed by the peasants themselves is a handicap for agricultural and overall economic development. Reclamation of such areas is the easiest and the most economical method of increasing output under the economic and social conditions of Indian agriculture. The cost is low because most of the resources are furnished by human-bullock labour which is chronically underemployed; even a part of the capital requirement is met by savings which would otherwise be hoarded or used for unproductive purposes. Output can increase rapidly because no major change from traditional agricultural practices is involved. Increase of output by increasing productivity of cropland, on the other hand, requires large external investment—in irrigation works and for production and supply of chemical fertilizers and high-yielding seed, for instance—and also involves major changes in traditional farming practices. Such changes depend in turn on an increase in knowledge among the farmers and changes in attitudes and socio-economic structures; these are slow in getting started. Increase of agricultural output in the early 1950s, to which expansion of cropped area by the farmers themselves made the major contribution was relatively rapid and painless; indeed it occurred faster than expected, because the targets of the First Five-Year Plan were over fulfilled. But output increase during the 1960s, which is dependent upon increase in productivity, has proved to be slower, and much more difficult; it has already led to a reappraisal of official development policies and may lead to major socio-economic changes within village society before it becomes established as a process.

Increase in productivity is linked with irrigation and adoption of improved agricultural techniques including use of modern inputs. Concentration of resources in selected areas is a strategy, based on evaluation of the relative efficiency of application of resources in different areas.

Irrigation

Nearly one-fifth of the cropped area of India is irrigated (Table 17.13) but the contribution of the irrigated area to total agricultural output is much larger because average productivity of the irrigated lands is higher than that of the unirrigated lands. Average yield of rice is 58 per cent higher and that of wheat 77 per cent higher (Planning Commission, 1969, Appendix 4, p. 7). Also, high-yield crops, such as sugarcane are grown mainly on irrigated lands. Development of irrigation has formed an important part of agricultural development programmes during the period of the Plans. In the first three Five-Year Plans, more than 40 per cent of the expenditure on agricultural development programmes has been for extension or improvement of irrigation facilities (Saran and Chawla, 1967, pp. 467-483). The irrigated area has increased from 22.56 million hectares in 1950-51 to 29.60 million hectares in 1962-63 or by 2 per cent annually (Table 17.13). Large increases in the irrigated area are projected both by the Planning Commission and the USPSAC Panel. The Commission has projected a doubling of gross irrigated area between 1960-61 and 1975-76; the Panel has projected a somewhat larger increase over the 22-year period 1964-86 (Tables 17.14 and 17.15). But the rates of increase in both projections—4.9 and 3.3 per cent per year respectively—are much higher than the actual rate of increase between 1950-51 and 1962-63. The rate of increase could be faster in the future—the potential of a number of irrigation projects completed under the Plans, or in advanced stages of construction, remains to be utilized (Planning Commission, 1966, pp. 216, 232-35). But realization of the projected rates of increase is quite unlikely.

Table 17.15 : Projections of USPSAC Panel Report

A. Growth of population and production

	1964	*1967*	*1971*	*1976*	*1986*
Population (million)	*471.3*	*509.0*	*565.4*	*647.5*	*853.5*
Growth rates (% per year)					
Population		2.52	2.66	2.75	2.80
National income		3.80	4.50	4.40	4.30 to 4.20
Per capita income		1.22	1.78	1.60	1.46 to 1.36
Agricultural production		3.33	6.8	3.4	3.6 to 2.3
Industrial production		3.4	2.6	4.8	4.8 to 5.4
Foodgrains production		3.28	6.75	3.61	3.22 to 3.03
Gross cropped area (million ha)	157.5	160.3	163.0	166.0	172.0
Gross integrated area (million ha)	30.2	32.7	36.5	45.0	63.0
Cropped area under food-grains (million ha)	116.3	118.7	121.0	123.5	128.5
Production of foodgrains million t.)	79.4	87.4	113.5	135.5	184.4
Consumption of chemical fertilizers (million t. NPK)	0.60	1.40	4.25	6.81	11.06

Table 17.15 B. Intensive and General Cultivation of Foodgrains.

	1967		1971		1976		1986	
	I.C.*	G.C.*	I.C.	G.C.	I.C.	G.C.	I.C.	G.C.
Cropped area (million ha.)	2.0**	116.7	12.0	109.0	22.0	101.5	42.0	86.5
Production (million t.)	3.4	84.0	23.0	90.5	45.9	89.6	108.6	75.8
Yield per ha. (kg.)	1716	720	1916	830	2085	883	2586	876
Consumption of chemical fertili-zers (NPK): Total million t.)	0.10	0.88	0.90	2.51	1.98	3.55	5.25	3.64
Per ha. (kg.)	50	7.5	75	23	90	35	125	42

*I.C. = Intensive Cultivation; G.C. +General Cultivation.
**The original target was 3 million acres but was later reduced to 2 million acres.
Source: Holst, W: Evaluation of population and food problems of India in : *The World Food Problem.* A Report of the President's Science Advisory Committee, Panel on the World Food Supply. The White House, May 1967, pp. 703-6.

Development of irrigation has particular importance for the development programmes of the USPSAC Panel and the New Agricultural Strategy, because the "intensive cultivation" areas which will account for most of the increase in output under these programmes must be provided with facilities of assured and adequate irrigation ("100 per cent irrigation" according to the Panel). Efficient water management is an essential counterpart to use of high-yielding seed, chemical fertilizers, and other inputs. The strategy is based on experimental evidence which indicates that very high crop yields can be obtained with intensive use of these inputs under conditions of controlled and adequate moisture (Holst, 1967, p. 695). But all irrigated areas do not fulfil the condition of assured and adequate irrigation; large areas, especially those irrigated from tanks and other sources of surface irrigation, have inadequate supplies of water which, moreover, fail during periods of drought. The USPSAC Panel has limited the ultimate extension of the "intensive cultivation" areas to 42 million hectares apparently on the assessment that not more than 2/3rds of the total irrigated area of 63 million hectares will meet the exacting requirement of "100 per cent irrigation". But the "New Agricultural Strategy" has assumed that the requirement will be met inasmuch as 25.3 million out of a total of 32.4 million hectares of irrigated area under foodgrains by 1970-71 (Table 17.16). Against the background of widespread failure of irrigation in 1965-67 from water sources which had been considered to be “safe for agriculture” (Sivaraman 1963, p. 438), such an assumption seems quite unrealistic.

Table 17.16 : Targets under the programme of the New Agricultural Strategy 1970-71.

Irrigated area	*Cropped area under food Million ha.*	*Production of foodgrains Million t.*
High-yielding seed varieties	13.16	40.95
Double cropping with use of short-term varieties	12.14	22.40
Other irrigated area	7.09	9.20
Total	32.39	72.55
Unirrigated area	105.26	47.45
Grand Total	137.65	120

Note: Consumption of chemical fertilizers 4.1 million tonnes of which 75 per cent in areas under high-yielding and quick-maturing varieties.

Source : Sivaraman, B., "The Strategy of Food Production," *Indian Journal of Public Administration*, 13, 1967, 3, p. 440.

In 1961 the ultimate potential irrigation development was an estimated 71 million hectares (Planning Commission 1961, p. 189). It now is being revised upwards because of recent experience indicating that two or more crops can be grown each year on much of the irrigated land with the use of new, quick-maturing varieties. Sivaraman has estimated that nearly half of the irrigated land may ultimately be multiple-cropped and that the gross cropped area may as a result reach 81 million hectares (Sivaraman, 1963, p. 441). The latter is a little less than half of the ultimate gross cropped area of 168 million hectares, projected by him.

Use of Modern Inputs

In the agricultural development programmes preceding the adoption of the “New Agricultural Strategy (NAS),” improvement of agricultural techniques included both the use of modern inputs and the adoption of traditional good farming practices, such as use of compost and green manure, deep ploughing, and systematic crop rotation. Considerable emphasis was given to more extensive adoption of the latter which, it was thought, could bring large gains in productivity without much capital investment. The development effort itself could be considered “organization-intensive”, because apart from expenditures on irrigation, land reclamation, and soil conservation, the expenditure was largely for agricultural extensions and credit and supplies organizations.

This approach was continued in the Perspective Plan of the Planning Commission. Of the projected increases in output under this Plan, only 36 per cent would come from use of improved seed and chemical fertilizers, while as much as 40 per cent would be contributed by "other inputs", including both traditional improvements and more efficient use of inputs (Planning Commission, 1969, p. 24). However, the programmes of both the USPSAC Panel and the NAS emphasize use of modern inputs. Under the programme of the Panel, two-thirds of the projected increase between 1964 and 1986 will come from chemical fertilizers and high-yielding seed; the balance will come mainly from irrigation (Holst, 1967, p. 700). Under the NAS programme, the entire increase will come from areas sown to high-yielding and quick-maturing varieties and receiving intensive application of chemical fertilizers and pesticides. These programmes were patterned after highly successful projects in Mexico, Taiwan, and the Philippines (*Ibid,* 693-95). But use of modern inputs is capital-intensive and technology-intensive. It requires large investment in seed farms and factories and also agricultural research organizations staffed by qualified plant breeders, agronomists, and other specialists. These requirements have been clearly stated by the Panel, which has recommended allocation of adequate resources for their implementation. The Panel has estimated the investment needs of the programme at $29 billion over a 22-year period—an average of $1.32 billon per year (*Ibid*, 700-701).

Total investment in the Indian economy was estimated at $3 billion in 1965-66,[6] and will undoubtedly increase over the 22-year period covered by the programme. Yet it is clear that the programme will take a very large share, especially in the early years (late 1960s and early 1970s) when the major investments will have to be made.

Concentration of Resources in Selected Areas

Under the programme of the USPSAC Panel, as well as under the NAS, most of the increase in output will come from areas selected for "intensive cultivation". As mentioned above, the strategy is based on experimental evidence which shows that very high-yields can be obtained with intensive use of these inputs under conditions of controlled and adequate moisture.

It is also implied that the possibility of increasing agricultural output in much of the unirrigated area is meagre. The Panel has proposed that areas having "100 per cent irrigation" and other favourable conditions should be selected for "intensive cultivation" of foodgrains. It predicts a progressive increase of the extent of such areas from 2.0 million hectares in 1967 to 12.0 million hectares in 1971, and 42.0 million in 1986 (Table 17.15). The corresponding production targets are 3.5 m.t., 23.0 m.t., and 108.6 m.t. respectively. In 1971 these areas will account for about 10 per cent of the total area under foodgrains but contribute nearly 20 per cent of the output; the corresponding figures for 1986 are 32 per cent and 59 per cent. Also in 1986 the intensive cultivation areas will account for 60 per cent of the total consumption of chemical fertilizers for foodgrain production, and average yields will be nearly three times those in the general cultivation areas (Table 17.15).

Concentration of resources and output increases has been carried even further under the programme of the New Agricultural Strategy. A proposed total area of 25.3 million hectares for high-yielding or quick-maturing seed varieties by 1970-71 is expected to account for three-fourths of the total consumption of chemical fertilizers and to contribute more than half of the projected output of foodgrains in that year (Table 17.16). The unirrigated areas appear to have been entirely ignored; indeed, total output projected for them in 1970-71 is lower than the actual output of 1964-65 (Sivaraman, 1967, pp. 438 and 440).

The idea of concentrating resources in favourable areas to obtain rapid increase in output is not new, although both programmes present it in a more extreme form than had been done earlier. It can be traced back to the early 1950s when a number of community development blocks were located in areas having a good potential for increasing agricultural output (i.e., irrigation projects). But a decision to extend the community development programmes to the whole country in about 10 years soon relegated it to the background. It was reviewed in 1959 by a team of American Agricultural experts invited by the Government of India to review its agricultural development programmes and suggest measures to increase agricultural output more rapidly. The team recommended selection of "promising areas" for increased production of wheat and rice, and seven districts (out of a total of more than 300) were selected accordingly in 1960 for an "intensive agricultural development programme" (IADP) of five years in duration. In 1962 the number of districts was increased to 15 and from that time on new areas continued to be selected until by the end of the Third Five-Year Plan (March 1966) nearly a third of the cropped area of the country was covered by either IADP districts or "intensive areas" (Planning Commission, 1966, p. 175). Such rapid expansion could only mean dilution of effort, because trained personnel, finance, and materials were limited.

The feasibility of the principal features of both programmes can be questioned. It can be argued that exclusive reliance on use of capital-intensive inputs, ignoring the possibilities of production increase without large investment, through improvements in farm management and adoption of traditional good farming practices, unduly raises the investment requirements. It can also be argued that it will not be possible to sustain concentration of resources in limited areas for long because the same pressures which caused a retreat from it earlier will again operate in the future. Resource-concentration in particular areas involves discrimination in their favour; increasing inter-regional and inter-farm disparities in income soon become evident. In periods of scarcity of inputs such as chemical fertilizers, reservation of large proportions of supplies for "intensive cultivation" areas is particularly resented by farmers in other areas. The pressures against resources concentration are strong.

Other difficulties arise as a result of land tenure and because of administrative deficiencies. The feasibility of achieving "intensive cultivation" in areas which are cultivated by tenants can be questioned on the ground that tenants are not sure of their status, are subject to extortionate rents, and have little incentive to increase production (Ledjinsky, 1965). Administrative agencies have been inefficient and the performance of the existing IADP districts has been much below expectations (Kieloch, 1967, pp. 486-87), and indeed, it can be argued that no present administrative agency is capable of carrying forward either of the intensive programmes.

Finally, the desirability of leaving much of the agricultural area in virtual stagnation is open to serious question. As mentioned above, the non-intensive areas have been entirely ignored in the programme of the New Agricultural Strategy. The projection of the USPSAC Panel envisages an increase in average yield of foodgrains in the "general cultivation" areas of about 1/3rd between 1964 and 1986. But they will include comparatively well-watered areas where irrigation is below 100 per cent, and unirrigated areas in the zones of moderate to heavy rainfall (1140 mm per year and above)—as well as moisture-deficient areas. If one assumes that the well-watered areas will receive higher inputs and experience larger productivity increase than the moisture-deficient areas, it is clear that the latter will be left to stagnate. The extent of such areas is not small : in 1960-61, about 60 per cent of the total cropped area of India was unirrigated and located in zones with rainfall below 1140 mm per year. Providing for little or no growth in such a large proportion of the cropped area constitutes wasteful use of resources. Indeed, average productivity per agricultural worker will decline in these areas, unless the increase in the labour force is offset by emigration—an extremely unlikely prospect in a country with such pronounced geographical immobility of population.

Population Growth and the Prospects of Increasing Food Output—Some Earlier Assessments

We have selected three assessments made since 1950 : the 1951 Report of the Census of India (Census of India 1953), Coale and Hoover in 1958, and Sukhatme in 1965. These reports not only illustrate different points of view, but changes in thinking on the subject within a very short period. The Perspective Plan of the Planning Commission and the Report of the USPSAC Panel might also be considered here, even though their primary object is to outline development programmes needed to meet pre-determined targets of output. Both arrive at the conclusion that increases in food output, required to meet the needs of population growth and economic development, are possible. Similar confidence has not existed in some of the earlier assessments. The Reports of the Census of 1951 was particularly pessimistic. In Malthusian style, it prescribed a rigid upper limit to the possibilities of expansion of agricultural (and food) output and forecast "catastrophe" if population outgrew that limit. The difference between the pessimism of this Report and the confidence of the latest assessments, even with their forecast of much higher populations, is due to two reasons :

(i) A much better record of increase in agricultural output during the period of the three Plans than in the previous half-century, and
(ii) Technological advance which has made possible large increases in agricultural output by increasing productivity of croplands.

1951 Census Report

Based on a continuation of the 1941-51 rate of growth for the next 30 years, the 1951 Census Report forecast a population of between 527.6 million and 535.5 million in 1981 (Table 17.17). A higher rate of growth was considered possible, but no estimate was given. It was estimated that agricultural output would have to increase by 55 per cent between 1951 and 1981 in order to maintain the existing levels of consumption; but the possibilities of increasing output were put at a maximum of 35 per cent. This pessimistic view was based on a detailed analysis of the prospects of increasing both cropped and irrigated areas and raising productivity through improvements in agricultural techniques. It was influenced undoubtedly, by the results of an analysis of the performance of Indian agriculture in the 60 years preceding 1951 which revealed declining cultivated and irrigated areas per capita, and stagnant or declining per acre yields. On the basis of this analysis, the Census Commissioner concluded : "Our effort to keep pace with unchecked growth of population is bound to fail at some point... and we should be able to go one step further and fix this point by saying that it is the time at which our total number reaches and passes 45 crores (450 million)" (Census of India, 1953, p. 207). He estimated that this number would be reached by 1969.

Increase of population beyond this number could, in the view of the Census Commissioner, only result in catastrophe. His prescription for averting catastrophe was a nation wide programme of family planning to limit the number of births so that they do not materially exceed the number of deaths and thus to achieve a substantially stationary population before our number exceeds 45 crores (450 million) (*ibid*, p. 216). The birth rate would have to fall in this period from 40 to 25 per cent and this would have to be achieved by reducing the incidence of "improvident maternity" from its present level of 40 per cent to under 5 per cent in 15 years (*ibid*, p. 218). Improvident maternity was defined as "child-birth occurring to a mother who has already given birth to three or more children of whom at least one is alive" (*ibid*, p. 217). It is interesting to note that while the Census Commissioner did not believe it possible for agricultural output to increase by 35 per cent in 30 years, he was extremely conscious of the difficulties of expanding output under conditions of peasant agriculture, he believed that Indian society could be transformed in 15 years from a stage in which few had heard about family planning to universal acceptance of the practice.

Coale and Hoover (1958)

Coale and Hoover selected India as a case example of their study of the relationship between population growth and economic development. The study is concerned primarily with projection of population growth and evaluation of the prospects of economic development in India; assessment of the agricultural prospects forms part of the larger evaluation.

In making their population projections, Coale and Hoover assumed growth rates of 2.0 to 2.5 per cent during the period 1951-86. (Table 17.17). These projections were much higher than the official projections of the time, and their publication immediately effected upward revision of the latter. But all projections made in the 1950s, including the highest projection by Coale and Hoover, were proved to be too low by the 1961 Census. Now projections are much higher; some of them, including the projection of the USPSAC Panel, assume increasing rate of population growth well into the 1980s (Table 17.17).

Table 17.17 : Selected Population Projection for India, 1961-86
(Population in Million, growth rate per cent per Year)

Source	*1961*	*1971*	*1976*	*1981*	*1986*
Census of India 1951 (4)	407	464		527.6 to 535.5	
Coale and Hoover 1958 (7)					
Projection II	**424.0**	**524.0**	**569.0**	**603.0**	**634.0**
Projection III	424.0	532.0	601.0	682.0	775.0
Sukhatme [1965 (44) Projection I]					
Population	438.0	535.0	585.0	630.0	
Growth rate		2.0	1.8	1.5	
Projection II					
Population	438.0	555.0	625.0	680.0	
Growth rate		2.5	2.5	2.0	
Planning Commission 1964	439.0	555.0	647.5	734.4	
USPSAC Panel 1967					
Population	439.0	565.4	647.5	734.4	835.5
Growth rate		2.4-2.6	2.75-2.80	2.80	

Source : V. Nath : Natural Resources of India, in *Gazetteer of India*, Vol. II, Chapter III (Ministry of Education, Government of India, New Delhi).

Coale and Hoover's assessment was not as detailed as that by the Census Commissioner; but it was based on the food consumption data of the National Sample Survey and other rural sample surveys and also the production results of the First Five-Year Plan. Their conclusion was more hopeful than that of the Census Commissioner. They expected that "India's output of food and other agricultural products can, for the next two or three decades, increase at least as fast as the maximum rate of growth of the consuming population (78 per cent in 25 years)" (Cole and Hoover, 1958, p. 110). They thought that the main difficulties in increasing output were in the area of social institutions and attitudes, and that the prime need was to overcome the apathy and inertia of the rural population.

Sukhatme (1965)

Sukhatme was concerned primarily with assessing the possibilities of meeting the food needs of India's growing population. He made two projections of population growth by 1981 (Table 17.17). The higher projection was similar to the government's official projection, but the lower one assumed a decline in fertility and growth rate beginning in the late 1960s when Sukhatme felt that the government's family planning programme could begin to have an effect. He was well aware of the difficulties of spreading family planning practices among a predominantly rural and illiterate population, but cited the experience of Japan and the East European countries, where birth rates fell by one-fourth to one-third in a decade, to support his assumption of an early decline (Sukhatme, 1965, p. 101). Sukhatme's work was notable for his very detailed assessment of existing consumption levels and the extent of "hunger" in India and the increases, quantitative and qualitative, needed to bring consumption to minimum nutritional requirements. His estimates of food consumption were based on data of nutrition surveys conducted by the State Governments, and the National Sample Survey. The "targets" of consumption requirements were based, similarly, on an exhaustive evaluation of recommendations of Indian and international (FAO) nutritionists. Sukhatme estimated food supplies needed to meet the requirements of the projected population of 1981 at "minimum" and "medium" targets, both of which envisaged specified quantitative and qualitative improvements over existing consumption levels. His conclusion was similar to that of Coale and Hoover, namely that it is possible to raise agricultural output sufficiently to meet the "minimum target" needs of the population of 1981, but not to provide for any major improvement in nutrition level, such as an appreciable increase in consumption of animal products (*ibid*, pp.154-55).

Population Growth and the Economic Prospect

The Perspective Plan of the Planning Commission and the Report of the USPSAC Panel also constitute in a sense assessments of the prospect of economic development. The Perspective Plan is based on the assumption that an annual population increase of 2.4 per cent can be combined with a growth rate of 2.6 to 5.0 per cent per year in per capita income (Table 17.14). The Panel has assumed a higher growth rate and a lower increase rate in per capita income; the latter falls as low as 1.36 per cent annually in the 1980s (Table 17.15). This lower rate is due only partly to assumption of a higher rate of population growth. The lower rate may also be the result of the development strategy followed by the Panel. The subject obviously needs detailed analysis; but the implication of the low rate is clear, namely that the effort to increase food output to meet the minimum needs of the rapidly growing population will take such large resources that economic development will be delayed for a long time. The Panel has explained the accelerated population growth in the 1960s on the ground that decline in death rate during this period will be more than the decline in birth rate and the spread between births and deaths will increase : there can hardly be any major difference on the forecast of a decline in the death rate. The rate of 22.8 per cent calculated for 1951-1960 by application of the reverse survival method to results of the 1951 and 1961 population censuses, is very high even by the standards of the developing countries—the rates in Ceylon, Jamaica, and a number of other countries are already between 8.0 and 9.0 per cent (United Nations, 1965, pp. 561-63)—and should fall with further improvements in health services and communications and increase in literacy. The Panel has assumed continuance of a high birth rate well into the 1980s because "it is not expected that population control will have such a downward impact on growth rates much before 1985 either in India or the World as a whole" (Holst, 1967, p. 683). This view is different from those of Sukhatme and a UN Mission which studied India's family planning programme in 1965, and from official expectations. Reference has been made above to Sukhatme's view that the family planning programme could have a noticeable effect on the birth rate even in the late 1960s. The UN Mission, after examining progress of the programme, stated that "population control measures could be sufficiently effective by 1975 to prevent the rate of increase from accelerating, but not falling" (Ohlin, 1967, p. 92). The object of the family planning programme has been stated officially as reducing the birth rate from 40 to 25 per cent "as expeditiously as possible," but it is expected that the reduction will be rapid enough to affect population growth in the late 1970s.

The prospect of population growth will remain somewhat uncertain until there is more information on the progress of the family planning programme. In existence since the 1950s, only during the last three years (1965-68) has the programme been implemented as a nationwide effort.

According to the latest official report, nearly 6 million couples, out of a total of 90 million in the reproductive age group, were practicing family planning in 1967-68 (Government of India, 1968). The practices included use of IUCD, condoms, and sterilization of both males and females. Of these, sterilization appears to be gaining in popularity while use of IUCD has declined somewhat. The number of people sterilized during 1967-68 was 1.4 million, which was double the number of the previous year, while the number of users of IUCD had decreased by 20 per cent (*ibid*).

Progress of the programme will depend in future on speed of change in attitudes, the resources allocated to it, and finally, adequacy of basic medical services. It is fortunate that there is no deep-seated prejudice against family planning among the majority of the population; and the main task is to propagate the attitude that something can be done about family size. The Fourth Five-Year Plan proposed to raise the resource allocation to the programme to nearly four times the level of the Third Plan (Planning Commission, 1966, p. 347). But lack of medical personnel is a serious handicap. There were less than 100,000 doctors in India in 1961, and 2/3rd of them were concentrated in the towns (Institute of Applied Manpower Research, 1965, No. 6, pp. 20-21). The total number of female doctors, whose role is critical in the spread of practices such as use of IUCD, was only about 8500, and only 1082 of them were in the rural areas. The female doctor-female population ratio was as low as 6 per million in the rural areas. The number of trained nurses and mid-wives was equally small—about 109,000 (*ibid*, No. 5, p. 24). The popularity of sterilization of males, an irreversible operation, frequently performed in camps organized by peripatetic medical teams, and the slow acceptance of IUCD, which requires follow-up advice and medical assistance in a percentage of cases, reflects, in our view, this shortage of medical and nursing personnel.

Economically, the recent record of stagnation and instability in agricultural output does impart a degree of uncertainty. But given continuance of adequate emphasis on increasing agricultural output, it should not be difficult to resume the steady growth of output ahead of population growth achieved during the 1950s. The resources of capital, organization, and technology are much larger now than in the 1950s, and reappraisal of official policies to ensure more effective use of resources is well under way. Investment rates have gone up steadily—from 5.5 per cent in 1950-51 to 14-15 per cent in 1965-66. The industrial base is larger and more diversified than at the beginning of the First Plan; the number of trained technicians is much higher; and further development of industry, transport and other modern sectors can be based much more on domestic resources than in the past. In agriculture, the basic extension, supplies, and credit organizations needed for modernization exist, and have only to be strengthened and reoriented. Forecasts of large increases in agricultural output within three or four years, such as the one made under the programme of the "New Agricultural Strategy", are possible only because of the existence of the basic organizations. The strategy, for all its excesses and limitations does represent an effort toward reappraisal of policies, which take into account the potential of rapidly advancing technology on the one hand and natural-resource-based limitations on the other. The rate of economic growth can be faster (than in the 1950s) with more efficient utilization of resources. Among these, particular mention needs to be made of the very large resource of underemployed manpower. We have referred earlier to the difficulties in utilization of this resource. But the difficulties are not insuperable: they can be overcome with good organization and leadership.

Post Script 2002

The postscript written in July 2002, 35 years after the paper (contents of which constitute this chapter) was presented at a Seminar in Penn State University in 1967.

The paper when presented, at the Seminar, was severely criticized by many participants. They said that the paper presented a grossly over-optimistic assessment of India's capacity to provide enough food, clothing and acceptable level of living to its rapidly increasing population.

The only support gratefully received, came from a Danish Economist, Mrs. Ester Boserup whose book *The Economics of Agricultural Growth* had made economists, geographers and other social scientists sit up and rethink the prospects of economic development in poor countries of south, south-east and east Asia, Sub-Saharan Africa and Latin America.

The main point of criticism was that India was already putting unsustainable pressure on its resources of cropped and irrigated areas, forests and minerals; that these were limited and could not support an increasing population at rising levels of living. The data, however, on increase in population, per capita income, nutrition intake, education and health of the population, of the last 40 years corroborate and vindicate the opinion of the author as was presented in his paper (included in this chapter) in 1967.

The population of India increased from 422 million in 1961 to 1,027 million in 2001 or about 2½ times, almost on average at 2% annually. However, the data show that the average Indian was better fed, better clothed, better educated, better informed and entertained and healthier, than his predecessor of four decades. (See Table 1 in Chapter 21 in this volume: Decennial Census of Population 2001, "First Results of the Decennial Census of Population 2001: A Regional Analysis".

The cultivated area in 1951-52 was 133.2 million hectares (m.h.) and the irrigated area 23.2 m.h. By 1996-97 the cropped area had increased to 189.5 m.h. and the irrigated area to 73.5 m.h., which was nearly 37 per cent of the total cropped area. In other words while the cropped area increased by just over 40 per cent, the irrigated area had increased by more than three times. Field surveys indicate that the biggest contribution to the increase was made not by canals constructed by the government but by wells and tube-wells owned and operated by farmers. Production of foodgrains increased from 60 million tonnes in 1950s to 200 million tonnes in 1991.

The first breakthrough in this process of development was made with arrival of dwarf very high-yielding varieties of wheat, in the late 1960s and of rice in the 1970s. Yields of wheat, in conditions of assured water supply provided by irrigation from canals or pump sets worked by electricity or diesel oil or tube-wells owned by the State Electricity Board in Punjab, Haryana and western Uttar Pradesh went up by two to three times in the 1970s. A similar increase in yields per hectare from high-yield varieties of seeds grown under irrigation provided by canals or a dependable rainfall have been experienced also in Andhra Pradesh and Tamil Nadu, Southern Karnataka and West Bengal.

These varieties needed high doses of chemical fertilizer and pesticides; the increased returns though in terms of much higher production justified the high costs of using these chemicals. In course of time farmers in Eastern Rajasthan and north-western Madhya Pradesh found that they too could grow high-yield wheat if they fitted their wells with pumps driven by electricity or diesel oil.

Farmers also found that cultivation by tractors is more efficient than by bullocks. Even farmers with small land holdings of 2-5 hacters, who could not own tractors, found it economic to get their lands cultivated by hiring them from tractor owners at a fixed rate for their use.

This development contributed not only to dramatic increase in the traditional canal irrigated areas of Punjab, Haryana, and western U.P. (for wheat) and coastal Tamil Nadu, coastal Andhra Pradesh and West Bengal (for rice), but also led to extension of cultivation in areas in which these crops were not grown earlier. There has been major extension of the irrigated area by small canals, and wells fitted with diesel oil operated pumps over very large areas. There has been selective change in the area of production of some crops. Production of wheat has increased greatly in eastern Rajasthan and western Madhya Pradesh in which only coarse grains (sorghum or millets) were produced earlier. Rice produced on irrigated lands has taken the place of coarse grain in western Maharashtra, Andhra Pradesh and western Tamil Nadu.

There was major change also in the geography of crop production. In the 1950s and the 1960s, most of the sugar was produced from cane grown in Uttar Pradesh and Bihar. The cane was thin and its sucrose content was much lower than that of cane grown in Indonesia, the Caribbean or Southern USA. Now, however, most of the cane is grown in coastal Andhra Pradesh, Western Maharashtra and Southern Karnataka under irrigation provided by canals taken from rivers or wells fitted with pumps driven by diesel oil. The yield of cane and its sucrose content are now comparable to that in the tropical lands mentioned above.

Medium staple cotton used for making fine cloth was grown until the 1950s only in the canal irrigated areas of West Punjab and Sindh; which were included in Pakistan in 1947. Now all that is needed for our requirements is grown in western Haryana in northern India and western Tamil Nadu in the south around Coimbatore. As a result India is self-sufficient in medium staple cotton needed for making fine fabrics. The quality of staple cotton grown over large areas in Maharashtra, Gujarat and Karnataka has also been improved so much that when mixed with polyester fibre it makes cloth, which wears well and is comfortable to wear in the Indian summer.

As a result the per capita consumption of cloth has gone up by 70 per cent. The per capita consumption of cereals has gone up by 10 per cent that of cooking oil by two-and-half times and of sugar by nearly 100 per cent.

The literacy rate has gone up by 25 per cent (from 45.2 per cent in 1991 to 67.2 per cent in 2001). Children are being sent to schools by farmers and agricultural labourers as well as by all groups in cities. The farmers have to be literate so that they can read the instructions on use of chemical fertilizers and pesticides. They must be literate also so that they understand the terms on which short-term loans are given to them by cooperative societies for current construction and medium-term loans are given by the land mortgage or nationalized banks for buying tractors, pump sets and fuel for these or for land reclamation. The agricultural labourers have to be literate so that they are not paid lower wages than those fixed by the Government when they work on farms or in the market.

Improved health is due partly to access to safe and adequate water and partly to effective coverage by primary health centres (small hospitals) in *talukas* or community development blocks and/or dispensaries in large villages and large hospitals in district headquarters towns/cities.

UNDP, New York estimates that as many as 88 per cent of the population had access to improved water supply sources in 2000. Infant mortality per 1000 births has gone down from 129 live births in 1971 to 72 in 1998. Expectation of life at birth has gone up from 44.7 years in 1969-70 to 58.7 years in 1990-1991 and further to 63.3 years in 1999-2000.

The resources of coal, iron ore, bauxite and other minerals have proved on detailed exploration to be much higher than had been estimated up to the 1960s. As a result India has a large and developed industrial sector which has exportable surpluses of steel, and cement to neighbouring countries. The country meets all its needs of heavy and light machine tools and of consumer durables—motor bicycles, passenger cars, heavy and light commercial vehicles, air-conditioners, refrigerators and electrically operated kitchen gadgets and television and radio receivers.

Proved resources of crude oil discovered after explorations in the late 1950s and the 1960s have proved to be much higher. As a result refining capacity for producing motor spirit and diesel for motor vehicles, production of electricity and other needs and LPG for cooking in homes has been expanded so much that more than half of the needs are met from domestic sources.

The rural development programmes undertaken since the 1950s have led to creation of not only the infrastructures of rapid agricultural development but also their connection with the regional and national economy and rapid spread of education and improvement in health and productivity, (through network of Primary and Secondary schools and hospitals and dispensaries). Rural telephone and broadcasting had broken the isolation of the villages and have been positive instruments of providing information on development as much or more than construction of roads, besides entertainment.

The Human Development Report, 2002 issued by UNDP, New Delhi states that telephone connections increased five time between 1980 and 2000 and consumptions of electricity up three-times in the same period.

The data indicate the extent of improvement in level of living of the population with increase in agricultural and industrial production, access to education and health facilities, rapid increase in use of means of communication, travel, electricity and telephones.

NOTES

1. The views expressed in this paper are the author's own, and the United Nations or the Indian Planning Commission are in no way responsible for them.
2. Male workers alone have been considered for this comparison; female workers have been excluded because the method of classifying (changes in the definition of "worker") and consequently the number of the latter has fluctuated greatly from Census to Census. Most female workers are women from agricultural households who do farm-work in addition to their domestic duties.
3. Schultz (39) has argued that supply of foodgrains under PL 480 assistance to India and other countries has depressed production because it "has had the effect of reducing farm product prices below what they would have been without such forms of aid." It is true that the period of stagnation of domestic output in India has coincided with the period of heavy imports of foodgrains under PL 480; and the increasing difficulty of obtaining such imports since 1966 has been followed by intensified official efforts to increases domestic production of foodgrains.
4. This rate is lower than the rate of 2.98 per cent per year calculated for 1949-50 to 1964-65 by the Economic and Statistical Adviser to the Ministry of Food and Agriculture, Government of India, and given in Table 10.
5. *Zamindari, Jagirdari* and other feudal systems of land tenure were abolished in the early 1950s as part of the land reform programme of the Indian Government.
6. The Planning Commission estimated the national income in 1965-66 at 159, 300 million rupees and the investment ratio at 14-15 per cent of the national income (Planning Commission 1966, pp. 420 and 28). At the current conversion rate of US $1—Rs. 7.5, total investment works out to between 2.97 million and 3.18 billion US $.

REFERENCES

Ackerman, E.A. : *Population and National Resources,* pp. 717-727 in : P.M. Hauser and O.D. Duncan, eds. : The Study of Population (Chicago 1959). Reprinted, pp. 127-152 in : I. Burton and R.W. Kates, eds. : Readings in Resource Management and Conservation (Chicago, 1965).

Bhattacharjee, J.P. ed.: *Studies in Indian Agricultural Economics.* (Indian Society of Agricultural Economics, Bombay, 1958).

Blyn, G.: *Agricultural Trends in India, 1891-1947: Output Availability and Productivity.* (Philadelphia, University of Pennsylvania Press, 1966).

Census of India, 1951: Vol. 1 India. *Part I-A—Report Delhi,* 1953.

Census of India, 1951: Vol. 1 India. *Part I-B—Appendices to the Census Report,* 1951, Delhi, 1955.

Census of India, 1961: Paper No. 1 of 1962. *Final Population Totals,* Delhi, 1962.

Coale A.J., and Hoover, E.M.: *Population Growth and Economic Development in Low-Income Countries—A Case Study of India's Prospects* (Princeton, N. J., 1958).

Darling, M.: *The Punjab Peasant in Prosperity and Debt.* 4th ed. (Bombay, 1947).

Datar, B.N.: The Second Five-Year Plan—*Employment Approach, in Papers relating to the formulation of the Second Five-Year Plan, Panel of Economists, Planning Commission* (New Delhi, 1955).

Epstein, S.T.: *Economic Development and Social Change in South India* (Bombay, 1962).

Gadgil, D.R.: *The Industrial Evolution of India in recent Times* (Calcutta, 1942).

Ginsburg, N.: *Natural Resources and Economic Development,* Annals of the Association of American Geographers, Vol. 47, 1957, pp. 197-212.

Reprinted in: I. Burton and R.W. Kates, eds. : *Readings in Resource Management and Conservation* (Chicago, 1965).

Government of India :

- *Report of the Energy Survey Committee* (New Delhi, 1965).
- Ministry of Food and Agriculture Economic and Statistical Adviser : *Growth Rates in Agriculture* (New Delhi, March 1966), mimeographed.
- Ministry of Finance : *Economic Survey 1967-68* (New Delhi, 1968).
- Ministry of Health: *Annual Report 1967-68* (New Delhi, 1968).
- Ministry of Labour: *Report on Intensive Survey of Agricultural Labour : All India, Vol. 1* (Delhi, 1954).

Holst, W.: *Evaluation of Population and Food Production Problems of India, in:* The World Food Problems—Report of the Panel on the World Food Supply of the President's Science Advisory Committee (Washington, 1967).

Institute of Applied Manpower Research and National Institute of Health Administration and Education : *Manpower Group Survey. IAMR Working Papers No. 5 and 6. Stock of Nursing Personnel in India and Stock of Health and Medical Manpower* (New Delhi, 1965), mimeographed.

Kieloch, E.A.: Some Administrative Shortcomings of Intensive Agricultural Development Efforts, *Indian Journal of Public Administration.,* Vol. 18, No. 3, July-September 1967, pp. 484-492.

Ledjinsky, Wolf: *A Study on Tenurial Conditions in Package Districts.* Planning Commission, Government of India (New Delhi, 1965).

Leibenstein, H.: *Economic Backwardness and Economic Growth (*New York & London, 1957).

Lewis, W.A.: Economic Development with Unlimited Supplies of Labour (The Manchester School, May 1954). Reproduced in : Agarwala and Singh : *The Economics of Under development* (Oxford University Press, 1963), pp. 400-449.

Madalgi, S.S.: Hunger in Rural India : 1960-61 to 1964-65, *Economic and Political Weekly*, Bombay. Vol. 3, Annual Number 1968. pp. 61-67.

Malenbaum, W. : *Prospects for Indian Development* (London, 1962).

Nath, V.: Natural Resourccs of India, in : *Gazetteer of India,* Vol. II, Chapter III. (Ministry of Education, Government of India, New Delhi).

Nurkse, R.: *Problems of Capital Formation in Underdeveloped Countries* (Oxford, 1953).

Ohlin, G.: *Population Control and Economic Development* (Development Centre, Organization for Economic Cooperation and Development, Paris, 1967).

Planning Commission, Government of India, Committee on Natural Resources: *Study on Wastelands including Saline, Alkali and Waterlogged Lands and their Reclamation Measures* (New Delhi, 1963).

Planning Commission, Government of India:

- *Notes on Perspective of Development India: 1960-61 to 1975-76* (New Delhi, April 1964).
- *Development of Agriculture India: 1960-61 to 1975-76* (New Delhi, January 1964), mimeographed.
- *First Five-Year Plan—A Draft Outline* (New Delhi, 1951).
- *First Five-Year Plan* (New Delhi, 1952).
- *Second Five-Year Plan* (New Delhi, 1956).
- *Third Five-Year Plan* (New Delhi, 1961).
- *Fourth Five-Year Plan—A Draft Outline* (New Delhi, 1966).
- *Reports of the Committee of the Panel on Land Reforms* (New Delhi, 1959).

Saran, R. and Chawla, H.L. : Food Production Policies and Programme since Independence: A Historical Review, *The Indian Journal of Public Administration*, Vol. 13, No. 3, 1967, pp. 461-483.

Schultz, T.W.: What Ails World Agriculture? *Bulletin of Atomic Scientists*, 1968.

Sivaraman, B.: The Strategy of Food Production, *The Indian Journal of Public Administration*, Vol. 13, No. 3, 1967, pp. 433-447.

Sivasubramonian, S. : *National Income of India, 1900-01 to 1946-47.* Ph.D. Thesis, Delhi School of Economics (Delhi, 1965), unpublish.

Sukhatme, P.V.: *Feeding India's Growing Millions,* Asia Publishing House, Bombay, 1965.

United Nations: *Demographic Year Book 1964,* New York, 1965.

United Nations: *Year Book of National Accounts Statistics—1966,* New York, 1967.

Zelinsky, W.: *The Geographer and His Crowding World,* Revista Geografica, Vol. 65, 1966, pp. 7-28.

18

Growth of Population and Labour Force : Some Problems and Strategies for the Future (1993)*

Introduction

This chapter focuses attention on two problems which relate to:

(i) Rapid growth of population, and
(ii) Continued concentration of the labour force in agriculture in which productivity per worker is much lower than in the non-agricultural sectors.

The source materials are Censuses of Population of 1951 and 1991 and the Eighth Five-Year Plan, 1992-1997, Vol. 1. The analysis is limited to 14 major States which accounted for 94 per cent of the population of India in 1991. Excluded from it are : (i) small states and Union territories with populations below 10 million, and (ii) the states of Jammu and Kashmir and Assam in which a census was not taken either in 1981 or 1991.

Growth of Population

The growth rate of population continues to be high. It was 2.1 per cent per annum (p.a.) during 1981-1991 and had remained almost unchanged since 1951-1961 when it was 2.0 per cent. The p.a. growth rates for this period are given below :—

	Per cent
1951-1961	1.96 p.a.
1961-1971	2.20 p.a.
1971-1981	2.22 p.a.
1981-1991	2.11 p.a.

* Paper presented at Indian Association for The Study of Population, New Delhi (Annual Meeting 1993).

There are large inter-state differences, however, in the population growth rates during both 1971-1981 and 1981-1991 with Kerala and Tamil Nadu at the lower end and Rajasthan, Haryana, Madhya Pradesh, U.P., Karnataka and Maharashtra at the higher end (Table 18.1). It will also be seen from this table that except for Maharashtra and Karnataka the growth rate of population is inversely related to female literacy. In Maharashtra and Karnataka high growth rates of population could be due to in-migration from other states. Both states are highly urbanized—38.7 per cent of the total population of Maharashtra and 30.9 per cent of that of Karnataka was urban in 1991—and there has been considerable migration into their rapidly growing cities, especially the metropolitan cities of Bombay and Pune in Maharashtra and Bangalore in Karnataka.

A high female literacy rate of 86.9 per cent sets Kerala apart from the other states so much that female literacy appears to be the key variable in successful practice of family planning and improvement of health status in this state. This is brought out by the various indicators for which data is presented in Table 18.1. The State has the lowest birth, death, infant mortality and total fertility rates and the highest life expectancy and age at marriage of females. In respect of all these, Kerala already has the rates, which other states should aim at achieving by the turn of the century or during the first decade of the next century. Furthermore, while the growth rates of population have fallen sharply between 1971-1981 and 1981-1991 in Kerala and Tamil Nadu there has not been a similar fall in the states with high growth rates of population.

Table 18.1 : Growth Rate of Population 1951-2001

Decade	*Population (millions)*	*Decade growth rate (per cent)*	*Average annual exponential growth rate (per cent)*
1951	361.1	13.3	1.25
1961	439.2	21.6	1.96
1971	548.2	24.8	2.20
1981	683.3	24.7	2.22
1991	843.4	23.9	2.14
2001	1027.0	21.3	1.93

Source : Registrar General and Census Commissioner India : Census of India 2001 Paper 1 of 2001: Provisional Population Totals, p. 34, New Delhi, 2001.

The policy implication of these findings is that efforts, both official and by Non-Governmental Organizations (NGOs) to reduce growth rate of population, should be concentrated on increasing female literacy. The efforts would need to form part of larger programmes of increasing literacy among both males and females and ensuring that all children in the age-group 6 to 14 years, complete primary school education. The total literacy programme successfully completed in Kerala by 1991 as well as the adult literacy programme undertaken in the Panipat area of Haryana in 1992 indicate that : (i) such programmes can be undertaken successfully if there is the needed political will and administrative support from them, (ii) the NGOs are better equipped to undertake the programmes than official agencies, and (iii) the programmes should offer the minimum financial incentives to the educators (*Economic and Political Weekly*, October 9, 1993, pp. 2187-91 and October 2, 1993, pp. 2112-15).

This recommendation is reinforced by the fact that female literacy is very low in Bihar, Rajasthan, U.P., and Madhya Pradesh which had not only high rates of growth of population but also of birth, death, infant mortality and total fertility and low life expectancy.

A recent study by the Institute of Development Studies, Thiruvananthapuram shows "that Tamil Nadu, Goa, Gujarat and West Bengal are moving fast towards a two-child family norm. Though still way behind Kerala in achieving a demographic transition, these states promise to accept the small family norm .... and that total fertility rate in Kerala has fallen sharply from 1981 to 1991 not only among the Hindus but also among the Muslims and Christians" (*Times of India,* October 15, 1993, p. 16).

Slowing Down of Population Growth

The need to reduce the growth of population was recognized as early as 1950 and a family limitation programme was initiated by the then Ministry of Health under the First Five-Year Plan, 1951-1956. The programme has evolved during the last four decades through changes in the methods of contraception and increasing coverage of facilities of delivery of the needed services. It may be added that except for the brief three-year period of Emergency (1975-77) acceptance of family limitation services by the beneficiaries has been entirely voluntary.

A family limitation programme is most effective when it forms part of a wider programme of delivery of health service. This means a high coverage with hospitals, dispensaries, primary health centres and sub-centres which are adequately staffed by doctors and para-medical personnel especially those specializing in diseases of women and children. It has been well documented that a woman is prepared to practice family planning methods on the advice of a lady doctor or para-medical person (nurse/mid-wife) or even a *dai* after she has received satisfactory ante-natal and post-natal service relating to family planning.

Inter-state differences in availability of health infrastructure are given in Table 18.2A. It will be seen that the number of hospitals and dispensary beds (including both government and private) per lakh of population is the highest in Kerala. It is twice the number in the next ranking states—Maharashtra—and more than 7 times the numbers in Madhya Pradesh and Bihar. The Hindi speaking states such as Bihar, Madhya Pradesh, Rajasthan, U.P. and Haryana in which the rates of growth of population, birth, death, and infant mortality are the highest, are also the ones in which the number of hospital and dispensary beds (per lakh of population) is the lowest. The same doesn't hold, however, of rural health infrastructures (primary health centres, sub-centres and community health centres) per lakh of population (Table 18.2B). Almost all of these facilities are official and private sector participation in them is generally lacking. Kerala is almost near the bottom in respect of the facilities per lakh of population. And while Rajasthan and Bihar are also at the bottom, U.P., Haryana and Madhya Pradesh are in the middle. However, a large proportion of the rural health facilities in the Hindi speaking states, except Haryana, remain unstaffed or only partially staffed because they are most deficient in facilities, in the rural areas, for transport and communication and education for children, with the result that doctors and para-medical personnel are unwilling to work in rural areas. This, however, is no problem in Kerala and all the other States, except Orissa, because the rural infrastructures, mentioned above, are well developed in them.

Raising Productivity per Worker in Agriculture Increase in Agricultural Production

Agricultural production has increased by 228 per cent during the four decades, 1950-51—1990-91; the index of agricultural production having increased in this period from 58.5 to 191.8 (Tata Services Ltd.Table 18.1). The number of main agricultural workers (cultivators plus agricultural labourers) has increased during the same period from 71.0 million to 185.5 million [Registrar General and Census Commissioner, India : (i) Table 8, pp. 98-99 and (ii) Statement 6, p. 18]. As a result productivity per agricultural worker has gone up by 25.6 per cent.

Table 18.2 : Average exponential growth rates of population 1971-1991 and important socio-economic indicators : India and 14 major States

States	Birth Rate 1990	Death Rate 1990	Infant Mortality rate (IMR) 1990	Couple protection rate (CPR) 1-4-91	Total fertility rate (TFR) 1985	Life Expectancy Females (1986-91)	Female Literacy Rate (1991)	Mean age at Marriage (females) 1981	Percentage of Women Employed in Organized Sector	Average Exponential Growth Rate	
										1971-81	1981-91
	(1)	(2)	(3)	(4)	(5)	(6)	(7)	(8)	(9)		
Andhra Pradesh	25.60	8.70	70	44.30	3.70	62.23	33.70	17.26	12.47	2.10	2.14
Bihar	32.90	10.60	75	26.00	5.40	57.00	23.10	16.55	6.73	2.17	2.11
Gujarat	29.50	8.90	72	57.80	3.90	61.49	48.50	19.52	12.44	2.46	1.89
Haryana	31.80	8.50	69	56.60	4.60	61.97	40.94	17.84	11.39	2.55	2.33
Karnataka	27.80	8.10	71	46.90	3.60	63.31	44.30	19.21	17.06	2.39	1.88
Kerala	19.00	5.90	17	55.60	2.40	73.80	86.90	21.82	38.97	1.77	1.31
Madhya Pradesh	36.90	12.50	111	40.30	4.60	54.71	28.40	16.56	10.24	2.27	2.37
Maharashtra	27.50	7.30	58	56.20	3.50	64.30	50.50	18.77	13.24	2.21	2.26
Orissa	29.90	11.60	123	41.00	3.80	55.15	34.40	19.08	8.80	1.85	1.78
Punjab	27.60	7.80	55	75.80	3.50	65.30	49.70	21.07	13.56	2.16	1.85
Rajasthan	33.10	9.40	83	29.00	5.50	58.69	20.80	16.10	11.67	2.87	2.47
Tamil Nadu	22.40	8.70	67	57.30	2.80	60.80	52.30	20.25	22.00	1.63	1.39
Uttar Pradesh	35.70	12.00	98	35.50	5.60	49.64	26.00	16.71	7.92	2.29	2.24
West Bengal	27.30	8.10	63	33.70	3.70	59.53	47.10	19.23	9.82	2.10	2.20
India	29.90	9.60	80	44.10	4.30	59.10	39.40	18.33	14.22	2.22	2.11

Source: Col. 1, 2, 3 and 5 - SRS Estimates, Registrar General, India.
Col. 4 - Department of Family Welfare.
Col. 6 - Report of Standing Committee of Experts on Population Projections.
Col. 7 - Census 1991 (Provisional Totals).
Col. 8 - Census 1981.
Col. 9 - Directorate General of Employment and Training, Ministry of Labour.

Table 18.2A : Hospital and Dispensary Beds : 1 January, 1989

Major States	*Hospital beds Total*		*Dispensary beds Total*		*Hospital and Dispensary Beds*	
	Number	*of which: rural (%)*	*Number*	*of which: rural (%)*	*Total*	*Per lakh persons*
Kerala	73,684	55.7	803	94.5	74,487	254
Maharashtra	92,975	9.8	2,351	17.1	95,326	132
Gujarat	46,374	10.8	4,650	13.7	51,024	129
Punjab	16,084	22.0	6,238	91.7	22,322	117
Tamil Nadu	46,993	9.0	278	49.6	47,271	86
West Bengal	53,897	14.8	—	—	53,847	85
Karnataka	33,833	7.5	1,208	74.7	35,041	80
Andhra Pradesh	36,400	10.2	277	61.7	36,677	82
Rajasthan	20,250	5.8	1,538	44.7	21,788	51
Haryana	7,443	7.3	378	7.7	7,821	50
Orissa	12,859	15.8	79	94.9	12,938	43
Uttar Pradesh	47,278	5.5	5,729	89.7	53,007	43
Madhya Pradesh	22,103	8.9	215	61.4	22,318	36
Bihar	28,137	8.2	96	—	28,233	35

Source: Centre for Monitoring Indian Economy : Basic Statistics relating to the Indian Economy, Vol. 2 : States, Bombay, September 1991.

Most of the increase in agricultural production has been achieved through increase in output of foodgrains, from 50.8 million tonnes in 1950-51 to 176.2 million tonnes in 1990-91 (Tata Services Ltd., 1992-93, Table 18.1). The area under foodgrains is nearly 80 per cent of the total cropped area and maximum attention has been paid to it under the agricultural development programmes of the Five-Year Plans. The primary goal of agricultural policy under the plans especially since the mid-1960s has been to achieve "self-sufficiency" in supply of foodgrains in order to avoid large and rising imports. "Self-sufficiency" was achieved by 1971 and thereafter production of foodgrains has increased steadily in step with the increase in demand with the result that there have been only small imports of foodgrains even in years of widespread drought such as 1987-88.

Table 18.2B : Rural Health Services : 31 December, 1988*

Major States	*Primary Health Centre (PHC)*	*Sub-Centre*	*Community Health Centres*	*Total*	
				Number	*Per lakh of rural population 1981*
Punjab	1,856	2,753	44	4,653	38.5
Gujarat	668	6,366	106	7,140	30.5
Tamil Nadu	838	8,200	72	9,110	28.0
Maharashtra	1,539	9,238	277	11,054	27.1
Uttar Pradesh	2,476	20,153	142	22,771	25.0
Haryana	304	2,186	32	2,522	25.0
Karnataka	629	5,714	126	6,469	24.5
Madhya Pradesh	1,034	8,915	115	10,064	24.2
West Bengal	1,411	7,873	81	9,365	23.4
Orissa	789	5,291	83	6,163	26.5
Andhra Pradesh (a)	1,283	7,894	46	9,223	22.5
Kerala (b)	585	3,874	29	4,488	21.7
Rajasthan	588	4,792	86	5,466	20.2
Bihar	1,555	10,449	78	12,082	19.7

Highlights:

* Many Studies are reported to have indicated that people in rural areas generally prefer private doctors for treatment. Besides physical inaccessibility of a PHC, other reasons for poor utilization of government health services include : "PHC doctors/staff are not always available/do not help in time", "good/standard medicines are not available at PHCs", etc.
* It is difficult to expect an initiative for radical changes would come from political leaders unless strong pressures are brought in by voluntary agencies or professional associations.

Source : Centre for Monitoring Indian Economy : Basic Statistics relating to the Indian Economy, Vol. 2 : States, Bombay, September 1991.

The increase in agricultural production has not been confined, however, to food grains alone. There have been increases also in production of other important crops—cotton, jute, oilseeds, sugarcane and beverages, and livestock products—milk, meat and poultry. The increase in the crops during the two decades, 1970-71 to 1990-91, are given in Table 18.3.

Table 18.3 : Increase in Production of Various Crops during 1970-71—1990-91

(In million tonnes)

Crops	1970-71	1990-91
Food grains	108.4	176.2
Cereals	96.6	162.2
Pulses	11.8	14.0
Oilseeds@	9.6	18.4
Tobacco	0.36	0.45
Cotton (lint)#	4.8	9.8
Jute#	4.9	7.8
Sugarcane (cane-weight)	126.4	240.3
Tea*	0.42	0.71
Coffee	0.11	0.17

@ Comprising groundnut, rape seed & mustard, sesame, linseed, castor seed, sunflower and soyabean.

Cotton in million bales of 170 k.g. each and jute in million bales of 180 kg. each

* Calendar years.

Source :Statistical Outline of India 1992-93, p. 50.
Tata Services Ltd., Department of Economics and Statistics, Bombay, 1992.

The "self-sufficiency" has been achieved only because a large proportion of the population, estimated at 40 per cent of the total in 1983-84 was still below the poverty line which is defined by deficiency in calorie intake below the level needed for subsistence (Krishnaswamy p.6). This population suffers from various diseases resulting from the deficiency of calorie intake. In order to eliminate this deficiency and to provide adequate calories to the entire population the output of foodgrains must be much higher than 176.2 million tonnes produced in 1990-91. Furthermore, if the entire population is to have a balanced diet, essential for maintaining health and productivity, production of protective foods—oil, vegetables, fruit and livestock products (milk, poultry products, meat and fish) must also increase much faster than hitherto. In other words, there must be faster growth of production in both agriculture and animal husbandry.

Disparity in Productivity between Workers in Agriculture and Non-agricultural Sectors

According to the Census of India 1991, two-thirds (66.9 per cent) of the main workers were engaged in agriculture and allied industries (Registrar

General and Census Commissioner, India, Paper 3, p. 5). At the same time, data given in the Eighth Five-Year Plan 1992-97 (Planning Commission 1992, p. 5), indicate that agriculture contributed during 1985-86 to 1989-90, one-third (32.8 per cent) of the GDP. Thus, productivity per worker in agriculture is one-fourth of productivity per worker in the non-agricultural sectors. Furthermore, the difference has increased progressively over the years. During the five-year period, 1951-52—1955-56, 55 per cent of the GDP was generated in agriculture which had 68.1 per cent of the main workers (Planning Commission, 1992, p. 5 and Registrar General and Census Commissioner, India, 1953, p. 7). This is because growth rates of GDP in Agriculture during this period of almost 40 years have varied between 0 and 5.4 per cent while those in the non-agricultural sectors have varied between 6 and 9 per cent (Planning Commission, 1992, p. 4). It should be added that the difference in sectoral growth rates would continue during the period of the Eighth Five-Year Plan so that by its end in 1996-97, agriculture would contribute only one-fourth (24.6 per cent) of the GDP (Planning Commission, 1992, p. 54).

The difference in growth rates between agriculture and the non-agricultural sectors forms part of structural transformation of developing economies. However, it is also accompanied in most countries by shifts of workers from agriculture to the non-agricultural sectors. Why that has not occurred in India is an important question which needs in-depth investigation by demographers and development economists.

Since agriculture is concentrated in the rural areas while the non-agricultural sectors are concentrated in urban areas, the differences in productivity per worker between agriculture and the non-agricultural sectors lead to differences in productivity per worker (and per capita income) between the rural and urban areas. Mohan (1985, p. 639) has calculated that the ratio of urban/rural income per capita had increased from 2.87 in 1980-81 to 3.19 in 1989-90 and would increase further to 3.35 by 1994-95. His figures are reproduced below:

Year	*Rural/Urban ratio of income per capita*
1980-81	1: 2.87
1984-85	1: 3.05
1989-90	1: 3.19
1994-95	1: 3.35

The large and increasing difference in per capita income between rural and urban areas is the principal driving force behind rural-to urban migration.

Since productivity of Indian workers in agricultural sector is already much lower than productivity in both the developed countries and the newly industrialized countries of East Asia—Singapore, Taiwan, Hong Kong and South Korea—the policy implication of these findings is that efforts should be concentrated on increasing productivity per worker in agriculture. The increase can be achieved through a variety of measures, which are discussed in the following paragraphs.

The measures would be more successful in the short term in the irrigated areas, which constitute 33 per cent of the total cropped areas, than in the unirrigated areas. The gross irrigated area is considerably lower, however, than the irrigation potential created by various irrigation projects. The figures for 1990-91 are given below :

1.	Gross cropped area	182.5 m.h.
2.	Gross irrigated area	59.0 m.h.
3.	Gross irrigated area as per cent Gross Cropped area	32.3 per cent
4.	Irrigation potential	82.8 m.h.
5.	Gross irrigated area as per cent Irrigation potential	71.3 per cent

Source : Tata Services Ltd. 1992, pp. 56 and 58.

Thus, a beginning has to be made by reducing the gap between the gross irrigated area and the irrigation potential. This involves : (i) greater speed in construction of tributaries and water courses from major and medium irrigation projects in order to ensure that irrigation water reaches the fields at the earliest, and (ii) greater efficiency in use of irrigation water.

Some measures such as brick lining of canals, taking off from major irrigation works, have been taken already in this direction. Brick-lining of canals reduces percolation from them. A second measure is effective drainage of irrigated areas. Both measures contribute to reducing salinity and alkalinity in areas, which have been irrigated for some decades. A third measure would be better allocation of water within the command areas of distributaries and watercourses. This will reduce wastage of water through flooding at the beginning of a channel and of shortage at its tail. This can be done most effectively by cooperative self-management of command areas by the farmers.

Higher pricing of irrigation water should also increase efficiency in its usage because both irrigation engineers and farmers would try to reduce wastage of water. In the irrigated areas of south-western United States and in Israel highly capital-intensive irrigation techniques, such as conveying water to the fields by PVC pipes and drip irrigation, are used. The techniques would not be economic in irrigated areas, which produce cereals or oilseeds, but they could prove economic in some areas which produce high value perishable crops, such as vegetables, fruit and flowers.

Increasing production of these crops for meeting both domestic demand and for export is an important measure for increasing value added in agriculture and productivity per agricultural worker. There is considerable scope for the increase because there is increasing demand for these crops in both rural and urban areas of the country and also in the Gulf countries which have large numbers of Indians.

Another area of advance is in increasing efficiency of HYV techniques to increase productivity per hectare and per worker. India has a long way to go in this direction because yields per hectare for most irrigated crops in India are lower than those in the other major producing countries.

Since two-thirds of the cropped area remains unirrigated, increasing productivity in unirrigated areas is of crucial importance. Some advance has been made in this direction in recent decades with research focused on development of drought-resistant seeds, and propagating the results through the agricultural extension organization. The efforts would need to be continued over a long period so that productivity per worker increases steadily.

Increase in agricultural production would also contribute to reduction of rural poverty because most of the rural poor are landless labourers and small, marginal farmers who rely on cultivation of small holdings of unirrigated lands.

Checking deforestation in the Himalayas and the Western Ghats and other hilly or mountainous areas, and undertaking forestation and related soil and water conservation measures in them would also make a major contribution to increase agricultural production and productivity per worker in both the irrigated and unirrigated areas. These measures would reduce the frequency and intensity of floods and coverage of fertile fields with coarse sands rendering them unproductive. Droughts would also be less frequent and less severe. Finally, there would be greater recharging of ground water which would increase the area irrigated by wells and tube-wells. The latter, accounted for 50 per cent of the gross irrigated area in 1987-88 (Tata Services Ltd., 1992, p. 57). It should be added that yields per hectare in areas irrigated by wells and tube-wells are generally higher than those irrigated by canals and tanks because watering of fields can be controlled by the farmers to meet the needs of the crops most efficiently.

The Indian Meteorological Department has made a remarkable advance in recent years in forecasting the size of the monsoon in India and its various regions. This has been done with the aid of super-computers. Further advance by it have to be in two directions :

(i) Forecasting accurately the distribution of rainfall within the monsoon season by weeks and months in every region. This will enable farmers in different regions to plan their agricultural operations within the monsoon season with minimum risk of loss, and

(ii) Making similar advances for the inter-monsoon period. These will be of particular value to farmers producing wheat, rice or other crops in this period. The principal regions are wheat-producing regions of Punjab, Haryana, western U.P. and parts of Rajasthan and rice-producing regions of Andhra Pradesh and Tamil Nadu.

It should be recognized that employment generation programmes such as the Jawahar Rozgar Yojana and the National Employment Programme would continue in the foreseeable future. The programmes reduce rural-unemployment or underemployment and increase rural incomes. Furthermore, they contribute to construction of much needed works relating to minor irrigation, rural roads and soil conservation. There is much inefficiency and widespread corruption, however, in implementation of the programmes because the programmes are considered temporary and are implemented on an *ad hoc* basis. The inefficiency and corruption could be greatly reduced so that the programmes yield the maximum benefit by recognizing their semi-permanent nature which would lead to establishment of suitable institutional structure for efficient implementation of the programmes that would also reduce corruption.

Development of Industries in Small Towns

It has been stated by the Finance Minister in a recent speech that the Government would soon launch a special strategy to promote rural industrialization and that more than 50 per cent of foreign investment proposals cleared so far is for promotion of agro-industries (Radio report, October 14, 1993). The industries would be concentrated, however, in small and medium sized towns although a large proportion of the workers in them could be drawn from surrounding villages. The main categories of agro-industries are :

(i) Manufacture, repair and servicing of modern agricultural implements, such as improved ploughs, tractors and electrical or diesel-driven pumps for irrigation, and
(ii) Processing of crops ranging from foodgrains, fibres and oil seeds to the high value perishable crops, mentioned earlier.

There is considerable scope for expansion of these industries because of the high priority given to them in the official industrialization strategy and the keen interest of foreign investors in them. It may be added that expansion and improvement of food processing industries is one of the most important objective of the Ministry of Food of the Government of India. Cold storage of fruit, potatoes and other vegetables and canning of fruits and vegetables would be important components of the agro-industries. They will reduce wastage of the products and increase rural employment and income.

The small town industrialization programme would not be limited, however, to agro-industries. Other industries, such as manufacture of components for machines and transport equipment—refrigerators, air-conditioners, kitchen appliances and automotive vehicles, could be located in them, with assembly of finished products being located in the larger towns or cities. The assemblers would also maintain strict quality control. This practice is widespread in Japan, the newly industrialized countries of East Asia, and is expanding in India.

Programmes of diffusion of marketable skills among the rural workers would contribute to success of small town industrialization because skilled worker for the industries could be drawn from neighbouring villages instead of being imported from distant areas.

The skill formation programmes would also reduce pressure of rural-to-urban migration. This has been demonstrated by the experience of migration into Delhi from neighbouring states during the period from before 1961 to 1981. The proportion of migrants to the city from Haryana and Punjab declined during this period while that of from U.P. increased. The figures given in the Regional Plan NCR 2001 are reproduced in Table 18.4.

Table 18.4 : Migrants to Delhi by States of their Origin

State	*Before 1961*	*1961-71*	*1971-81*	*Period not known*	*Total*
Haryana	98324 (22.1)	85945 (16.4)	159028 (12.9)	14412	357709 (15.5)
Madhya Pradesh	5585 (1.2)	8860 (1.7)	37709 (3.1)	2496	54650 (2.4)
Punjab	74944 (16.8)	59503 (11.3)	78671 (6.4)	11447	224565 (9.8)
Rajasthan	33341 (7.5)	39885 (7.6)	93836 (7.6)	7603	174665 (7.6)
Uttar Pradesh	185550 (41.7)	260748 (49.6)	616021 (50.1)	54362	1107681 (48.2)
Others (Including outside India)	47311 (10.7)	70368 (13.4)	244480 (19.9)	17823	379982 (16.5)
Total	445055 (100.0)	525309 (100.0)	1229745 (100.0)	99143	2299252 (100.0)

Note : Figures in brackets indicate per cent to the respective totals.
*Source :*Regional Plan 2001, National Capital Region, Table 3, p. 138.

Most of the present migrants from Punjab and Haryana take up jobs in the formal and informal sectors in the city which require marketable skills or education up to high schools or higher levels. Those with skills of masons, carpenters and repairmen of mechanical, electrical or electronic equipment find work readily on commuting to the city. Those with high school or higher level education seek and generally succeed in getting employment as white-collar workers though they may have to wait for the jobs for sometime. They are better paid and have a higher standard of living, including living in brick and mortar houses which have running water, electricity and surface drainage, than most of the migrants from U.P. and other states, such as Bihar and Rajasthan. The latter are unskilled and take up low paid jobs as construction workers, gardeners, watch men and live in slums. Migrants from Rajasthan tend to concentrate in the construction industry while those from the other states take up the other low paid jobs.

Conclusion

This chapter has emphasized the importance of education in its broadest sense, consisting of universal adult literacy, primary education, and education in environmental sanitation, health care and nutrition, agricultural extension and diffusion of marketable skills. Furthermore, it brings out that the educational programmes should give equal, if not greater, emphasis to females as to males. The importance of female literacy in lowering the growth rates of population, birth, death and infant mortality and raising life expectancy at birth has been demonstrated by the experience of Kerala. It may be added that Kerala could also have a higher proportion of women possessing marketable skills than women of other states. The most visible evidence of this is the presence of large numbers of nurses from Kerala in hospitals in India and abroad, especially in the Gulf countries.

The experience with the programmes of achieving total literacy, undertaken in Kerala and Panipat area of Haryana between 1990 and 1992, demonstrate that the programmes do not require large public investment or involvement of officials, but they do require strong political and administrative support from the government. Both programmes were implemented quite efficiently by NGOs who recruited volunteer educators for them and gave them small financial incentives in comparison with the salaries of officials executing such programmes.

Skill formation programmes should also not require large public investment. The skills of carpentry, smithy, masonry, tailoring and repair of electrical or electronic equipments are acquired largely through the traditional apprentice system; vocational institutions run by the government or by NGOs have only a supplementary role in them. Training for nursing or teaching are exceptions to this rule because a diploma or a degree from a recognized institution is required for acquiring the needed proficiency and getting suitable job in these professions.

There is need for in-depth investigation of the economic, social and cultural factors in various states and regions of India which account for the wide differences in literacy and education. Similar in-depth investigations are needed to ascertain why particular skills are concentrated among particular groups and regions.

An important role of the government is (i) to sponsor, through the Universities and research institutions, investigations into the historical, social, cultural and economic reasons that account for the large inter-state and inter-group differences in literacy, education and skills, and (ii) to convince the rural population through the Panchayati Raj institutions that literacy and skills can be useful in modernization or diversification of agriculture and increase in the income and level of living of the farmers. The investigations should focus on answering questions such as the following :

- What role have the traditional matriarchal system and the educational efforts of the Churches had in the very high level of female (and male) literacy in the state?
- Why is literacy so much lower in the northern and central Hindi speaking states than in other states?
- Why are skills of carpenter, smith, electrician etc., so much greater among certain caste groups than among others?
- What influence has the caste system or experience like service in the Armed Forces has had in contributing to possession of these skills?

The linkage between literacy and modernization or diversification of agriculture can be demonstrated by the fact that a literate farmer can read literature about use of improved seed, chemical fertilizers and pesticides distributed by the agricultural extension organization or the marketing companies and does not have to rely exclusively on demonstrations and related efforts of the extension staff. He and his wife can read the literature about poultry-keeping and production of milk. Through the literature they can know the common diseases of poultry and cattle and how to avoid them. Furthermore, they will know the elements of environmental sanitation and treatment of minor ailments in the family and need not rely exclusively on folk medicine.

Table 18.5 : Population, Literacy rates, per cent of rural population, Principal exports to towns—Sawai Madhopur and Pali 1961-1991

	Sawai Madhopur		*Pali*	
Area (sq. k.m.)	*10,527*		*12,387*	
	1961	*1991*	*1961*	*1991*
Population ('000)	944	1954	806	1485
Rural	847	1663	729	1162
Urban	96	291	77	323
Principal towns (Population of Urban Areas in '000)				
Sawai Madhopur	21.0	77.6	33.3	136.8
Karauli	23.7	49.0	46.5*	30.0*
Gangapur	22.6	69.0		
Hindaun	20.2	60.7		
Literacy rate (per cent)				
Total	12.6	28.7	13.6	33.3
Male	21.0	43.3	21.9	43.7
Female	3.0	11.7	4.9	25.4
Percentage of Rural Population served in 1981 by :				
Electric supply		49.5		74.3
Pucca roads		35.0		22.1
Primary schools		89.1		96.0
Health centres		36.6		47.7
Post and telegraph centres		60.7		70.1
Principal exports from towns				
Sawai Madhopur	*Biris*, raw cotton, foodgrains			
Gangapur City	Groundnuts, rice, other foodgrains			
Hindaun	Sandstone, slate, foodgrains			
Karauli	Lac bangles, sandstone and *gur* (brown sugar)			
Pali	Coarse cotton yarn and cloth, printed sarees, plastic bangles			
Sajot	Limestone, chemicals and foodgrains			

Sources:

1. Census of India 1961—District Census Handbooks for Sawai Madhopur and Pali. District Primary Census Abstracts. (pp. 8-9).
2. Census of India 1981—District Census Handbooks for Sawai Madhopur and Pali. District Primary Census Abstracts (pp. 8-9).
3. Census of India 1991, Series-1 India. Paper 2 of 1991: Provisional Population Totals : Rural-Urban Distribution. (pp. 132-133 & 290-291).

REFERENCES

Economic and Political Weekly, Bombay, India.

Government of India, National Capital Region Planning Board, Ministry of Urban Development: *Regional Plan 2001, National Capital Region*, New Delhi 1988.

Government of India, Planning Commission, *Eighth Five-Year Plan 1992-97*. Vol. 1, New Delhi 1992.

Krishnaswami, K.S. (Ed): *Poverty and Income Distribution.* Oxford University Press, Bombay 1990.

Mohan, R.: Urbanization in India's Future. *Population and Development Review*, New York, Vol. 11, No. 4 (December 1985).

Registrar General and Census Commissioner, India, New Delhi:

(i) Census of India 1991, Paper-1 of 1991: Provisional Population Totals.

(ii) Paper-3 of 1991: Provisional Population Totals : Workers and their Distribution, New Delhi, 1992.

Tata Service Ltd. Department of Economic and Statistics : *Statistical Outline of India 1992-93*, Bombay, October 1992.

Times of India, New Delhi.

19

Agricultural Growth Under High Population Pressure : The Case of India*

Introduction

This chapter brings out, with India as the case example, the constraints and the potential of agricultural growth in underdeveloped countries with high population pressure on agricultural resources, using the technology of the 1970s, but without break-up of the socio-economic organization of peasant agriculture.

On the relationship between growth of population and agricultural output, there are two, almost opposite views. In the classical Malthusian view, the limits to population growth are set by the capacity to produce food. The view has been revived in the post-War period by the neo-Malthusians in the wake of the spectacular population growth in the under-developed countries and return of the Malthusian checks of war, pestilence and famine have been held up as the inevitable prospects for the countries (Census of India 1951). On the other hand, Boserup has recently advanced the contrary view under which population growth is the autonomous variable and the dominant cause of agricultural growth which takes place through expansion of cropped area (principally through shortening of fallows), intensification of agriculture and improvement of techniques (Boserup, 1965). According to this author India's experience, apart from its intrinsic importance to the current world agricultural and demographic outlook because of the large size of the country, is useful in understanding the prospects and problems of agricultural growth in these countries. The

* This paper was presented by V. Nath at the South Eastern Division of American Association of Geographers held at Lexington, Kentucky on November 22, 1971 in the Asia Session.

pressure of population is very high and the trends in agricultural output, including those under the influence of the post-War official efforts to accelerate agricultural growth under the Five Year Plans, are very well documented. After a brief reference to earlier trends, the author focuses on analysis of some aspects of the recent increase in food output with use of the high-yielding (dwarf) varieties of cereals, in association with intensive use of chemical fertilizers and other inputs, the so called 'Green Revolution'. The author examines the current official strategy of agricultural growth with reference to the constraints on growth in the Indian situation, and concludes that (i) suitable, modern capital-and-technology-intensive techniques can be successfully introduced in peasant economies with high population pressure; (ii) diffusion of the techniques can be rapid; (iii) the employment-reducing and social-polarization effects of the techniques, about which much concern has been expressed, may have been overestimated; and (iv) on the contrary, the increase in agricultural output and incomes resulting from use of the techniques have created significant new opportunities for raising the economic levels of the poorer groups within agriculture.

Expressions of High Population Pressure (HPP)

Existence of HPP on land in India is indicated in a variety of ways—(i) extremely low average per capita income of $73 and only $53.5 in the agricultural sector (Planning Commission, First Five-Year Plan, 1952); (ii) very low consumption levels, with large sections of the population, an estimated 13 per cent of the rural and 50 per cent of the urban below the minimum calorie intake level (Dandekar, 1971); and (iii) the difficulty of meeting the demand for food even at such low consumption levels, although as much as 45 per cent (44.8 per cent in 1966-67) of the geographical area is under crops and 75 per cent (73.5 per cent in 1966-67) of the cropland is under foodgrains (Government of India Growth Rates in Agricultural, 1966). Another set of indicators relate to the large labour surplus in agriculture, which contains 70 per cent of the labour force (Census of Population, 1991, p. 30). The great majority of the cultivated holdings are extremely small. In 1960-61, 63 per cent are below 5 acres, and as many as 20 per cent are below 1 acre (Sharma, 1967, p. 228, Table 13), and there are large numbers of landless agricultural workers; more than one-third of the agricultural workers reported agricultural labour, rather than cultivation, as their main occupation (Population Census, 1961, p. 30). At the lower end of the agricultural scale, the households combine cultivation of tiny bits of land (often as tenants or sharecroppers) with labour, agricultural and non-agricultural. Underemployment is widespread, with a large proportion of the labour force without employment for varying periods of the year. It is clear that at the present levels of technology and organization, agriculture can neither provide adequate employment to the large numbers dependent upon it, nor yield the output needed for attaining even the minimum consumption levels by the population. Some of the phenomena—low level of technique and existence of large labour surplus are characteristic of agriculture in densely populated, underdeveloped countries; but others, such as the very low socio-religious status of the small agriculturists-*cum*-labourers, most of them belong to the Scheduled Castes, Scheduled Tribes and other socially depressed groups are distinctive to India.

Inter-group Disparities within Agriculture-Rural Tensions

Since the adoption of the New Agricultural Strategy (NAS) by the Indian Government it has been argued that it will greatly increase economic disparities within the agricultural sector and lead to a growing polarization of the rural society. It is argued that (i) only the richer, larger-size farmers will have the resources and the incentives to adopt the new technology and to increase output while the small farmers, unable to adopt the new technology and to compete with them, will be progressively squeezed out of agriculture. (ii) Second, mechanization of agriculture, essential for successful adoption of the new technology, will throw large numbers of agricultural labourers out of work; the two together will create a problem of unemployment of small farmers and agricultural labourers of colossal proportions. The growing agrarian unrest in some parts of India is also attributed to introduction of the new capital-and-technology intensive programmes. These fears, expressed by a large number of observers of Indian agriculture, reflect a basic problem in introduction of modern-capital intensive technology in a situation of high population pressure on agricultural resources. But the fears were expressed mainly within the first 1-2 years of adoption of the NAS, and are not based on evidence of field experience of operation of the HYV (High Yielding Variety) programme. Such evidence is very meagre, despite the keen interest in these issues.

The evidence, reviewed in this chapter, relates to Punjab in which diffusion of HYV and consequent increase in yields has been most rapid. The evidence indicates that :

(i) Adoption of the HYV is already nearly universal, benefiting both large and small cultivators;

(ii) A number of technical innovations, such as electric irrigation pumps and mechanical threshers are available equally to the large and small cultivators; the practice of customary sales of services contributes significantly to wider availability of modern innovations; and

(iii) The reduction in the demand for human energy, consequent on adoption of HYV and a package of mechanization is marginal and is compensated to some extent by a better seasonal distribution of demand, which results in reduction of peak period shortage of labour.

It has been pointed also by some observers that agrarian unrest has been far more pronounced in West Bengal, Andhra Pradesh and Kerala, in which agricultural growth has been much slower than in Punjab.

The experience of Punjab, limited and perhaps not typical, does not substantiate the fears about polarization and unemployment-creating effects of adoption of the new technology. Further evidence, based on longer experience and experience of other states, needs to be obtained.

The plan programmes for increasing agricultural output have had four main components :

(i) Extension of irrigation through programmes ranging from construction of large storage reservoir-and-canal projects, such as the Bhakra-Nangal on the river Satluj in Punjab which irrigates millions of hectares, to assistance to farmers and rural communities to construct, renovate or modernize small irrigation works, such as tanks, wells, tube-wells and others. The small works are a very important part of the irrigation systems of India; nearly 60 per cent of the total irrigated area (in 1970-71) is benefited from them (Tata Consultancy Services, 1998-99, p. 64).

(ii) Creation of a countrywide extension, and supplies organizations to take to the farmers knowledge of improved technique and supplies of essential inputs such as good seeds, chemical fertilizers and pesticides;

(iii) A major expansion of cooperative credit to provide to the farmers credit at low rates of interest; and

(iv) Land reforms, specifically abolition of intermediary tenure such as *zamindari* and giving rights in lands to the actual cultivators, and increasing security of tenures.

Aided in part by good monsoons in the early 1950s, agricultural and food output increased steadily during the decade (see Table 10 of Chapter 17 'Population, Natural Resources and Economic Development in India'); the rate of increase of food output, 3 per cent a year during 1949-50—1964-65 was appreciably higher than the rate of population increase of 2.5 per cent a year. The food shortage was overcome by the mid-1950s, and although imports of foodgrains continued, they were not too large—an average of 2.5 m.t. during 1951-55 and 3.5 m.t. during 1956-60 (*Ibid*, Table 11). The planners felt reassured enough by the progress to shift the focus of their attention from agricultural growth to industrialization; the proportion of total public investment in agricultural programmes which had been as high as 40 per cent in the First Five-Year Plan was reduced to 20-22 per cent during the Second and Third Five-Year Plans.

The Indian agricultural development effort under the Five Year Plans has been dominated by the need to maintain an adequate rate of increase of food output in order to meet the increases in demand for food resulting from growth of population of nearly 2.5 per cent a year and increase in incomes with the economy growing at almost 5 per cent per annum (*Ibid*, Table 14). Successive Five Year Plans have reiterated the objective of raising food output rapidly and attaining self-sufficiency in food supplies (elimination of food import). But achieving an adequate rate of increase in food output has proved to be difficult and food shortages caused by shortfalls in output have been frequent; those during the drought years, 1965-67, when widespread famine could be averted only by very large imports of foodgrains, 9-10 m.t. a year (*Ibid*, Table 11), being the most serious. India inherited a food shortage at Independence. Its immediate causes were disruption of rice imports from Burma since 1942 (and the difficulty of obtaining adequate quantities of rice in the post-war situation of worldwide shortage) and loss of the food surplus areas of Punjab and Sindh to Pakistan. But the longer-term and more fundamental causes were secular stagnation in agriculture and increasing pressure of a growing population on agricultural resources, extending over several decades before Independence. Blyn's (1966) analysis of trends in crop output and population growth during the period, 1891-92 to 1945-46, shows that while the population of British India increased at an average annual rate of 0.67 per cent, the rates of increase of crop output and foodgrains output were 0.37 per cent and 0.11 per cent respectively. The rates of increase of output are lower still if Punjab and Sindh (now in Pakistan) in which there was fairly rapid growth of agricultural output in the wake of extension of canal irrigation are excluded. The agricultural stagnation, resulted in replacement of food exports by imports, despite progressive decline in per capita consumption, from the 1920s, when population began to increase steadily at 1.00 to 1.25 per cent a year; the earlier demographic experience had been one of intermittent and in the aggregate a low net increase in population.

Problems associated with addition of the New Agricultural Strategy Inter-group disparities-rural tensions:

(i) Since the adoption of the New Agricultural Strategy (NAS) by the Indian Government, fears have been expressed that it will greatly increase economic disparities within the agricultural sector and lead to increasing polarization of the rural society. It is argued that only the richer, larger-size farmers will have the resources and the incentives to adopt the new technology and increase output, while the small farmers, unable to adopt the new technology and to compete with them, will be progressively squeezed out of agriculture.

(ii) A second fear concerns large numbers of tenants and sharecroppers being dispossessed because the owners of the lands which they cultivated, finding that self-cultivation of the lands by using the new technology and hired labour was more profitable than giving it out for cultivation, would resume the lands. Ladejinsky (1965) lists increase in price of land and in rents, as a result of the greatly increased profitability of agriculture as another factor contributing to the squeeze on the sharecroppers.

(iii) It is stated that mechanization of agriculture, essential for successful adoption of the new technology, will throw large numbers of agricultural workers out of work and will greatly aggravate an already difficult employment situation. Dandekar and Rath (1971) sum up with the statement, "The fact which is concealed today will become evident, namely, that there is not room enough in agriculture for so many people." The HYV and the earlier Intensive Agricultural Development Programme (IADP) are also believed to have contributed to increasing social polarization and agrarian tensions.

These fears, which have been expressed by a number of observers of the 'Green Revolution' in India and other Asian countries bring out what is perhaps the most difficult problem in introducing high productivity capital-intensive, technology under conditions of high population pressure, and the large economic and social disparities that are generally associated with the latter. The Indian policy makers' concern with these issues is apparent from special programmes for the small farmers and agricultural labourers included in the Fourth Plan and the exhortation by the Central Government on the governments of the states for speedier and more effective implementation of land reforms.

But, despite the keen interest in these issues, hard data based on field experience of the effects of the HYV programme on small farmers and agricultural labourers or on inter-group relations within agriculture are scarce and one must rely on a very few field studies to get an indication of the effects. Ladejinsky, Wolf (1965), perhaps the most influential observer of the programme has based his opinion on two brief field trips in Punjab and Bihar. The following discussion relates mainly to the Punjab for which field data are somewhat more reliable than for the other states. The average holding size is somewhat larger and the proportions of small farmers and agricultural labourers are lower in the state than the all-India averages; on the other hand, the proportion of land held under pure and mixed tenancies is higher than the national average. But the differences are not such as would materially alter the effect of adoption of the new technology on the small farmers, tenants or agricultural labourers.

Among the components of the new technology, use of high-yielding seed and chemical fertilizers is scale-neutral. This is brought out by the very large proportion of the wheat area already under the HYV. The small farmers are at no disadvantage also in electrification of irrigation wells, because "Typically farms large enough to support a team of bullocks (7 to 10 acres) appear equally able to support a pump set (although not a tube-well) which may be put upon a dug well or channel." Any disadvantage that the small farmers may have in this respect is mitigated by the existence of the large and rapidly expanding network of state tube-wells, and by the practice of sale of water, in excess of their own requirements, by the owners of pump sets and tube-wells. Small farmers do have a disadvantage in use of farm machinery, especially tractors. Billing and Singh (1970) estimated that for efficient and economical utilization of a medium-sized (35 h.p.) tractor, which is the most popular in the state, an operating unit of 30 acres of net sown area or 50 acres of gross cropped area is needed. As for the need (or advantage) of using farm machinery along with the HYV, they say, "Practically however their (HYVs) presence means intensive mechanized irrigation and later mechanized harvesting and threshing. The HYV demands faster seedbed preparation to gain full benefit from their shorter duration through multiple cropping. In the context of proper economic incentives, the HYV are the thin end of the wedge which will very likely lead to progressive mechanization of agriculture although their short-run effect is labour-intensive." The disadvantage of the small farmers is reduced somewhat by the practice of custom ploughing of their lands by the owners of tractors—many are non-farmers—and will be greatly reduced if suitable, small, garden tractors become available. The practice of custom—sale of service has become very widespread in case of another machine, the grain thresher, so much so that an estimated 50 per cent of the wheat crop was threshed by it in 1968-69 and the proportion is expected to go up to 90 per cent by 1973-74. In this case, "owners usually set up their machines along highways in the fields and farmers bring their crop to the site. The operation is therefore both custom and entirely neutral to scale." Thus the small farmers of Punjab do not appear to be at a serious disadvantage in adoption of the new technology.

Of course, economic disparities between the large and small farmers would increase even if the two groups raised their output in the same proportion, because the absolute increments of the large farmers would be so much greater. The saving differentials between the groups would be larger still because a smaller proportion of the output of the large farmers would need to be devoted to current consumption. On the other hand, adoption of the new technology lowers the minimum holding size needed for economic viability, thus converting large numbers of non-viable farmers into viable ones. A study in Gujarat indicates that the minimum size of the viable farm was reduced with use of hybrid *bajra* (a millet) from 9-10 acres to 4.5 to 7 acres. Viability was defined in the study as having an adequate income to maintain the family at its customary level of living.

Eviction of Tenants and Agrarian Tensions

Eviction of tenants and resumption of lands by the owners has been reported from several states since the 1950s, when land reforms, such as abolition of *zamindari*, aimed at giving land rights to the actual cultivators were undertaken; a detailed account appears in an official report on implementation of land reforms (Planning Commission, 1959). The

National Sample Survey revealed a marked decline in the areas cultivated under tenancies between the 8th (1953-54) and the 16th (1960-61) rounds of the Survey :

		Area leased as per cent of total operated area
N.S.S: 8th round (1953-54)	–	20.34 per cent
N.S.S: 16th round (1960-61)	–	12.53 per cent

The validity of these figures has been questioned. Reporting on tenancy is undoubtedly vitiated in a complex situation in which both the land-owners and the tenants are afraid to report the true facts, the farmer for fear of losing their rights to land and the latter the opportunity to cultivate it, often based on an oral lens. But resumption of lands by the owners and decline in tenancy, if any, would thus appear to be related primarily to land reform legislation and not to the adoption of the new technology. Ladejinsky, Wolf (1965) refers in his Bihar field note to the "mounting determination among owners not to permit the tenants to share in the rights of lands they cultivate. Their preference is to be rid of them", but gives no instances of rejection of tenants or other evidence in support of the statement. The linkage between adoption of the new technology and agrarian unrest has been questioned by scholars who point out that the unrest has been far more pronounced in recent years in West Bengal, Andhra Pradesh and Kerala, in which agricultural growth has been slow than in Punjab.

Several of the areas of acute unrest listed, e.g. the Naxalbari area of West Bengal in which the Naxalite movement originated, are those in which a large proportion of the cultivators are of Scheduled Tribes and it would appear that the particular difficulties faced by these people are a factor in the unrest and impediment to agricultural growth in the Eastern States. These are also the rice growing areas, a crop in which the increase in rice output has been modest, less than 10 per cent, due mainly to the failure of the new rice varieties to withstand pests and diseases. This has been the major disappointment in the HYV programme. The increases in output of wheat and maize are confined, moreover, to the northern states of Punjab and Uttar Pradesh in which most of the area under the crops are irrigated; outputs have increased little in other states (such as Madhya Pradesh, Rajasthan) in which most of the areas under the crops are unirrigated. Finally, the increase in foodgrain output is barely adequate to meet the needs of population growth at current consumption level, any improvement in the level, to alleviate widespread undernutrition, will require faster growth. Even with the record output in 1970-71 of 107.8 m.t. and a total supply, including imports, of 111.4 m.t. net per capita availability of foodgrains was only marginally higher than the pre-drought (1965) figure of 173 kg. The Fourth Plan Projects an increase in per capita availability to nearly 200 kg. by 1973-74; but achievement of its foodgrains output target of 129 m.t. will require acceleration.

Accentuation of inter-state differences in agricultural growth will create difficult problems of allocation of scarce resources (finance, scarce inputs such as chemical fertilizers and pesticides) by the Central Government, and of pricing and movement of foodgrains because the rapid growth of food-surplus states and the slow growth of food-deficit states will be ranged on opposite sides on these issues. Second, since agricultural growth and overall economic growth are closely related in a predominantly agricultural economy, the increasing agricultural growth differentials will have corresponding effects on economic growth. The latter will, in turn, make achievement of the planners' objectives of reduction of regional disparities in development increasingly difficult and also increase regional tensions.

Effects on Agricultural Labour

Billing and Singh made a detailed estimate of the demand for human energy in agriculture of Punjab in 1968-69, and also a projection of the demand to 1983-84 (*Economic and Political Weekly,* 1969). Three sets of estimates were made for each year, based on assumptions respectively of: (i) use of conventional technology; (ii) use of HYV without mechanization; and (iii) use of HYV with mechanization. The last estimates are based on estimates of the numbers of power driven implements actually in use in 1968-69 and projections of increase to 1983-84. The estimates indicated that in 1968-69, the shift from conventional technology to HYV would have increased demand for human energy by 6 per cent, but the power-driven implements that were in use, had led to labour saving equivalent to 12 per cent of the total demand so that there was a net reduction of 6 per cent in the demand for human energy. For 1983-84 similarly, use of HYV alone, would increase human energy requirement by 18 per cent, but as a result of the projected increase in mechanization, the net demand would be lower than with conventional technology by 17 per cent. As against this reduction in total demand for human energy, use of HYV and mechanization make for a somewhat better seasonal distribution; the duration of the periods of peak demand is increased and the peak-period shortage of labour is reduced. The shortage has been experienced in the state since the introduction of HYV and during the first two years, 1967-68 and 1968-69, wages of agricultural labourers rose sharply during the peak demand periods (Ladejinsky: from 10 rupees to 15 rupees a day).

The average wage level has also increased significantly, but since foodgrains prices have risen sharply also, the net benefit to agricultural labourers has been in doubt. One recent study indicates, however, a net gain to agricultural labourers (after discounting the effects of rise in foodgrain prices) of 25 per cent between 1963-64—1964-65 (average) and 1968-69—1969-70 (average).

In this context, it is necessary also to refer to the new opportunities for non-agricultural labour resulting from increases in farm output and income with adoption of the new technology. The opportunities arise mainly in (i) distribution of new inputs, such as HYV seed, chemical fertilizers, and implements, and servicing and repair of the latter; (ii) marketing, transport and processing of the output; and (iii) construction and related activities.

The opportunities have particular significance in Punjab because relatively rapid agricultural growth has been accompanied in it from the mid-1950s with vigorous growth of small industries, which are located frequently in small towns and even large villages. The penetration of industry into rural areas has resulted in diffusion of industrial skills in the rural population which had led to vigorous technological change in agriculture and could be an important factor in rapid diffusion of HYV and the associated modern technology. Furthermore, increase in food output, resulting from adoption of HYV has removed a major constraint on undertaking large programmes of employment of surplus agricultural labour in capital-creation programmes.

The contribution of the programmes to capital formation and even more to welfare of agricultural labourers has been recognized in India and they have been included in every Five Year Plan. But their size has been limited, particularly during the 1960s by the food shortage. The programmes increase demand for food, because income elasticity of demand for food is very high among the rural population—almost 0.8 per cent. The large programme included in the Fourth Five-Year Plan, and the recent plea by Dandekar and Rath (1971) for undertaking a much larger programme as the principal measure for relief of poverty in India reflects the linkage between the programmes and increase in food output.

But within the irrigated wheat region of the north-west, spread of the new HYVs has been very rapid—significantly more rapid than the spread, during the 1930s, of hybrid corn in Iowa, which was the most progressive state of US in adoption of the practice. In both Punjab and U.P., 90 per cent coverage of the irrigated wheat area by the HYVs was reached by the fifth year of adoption (1970-71), as against similar coverage by hybrid corn in Iowa, in the eighth year (1941). Furthermore, in Punjab, but not in U.P., the increase in yield consequent on adoption of the HYV (75 per cent by the fifth year) has been much greater than (38 per cent the fifth year) in Iowa. It should be mentioned that successful adoption of the HYVs requires much larger investment and changes in management practices, than did adoption of hybrid corn. High yields can be obtained with the HYV, only if it is accompanied by intensive use of chemical fertilizers and efficient water management; the latter may require considerable investment in improvement of irrigation facilities. The rapid increases in consumption of chemical fertilizers and in the numbers of irrigation pumps, after spread of the HYV, in both Punjab and U.P., indicates that these investments and changes in management practice are being made. It is true that adoption of the HYVs has been stimulated by an unusually favourable price situation; wholesale prices of wheat increased by about 50 per cent between 1965-66 and 1968-69, while adoption of hybrid corn had been retarded by the economic depression of the 1930s. But the experience does indicate that the rate of diffusion of new, decisively superior agricultural techniques among peasant communities can now be comparable, or higher than the rate in the most progressive areas of the U.S.A. during the 1930s.

Resulting in replacement of food exports by imports, despite progressive decline in per capita consumption, from the 1920s, when population began to increase steadily at 1.00 to 1.25 per cent a year; the earlier demographic experience had been one of intermittent and a low net increase in population.

Conclusion

The conservatism and handicaps of the peasants' small scale of operations, meagre resources and limited capacity to take risks and the infrastructures of diffusion—agricultural extension, supplies and credit organizations or the efficiency of communication in densely populated rural communities are apparently effective enough to counter some of these handicaps.

These would lead one to conclude :

Either the peasants' handicaps of small scale of operations, meagre resources, limited capacity to take risks and 'conservatism' are not so serious as to prevent rapid acceptance of decisively superior new practices,

Or the infrastructures of diffusion—the agricultural extension, supplies and credit organizations built up in India (and other countries) in the post-Independence period and the efficiency of communications in densely populated rural communities are effective enough to offset the handicaps.

REFERENCES

Billing and Singh :

(i) Labour and the Green Revolution : *Economic and Political Weekly*, Bombay Vol. 52, 1969.

(ii) Mechanization and Rural Employment with some Implications for Rural Income and Distribution. *Economic and Political Weekly*, Bombay. June 27, 1970.

Blyn, G : *Trends in Crop Output and Population Growth in Agricultural Trends in India, 1891-1947: Output Availability and Productivity*. Philadelphia, Pennsylvania, 1966.

Boserup, E. : *Conditions of Agricultural Growth:* The Economics of Agrarian Change Under Population Pressures, London; George Allen & Unwin, 1965.

Chakraborty, D.: "From Green Revolution to Liberalization", *Growth of Agrarian Capitalism in Punjab*, Jawahar Lal Nehru University, New Delhi, JNU.

Dandekar, V.M.: "Poverty in India", Bombay, *Indian School of Political Economy*, 1971. Levels of Poverty measured through calories intake, 1970-71. (*Source : Economic and Political Weekly*, Vol. 6, January 2nd to 9th, 1971).

Government of India :

(i) Ministry of Food and Agriculture : *Growth Rates in Agriculture.Economic and Statistical Adviser* (New Delhi March 1966) mimeographed.

(ii) Planning Commission : *First Five Year Plan—A Draft Outline* (New Delhi 1952).

(iii) Planning Commission : *Report of the Committee of the Panel on Land Reforms*, New Delhi, 1959.

Ladedjinsky, Wolf: A Study of Tenurial Conditions in Package Districts. Planning Commission, Government of India (New Delhi 1965).

Registrar General India :

(i) *Census of India,* 1951, Vol. I, India. Part 1 A Report (Delhi 1953).

(ii) *Census of India*, 1951 : Vol. I, India Part-1-Appendices to the Census Report, 1951 (Delhi 1955).

(iii) *Census of India*, 1961: Paper No. 1 of 1962. Final Population Totals (Delhi 1962).

(iv) *Census of Population* 1991: Provisional Population Totals.

Sharma, P.S.: A Study of the Structural and Tenurial Aspects of Rural Economy in the light of the 1961 Census. In *Patterns of Population Change in India* 1951-61. ed. Bose Ashish 1967, p. 228.

Tata Consultancy Services 1998-99.

20

1991 Population Census: Some Facts and Policy Issues

I.* Registrar General and Census Commissioner, India, Census of India 1991. Series-1 India. Paper 1 of 1991. Provisional Population Totals, New Delhi March 1991, pp. 103 + iv.

Interest in the decennial censuses of population is mainly on account of their being the most comprehensive and authoritative records of demographic and associated socio-economics changes in the nation during a decade. However, the census is also an administrative undertaking of enormous magnitude and complexity. The 1991 census of population involved participation of 1.7 million volunteer enumerators and their supervisors in conducting the enumeration and staff numbering thousands in the offices of the Registrar General and Census Commissioner, India and Directors of Census Operation in the States and Union Territories for compilation and analysis of the census data and preparation of various reports and other publications. Furthermore, it involved willing co-operation of about 200 million heads of household in furnishing the data about themselves, their household and their houses, required by the census.

The census of 1991 was the fifth to be conducted since independence and the 13th since the beginning of census operations in 1872. Thus the censuses have been conducted without a break despite two world wars, famines over large parts of India during the last quarter of the 19th century, and the partition of former British India into the Indian Union and the West and East Pakistan (present Bangladesh) in 1947, which was followed by the migration of over 12 million persons across their borders. No other

* Published in *Economic and Political Weekly*, September 14, 1991, pp. 2148-2152.

developing country and few even among the developed countries can claim a comparable record in census taking. It is hoped that this record will be maintained and censuses will continue to be conducted, freely and fairly, despite the political and socio-economics changes that India may experiences during the coming decades.

The publication, *Census of India 1991 Series-1: India. Paper 1 of 1991. Provisional Population Totals*, towards the end of March 1991, barely four weeks after the end of the enumeration on March 1, of the first results of the census in the paper under review speaks highly of the speed and efficiency of processing of the census data in the offices of the Registrar General and Census Commissioner, India and of the directors of census operations in the States and Union Territories, several of whom have published similar papers. The paper presents data on the size of the population, its growth rate during 1981-1991, density of population, sex ratio, and literacy rates for males and females, in six main tables entitled 'Provisional Population Totals' in addition the paper under review contains :

16 analytical tables, 8 coloured maps of India showing the values of these variables by States and Union Territories, 9 graphs and charts, and three appendices; these reproduce the three census schedules, relating respectively to the individual, the household and the house; list the tables of various series to be generated as a result of census, village and town directories, and other proposed publications of the census.

Planning for the 1991 census had started in 1987. A number of advisory and consultative committees had been constituted to assist the Registrar General and Census Commissioner in it. The three schedules were finalized on the advice of the Data Users' Committee, which included representatives of the Planning Commission and the Central Ministries, such as Education and Health and Family Planning, which are most interested in the results of census. Special attention was given in designing the schedules to obtaining detailed and accurate information on women's participation in economic activities and on the size and type of the construction of the house, and existence within it of facilities like a latrine. The first chapter of the paper describes the organization of the census, the process of planning for conducting it, beginning with the house—listing which was done in various States and Union Territories between April and September 1990, six to nine months ahead of enumeration. The second chapter presents a summary of the census results in narrative form. Since most of the information contained in the two chapters and the three appendices is not likely to be published later, this paper needs to be obtained by all students of the census and retained as a reference document.

The large number of maps, diagrams and charts in this paper, its attractive art paper, cover and its simple, non-technical language, all appear to be aimed at presenting the results of the census in a form in which they can be easily understood by an average Legislator or an undergraduate student. But achievement of this objective will be frustrated by the fact that only 5,000 copies of the paper have been printed and since it is not priced publication, it is not available to the general public.

In order that the Census Commissioner's objective of creating widespread understanding of the facts of population and the population problems among the general public is achieved, the paper or a revised version of it, needs to be reprinted in tens of thousands of copies and distributed at a nominal price to all its potential readers. It could then be used as a text or reference material for short courses on population in colleges and high schools, besides being used for discussions by legislators and in various citizens'associations. Meanwhile a second edition of 5,000-10,000 copies should be printed immediately so that the paper can be distributed beyond the restricted circle of Legislators, senior official of the Central Government and their counterparts in the states and the Union Territories, members of social science faculties of universities and colleges and staffs of social science research institutions.

As mentioned earlier, planning for conducting the census had begun in 1987. Processing of the census data and publication of the large number of tables of various series and of other publications is expected by the Census Commissioner to continue to 1995. Thus census related activities would extend over almost a decade. This is possible because the census organization was made permanent in 1961 thus ending its earlier phoenix-like existence of three to five year before, during and after every census. The permanent status has also enabled the organization to achieve a high degree of accuracy in projecting the size and growth rate of the population, and so to attain the speed and efficiency in processing the census results. The provisional population total of 843.9 million is only 0.04 per cent higher than the estimate of 843.6 million made by the Expert Committee on projections (Table 20.1).

Table 20.1: Provisional and Projected Population of India, States and Union Territories as on March 1, 1991

(in '000s)

India/State/ Union Territory	*Projected population 1991[1]*	*Provisional Population 1991*	*Difference[2]*	*Per Cent Difference[3]*
1	*2*	*3*	*4*	*5*
India	*8,43,596*	*8,43,931*	*+335*	*+0.04*
States				
1. Andhra Pradesh	65,139	66,305	+986	+1.51
2. Arunachal Pradesh	836	858	+22	+2.63
3. Assam	24,802	22,294	-2,507	-10.11
4. Bihar	88,254	86,339	-1,915	-2.17
5. Goa	1,268	1,169	-99	-7.81
6. Gujarat	42,171	41,174	-997	-2.36
7. Haryana	16,747	16,318	-429	-2.56
8. Himachal Pradesh	5,340	5,111	-229	-4.29
9. Jammu and Kashmir[4]	7,719	7,719	—	—
10. Karnataka	44,855	44,817	-38	-0.08
11. Kerala	30,065	29,011	-1,054	-3.51
12. Madhya Pradesh	65,375	66,136	+761	+1.16
13. Maharashtra	77,833	78,707	+874	+1.12
14. Manipur	1850	1827	-223	-1.24
15. Meghalaya	1736	1761	+25	+1.44
16. Mizoram	695	686	-9	-1.29
17. Nagaland	1097	1216	+119	+10.85
18. Orissa	31,979	31,512	-467	-1.46
19. Punjab	20,347	20,191	-156	-0.77
20. Rajasthan	43,728	43,881	+163	+0.37
21. Sikkim	454	404	-50	-11.01
22. Tamil Nadu	55,742	55,638	-104	-0.19
23. Tripura	2667	2745	+78	-2.92
24. Uttar Pradesh	135,318	13,8760	+3442	+2.54
25. West Bengal	66,300	67,983	+1683	+2.54
Union Territories				
1. Andaman and Nicobar Islands	281	278	-3	-1.07
2. Chandigarh	711	641	-7.0	-9.85
3. Dadra and Nagar Haveli	142	138	-3	-2.11
4. Daman and Diu	100	101	+1	+1.0
5. Delhi	9054	9370	+316	+3.49
6. Lakshadweep	54	52	-2	-3.70
7. Pondicherry	368	789	+21	+2.73

Notes : (1) According to the report of the Standing Committee of Experts on Population Projection (mimeographed), October 1989.

(2) Provisional population minus projected population.

(3) Provisional minus Projected/Projected × 100 projected.

(4) The 1991 Census has not yet been conducted in Jammu and Kashmir. The figures are as per Projection made by Standing Committee of Experts on Population Projection, October 1989.

Size and Growth Rates of the Population

Perhaps the most important result of the census relates to the size and growth rate of the total population. The provisional total of 843.9 million is 9.1 million below the projection of 853 million, made by population division of the United Nations in 1988. However, after providing the possible under count of 1 to 2 per cent the revised total would approximate or exceed the projection of the United Nations. The average annual exponential growth rate of 2.11 per cent during 1981-91 is marginally lower than the rates of 2.20 per cent and 2.22 per cent recorded during the two previous decades (p. 21)*.

The committee on projections has projected decline in the growth rate of the total population from 20.1 per thousand during 1986-91 to 15.2 per thousand by 2006. The reduction would be realized through more rapid decline in the birth and fertility rates than in the death rate. Whereas the crude birth rate would fall by almost 8 percentage points—from 30.9 per thousand during 1986-91 to 23 per thousand by 2006—the corresponding reduction in the crude death rate would be by 3 percentage points, from 10.8 per thousand to 7.8 per thousand. The reduction in general fertility rate (GFR) during the period would be from 140.9 to 98.1 and in the maternal fertility rate (GMFR) from 178.7 to 132.3 per thousand (p. 40).

There is large inter-state variation in the average annual exponential growth rate. Among the 15 large states, which have 96 per cent of the total population of the country, the variation is from 1.31 per cent in Kerala and 1.39 per cent in Tamil Nadu to 2.37 per cent in Madhya Pradesh and 2.47 per cent in Rajasthan. The rates of Kerala and Tamil Nadu are 30 to 50 per cent higher than the rates in most developed countries : the rate for the US estimated at 1.0 per cent and those for most European countries at between 0.8 and 1.0 per cent.

The reasons for the relatively low growth rates in Kerala and Tamil Nadu, and also the small state of Goa (1.48 per cent), need to be carefully investigated. It would be erroneous to ascribe them to any single cause such as high female literacy rate although the latter may be an important contributory factor in some states. Kerala has a female literacy rate of 87 per cent, but in Tamil Nadu the rate is only 52.3 per cent. Among the small states, while Goa has a high female literacy rate of almost 70 per cent and a low population growth rate, Mizoram has a high female literacy rate of 78 per cent has a very high population growth rate of 3.3 per cent (pp. 29 and 62).

---

* The page numbering given in brackets in this chapter relate to the page numbering as given in the publications under review.

Progressive Decline in Sex Ratio

Progressive decline in the sex ratio (females per 1000 males) throughout this century is perhaps the most depressing statistics of the censuses. The ratio, which was already unfavourable (972) in 1901, had fallen to 946 by 1951, and the provisional figure of 929 in 1991 indicates a further fall of 17 points over four decades (p. 51). The reasons for the decline have to be investigated in much greater detail than has been done so far. The Census Commissioner refers to several explanations for it that have been given in the past. Some of them were : "a preference for male children resulting in neglect of female babies, the relative gap in health conditions between males and females and certain types of mortality which are sex selective. The adverse sex ratio is also due to lower expectation of life at birth for females compared to males, part of which is due to high maternal mortality. It is, however, difficult to pinpoint any particular reason for the declining sex ratio, which requires a detailed analysis" (p. 55).

The Literacy Rate

There has been some increase in the literacy rate as indicated by the figure in Table 20.2. However, increase in the literacy rate has been so slow that the number of illiterates increased during the decade 1981-1991 from 302 million to 324 million.

Table 20.2 : Literacy Rates

Year	*Persons*	*Males*	*Females*	*Inter-Decadal Increase (Persons)*
1991	52.11	63.86	39.42	8.55
1981	43.56	56.37	29.75	9.11
	(41.52)	(53.45)	(28.46)	(7.07)
1971	34.45	45.95	21.97	—

Note : Figures in brackets for 1981 and those for 1991 relate to the population 5 years and above, while those for 1981 and 1991 relate to the population 7 years above. This change in the calculation of the literacy rate was made in 1981.

There is very large inter-state variation in the literacy rate—from more than 90 per cent in Kerala to less than 40 per cent in Bihar and

Rajasthan, and only slightly higher, 41.7 per cent in U.P. and 43.5 per cent in Madhya Pradesh. Thus while Kerala is approaching the goal of universal literacy, almost 60 per cent of the population of the large Hindi speaking states of North and Central India remains mire in illiteracy. Variation in the female literacy are—from 86.9 per cent in Kerala to 20.8 per cent in Rajasthan and 23.1 per cent in Bihar—are even greater than in the overall or male literacy rates. Indeed the overall rates of the Hindi speaking states are due in large part to their very low female literacy rates.

In view of the crucial importance of high literacy, particularly high female literacy, in achieving more rapid economic growth and improvement in levels of health, nutrition and education of the population, a concerted national effort needs to be made to raise the level of literacy. The objective should be to achieve universal literacy by 2010; an earlier target date appears to be difficult to achieve considering past trends. The effort should focus on increasing female literacy in the Hindi speaking states. The socio-cultural factors that contribute to low female literacy in these states need to be identified and progressively weakened as part of the effort.

Population of Metropolitan Cities

The press release issued by the Census Commissioner, along with publication of the paper had mentioned the provisional population of the four largest metropolitan cities—Bombay, Calcutta, Delhi, and Madras. This paper does not include these figures however, or any other data on urbanization. But figures on the provisional populations of the 21 metropolitan cities (with population of one million and above in 1991) could be obtained from the office of the Census Commissioner on special request. They are presented in Table 20.3, along with the data on the number and populations of these cities from 1951 to 1991. In this table the cities are listed in descending order of their provisional populations in 1991.

The number of metropolitan cities had been increasing slowly from five in 1951 to six in 1961, nine in 1971 and twelve in 1981. But it has taken a quantum jump to 21 in 1991. The proportion of the urban population living in the metropolitan cities has increased progressively from 17.3 per cent in 1951 to almost 30 per cent in 1991(Table 20.3). The corresponding increase in the proportion of the total population of the country living in the cities has been from 3.23 per cent in 1951 to 8.12 per cent in 1991.

Table 20.3 : Trends in Growth of Population of the Metropolitan Cities, 1951-1991

*(Population figures in lakhs)**

Sl. No.	*City*	*1951*	*1961*	*1971*	*1981*	*1991 (Provisional)*
1.	Calcutta	45.89 (28.3)	57.37 (25.0)	70.31 (22.6)	91.9 (30.4)	108.6 (18.1)
2.	Bombay	29.69 (76.0)	41.52 (39.9)	59.71 (43.8)	82.43 (37.8)	125.7 (52.4)
3.	Delhi	14.37 (106.5)	23.59 (64.2)	36.47 (54.6)	57.29 (56.7)	83.8 (46.2)
4.	Madras	15.42 (65.8)	19.44 (26.1)	31.70 (63.1)	42.89 (34.9)	53.6 (25.0)
5.	Hyderabad	11.28 (52.6)	12.49 (10.7)	17.96 (43.8)	25.46 (40.7)	42.7 (67.8)
6.	Ahmedabad	8.77 (47.0)	12.06 (37.5)	17.41 (44.4)	25.48 (43.5)	32.8 (28.7)
7.	Bangalore	7.79 (91.4)	12.00 (54.0)	16.54 (37.8)	29.22 (76.2)	41.1 (40.6)
8.	Kanpur	7.05 (44.8)	9.71 (37.7)	12.75 (31.3)	16.39 (32.4)	21.0 (24.5)
9.	Pune	6.06 (87.0)	7.91 (30.5)	11.35 (43.5)	16.86 (48.5)	24.4 (45.0)
10.	Nagpur			9.33	13.02 (39.5)	16.05 (26.8)
11.	Jaipur			6.43	10.15 (57.8)	15.1 ((50.2)
12.	Lucknow			8.15	10.08 (23.7)	16.7 (65.6)
13.	Surat				9.1	15.2 (66.0)
14.	Coimbatore				9.2	11.4 (23.4)
15.	Vadodara				7.5	11.2 (49.7)
16.	Indore				8.3	11.7 (33.3)
17.	Patna				9.2	11.0 (19.5)
18.	Madurai				9.1	10.9 (20.5)
19.	Bhopal				6.7	10.6 (58.6)
20.	Varanasi				8.0	10.2 (27.7)
21.	Visakhapatnan				6.0	10.5 (75.0)
22.	Population of the Metropolitan cities	11.66	17.85	27.42	42.11	68.56
23.	Total Urban population	65.44	78.90	109.11	159.72	231.60
24.	Total Population	361.0	439.23	548.2	683.3	843.9
25.	Proportion of population of metropolitan cities to :					
	(a) Urban population (per cent)	17.8	22.6	25.1	26.4	29.6
	(b) Total population per cent	3.23	4.06	5.00	6.16	8.12

* Decennial growth rates are given in bracket.

Greater Bombay, with an estimated population of 12.57 million in 1991, is the most populous metropolitan city, having overtaken Calcutta which had been the must populous until 1981 but had a population of 10.86 million in 1991. The change in rank is due to Greater Bombay experiencing much faster growth (52.4 per cent) during the decade than Calcutta (18.1 per cent). The ranks of several other cities have also changed because of differences in the growth rate of population during 1981-1991. Thus, Hyderabad has overtaken Bangalore for the fifth rank.

However Delhi and Madras have retained their third and fourth rank respectively. The nine cities which were added to the metropolitan list during 1981-1991 had populations in 1981 ranging from 604,000 (Visakhapatnam) to 920,000 (Coimbatore).

The trend towards increasing concentration of the urban and total population in large cities in India is in accord with similar trends in the low income developing countries and regions. This is revealed by figures on the proportion of population of the low income countries, including India and China, living in the large cities (with population of 500,000 and above) in 1960 and 1980, presented in the Table 20.4. The proportions increased in India by 50 per cent, from 26 per cent to 39 per cent, in contrast with an increase by 2 ½ times, from 17 per cent to 43 per cent, in the other low income countries. The increase was marginal, however from 42 per cent to 45 per cent, in China, a result undoubtedly, of the severe restriction imposed by the government on migration into the large cities.

Table 20.4 : Percentage of Urban Population in Large Cities of Low Income Economies.

	Proportion of Population Living in Cities with over 50,000 Persons		*No of Cities with 50,000+ Persons*	
	1960	*1980*	*960*	*1980*
Low income economies	59	165	30	43
China and India	49	14	36	43
Other low income economies	10	51	17	43
China	38	78	42	45
India	11	36	26	39

Source : World Development Report 1990, Appendix Table 31, Urbanization, p. 238.

Variation in Population of States and Union Territories

There is a very large variation in the populations of various states and Union Territories. Among the 15 large states, as many as seven had populations of more than 50 million in 1991 and as many as 11 had populations of more than 30 million. Uttar Pradesh (138.8 million), Bihar (86.3 million) and Maharashtra (78.7 million) were the most population states (Table 20.1). The three states together with West Bengal (86 million) and Andhra Pradesh (66.3 million) had more than half (52 per cent) of the total population of the country. The population of U.P. was almost 75 per cent of the combined populations of the 14 Arab states, more than half the population of US (249 million in 1990) and almost half the population of the USSR (187 million in 1989). At the other extreme from these very large states, as many as nine political units (both States and Union Territories) had populations of less than one million.

Furthermore, there is great disparity in the levels of economic development among the different regions of large states, or differences in ethnic composition of their populations, The western U.P. plain, with its highly productive agriculture (because of extensive coverage with irrigation by canals, tube-wells and wells and intensive use of modern inputs) and significant development of agro-processing and other industries and handicrafts is among the must prosperous regions of the country. At the other extreme eastern U.P. is among the poorest and most backward regions. Western Maharashtra which includes the large metropolises of Bombay and Poona, besides smaller industrial cities like Sholapur, is at a much higher level of economic development than Marathwada. In Bihar and Madhya Pradesh, there are large areas inhabited predominantly by tribal, who are at lower levels of economic and social-cultural development than the rest of the population.

As a result of this very large variation in the population of the different States and Union Territories and the disparities in the levels of economic development or differences in ethnic composition of the populations of the large states, the question arises : Is the present territorial division of the country optimal or even efficient for the needs of economics development, delivery of developmental and social services to the population, or economy in public expenditure, or would these objectives be better served through a territorial reorganization?

We recognize that geographical and political issues have to be kept prominently in view when considering any scheme of territorial reorganization. Lakshadweep and Andaman and Nikobar Islands, located in the midst of the Arabian Sea and the Bay of Bengal respectively, at long distances from the nearest states on the main land of India, need to be administered as Union Territories because of their location and strategic importance. The separate political identity of Nagaland, Mizoram and other small states of north-east has to be maintained for politico-institutional or strategic reasons. But there are a few cases in which no such consideration obtains. Thus the tiny administrative enclaves of Dadra and Nagar Haveli (population 138,500) and Daman and Diu (population 101,400) can be easily merged with the neighbouring state of Gujarat. The present political status of Chandigarh as a Union Territory must be ended at the earliest as part of the settlement of the Punjab issue which has caused so much bloodshed and suffering and had such disturbing implications for the territorial integrity of the country.

For the large states U.P., Bihar and others, the optimum solution would be division into a number of smaller states. Thus U.P. could be divided into five smaller states keeping in view topographical or agro-climatic factors. Three of them located in the Gangetic plain, would have larger populations than the populations of several medium-sized states such as Punjab and Haryana. Bihar, similarly, could be divided into three or more smaller states. These smaller states would be administered more efficiently and would also serve the needs and aspirations of their populations better than the present mammoth states. And, as the experience of Punjab and Haryana, formed in 1966 by division of the then state of Punjab brings out, economic development could also be more rapid in them than the present states.

However, since such a division of the large states into smaller states is not likely to be considered at present or in the foreseeable future, an **administrative solution to the problem has to be sought**. The most feasible solutuion would be very large and effective devolution of powers and functions along with transfer of funds from the State Government to lower level institutions established at the levels of district, and the multi-district division.

In case of the district, revival of the three-tier structure of Panchayati Raj Institutions, in states in which it was abolished during the 1960s or the 1970s, and revitalization of the institutions with greatly increased functions and resources, in states such as Gujarat and Maharashtra, in which the three-tier structure has continued would meet all the three objectives mentioned earlier. However, since the number of districts is very large in the large states—almost 60 in U.P. and about 40 each in Madhya Pradesh and Bihar—the needed devolution of powers and functions to the district level institutions is not likely to be made by the Governments of these states, because of difficulties experienced by them in supervising effectively delivery of services or implementation of development programmes in such a large number of districts.

There is need therefore for creation of a politico-administrative institution such as a Divisional Development Committee (DDC), with a wide range of powers in the areas of general administration and delivery of services at the multi-district level. U.P. could be divided into 8 or 10 such divisions. Bihar, Maharashtra and other large states could all have appropriately smaller number of divisions. The DDC for each division should have a Senior Minister from the division as its Chairman, other Ministers, MLAs, Collectors and divisional level officials of the principal development departments as the members and a senior official of the rank of a Divisional Commissioner as the Member Secretary. The functions and powers of the DDC should extend over the entire range of administration and delivery of social and developmental services.

With such a structure at the division level, the state administration would be concerned mainly with formulation of policies and programmes and implementation of large multi-division projects such as irrigation, power and state highway projects.

We recognize that it would not be easy to achieve such wide ranging and effective devolution of powers and functions from the state to the division level; the devolution would be against the strong trend towards centralization of powers and functions with the State and Central Government during the post-independence period. The failure in most states of the Panchayati Raj Institution created in 1960s, culminating in their abolition in the 1970s; existence of week and ineffective municipal bodies and their suspension for indefinite periods in several states are all due to the unwillingness of the State Governments to decentralize powers and functions to lower level institutions. The Central Government itself has assumed an increasingly important role in formulation of policies and programmes relating to economic development and delivery of social services which are responsibility of the State Governments under the Constitution of India. An extreme case of such centralization was assumption by the Central Government of direct responsibility in 1989 for financing and overseeing implementation of the Jawaharlal Rozgar Yojana, bypassing the State Governments, which have both the responsibility of implementing such projects and the organization for overseeing their implementation.

However, we see no alternative to wide-ranging and effective devolution to the Divisional Development Committees proposed above (or a similar other structure) to reverse the trend towards progressive deterioration in general administration, the most visible symptoms of which are deterioration in law and order, and inefficient delivery of social and developmental services in several states.

II.* 1991 Population Census : Some Facts and Policy Issues

The Census of India 1991: Series—1 India. Paper 2 of 1991—Provisional Population Totals : Rural-Urban Distribution, August 1991: pp. 425 +vi; Registrar General and Census Commissioner, India, is the second paper in the series on provisional population totals of the 1991 Census, to be published by the Registrar General and Census Commissioner, India. A third paper, which will present provisional data on main and marginal workers is proposed to be published, and judging by the speed with which the first two papers have been published, it should also be out by the end of the year. With the publication of the three papers, the most important demographic and economic data of the 1991 Census, based on a quick count of a sample of census schedules, will have been published in less than a year of the conduct of the census.

In this paper, as in Paper I, the Census Commissioner has aimed on the one hand, at presenting the most important data on urban growth and urbanization in a form in which they can be easily understood by the lay reader and, on the other, to provide adequate scope to the specialist to dig deeper and analyze the data by states, Union Territories, districts and cities and towns of different size classes. This paper too has an attractive art paper cover and its six-chapter text, written in succinct and lucid language, is interspersed with 34 tables (called statements), a dozen colour maps and an equal number of charts and diagrams. The statements provide adequate support for the main points made in the text while the charts and diagrams present the points to the reader in a vivid form. The statements and the ten Provisional Population Tables (listed in the appendix) which cover almost 350 pages of the paper, provide adequate scope to the specialist to undertake detailed analyses of the data.

Special attention has been given to presenting data on large cities with populations of a million or more (pp. 23-44 including Figures 9 and 10).[1] The four mega cities—Bombay, Calcutta, Delhi and Madras—with populations of five million or more in 1991, receive even greater attention through a number of statements, historical reviews of their growth, their ranks (by size of population) among the world's 34 mega cities[2] and two or more maps each. The latter show spatial expansion of their agglomerations during the two decades, 1971-91 (pp. 43-49). There is a short section (pp.

---

* Published in *Economic and Political Weekly*, Bombay. Vol. xxxvi, No. Dec. 21, 1991.

49-50) also on the National Capital Region, which indicates its area and population in 1991 by states and districts and the Union Territory of Delhi, the number of towns of different size classes in it and growth of population during 1971-91 of the Class-I and Class-II towns.

Two Definitions

Before going into discussion of the data presented in the paper, it is useful to reproduce the definitions of an urban area and an urban agglomeration, used in it. The definitions have remained essentially unchanged since the census of 1971, although some refinements were made in them in the censuses of both 1981 and 1991.

(1) Urban Area

"(a) All places with a municipality, corporation, cantonment board or notified town area committee, etc.

(b) All other places which satisfy the following criteria :

- A minimum population of 5,000;
- At least 75 per cent of male working population engaged in non-agricultural pursuits; and
- A density of population of at least 400 persons per sq. km." (p. 7).[3]

(2) Urban Agglomeration

"An urban agglomeration, therefore, constitutes :

- A city or a town with a continuous outgrowth, the outgrowth being outside the statutory limits but falling within the boundaries of the adjoining village or villages; or
- Two or more adjoining towns with their outgrowths, if any, as in (i) above; or
- A city and one or more adjoining towns with or without outgrowing, all of which form a continuous spread." (p. 8).

In chapters 5 and 6 of the text (pp. 51-61), the Census Commissioner discusses comparative growth Rates of urban and rural populations and the Urban-Rural Growth rate Differentials (URGD) for India, States and Union Territories during the three decades, 1961-1991. The discussion is based on data of the sample registration system. One objective of the discussion is to arrive at some explanation of slower average annual growth rate (3.09 per cent) of the urban population during 1981-91 than during the two previous decades, the figures for which were 3.21 per cent (1961-71) and 3.83 per cent (1971-81) respectively.

Urban and rural birth and death rates and rates of natural increase, based on the sample registration system, are compared for two periods—1971-80 and 1981-89 in Statement 29 on p. 52 which is reproduced here as Table 20.5. It is interesting to note that although urban birth and death rates were much lower than the rural rates in both periods, the urban rates of natural increase were only marginally lower than the rural rates.

Table 20.5 : Average Birth Rate, Death Rate and Rate of Natural Increase Per 1,000 Population, as per SRS-India : 1971-1980, 1981-1989.

Period		*Urban*	*Rural*	*Difference (Col. 2–3)*
1		*2*	*3*	*4*
1971–80	Birth Rate	28.5	35.8	-7.3
	Death Rate	9.2	15.8	-6.6
	Rate of natural increase*	19.3	20.0	-0.7
1981–89	Birth Rate	27.3	34.2	-6.9
	Death Rate	7.7	12.8	-5.1
	Rate of Natural Increase*	19.6	21.4	-1.8

* Rate of natural increase is defined as birth rate minus death rate.

Main Facts

Growth of Urban Population

The census figures for 1981 and 1991 and projections of the total and urban population to 2001 are given in Table 20.6 along with those of three projections made respectively by the Census Commissioner in 1985 for inclusion in the Seventh Five-Year Plan 1986-90, the World Bank and Mohan. The census projection of the total population in 2001 is based on an annual growth rate of 2 per cent during 1991-2001, slightly lower than the provisional growth rate of 2.1 per cent during 1981-91, but the projection of the urban population during 1991-2001 is based on the provisional 1981-1991 growth rate of 3.09 per cent per annum.

The urban population of 217.2 million in 1991 constituted 25.7 per cent of the total population of 844.4 million. The increases during 1981-91 of nearly 57 million in the urban population and of 2.4 percentage points (from 23.3 per cent to 25.7 per cent) in the proportion, urban/total population, have both been significantly lower than the projections made during the early or mid-1980s.

The provisional 1991 Census figure of the urban population is 13 to 19 million lower than the figures of the earlier projections, while the urban/rural population ratio is 1.6 to 1.8 percentage points lower. The growth rate of the urban population of 3.09 per cent per annum during 1981-1991 is also significantly lower than the rates of 3.7 per cent to 4.2 per cent per annum during 1981-2001 that had been projected earlier (Table 20.6). Furthermore, contrary to the expectations of the World Bank, which had forecast acceleration of urban growth with acceleration of economic growth, slower growth of the urban population has been experienced during 1981-91, although the rate of economic growth of 5 per cent per annum or more, during most of the decade was significantly higher than the average growth rates of 3.6 to 3.8 per cent per annum experienced during the two earlier decades, 1961-1971 and 1971-1981 (World Bank Development Report 1991, pp. 206-207).

The latter fact has an important implication for public policies : it indicates that efforts to accelerate economic growth need not be inhibited unduly by fear of accelerating growth of the urban population. During the next five years while the effects on economic growth of the economic liberalization policies, initiated with the Budget of 1991-92, would be the primary focus of attention of economists and other policy-makers, the effects of the policies on growth of the urban population and on urbanization should also be studied by the Census Commissioner and other analysts of population to see the relationship between the rate of economic growth and the growth rate of the urban population.

If the slower growth rate of the urban population observed during 1981-91 continues (with marginal variations) during the early 1990s, both the total urban-population and the proportion of urban/total population in 2001 would be significantly lower than the figures of 320-350 million and 32-35 per cent respectively projected in the 1980s (Table 20.6). The urban population would be in the neighbourhood of 300 million, and the urban/total population ratio would be about 29 per cent.

Revised projections of the urban population and of the urban/total population ratio in 2001 should be made in the mid-1990s. By that time, the final figures of the 1991 Census (including figures on rural-to-urban migration) would have been published and there would also be sufficient data on the effects of the economic liberalization policies on economic growth.

Table 20.6 : Projections of Total and Urban Population, and Growth of GDP per Capita 1981-2001

	1981 Census (Actual)	1991 Census (Provisional)	2001 (Projected)*	World Development Report, 1984			Seventh Five-Year Plan, 1986-90			Mohan		
				1980	1990	2000	1981	1991	2001	1981	1991	2001
1	2	3	4	5	6	7	8	9	10	11	12	13
Total population*	685	844	1029	685		994	685	837	986	697	850-856	993-1018
										(2.2 during 1981-86, falling to 1.47—1.68 during 1996-2001)		
Average growth rate**	2.1		2.0		1.9		2.0		1.65			
Urban population*	160	217.2	294	160		353	160	230	326	164	234-236	315-320
Average growth rate**	3.09		3.09		4.2		3.7		3.5	3.8	3.1	
Urban population/ total population (per cent)	23.3	25.7	28.6	23.3	—	35.5	23.3	27.5	33.1	23.5	27.3-27.5	31.0-31.5
Growth Rate of GDP Per capita												
High-case scenario		3.2***			3.2****		3.35				n.a.	
Low-case scenario		2.5***										

1	2	3	4	5	6	7	8	9	10	11	12	13
Growth Rate of GDP Per capita												
High-case scenario	3.2***		3.2****		3.35			n.a.				
Low-case scenario	2.5***											

Note: * Figures for population are in millions, and

** Figures for growth rate are in per cent per annum.

*** 1985-95.

**** 1986-91 Growth rate of GDP per capita for India is projected at 2.5 per cent under the low case scenario. The rate for the high case scenario is not projected in the WDR, but is inferred as being lower than the rate for 'low income Asia' by 0.5 per cent per annum, as under the low case scenario.

Total population is projected under three variants of decline in fertility, while growth of the urban population is projected under two variants. The methodology of the projections is explained in the Appendix (pp. 642-43).

Sources: (i) Census of India 1991, Series I, India, and Paper 2 of 1991 Provisional Population Tables : Rural- Urban Distribution, p. 1.

(ii) World Bank (1984: 36, 67, 254-55).

(iii) Government of India, Planning Commission (1985 : 11-12).

(iv) Mohan (1985 : 630-31).

Table 20.6a : Growth Rates of Total and Urban Population 1960-2000: India and Other Low Income Economies Other than India and China.

(Projected)		*India*			*Low income economies other than India*			
	1960	*1970*	*1980*	*2000*	*1960*	*1970*	*1980*	*2000*
	(1)	*(2)*	*(3)*	*(4)*	*(5)*	*(6)*	*(7)*	*(8)*
Total Population (millions)	439	548	685	994	329	421	544	907
Growth Rate (% per annum		2.3	2.3	1.9	2.5	2.6	2.9	n.a.
Urban Population (millions)	79	109	156	353	n.a.	n.a	109	n.a.
Urban/Total Population (per cent)	18.0	18.0	23.3	35.5	12	n.a.	20	n.a.
Growth Rates (% per annum):								
Urban Population	3.3	3.7	4.27	n.a.	5.2	5.2	n.a.	n.a.
Rural Population	—	1.8	1.1	n.a.	n.a.	n.a.	n.a.	n.a.
Proportion of urban population in cities of 500,000 and above *1950-80	25,6	31.3	39.7	n.a.	19	n.a.	400	n.a.

Note: Figures of total and urban population for India are for 1961 to 1981, and are from Population Censuses of India.1961-1981. All other figures are from World Development Report1984—Appendix Tables 20.22, pp. 260-61 and 19, pp. 254-55, and Text Table 4.3, p. 67.

The revision should be based on the trend line derived from the growth rates of the urban population during the three decades, 1961-91. This is essential in view of the large fluctuations in the rates during the three decades.

Concentration of Urban Population in Larger Urban Places

There is a pronounced tendency for the urban population to concentrate in the large cities and towns. Almost 65 per cent of the urban population lived in 1991 in 300 cities (with populations of 100,000 or more) and only about 35 per cent lived in the almost 3,400 smaller urban places designated as towns (Table 20.7). In 1981 the figures had been 60 per cent and 40 per cent respectively.

Table 20.6b : Growth Rates of GDP Per Capita, 1960-95—India and low income developing countries (L)
Average Annual Growth Rates of GDP Per Capita (per cent)

Country/Group	*1960-73*	*1973-79*	*1980-85*	*1985-95 (Projected)*	
				Low Case Scenario	*High Case Scenario*
Low income developing countries	3.0	2.9	3.2	2.7	3.4
Low incomes :					
Asia*	3.4	3.3	3.7	3.0	3.7
Africa	1.0	-1.0	-1.6	2.5	3.2[c]
India**	3.2**	1.3[b]			

a Includes China, Indonesia and all countries of South Asia (Afghanistan, Bangladesh, Bhutan, Burma, India, Nepal, Pakistan and Sri Lanka).

b 1960-1982

c Assuming India's growth rate to be 0.5% p.a. lower than that for Low Income Asia, as under the Low Case Scenario.

Source : World Development Report. 1984. Text Table 3.2, p. 36 and Appendix Table 1, pp . 218-19.

Almost half of the city population or one-third of the urban population lived in 1991 in the 23 million-plus cities; more than 17 per cent of it lived in the four mega cities—Bombay, Calcutta, Delhi and Madras. There is similar concentration in the larger towns. While the towns in the two larger size classes with populations of 20,000-49,999 and 50,000-99,999 had almost one-fourth (24.3 per cent) of the urban population, the smaller towns with populations below 20,000 had only 10.8 per cent of it. Finally, the 197 towns of the smallest size class (population below 5,000) had only 0.4 per cent of the urban population.

Increasing concentration of the urban population in larger cities is due mainly to progressive increase in the numbers of both the cities and the million-plus cities. The number of cities increased from 216 in 1981 to 300 in 1991 while the number of million-plus cities almost doubled, from 12 to 23, during the decade as six cities with populations between 750,000 and 1 million in 1981 and 5 with population below 750,000 became million-plus cities (Statement 23, p. 39). The numbers will increase further during the 1990s : that of the million-plus cities could reach (or exceed) 36 by 2,000 as estimated by the National Commission on Urbanization in 1988

(Ministry of Urban Development, 1988, Table A p. 26), because a significant number of the 30 cities which had populations of 500,000-1 million in 1991 would become million-plus cities.

Table 20.7 : Distribution of Urban Population among Cities and Towns of Different Size Classes, 1991

Census Symbol of Size Class	*Cities/Towns with Populations of*	*No. of Cities/ Towns*	*Total Population (millions)*	*Per Cent of Total Urban Population*	*Cumulative Percentage*
1	*2*	*3*	*4*	*5*	*6*
	Cities 5,000,000 and above (Mega cities)	4	37.22	17.13	17.13
M5	10,00,000	19	33.46	15.41	32.54
M2	5,00,000	30	20.94	9.6	43.18
n.a.	1,00,000	247	47.11	21.69	64.87*
I	All cities (Class I)	300	139.73	64.89	64.89*
	Towns of class:				
II	50,000	345	24.00	10.96	75.85
III	20,000	947	28.71	13.33	89.18
IV	10,000	1167	17.00	7.89	97.07
V	5,000	740	5.64	2.62	99.69
VI	Less than 5,000	197	0.66	0.37	100.06*
	All cities and towns	3696	215.34	100.00	100.00*

**Note :* Small differences are due to rounding up of various percentage figures. Figures exclude Assam and Jammu and Kashmir.

Source : Adapted from Statements 11, pp. 22-23 and 13, p. 29. Figures exclude Assam and Jammu and Kashmir.

Table 20.7a : Distribution of Urban Population by size of Urban Place, 1951-1981

(Percentage of Urban Population in Urban Places)

Places with population of :	*1951*	*1961*	*1971*	*1981*
1 million and above	n.a	22.5	25.1	26.3
500,000 – 1 million	n.a	3.1	6.2	13.4
100,000 – 500,000	n.a	18.1	17.6	20.7
50,000 – 100,000	12.0	12.1	13.5	11.6
20,000 – 50,000	17.8	20.0	18.3	14.4
Below 20,000	31.9	23.4	19.5	13.6

Source: Population Censuses of India - 1951, 1961, 1971 and 1981

Table 20.7b : Actual and Projected distribution of the Urban Population in India of various size classes of Urban Places : 1971-2001

Year	*Class size*						*Total*	*Projected*	*Proje-cted*
	Metropolitan	*I*	*II*	*III*	*IV*	*V*	*Urban*	*Urban*	*Rural*
	(Per cent of total urban population)							*(millions)*	
1971	(i) 25.4	30.2	11.3	15.6	11.3	4.7	108.3		423
	(ii) 25.5	28.6	11.6	18.1	12.5	4.1	100.4		429
	(A) 25.7	30.6	11.3	16.4	11.3	4.7	106.6		422
1981	(i) 27.6	29.7	11.2	14.6	12.9	4.1	152.3		506
	(ii) 28.2	33.1	11.2	14.9	9.5	3.2	145.9		506
	(A) 26.9	33.5	11.6	14.3	9.5	4.1	156.1		502
1991 (Projected)	(i) 28.1	36.3	12.0	12.4	7.9	3.3	235.7	236	604
	(ii) 28.3	36.5	11.7	12.4	7.9	3.4	235.6	236	605
2001	(i) 29.1	39.6	11.8	10.3	6.4	2.8	333.6	315	704
	(ii) 29.2	40.1	11.4	10.3	6.4	2.8	333.4	315	703

Notes : Percentages calculated from figures given in Mohan (1985 : 633). The size classes are : Metropolitan : 1 million and above; class I : 100 000-1 million; Class II: 50,000-100,000; Class III: 20,000-50,000; Class IV: 10,000-20,000; Class V: below 10,000.

A is the actual population according to the Census of India; (i) and (ii) are calculated from Mohan's two projections, which are explained in the Appendix on (pp. 642-643).

Another significant fact is that in both 1971-81 and 1981-91, the growth rates of cities and large towns has been significantly higher than the rates of growth of small towns (Table 20.8). In 1981-91, the decline was from a growth rate of 46.87 per cent for cities to negative growth rates of –1.27 per cent and –21.70 per cent for towns of the two smallest size classes, V and VI, with populations of 5,000-9,999 and below 5,000 respectively. The decline in the growth rate with decrease in the size of the urban place during 1971-81 was from about 55 per cent for cities and large towns in the 50,000-99,999—population range, to about 18 per cent for class V towns. However, towns of the smallest size class (VI) had shown the highest growth rate of 65.73 per cent during the decade (Table 20.8).

The reasons for the sharp differences in the growth rate of towns of the smallest size class during the two decades need to be investigated. One reason for the difference appears to be in the way in which the definition of a town was applied by the field staff in the three censuses of

Table 20.8: Trends in Growth of Population in Cities and Towns of Different Size Classes, 1971-91

Size Classes	*No. of Cities & Towns*	*Growth rate of Population (Per cent)*	
		1971-1981	*1981-1991*
All Classes	3696	46.23	36.09
I	300	54.35	46.87
II	345	55.73	28.14
III	947	30.85	25.30
IV	1167	27.54	10.72
V	740	17.82	-1.27
VI	197	65.73	-21.70

The World Bank Report, 1984 contained the following projections of growth of the population of the four cities by the year 2000:

Table. 20.8a : Projected Population Growth and Growth Rates of Mumbai, Kolkata, Chennai and Delhi.

	Population (millions)		*Growth Rate (per cent p.a.)*	
	Actual 1980	*Projected 2000*	*Actual 1980-2000*	*Projected 1961-1981*
Bombay	8.2	17.1	3.7	3.5
Calcutta	9.2	16.7	3.0	2.3
Madras	4.3	12.9	5.7	4.0
Delhi	5.7	11.7	3.7	4.5

1971, 1981 and 1991. The number of towns of the smallest size class which was only 147 in 1971 went up to 229 in 1981, to come down again to 185 in 1991 (Statement 14, p. 30).

Spatial Expansion of Large Urban Agglomerations

Part of the increase in the populations of large cities is due to spatial expansion of their agglomerations to include large numbers of towns and villages. The paper contains eight maps (Nos. 5 to 12) which show expansion during the 20-year period, 1971-91, of the agglomerations of the four mega cities. The area of the Bombay urban agglomeration, for instance, more than doubled during this period. By 1991, the agglomeration had expanded to include the whole of Bombay Island and a large area of Thane district on the main land (map 5). It contained within it three Municipal Corporations (Bombay, Kalyan and Thane) and three other municipal bodies (p. 74).

Table 20.8b: Total Number of Cities with Population one Million+ Cities Growth rates of urban places of different size classes, 1961-81

(Population figures in millions)

	1961	Growth rate (% p. a.)	1971	Growth rate (% p. a.)	1981
A. Four metropolitan cities— Bombay, Calcutta, Madras and Delhi	14.2	3.3	19.8	3.3	27.5
Other cities with population of: 1 million or more.	3.5	8.1	7.6	6.0	13.6
500,000 - 1 million	3.9	5.6	6.8	12.0	20.9
100,000-500,000	14.3	2.9	19.6	5.3	32.3
All cities	35.1	4.3	53.4	5.9	94.3
Towns with population of :					
50,000-100,000	9.5	4.5	14.7	2.2	18.2
20,000-50,000	15.7	2.4	19.9	1.2	22.4
Below 20,000	18.5	1.3	21.1	0.1	21.3
Total Urban population	78.9	3.7	109.1	3.7	156.2
B. All cities with population of 500,000	20.8 (11)*	5.1	34.2 (19)*	6.1	61.0 (42)*
Population of the 11 cities which had population of 500,000 or more in 1961	20.8	3.1	28.3	3.8	41.1

* Number of cities.

Source : Population Census of India 1951-1981.

The Delhi urban agglomeration had expanded during the same 20-year period to cover most of the area of the Union territory of Delhi, absorbing within it almost 150 villages of 1971 besides, 23 towns, and was expanding by 1991 into the adjoining states of Uttar Pradesh and Haryana. The new industrial-residential city of NOIDA, located across the river Yamuna in U.P., which had been established during the 1980s and had a population of 174,000 in 1991, had become part of the agglomeration. This city is growing so rapidly that it could double its population during the 1990s. Industrial and residential developments along the Delhi-Faridabad and the Delhi-Gurgaon roads have gone so far that both these Haryana cities, situated at distances of about 30 k.m. and 20 k.m. respectively from Delhi would become part of the Delhi urban agglomeration by the late 1990s. The agglomeration contained already in 1991, 26 administrative units—the Municipal Corporation of Delhi, the New Delhi Municipal Committee, the Delhi Cantonment Board and 23 towns of Delhi state. The number of administrative units (cities and towns) was much larger in case of both Calcutta (129) and Madras (57) urban agglomerations.

Policy Implications

The large number of administrative units within the agglomerations of the mega cities, constitutes a serious problem in planning for them. Long-or-medium-term development plans for the agglomerations of these cities and the million-plus cities must be formulated in agreement with all the administrative units (municipalities and panchayats) or at least the larger ones among them. The administrative units must also extend their full co-operation in implementing the projects and programmes included in the plans and enforcing measures, ranging from control over land use to reducing pollution of water and air recommended by them within their respective areas. In particular, the municipal bodies and panchayats within the agglomerations must resist (or be required by the State Government to resist) the temptation to pre-empt the land use component of the plans by allowing conversion of agricultural and other lands to non-agricultural (residential, industrial or commercial) uses in anticipation of enforcement of the plans. This happens often when the areas designated in the plans for schools, colleges, other public utilities or for recreation, are sold to developers, industrialists and other individuals for residential, industrial or other non-agricultural uses.

The proportion of urban population living in the towns of the three smallest size classes, IV, V and VI, with populations 5,000-9,999 and under 5,000, is small and has tended to decline progressively during the period, 1951-91 (Statement 17, p. 32). This has two implications :

(i) The size of the urban population and the proportion, urban/total population, would be affected little if the minimum population of a town was fixed at 10,000. Even fixing the minimum at 20,000, as is done in some publications of the international agencies, would not affect the total size of the urban population and the proportion, urban/total population significantly.

(ii) It suggests the need for refining and reformulating the strategy of encouraging growth of a large number of small towns for integrated rural-urban development and accelerating economic growth in backward states, such as Bihar, Orissa, Assam and other hill states of the north-east, or regions such as eastern

U.P., and Eastern Madhya Pradesh. In most of these states and regions, the number of small towns has either remained stationary or has increased progressively during the period 1951-91 (Table 20.9). It could increase even more rapidly if a large number of the larger villages could be upgraded to become small towns performing functions of micro-regional service centres. This would require expanding and improving the physical and social infrastructures within the villages and their transport and communication links particularly roads, with the micro-regions served by them.

Table 20.9 : Number of Towns of Classes V and VI in 15 States at Relatively High, Medium and Low Levels of Urbanization, 1951-1991

States at Level of Urbanization/Economic Development	*Percentage Urban/Total Population in 1991*	*No. of Class V and VI Towns in*				
		1951	*1961*	*1971*	*1981*	*1991*
High						
1. Maharashtra	38.73	224	87	74	58	49
2. Gujarat	34.40	150	64	70	60	53
3. Tamil Nadu	34.20	114	89	54	43	42
4. Karnataka	30.91	204	92	71	58	64
5. Punjab	29.72	68	54	40	54	23
Medium						
6. West Bengal	27.39	27	30	27	27	40
7. Andhra Pradesh	26.84	145	71	41	32	17
8. Kerala*	26.44	44	10*	9	4*	6*
9. Haryana	24.79	31	26	24	24	22
10. Madhya Pradesh	23.21	127	109	95	107	135
11. Rajasthan	22.88	156	67	42	23	23
Low						
12. Uttar Pradesh	19.89	317	80	88	311	250
13. Orissa	13.43	24	27	32	28	25
14. Bihar	13.17	37	40	46	28	34
15. Himachal Pradesh	8.70	27	24	28	38	43

Note : Figures are not available for Assam and Jammu and Kashmir.
Figures for Kerala are for Class IV and VI towns in 1951 and 1971 and for class V towns only in 1961, 1981 and 1991.

Source : Statement 33, p. 57 and Provisional Population Table 5, pp. 372-73 in paper under review.

In the more urbanized states, such as Maharashtra, Gujarat, Tamil Nadu, Karnataka and Kerala, however, the number of such towns has declined sharply during this period. The reasons for this need to be investigated. One reason could be the spatial expansion of the agglomerations of the mega cities, such as Bombay and Madras and other large cities like Bangalore, Ahmedabad and Pune, to absorb a number of these towns. Another possible reason could be that the rural populations of the more developed states prefer to obtain the various services required by them ranging from obtaining essential inputs such as seed, chemical fertilizers, pesticides and marketing of produce to social service facilities, such as schools, high schools, colleges and hospitals located in large towns with populations of 20,000 or more. In these states, both the size of the micro-regional centres and of the micro-regions should be larger than in the backward states.

Regional Variation in Urbanization

There is large variation among the States and Union territories in the level of urbanization as indicated by the figures on the percentage of urban to total population in Statements 7 and 8 (pp. 15-16) of the paper. The range of variation in 1991 was from almost 90 per cent in Chandigarh and Delhi to less than 10 per cent in Himachal Pradesh, Sikkim and Dadra and Nagar Haveli. Among the 16 large states, which had more than 98 per cent of the total population of the country in 1991, the variation was from 38.7 per cent in Maharashtra to 11.1 per cent in Assam (Table 20.10). Maharashtra, Gujarat and Tamil Nadu are the most urbanized states while Assam, Bihar and Orissa are the least urbanized.

This pattern has changed little from 1981 and indeed from 1961, although there have been changes in the ranks of individual states. West Bengal, which had the fourth rank in 1961, had been relegated to the sixth rank by 1981 (which it has retained in 1991) because of more rapid urbanization during 1961-1981 of Karnataka and Punjab. On the other hand, Kerala which had ranked 11th during 1961-81 has risen to the eighth rank in 1991.

The high level of urbanization of several states is due to location in them of a mega city and one or more million-plus cities. This is best illustrated by West Bengal : almost 60 per cent of its urban population—10.9 million out of 18.62 million—is concentrated in the Calcutta urban agglomeration. Similarly, almost half of the urban population of Maharashtra—15.1 million out of 30.5 million—is concentrated in the Bombay and Pune urban agglomerations. The pattern is visible also,

Table 20.10 : Percentage of Urban to Total Population, 1961-1991, by States, Ranked according to Level of Urbanization in 1991

Rank	*State*	*1991 (Provisional)*	*1981*	*1971*	*1961*
	India	*25.72*	*23.70*	*20.21*	*18.24*
	States				
	Maharashtra	38.73	35.03	31.17	28.22
	Gujarat	34.40	31.10	28.08	25.77
	Tamil Nadu	34.20	32.95	30.26	26.69
	Karnataka	30.91	28.89	24.31	22.33
	Punjab	29.72	27.68	23.73	23.06
	West Bengal	27.89	26.47	24.75	24.45
	Andhra Pradesh	26.84	23.82	19.31	17.44
	Kerala	26.44	18.74	16.24	15.11
	Haryana	24.79	21.88	17.66	17.23
	Jammu and Kashmir	23.83	21.05	18.59	16.66
	Madhya Pradesh	23.21	20.29	16.29	14.29
	Rajasthan	22.88	21.94	17.63	16.28
	Uttar Pradesh	19.89	17.95	14.02	12.85
	Orissa	13.43	11.79	8.41	6.32
	Bihar	13.17	12.47	10.00	8.11
	Assam	11.80	n.a	n.a	n.a

Source : Census of India 1981 and 1991, Statement 32. p. 57.

although it is less pronounced in Gujarat and Karnataka. Forty-two per cent—5.9 out of 14.2 million—of the urban population of Gujarat is concentrated in the agglomerations of its three million-plus cities—Ahmedabad, Surat, Vadodara. The Bangalore urban agglomeration alone has 30 per cent of the urban population of Karnataka.

Detailed discussion of the sub-regional and inter-district variations in the level of urbanization within individual states or across states would be beyond the limited scope of this review. It may only be mentioned that the variations, both within and across states, are much higher than inter-state variations. This is illustrated very well by map 3 of the paper which shows levels of urbanization by districts. The districts are divided into eight categories, with the percentages of urban to total population ranging more than 60 per cent to 0 (entirely rural). The 60 per cent plus group has nine districts, almost all of which contain very large metropolitan cities such as Bombay, Delhi, Ahmedabad, Kanpur and

Lucknow. There are six entirely rural districts, three each in Arunachal Pradesh and Manipur.

The great majority of the districts are at lower levels of urbanization than the national average with the proportion, urban/total population below 25.72 per cent. The districts at higher levels than the national average are concentrated in the more urbanized states—Maharashtra, Gujarat, Tamil Nadu, Karnataka, Kerala and Punjab. On the other hand, most districts of U.P., Bihar, Orissa and West Bengal are at a low level of urbanization with the proportion of urban/total population below 10 per cent.

The map does not show any clear pattern of sub-regional variations within or across states. On the contrary, districts at high and low levels of urbanization are frequently interspersed. An example is provided by the coastal areas of Gujarat and Maharashtra in which the two types of districts are interspersed.

Levels of Urbanization and Per Capita Domestic Product

In order to see the relationship between urbanization and per capita domestic product, the 16 major states have been ranked in Table 20.11 by both indicators of economic development. Maharashtra, Gujarat, Tamil Nadu, the three most urbanized states, ranked third, fourth and sixth in per capita domestic product : the first two ranks were taken by Punjab and Haryana which ranked fifth and ninth in the level of urbanization. But, when the 16 states were divided into two halves of eight states each, almost all of those in the upper half of one indicator were also in the upper half of the other and *vice versa*. Thus, of the eight more urbanized states as many as seven were also among the eight states with relatively high per capita domestic product. Accordingly, a rough correlation between the two indicators can be inferred, and it can be stated that the more urbanized states generally have higher per capita domestic product than the less urbanized states.

Policy Issues

Recommendations on the following three policy issues have been made earlier to repeat in this paper :

- The effort to achieve more rapid economic growth need not be inhibited by the fear of too much urbanization.

Table 20.11: Ranking of States by Levels of Urbanization and Per Capita Domestic Product

State	*Urban/Total Population in 1991 (Per cent)*	*Rank by Level of Urbanization*	*Per Capita Domestic Product in 1986-87 (Rs. at 1970-71 Prices)*	*Rank by Per Capita Domestic Product*
1	*2*	*3*	*4*	*5*
India	25.72	—	n.a	—
Maharashtra	38.73	1	1036	3
Gujarat	34.40	2	936	4
Tamil Nadu	34.20	3	825	6
Karnataka	30.91	4	799	7
Punjab	29.72	5	1702	1
West Bengal	27.89	6	855	5
Andhra Pradesh	26.84	7	758	8
Kerala	26.44	8	639	10
Haryana	29.79	9	1233	2
Jammu and Kashmir	23.83	10	684	9
Madhya Pradesh	23.21	11	590	14
Rajasthan	22.88	12	634	11
Uttar Pradesh	19.89	13	607	13
Orissa	13.43	14	538	15
Bihar	13.17	15	482	16
Assam	11.08	16	619	12

- Long- or medium-term development plans for the agglomerations of the mega cities and the larger million-plus cities must be formulated in agreement with all the administrative units (municipalities and panchayats) or at least the larger ones among them. The administrative units must also extend their full cooperation in implementing the projects and programmes included in the plans and enforcing measures, ranging from control over land use to reducing pollution of water and air rccommended by them within their respective areas. In particular, the municipal bodies and panchayats within the agglomerations must resist (or be required by the State Government to resist) the temptation to pre-empt the land use component of the plans by allowing conversion of agricultural and other lands to non-agricultural (residential, industrial or commercial) uses in anticipation of enforcement of the plans.

This happens often when the areas designated in the plans for schools, colleges, and other public utilities or for recreation, are sold to developers, industrialists and individuals for residential, industrial or other non-agricultural uses.

- The need to confine the strategy of developing a large number of small towns for accelerating economic growth in the less urbanized, relatively backward states and regions. The towns would be developed primarily by upgrading larger villages and encouraging their growth to become micro-regional service centres. In the more urbanized states, however, in which the number of small towns has declined sharply between 1951 and 1991, efforts should be concentrated on developing somewhat larger towns, with populations between 20,000—50,000, as micro-regional service centres. These towns would also be important '*mandi*' towns.

Investment in Urban Development Programmes

Slower than projected growth of the urban population would have meant lower need for public and private investment in urban development programmes. However, increasing concentration of the urban population in the cities and the million-plus cities, in particular, has the opposite effect. The needs for investment, total and per capita, are much larger in the large cities than in smaller cities and towns for several reasons, including :

(i) higher costs of land acquisition and development and of housing, and
(ii) larger needs for investment in physical and social infrastructures.

There is a difference of view on whether the per capita costs of expansion/improvement of housing and infrastructure facilities, providing basic services such as water supply, sanitation, electricity, transport, telecommunications, education and health care, are higher or lower in the large cities than in smaller urban places (Johnson, 1965, pp. 11-13).

However, there is no question that problems, such as control of pollution of air and water, traffic congestion and providing security of life and property to the residents, are much greater in large cities than in smaller cities and towns. Furthermore, services such as intra-urban transport (by buses, taxis or other means) which are essential in large cities and which involve high costs of investment and maintenance are either not needed in small cities or can be provided at a comparatively low cost. Most of the investment would be public investment by the richer municipal bodies, such as the Bombay Municipal Corporation, urban development authorities and the State or Central Government. Funds for the investment would need to be borrowed from HUDCO, the National Housing Bank, the nationalized banks and other public sector financial institutions. However, the demands on public investment can be reduced significantly through larger private investment, by companies in providing services such as electricity and intra-urban transport and by households, principally for housing.

Effect of Economic Liberalization Policies on Growth of Large Cities

It is difficult to forecast the effect. However, we can advance the following hypothesis to be proved (or disproved) by studies undertaken in the mid-1990s, when there is sufficient evidence to indicate the effect.

The liberal policy framework could provide further stimulus to growth of large cities with populations of a million or more and within them of cities with populations of two to five million or more. With the abolition of licensing for the great majority of manufacturing industries, the owners or managers of industrial units would be free to locate the units in places which are most economic or convenient for them. Most of them could find that the peripheral areas of the large cities constitute the best locations. The cost of land, needed for the units and for housing staff and workers, which is so high in the central areas of cities, is comparatively low in these areas. Physical and social infrastructures providing essential services can be extended from the cities at much lower costs than those of creating them in other locations. There is also easy access to the pools of trained and experienced managers, professionals and skilled workers available in the cities. The workers and the professionals can commute from their existing houses to the industrial units at comparatively low cost. Furthermore, the owners or top managers can exercise personal supervision and control over the working of the units. Access to sources of finance is also much greater in the large cities than in other locations, because of location of branches of nationalized banks and other financial institutions in the cities. There is ready access to information about changes in policies of the Central and State Governments which remain important even within the liberal policy framework.

Finally, the cities themselves are large markets for the outputs of the units and provide the best facilities for export of outputs to regional, national and international markets.

The effect on migration to the cities is less certain, however, because the stimulus to migration provided by rapid growth of jobs in the manufacturing and service sector units could be offset to a large extent by increase in commuting from villages or small towns located near the units or at more distant locations which are, however, within daily commuting range. Improvements in transport and communications, which reduce the time and cost of commuting, could increase the numbers of commuters significantly. A large proportion of the commuters would be unskilled in the beginning; but the proportion of skilled workers among them would increase progressively through unskilled commuters acquiring the needed skills and entry of young men possessing the skills.

Provisional Population Tables

Almost three-fourth of the space in the paper is occupied by the Ten Provisional Population Tables. A list of the tables is attached. The first two tables present data on the total and literate population by states, Union territories and districts, by sex and by residence (rural-urban). Table 20.3 presents data by States, Union Territories and districts on the proportion of urban/total population, in 1981 and 1991; the density of population in 1991, the sex ratio (female per 1000 males) and the growth rate of the population during 1981-91. For the latter two, rural-urban breakdown of the data is also given.

From Table 20.4 onwards there is a series of tables on urban agglomerations, cities and towns of different size classes by States, Union Territories and districts. Provisional Table 4, in which these data are presented for individual urban places, is perhaps of greatest interest. It indicates also the civic status of each urban unit by appropriate acronyms which are listed at the beginning of the table on page 170. Another noteworthy table is no. 6 in which historical data on growth of urban population during 1951-91 are given by States and Union Territories, and by cities and towns of different size classes.

III. Growth of Urban Population: An Analysis*

The World Development Report 1984 projects an annual growth rate of 4.2 per cent for the urban population of India during 1980-2000,

* The author had published several articles dealing with issues relating to *Urbanization, Urban Development and Metropolitan Cities in India*, which have been published in Volume 1 of his works in 2007 by Concept Publishing Co. Pvt. Ltd.. This section of the Chapter analyzes the latest data available on the subject up to 2002.

significantly higher than the growth rate of 3.5 per cent experienced during 1961-1981 (Table 20.6). The acceleration is projected along with projection of slower growth of the total population—from an average of 2.3 per cent p.a. during 1961-1981 to 1.9 per cent p.a. during 1980-2000. The growth rate of the rural population is projected to be reduced accordingly, from 1.8 per cent p.a. to 1.1 per cent. The proportion of urban population to the total population which had increased slowly from 16.8 per cent in 1951 to 23.3 per cent by 1981 is projected to increase rapidly to 35.5 per cent by the year 2000; more than one-third of the total population would be urban by the end of the century. On the basis of the median projection of 994 million for the total population in the year 2000, the urban population would exceed 350 million; more than double the figure of 156 million for 1981. Increasing urbanization in India is part of an LDC-wide process, but the rates of growth of both the total population and the urban population, projected for India for the period 1980-2000, are lower than the rates projected for all 'low income economies other than India and China' (Table. 20.4).

The WDR's projection of growth of the urban population is much higher than the official projection contained in the Sixth Five-Year Plan 1980-85. According to the latter, the urban population was expected to increase by 2.9 per cent p.a. during 1980-96 and to rise to 25.4 per cent of the total population by 1996. The rate of growth of the total population projected in it was lower than that in the WDR's projection, but of growth of GDP per capita was higher. The comparative figures of the two projections are given in Table 20.6.

Both the rate of growth of the urban population and increase in the proportion of urban population to the total population in the Sixth/Seventh Plan projections were lower than those observed during the 20 years 1961-1981, and appear too low in the context of the major acceleration of growth of GDP per capita projected in the Plan. The WDR's projection of growth of the urban population may on the other hand prove to be too high; it is related to the acceleration of economic growth projected by it. During 1965-1990, the growth rate of GDP had averaged 3.9 per cent, and of Gross National Product (GNP) per capita 1.9 per cent p.a. (World Development Report 1992, p. 218). During 1985-95, however the growth rate of GDP per capita is projected in the WDR to average 2.5 per cent p.a. under the 'low case scenario', which is based on assumptions of relatively unfavourable conditions for economic growth in the industrial market economy countries and of world trade. Under the 'high case scenario', which is based on more favourable assumptions about the two variables; significantly higher rates of economic growth are projected for the LDCs. Thus the rate of growth for 'Low Income Asia' of which India forms part is projected to increase from 3.0 per cent p.a. under the 'low case scenario' to 3.7 per cent p.a. under the 'high case scenario'. Although the rate for India under the latter is not mentioned in the WDR, the figure of somewhat over 3 per cent p.a. can be assumed by keeping the Indian rate about 0.5 per cent p.a. lower than the average for 'low income Asia'. The projections of the WDR thus assume a radical change in the performance of the Indian economy during 1985-1995 from that during 1960-1982, even the growth rate projected under the 'low case scenario' is almost double the rate actually achieved during 1960-1982 (Table 20.6a).

The performance of the Indian economy during the past five years has been relatively good. Average economic growth for 1980-1985 is estimated at around 5.4 per cent p.a. which translates into a growth rate of GDP per capita of well over 3 per cent p.a. But the experience of five years is too short to provide a basis for projection of economic growth over a decade because the performance of the Indian economy is still influenced so much by the monsoons. The five years, 1980-1985, included two years, 1983-84 and 1984-85, of favourable monsoons. The rain gods are not always so kind. One or more bad monsoons would lead to sharp fall in both agricultural and industrial output and also to severe pressure on foreign exchange resources because of the need, mentioned earlier, for large imports of food and of petroleum.

The second critical factor will be experience with the economic liberalization policies, which have been followed since the late 1970s but which have been given much greater emphasis by the new Government. Reference has been made earlier to the risk of failure of the policies, and the possibility of their reversal leading to serious economic dislocation and a period of stagnation.

Distribution of the Urban Population by Towns of Different Sizes

By 1981, more than 60 per cent of the urban population was living in cities (towns with population of 100,000 or more), the proportion having gone up progressively from 38 per cent in 1951 (Table 20.7a). On the other hand, the proportion of urban population living in the smallest urban places (with population below 20,000) had gone down progressively from 32 per cent in 1951 to 13.6 per cent in 1981 and less than 11 per cent in 1991. Of the city population, as much as 60 per cent in 1981 and

64 per cent in 1991 was living in the larger cities with population of 500,000 or more. The number of such cities had gone up rapidly from 11 in 1961 to 42 in 1981[4] whereas the number of million+ cities had gone up from 5 in 1951 to 45 in 2001; their number doubled every ten years between 1981 and 2001.

Data on growth of population during 1961-81 of urban places of different size classes, given in Table 20.8, indicate more rapid growth rates for the cities, particularly the larger cities than for the smaller urban places. The fastest growth rates were recorded by the cities with population of 500,000 or more, excluding, however, the four metropolitan cities of Kolkata, Mumbai, Chennai and Delhi. The latter registered as a group, an average growth rate of 3.5 per cent p.a. in 1961-1981 and 4 per cent between 1980-2000 (Table 20.8a), lower than the growth rates recorded by most other cities. The lowest growth rates were recorded by the small urban places, with population below 50,000 and especially those with population below 20,000.

Four factors contributed to rapid growth of the larger urban places :

(i) Natural increase of the population already resident in them;
(ii) In-migration from villages or smaller urban places;
(iii) Expansion of administrative areas to include villages and small towns, located in their peripheral zones, and
(iv) Increase in the number of larger urban places by inclusion in them of smaller places after they crossed the threshold population for the larger place.

The last factor appears to have been particularly important in case of cities with population of 500,000 or more. The increase in the number of such cities, from 11 in 1961 to 42 in 1981, contributed half of the population increase recorded during this period—20.8 million out of 41.2 million. If the number of cities were held constant at the 1961 figure of 11, the rates of increase for this size class would be 3.1 per cent during 1961-1971 and 3.8 per cent during 1971-1981 (Table 20.8b).

Slow growth of the smallest urban places appears to have been due in part to a definitional change—adoption in the Census of 1961 of more restrictive criteria for designating a place as 'urban'. Mitra, who as Census Commissioner had responsibility for overseeing application of the new criteria writes "The application of new tests on the eve of the 1961 Census disqualified 812 places with a total population of 4.4 million...... on the other hand, 483 million were treated as living in towns for the first time." (Population Census Report, 1961).

Rapid increase in the population of cities, especially the larger cities with population of 500,000 or more, may be expected to continue. Extrapolation to the year 2000 of the average growth rate of 5.5 per cent recorded by the cities during 1961-81 would take their total population to 178 million, more than half of the projected total urban population of 353 million. All the four factors listed above including increase in the number of cities with population of 500,000 or more, which have contributed to rapid growth of such cities in the recent past, will be operative during this period. The 1981 Census listed 28 cities with populations of 300,000-500,000 which could enter this class with an average annual growth rate of only 2.7 per cent; most of them had experienced much higher growth rates during 1961-1981.

The Spatial Pattern of Urbanization

There was much discussion during the early 1960s on the most appropriate spatial pattern of urbanization for India. The impetus for the discussion came both from industrial planners and economists who were concerned with location of industries, and from urban planners who were engaged in preparing urban development plans. The background to the discussion was provided by the following :

(i) Increased interest by the Central Government in urban planning and development as evidenced by the establishment of the Town and Country Planning Organization within the Central Government;

(ii) Encouragement given by it to the State Governments to establish similar planning organizations and to prepare development plans, particularly for the large cities; the Master Plan for Delhi had been completed by 1960;

(iii) Emphasis given in the Second and Third Five Year Plans to industrialization, particularly establishment of basic, heavy industries, such as steel, heavy machinery, chemicals etc., in the public sector; and

(iv) Building by the Central Government of new towns, or virtually new towns in the vicinity of cities like Bhopal and Ranchi, to locate large public sector industrial units.

It is of interest to mention that industrialization was seen as the key element in urbanization despite mounting evidence that the needs of modern industry for labour were relatively limited—far less than they had been in the 19th century when the countries of Europe and North America were undergoing industrialization, and that the rate of post-war urbanization in India and in most other LDCs were far in excess of those required to meet the demands of modern industry for labour.

Dispersed Industrial Development and Urbanization

The consensus of opinion was in favour of dispersed development of industries which would contribute to dispersed urbanization; it is reflected very well in the papers presented at the seminar on the prospects and strategies for urbanization in India held in 1960 at the University of California, Berkeley and included in the volume *India's Urban Future* mentioned earlier. Several strands of thought converged to form the consensus (Turner, 1962).

(i) *Cost of Urbanization* : The realization that urbanization with focus on rapid growth of the large metropolitan cities would involve such high costs of expansion of housing, and of urban infrastructures as could not be incurred by a low income country, such as India. The failure to incur the costs because of resource constraints would lead to further aggravation of the problems of congestion, proliferation of slums and pressures on essential service facilities—transport, water and sanitation, electricity, education, health and others—which were already acute in the large cities. These costs would be much lower, however, in smaller urban places and on the outskirts of the large cities. There would also be greater scope for use of simpler technology, and cheaper, locally available materials. Self-help by the beneficiaries could reduce the costs further. The data, then available, indicated that the unit costs of providing housing in the central, maximum density area of Mumbai and Kolkata were 2 to 3 times higher than those in the smaller towns, or on the outskirts of these cities, and that the use of simpler technology and self-help by the beneficiaries could raise the differential to 5 or 6 times, i.e. a ratio of 1 : 6. (Nath, 2007, Chapter 1, pp. 7-8). Costs of transport were also much lower with dispersed urbanization because long journeys for work in the large cities, which required use of mass transport facilities, could be avoided; the workers could travel the short distances to their work places by bicycles or on foot.

(ii) *Promotion of Small Scale and Agro-based Industries* : It was argued that the employment generation potential of such industries was much larger than that of large, capital-intensive industries. Furthermore, growth of small and agro-based industries in medium-sized or small towns would promote growth of entrepreneurship and diffusion of industrial skills. It would also provide a strong stimulus to improvement of agricultural techniques and increase in agricultural output because of the linkages between these industries and agriculture.

It is noteworthy that while the relationship between dispersed development of small and agro-based industries and expansion of employment and development of agriculture was clearly seen, the perception of a wider relationship between dispersed urbanization and rural development, of small towns, such as market centres, serving as foci of economic growth in micro-regions through their various functions—marketing and processing of agriculture produce, distribution of consumer goods, and agricultural inputs, servicing and repair of implements and manufacture of a limited range of consumer goods for the micro-regional market, etc., was not common. One reason for lack of interest in the latter relationship was dominance, especially in the states of rural-based, tradition oriented political leaders who did not see the linkages between rural and urban development. They viewed towns and villages primarily as competitors for scarce resources of finance and manpower and were concerned with obtaining the maximum resources for the villages, which they felt had long been neglected (Nath, 2007, Table 7.5B, p. 132).

(iii) *The Need to Accelerate Development of Backward Regions* : The political leaders of these regions first concentrated their efforts on securing location in them of large, centrally financed resource development or industrial projects—irrigation or irrigation-*cum*-hydroelectric projects in the early 1950s and public sector industrial projects in the late 1950s and the early 1960s. The projects were seen by them, as also by the national planners, as 'nuclei of regional growth' location of which would through their multiple backward and forward linkages set in motion a process of rapid economic growth in the regions. But by the late 1960s, when decisions on location of most large projects had already been taken and there had been experience of limited (and in some cases negative) economic impact of the projects, the leaders turned their attention to pressing the Central or State Governments for undertaking in their regions broad-based regional development programmes. Location of industries supplying the regional market, or of footloose industries which though supplying much larger markets could be located within the regions, was regarded as an important component of the programmes.

(iv) *Interest in the Relationship between Rural and Urban Economic Development* and in using it in formulation of spatial development strategies was confirmed by a few economists with interest in the spatial aspect of economic development. Starting from the rural end of the relationship, the author emphasized the emerging role of small towns and large villages as multi-service centres for groups of villages, and referred to the prospect of gradual emergence of a new rural community consisting of the service centres and the group of villages served by it (Nath, 2007, Chapter 4, pp. 67-90). For Johnson (1965), the market town was the service centre; he recommended building of about 5000 new market towns as an essential element of India's development strategy. Lewis (1962) advocated promoting development of towns with populations of 20,000—300,000. The towns at the lower end of the population range would be micro-regional service centres; Lewis emphasized the importance of a rural-urban continuum in economic development. As regards towns at the upper end of the population range, he argued that they were large enough to provide to the industries located in them all the facilities—physical and economic infrastructures, skilled labour, entrepreneurship, and active interaction with ancillary and other linked industries—which were provided by the big cities, but were at the same time small enough to escape the latter's disadvantages of excessive costs of housing and urban services and existence of difficult social problems. His view found considerable support among urban planners although it had few adherents among official policy-makers.

The strategies of promoting growth of micro-regional service centres on the one hand and medium-sized cities with populations of about 300,000 on the other, need to be re-examined keeping in view particularly the growth experience of the past 25 years. It will be recalled that the smallest size urban places, with populations below 20,000 experienced very slow growth during 1961-1981 and that the smaller cities with population in the 100,000—500,000 range had significantly lower growth rates than the larger cities, in the 500,000 to 1 million and 1 million and above size classes (Table 20.8). The reasons for slow growth of the smallest urban places need to be investigated. If it is revealed that growth of non-agricultural employment in them had been much faster than the growth of population and that the latter was slow because a large proportion of the non-agricultural workers in them were commuters from neighbouring villages, there would be a good case for promoting growth of small towns as industrial-*cum*-service centres. If on the other hand, growth of non-agricultural employment had also been slow, the finding would indicate the limited growth potential of the small towns. It may be mentioned that the multi-service role of the small towns becomes progressively more important with agricultural development and increases in rural incomes; because it is only with these that the rural population has increasing need and capacity to pay for the variety of services and goods that are provided by such towns.

As regards the medium sized cities, keeping the upper limit for support of growth to a population size of 300,000 or even 500,000 would mean withdrawal of support when they were in their most active growth phase. The limit will need to be much higher, perhaps in the region of a population of one million or even higher. It should be a range of population, in which the disadvantages of large size, such as rapid increase in costs of expansion of housing and urban housing, and social problems become pronounced.

Official Interventions to Promote Dispersed Industrial Development

Official interventions for promoting dispersed industrial development included both incentives and sanctions, with emphasis from the outset on the former. The principal incentives were providing (a) land and various infrastructure facilities (electricity, water, road and/or railway connections, drainage etc.,) needed by the industrial units, rapidly and at low cost; (b) concessional loans and other fiscal incentives to the entrepreneurs, and (c) technical assistance to them, e.g. for project appraisal and selection of equipment, or in some areas of management. These facilities were provided typically for industries locating in the industrial estates in the mid-1950s under a programme sponsored by the Central Government. While promoting development of small industries and industrial dispersal remained the professed objectives of building of the industrial estates and areas, the actual locations of these indicated that the State Governments attached equal or greater importance to promoting the industrial development of the state. Thus while a large number of industrial estates and areas were built in backward regions or near medium-sized or small towns, some of the largest and most successful ones were located in the vicinity of large cities, including the state capitals, and metropolitan cities like Delhi, Chennai and Mumbai. In their anxiety to promote development of industries, the State Governments were ready to provide these facilities, wherever the prospective industrialists wanted them.

The principal sanction, denying permission to locate industries within the municipal areas of large cities—is applied through local zoning regulations. But under the system of industrial licensing, which has been an important instrument of controlling industrial development by the Central and State Governments, both sanctions and incentives have been combined to promote location of industries in backward regions or other areas preferred by the government. Location of the industrial unit is specified in the licence permitting its establishment; concessional loans by official credit agencies—banks and industrial finance corporations—are provided for the licensed units. The concessions are particularly generous for industrial units locating in backward regions.

Waning of Official Interest in Industrial Location and Urbanization

Official interest in the strategies of industrial location and urbanization had waned, however, by the late 1960s because the attention of the policy-makers and planners had shifted to the urgent tasks of overcoming the serious imbalances in the economy, particularly an acute food shortage and large external payments deficits, that had appeared. Growth of agricultural and cereal output which had been well ahead of the growth of population in the 1950s had slowed down in the 1960s, partly because agricultural development had not received under the Second and Third Five Year Plan (1956-1966) the top priority attention and the resources, that it had received under the First Plan (1951-1956): the development strategy of both plans had focused as mentioned earlier on industrialization, particularly development of basic, heavy industries in the public sector. Widespread and severe drought, during both 1965-66 and 1966-67 led to a steep fall in agricultural output and famines could be avoided only by massive imports of cereals, of about 10 m.t. in each year. The balance of payments deficits were due partly to the large investment needs of the new industrial units. Furthermore, the returns in terms of increased output from the heavy investments in the units and related infrastructures were being delayed because of the nature of the lumpy investments and the serious gestation problems that some of the largest units were facing.

Although the imbalances had been reduced by the end of the decade—food production increased rapidly during the late 1960s with the green revolution in the wheat-producing region of northwestern India—interest in industrial location or urbanization was not revived. The policy-makers remained preoccupied throughout the 1970s with current economic problems, such as coping with: (a) the effects on the balance of payments and domestic costs and prices of the steep increases in petroleum price during 1973-74 and again in 1979-80; and (b) the shifts in economic policies that accompanied the political changes of latter half of the decade—the Emergency (1975-76), coming to power of the Janata Party in 1977 after the defeat of the Congress (I) party in the General Election of 1977, and the return of Congress (I) to power in 1980.

Despite this lack of interest, however, one element of the strategy of industrial location, viz. encouraging location at the outskirts of the cities (including satellite towns of the large metropolitan cities), and in backward regions, has remained. Such locations have continued to be encouraged through substantial capital investment by the State Governments in developing industrial areas and estates, and by the other measures mentioned above. Particularly generous fiscal incentives have continued to be given, and the powers of the Central and State Governments for licensing of industries have been used to promote location of industries in the backward regions. On the other hand, there has been little action towards checking rapid growth of the large cities despite evidence of increasing deterioration in urban conditions. The inevitability of rapid growth of the cities, including the largest like Mumbai and Delhi, has been accepted and not only has the growth not been discouraged, but it has at times been encouraged by official actions. Thus in Mumbai, the proposals, to concentrate further development on the mainland across the bay from the present city, including by shifting progressively the offices of the Maharashtra Government to this area, in order to relieve the congestion in the central business district of the city, and to connect the two parts by a number of bridges, which had been accepted in the mid-1960s were not implemented. On the contrary, further concentration of population and economic activities in the central area of the city was allowed and even encouraged by permitting construction of high-rise residential and commercial buildings and by the Maharashtra Government itself which sold land reclaimed from the sea in the Nariman Point area for construction of such buildings.

The current policy of economic liberalization gives the private sector much greater latitude in industrial decisions, including those on location of industries. Licensing of industries is now restricted to industrial units of large size with projected investment of Rs. 250 million or more. This latitude should favour location of industries near the large cities because such location continues to be the most attractive for all entrepreneurs except those wishing to establish very large industrial units. The reasons for the attraction of near-city location range from ease of effective supervision of the unit by the owners or managers from their homes in the cities, to access to capital and skilled labour, and the output of ancillary industries. The wider range and higher quality of infrastructure and social services (from telecommunications to education and health) in or near the cities is itself a very important attraction, because the range of such services is very restricted away from the cities and their functional efficiency is very low. States like Maharashtra may continue their policy of diverting industries away from the over urbanized Mumbai-Poona region to the less developed regions of the state, but the dominant trend among the State Governments will be towards further backpedaling on the industrial location issue and encouraging the prospective investors to locate industries almost wherever they want. Indeed, the efforts of the State Governments to attract industrial investment in their states are expected to become aggressive in the future, culminating at times in intense competition among the governments to attract large industrial units.

Density Gradients and Zones of Urban Influence

Brush (1962, pp. 57-70) and Ellefsen (1962, pp. 94-116) had described the steep gradients in population density from the central areas of Indian cities to the peripheral zones. Brush had presented data for a large number of cities, based on studies conducted by him during the 1960s. Ellefsen had developed a generalized density gradient based on his studies, conducted during 1959-60 in five large cities—Mumbai, Chennai, Delhi, Hyderabad and Baroda—and also a generalized schematic map showing the extension of urban influence into the hinterland. The map showed a narrow belt of urban influence surrounding the suburbs of the city and ribbons of urban influence extending into the hinterland along the principal lines of communications. The width of the belt was fixed by him at 2 miles and of the ribbons at 1 mile on either side of all-weather roads. For villages along a railway line, location within one mile of the railway station was an essential condition for being included within the ribbon. Thus the zone of significant urban influence, marked by active urban-rural interactions, was quite small. A similar conclusion had emerged from several studies conducted during the 1950s. One study had revealed that the zone of effective impact of Nasik, a city with a population of almost 100,000 located almost 100 miles north of Mumbai was only about six miles; villages located beyond this distance were relatively untouched by the city.

But Ellefsen had conducted his study in 1959-60 and the other studies mentioned above are of the mid-fifties. Since then there has been tremendous expansion of rural communications and extension to the villages of other modernizing infrastructures, such as electricity. The length of surfaced roads increased by nearly three times between 1961 and 1981—from 263,000 k.m. to 692,000 k.m. and of passenger traffic by road nearly 5 times—from 57 billion to 270 billion passenger k.m. by 1982, almost half of all the villages of India, and more than 80 per cent of those with population of 1500 or more, were connected with roads. The progress of rural electrification has been even more rapid. In 1961, less than 2 per cent of India's villages were electrified. By 1982 the proportion had risen to 56 per cent. In 4 states—Punjab, Haryana, Kerala and Tamil Nadu all the villages were reported to be electrified and the proportion were 70-90 per cent in another five small states.

One would expect, therefore, a marked increase in urban-rural interactions since the late 1950s, and both broadening of Ellefsen's belt of urban influences and lengthening and broadening of the 'fingers of urban influence'.

Rurban Corridors

In relatively developed regions of high population density, in which several cities or smaller towns are located at short distances from one another, the fingers of urban influence radiating from several adjacent cities or towns could coalesce to form a continuous zone of urban influence. Such zones had begun to appear by the late 1960s in a few regions, notably the Central Gujarat plain, along the highway and the railway line connecting the cities of Ahmedabad and Baroda, and in Punjab and Haryana along the highway linking Amritsar and Delhi. Each zone included a number of urban places, and the villages located with them were being progressively urbanized with locations in or near them of industrial units or various services facilities such as training centres and colleges. The zones could be designated as 'rurban corridors' because of the intermixture of villages and towns in them and because they extended corridor—like along the lines of communications. Both 'corridors' were located within regions in which infrastructures and service facilities were relatively developed and the levels of agricultural productivity and rural incomes were high. They provided a good example not only of vigorous urban-rural interaction but also of successful industrial dispersal and development of agro-industries. The cities and towns located within them provided to the villagers, non-agricultural employment, markets for high value perishable agricultural products such as milk, vegetables and fruit and a variety of services ranging from marketing and processing of agricultural products and distribution of goods, to education and recreation. They also served as centres for diffusion of new ideas, techniques and skills. The villages provided cheap land and labour for the various industrial and service units.

Because of the importance given to industrial dispersal, development of agro-industries and vigorous rural-urban interaction in India's development strategy, detailed studies of these aspects in these rurban corridors—several others should have developed since then in the other parts of the country—will be of interest to development planners, economists and other social scientists. The studies will reveal the details of rural-urban interactions and of the linkages between agricultural, industrial and service activities. Furthermore, they could provide useful insights into the conditions essential for dispersed development, and the relationship between agricultural and overall regional economic development.

List of Provisional Population Tables

Provisional Population Table	*Title*	*Level of Presentation*	*Page Nos.*
1.	Population and literates in States and Union territories by residence and sex, 1991	India, State/Union territory	91-95
2.	Population and literates in districts by residence and sex, 1991	India, State/Union territory, district and urban agglomeration/city with a population of 1,00,000 and above	96-149
3.	Percentage of urban population, decennial growth rate, sex ratio by residence and density	India, State/Union territory and district	150-168
4.	Population of urban agglomerations, cities and towns, 1991	Urban agglomeration/city/ town and constituent units of urban agglomeration	169-369
5.	Number of urban agglomerations/towns in States and Union territories by size class, 1951-1991	India and State/Union territory	371-373
6.	Population of urban agglomerations/towns in States and Union territories by size class, 1951-1991	India and State/Union territory	375-383
7.	Urban population by size class of urban agglomerations/towns, 1971-1991	India, State/Union territory and size classes I to VI	385-393
8.	Urban population by size class of urban agglomerations/towns by sex, 1991	India, State/Union territory and size classes I to VI	395-403
9.	Population, growth rate and sex ratio of urban agglomerations/cities with a population of 100,000 and above arranged in descending order of population, 1991	Urban agglomeration/city with more than 100,000 population	405-415
10.	Population of urban agglomerations/towns (a) common in 1971 and 1981 by their size class in 1971; and (b) common in 1981 and 1991 by their size class in 1981	India, State/Union territory and size classes I to VI	416-425

NOTES

1. In the review of 'Census of India Paper I Provisional Population Totals' (*EPW* September 14), the number of million-plus cities was stated to be 21. It has since been revised to 23 with the addition of Kochi (formerly Cochin) in Kerala and Ludhiana in Punjab. The other changes resulting from the addition are as follows :

	Provisional Population Totals	*Revised*
No. of million-plus cities	21	23
Total population of the cities (millions)	68.56	70.66
Percentage of population to million-plus cities to :		
(a) urban population	29.6	32.5
(b) total population	8.12	8.37

2. Statement 25, p. 47. Only cities with population of 5 million or more were ranked. The ranks varied from 6th for Greater Bombay to 31st for Madras. Mexico City with a population, estimated at 20.2 million ranked first and Leningrad with a population of 5.1 million ranked last. As many as 14 of the 34 mega cities were from the LDCs of Asia.
3. "Besides, the Directors of Census Operations in States/Union Territories were allowed to include in consultation with the concerned State Governments/Union Territory Administrations and the Census Commissioner of India, some places having distinct urban characteristics as urban even if such places did not strictly satisfy all the criteria mentioned under category (b). Such marginal cases include major project colonies, areas of important tourist centres etc." (p. 7).
4. According to a paper prepared by the Asian Development Bank "India Country Paper" for Regional Seminar on Major Policy Issues held in Manila, 3-7 February, 1987 "The large cities are not growing at rates significantly higher than the others; the secondary cities are growing fast; the small and medium towns are not languishing:" (p. 399).

REFERENCES

Brush, John: *The* Morphology of Indian Cities in *Turner Roy*: *India's Urban Future*. University of California Press 1962.

Ellefsen, Richard A: City-Hinterland Relationship in India in Turner Roy 1962. *India's Urban Future*. University of California Press 1962.

Johnson, E.A.J.: '*Market Towns and Spatial Development in India*', National Council of Applied Economic Research, New Delhi, October 1965.

Lewis, J.P.: *Quiet Crisis in India*; The Brookings Institution, Washington, D.C., 1965.

Ministry of Urban Development, *Report of the National Commission on Urbanization,* Vol. II, New Delhi, August 1988, Table A22, p. 26.

Mohan, R. (1985) : Urbaniztion in India's Future. *Population and Development Review* 2 (4) December 1985, Table 7, p. 63 and Table 8, p. 631.

Nath, V.: *Urbanization, Urban Development & Metropolitan Cities in India.* Concept Publishing Company Pvt. Ltd., New Delhi, 2007.

Turner, Roy: *India's Urban Future*, University of California Press, 1962.

World Bank, *World Development Report*, 1991, Appendix Table 2, pp. 206-7.

21

The Decennial Census of Population 2001 : A Research Note and First Results of Census 2001—A Regional Analysis

I

The decennial census of population is the largest administrative undertaking in India and one of the largest in the world. Employed in it are hundreds of thousands of enumerators, usually school teachers or other educated persons, such as secretaries of *panchayats* and cooperative societies. In addition, thousands are engaged in offices of Census Commissioner of India and Superintendents (Directors) of Census in the States and Union Territories. They analyze the data collected in the census and prepare reports on the demographic, social and economic characteristics of the population.

The enumerators who interview the people often do not understand the significance of many questions that they ask them. The people who respond to the questions may, because of political reasons or social inhibitions, be reluctant to give correct answers to various questions. Despite these limitations, various surveys conducted after every census since 1951 have revealed that the margin of error in the data collected in the census is no more than $1–1\frac{1}{2}$ per cent.

In most developed countries of the world the census is a technical undertaking; the Census Commissioner is an eminent demographer or other social scientist. In India, however, it is an administrative undertaking; the Census Commissioner of India and the Superintendents/Directors of Census in the States and Union Territories are senior officers of the Indian

---

* Published in "*Population Geography*", Vol. 20, Nos. 1 and 2, June-December 1998.

Administrative Service. There is a valid reason for this preference for administrative officers.

The enumerators get very little money for the time that they spend in filling the questionnaires. However, they cannot refuse to do so because a refusal would make them liable for punishment which may extend to being sent to prison. The Census Commissioner is advised however by an Advisory Committee consisting of demographers, economists and other social scientists. They assist the Census Commissioner in drafting the questionnaire and preparing a plan for analyzing the data so that the census yields results which are most important for formulating policies for economic development and social progress of the people.

Another important characteristic of the census of population is that it has been taken without break since 1872. The census of 2001 will be the 14th in a series that began in that year. During this period, the country was visited by two famines in the last two decades of the 19th century and again in 1943 in which millions died. Millions perished also in the epidemics of bubonic plague in the first decade of the 20th century and again in the influenza epidemic of 1918-19. The country was partitioned into India and Pakistan in 1947. The partition was followed by the largest and bloodiest migration in human history in which hundreds of thousands died or were wounded. Despite these man-made and natural calamities, the decennial censuses have been conducted in the first year of every decade with regularity since 1872. Maintain such an unbroken record through all these natural and man-made calamities is a record of which the nation may well be proud.

The census of population is conducted over a period of 3 weeks during February of the census year. In mountainous areas it is conducted in early summer.

Census of Housing

Six to nine months before the population census, a census of housing is conducted. In it, data is collected about the type of house in which a census household lives. The house may be *Pucca* (built of brick and mortar with roof of concrete or baked tiles), Semi-*Pucca* (built of stone or other locally available strong material which would withstand the onslaught of the monsoon rains) or *kutcha* (with roofs of thatch and/or corrugated iron sheets and walls of bricks of unbaked clay, thatch and mud floors). Such houses are likely to be damaged or even destroyed during heavy monsoon rains or cyclones that visit various areas along the coasts from time to time. The amenities available in the house such as adequate supplies of water and electricity and arrangements for disposal of solid and liquid waste and the number of persons per room are also indicated. Finally, the housing census collects data about homeless persons and inmates of institutions such as hostels.

Census Monographs

The detailed reports prepared by the Census Commissioner of India and the Superintendents of Census of the States/Union Territories are published 1-3 years after the census. Before them however, short monographs are published which contain preliminary population totals; distribution of the population by age and sex, the literacy rate, crude birth, death and infant mortality rates and other details. In 1951 one such paper was published within a few weeks of conduct of the census. It contained preliminary estimates of total population, its growth during the previous decade; its distribution by sex; birth, death and infant mortality rates; literacy rate by sex; distribution of population by rural and urban areas and by urban places of different sizes. All this data was given by States and Union Territories.

In 1991, three such papers were published. The first, published within a few weeks of conduct of the census contained preliminary population totals, its distribution by sex; its growth during 1981-1991; comparative data on growth rates during the three previous decades; birth, death and infant mortality rates; literacy rate by sex, life expectancy at birth by sex, distribution by rural and urban areas and population of urban places of different sizes. All these data were given by States and Union Territories and contained, besides the detailed data, explanatory notes, a few shorter tables and some pictogrammes and maps.

Two other papers were published within 18 months of conduct of the 1991 census. The first contained detailed data by States and Union Territories on rural and urban distribution of the population and populations of urban places of different sizes. The second paper contained detailed data on workers and non-workers and the distribution of workers by 10 major occupational categories. Besides the detailed tables, both papers contained a number of shorter tables, maps and pictograms and detailed explanatory notes in order to make the data presented in them easily intelligible to Members of Parliament and Legislatures of states and other policy-makers. Demographers, economists and other social scientists have been using them extensively for their analysis of the census data.

The Census Commissioner of 1951 cautioned the government against too rapid growth of population and recommended that it should initiate immediately a vigorous programme of family planning in order to slow it down. The recommendation was accepted by the government and a programme to propagate family planning was started. The programme, rather ineffective at first, has become increasingly effective. It now forms the basis of the national population policy. Its results are noticeable. In Kerala and Goa, for instance, where total and female literacy rates are high, the rates of natural increase of population are only marginally higher than replacement rates.

The Census of 1991 has revealed increasing urbanization of the population and its concentration in cities with a population of 1 million or more. From various projections made by demographers it appears that the Census of 2001 will show accentuation of these trends. The number of metropolitan cities is expected to nearly double from 23 in 1991 to about 40 in 2001. Since most of the factories and small scale industries and modern services are concentrated in these cities or their peri-urban areas, there is need for very large investment for expansion of facilities for electricity, water supply, disposal of solid and liquid waste, intra-city management of traffic, adequacy of housing and ensuring effectiveness of measures for providing security of life and property to the citizens to ensure that the cities perform their role efficiently.

It is of interest to note that the official definition of many terms that geographers and other social scientists use are given by the census. Take village, town, city, house and household as examples. In many states, the village is a tightly nucleated settlement with a population of not more than 5,000. However, in Kerala where most rural households live in houses surrounded by fields of rice and tapioca and a grove of coconut or other trees, the village is a purely administrative unit, which may have a population of 10,000 or more. In Tamil Nadu, Karnataka, Andhra Pradesh, West Bengal, Bihar, Orissa, Eastern and Central Uttar Pradesh, the village includes a central settlement in which the majority of the population consists of high castes and one or more hamlets inhabited by people of the Scheduled Castes. In Himachal Pradesh and adjoining Uttaranchal (now Uttarakhand) and in the seven states of the eastern Himalayan region, the population of a village may be 500 or less.

A town is an urban area with a population of between 5,000 and 100,000 which has a municipal committee, notified area committee or other such administrative body, with powers of taxation of households and responsibility for provision of essential services to the residents. A city is a settlement unit of 100,000 or more.

A house, defined by the Census is a residential structure. Any attachments to the house for tying livestock or for storing grain or fodder are considered to be part of the house. A census household consists of persons of one or more nuclear families who have a common kitchen. A census house may contain in rural areas, two or more households each of which has a separate kitchen. In cities, however, a multi-storey flat which houses a number of households is not considered a house. It is considered a collection of houses depending upon the number of households that are living in it.

The reports of the Census Commissioners are masterly treatises, several of which have had great influence on social and economic policies. The report of the Census of Population of 1931 is the most authoritative treatise on castes of India and Pakistan.

The Census of 1951 presented data of the census by both States and Union Territories and by resource development regions. This practice was continued in the Census of 1961; the Commissioner refined the scheme of resource development regions and made it more scientific. The regions, now called agro-climatic regions, are used by the Ministry of Agriculture to present forecasts of production of cereals and other food and cash crops every year. The Census Commissioner of 1951 warned the policy-makers of the danger of rapid growth of population and the absolute need to undertake an effective programme of family limitation in order to reduce the rate. The rate in 1941-1951 was only 12.5 per cent as against 19.5 per cent during 1981-1991.

The reports of the 1991 census have revealed large inter-state differences in rates of literacy, female literacy and growth rate of population. In Kerala and Goa, overall and female literacy were very high and rates of growth of population were 1.3 to 1.4 per cent per annum respectively, slightly above the replacement rate of 1.2 per cent per annum. On the other hand, in Rajasthan, U.P., Bihar and Madhya Pradesh the overall and female literacy rates were very low, and rates of population growth were 2.2 to 2.5 per cent per annum. The rates were even higher in Jammu and Kashmir and some states inhabited mainly by tribal in the north east.

The Census of 2001 will reveal the results of campaigns for increasing literacy launched in the 1990s by Madhya Pradesh and other states.

The report of the 2001 census together with data collected by the National Sample Survey will indicate the progress, if any, made in reduction of poverty as a result of the economic liberalization programme undertaken since 1991. The result should form the basis for significant modification of the anti-poverty programmes in order to make them more effective.

II
First Results of the Decennial Census of Population 2001

A Regional Analysis

The first results of Census of Population of 2001 show an unmistakable trend towards a decline in growth rate of population. The rate 21.4 per cent during 1991-2001 has declined for two successive decades 1981-2001 after having peaked at 25 per cent during 1961-1981. Thus, the cumulative decline between 1981 and 2001 is about 12 per cent. In several states, the rates of growth in 1991-2001 were lower than the rate needed to hold a stationary population or just above it.

Projecting the trend over the next 15 years UNDP, New Delhi has forecast a total population of 1235 million by 2015. The Census Commissioner's estimate is slightly higher, 1263 million. In both estimates, the annual rate of growth of population is estimated at 1.3 per cent p.a. The decline in the growth rate during 1991-2001, has occurred in a decade in which per capita income has been rising by 3-4 per cent per annum. On the other hand increasing growth rate during 1951-1981 had occurred in a period in which per capita income had increased by only 0.5 to 1.5 per cent per annum.

If, as expected, per capita income continues to increase at the same or a higher rate during the next decade, India could be considered to have made the demographic transition in which population declines, while per capita income increases steadily.

The decline in growth rate has been caused by the voluntary decision of couples in the reproductive age group to limit the size of their families. The total fertility rate has fallen from 4.6 in 1991 to 3.1 in 2001, i.e. by 1/3rd during the course of a decade. It is projected to decline further to 2.5 by 2011-2016. The couples have made the decision to limit the size of their families after seeing that the survival rate of children is much higher than it used to be. This is the cumulative result of better nutrition, access to adequate and safe water supply and easy access to facilities for treatment of diseases of the digestive and respiratory tracts.

India may have the largest number of illiterates in the world. But progress in reducing illiteracy has been noteworthy. The national literacy rate has increased steadily from 18 per cent in 1951 to 65 per cent in 2001. In several large and populous states, literacy among males is between 70 and 80 per cent and that among females is also between 55 and 70 per cent. In Kerala, the rate is over 90 per cent for males and 88 per cent for females.

Some data on rural/urban distribution of population released by the Census Commissioner indicate that the proportion, urban/total population increased nearly 10 per cent from 25.7 per cent in 1991 to 27.8 per cent in 2001. UNDP has projected that the proportion would rise to 35 per cent by 2015, i.e. by about 20 per cent. The estimate of the Census Commissioner is not yet available. The number of metropolitan cities, i.e. cities with population of 1 million or more has increased from 23 in 1991 to 35 in 2001, i.e. by 50 per cent.

Tamil Nadu, Maharashtra and Gujarat are the most urbanized states with 43.9, 42.4 and 37.4 per cent respectively of their populations living in urban areas. Bihar and Assam are the least urbanized states with 10.5 and 12.7 per cent respectively of their population living in urban areas. The 41 million residents of urban areas of Maharashtra constitute 14 per cent of the total urban residents of the country. It has also the largest number of metropolitan cities, four. Tamil Nadu and Gujarat have three such cities, U.P., the most populous state has six such cities.

Growth of Population

The total population of India was 1027 million in 2001. The rate of growth during 1991-2001 was 21.43 per cent; almost 11 per cent lower than the rate of 23.9 per cent during the previous decade. The average annual exponential growth rate is estimated at 1.93 per annum during 1991-2001. (Population Census, 2001 p. 34). The growth rate has been falling for two successive decades; it had peaked at about 25 per cent during 1961-1981 (Table 21.1). The rate 13.3 per cent during 1941-1951, increased steadily during the next 4 decades (*Ibid*). The increase was due to various measures taken by the government to reduce mortality: (i) assured supply of adequate and safe drinking water to an increasing number of villages and towns and providing facilities for preventive health and medical care to their residents; (ii) eradication of malaria, the great killer during the late 1950s; (iii) reduction of mortality from diseases of the digestive and respiratory tracts due to access to cleaner water supply and also to facilities for primary health and medical care to all the villages and towns in several progressive states; and (iv) better nutrition due to larger availability of cereals. Output of cereals has been increasing steadily thanks to use of dwarf, high-yielding seed varieties of wheat and rice along with recommended dosages of chemical fertilizers and pesticides in areas irrigated by canals or by deep tube-wells, or surface wells fitted with pumps operated by diesel oil or electricity. Output of cereals was 203 m.t. in 1998-99 as against about 60 m.t. during the mid- 1950s. In the past two decades itself it increased from 120 m.t. in 1980-81 to 203 m.t. in 1998-99 (Tata Consultancy Services 2001, Table 35, p. 39).

Table 21.1 : Growth Rate of Population 1951-2001

Decade	*Population (millions)*	*Decade growth rate (per cent)*	*Average annual exponential growth rate (per cent)*
1951	361.1	13.3	1.25
1961	439.2	21.6	1.96
1971	548.2	24.8	2.20
1981	683.3	24.7	2.22
1991	843.4	23.9	2.14
2001	1027.0	21.3	1.93

Source : Registrar General and Census Commissioner, India : Census of India 2001 Paper 1 of 2001: Provisional Population Totals, p. 34, New Delhi, 2001.

The decline in growth rate of population is accompanied by progressive decline in total fertility rate of women in the reproductive age group. The rate in 2000—2001, 3.1 was one-third lower than the rate 4.6 in the previous decade (Population Census 2001, Statement 11, p. 65). The Census Commissioner has projected a further decline to 2.5 by 2011—2016. Projecting continuation of the decline in the growth rate for another 15 years the Census Commissioner has estimated that the population during 2015-16 would be 1263 million (*Ibid* Statement 4, pp. 42-43). UNDP, New Delhi has projected a slightly lower population, 1235 million by 2015 (UNDP 2001, Statement on India).

There was great variation among states in the annual exponential rates of growth of population during 1991-2001, Census of India 2001, Statement 11, pp. 42-43). The annual rate in Kerala (0.9 per cent) and Tamil Nadu (1.0 per cent) were lower than the rate needed to maintain a stationary population. The rate in Andhra Pradesh (1.3 per cent) was just enough to maintain a stationary population. The rates were lower than the national average also in Karnataka (1.6 per cent), Orissa (1.5 per cent), West Bengal (1.6 per cent) and Assam (1.7 per cent). Except, Orissa and Assam all these are relatively developed states with high rates of total male and female literacy (Table 21.2).

Table 21.2 : Growth Rate of Population, 1981-1991 and 1991-2001 and Growth Rate of Per Capita Income 1980-81 to 1996-97 by States

India & States	*Population in 1990-91*	*Population in 2000-01*	*Growth rate of population Per cent per annum*		*Literacy rate (per cent)*			*Per capita income rupees at 1980-81 prices (Rupees)*		
	(millions)	*(millions)*	*1981-91*	*1991-2001*	*Total*	*Male*	*Female*	*1980-81*	*1996-97*	*Increase (%)*
India	846.4	1027.5	2.01	1.93	65.4	75.4	54.16	1625	2814	70.5
Andhra Pradesh	66.5	75.7	2.37	1.30	61.1	70.9	51.5	1380	2134	54.6
Assam	22.4	26.5	2.17	1.73	64.3	71.9	56.0	—	—	—
Bihar	64.5	82.9	2.10	2.50	47.5	60.3	33.6	917	1010	10.1
Goa	1.2	1.3	1.47	1.39	82.5	88.4	75.5	3145	6220	97.8
Gujarat	41.3	50.6	1.92	2.03	70.0	80.0	58.6	1940	3717	91.6
Haryana	16.5	21.0	2.42	2.47	68.6	79.3	56.3	2330	3996	71.5
Karnataka	45.0	52.7	1.92	1.59	67.0	57.0	57.5	1380	2518	64.5
Kerala	29.1	31.8	1.34	0.90	90.9	94.2	87.9	1568	2274	45.0
Madhya Pradesh	48.6	60.4	2.41	2.18	64.1	76.8	50.3	1358	1877	38.0
Maharashtra	78.9	96.8	2.29	2.04	77	87	67.5	2425	4853	100.1
Orissa	31.7	36.7	1.83	1.48	63.6	76.0	50.1	1314	1595	21.4
Punjab	20.3	24.3	1.89	1.80	70.76	63.0	63.5	2674	4171	56.0
Rajasthan	44.0	56.5	2.50	2.49	61.0	76.5	44..	1228	2247	83.0
Tamil Nadu	55.9	62.1	1.43	1.06	73.5	82.1	64.5	1448	2876	98.6
Uttar Pradesh	132.0	166.0	2.28	2.30	57.4	70.0	43.0	1278	1628	27.4
West Bengal	68.0	80.2	2.14	1.64	69.2	70.72	60.2	1773	2641	49.0

The 1991 populations of Uttar Pradesh, Bihar and Madhya Pradesh have been reduced to take into account the separation of Uttaranchal, Jharkhand and Chhattisgarh respectively from the three states.

Sources : Registrar General India : Provisional Population Totals 1990-91, Paper No. 1 of 1991 and Provisional Population Totals, paper 1 of 2001, New Delhi, India.

For per capita income : *Economic and Political Weekly Research Foundation* : National Accounts Statistics of India 1950-51 - 1996-97, Mumbai, 1998 pp. 84.

There has been significant decline in infant mortality and increase in expectation of life at birth. The expectation of life at birth during 1996-2001 was 62.3 years for males and 65.3 years for females (*Ibid* Statement 11, p. 65). The Census Commissioner has projected that the life span will continue to increase during the next 15 years and during 2011-2016, it will be 67.1 years for males and 69.2 years for females. These figures are close to those for many rapidly developing countries of South East Asia at present.

Literacy Rate

India has the dubious distinction of having a larger number of illiterates (296 million) than any other country in the world. However, as the figures presented in the foregoing paragraphs and below indicate, progress in increasing literacy has been noteworthy. The number of literates has increased by 204 million between 1991 and 2001 (Statement 25, p.106).

The rate 65.4 per cent during 2000-01 was nearly 25 per cent higher than the 1990-91 rates of 52 per cent (Census of India, 2001, pp. 113-114). The literacy rate has increased steadily during the last half a century; it was only 18.3 per cent in 1951. The highest rates are in Kerala (90.9 per cent) in the extreme south-west and Mizoram (88.5 per cent) a small state in the north-eastern Himalayan region (*Ibid,* pp. 115-116). The rate is higher than the national average also in Goa (82.3 per cent), Maharashtra (77.3 per cent), Himachal Pradesh (77 per cent), Tamil Nadu (73.5 per cent) and Gujarat, Punjab and Sikkim (70 per cent), [*Ibid,* pp. 117-118]. It is slightly lower in West Bengal and Haryana (69 per cent). In most of these states, literacy rate among males is 80 per cent or higher. In several other large states, the average rates are 65 per cent and above for females and 75 per cent and above for males. In Madhya Pradesh and Rajasthan, states which had very low levels of literacy earlier, the rates in 2001 in Madhya Pradesh were 76 per cent for males and 50.3 per cent for females. In Rajasthan the corresponding figures were 76.5 per cent and 44.3 per cent respectively. In Madhya Pradesh, the female literacy rate has nearly doubled and in Rajasthan it has more than doubled during the decade. The rate in Rajasthan in 1990-91 was only 20.8 per cent, the lowest in the country (*Ibid*, Statement 34, pp. 123-124).

The lowest rates are in U.P. (57.4 per cent) and Bihar (47.5 per cent). Female literacy rates, 43 per cent in U.P. and 31.6 per cent in Bihar are also low. The national literacy rate would be much higher if literacy rates in these two states, which together have about 25 per cent of the population of the country, were higher (Table 21.3).

Table 21.3 : Literacy Rates

Sl. No.	*State*	*Literacy rate in 1991 (per cent)*			*Literacy rate in 2001 (per cent)*		
		Total	*Male*	*Female*	*Total*	*Male*	*Female*
1.	Bihar	38.5	52.6	23.5	47.5	60.3	31.6
2.	U.P.	41.7	55.4	26.0	57.4	70.2	43.0
3.	Rajasthan	38.5	55.1	20.8	61.0	76.5	44.3
4.	M.P.	43.4	57.4	28.4	64.1	76.8	50.3

Source : Registrar General India : Census of India, 2001. Paper No. 1, Provisional Population Tables. New Delhi, 2001.

One result of increase in literacy has been phenomenal growth of the print media—weekly and daily newspapers, magazines and books. The fastest growth of these has been in the regional languages because most of the literates can read and write only in their regional language. The quality of books in regional languages has improved so much that in many years, the national award for the best book is given to a book in a regional language. Films and television serials in regional languages—Marathi, Bengali, Tamil, Telugu, Malayalam and Kannada produced in studios located in these states—have altogether far larger audiences than those for Hindi movies produced in Mumbai.

Sex Ratio

Number of females per 1000 males has been declining steadily through the last century from 972 in 1901 to 927 in 1991. There was a marginal increase to 933 in 2001 (Statement 19, pp. 92-94).The cumulative decline during the 90 years 1901 to 1991 was about 5 per cent. Among states with populations above 20 million the highest ratios are in Kerala (1071), Tamil Nadu (992), Andhra Pradesh (980), Chhattisgarh (990), Maharashtra (923), Karnataka (966), Orissa (976), West Bengal (929), Assam (926), Jharkhand (936) and Gujarat (927). The lowest ratios are in Punjab (886), Haryana (869), Bihar (916), U.P. (895) and Rajasthan (925). Among the states dominated by cities Delhi (813) and Chandigarh (763) have very low sex ratios. The ratio in Maharashtra (923) is also relatively low (*Ibid*).

Among the reasons for low sex ratio, widespread prevalence of infanticide and also feticide in recent years are considered to be the most important. Apparently these are prevalent more in a group of states extending from Punjab and Haryana to Bihar than in the rest of the country. Very low ratios in Chandigarh and Delhi are due mainly to male selective migration to these cities.

Density of Population

Data on density of population is of much interest to geographers, demographers, policy-makers and administrators in various states. Average density of population has increased from 267 in 1991 to 324 in 2001, i.e. by more than 20 per cent (*ibid*, Statement 14, pp. 73). It increased by about 4 times in the course of the last century; the density was only 77 in 1901 (Statement 15, pp. 75-76). Among the states with population above 20 million, the highest densities are in West Bengal (904), Bihar (880), Kerala (819), and U.P. (689) [*ibid*, Chart 1]. A belt of states with high density (500 per sq. km. and above) extends from Delhi in the west to West Bengal in the east. The only southern state with a high density is Kerala (819)[*ibid*, Chart 1].

A medium density belt (281-500 per sq. km.) extends from Gujarat on the west coast through Maharashtra, Andhra Pradesh and Karnataka to Tamil Nadu in the extreme south. Punjab, Haryana, Assam (340) and Jharkhand (335) also have densities above 281. A low density (101-280 per sq. kms.) belt extends from Rajasthan in the west to Chhattisgarh and Orissa in the east. About half of Rajasthan is arid or semi-arid and the remaining three states which include Madhya Pradesh have large populations of tribal. Himachal Pradesh and Uttaranchal in the Western Himalayan region and Nagaland, Manipur and Meghalaya in the Eastern Himalayan region also have low densities (101—280 per sq. km.). The lowest densities (100 and below) are in Jammu and Kashmir, Arunachal Pradesh, Mizoram and Sikkim all of which consist of high mountains and narrow valleys (*ibid*).

Number of Districts

The Census gives information also on the number of districts in every State and Union Territory. Provisional paper No. 1 contains a large map showing boundaries of districts in every State and Union Territory (*ibid*, Map 21.1). It does not mention however that the number of districts has increased greatly since independence. The increase has become necessary on account of (i) growth of population, and (ii) the fact the some districts in several states were too large and had to be divided into two or more districts for efficient administration. A large increase in the number of districts was affected after the reorganization of states in 1958. Thereafter, there has been slow but steady increase in the number in response to political pressure. The best example of this is in two very small states of the north-east. Sikkim with a population of 540,000 has four districts, while Manipur with a population of 2.64 million has nine districts. The map gives a list of 39 districts which are so small that their names could not be written on the map (*ibid*, Map 21.1).

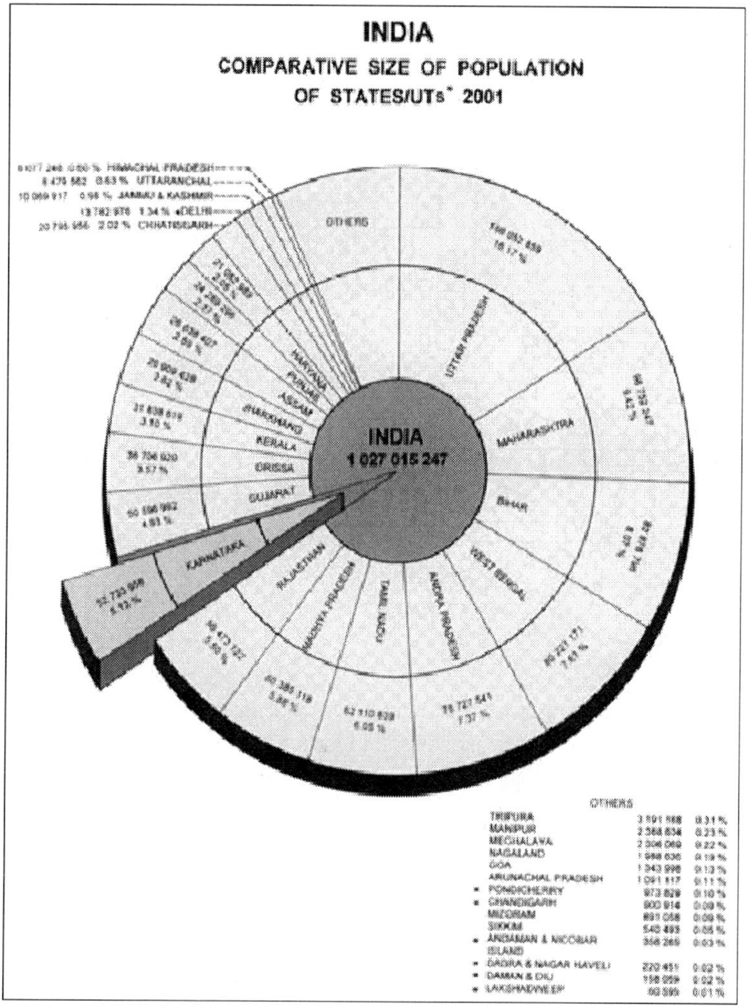

Fatehgarh Sahib in Punjab and Udham Singh Nagar in Uttaranchal were created into districts in response to pressure from Sikhs. The former is tiny in size but has an important Gurudwara (temple) which is visited by large numbers of pilgrims every year. In Udham Singh Nagar in Uttaranchal, Sikhs from Punjab have established relatively large farms (20 ha. and above) by clearing the jungle. They produce large crops of wheat, rice and sugarcane; the district has a number of mills processing the crops. The Sikhs did not wish to be included in the new State of

Map 21.1 : Territories of Indian states as in 2000

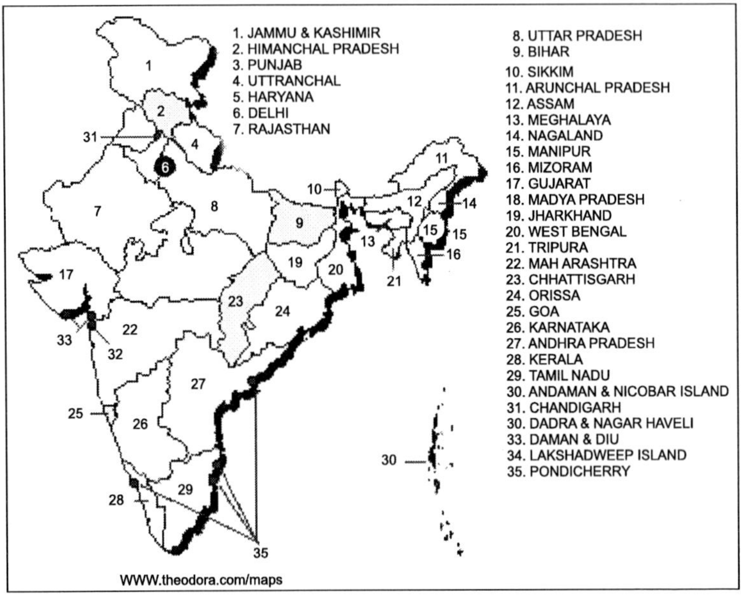

Uttaranchal because they were afraid that the government of the new state would break up their farms into small farms to bring them in line with size of farms (2-4 ha.) in the rest of the state. The creation of the new district has given them some re-assurance that this would not be done in the near future.

Growth Rate of Population and of Per Capita Income

Growth rate of population has declined during 1991-2001 while there has been rapid increase in per capita income. The latter, which had been increasing by 3-4 per cent p.a. during the previous 3 decades (1960-1990), increased by 5-6 per cent or higher during the 1990s. Per capita income, which had been increasing by half to one-and-half (1½) per cent p.a. during the earlier 3 decades, increased by 3-4 per cent p.a. during the 1990s. It was estimated at Rs. 2814 in 1996-97, about 70 per cent higher than the income of Rs. 1625 in 1980-81 prices. (Table 21.2).

Despite the recession in the economies of the U.S.A. Western Europe and Japan during the last two years, per capita income increased by over 5 per cent in India during 2000-2001(Tata Consultancy Services

p. 12, based on estimates of the Central Statistical Organization of the Government of India). If falling rate of growth of population and rising per capita income continue during the next two decades, India should have finally entered an era in which per capita income continues to increase despite fall in the rate of growth of population.

Rural-Urban Distribution of Population

Detailed data on the distribution will become available probably later during the current year. However, the Census Commissioner has through a press note dated July 20, 2001 published summary data for 2001 (Census Commissioner Note : Rural-Urban Distribution of Population, (Press Note, dated July 20,2001). They are summarized below :

Total urban population increased from 217.5 million in 1990-91 to 285 million in 2000-2001. The urban population in 2000-2001 was 27.8 per cent of the total population; the corresponding ratio in 1990-91 was 25.7 per cent. Total urban population increased by 68 million during the decade or by about 32 per cent. UNDP has projected that total urban population in 2015 would be 434.5 million almost 36 per cent of the total population (UNDP, *op cit*, p. 5.). The estimate of the Census Commissioner is not available so far.

Table 21.4 : Rural/Urban Distribution of Population—India and Selected States/Union Territories, 2001

Sl. No.	*States/UTs*	*Total population (million)*	*Urban Population (million)*	*Per cent Urban/ Total*
1.	Tamil Nadu	62.1	27.4	43.9
2.	Maharashtra	96.8	41.0	42.4
3.	Gujarat	50.6	18.8	37.4
4.	Karnataka	52.7	17.9	34.8
5.	Punjab	24.3	8.2	34.0
6.	Haryana	21.0	6.1	29.0
7.	West Bengal	80.2	22.5	28.0
8.	Andhra Pradesh	75.2	20.5	27.0
9.	Kerala	31.8	8.3	26.0
10.	Madhya Pradesh	60.4	16.1	26.6
11.	Jharkhand	26.9	6.0	22.3
12.	Rajasthan	56.5	13.2	23.4
13.	Uttar Pradesh	166.0	34.5	20.8
14.	Orissa	36.7	5.5	15.0
15.	Assam	26.6	3.4	12.7
16.	Bihar	82.9	8.7	10.5

Source : Rural/Urban Distribution of Population—India States and Union Territories, 2001, Registrar General of India : Press Note, New Delhi, July 20, 2001.

The number of metropolitan cities i.e. cities with populations of one million and above had increased from 23 in 1990-91 to 35 in 2000-2001, i.e. by 50 per cent during the decade (Registrar General and Census Commissioner Note : Rural-Urban Distribution of Population, Press Note, dated July 20, 2001). The total population of the metropolitan cities was estimated at 108 million, just over 38 per cent of the total urban population. Population of the three largest cities—Greater Mumbai, Kolkata and Delhi—was 42 million in 2001, i.e. about 15 per cent of the total urban population. The total population of the 7 large cities with populations above 4 million was about 64 million, 22 per cent of the total urban population (*ibid*). Maharashtra had the largest urban population (41.0 million which constituted 42.4 per cent of its total population); its urban population constituted 14 per cent of the total urban population. It had also the largest number (4) of metropolitan cities. Gujarat, Tamil Nadu, Punjab and Karnataka are the other states with relatively high proportions of urban population. Gujarat and Tamil Nadu have three million-plus cities each. U.P. the most populous state has 6 such cities.

Population : Resource or Liability

The Census Commissioner of 1951 had warned that the rate of growth of population was too high (13.3 per cent) and must be reduced to 5 per cent per decade by 1969-70; otherwise Malthusian checks—widespread famine and pestilence—would prevail to bring population down to sustainable level. The population in 1951 was 361 million; the Commissioner held the opinion that at this rate of growth total population would be 500 million by 1969-70. He stated that with all known means of increasing agricultural output including increase in the irrigated area, India could not feed more than 500 million people. The population has increased to more than one billion in 2001; at the same time output of foodgrains has increased from less than 60 m.t. during the mid-1950s to over 200 m.t. by the late 1990s, i.e. by more than 3 times. Output of other important foods—sugar, cooking oil, milk and vegetables—has also increased so rapidly that an average villager can afford to buy them. As a result, the average Indian was better fed and healthier in 2000-2001 than he/she were in 1950-51. As the data in Table 21.5 show he/she were also better clothed. The data for the housing census of 2000-2001 could show that he/she were also better housed.

Table 21.5: Per Capita Consumption of Food and Cloth, use of Electricity and Growth Rate of Population.

Consumption	*1980-81*	*1998-99*	*Increase (+) Decrease (-)*
Food grains (grams per day)	410.4	450.71	10%
Edible oils (kg. per annum)	3.8	9.5	2½ times
Sugar (kg. per annum)	7.3	14.0	Nearly twice
Tea (grams per annum)	571	676	Nearly 20%
Cloth of cotton and man made fibres (metres per annum)	17.3	28.2	Over 63%
Electricity consumption (kWh p.a.)	13.5	64.5	(+) Nearly 5 times
Population below poverty line (per cent)	1974-75 54.9%	1987-88 37.9%	2001-2002 18.0% Declined to 1/3rd from 1974/75
Per capita income at 1993-94 prices	1950-51 3940	1960-61 5950	1998-99 10801
Growth rate of population (per cent, per annum)	1941-51 1.25	1981-91 2.14	1990-2001 1.93

For per capita income—*Economic and Political Weekly Research Foundation* : National Accounts Statistics of India 1950-51-1996-97, Mumbai, 1998, pp. 84.

For other statements—Tata Consultancy Services : *Statistical Outline of India 2000-2001*, Bombay House, Mumbai-2001, (p. 213).

We cannot blame the Census Commissioner of 1951 for his gloomy forecast. The dwarf, high-yielding varieties of wheat and rice, use of which by farmers in areas irrigated by canals, tube-wells or surface wells fitted with pumps operated by diesel oil or electricity; or in those having adequate and dependable rainfall which have led to such remarkable increases in cereal output, were unknown in the 1950s. Polyester fibre, use of which in textiles has resulted in similar increase in production of cloth was also unknown in the 1950s.

The Government of India did launch a programme which propagated limitation of families by couples in the reproductive age group. The programme was completely ineffective however; on the contrary use of coercive methods to induce such couples to limit the number of their children during 1975-77, i.e. years of the national emergency gave a serious setback to the programme from which it recovered only during the late 1980s. The decline in the rate of growth of population during 1990-91—2000-2001 is due entirely to the voluntary decision of couples in the reproductive age group to reduce the number of children that they bear. This decision is the outcome of perception of a marked increase in the survival rate of children due to various measures taken by Governments of various states and mentioned above.

The National Population Policy aims now at reducing the total fertility rate and the Census Commissioner has forecast that the total fertility rate which has fallen from 4.6 in 1990-91 to 3.1 in 2000-2001, i.e. by 1/3rd during the last decade and will fall further to 2.5 or about 30 per cent during the next 15 years.

Thus, during the 50 years 1951-2001, a growing population has produced its own means of subsistence. The prospects for its continuing to do the same during the next 15 years are bright given the projected decline in growth rate of population and increase in agricultural and industrial output.

Conclusions

The conclusions of the foregoing discussion are:

1. Growth rate of population would continue to decline during the next 15 years and would average 1.3 per cent p.a. during this period. Total population in 2015 would be between 1235 and 1263 million.
2. The growth rate in some large and comparatively developed states would be lower or just above the rate needed to maintain a stationary population. These states with some notable exception have also the highest rates of literacy and per capita income.
3. U.P. and Bihar, two large and populous states which have a population of about 25 per cent of the total population of the country, could continue to have comparatively high rates of growth of population during the next 15 years, low levels of literacy and low per capita income (Table 21.3). Some other states with the above characteristics would be those which have large populations of tribal people.
4. The proportion urban/total population is expected to increase from 28 per cent in 2000-2001 to 35-36 per cent during 2015-2016. The proportion will continue to be high in most of the states which have high rates of urbanization at present. These states will have also higher levels of literacy and higher per capita income than states with low levels of urban population.

5. Maharashtra is expected to remain the state with the highest level of urbanization and to have the largest number of metropolitan cities (four), relatively high rate of literacy (77%) and high levels of per capita income (Tables 21.2 and 21.4). Its urban population (41 million) was just over 14 per cent of the total urban population in 2001. The per capita income of the state Rs. 4853 in 1996-97 was double the figure for 1980-81, the highest among states with population above 20 million. Other states with these characteristics are Tamil Nadu and Gujarat.
6. The high levels of Per Capita Income (PCI) of these states were due to their leadership in industrial development. Relatively high level of urbanization, literacy and per capita income in Punjab are due mainly to its leadership in agricultural output. Haryana also has a relatively high per capita income but relatively low level of urbanization and literacy. Its high per capita income is due to high agricultural output. The highest per capita income (Rs. 6550 in 1996-97) was in Goa. It had doubled during the period.
7. The sex ratio has been falling consistently during the last century. The cumulative fall in the course of the century was 42 per 1000 or over 4 per cent. The reasons for the low sex ratio are believed to be widespread prevalence of infanticide and also of feticide in recent decades in states with low sex ratio. The sex ratio is far higher in the southern states than in the rest of the country.
8. The prospect for the next 15 years (2001-2015) is for significant decline in growth rate of population, progressive increase in literacy rate and in per capita income. As a result, the average Indian will be living longer, will be better fed, better clothed and probably better housed and much more informed than his/ her predecessor of 15 years ago.

Appendix I

Migration

The Census of India classifies migrants into two categories: (i) life-time migrants whose place of enumeration during the Census was different from their place of birth and (ii) others whose place of enumeration was different from place of last residence. The latter are classified by duration of residence in the place of enumeration. Migrants of both types are further classified into intra-district, inter-district, inter-state and international migrants. Further, they are separated by rural-to-rural, rural-to-urban and urban-to-rural migrants. Within rural-to-urban migrants, those migrating to million-plus cities are tabulated separately. All migrants, male and female, are classified by reasons for migration.

It will be seen from Migration Tables (Population Census, 1981, Series 1, Part V, a & b Migration Tables D4-D8) that migrants constituted a little over 30 per cent of the total population in 1981. The proportion fell by one per centage point after excluding migrants from abroad. The proportion of migrants to total population by place of last residence was also similar.

Females heavily out-numbered males among migrants in the country as a whole in both 1971 and 1981. Among the migrants to the million-plus cities, however, males out-numbered females.

There were 12 million-plus cities in 1981. The proportion of migrants in their population was highest in case of Bombay (51.46 per cent), followed by Pune (48.40 per cent) and Delhi (44.56 per cent). The proportions were lower in the remaining cities, the lowest being in Hyderabad in which about 20 per cent of the population consisted of migrants.

Reasons for Migration

There are five reasons for migration for which data are tabulated by the population census : employment, education, family moved, marriage and others. These are given by males and females and by rural and urban areas for India and for males and females in the 12 million-plus cities. Employment was the principal reason in case of males accounting for 45 to 50 per cent of the total migrants in all cities except Nagpur. Among the females, however, the principal reasons were marriage and movement of the family.

There is no early prospect of reduction in the number of migrants into the million-plus cities. An indication of this was provided by the campaign for the November 1993 election to the Delhi State Assembly. The two major contending parties—the Congress and the Bhartiya Janata Party (BJP)—vied with one another in promising measures for promoting the welfare of the *jhuggi* (huts in slums) dwellers. Beginning with regularization of the slum colonies in their present (unauthorized) locations, they promised that they would provide the colonies with electricity, water, surface drainage, schools, clinics, i.e. all the facilities that would make them comfortable and would attract others to come and settle in Delhi's slums. The principal reason for this was that nearly 50 per cent of the voters in 25 out of the 70 constituencies were concentrated in the slums and winning their support was crucial to the success of the parties in the election. (*Times of India,* November 3, 1993).

Since most of the migrants to the large cities come in search of employment, their inflow can be checked by a combination of measures of which the following are the most important :

(i) Decentralization of employment to growth centres in regions, such as the National Capital Region for Delhi and the Bombay Metropolitan Region (which includes New Bombay across the Bay from the main Bombay City). This would mean that a significant proportion of the potential migrants to the metropolitan cities would be induced to go instead to the growth centres.

(ii) Implementing large programmes of small town industrialization and skill formation among the rural workers. These will reduce the incentives for them to migrate to large cities because remunerative employment would be available to them in towns that are within commuting distance from their villages.

That this strategy would be successful is illustrated by the change in the pattern of migration into Delhi from neighbouring states of Punjab, Haryana and U.P. during the period before 1961 and 1981. As mentioned earlier, the proportion of migrants from Punjab and Haryana declined and that from U.P. increased. Both Punjab and Haryana are foremost in the Green Revolution and have besides, successful small-town industries. Indeed, there is significant in-migration into them from other states particularly Eastern U.P. and Bihar.

Appendix II

Tabulation of Data of the Census of 2001 by Castes

There has been much discussion in recent months about the decision of the present Government to tabulate the data of the Census of 2001 by castes. The decision, unprecedented in the Censuses of the post-Independence years, has been taken explicitly for political reasons, in order to meet the demands of leaders of other backward classes who form the most numerous middle level groups between the high castes—Brahmin, Kshatriya and Vaishyas or traders—on the one hand and the Scheduled Castes and the Scheduled Tribes on the other. The leaders of these castes have assumed political power during the past two decades or more. They are anxious to maintain their position. The controversy is mainly about inclusion or otherwise of particular castes in the list of OBCs in Uttar Pradesh and Bihar where the OBCs have assumed power during the last two decades.

The object of this note is to give a historical perspective to such tabulation. The Census of 1931 was the last among the Censuses of pre-Independence period in which tabulation of data by castes was undertaken. The report on the census, written by the then Census Commissioner, E.W. Hutton, is perhaps the best treatise on the social status, economic activities and customs of different castes and sub-castes in the British India, viz. India, Pakistan and Bangladesh. Since the report is out of print, it should be reprinted and made available to the academic community and the interested political leaders so that the facts reported in it are not forgotten for ever.

Three interesting facts mentioned by Hutton are :

(i) The caste hierarchy is not confined to Hindus but extends to Moslems, and Christians. This is accepted by Indian Sociologists and there is considerable literature on non-Hindu castes.

(ii) Relative social status of different castes is not fixed but is subject to change with change in the economic status of particular castes or smaller groups within them. Thus, when the members of a particular caste or sub-caste become more prosperous for some reason, they begin to regard themselves superior to other castes who were their equals earlier.

(iii) Most of the non-high castes, i.e. castes other than Brahmins, Kshatriyas and Vaishyas are constantly trying to raise their social status.

The last fact was noticed by the present writer during his stay in a district in Rajasthan during the 1960s. He noticed that the *Berwa Chamars*, the most numerous Scheduled Castes in the area who had flaying of hides of dead animals and making of leather goods and agricultural labour as their principal occupation had given up both these and were strivinghard to become peasant proprietors by cultivation of cultivable waste lands, owned earlier by the Jagirdars, which became available for allotment to landless labourers after the abolition of *Jagirdari* system of land tenure in the early 1950s. Flaying of hides and skins and making of leather goods had been taken up by a caste lower than the *Chamaars* in the caste hierarchy. Labour for agriculture was performed by members of various other landless castes (Nath : *Rural Development and Planning in India,* Chapter 17).

Meenas, the principal peasant proprietor caste in the area were desperately trying to adopt the customs of the high castes in order to raise their social status. Thus payment of bride price by the husband for marrying a girl, a custom eminently suitable in a situation in which wife was also a valuable agricultural worker, was being replaced by payment of a dowry by her parents if they had the income for it. The leaders of the Meenas referred to this change with great pride. They also mentioned that they were also meeting all the expenses of feeding a marriage party. This change was mentioned as *Roti Beti.* Hutton mentions also the reasons for the esteem or lack of it in which a particular caste is held by other castes. A caste may be held in esteem or contempt for some particular characteristic which is accepted by itself and the other castes.

There is no controversy about the classification of OBCs in the Southern states or those of Western and Eastern India. The governments in the Southern states, in the western states of Maharashtra and Gujarat and in Punjab and Haryana are all formed by leaders of the cultivating castes (or group of castes). Among the eastern states, all Governments in West Bengal have been formed in the post-Independence years by leaders of the *Bhadra Loke* (usually Kayasthas); the labouring classes have not yet got up to assume the leadership of governments. In Assam, governments are formed by the leaders of the Assamese who are the dominant cultivating caste in the area. In Punjab and Haryana, formation of governments by leaders of Sikh and Hindu Jats respectively, and in Maharashtra by leaders of Maharathas is taken for granted. The controversy is mainly about governments in Uttar Pradesh and Bihar, the two most populous and economically most backward states of India. The leaders of 'other backward castes' in these states have got up to assume positions of political power only during the last two decades; earlier governments in these states were formed invariably by leaders of the high castes. Since the leaders of the OBCs are anxious to consolidate their newly won position of political power, they are anxious to ensure that the maximum number of castes is included in the list of OBCs so that their numerical dominance in the caste hierarchy and consequent position of political power is maintained.

Formation of most governments by leaders of OBCs in the two states can now be regarded as a fact which is unlikely to change in the foreseeable future. The real need in these states is for better governance, including particularly improving the law and order situation and more rapid economic development through more efficient utilization of the available resources of finance and manpower. The law and order situation in Bihar is so bad—there is virtually a class war in parts of the state between the high castes—Brahmins, Rajputs and Bhumihaars—and the former backward castes, such as Paswans (traditionally toddy tappers) and 'Yadavs'—that the present Central Government decided recently to suspend the government and was restrained from doing so only on the advice of the President of India. The situation in Uttar Pradesh can be considered only as marginally better, although in parts of the state, conditions are similar to those in Bihar.

The need in the two states is for better governance including in particular improvement in the law and order situation and more rapid economic development through more efficient utilization of finance and manpower available for economic development.

REFERENCES

Economic and Political Weekly, Mumbai, India 1998.

Tata Consultancy Services:

- Statistical Outline of India 2000-2001, Bombay House, Mumbai 2001.
- Statistical Outline of India 1999-2000.

Nath, V.: *Rural Development and Planning in India*. Concept Publishing Co. Pvt Ltd. (Forthcoming).

Registrar General and Census Commissioner India :

Census of India 2001 Paper 1 of 2001: Provisional Population Totals.

Census of India 1991: Provisional Population Totals 1990-91 Paper No. 1 of 1991.

Press Note, New Delhi, July 20, 2001 : *Rural/Urban Distribution of Population*.

Times of India, Thiruvananthapuram October 15, 1993.

UNDP, New Delhi : *Human Development Report*, 2001, Statement on India 2001.

Section V

Development Planning and Administration: Theory and Practice in Developing Countries

22

Looking Back on Fifty Years of Development and Planning in India : The Experience 1950-2000 and Prospects 2020*

This chapter reviews the half a century of experience of economic development and planning in India, with a view to achieving self-sustainable development. It reviews the goals set by the Government of India in planning for development and its achievements in (i) economic, (ii) social development, (iii) political development, (iv) the growth poles in the economy, and (v) the role of the Planning Commission, bureaucrats, entrepreneurs, Judiciary and the non-governmental organizations. It touches on increase in corruption and inefficiency as a major hindrance in equitable economic and social development. The last section gives author's projection of changes in he goals in the future and prospects for India's Development into 2020.

Economic Development

Economic development is a tumultuous, stressful process in which although the GDP increases at a faster rate than earlier, some economic or social groups gain at the expense or *vis-a-vis* the others. It is important, however, that the planned development undertaken by any country should lead to equity and should be self-sustaining. Self-sustaining development according to Rostow (Stages of Economic Growth, 1960, Cambridge University Press) is that economic and social development should reach a stage when the economy and society propel themselves to further progress. Furthermore, it means development that does not lead to environment deterioration or depletion of natural resources of soil, water, vegetation or minerals.

India has reached that stage in some areas of social development but not yet in economic or political development. Disparities in income have widened and the condition of the poor particularly the urban poor has not improved.

The Government of India undertook, soon after the Independence of the country, planning as a means of promoting economic and social development. The first Prime Minister of India, Pandit Jawahar Lal Nehru was an ardent believer in planning after he had seen, during his visit to the Soviet Union, the very rapid progress that the country had made after it undertook the implementation of its First and Second Five Year Plans in the early 1930s.

Goals of Development

The goals of development as set out by the government for newly independent India were :

1. Provide security of life and property to all the people.
2. Self-sustaining development. In other words raising income and consumption of all the people without overdraft on natural resources of soil, surface and ground water, forests and minerals.
3. Ensuring that all the people have adequate food with adequate quantities of cereals and protective foods (milk, vegetables, fruit, poultry products and fish in coastal areas).
4. Providing expansion of primary education to all students (boys and girls) of school going age (6-14 years) and preventive and curative health care to all. Secondary school education to a large proportion of the children.

   An educated and healthy population is an indispensable resource for rapid economic growth as indicated by the post-Second World War experience in several east and south-east Asian countries.
5. Fostering growth of a population with keen awareness of their rights as citizens and as electors of Legislators. Ensuring that the electors advance the people's welfare through their action in representative institutions.

Planning in India—The Experience 1950-2000

Several efforts at planning the economic and social change had been made prior to the Independence of India. One such attempt was made by a group of industrialists and big businessmen, based in Mumbai who produced in 1945, a 20 year plan, 1945-65, for economic development of the country known as the Bombay Plan. The plan emphasized the need for modernization and expansion of existing industries. It emphasized also the need for providing basic infrastructures such as approach roads, safe and adequate water supplies to villages and cities, opening schools and health centres and increasing agricultural output by modernization of techniques to meet the food needs of the people and fibre needs of industries. Veterinary hospitals and dispensaries were to be built in order to provide facilities to farmers for preventing and curing diseases of livestock.

The British Government joined the movement by producing a 10-year plan for reconstruction of the economy after the war. Emphasis in this plan was on construction of roads to break the isolation of villages so that a large proportion of them could be reached by motorable roads and improving national and state highways to match the existing network of railways.

The Planning Commission was established in January 1950, almost immediately after the Government of India had got over the daunting tasks of providing relief to and ensuring rehabilitation of millions of displaced persons that had migrated from Pakistan to India.

The Commission produced the First Five Year Plan 1951-56 in December 1951, two years after its establishment. Emphasis in the Plan was on agriculture and rural development. The investment envisaged under it was modest and could be financed easily from domestic funds without need for foreign aid.

Priorities in the Plan were dictated by the problems that the Government of India had faced in the 3-5 years following independence due to partition of the country, i.e. rehabilitation of the refugees and to meet the food deficit of the country.

The Plan was successful. Output of cereals and medium staple cotton increased enough to eliminate the need for imports of these. Two favourable monsoons in 1954-55 and 1955-56 together with extension of irrigation by canals, tube-wells and surface wells helped in achievement of these targets. The Community Development Programme, launched by the Government of India in October 1952, provided funds from the State Governments to villages to construct thousands of kms. of approach roads, improvement of water supplies for drinking and for irrigation, opening of tens of thousands of primary schools in villages and thousands of secondary schools in large villages to increase the proportion of children going to schools. Primary health care centre established under the programme provided facilities for preventive and curative health care. Similar facilities were created at the community development block/taluka levels to advice farmers on prevention of diseases of animals and curing sick animals.

The Second Five Year Plan 1956-61 and the Third Five Year Plan 1961-66

Buoyed by this experience, the Planning Commission prepared these two plans. Emphasis in them was on industrialization. Five large integrated steel mills were established as were two mills for processing bauxite to make alumina and aluminium metal. Also established were a factory for making heavy machine tools, factories for making machines for generation, transmission and distribution of electricity, two factories for making light machine tools, another for making telephone receivers and other telecommunication equipment. A factory for making electric and diesel locomotives for the railways had already been established during the First Five Year Plan. Factories for manufacturing rails, wagons and coaches were also established during this period.

After the discovery of oil off the coasts of Mumbai and off-shore and on-shore Gujarat, large investment were made in exploration and development of the oilfields establishing refineries for processing crude oil to produce petrol, diesel oil, kerosine and cooking gas; the two former for providing fuel for motor vehicles and the two latter for cooking or to provide light in villages in some parts of the country, cooking fuel in the cities. Some of the refineries were established in collaboration with companies based in oil producing countries of the Gulf. Large investments were made also for constructing pipelines for carrying petroleum products from the oilfields to the consuming centres.

Technical and financial assistance for establishing these factories was given by the Soviet Union, Germany and Britain and to a much smaller extent by Canada. Technical assistance was given on a commercial basis by Switzerland and the U.S.A.

The light machine tools and telecommunication equipment factories were profit generating from the beginning. Similarly, petroleum refining and construction of pipelines and distribution of petroleum products had been self-financing or profit generating from the beginning. The factories manufacturing machines for generation, transmission and distribution of electricity became profit-making after a period of suffering losses. But the steel and aluminium processing mills and several other factories incurred large losses due to difficulties of management and infrastructures.

It is significant that in this period when national control of means of production was the rage, the Tatas were allowed to expand capacity and modernize their steel mill at Jamshedpur with loans guaranteed by the Government of India. They were assisted also to expand capacity of their hydro-electric and water supply capacity units in order to meet the increasing demands of electricity and water of the rapidly growing metropolis. The two foreign oil companies that had been distributing petroleum products in India for decades were also allowed to establish oil refineries in a suburb of Mumbai and were allowed to expand their network of dealers throughout India.

No new large industrial investments were made in subsequent plans. However, diversion of such large investment to industrial projects which were slow in yielding returns had resulted in neglect of agricultural development. As a result, there was a food crisis in the mid-1960s when famine was averted only by large imports of cereals (wheat and milo) from the U.S.A. under its PL 480 Programme. Cessation of the imports by order of President Johnson coincided with rapid use of high-yielding dwarf varieties of wheat developed first in Mexico and adapted to Indian conditions by Indian research scientists. Extensive use of these varieties increased production of wheat so rapidly that the country did not need to import any cereals by 1970-71. Subsequent arrival of high-yield dwarf varieties of rice, developed at the International Rice Research Institute in Mumbai and adapted to Indian conditions by Indian research scientists to the variety of conditions under which rice is grown in different regions has increased yield so much that the country became self-sufficient in rice also.

Production of both cereals has been increasing steadily with increasing areas brought under conditions of assured and adequate supplies of water provided by dependable rainfall or rainfall-*cum*-irrigation. By the mid-1990s production of cereals had increased to nearly 200 million tonnes—3½ times the production in the mid-1950s. The production has been adequate to meet the increasing needs of the population which in 1991 was 2½ times the population in 1951. Production of sugar and medium staple cotton has also been increasing steadily so that there has been no need for import of these. Production of tea and jute has increased rapidly enough to increase in exports despite increase in domestic consumption of tea. The only food for which there is a shortage met by import is cooking oil.

The fever of nationalization continued during the 1960s despite the losses of the industrial projects. Twenty largest banks were nationalized in 1969; life and general insurance companies had already been nationalized; Air India, the profit-making international air line, established by the Tatas was nationalized at the same time and the Indian Airlines was established to cater to the needs of the increasing volume of air travel between metropolitan cities. Although the life and general insurance companies remained profitable, the losses of nationalized banks mounted because they were forced to open branches in villages and lend to non-creditworthy borrowers under the slogan of *Gharibi Hatao* (Remove Poverty).

By 1991, when the country was faced with a balance of payments crisis all these policies were reversed in order to get bridging loans from the IMF and the World Bank.

The policy now is to abolish most of the controls on imports and exports in order to enable private industrialists to improve quality of their products in order to make their goods internationally competitive. Increased exports of products such as garments, leather goods, consumer durables ranging from furnishing for home and office to chasses for buses and trucks and a variety of other goods and finally rapidly expanding exports of computer software have enabled India to have a positive balance of payments. Fiscal, monetary and development policies are now made by the Ministry of Finance in consultation with the chambers of Commerce and Industry and planning is reduced to incorporating the results in various plans. The Plans still serve as instruments of fixing targets for increasing production of products ranging from foodgrains to consumer durables and coordinating the plan of the Centre and State Governments. But planning has lost the glamour that it had earlier. It is felt now that in the rapidly changing economic and political situation in the world, five years is too long a period to be useful for projecting trends of investment or its allocation between different sectors of the economy.

In India, there is now a consensus that most of the industries and infrastructure such as distribution and transmission of electricity and water supply and telecommunications are better managed by companies than by the government. Denationalization of the banks that have started making profits is being considered actively; certain areas of insurance have been thrown open to foreign insurance companies in order to provide competition to the domestic life and general insurance corporations.

This review of planning in India during the last 50 years has demonstrated that the government has played its role in initiating agricultural and rural development, industrial development as also providing electric and water supplies to cities and to villages, running banks, economic services, insurance companies, airlines and tourist hotels.

These industries and services are best run by private entrepreneurs. The government should concentrate now on assisting increase in agricultural production in cooperation with producers' cooperatives for sugar, vegetables and fruit and finally to alleviating poverty by food for work programmes and other means aimed at removing poverty. Private enterprise should provide jobs by aggressively improving its products and services such as information technology to make them internationally competitive. This is the essence of the Structural Adjustment Programmes advocated by IMF and the World Bank. India had to follow this formula in 1991 with consequent increase in growth rate from 3-4 per cent p.a. to 5-6 per cent p.a. wiping out its foreign exchange and government's fiscal policy deficits.

Impact of Development Planning and Social Change Policies

I. Social Development

(a) The Scheduled Castes

Consider the position of the Scheduled Castes. After abolition of *Jagirdari* in the princely states and of *zamindari* in British ruled provinces, millions of members of the Scheduled Castes have become peasant proprietors by getting allotted cultivable land which was held by the jagirdars and *zamindars* as pastures or woodland. With this change, they have ceased to do their dirty work such as flaying the hides and skins of dead animals and making shoes and other leather goods used on the farms. They have stopped doing also their traditional duties on the occasion of life cycle events such as births and marriages in the homes of the *jagirdars* and *zamindars*. The latter have taken the change in their stride regarding this as the inescapable result of the abolition of *jagirdari* and *zamindari*. Furthermore with increasing numbers of young men in white-collar jobs, including those in the offices of the Government of India and of the State Governments, it is no longer possible for the high castes to discriminate against them or exploit them as they used to do. Since their support is essential for election of many candidates, of the high casts, the candidates must do all that is possible to win it. Since one-fourth of the seats in Parliament and Legislatures of most of the states are reserved for the Scheduled Castes and the Scheduled Tribes, the support of their representatives is essential for continuation of the governments in power or for enactment of important legislation. Even in Panchayati Raj Institutions, there is adequate representation for these groups so that discrimination against them is difficult to maintain in these institutions also.

(b) Position of Women

The position of women has also improved greatly. Illiteracy and ignorance about prevention and cure of common diseases of children and themselves is appreciably less than in the 1950s, thanks to the work of the school teachers and physicians (including women doctors) nurses and family planning advisers posted at the community development block/taluka level health centres for rural women and of private practitioners and health centres run by the municipalities in the urban areas. Although the birth rate and the rate of population growth continue to be high in several states, they are falling in an increasing number. The two or three child norm has been adopted by low income group women such as domestic servants in Delhi and other metropolitan cities. In Kerala and Goa where female literacy and acceptance of family planning are both high, rates of population growth are marginally higher than replacement levels.

There has emerged in the metropolitan cities an expanding class of educated and trained women who combine home making with work outside the home. That all the telephone operators and receptionists and most of the secretaries in offices of companies and in many offices of the Central Government and of governments of some states, women are accepted as a matter of course. Educated women are in the forefront of the movement for preventing violence and crime against women. An increasing number of those guilty of such offences are prosecuted.

(c) The Growth and Role of Middle Class

The middle class has an enormous influence on economic policies for several reasons. First, most of the Ministers, Legislators, government employees as well as executives and employees of Panchayati Raj Institutions belong to the class. They run the electronic and print media and mould public opinion. They constitute the largest group of voters and consumers. No government can stay in power without their support.

The rise in size and influence of the middle class is in line with development during the last century or 150 years in the countries that are now developed. The number of the middle class and its power and influence are bound to increase as a result of successful implementation of anti-poverty programmes.

II. Economic Development

The rate of economic growth has increased progressively from 3-4 per cent per annum during the period 1960-80, just about 1-2 per cent above the rate of increase of population to 5-6 per cent per annum and 3-4 per cent above the rate of population growth during the 1990s. As a result, per capita income of an average Indian is significantly higher today than it was during 1960-80. It is not certain if it will be possible to maintain this growth given the large oil pool deficit and the government's difficulty in reducing its fiscal deficit. However, since rate of inflation is also high, the impact of increase in per capita income on levels of living gets eroded some what; there is need to have a rigorous policy for control in inflation (cost of living).

The economy has not yet reached the stage at which maintenance of average growth rate of GDP of 5-7 per cent per annum attained in the 1990s would be automatic. It is very much dependent upon a favourable external environment and the government not making any serious mistakes in formulation or implementation of macro-economic or fiscal policies. The growth rate of the 1990s was achieved because prices of crude oil, import of which forms a significant proportion of the country's foreign exchange expenditure, were stable at a rather low level. Furthermore, exports increased rapidly because the rupee was undervalued, keeping in view its domestic purchasing power. Keeping bureaucratic red tape in check also encouraged the exporters and other entrepreneurs. These favourable factors are no longer operating. Steep rise in prices of crude oil, is making such a large demand on foreign exchange earnings of the country that the exchange rate of the rupee has already depreciated by more than 25 per cent against the dollar during the last 3 years (1999-2002). Furthermore, India's exports are facing increasing competition from China and Western developed market economies. Foreign direct investment remains much lower than projected. It is concentrated in production of goods and rendering services such as banking in which large profits can be made quickly. There has been little investment in capital industries infrastructures such as construction of high-speed 4 or 6 lane expressways, improvement or reconstruction of ports.

The increase in rate of economic growth has been due also to increasing efficiency of information technology industries which has made it competitive in foreign markets. It is not clear whether the benefits of economic growth have tickled down to the poor. The percentage of population below the poverty line is estimated to have declined steadily from about 55 per cent in 1973-74 to a projected 18.00 per cent during 2001-02. There has been sharp decline in 1990s; the rate was 36.0 per cent in 1993-94 and is estimated at 26 per cent in 1999-2000. The decline is being attributed to the trickle down effect of the rapid growth of gross domestic product achieved during the 1990s. There are, however, large inter-state and intra-state sub-regional variations in rural poverty due to environmental and/or man-made reasons (Nath, 2009, Chapter 11).

A second change has been in the agents of accelerating economic growth. During the late 1950s to the 1980s the Government of India and of the states made large investments aimed at increasing agricultural production, in establishing industries and expansion of infrastructures. Private entrepreneurs with some notable exceptions concentrated on production of consumer goods and consumer durables in production of which large profits were made in satisfying domestic demand. In the 1990s, large investments in some basic industries such as petroleum refining and manufacture of petro-chemicals and expansion of power supplies is being made by private entrepreneurs. Furthermore, some of the largest private companies are offering to takeover loss making public enterprises such as airlines, tourist hotels, banks and state electricity boards. The IT industries that have grown exponentially during the last three decades are the product entirely of private entrepreneurs.

Consistent with this change, there has been a major shift in the groups that influence economic policies of the government. Earlier, the most powerful pressure group was labour unions of public enterprises—Railways, Post and Telecommunications, Nationalized Banks and Life and General Insurance Corporations and Public Sector Industrial Enterprises. They insisted on preservation of their employment, pay and other perquisites in order to reduce losses of public sector units. Their influence remains strong. However, the chambers of commerce and industry have acquired an influence on economic policies that they did not have before. Foreign investors including non-resident Indians have also emerged as an important pressure group influencing economic policies of the government.

In the 1950s and 1960s, the government established institutes of technology and management. Now, the products of these institutions who have become multi-millionaires abroad as software professionals and information service providers are offering to takeover the responsibility for management, expansion and modernization of these institutes. The most affluent alumni of the best universities are offering to takeover expansion and modernization of some departments of their *alma maters*. Earlier, the government established some world-class hospitals in Delhi, Chandigarh and some other cities. Now physicians/surgeons trained abroad have established hospitals that are both efficient and profitable in several metropolitan cities and are planning to open them in others. Benefits of newly established hospitals are not reaching to the poor, accessibility of the poor to these institutions should be ensured. The unions of employees of public sector enterprises still have enormous power. But they are acquiescing with the fact that they have to accept voluntary retirement packages. Furthermore, they have accepted the fact that the employees that are retained after privatization of the enterprises must improve their productivity in order to remain in employment. With the increasing privatization unemployment is growing and living and working conditions of the workers are deteriorating. The policy-makers should make an attempt to avert this situation.

Growth Poles in the Indian Economy 1950-2000 (Nath, 2010, Chapter 11)

The concept of growth pole was first advanced and elaborated by the French Economist, Francois Perroux soon after Second World War. He defined a growth pole as an innovation or industry or discovery of a natural resource, exploitation of which propels a region and the nation to a higher growth path or aids development of a backward region. Perroux advanced the concept to justify the efforts of the French government to develop industries in the backward south based on use of natural gas which had been discovered in the region in the 1950s.

The effort failed because the power stations and industries using natural gas remained isolated developments and did not lead to regional development. Winter and summer tourism, rather than industries processing natural gas, remain the dominant providers of employment and source of foreign exchange since the last quarter of the 19th century and especially after First World War. However the concept became popular among economic geographers and those interested in development of backward regions.

It is possible to identify four growth poles in India's economic development during the 50 years, 1950 to 2000.

The first was start of the community development programme of integrated rural development in October 1952, which was extended to the whole country in the next ten years. Under the programme hundreds of thousands of kilometres of approach roads were built to connect villages in all parts of the country with towns. The isolation of villages was broken. The roads which were heavily travelled, were metalled by the Public Works Departments of the State Government to make them fit to be used by buses and trucks so that dependence on the slow and cumbersome bullock cart as the sole means of rural transport ended.

Tens of thousands of primary schools were opened in villages and thousands of secondary schools were opened in large villages so that increasing numbers of children, boys and girls, could go to primary and secondary schools. Adult literacy programmes were organized in order to eradicate illiteracy among adults. Primary health centres (mini hospitals) with 6 beds, one or more doctors, nurses and dispensers were opened at the community development block/taluka level, usually small or medium sized towns to provide treatment to the sick and disseminate principles of clean living so that incidence of disease among rural men, women and children was reduced. Construction or improvement of tens of thousands of drinking water wells, tanks and other water supply sources had the same object besides reducing the hardship of rural women in fetching water from distant wells and tanks. Thousands of veterinary dispensaries were opened for treatment of and prevention of diseases among livestock. The agricultural extension programme promoted use of improved seed, manure and/or chemical fertilizers and pesticides to increase yields of crops. As a result, production of cereals increased rapidly as also of other crops.

Discovery of Large Deposits of Crude Oil

The second growth pole was discovery of large deposits of crude oil off the coasts of Mumbai and off-shore and on-shore Gujarat. To process the oil, petroleum refineries were opened near Mumbai, in coastal Gujarat and near centres of consumption of products. Technical assistance for exploration and development of the oilfields was given by the Soviet Union. However, construction of pipelines to centres of consumption usually cities and comparatively prosperous agricultural regions was done through India's own funds.

These developments had the effect of large increase in use of motor vehicles for transport. Several plants were opened to manufacture motor vehicles—buses and trucks, passenger cars, 3-wheeler and 2-wheeler scooters and motor bicycles. The plants were located in the peri-urban areas of large cities—Mumbai, Kolkata, Chennai, Pune, Kanpur and Delhi. The availability of petroleum products within the country enabled India to survive the shocks in 1973 and 1979 given by sharp increase in the prices of crude oil, made by the principal oil producing countries of the world. Technical assistance for establishing plants of motor vehicles was given on a strictly commercial basis by Germany, Britain, Japan and Italy. India could motorize its transport and produce petro-chemical products ranging from polyester fibre to a variety of goods made of plastics.

The third growth pole was availability of dwarf, high-yielding varieties of seeds for the most widely consumed cereals—wheat and rice from the mid-1960s to the mid-1970s. With use of these varieties under conditions of assured and controlled moisture provided by an assured and dependable rainfall and/or irrigation, along with the use of recommended doses of chemical fertilizers/organic manure and pesticides gave 2-3 times the yields of the older varieties. Use of these varieties spread like wild fire in Punjab, Haryana, western U.P. and three districts of northern Rajasthan (for wheat); coastal Andhra Pradesh, coastal Tamil Nadu, south-west Karnataka and parts of West Bengal in which rice is grown under conditions of assured moisture. As a result, India became self-sufficient in cereals by 1971. Output of cereals has been increasing steadily ever since so much so that by the mid and late 1990s, their output was about 200 m. tonnes, 3 ½ times the output of less than 60 mt. in the 1950s. Furthermore, their widesprcad use has created regions of agricultural prosperity in Punjab, Haryana, western Uttar Pradesh and other regions which are mentioned below. In this area, high-yield wheat is grown along with other crops. In Punjab, it is produced along with high-yield rice; in Haryana, it is grown with medium staple cotton and oilseeds. In western U.P., it is grown with sugarcane and oilseeds.

In coastal Andhra Pradesh, especially the deltas of the Godavari and Krishna rivers, high-yield rice is grown along with sugarcane. There is a large number of rice and sugar mills. In one district, flue cured tobacco used for making cigarettes is the principal crop which is both labour intensive and highly remunerative. In West Bengal as also in the delta of the Kaveri River in Tamil Nadu 2 or 3 crops of paddy are harvested. In south-west Karnataka high-yield varieties of rice are grown along with high-yield sugarcane. There is a number of sugar and rice mills. In the area located around Coimbatore which is irrigated by a canal from the Pykara river, high yield medium staple cotton is grown. There is a large number of textile mills and various industrial units producing machine tools for the mills and other industrial goods.

In western Maharashtra a large area is irrigated by a number of streams flowing from the Western Ghats to the Arabian sea. High-yield sugarcane with high sugar content is the principal crop. There is a number of sugar mills, and a number of industrial units produce a variety of machine tools for the mills. In Mumbai and Pune and the 170 km. rail-*cum*-road strip, there is a very large number of industrial units which produce everything from textiles, garments, shoes and other leather, consumer durables, toiletries, pharmaceutical drugs and motor vehicles. In the area around

Nasik are produced high-yield grapes, mosambi oranges and a variety of vegetables. A large number of farmers and agricultural labourers are busy growing the crops and crating them for consumption in northern and western India and for export to countries of the Gulf primarily for consumption of Indians settled there.

Coastal Gujarat: The farmers grow high-yield oilseed and sorghum and millets. There is a very large number of industrial units manufacturing everything from cloth and garments to consumer durable such as air-conditioners and refrigerators and a variety of machine tools. Because of location of off-shore and on-shore deposits of crude oil there are petroleum refineries and industrial units manufacturing petro-chemical products such as polyester fibre for textiles and plastics for a variety of domestic goods.

In the area around Anand in central Gujarat large employment is available to wives of farmers and agricultural labourers in producing liquid milk for Mumbai and other cities in Gujarat. Amul Dairy, located in Anand provides large employment in shipping milk to the cities mentioned above and processing surplus milk to produce butter, cheese and baby food. It is the largest producer of these products in India. The farmers grow fodder crops for the animals and their wives and daughters look after 1-3 buffaloes to produce liquid milk.

The fourth growth point in the economy is expansion from the early 1970s of information technology industries, use of computer software for export and domestic use, e-mail and internet. The export makes a valuable contribution to India's foreign exchange while its domestic use in industries increases efficiency and makes the products competitive in foreign markets.

Their use in modern service institutions has had two beneficial results. The nationalized banks and insurance corporations have become competitive with foreign institutions. Besides, they can mobilize large savings from households within the country and from non-resident Indians to finance economic growth within the country. The increase of growth of GDP from 3-4 per cent p.a. (1-2 per cent above the rate of growth of population) from the early 1960s to the end of the 1980s to 5-7 per cent in the 1990s is due in large part to India's success in export of computer software.

The prospect for the next 20 years is for further growth of the information technology industries and of pharmaceutical drug industries. Development of drugs based on original research, some of them on the principles of the ancient Ayurvedic system of medicine, that are effective in treatment of the aged, as well as women and children have large sales within India and abroad. Two companies, one based in Hyderabad and the other in Delhi, that have developed these drugs have a turnover of several hundred million dollars and are poised for rapid growth.

The prospect for the next 20 years is for rapid increase in use of these drugs especially in southern India and Sri Lanka because Ayurvedic medicines are more popular in southern India and Sri Lanka than in northern India. The likely future centres of production of these drugs are Vadodara in Gujarat in which there are two companies which make already highly popular Ayurvedic drugs, Lucknow where the Central Drug Research Institute in U.P. is located and Chennai or Trivandrum in southern India.

The country has been able to maintain a growth rate of 5-7 per cent per annum which was achieved in 1991, due to a favourable economic environment. Prices of crude oil import of which makes a large dent in India's foreign exchange resources were low. Bureaucratic controls on export of domestic producers and import of raw material was relaxed so that they could export products and import raw materials.

The international environment has been unfavourable during the last 2 years. International prices of crude oil have been extremely high. Indian manufacturers face increasing competition in foreign markets. Foreign direct investment has been less than 2 billion, less than 0.25 per cent of the GDP.

The growth has been maintained due to the contribution made by the information technology industries to earning foreign exchange. The bonds issued by nationalized banks such as State Bank of India and the Bank of Baroda has mobilised savings of non-resident Indians. Continuance of this position and privatization of loss making state enterprises such as Air India, Indian Airlines, steel and aluminum plants and others by finding strategic foreign partners will help India attain self-sustaining economic growth.

Improvement in District Administration

When revenue records are computerised, as is being considered by some State Governments, the present dependence on *patwaris* (called *karnams* or *talatis* in some states) would be eliminated. Most of them are corrupt because they are paid so little. Furthermore, most of them are inefficient because they are educated only to primary or (8-grade) middle school. They would be replaced by young men, educated to higher secondary school level, who are proficient in use of computers. They would live in relatively large villages and be provided bicycles or motor cycles to travel to 5 or more small villages within their jurisdiction to collect the information contained in the present land records. The computerised records would not only be permanent and easily accessible but the cost of storing them at the district or taluka headquarters would be much less than of the mountains of books that contain them at present.

With basic equipment—a telephone, a computer and a fax machine—provided in the office of every Collector, information on progress of various development programmes being implemented in a district could be provided to the concerned departments of the State Governments much faster and in much greater detail than is possible at present with dependence on the use of post, telegraph and telephones. Modifications in policies and programmes, after recognising problems in implementation could be done more rapidly than is possible at present. One of the effects of use of these techniques is that every Collector in Rajasthan produces every year, a handbook of statistics about his district. It presents all informations about climate, topography, crops, cottage and other industries, population, coverage with facilities for education and health service etc. The problems and potential for economic development and social change in the district are described by short notes.

Possible Effects on Inter-State Disparities in Economic Development

The principal centres of the information technology industries are all located in states which have higher levels of economic development than the all India average. Bangalore in Karnataka is the most important centre of these industries at present. Other important centres are Chennai in Tamil Nadu, Hyderabad in Andhra Pradesh, Mumbai and Pune in Maharashtra, Ahmedabad in Gujarat, Gurgaon in Haryana and Noida in U.P. Both the latter are satellite cities of Delhi. Growth of these industries will in the foreseeable future also be concentrated in these centres so that the total domestic product of the states in which they are located will increase faster than in states in which industries are not located.

Possible new centres are Kolkata in West Bengal and Kanpur or Lucknow in Uttar Pradesh. Development in Kolkata would be assisted by location of the Indian Statistical Institute in Barrackpur, a suburb of Kolkata, and by location in Kolkata itself of two Universities which have strong departments of science; one has a college of engineering. The possible development of Kanpur or Lucknow would be encouraged by location near an Institute of Technology in the former and of a good university in the latter.

Chandigarh in Punjab should also emerge as a Centre. It has a University, a Regional Engineering College and a world-class medical college and a hospital. It would attract a large number of Punjabi computer software specialists who are now settled in the U.S.A. Another favourable factor is access to venture capital because of the strong entrepreneurial tradition among the Punjabis. Furthermore it has a salubrious climate, and relatively low levels of pollution of air and water pollution.

With the exception of Uttar Pradesh, all the states in which the IT centres are located or are expected to come up in the foreseeable future have higher per capita income than the all India averages (Table 21.2) so that inter-state disparities in economic development could increase with rapid growth of these industries.

Effect on the Settlement Pattern

The effect of these techniques on the rural and urban settlement patterns cannot be forecast with any degree of accuracy but it is likely that the long-term trend towards concentration of the rural population in large village will be accentuated. There are several reasons for this.

The agricultural extension officers that advise farmers in adoption of high productivity techniques concentrate their attention on farmers, who live in large villages. These villages are easily approached by motorable roads; so that large farmers who market most of their produce live in them. Branches of cooperative societies and of land mortgage banks that provide short and medium-term credit for buying inputs of high productivity agriculture are located in them—stores that sell, improved seed, chemical fertilizers pesticides and medicines (tractors, pump sets driven by diesel oil or electricity) fuel for the machines and facilities for their repair and spare parts are located in them. With use of long distance telephones up-to-date information on prices of crops is available to farmers living in them. Secondary schools for boys and girls and primary health centres that provide advice on preventive health and nutrition and treatment in case of sickness are located there. Farmers who live in them have better health and productivity and have access to education of facilities for their children so that some of them can become white-collar workers. Agricultural labourers will live in or near them so that they will have opportunity for employment on the farms, in the states mentioned above, or those which send crops to regional markets.

Probable Effects on the Rural and Urban Settlement Patterns

These effects are more difficult to foresee because of the great diversity in the present settlement pattern in different states of India. The variation in the rural pattern is all the way from most farm households living in their own compounds with a drinking water well, and a small patch growing vegetables and tapioca and the family's rice field in the back in Kerala, to most of the rural people living in relatively large villages with populations of 1000 or more in Punjab, Haryana, western U.P., northern Rajasthan, Gujarat and north-western Madhya Pradesh.

Information on weather and prices of crops can be broadcast to farmers in small villages as well as in large ones. Similarly, because of near universal rural electrification in several states, electrically operated pumps on irrigation wells and electrically operated machines for de-husking rice and wheat, shelling maize, pressing sugarcane to make *khandsari* or brown sugar for local consumption or processing oilseeds to make cooking oil for similar use can be done just as well in small villages as in large ones.

However, residents of relatively large villages have an advantage over those of small villages in a number of ways. Approach roads to them are better because the large farmers who are the principal sellers of crops are concentrated in them. Furthermore, the villages have an advantage in production of high value perishable foods—milk, vegetables, fruit and poultry products (chicken and eggs) for urban and local markets. Output and consumption of these foods is increasing rapidly and they are providing remunerative employment and income to those—small farmers and rural women—who would otherwise be unemployed. Residents of large villages have access to better roads to take their produce to markets. Furthermore, offices of producers' cooperatives which supply essential inputs—chemical fertilizers and pesticides needed for production of crops, medicines for livestock and vaccines for birds are all located in relatively large villages. Thus, in states and regions mentioned earlier, concentration of the rural population in relatively large villages will be accentuated. This trend can be confirmed or contradicted, however, only when data of the subsequent census of population become available. Another advantage for residents of large villages is that one or more public telephone booths and several private telephones are installed in relatively large villages. Their residents will therefore, have access to telecommunication with relatives and friends living at long distances, which residents of small village do not have.

The principal foreseeable future effect on the urban settlement pattern is to accelerate spatial expansion of the large metropolitan cities in the peri-urban areas of which the information technology industries are located. This is because the infrastructures needed for location and growth of these industries—dependable (preferably captive) supplies of electricity and water, freedom from noise and dust pollution, enough space for foreseeable expansion of the IT companies and suitable housing and various service facilities for their executives and employees can be located in the peri-urban areas of the cities. In Hyderabad, the industries are concentrated in Cybercity, which is located about 30 kilometres from the city and in which all facilities for their location and growth have been provided by the Government of Andhra Pradesh. In Chennai, they are located in the vicinity of the Institute of Technology—at Guindy about 30 kilometres north of the city. In Mumbai they are located in the vicinity of the Institute of Technology in Pawai, also located about 30 kilometres north of the city. This is because; most of the investors in these industries are graduates of the IITs. In Delhi, however, they are located in Gurgaon and NOIDA, both of which are satellite cities located 20-30 kilometres from New Delhi.

Architects of Economic Growth (Nath, 2010, Chapter 12)

(a) The Bureaucrat (1950-1990)

The entrepreneur has become the most important person who has been responsible for accelerating growth of GDP in India from 3-4 per cent per annum during the 30 years 1960-1980 to 5-7 per cent per annum during the 1990s.

In the former period, the Government of India made large investments in establishing five large integrated steel mills, mills for converting bauxite into alumina and metallic aluminium, irrigation-*cum*-hydropower-*cum*-flood control projects, thermal power plants, a heavy machine tool factory, a factory for making light machine tools, two more factories for making machines for generating, transmission of electricity, factory for making diesel driven electric locomotives wagons and coaches for the railways and a factory for making penicillin and other basic pharmaceutical drugs.

After the discovery of oil off the coasts of Mumbai and Gujarat, large investments were made in exploration and development of the oilfields, refining of crude oil into motor spirit, diesel oil, kerosene and liquefied natural gas for cooking. Large investment was made also for constructing pipelines from the refineries to metropolitan cities which were the principal consuming centres.

Quasi-independent public sector companies were established for managing each of these investments. Thus the Oil and Natural Gas Commission was established for exploration and development of the oilfields and the Indian Oil Corporation was established for establishing refineries, constructing pipelines for taking petroleum products and gas from the refineries to the metropolitan cities and rural areas of high consumption of these. It has responsibility for managing the network of dealers of its products. Technical and financial assistance for establishing these factories was obtained from the Soviet Union, Germany and Britain and to a much smaller extent from Canada. Technical assistance was obtained also from the United States and Switzerland.

After establishing the enterprises the efforts of the Government of India have been concentrated on reducing the loss of the steel mills and other loss making enterprises, by over carrying deficiencies of management and infrastructure. The petroleum related enterprises were generating large profits from the beginning and the light machine tools factories started making profits after a few years, as did the factories, which made machines for generation of transmission and distribution of electricity. However, the steel mills and heavy machine tools factory are still making losses.

During this period, the bureaucrats had great power. The managers of the plants came to the Secretaries and Joint Secretaries of the Ministries of Steel, Power, Petroleum and Railways for funds needed to reduce the loss of the enterprises or for expansion of capacity or for modernisation of the plants making locomotives, wagons or coaches for the railways, the changes needed in pricing of various products, etc. The Ministers in charge of these Ministries relied on their senior bureaucrats for advice on sanctioning additional funds or for changes in policies.

(b) Intellectual or Visionary Entrepreneur

The information technology industries have been the fastest expanding industries during the last 3 decades and are expected to maintain such growth during the next two decades.

The founders of the best companies such as Wipro, Infosys and HCL are outstanding computer engineers. The non-resident Indians who have made millions in Silicon Valley in the U.S.A. are young men who have become affluent as successful owners of IT companies. They now are wanting to set up these companies in their home states. Some of them are offering to share the cost of running their *alma mater*—Institutes of Science and Technology; Schools of Management and of Universities such as Delhi to ensure that they maintain high standards.

Groups of outstanding physicians and surgeons have established a chain of world-class hospitals in several Indian's metropolitan. The heads of the pharmaceutical companies that have developed drugs based on original research are also outstanding students of pharmaceutical science who have had brilliant ideas to develop these drugs. The companies that manufacture highly effective Ayurvedic drugs are managed by entrepreneurs who are highly knowledgeable in pharmacy. Other companies which succeed in this rapid growth industry would also be established by such pharmaceuticals.

The intellectual entrepreneurs or businessmen are likely to remain the dominant players in the information revolution that is sweeping the world. An enterprising entrepreneur was one of the first to establish world-class hotels in several metropolitan cities in India. Furthermore, in collaboration with hotel chains in the U.S.A. in several cities in neighbouring countries of South, South East and in East Africa, a group of enterprising young men have established restaurants serving north Indian and south Indian foods in the countries of the Gulf, the U.S.A. and Britain. There are several such restaurants in London, besides those in other cities in which there are large Indian or Pakistani communities. The Tatas have set up world-class hotels in several metropolitan cities in India and in places, which are visited by large numbers of foreign tourists. Their hotels were established in collaboration with foreign chains in some of the American and British cities. Some of the businessmen who have become multi-billionaires in Britain are offering to takeover India's sinking public sector enterprises such as air lines. One group has already bought India's largest company whose activities ranging from mining of coal to manufacture of liquor.

(c) Efficient Managers

Rapid and accelerating economic growth is dependent upon having efficient managers. All the big industrial houses realize this. The Tatas were the first to realize this truth. Although the head of Tata's always a relative of the founding family, the directors and managers of different enterprises in the group are people belonging to various communities and provinces.

They are chosen for the top posts on the basis of outstanding performance in various positions in the company that they have held since they joined it. The result of this policy has been that every company floated by the Tatas has become a major profit centre over the long term. Any company that does not make the growth is sold off. Other leading companies Reliance, Godrej, Kirloskars and Bajaj Auto are following the same policy. Although the chairman continue to belong to the founding family and the heads of various enterprises are controlled by the efficient managers. Multi-nationals such as Hindustan Lever and

Indian Tobacco Company doing business in India for decades are following the same policy.

Furthermore the heads of the biggest companies are sending their sons to the best business schools in the U.S.A. so that they know the essentials of good management and make profit-making new investments.

The best managers are paid high salaries and have perquisites such as car and a furnished house both paid for by the company. Even after deduction of income tax they live extremely well. They too ensure that their sons attend the best business schools so that they become efficient managers. However, if the manager fails to deliver high and increasing profits through adverse market conditions, he may be summarily dismissed. Thus a trained and talented man may find himself out of a job in mid-career, unless he is picked up for a management position in another company.

Thus the job of an efficient manager carries high rewards and trust. If he is not successful and lucky he may end up using his skill to float an enterprise of his own and if he is really good, he must be successful in it. Otherwise he becomes a management consultant with a consulting firm or set up his own agency to advice small but growing industrial enterprises.

Thus, almost all efficient managers are affluent through most of their working life and also after retirement. Indeed the habit of hard work is so strong among them that their periods of complete retirement are brief.

(d) The Role of Foreign Aid and Foreign Direct Investment

When the former colonies of Britain, France and the Netherlands became independent in the 1950s and the 1960s, there was much discussion of aid by the former colonial powers and by the U.S.A. to aid their economic development.

This was based on the American experience of aid towards rebuilding quickly the industries, agriculture and cities of its allies—France and Britain and former enemies Germany, Italy and Japan which had suffered severe damage or had been destroyed during Second World War. American aid had within 15 years, i.e. by the beginning of the 1960s rebuilt these war-ravaged economies so well that their traditional exports were flooding the markets of the world. Japanese had, with American aid, built such state-of-the-art steel plants and shipyards that import of their steel led to closure of many steel mills in U.S.A. and Britain, and import of their ships led to closure of some American shipyards. Furthermore, Japanese T.V. receivers and music systems and cars were the rage in U.S.A., Britain and west European countries.

Motives of Aid

The motives of giving aid to the developing countries were mixed. The former colonial countries Britain, France and the Netherlands wanted that their influence should remain strong in their former colonies and dependencies. The British, the Dutch and the French wanted that the ruling elites of newly independent Malaysia, Indonesia and former colonies in Africa and Asia should not nationalize the plantations of oil palm and coffee or mines or tin and other minerals but should be partners with the erstwhile colonial planters and mining companies to exploit these resources.

All these countries wanted also that they should be free to exploit the newly discovered oilfields of Nigeria and the Republic of Congo in Africa and Malaysia and Indonesia in Asia. The British and the French succeeded in their efforts. The newly independent elites of African countries retained English as the language of communication with foreigners and adopted Parliamentary Democracy as their mode of government. However, the plantations of oil palm, cocoa and coffee in Ghana, tea and coffee in Kenya, Uganda and Tanzania were nationalized. The Nigerians invited all the seven oil potential major African countries to explore their oil fields.

The newly independent elites of the former French colonies retained similarly French as the language of communication with foreigners, shopped in Paris during the summer and patterned their Legislatures after the Chamber of Deputies in Paris. They did not nationalize the mines but ensured that a part of the profits went into supporting their French style mode of living, building approach roads, and to finance essential consumer goods.

The Kenyans quickly decided that they had better retain the British as managers of plantations, but the Ghanaians, the Ugandans and Tanzanians decided otherwise. They were all victims of grinding poverty and a succession of *coup d' etat* in Ghana and Uganda and it was years before their economies reverted to the position at independence. Furthermore, improvement of communications in all African countries brought to the cities, millions of young men and women who wanted jobs of domestic servants and other unskilled workers, because they no longer wanted to do the back breaking work in subsistence agriculture.

Moreover the amounts given in aid were too small to have any tangible effect on the economies of these countries and was absorbed in salaries and perquisites of the technical assistance experts and expenditure on equipment bought in the aid giving country. Aid with such mixed motives was severely criticized as evinced by Sameer Amin an Egyptian economist and many other political economists. They described it as neo-colonialism in another form. (Samir Amin)

Foreign Aid to India

Aid was given by the Soviet Union, Britain and Germany and to a much smaller extent by Canada and the U.S.A. Aid from the first three countries was utilized principally in building five large steel mills, mills for processing bauxite into aluminium and metallic aluminium, a factory for making heavy machine tools, factories for making locomotives, wagons and coaches for railways, two factories each for making light machine tools and for producing machine for generation, transmission and distribution of electricity, three factories for making motor vehicles including passenger cars and chasses for buses and trucks and several factories for making motor bicycles and scooters. Technical assistance for establishing them was given on a commercial basis by companies in Germany, Japan and Italy.

After discovery of large deposits of crude oil off the coasts of Mumbai and off-shore and on-shore Gujarat, large investments were made also in exploration and development of the oilfields, establishing refineries and a country-wide network of vendors for distribution of products—motor spirit and diesel as fuel for motor vehicles and kerosene and natural gas for cooking. Assistance for such development was given by the Soviet Union and on a commercial basis by other countries.

American assistance for development of agriculture and rural development began with start of the community development programme in 1952. However, it was terminated soon because the Administrator of the programme and the Development Commissioners who implemented the programme in the states found that they knew more about agriculture and rural development than did the experts and the equipment that they brought was not too useful. Later, in the mid-1960s US assistance was given mainly as surplus cereals, (wheat and milo) under its PL 480 programme when there was a severe shortage of grains in the country.

In later years, there has been little assistancc from America, Britain or Germany. The principal role of these countries has been to support assistance from the World Bank for some poverty eradication programmes and from the IMF for balance of payments support.

The acceleration of economic growth from 3-4 per cent per annum during 1960-90 to 5-7 per cent of GDP per capita in the 1990 has been due entirely to India's own developmental effort. Foreign direct investment has come in running tourist hotels and banks in which large profits are assured and can be recaptured. There has been little assistance in construction of essential infrastructures such as 4-6 lane highways or for construction or modernization of ports.

In 2000-2001 with all the facilities extended to foreign investors, foreign direct investment was estimated at less than 2 million dollars, scarcely more than 4-5 per cent of the GDP. India's economic development would be the result of India's own economic development effort.

Foreign aid amounts to about 6 billion dollars per year. Some of it is in aid of poverty eradication programme from the World Bank the rest is to finance equipment for industrial or infrastructure projects assisted by the aid giving countries.

Foreign aid and foreign direct investment has been too small to assist India's economic development after its initial role in establishing India's basic industries. Most of the amounts given as 'aid' have had to be repaid over the decades. Foreign aid and foreign direct investment in less developed countries of sub-Saharan Africa has only brought to them the serious problems of over-urbanization and political instability due to too rapid migration of youth to cities where there were no jobs for them.

The ruling elites of the resource rich countries are cooperating with the former colonial power to build their cities and provide education and health to their populations. They have also made peace on their own terms with the Chinese who provide most of the skilled labour force for mining the mines and plantations.

Issues of Sustainable Economic Development (Nath, 2010, Chapter 13)

(a) Development and Environment Preservation

Self-sustaining development means also development that does not lead to environmental deterioration or depletion of natural resources of soil, water, vegetation or minerals. Consider two examples. The grasses in the pasture lands of semi-desert or desert areas of Rajasthan were self re-generating as long as the number of livestock (cattle, sheep and goats) was not too large, so that grazing by livestock during the dry season was followed by restoration of the grass in the monsoon season. Furthermore, the thin cover of thorn forest in these areas checked wind erosion and allowed the pastures to regenerate themselves. Leaves of certain trees served as food for sheep and goats. However, increase in livestock numbers now exhausts the grass a few months after the rains so that annual migration of herds to pasture lands of eastern Rajasthan has become an annual phenomenon. Thousands of livestock (cattle, sheep and goats) die and the pastures are impoverished in years of drought, which came once or twice in three years.

Second, consider production of wheat and rice in the areas with assured and regulated supplies of water provided by rainfall and/or irrigation sources, mainly surface wells fitted with electric pumps in Punjab. Yields per hectare of both crops are high with application of heavy doses of chemical fertilizers and pesticides. However, there have been increasingly frequent disturbing reports about a steep fall in ground water table in some areas and increasing areas suffering from salinity.

In Punjab, paddy rice is followed by wheat; in Haryana winter wheat is followed by cotton or an oilseed; in western U.P. wheat is followed by an oilseed. In U.P. farmers grow also sugarcane, which occupies the cropped area for almost a year or even more. These have become the normal cropping patterns. Earlier, in all these areas, wheat used to be followed by summer fallow or a fodder crop in the monsoon season. The latter provided food for livestock which were used for farm work. They provided also manure and fuel. The females provided milk which together with milk products (ghee, curds and butter) is an important component of the food of the people. Besides certain fodder crops enriched the soil by fixing nitrogen from the air.

Apparently, the new cropping pattern is not self-sustaining and will need to be changed either by reversion to the old self-sustaining pattern or by evolving a new self-sustaining pattern. The farmers' income would not be lower if they reverted to the old pattern of wheat, rice or sugarcane followed by a period of fallow or growing fodder crops. The yield of wheat would increase and the livestock would enrich the soil. Production by the farmers and of milk, butter, cheese and *ghee* would also have a ready market in the cities. Farmers with small holdings could grow vegetables and produce milk for urban markets. They could also take up poultry keeping, to produce chicken and eggs for which there is a very large demand in Delhi and other cities in the region. Their income would not be lower than in the present cropping pattern which reduces fertility of the soil and raises the water tables.

(b) Reducing Growth Rate of Population

Rapid growth of population is viewed as a problem which must be solved if sustainable economic development is to be achieved. Kerala and Goa in which rate of increase of population are little more than replacement rates are considered ideals to be achieved by the other states within the next 2 decades, if sustainable economic development is to be achieved. In this discussion, it is forgotten by the theorists that population is also a resource which produces up to a period its own means of subsistence.

The danger of too rapid growth of population was emphasized by the Census Commissioner of 1951. He wrote in his report that with all the known means of increasing food production, India could not sustain a population of more than 500 million, which at the 1941-1951 growth rate of population of 12.5 per cent per decade would be reached by 1969-70. Thereafter, Malthusian checks, famine and pestilence would apply. The population in 1951 was 361 million. The population in 2001 is expected to exceed 1 billion—almost 3 times, the number in 1951. Production of cereals at the end of the 1990s was about 200 million tonnes, $3^1/_3$ times the production of about 60 million tonnes in the mid 1950s. Per capita consumption of cloth has doubled. In other words, the average Indian is somewhat better fed and better clothed now than he was in 1951.

Reducing growth rate of population is the basis of the national population policy which was adopted by the Government of India in January 2001. The chances of reducing it from the estimated current rate of increase of 1.9 per cent per annum are much greater now than ever before because birth rates in several large and relatively developed states—Tamil Nadu, Karnataka, Andhra Pradesh, Maharashtra and Gujarat are falling already. A recent study in a backward area of Rajasthan, a state with one of the highest rate of population growth shows that family planning, very mention of which was anathema to rural women in 1961, is so acceptable now that a auxiliary nurse midwife whose main business is to advise on family planning is stationed permanently in a large village. A variety of contraceptives are being used by men and women and it is reported that 100 'operations' are performed (on women) every month. The principal reason for this change is that survival rate of children is much higher now than it was in 1961. The women have access to clean water for bathing and drinking and access to a private medical practitioner in a neighbouring village and a well-equipped hospital at the district headquarter, located about 5 kilometres from the village. They and their children are much cleaner and better nourished than they were in 1961. Furthermore, in case of any sickness of themselves or their children, they can go to the physician for treatment of ordinary sickness and to the hospital in case of serious sickness of themselves, their men or the children. Their children, most of the young boys and a few girls are cleaner because they go to school where the teachers insist that they come to school after a bath using soap and hair oil and in a uniform which is washed at least once in two days. In 1961 most of the girls never went to school because they were busy taking care of their younger siblings while the mothers worked in the fields. Now the mothers have less work in the fields because their fields are ploughed by tractors and there are machines for dehusking wheat and shelling sorghum and millets. Oilseeds grown in the village are sold to dealers in the market except the small quantities required for local consumption.

Most of the women and men interviewed by the researchers[1] said that they want no more than 3 children of which one must be a son; in 1961 this question could not be asked at all. Although the number of children borne by the women is higher than 2 or 3 (the state-wise average was 4.6 live births per woman in the 1980s) the desire for fewer children would be reflected in smaller number of live births in the state during the next decade which would in turn be reflected in a fall in the rate of growth of population in the forth-coming Population Censuses.

The field experience in this study only confirms the experience of Kerala and Goa in India and of countries in which there has been rapid decline in growth of population in the last 2-3 decades and shows that :

(i) With increase in literacy and female literacy in particular and decline in infant, child and maternal mortality, the rate of population growth declines. The principal reason for this is that with increase in survival rate of children, there is less desire among women to have more children.

(ii) Success in achieving a rapid decline in growth of population is through greater investment, in providing adequate and clean drinking water, facilities for primary health care and education to avoid common diseases and facilities for medical care in case of sickness and for education of both boys and girls.

Political Development

(a) Inefficiency and Corruption

A major weakness of our political development is increase in inefficiency and corruption among officials and workers in municipal, state and even some national services. It has affected also the Legislators and Ministers in many State Governments. A detailed analysis of this problem has been done in Chapter 14, "Changes in political culture between 1950s and the 1990s" in this volume.

Main Causes of Deterioration in Corruption

One of the main causes of corruption in the political executives is that the practice of duly recording contributions to the election expenses of political parties by companies was abandoned in 1969 for political expediency and has not been restored. The result is that moneys for fighting elections are obtained from various sources—companies, big businessmen and even smugglers and other criminals. After having financed the elections of various parties and of the Ministers these criminals have no hesitation in continuing their criminal activities. The Chief Minister of one large state has been in and out of jail during the last 3 years because there are proved charges of corruption against him. However, when in jail he runs the administration through his wife who has been elected as the Chief Minister.[2] His following among the poor people of the states is so large that every time he is sent to jail his followers start riots.

A former Chief Minister of another large state has been convicted of massive corruption. However her political following is so large that every time her case came up for trial in the courts, her followers started a riot which was curbed with some difficulty.

Both the Chief Ministers are secure in their positions;[3] there is no strong movement for their resignation. On the other hand there is great instability among the Chief Ministers of U.P. which is one of the most inefficiently administered state in India.

Corruption in some departments of the Central Government, such as Income Tax and Excise, and of State Governments, such as sales tax is so widespread that all officers from the Inspectors to the Assistant Commissioners or even many Commissioners are presumed to be corrupt. The lowest officers in these departments can line their pockets without any fear of being persecuted by their superiors. The position is worse among employees of the municipal bodies and state electricity boards which supply electricity to both urban and rural areas. Under-payment or non-payment of municipal taxes or not attending to their duties for days together by the lowest staff such as sanitation workers is common. They do it because they have protection of influential Councillors. Many Councillors connive with the staff to permit encroachment on municipal lands by the slum dwellers. Theft of electricity by the slum dwellers as also by high income households, by farmers who use electric motors on surface wells is so great that most of the state electricity boards incur large losses every year. As a result, privatisation of transmission and distribution of electricity is being actively considered by the Central Government. The argument is that the companies which takeover the responsibility for transmission and distribution of electricity will curb theft in order to earn an adequate return on their investment. Privatisation of other municipal services such as water supply and waste disposal is also being advocated for the same reason.

Competent, well-paid, well-trained and uncorrupted administrative and technical services are essential for efficiency in government and avoidance of serious errors of policy and programme formulation and implementation.

Effects of Economic Development

Economic Imbalance

But with increase in output of these crops, there developed a marked imbalance between incomes and employment of farmers and agricultural labourers in the more than 35 per cent of cropland which had assured and controlled water supply and the remaining 65 per cent of cropland in which crop production depended only on rainfall.

In the former, employment and income of farmers increased and they had almost full time work because they could produce at least 2 crops in the year. Agricultural labourers found employment both in farms (in sowing, weeding or harvesting of the crops), in handling produce in the markets in construction or repair of farm buildings and building brick and mortar houses in villages for the farmers and for themselves and working as labourers in wheat flour and rice mills, sugar mills and oil mills. Indeed in parts of Punjab and Haryana there was seasonal shortage of labour which was met by in-migration by labourers from eastern U.P. and adjoining areas of Bihar.

In the areas dependent only upon rainfall the output of the principal crops (wheat, rice, pulses, oilseeds, etc.) remains dependent upon the adequacy and timely distribution of rain within the rainy season. In most of Kerala, Assam and a large part of West Bengal and Coastal Orissa while rainfall is adequate and dependable for producing one or two crops of rice, besides those of jute in West Bengal, of rice, tapioca (a fibrous root pulp is used for food) and spices in Kerala; of rice and tea in Assam. However, in the rest of the country, comprising the hilly forested or moisture deficient areas of peninsular India, comprising most of Madhya Pradesh, the Telengana (inland area) of Andhra Pradesh, inland Tamil Nadu, parts of Karnataka, Maharashtra, Gujarat and Southern Rajasthan crop production remains dependent upon adequacy of rainfall. The same is true of a large part of U.P. and Bihar. In large parts of these states otherwise fertile land is destroyed by deposit of coastal sand and boulders during the monsoon floods. In the semi arid and arid areas of Rajasthan, crops fail and a large numbers of poultry and livestock have to be evacuated once or twice in three years. Thousands of livestock died despite the efforts of the government to save them.

The imbalance between the irrigated and un-irrigated areas is one for which there has been no remedy so far. The state has helped the farmers and agricultural labourers by undertaking food for work programmes and supplying balanced food—cereals, pulses, sugar and powdered milk as part of the wages for the work.

The Managers and Entrepreneurs

A major change during the last 50 years is transformation of the Indian economy from a dominantly agricultural economy to a diversified agricultural-industrial-service economy. At the beginning of the process, agriculture contributed more than half of (56%) of the GDP while industries and services contributed the remainder. However, by the end of the 1990s, factory industries and handicrafts and services contributed more than 75 per cent of the GDP while agriculture contributed 25 per cent or less.

Furthermore, the rate of increase in GDP had increased from 3-4 per cent per annum which was 1-2 per cent above the rate of increase in population, to 5-6 per cent in the 1990s or 3-4 per cent more than the rate of increase in population. In the beginning of industrial development in the late 1950s, large investment were made by Government of India in establishing steel mills, plants for making heavy and light machine tools, basic pharmaceutical drugs and even photographic films. After discovery of large deposits of oil off the coasts of Mumbai and Gujarat, large investments were made in exploration and development of oil fields, establishing oil refineries and developing a network of distributors of products-motor spirit, diesel, kerosene and cooking gas.

The investment was managed and supervised by the Ministers and senior officials of the Government of India. The industrial units were controlled by the managers and engineers and other technicians. Most of them belonged to the high castes. Other beneficiaries were highly qualified and skilled workers who earned high wages for the highly specialized work that they did. Most of them were trained by the management of the mills themselves. Most of them also belong to the high castes.

By the 1980s, the Government decided to withdraw from development of industries and services and leave it to private entrepreneurs. The government would reduce losses of loss making enterprises by eliminating deficiencies of management and infrastructure and concentrate its efforts on programmes of alleviation of poverty, illiteracy and disease and providing security of life and property to the citizens. However, because of strong opposition to this policy in Parliament and by unions of workers there has been little dis-investment so far. Meanwhile private entrepreneurs who had earlier confined themselves to making consumer goods and consumer durables from T.V. and video receivers to motor vehicles and construction materials—cement, steel rods and corrugated iron sheets have established oil refineries, plants for manufacture of petro-chemicals and are also trying to establish steel plants, with technical assistance as needed from Western developed countries. The information technology industries which have experienced exponential growth during the last three decades and are expected to maintain the growth for the next two decades is the creation of private entrepreneurs.

The principal beneficiaries of development of industries and modern services have been the entrepreneurs who belong mainly or exclusively to the high castes—Brahmins, Mahajans and a few Rajputs. Their income is much higher than that of farmers and other workers. The managers, senior technicians and skilled workers in these plants also belong mainly to the high castes.

The country has witnessed rapid urbanization. The greatest beneficiaries of this process are professionals—physicians, engineers, lawyers, architects and owners and managers of small and medium sized industrial units. The professionals perform highly specialized services. They are sought after for their specialized skills and paid high wages for these. Most of them belong to the high castes.

However, regardless of caste, the entrepreneur, the managers and highly trained professionals have been the greatest gainers of this process which will continue in the foreseeable future. The political process could reduce the disparity between their income and consumption and those of other groups in society through high taxes on high income and conspicuous consumption; but it would not reduce their high social status and the value that society attaches to their services. Conspicuous consumption by them is being cautioned at present but it will not be long before social pressure makes it increasingly unacceptable.

These processes are in many ways very similar to those in Western developed countries or in that of East and South East Asia which have experienced rapid growth in GDP during the last 50 years.

Social Imbalance

Another feature of Indian development has been improvement in economic and social conditions and political power of the Scheduled Castes and other backward castes at the expense of the high castes—Brahmins, Rajputs and Mahajans (traders). In the areas in which *zamindari, jagirdari* and other similar system of land tenure prevailed, abolition of these has released large areas of land which had been kept by the *zamindars* and *jagirdars* (all of high castes) as woodland and pasture. These areas have been allotted to landless labourers of the Scheduled Castes or marginal farmers so that the former could become peasant proprietors and the land holdings of the latter could become of viable size.

The state helped them with loan or grants for construction of drinking water wells and buildings for primary schools (and secondary schools in larger villages) and teachers and equipment for their operation. Furthermore, the Scheduled Castes ceased to perform their customary duties at life cycle events such as birth, marriage and death in the houses of *zamindars* and *jagirdars* which they used to perform earlier. The *chamaars* (leather workers) ceased to flay the hides and skins of dead animals and making shoes and leather goods for some farm operations. Furthermore, 25 per cent of the seats in schools and colleges (including professional colleges) were reserved for candidates of the Scheduled Castes, large numbers of their young men became white collar workers including junior and senior officers in the governments of the States and the Government of India.

The political process has also helped the Scheduled Castes and the Scheduled Tribes at the expense of the high castes. Untouchability has been abolished through a directive principle of the Constitution and is disappearing in both rural and urban areas. Since one-fourth of the seats in State Legislatures and in the Parliament are reserved for their representatives, their support is essential for enactment of important legislation and often even for continuation of the ruling party in power.

Thus one major effect of the economic, social and political developments of the last half a century is improvement of economic, social and political position of the Scheduled Castes and other backward castes *vis-à-vis* the high castes.

The most visible effect of the political change is in the caste composition of the cabinets in the Government of India and of the states. In the first cabinets formed after India became independent, the Prime Minister and most of the Ministers belonged to the high castes because most of the leaders of the independence movement had belonged to these castes. However, the pattern changed radically within one or two decades. While the Prime Minister and most of the Ministers in the Government of India continued to belong to the high castes, in the states the Chief Ministers belonged to the dominant cultivating castes. This position exists even today. The Chief Ministers of most of the states belong to these castes. In two states, the Chief Ministers belongs to "the other" backward castes.

Pluralist or Competitive Democracy

India selected the system of Parliamentary Democracy for government of the people. This means that different political parties compete for control of the government. The legislators are those selected by the people to represent them in the State Legislatures and the National Parliament. Although the majority of the electors are poor and illiterate they have exercised their vote with the ultimate care. They consider their vote a valuable gift of independence.

Fourteen elections have been fought since the Constitution of India was enforced in 1950, without too much violence. Although Congress Party has been in power in majority of the elected governments, there have been brief periods when opposition parties tookover the control. However, it is significant that almost the same economic and fiscal policies have continued that were introduced by the government formed by the Congress Party in 1991 in order to avert the balance of payments crisis that faced the country in that year because it feels that they are in the best interests of the country. Certain important features of its foreign policy, i.e. relations with the neighbouring and other countries are not too different from those policies initiated by Pandit Nehru in 1952 or earlier. Thus, there is both continuity and change in policies and programmes in India's Parliamentary System of Government.

The Prospects of Self-sustaining Economic Growth

The Prospect 2000-2020

If despite adverse foreign economic conditions, the country can maintain a growth rate of GDP of 5-6 per cent per annum for several years in the current decade, it will be considered to have reached self-sustaining economic growth. The principal influences contributing to it will be :

(a) Information Technology Industries

Further growth of information technology industries for export and use in manufacturing industries and modern services will contribute to India's foreign exchange earnings, while use of these techniques in manufacturing industries within India will improve the quality of the products, reduce their prices and make them more competitive in international markets. The growth of pharmaceutical drug industries based on original research, some based on principles of Ayurveda (the ancient Hindu system of medicine), will also make a significant contribution to increasing export earnings if the drugs are effective in treatment of diseases of the aged, or women and children. There is a very large demand for such drugs in the developed countries and also in India.

(b) Public Sector Enterprises

A more important influence will be reduction in losses of public sector enterprises which are loss making such as steel plants, domestic and international airlines and hotels. The government has an active programme of finding strategic partners who will takeover shares in these enterprises and make them profitable by better management and infusion of much needed funds to buy additional machines and spare parts and giving surplus staff voluntary retirement packages. There is strong opposition to such disinvestment at present but it is bound to be progressively reduced. On the other hand profit-making public enterprises should be given additional funds to enable them to grow for domestic and international markets. Two groups of hotel operators—the Taj and the Oberois—are already strong enough to open profit-making hotels in various cities and places of tourist interest in India. They have established also, in collaboration with international hotel operators or by themselves profit-making hotels in the U.S.A. and developing countries of South Asia and Africa.

(c) Banking and Insurance

A number of nationalized banks such as the State Bank of India, the Punjab National Bank and the Bank of Baroda have already become profit-making. They would progressively reduce their non-performing assets (bad debts) and staff and reduce costs by closing down branches in villages and small towns which are running at a loss.

The bonds of various derivation issued by these banks are making major contribution to mobilizing small savings for economic growth. Similarly, the Unit Trust of India has become profit-making after a period. Since the dividends earned by investing in these investments is tax exempt up to a certain limit, they will make a major contribution to mobilizing domestic savings, which can be used for financing infrastructures. Efficiency in them could be increased progressively so that they can mobilize more funds. The LIC should be encouraged to enter areas like health insurance by itself or in partnership with well-established companies abroad. The consumer's interests will be served and part of the large profits in this area will accrue to a domestic company. Similarly the General Insurance Corporation should in collaboration with reputed foreign companies enter areas such as marine insurance, which it has avoided so far. The dollar bonds of the State Bank of India are mobilising savings of non-resident Indians.

The voluntary retirement packages being offered by the banks and which have proved very popular have two benefits. Productivity per worker employed in the banks will increase so that they become more efficient and can compete with foreign banks which are making large profits. The employees who retire are generally efficient managers and those with good knowledge of banking. These will start their own new banking, financial institutions such as chit funds to mobilize savings of the poor. They could also with the help of the loans given by the banks start successful industrial enterprises.

(d) Infrastructure Development

The Maharashtra and Gujarat Governments which are among the most developed states in India have already constructed 4 and 6-lane expressways on stretches of roads along which traffic is heavy. The two governments have developed also small ports which are being used for developing 'Special Enterprise Zones' (SEZs) in which multi-nationals and non-resident Indians, who have established industrial or trading enterprises abroad, can establish manufacturing facilities. The Mittals, an Indian group based in Britain, which has acquired control of a large number of steel plants round the world and made them profitable by improving management should be encouraged to takeover management of loss making steel plants so that their losses can be progressively eliminated and they become profit-making.

(e) Agricultural Production and Growth

Agricultural output could continue to increase by 3-4 per cent per annum. Cereal production can be increased in rain-fed areas in which potentially fertile lands are rendered infertile because they are covered every year by coarse sand and boulders brought down by monsoon floods. This can be avoided by a forestation in the hill slopes and reclamation of lands in the plains by farmers with financial assistance from the State Governments. Punjab Sikhs have developed highly productive farms which produce rice and wheat by reclaiming some of these areas in the sub-mountainous area of western U.P. The small holders of the lands should be provided loans for reclamation of land, buying livestock and improved seed for cultivation. The Government of West Bengal has reclaimed large areas of such lands by land reforms to make actual farmers owners of the lands and controlling floods through check dams and giving loans to farmers to buy improved seed and bullocks, if needed. The Government of U.P. and Bihar can do the same. The new states of Uttaranchal (now Uttarakhand) and Jharkhand, in which there are larger numbers of educated and skilled people, could do the same, thus ending the food deficit of these states.

Encouraging production of milk, vegetables and chicken and eggs in areas which produce most of the cereals in the country will make a further contribution to increase in agriculture output. Production of fruit and vegetables can be increased also in areas which already produce these by giving loans to the producer cooperatives to establish cold storage facilities, arranging marketing of products and for establishing facilities for processing fruit and vegetables.

(f) Education and Skill Formation

Education and skill formation among men and young women will enable tribal youth of Jharkhand to take up jobs of white collar workers and skilled workers in the numerous industrial units which are at present held by outsiders. The list could be extended but the thrust of the argument is clear from the above notes.

Conclusion

The management of loss making public sector enterprises such as the steel plants should be entrusted to non-resident Indian groups like the Mittals, which has a proven record of making loss making steel mills profitable by using their capital and expertise. The loss making modern service enterprises such as Air India, Indian Airlines and hotels should be entrusted to Indian multi-nationals or partners in Indian and foreign companies which have a proven record of turning around loss making enterprises like the Tata Singapur Airlines consortium. The management of loss making public sector hotels could be entrusted to the Taj and Oberoi groups of hotel operators which are operating hotels in various cities and places of tourist interest in India and in collaboration with foreign multi-national in various cities in Britain and the U.S.A.

On the other hand, profit-making public sector enterprises such as Hindustan Machine Tools and Bharat Heavy Electricals should be given all facilities especially allowing to expand their operations within India and in neighbouring countries as far as possible.

All these steps and related others will contribute to India attaining self-sustaining economic growth. Reference has been made already to increasing production of cereals in the irrigated lands which are inherently fertile but are rendered unproductive by deposits of coarse sands and boulders in the monsoon. Two examples have been given to illustrate this fact.

Increase in production of protective foods—milk, vegetables, fruit, chicken and eggs and meat will contribute to further increase in agricultural production. Producers' cooperatives or individual small holders which produce and market these products successfully should be enabled to expand their operations.

Industrial production would be increased by undertaking some of the steps mentioned above. The rapid growth of IT and pharmaceutical drug industries should be given all facilities to expand their operations. The country has been able to maintain a growth rate in GDP of 5-6 per cent per annum[4] despite adverse foreign conditions such as steep increase in prices of crude oil and its inability to reduce its fiscal deficit. The increase has been possible despite meagre foreign aid or foreign direct investment.

The Goals and Strategies of Development : 2000-2020

There should be no major change in the most important goals of development, viz. eradication of poverty, illiteracy and disease and reducing to the extent possible the imbalances that have developed among regions and various economic group of society.

During the last 50 years the rate of growth of gross domestic product has increased progressively from an average of 3-4 per cent per annum during 1960-80 to 5-7 per cent per annum in the 1990s. After allowing for increase in population of about 2 per cent per annum, this means an increase in GDP per capita from 1-2 per cent per annum to 3-4 per cent per annum. Economic policies should be so designed that the latter rate is maintained and if possible increased in the next two decades. Emphasis should be on poverty elimination rather than raising the GDP. Increase in GDP will not ensure improvement of poor sections. The goals of development mentioned above could not be achieved if this condition is not fulfilled.

The principal regional imbalance is in employment and income of the farmers and agricultural labourers in the nearly 35 per cent of the cropland that has assured and controlled water supply provided by an adequate and dependable rainfall and/or irrigation. These areas contribute most of the output of foodgrains (wheat and rice), sugar, cotton, jute, tea, coffee and spices. Both farmers and agricultural labourers have employment for most of the year and their income and levels of living are far higher than those in the areas, which do not have these advantages. The latter, which contribute almost 65 per cent of the cropland contribute much less than this percentage of agricultural output. Despite all the measures the regional imbalance between income and employment for farmers and agricultural workers in the areas having assured water supply provided by a dependable rainfall and those which do not have this advantage shall remain. This should be accepted and the measures mentioned earlier in this section should be taken to provide productive work in areas lacking these advantages. Most of the poor are concentrated in the following areas :

- (i) The hilly, forested areas, inhabited mainly by tribal people in Madhya Pradesh, Jharkhand region of Bihar, inland Orissa and small areas in West Bengal, the Telengana region of Andhra Pradesh, Maharashtra, Gujarat and Rajasthan.
- (ii) The mountainous areas of Uttaranchal, Himachal Pradesh and parts of Jammu and Kashmir and some of the hill states of the north-east.
- (iii) The drought-prone areas of peninsular U.P. (south-west U.P.), Madhya Pradesh, Saurashtra and Kutch in Gujarat, a large part of Maharashtra, the Telengana region of Andhra Pradesh and inland areas of Karnataka and Tamil Nadu.
- (iv) The desert and semi-desert areas of western Rajasthan.
- (v) The plains of central and eastern U.P., Bihar, parts of West Bengal and coastal Orissa.

The Jharkhand area of Bihar and adjoining areas of West Bengal, inland Orissa and Madhya Pradesh is rich in mineral, power and forest resources. There are a number of large industrial units, owned principally by the Government of India but also by private entrepreneurs. The tribal youth could be educated and trained to work in the industrial units as skilled, semi-skilled or white-collar workers. A major effort must be made in all the areas to be mentioned to increase agricultural output by adoption of suitable improved agricultural practices. Soil conservation works must be undertaken to prevent loss of fertility by wind and water erosion. Re-forestation to restore the greatly depleted forest resource would provide the tribal and non-tribal people with fuel, fodder, medicinal herbs and food.

In the other areas mentioned above, agricultural output could be increased slowly by evolving varieties of seed of foodgrains (rice and coarse grains) and oilseeds that give higher yields than those sown by the farmers at present. In parts of U.P. and Bihar large areas of inherently fertile soil get covered every year by deposits of coarse sand, boulders and silt by monsoon floods. The fertility of land can be restored by flood control and reclamation of land by suitable measures financed by the State and Central Governments. A beginning should be made by re-afforastation on the hill slopes that are continually eroded in the monsoon because of lack of forest cover.

The present Government of West Bengal has improved productivity of such lands by control measures and providing loans and subsidies to farmers for installation of electric motors on irrigation wells.

Food for work programme must be undertaken in all these areas from time to time to avert starvation in years when the rains fail. These programmes can be used also as an educational tool. Balanced food (cereals, pulses, sugar, cooking oil and powdered milk) should be given to the workers along with instruction on the principles of nutrition and child care to reduce the incidence of epidemic diseases among the recipients. Stores of Food Corporation of India have surplus foodgrains and their problem is of maintenance of the stored grains. The maintenance cost is more than its total value. So, it will be better to distribute this foodgrain to the poor section on subsidized rate and not to sell it to foreign country at prices lower than the cost, as the government has decided to do so. Or government can start the food-for-work programme to dispose of the surplus grains. In this way food prices can be raised to some satisfactory level and the continuing scenario of the suicides of farmers can be averted. The Government of India and of various States have implemented successfully for almost 50 years programmes aimed at assuring employment and reasonable earnings to handloom weavers and handicraft workers. These programmes will need to be continued. Emphasis in the programmes for assistance to handicraft workers should be on those who manufacture goods, a proportion of which is exported. Carpet weaving around Mirzapur, the manufacture of decorative brassware in Moradabad and weaving of silk *saris* and other garments for festive occasions in a suburb of Varanasi in U.P., in Kanchipuram in Tamil Nadu and in various other temple towns in the south provide examples. Use of child labour in carpet weaving should be banned so that the products have a large export market. Furthermore, the workers should be given higher wages and trained to use modern high productivity looms and modern designs to make the products more acceptable in both domestic and foreign markets. Government should provide the market facilities to the organized sector and the entry of multi-national should be checked in the household and small-scale industries, as our small-scale industries cannot stand before MNCs in the market.

In most of the handicraft industries, the Government of India and of the States have encouraged formation of cooperatives which procure raw materials, provide training to workers to improve productivity, modernize designs and market products. Experiences of cooperatives have been disappointing in India. There is huge corruption among the cooperatives. If we have to continue with cooperatives, transparency must be ensured.

Role of Producers' Cooperatives

Milk producers' cooperatives organized by the National Dairy Development Board on the pattern of Amul in Gujarat are supplying most of the milk used in metropolitan cities—Mumbai, Delhi, Hyderabad, Ludhiana, Chandigarh and cities in Gujarat. They provide year round employment to men and wives of producers most of whom are small farmers with bare subsistence holdings and contribute a significant proportion to their income. Government has made a deal with Denmark to import milk, which will be sold in India at a price lower than the cost of the Indian milk production. It will result in the destruction of Indian dairying. Hence this trend must be checked.

Producers' cooperatives have proved to be the best organizations for providing fruit, vegetables and poultry products for the cities. In the areas of production, they organize supplies of fertilizers and pesticides to the growers needed to increase yield among fruit and vegetables and vaccines to poultry farmers to immunize the birds against diseases. They also organize shipment of products to markets in order to obtain the best prices for the producers. The cooperatives in area around Nasik in Maharashtra, which supply onions and other vegetables, crate them for supply to Indian cities and for export to countries of the Gulf, are rich and have constructed large storage facilities in order to supply the markets throughout the year.

A large proportion of the country's sugar is produced by sugarcane growers cooperatives in valleys irrigated by small streams in Maharashtra and rivers in Andhra Pradesh and South Karnataka. In Maharashtra, these cooperatives own also sugar mills. Their members are affluent enough to dominate the politics of Maharashtra. Producers' cooperatives should be organized wherever possible.

Role of Non-Governmental Organizations/Civil Societies

Non-governmental organizations such as *Sewa* in Ahmedabad, which has implemented successfully an employment generation programme for poor women for some decades, should be provided financial assistance to encourage them to expand their activities. There is a need of some statistical data of the performance of *Sewa*. There are several other such organizations in different parts of the country. They should be given funds to expand their activities. Other non-governmental organisations have been active in preventing crime and violence against women. They should also be assisted, after due evaluation of their motives and sources of finance. Financial assistance by foreign governments should be scrutinized in order to ensure that its motivation is genuine.

Increased Importance of Business and Industry

Whereas agriculture contributed more than half of the GDP in the 1950's, 75 per cent of the output was produced in industries and modern services by the mid-1990s. The latter proportion will increase progressively in the next two decades. This is because while agriculture output would increase by a maximum of 3-4 per cent per annum, output in industries and modern services would increase 6-8 per cent per annum or faster.

Consistent with this trend is the increased influence of organizations of industrialists or associations of modern service providers have a strong influence on policies of the present government. The Federation of Indian Chambers of Commerce and Industry, the Confederation of Indian Industries, Chambers of Business and Industries in several states, associations of tourist operators and of owners of hotels are examples. These associations have a strong influence on the present government's policies for encouraging growth of industries and services. This influence is bound to grow. While the reform of economic policies suggested by them must be implemented by the World Bank and IMF must be implemented by the Government to improve modern service and competitiveness of modern industries, the interests of the consumers has to be guarded.

The organizations of affluent farmer's which produce most of the wheat, rice, sugarcane, high quality cotton and groundnut have a strong influence on procurement prices fixed by the Government of India. They are so strong in pressing for protection of their incomes that government has to placate them regardless of the effect that they have had on the consumers' cost of living. This cannot continue for too long, however. The government succumbing to the pressure of farmers' lobbies is being widely criticized. It is unlikely that the body will have a lasting impact on government policies, this criticism will increase and the government will have to pay economic prices in the interest of the consumers.

Since the information technology industries have experienced most rapid growth during the last two decades, the principal producers of services such as telecommunications have a strong influence on government policies. Such influence is bound to remain high during the next two decades. The Government should guard the interest of small and marginal farmers. After GATT farmers cannot compete with the farming of big business companies and of MNCs of developed countries which all getting very high subsidies from the respective government.

The heads of the most progressive information technology companies make their agreements for export of IT services in the USA and Western Europe first and ask for approval of the government later, if necessary.

Corruption: One negative social change is increase in monetary corruption by the bureaucrats, who with the public—whether in the departments that provide electricity, water and other services or medical care in hospitals and health centres opened by the government in cities, the dispensaries and primary health centres in block/taluka headquarter towns. This must be reduced to the maximum extent—Government hospitals are the only medical care facilities that are open to the rural and urban poor. Private charitable organizations cannot be expected to assume this role. They can provide at most a small percentage of the needs.

Many of the development programmes mentioned earlier, are not implemented successfully because most of the funds provided for them are in fact pocketed by the MPs or MLAs of the areas and the district and lower level officials responsible for implementation of these programmes. Panchayati Raj Institutions, which should be ensured proper utilization of funds are weak and are not allowed to become stronger. As a result, the poor people are frustrated and loose confidence in the ability of the Government to provide them with needed assistance.

It is only in crises such as an outbreak of an epidemic disease in a city or area that the governments mobilize efforts to check it. However, even in crisis like flood caused by excessive monsoon rains in Assam, parts of West Bengal, Bihar or U.P. and coastal areas of Orissa, Andhra Pradesh, and Tamil Nadu when millions lose their homes and are stranded for weeks, hundreds die and thousands of cattle die, funds for relief work sanctioned by the Central Government are not utilized quickly for rehabilitation of the affected people. Furthermore, there is much leakage in utilization of the funds. It is only in the relatively rich areas mentioned in Section II that these organizations are strong enough to ensure proper utilization of these funds. Thus the imbalance between the relatively developed and the poor and backward region increases.

Accordingly, a most urgent task is to mobilize public opinion in both rural and urban areas to check corruption. So that the effects of government programmes effectively reach the most deserving.

NOTES

1. Three senior researchers including the co-author visited the three villages of Sawai Madhopur district in January 2000 to capture the economic and social change studied by the author in 1961 when he was posted as Collector of the District.
2. She was displaced by her opponents but came back to power in spite of charges against her still to be proved or disproved.
3. Somehow the presumably corrupt Chief Minister has returned to power again in 2003.
4. The forecast for the coming fiscal year for growth rate of the Indian economy is expected to increase to 7 per cent in the year 2004.

Reference

Nath, V., "*Regional Dimensions of Rural Poverty in India*", *Regional Development and Planning in India*, Concept Publishing Co. Pvt. Ltd., 2009.

- *Economic Development and Planning in India*, Concept Publishing Co. Pvt. Ltd., 2010.

Perroux Francois : *Le Nation de Poles de Croissance Economic Applique* 1955 and *La Economic* due xxe. Siecle PUF 1961.

Rostow, W. W. : *Stages of Economic Growth*, Cambridge, Mass. 1960.

Samir Amin : *Neo-Colonialism in West Africa*, Penguin Books Ltd.